IMAGES OF NEPOTISM

JOHN BELDON SCOTT

Images of Nepotism

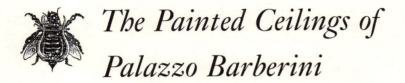 *The Painted Ceilings of Palazzo Barberini*

Princeton University Press, Princeton, New Jersey

Copyright © 1991 by Princeton University Press
Published by Princeton University Press, 41 William Street,
Princeton, New Jersey 08540
In the United Kingdom: Princeton University Press, Oxford

Library of Congress Cataloging-in-Publication Data
Scott, John Beldon, 1946–
Images of nepotism.
Includes bibliographical references.
1. Mural painting and decoration, Baroque—Italy—Rome.
2. Mural painting and decoration, Italian—Italy—Rome. 3. Allegories.
4. Authority in art. 5. Ceilings—Italy—Rome.
6. Urbanus VIII, Pope, 1568–1644—Art patronage.
7. Palazzo Barberini (Rome, Italy) I. Title.
ND2757.R6S38 1991   751.7′3′0945632   89-24313
ISBN 0-691-04075-3 (alk. paper)

Publication of this book has been aided by
a grant from the Millard Meiss Publication Fund of the
College Art Association of America

This book has been composed in Linotron Janson

Princeton University Press books are printed on
acid-free paper, and meet the guidelines for permanence
and durability of the Committee on Production Guidelines
for Book Longevity of the Council on Library Resources

Printed in the United States of America by
Princeton University Press,
Princeton, New Jersey
10   9   8   7   6   5   4   3   2   1

For John Lloyd and Rosa Nelle

CONTENTS

viii • CONTENTS

LIST OF ILLUSTRATIONS

ACKNOWLEDGMENTS

THIS STUDY has greatly benefited from the corrections, comments, and suggestions of a number of colleagues who read either all or part of the manuscript. I wish particularly, in this regard, to thank Olga Berendsen, Malcolm Campbell, Joseph Connors, Roger Hornsby, Ann Sutherland Harris, Irving Lavin, Laurie Nussdorfer, Claudia Rousseau, Katherine H. Tachau, and Patricia Waddy.

I am also indebted to R. Ward Bissell, Mary Jane Bright, Thomas Cerbu, Brian Copenhaver, Charles D. Cuttler, Karin Einaudi, Marcello Del Piazzo, Giovanna Della Chiesa, Mary Alice Lee, Frederick J. McGinness, John McManamon, Giuseppina Magnanimi, Fabrizio Mancinelli, Tod Marder, Jörg Martin Merz, Jennifer Montagu, Carole Paul, Harlan Sifford, Orietta Verdi, Patricia Westercamp, Marc Worsdale, and Simone Zurawski, all of whom contributed significantly to the research for the project. Alexandra Carpino and Christina McOmber assisted with the editing and proofing of the manuscript. At Princeton University Press, Elizabeth Powers, editor, and Cynthia Arbour, production editor, were ever patient and solicitous.

Four individuals deserve special acknowledgment: Barbara Bini, who gave photographic reality to my abstractions about how ceiling paintings ought to be seen; Arlette Klaric, who always reminded me to "go back and look again at the work of art"; Irving Lavin, who asked me, significantly, "By what means are popes elected?"; and Patricia Waddy, who has worked virtually as a collaborator and whose own research on the art and use of the plan in seventeenth-century Roman palace architecture has served as stimulus in the formulation of a methodology for the study of ceiling painting. Students in graduate seminars at the University of Pennsylvania and the University of Iowa provided valuable assistance in testing the conventions of Baroque ceiling painting through a variety of case studies.

The American Council of Learned Societies, American Philosophical Society, Gladys Krieble Delmas Foundation, University of Iowa, Andrew W. Mellon Foundation, National Endowment for the Humanities, and University of Pennsylvania all provided generous financial support. The solicitude of the staffs of the Vatican Library, Father Leonard Boyle, Prefect, and the Galleria Nazionale d'Arte Antica (Palazzo Barberini), Dott.ssa Lorenza Mochi Onori, Director, made possible work with the Barberini Archive and at the Barberini Palace. At the Library of the American Academy in Rome, Dott.ssa Lucilla Marino and her staff were perennially helpful; the Bibliotheca Hertziana—Christoph Frommel and Matthias Winner, Directors—was an invaluable resource throughout the period of research.

In the course of preparing this study I was fortunate to have the friendship and personal support of Virginia Bush, Steven Helmling, Frima Fox Hofrichter, Patricia Leighten, Marika Smith, Thomas Gordon Smith, and Wallace J. Tomasini. And I want to thank Joel H. Griffith, with whom I shared so many youthful travels and with whom I first saw the ceiling paintings of Palazzo Barberini.

ABBREVIATIONS

ACR	Archivio Storico Capitolino, Rome	ICCD	Istituto Centrale per il Catalogo e la Documentazione, Rome (formerly GFN)
Arch. Barb.	Archivio Barberini, BAV		
ASM	Archivio di Stato, Modena		
ASR	Archivio di Stato, Rome	ind.	*indice*
AVR	Archivio Storico del Vicariato, Rome	Istr.	*Istrumento*
BAV	Biblioteca Apostolica Vaticana, Rome	LM	*libro mastro*
BCJ	*Bibliothèque de la Compagnie de Jésus*, 12 vols. (Brussels-Paris-Louvain, 1890–1960)	*LTK*	*Lexikon für Theologie und Kirche*, 10 vols. (Freiburg-im-Breisgau, 1957–1965)
		mand.	*mandato*
BLF	Biblioteca Medicea Laurenziana, Florence	*ODCC*	*The Oxford Dictionary of the Christian Church*, 2d ed. (Oxford, 1974)
BMF	Biblioteca Moreniana, Florence	PBN	Palazzo Barberini, piano nobile
CE	*The Catholic Encyclopedia*, 15 vols. (New York, 1907–1912)	PBT	Palazzo Barberini, piano terreno
		PSN	Palazzo Sforza, piano nobile
comp.	*computisteria*	PST	Palazzo Sforza, piano terreno
DBI	*Dizionario biografico degli Italiani* (Rome, 1960–)	quad.	*quaderno*
		SC	*salariati et companatici*
EU	*entrate e uscite*	sc.	scudo
GFN	Gabinetto Fotografico Nazionale, Rome (see ICCD)	SCEP	Archivio Storico della Sacra Congregazione per Evangelizzazione dei Popoli, Rome (formerly Collegio Urbano della Propaganda Fide)
gior.	*giornale*		
giust.	*giustificazione*		

IMAGES OF NEPOTISM

INTRODUCTION

As Urban VIII Barberini lay dying, he thought of his nephews. The pope called before him a group of distinguished canonists for the purpose of asking their counsel on a matter of private moral concern. Urban had earlier provided these prelates with a list of all gifts and benefices given to his nephews during the previous twenty years of his pontificate and asked them to consider if, in any of these, he had exceeded papal prerogatives in dispensing the wealth of the Holy See.[1] The aged pope now requested the group to report to him on their findings, for he was intent on redressing any excesses in this area "that might burden his conscience before the tribunal of God." The commission quickly assuaged the contrite pontiff's conscience by declaring that they had found no illegal actions in his munificence toward his family.[2]

The exculpatory finding may be open to suspicion, for Urban has been judged at fault in this regard both by contemporaries and by posterity. In his diatribe on the subject, the seventeenth-century publicist Gregorio Leti declared the reign of Urban VIII to have been the "feast day of nepotism" and cited as visible proof of this the more than 10,000 painted and sculpted Barberini heraldic bees affixed to buildings and monuments throughout the Papal States.[3] Even the Roman diarist Giacinto Gigli, a more objective contemporary observer, was negatively impressed: "He [Urban] accumulated more riches for his nephews than any other pope has ever accumulated."[4] The program of social advancement and the ostentatious behavior of the three papal nephews gave rise to much discontent and hyperbolic accusations: "Avidity for accumulating wealth so blinded the Barberini nephews that night and day they thought of means to make themselves princes, how to render their family eternal, and how to redouble the filling of their storehouses."[5] On this matter the pontificate of the Barberini pope has also been the object of particular scholarly scrutiny.[6]

---

[1] This is the official version of events given by Urban's biographer. A. Nicoletti, "Della vita di papa Urbano ottavo," BAV, Barb. Lat. 4737, 755r–56r. Transcribed in L. v. Ranke, *History of the Popes*, trans. E. Fowler (New York, 1901), 3:380. J. Grisar, "Päpstliche Finanzen, Nepotismus und Kirchenrecht unter Urban VIII," in *Miscellanea Historiae Pontificiae* (Rome, 1943), 7:252–97.

[2] L. F. v. Pastor, *The History of the Popes*, trans. E. Graf (London, 1923–1953), 29:403; Grisar ("Päpstliche Finanzen," 294–96), calls into question the narrative of events as recounted by Nicoletti. See the synthetic account of T. Magnuson, *Rome in the Age of Bernini* (Stockholm, 1982), 1:236–37.

[3] G. Leti, *Il nipotismo di Roma, o vero relatione delle ragioni che muovono i pontifici all'aggrandimento de' nipoti* (Amsterdam, 1667), 1:208, 228. This publication consists of a variety of manuscripts of anonymous authors written in Rome. F. Barcia, *Bibliografia delle opere di Gregorio Leti* (Milan, 1981), 146–56.

[4] G. Gigli, *Diario romano*, ed. G. Ricciotti (Rome, 1958), 253. On Gigli and his diary, see A. Ademollo, *Giacinto Gigli ed i suoi diarii del secolo XVII* (Florence, 1877).

[5] Leti, *Il nipotismo di Roma*, 214–15.

[6] Grisar, "Päpstliche Finanzen," 207–366; A. Kraus, "Amt und Stellung des Kardinalnepoten zur Zeit Urbans VIII. (1623)," *Römische Quartalschrift* 53 (1958), 238–43; "Der Kardinal-Nepote Francesco Barberini und das Staatssekretariat Urbans VIII.," *Römische Quartalschrift* 64 (1969), 191–208; K. Repgen, "Finanzen, Kirchenrecht und Politik unter Urban VIII.," *Römische Quartalschrift* 56 (1961), 62–74. On the Barberini nephews in general—Francesco (1597–1679), Taddeo (1603–1647), and Antonio the Younger (1607–1671)—see the entries in *DBI* 6:166–70, 172–76, 180–82. For Urban's brothers, Carlo (1562–1630) and Antonio the Elder (1569–1646), ibid., 165–67, 170–72. Also, P. Pecchiai, *I Barberini* (Rome, 1959), 130–33, 151–52, 154–213. For Cardinal Francesco, the eldest and most powerful

Difficult though it may be for the modern viewer to credit, cynicism played little role in the commission's finding. If Urban practiced nepotism to the utmost, he had not invented it. From the earliest times of the papacy popes were accustomed to appointing relatives, usually brothers and nephews (*nipoti*), to high ecclesiastical offices and providing them through church benefices with the independent means to maintain their political and social station.[7] Although not without its critics, in the seventeenth century nepotism was an accepted institution of the papacy, and the justification given for its practice lay in the pope's need, as temporal prince, to surround himself with intimates of unquestionable personal loyalty. Ties of blood were seen as the guarantors against intrigue and factionalism.[8] Moreover, as Urban's authorized biographer, Andrea Nicoletti, argued, the riches showered upon the Barberini nephews found justification in the use to which they put that wealth. In providing support for newly created cardinals who were without independent financial means and in seeing to the welfare of the poor, the pope's nephews demonstrated their worthiness. Furthermore, having for the benefit of the Church exposed themselves to the enmity of many secular princes, Urban's relatives were deserving of some form of material compensation.[9]

The offices, honors, and wealth that Urban bestowed on his relatives were justifiable, according to this reasoning, if they were to be effective in fulfilling the political functions required of them by the pope. Public display of the newly found wealth and power of the family became an inseparable component of this process. Conspicuous consumption manifested the princely virtues of munificence and magnanimity.

When examining nepotism, modern investigators have emphasized the social aspects of the liberality shown by the popes of the sixteenth and seventeenth centuries toward their families.[10] Few scholars, however, have noticed that the elective character of the papacy was the engine of seventeenth-century nepotism.[11] The vagaries of the process by which popes were elected frequently produced surprising results. Families of modest social and financial means could suddenly, and sometimes quite unexpectedly, find themselves in effect the rulers of the Papal States, with much of the wealth from the income of that land virtually at their disposal. Whenever a newly elected pope was of relatively obscure background, as was the case with Urban VIII, whose family had become rich in the wool trade and held only a modest position among the nobility of Tuscany, more resistance than usual would be encountered in finding an appropriate position for the new family amid the old nobility of Rome and the already well-established papal families.

of the nephews, see M. G. Iodice, "Il Cardinale Francesco Barberini," thesis, Università degli Studi di Roma, 1964–1965 (copy in BAV).

[7] W. Reinhard, "Nepotismus: Der Funktionswandel einer papstgeschichtlichen Konstanten," *Zeitschrift für Kirchengeschichte* (1975), 86:145–85. For a detailed account of nepotism as it developed in the sixteenth century, B. M. Hallman, *Italian Cardinals, Reform, and the Church as Property* (Berkeley, 1985).

[8] M. Laurain-Portemer, "Absolutisme et népotisme: la surintendance de l'état ecclésiastique," *Bibliothèque de l'Ecole des Chartes* (1973), 131:489. For a restatement of the classic defense of nepotism, see G. Moroni Romani, *Dizionario di erudizione storico-ecclesiastica* (Venice,

1840–1861), 51:163–74, and W. Felten, "Nepotismus," in *Wetzer und Welte's Kirchenlexikon* (Freiburg-im-Breisgau, 1882–1901), 9:101–54, esp. 101–9.

[9] BAV, Barb. Lat. 4737, 755r–56r.

[10] Ranke, *History of the Popes*, 3:11–19; Reinhard, "Nepotismus," esp. 171; V. Reinhardt, *Kardinal Scipione Borghese (1605–1633): Vermögen, Finanzen und sozialer Aufsteig eines Papstnepoten* (Tübingen, 1984), 1–2, 117–19, 133–36; L. Nussdorfer, "City Politics in Baroque Rome: 1623–1644," Ph.D. diss., Princeton University, 1985, 154.

[11] See the comments of G. Schwaiger, "Nepotismus," in *LTK*, 7: col. 879.

For their part, the new pope and his family would strive to convince the world of the God-given nature of their good fortune. In this they were aided by the theory behind the conclaves, which allowed that the hand of God controlled the proceedings and that, however mysterious the outcome, the final choice was a matter of divine election. A whole new electoral system was put into effect for the first time in the conclave of 1623, which unexpectedly elevated Maffeo Barberini to the pontificate. He emerged from the conclave more the product of a truly elective system than had any previous pontiff. The theme of divine election—not only for the pope but also for his entire family—thus became a central subject in Barberini family iconography. The Barberini saw themselves as having been literally elected by God to rule the Church and the Papal States.

In this system of beliefs astrological practice was an important component. For seventeenth-century observers the movement of the heavenly spheres constituted nothing less than the open book of divine providence, revealing to humankind God's intentions in all matters mundane. Some popes retained astrologers to advise them on the most favorable moments for taking important actions and convening ecclesiastical bodies.[12] In art they celebrated as signs of divine favor the dominant astrological features of their natal and election charts. Cardinals, too, took care to have their nativities interpreted, always with an eye to discerning in advance what providence might have in store for them.

Since the death of a reigning pope usually produced a radical redistribution of offices and wealth, the length of a pontificate and the identity of the successor provided occasion for speculation, much of it based on astrological prognostications. The nephews of popes and cardinals, especially, concerned themselves with the destinies of their uncles, and rarely resisted the temptation to turn to astrology for some indication of future events. These were matters of high office, political power, and great wealth. And, because of the elective nature of the papal throne, even the most coveted destiny was potentially open to individuals and families of varied background and social status. In the heavens one could perhaps find indication of impending good fortune or, after the fact, evidence of divine sanction for one's exalted station. Nepotism fueled the practice of astrology in Baroque Rome, particularly, as we shall see, during the Barberini pontificate.

The death of a pope and the election of his successor encompassed not only the collapse of old fortunes and the acquisition of new ones but also, inextricably, the eclipse of one papal family and the exaltation of another. In this arena the nouveaux riches families and the older families they threatened to surpass, especially, regarded matters of social and political prestige with the highest degree of seriousness. Inflation of titles and disputes over precedence caused much concern during Urban's reign. The pope raised all cardinals to the rank just below that of kings and declared that henceforth they should be addressed "Eminence."[13] The decree occasioned some protest and considerable grumbling, since individuals with little or no claim to noble birthright now attained the status of princes—among them three Barberini cardinals who with one stroke thereby neutralized the claims of the more nobly born

[12] Paul III Farnese, for example, relied on the famous astrologer Luca Gaurico for such guidance. Pastor, *History of the Popes*, 11:38–39, and n. 4.

[13] Decree dated 14 May 1630. Ibid., 29:160–162; Gigli, *Diario romano*, 113, 115; P. Brayda di Soleto, "Il titolo di eminenza ai cardinali ed i Duchi di Savoia (tre documenti inediti del 1630)," *Bollettino storico-bibliografico subalpino* 24 (1922), 230–50, esp. 239–40, discusses the social implications of the decree.

cardinals and also trumped the pretensions of the old ducal families. The obsession over issues of rank was so pervasive it even appears in the pages of Cesare Ripa's popular iconographic handbook, the *Iconologia*, where the personifed figure of Precedence and Preeminence of Titles deflects the advances of an overambitious eagle who aspires to displace the Kingbird seated on her head (Fig. 114).[14] Urban's secular nephew, Taddeo, was particularly enmeshed in such disputes over precedence and titles.

Matters of rank and social prestige precipitated the War of Castro (1641–1644) with the Farnese and brought the Barberini papacy to an inglorious conclusion.[15] A new family aspiring to establish itself within the ranks of the exalted could choose no finer example than the one set by the Farnese, and Urban evidently regarded Paul III Farnese (1534–1549) as a role model in his campaign to empower his own family, as the pope acknowledged symbolically by repositioning the tomb of the Farnese pope in the left niche of the tribune of St. Peter's, just opposite the niche he planned for his own tomb.[16] Paul III provided his family with the highest offices at his disposal, appointing family members to the cardinalate and to the generalship of the papal army. As a symbol of worldly glory, he left behind Palazzo Farnese, one of the grandest monuments of post-antique Rome (Fig. 115). But most remarkable of all, from the patrimony of St. Peter he carved out lands over which he made his son, Pierluigi, duke, thus ensuring a permanent power base for his descendants.

Castro, one of the Farnese possessions held as a papal fief on the northern edge of the Papal States, ultimately became vulnerable because of its ambiguous legal status and because of Farnese financial difficulties. The Barberini nephews, with Urban's backing, at first sought to gain this territory for themselves by negotiating a marriage alliance with Duke Odoardo Farnese. When informed that the duke had no intention of marrying his family into the vulgar classes, the Barberini turned to more coercive means. The costly war that followed was seen by all sides as a disastrous manifestation of nepotism at its worst, a private concern of the Barberini family to which the pope had illegitimately committed the resources of the papacy.[17] When Odoardo invaded the Papal States with the backing of a league of Italian princes, he proclaimed that he had no quarrel with the people, or even with the pope, but that he sought only to punish the Barberini nephews for their arrogance.[18] The most successful nepotic family of the sixteenth century thus confronted the Tuscan newcomers.

The Barberini met with more opposition to their enterprise of aggrandizement than did many other similarly positioned families of the period. This resulted from the excessive length—by papal standards—of Urban's reign. Gigli lamented that Urban had lived so long, for if he had reigned for only fourteen or fifteen years, instead of twenty-one, he would have been remembered as a good and even great pope. As it happened, when Urban died on 29 July 1644—broken, it was said, by the humiliation he had suffered at the hands of the

[14] C. Ripa, *Della più che novissima iconologia . . .* (Padua, 1630), 583.

[15] G. DeMaria, "La Guerra di Castro e la spedizione de' presidii," in *Miscellanea di storia patria*, ser. 3, 4 (35) (1983), 200.

[16] Paul's tomb, designed by Guglielmo Della Porta (1551–1575), was moved in 1628–1629 from the crossing of the basilica when Bernini began reorganizing the pier niches. O. Pollak, *Die Kunsttätigkeit unter Urban VIII.* (Vienna, 1928, 1931), 2:589.

[17] L. Grottanelli, "Il Ducato di Castro: i Farnesi ed i Barberini," *La rassegna nazionale* 56 (1890), 476–504, 824–838; 57 (1891), 58–75, 554–585, 793–817; 58 (1891), 261–89; F. Borri, *Odoardo Farnese e i Barberini nella Guerra di Castro* (Parma, 1933), esp. 11–12.

[18] Ranke, *History of the Popes*, 3:23–24.

Farnese—and word of his death spread to the city, there was jubilation, and Bernini's monumental statue of the pope located on the Campidoglio narrowly escaped the wrath of the populace. The Barberini were now called the "Barbari."[19]

[19] Gigli, *Diario romano*, 252–54.

PART I

• The Patron and the Painted Ceiling

CHAPTER I

• The Art and Ideology of the Painted Ceiling

IN BAROQUE ROME art and architecture were signs of social status and political power. In order to demonstrate their rightful position in Roman society the Barberini therefore needed to build a larger and more opulently decorated palace than the one they possessed at the time of Urban's election, the Casa Grande in the Via de' Giubbonari (Fig. 116). This was to be accomplished not without reference to the nearby palace of their most admired rivals, the Farnese, designed by Antonio da Sangallo and Michelangelo (Fig. 115). Thus the Barberini soon acquired property on the slope of the Quirinal near the crossing of the Four Fountains, and a great architectural and pictorial project was initiated (Figs. 1–2). Palazzo Barberini became the principal monument of Roman Baroque nepotism, and critics of the period, inveighing against material ostentation, recognized it as such: "The palaces, for example that at the Four Fountains [which is] a royal work, the vineyards, the pictures, the statues, the wrought silver and gold, the precious stones, [all] heaped on that family, are of more amount than can be believed or expressed."[1] The indignant author might also have added to his list the ceiling paintings of the palace, for few manifestations of Barberini patronage reflected more directly the nepotism and social agenda of the family. The ensemble of painted vaults in Palazzo Barberini surpassed in number, extent, and programmatic purpose that of all other secular palaces in Rome.

The patronage of innovative works of art is a significant factor in gaining social prestige. In this regard, the Barberini were at the vanguard, seeking novelties, yet without neglecting tradition. Such is the hallmark of Barberini patronage, particularly in iconographic matters. As a poet himself, Urban encouraged every sort of literary endeavor that might add luster to his pontificate and to his family. While other families were content with pedestrian history scenes and clichéd personifications pilfered from Ripa for the walls and vaults of their palaces, the literary minions of the Barberini came forward with fresh allegorical programs based on exalted theological, astrological, and poetic conceits as ideological support for social and political preeminence. Themes unprecedented in secular palace decoration, such as Divine Wisdom, Divine Providence, and the Creation of the Angels, took pictorial form on the vaults of the Barberini Palace. The papal nephews commissioned the most sought-after architects, sculptors, and painters of the period to work at Palazzo Barberini to make visible these elevated conceptions. Carlo Maderno, Francesco Borromini, Gian Lorenzo Bernini, Pietro da Cortona, and Andrea Sacchi all worked on the new palace. For Sacchi and Cortona the commissions resulted in masterworks unparalleled elsewhere in their oeuvres.

The seventeenth century was the great age of the painted ceiling, and the Barberini

---

[1] "Conclave di Innocenzo X," BAV, Vat. Lat. 8781. Quoted in Ranke, *History of the Popes*, 3:17. The manuscript appears to date 1644, at the height of anti-Barberini sentiment.

contributed significantly to this phenomenon. Even the ceiling of Urban's ceremonial carriage was painted. There appeared a heavenly vision: the Dove of the Holy Spirit descending through clouds amid a burst of light.[2] More than any papal family before them, the Barberini exploited the surface of the vaults of their palace as a place for declaring to the world their high station. More than any previous cycle of ceiling paintings in a secular palace of Rome, that of the Barberini Palace made full use of the elevated position of the imagery for the expression of supramundane themes. That the fresco cycle of Palazzo Barberini embellishes the ceilings rather than the walls is integral to the message being conveyed to the visitor. In the celestial realm of the stars, in particular, the papal family saw proof of their divine election, and they sought to express God's sanction of their worldly status in the artificial heavens of their palatial chambers.

CONVENTIONS OF ITALIAN BAROQUE CEILING PAINTING

Our understanding of the imagery of these vaults thus rests on a conjunction of phenomena: the elective nature of the papacy, the ascendancy of nepotism, the uses of judicial astrology, and the exploitation of the painted ceiling as an ideal vehicle for political persuasion. Only through knowledge of the formal conventions of Baroque ceiling painting can we appreciate the unity of form and content displayed on the vaults of Palazzo Barberini. In retrospect these conventions may be seen as a set of mostly unstated principles operative in the aesthetic and iconographic decision-making processes followed by painters and patrons. Because of the practical, commonsense nature of the conventions, they were never set down in formulaic expression, yet study of major cycles of ceiling paintings in Baroque Italy indicates the efficacy of certain assumed guidelines. It is possible to deduce these from an analysis of the visual evidence and thereby reconstruct the assumptions that underlie the ceiling paintings of this epoch. The identification and enumeration of these conventions will provide a system and analytical procedure for the study of the ceiling paintings of Palazzo Barberini.

Each commission for the decoration of a ceiling gave rise to a unique set of problems according to the physical matrix of the painting. For this reason not all of the conventions were fully applicable in every instance, although they seem to have been the preferred ideal in the majority of cases. The essential fact that underlies all five conventions is an awareness of the architectural context of ceiling paintings and the function of the space they cover.[3] In

[2] The gilder Simone Lagi, who later worked at Palazzo Barberini, in 1624 received 250 scudi for gilding the coach and providing it with a ceiling depicting "the Holy Spirit with clouds of ground silver and with its rays roundabout." Payment document cited in E. Bonomelli, *I papi in campagna* (Rome, 1935), 64, n. 8. For seventeenth-century Roman monetary denominations, see Appendix A.

[3] P. Mora, L. Mora, and P. Philippot, *Conservation of Wall Paintings* (London, 1984), 1–7. Evaluation of the architectural context is the methodological sine qua non for the study of ceiling and mural painting. This fact has been explored in the recent studies of Cortona

by L. Kugler, *Studien zur Malerei und Architektur von Pietro Berrettini da Cortona: Versuch einer gattungsübergreifenden Analyse zum Illusionismus im römischen Barock* (Essen, 1985), and idem, "Zum Verhältnis von Malerei und Architektur in den Deckenfresken von Pietro (Berrettini) da Cortona," in *Studien zu Renaissance und Barock: Manfred Wundram zum 60. Geburtstag*, eds. M. Hesse and M. Imdahl (Frankfurt, 1986), 149–76. In a forthcoming study, M. A. Lavin [*The Place of Narrative: Mural Decoration in Italian Churches 431–1600* (Chicago, 1990)] has undertaken a quantitative computer-aided analysis of the disposition of narrative scenes in Italian mural painting.

the publication of scholarly studies of ceiling paintings, photographers and publishers have often seen fit to trim away every vestige of unsightly cornice or wall that might suggest the architectural setting of the imagery. Thus we are confronted with illustrations of ceiling paintings disembodied from their spatial context and made to appear as though they were easel paintings that happened to be inconveniently affixed to unseen vaults.[4] The present study will seek to avoid this misrepresentation and will attempt to convey some of the actual on-site spatial and temporal experience of overhead imagery. Investigation of the conventions of ceiling painting is also a means to assist us in looking at ceiling painting as a unique mode of pictorial expression.[5]

1. Programmatic Unity

The rooms of princely palaces like Palazzo Barberini were divided and grouped into various apartments according to the number and rank of the occupants. Series of ceiling paintings were conceived according to each independent apartment grouping. Consequently, artists and their patrons tended to think of ceiling paintings in such contexts, not just in terms of a succession of totally independent works, but as an ensemble. This was true even when the decorative project involved a number of different artists. Patrons often chose subject series such as the seasons, the elements, the virtues, or the planets—themes that provided sufficient subject material for three, four, five, or seven successive rooms according to the size of the apartment.[6]

2. Ideal Station Point

Formulating it as a general rule of Baroque ceiling painting, Wolfgang Schöne has demonstrated the validity of Hans Posse's neglected observation, made in 1919, that Cortona's Barberini salone ceiling must be seen at an oblique angle for its illusionism to be fully effective.[7] This means that the ideal point of view is in the vicinity of the main entrances. The principle can be observed by comparing a photograph of the fresco seen from directly below (Fig. 80), as are almost all published examples of the work, with an oblique-angle view (Colorplate III and Fig. 104). In Fig. 80, all imagery in the ceiling is flattened out onto a two-dimensional plane, while in the angle view the central figure of Divine Providence seems to rise up on a plane perpendicular to the floor and illusionistically penetrate the horizontal plane of the vault.[8] Artists designed their ceiling paintings with the position of the viewer in

[4] See the complaint of E. H. Gombrich, *Means and Ends: Reflections on the History of Fresco Painting* (London, 1976), 11.

[5] This endeavor was first undertaken by W. Mrazek, "Ikonologie der barocken Deckenmalerei," *Österreichische Akademie der Wissenschaften, philosophisch-historische Klasse, Sitzungsberichte* 228 (1953), 1–88, esp. 71–75, basing his analysis primarily on eighteenth-century French and German sources.

[6] In churches of the period this convention of ceiling painting takes the form of spatial and narrative connections between the various component divisions of the vault: nave, dome, and apse semi-dome.

[7] W. Schöne, "Zur Bedeutung der Schrägsicht für die Deckenmalerei des Barock," in *Festschrift Kurt Badt* (Berlin, 1961), 154–56; H. Posse, "Das Deckenfresko des Pietro da Cortona im Palazzo Barberini und die Deckenmalerei in Rom," *Jahrbuch der Preussischen Kunstsammlungen* 40 (1919), 117–18.

[8] In illusionistic ceilings where extensive use is made of fictive architecture (*quadratura*), the ideal station point for the viewer can be either at point of entry or directly beneath the center of the vault. The latter case can be seen in the well-known example of Pozzo's *Triumph of St. Ignatius*, where a marble disk marks the point in the center of the nave from which the spatial illusionism of the vault fresco is most effective. When the viewer moves away from this location, the *quadra-*

mind, and a correct reading of the spatial dynamics of the imagery will depend on an appreciation of this convention.

The location of windows represents a secondary factor that, in addition to point of entry, must frequently have affected the artist's choice in orienting the imagery. Ideal circumstances presupposed outside windows providing light from the viewer's back or side at the point of entry, thus allowing fullest illumination of the painted surface. Actual circumstances, however, sometimes prevented this or required a compromise arrangement.

3. Decorum

The subject matter of ceiling paintings was chosen for its appropriateness to the social station of the patrons, type of building, function of the room, and overhead location of the imagery.

The sixteenth-century theoreticians Armenini and Lomazzo advised artists to take into consideration the social status of the patron and function of the room in choosing themes for the decoration of palace walls and the ceilings.[9] For example, the scenes appropriate for the palace of a secular prince might not be suitable for the palace of a cardinal. The imagery of the apartments of noblewomen was of a distinct character from that of their husbands.

Building type was also an important consideration with regard to decorum. Villas and garden casinos have a different, less formal order of subject matter than urban palaces.

The rule of decorum also suggests that the iconography of a ceiling painting should reflect the specific function of the room. Audience halls and bedchambers have very different functions, and they require different types of pictorial themes.

Status of patron, building type, and function of room are three aspects of the rule of decorum applicable no less to mural painting than to ceilings, but the fourth item under this convention is unique to ceiling imagery. This aspect might be designated *di sotto in su* iconography. Subject matter appropriate to elevated placement dominates the painted ceilings of the late Renaissance and Baroque.[10] This might seem obvious when the treatment

---

tura architecture warps and the illusion of spatial depth dissipates. In this case the point of entry and the ideal station point are divergent. See the discussion of B. Kerber, *Andrea Pozzo* (Berlin, 1971), 94–98, and I. Sjöström, *Quadratura: Studies in Italian Ceiling Painting* (Stockholm, 1978), 64–67. On the history of *quadratura* painting, E. Guldan, *Die jochverschleifende Gewölbedekoration von Michelangelo bis Pozzo . . .* (Göttingen, 1954); R. Horstmann, *Die Entstehung der perspektivischen Deckenmalerei* (Munich, 1965); and F. De' Maffei, "Perspectivists," in *Encyclopedia of World Art* (New York, 1966), 11:221–43. For illusionism in general in Italian Baroque ceiling painting, N. Spinosa, "Spazio infinito e decorazione barocca," in *Storia dell'arte italiana dal cinquecento all'ottocento: cinquecento e seicento*, ed. P. Fossati (Turin, 1981), 1:278–343.

[9] G. P. Lomazzo, *Trattato dell'arte de la pittura* (Milan, 1584), 342–51 (bk. 6, chaps. 23–24); G. B. Armenini, *De' veri precetti della pittura* (Ravenna, 1587), 148–52, 167–89, 197–201 (bk. 3). Earlier formulations of the rule of decorum in relation to the pictorial imagery of palaces can be seen in the treatise of Paolo

Cortesi (published 1510) on the cardinalate and in the theoretical writings of Alberti. K. Weil-Garris and J. F. D'Amico, "The Renaissance Cardinal's Ideal Palace: A Chapter from Cortesi's *De Cardinalatu*," in *Studies in Italian Art and Architecture 15th through 18th Centuries*, *Memoirs of the American Academy in Rome* 35 (1980), 91–97; L. B. Alberti, *On Painting and On Sculpture*, trans. C. Grayson (London, 1972), 73–77. The concept apparently derives from a passage in Vitruvius, *The Ten Books on Architecture*, trans. M. H. Morgan (Cambridge, Mass., 1914 [rpt. 1960]), 210–11 (bk. 7, chap. 5, pars. 1–2). On the theory of decorum, see the discussion in E. H. Gombrich, "Aims and Limits of Iconology," in *Symbolic Images* (Oxford, 1972), 7–11.

[10] Leonardo had earlier identified the problem when he complained that too often artists paint mural narrative scenes in registers without regard for the angle of view of the observer standing within the space of the room. Leonardo da Vinci, *Treatise on Painting*, ed. A. P. McMahon (Princeton, 1956), no. 265, as analyzed in Gombrich (1976), 10–11.

calls for a miraculous illusionistic scene open to the sky, such as Apollo in the chariot of the sun, but it is also often true when the subject is treated as a simple easel painting or *quadro riportato*. This can be seen in Camassei's *Creation of the Angels* in Palazzo Barberini, a work that has little illusionism but nevertheless still depicts a celestial event appropriate to overhead placement (Fig. 59).

4. Heraldic Concetto

Emblematic of aristocratic pedigree and social status, heraldry was in the Baroque period held to be a matter of utmost importance. In the palaces of the early Renaissance sculpted coats of arms adorn the crowns of the vaults of important rooms, announcing the family of owner and occupant. By the late sixteenth and early seventeenth centuries, when painted ceilings had become more common in secular palaces, the arms and family imprese merge with the pictorial field. The salone ceiling of Palazzo Barberini represents the culmination of this development, where the bees from the family coat of arms appear flying across the open sky above the viewer's head.[11]

5. Optical Persuasion

This convention is the most subjective of the group, but no less operative in Roman Baroque ceiling painting. Historians have largely ignored the relationship between spatial illusionism and the subject content of ceiling painting, as though trompe l'oeil display carried no significance beyond titillation of the beholder's visual perception.[12] But optical deception could also be used for purposes of intellectual persuasion, and the artists of the Roman Baroque appreciated this potential. The precedent was Correggio's dome paintings in Parma, especially for the cathedral (1524–1530) (Fig. 158). There the artist sought to convince the worshiper of the reality of the miracle of the Assumption by painting away the real architecture and replacing it with a cloud-borne vision of radically foreshortened figures. In the squinches beneath the dome he depicted figures descending on clouds, who thus appear to enter the actual space of the viewer to become reality. The optical persuasiveness of the painted imagery metaphorically reinforces the viewer's intellectual acceptance of the Assumption as an actual historical event. Equating illusionism and verisimilitude, and citing the example of Correggio, Cortona makes the same point in his treatise when discussing the persuasive power of painting: "by deceiving the spectator, the power of fictive representation triumphs."[13] For the artist, the power to sway validates illusionism.

No schematic system such as this enumeration of conventions can ever be more than an oversimplification of actual practice. Exceptions abound. One must keep in mind that, according to the exigencies of a given artistic problem, some conventions may have taken pre-

[11] The heraldic concetto is no less applicable to the ceiling paintings of churches than to those in secular palaces. The heraldry of the institutional patron or the attributes of the titular saint serve as readily as any family shield as the point of departure for large-scale iconographic programs. The nave paintings of Gaulli at Il Gesù and Pozzo at S. Ignazio, where the heraldry and name of both the society and its founder are fun-

damental to the imagery, demonstrate the continuing validity of this convention.

[12] Spinosa's comments ("Spazio infinito," 290–94) on "Barocco e propaganda" are exceptionally to the point.

[13] G. D. Ottonelli and P. Berrettini, *Trattato della pittura e scultura uso et abuso loro*, ed. V. Casale (Treviso, 1973), 22–25.

cedence over others. Not all the conventions were operative at all times. They were thus quite malleable, with artists and patrons opting for solutions that would reflect their primary concerns. These qualifications notwithstanding, the system of re-created conventions can work to the benefit of the historian in providing a useful, if imperfect, methodological guideline to help penetrate the complexities of Baroque ceiling painting. For the immediate task, it will enable us to see and understand the painted ceilings of Palazzo Barberini afresh, in the manner anticipated by the patrons and artists who conceived and executed them.

PALAZZO BARBERINI, "A ROYAL WORK": PATRONS AND DESIGN (1627–1632)

In December 1625 Cardinal Francesco Barberini purchased the Sforza Palace and surrounding land on the northern slope of the Quirinal Hill, giving it to his younger brother Taddeo in January of the following year.[14] Taddeo was the logical titleholder because he had been chosen from among the pope's nephews, sons of Carlo Barberini, to be responsible for the continuation of the family name. These two figures, Taddeo and Francesco, one a secular and the other an ecclesiastical member of the family, were the most important patrons for the massive building program and decoration of the enlarged new palace, which began in 1627. If the hand of Urban could be seen intervening from afar, Taddeo and Francesco were the participants most immediately involved in design decisions at the newly acquired palace near the Four Fountains and the Quirinal Palace, summer residence of the popes.[15]

The earliest Barberini documents associated with the property date July and September 1626 and indicate that at first the new owners were satisfied with cosmetic alterations such as the whitewashing of walls and the changing and adding of coats of arms.[16] The heraldic shields of the Sforza cardinals in the corners of the room painted with the story of Joseph (Fig. 3, Palazzo Barberini Nobile 13), for example, were overpainted at this time with the devices of the Barberini cardinals, Francesco and Antonio the Elder, as can be seen in pre-restoration photographs (Fig. 18). The crossed arms of Christ and St. Francis, emblem of the Capuchin Order, positioned above the bees, distinguish the escutcheon of Cardinal Antonio from that of his nephew. With the marriage of Taddeo in 1627 and the appointment in 1628 of yet another Barberini cardinal, Antonio the Younger, it became evident that the small undistinguished structure on the Quirinal and the old family dwelling, the characterless Casa Grande ai Giubbonari (Fig. 116), were inadequate to the size and status of the papal family.[17] Grandiose plans began to emerge.

All early designs for Palazzo Barberini incorporate the old Palazzo Sforza into the

---

[14] Pollak, *Die Kunsttätigkeit*, 1:251–55; P. Waddy, "The Design and Designers of Palazzo Barberini," *Journal of the Society of Architectural Historians* 35 (1976), 154, n. 11.

[15] P. Waddy, *Seventeenth-Century Roman Palaces: Use and the Art of the Plan* (New York, 1990), 131, 179–80, 201–2.

[16] BAV, Arch. Barb., Giust. 501–625, 218r-v, 262r-v; BAV, Arch. Barb., Comp. 49, 130v (LM); BAV, Arch. Barb., Comp. 66, 133r (gior.). All pay-

ments are made by Cardinal Francesco. For a discussion of the Barberini household account books (types of documents, reliability, and usefulness), see F. Hammond, "Girolamo Frescobaldi and a Decade of Music in Casa Barberini: 1634–1643," *Analecta Musicologica* 19 (1980), 100.

[17] On the history of the Casa Grande, purchased in 1581 by Urban's uncle, Monsignor Francesco Barberini, see Waddy, *Seventeenth-Century Roman Palaces*, 132–72.

fabric of the new edifice. Some of these designs took the form of drawings, plans, and written suggestions made by amateurs such as Michelangelo Buonarroti the Younger.[18] Maderno produced a working plan and some basic ideas for the elevation before his death in 1629. Bernini, with the technical assistance of Maderno's protégé, Borromini, carried the project to completion, but not without some significant contributions by Cortona.[19] The patrons, too, actively participated in the design process. Francesco reports in his biography of the younger brother that Taddeo provided some fundamental design elements for the palace and was daily on site to oversee the construction and make immediate design decisions.[20] The unusual building that emerged from this collaborative effort expressed to contemporaries the new wealth and status of the papal family. As a contemporary critic complained, the Barberini Palace was "a royal work."[21]

The plan and elevation of the palace embody the two spheres within which the ambitions of the Barberini were manifested: the secular and the ecclesiastical (Figs. 1–3). The Sforza Palace was absorbed into the design to become the north (left) wing of the new structure. To the south, farther up the slope of the hill, an entirely new wing paralleled the old building, while a great recessed central block linked the two wings to form an H-shaped configuration. The older north wing contained the apartments of the secular members of the family, and the south wing would house the ecclesiastics. Taddeo himself contributed this fundamental idea to the design.[22] The vaulted salone of the central block (Fig. 3, PBN 2) served the two wings in common. This great hall, the largest in the palace, functioned as a *sala dei palafrenieri* or guardroom through which all visitors to the piano nobile apartments passed, whether they had business in the north or the south wing. Normally the visitor would ascend the square stairs on the left (PBN S1) and arrive at the salone by way of the vestibule (PBN 1).[23]

The elliptical stairs on the right (PBN S2) could also be climbed to arrive at the same destination, but this was more often used by visitors intending to proceed directly to the salotto (PBN 20) or to the library on the upper floor. In the ecclesiastical wing, rooms (PBN 20–26 and 27–31) formed the two main apartments for cardinals (one with a southern exposure for the winter months and the other facing east). These apartments were not adorned with ceiling imagery until beginning in the mid-1640s. Anna Colonna, Taddeo's wife, was to occupy the main apartment on the piano nobile of the north wing (PBN 3–11), while Taddeo himself lived in the comparable suite of rooms on the ground floor below (Fig. 5, Palazzo Barberini Terreno 3–11).[24] These two apartments of the north wing contain the major ensembles of ceiling paintings dating from the seventeenth century.

[18] P. Waddy, "Palazzo Barberini: Early Projects," Ph.D. diss., New York University, 1973; idem, "Design and Designers," and idem, "Michelangelo Buonarroti the Younger, Sprezzatura, and Palazzo Barberini," *Architectura* 5 (1975), 101–22.

[19] A. Blunt, "The Palazzo Barberini: The Contributions of Maderno, Bernini, and Pietro da Cortona," *Journal of the Warburg and Courtauld Institutes* 21 (1958), 256–87; H. Thelen, *Francesco Borromini, die Handzeichnungen* (Graz, 1967), 1:54–78.

[20] "Descrittione della vita del sig.e d. Taddeo Barberini," BAV, Arch. Barb., Ind. IV, 1254, unpaged.

[21] BAV, Vat. Lat. 8781. Quoted in Ranke, *History of the Popes*, 3:7.

[22] P. Waddy, "Taddeo Barberini as a Patron of Architecture," in *L'âge d'or du mécénat (1598–1661)* (Paris, 1985), 191–94; idem, *Seventeenth-Century Roman Palaces*, 219–20, 228–29, 231.

[23] The numbering of the rooms in Figures 3, 5, 8, and 9 follows, within each apartment, the sequence in which they would be entered by a visitor to the palace. For the seventeenth-century Roman unit of measurement, see Appendix A.

[24] Construction documents designate Taddeo's level

The same principle of bipartition operative in the plan of the palace appears also in the facades. Just as the Barberini family had two branches, one secular and one ecclesiastical, so does Palazzo Barberini have two wings and two main facades—the loggia-like recessed main facade facing west and the re-articulated but still rather austere facade of what was Palazzo Sforza facing north. The arched opening at the base of the northern facade (Fig. 1) led up to a landing (Fig. 5, PBT 2) and thence to the guardroom of Taddeo's apartment (PBT 3). A central block with cryptoporticus and fictive loggia (Fig. 2, PBT 1) united the separate wings.

Taddeo's facade on the north, with its emphatic horizontality, alternating triangular and segmental window pediments, and central balcony with arms above and arched opening below, recalls the main facade of Palazzo Farnese—the largest urban palace of Renaissance Rome (Fig. 115). By contrast, the recessed western facade, with its forceful plasticity and superimposition of loggia-like openings and arched windows, reminds the viewer of papal structures such as the benediction loggia at St. Peter's (1461–1508, destroyed 1616) and Bramante's loggia of the Cortile di San Damaso at the Vatican Palace (Fig. 117).[25] The recessed window aediculae flanking the frontispiece of the western facade were also inspired by those on Maderno's new facade at St. Peter's—and the massive papal coat of arms hanging in place above the central window on the piano nobile (Fig. 10) would serve as further stimuli for the recollection of papal monuments.[26] The balustraded balcony at the center of the facade seems to await the appearance of the Barberini pope. Thus the north and south wings—the secular and ecclesiastical components of the palace—unite in the central pontifical block.

The fresco cycles in the north wing and central salone, commissioned during the apogee of Urban's papacy and Barberini family fortunes, and modified by Cardinal Francesco in the 1670s, are the focus of the present study.[27] As an ensemble embellishing the newly aggrandized structure, the Barberini paintings, added to those preserved from the Sforza period, constituted the most extensive series of figural ceiling frescoes in Rome, excepting only that of the Vatican Palace (Figs. 4, 6). When the Barberini moved into their palace on the Quirinal in 1632, it contained twenty-three ceiling paintings, all of them in the north wing apartments of Taddeo and Anna. Completed in 1639, the last and largest of the group, Cortona's *Divine Providence* in the salone located at the core of the palace (PBN 2, Colorplate III, Fig. 80) became the principal pictorial component of the series as conceived in the period of the late 1620s and early 1630s. Surpassed in size only by Michelangelo's Sistine ceiling, the painted vault of the Barberini salone represented the most ambitious such enterprise undertaken in Rome since the time of Julius II. Among painted ceilings of secular palaces, it had no rival.

---

the "piano terreno nobile." Because the land sloped away on this side of the palace, there was yet another range of rooms beneath Taddeo's apartment. This lower floor thus became the true piano terreno of the north wing.

[25] Waddy, "Design and Designers," 176–77.

[26] The arms were sculpted by Agostino Radi. Payment of 216.90 scudi dated 6 July 1635. BAV, Arch. Barb., Comp. 68, 40 (gior., Card. Fran.). Taddeo's arms were to have been placed on the north facade, as indicated in the elevation drawing by Borromini. Thelen, *Francesco Borromini*, 74–75, cat. 63.

[27] The pictorial decoration of the south wing (PBN 21–26; PBT 23–28), accomplished mostly with canvas paintings of modest character, was not completed until the end of the century. It constitutes a less coherent statement of familial ambitions and falls outside the scope of the present study.

CHAPTER II

• The Painted Ceilings of Palazzo Sforza (1580–1612)

THE PALACE Francesco Barberini acquired in 1625 from the financially troubled Duke Alessandro Sforza already contained an ensemble of painted ceilings.[1] For the most part, however, it was a fragmentary and undistinguished group of works, the product of artists of conservative mind and modest talent. These works nevertheless serve to illustrate a characteristic approach to ceiling painting in Rome in the last decades of the sixteenth century and, by comparison, serve as an instructive foil for the formal and iconographic innovations of the later Barberini cycle. The Sforza and Barberini frescoes have a common denominator in that they reflect interests typical of noble families with ecclesiastical connections and conform to the conventions of ceiling painting. A brief examination of the ceilings from the Sforza period will therefore facilitate an analysis of the Barberini ceilings.

The new owners retained many of the older frescoes and took care to incorporate them into their own much more ambitious cycle of painted vaults. In some instances the Sforza imagery even influenced the Barberini in the choice of iconographic themes. Given our lack of precise documentary knowledge of the architectural history of the Sforza building, examination of the ceiling imagery will provide useful information about the genesis and development of the building up to the time of Barberini acquisition.[2]

The building and its painted ceilings appear to date from three distinct campaigns. The single ceiling surviving from the period of the earliest Sforza owner, Cardinal Alessandro (d. 1581),[3] is a modest and poorly preserved fresco divided into nine sections by prominent stucco enframements (Figs. 11–12). The painting, originally located in one of the rooms of the eastern arm of the palace (not on plan), was shifted in 1936 when this part of the building underwent reorganization as commercial offices.[4] The image of the central panel, the *Virgin Immaculate*, is stylistically close to the work of Antonio Tempesta ca. 1580.[5] The

[1] H. Hibbard, *Carlo Maderno and Roman Architecture, 1580–1630* (London, 1971), 222–23, summarizes the history of the property. Also, Waddy, "Palazzo Barberini," 7–8; Waddy, "Design and Designers," 152–56; C. Hülsen, *Römische Antikengärten des XVI. Jahrhunderts* (Heidelberg, 1917), 43–84; D. R. Coffin, *The Villa in the Life of Renaissance Rome* (Princeton, 1979), 195–200; S. Eiche, "Cardinal Giulio della Rovere and the Villa Carpi," *Journal of the Society of Architectural Historians* 45 (1986), 115–33.

[2] The lack of accessibility and disorder of the Sforza archive in Rome have long hampered the study of Sforza patronage. Until such time as the present conditions are corrected, we must rely on evidence intrinsic to the building, but much can be deduced from a direct study of the ceiling paintings.

[3] Cardinal Alessandro had acquired the property, known as the Villa Carpi, from Giulio della Rovere, the cardinal of Urbino, in 1578. Hibbard, *Carlo Maderno*, 223; Waddy, "Design and Designers," 153–54; Coffin, *The Villa in the Life of Renaissance Rome*, 199–200.

[4] The Società Finanziaria Marittima (Finmare). I owe this information to Avvocato Trizza of Finmare. See also Blunt, "The Palazzo Barberini" 257, n. 6.

[5] The figure style is particularly close to Tempesta's contemporaneous (1580–1585) fresco work in S. Stefano Rotondo. For comparative illustrations of the documented work there, see A. Vannugli, "Gli affreschi di Antonio Tempesta a S. Stefano Rotondo e l'emblematica nella cultura del martirio presso la Compagnia di Gesù," *Storia dell'arte* 48 (1983), 101–16.

surrounding landscape scenes depicting the Church Fathers traditionally associated with Marian theology[6] and the biblical narratives alluding to the iconography of the Virgin[7] suggest the intervention of a Flemish landscapist collaborator.[8] The four Old Testament prefiguration scenes in the side compartments—the *Moses and the Burning Bush*, the *Crushing of the Serpent*, the *Dream of Nebuchadnezzar*, and the *Jael and Sisera*—pertain to the iconography of the Virgin Immaculate (Fig. 12).[9] The lion heads, an emblem of Sforza patronage, appear on the tent of Jael in the compartment to the right of the Virgin, and the lone standing column on the right of the same scene must refer to the virtue of Fortitude as exemplified by Jael's action. This, too, was a favored Sforza symbol alluding to the strength implied in the family name. Although Sforza patronage of the *Virgin Immaculate* is secure, the painting exhibits a formal and conceptual character different from all other ceiling frescoes in the palace. The simple design of the ceiling, the use of prominent stucco moldings to isolate each of the individual scenes, and the unusual treatment of Marian iconography have no parallel in any of the other Sforza ceilings and may suggest the cardinal's involvement with the work.

Different in character from the *Virgin Immaculate* ceiling, the vault fresco in the room at what was then the extreme western end of this same range of rooms (Fig. 8, Palazzo Sforza Nobile 6) seems to have been executed by a different team of artists (Figs. 13–14). The landscape scenes again display a generic Flemish heritage, but the views of ruins and distant cities are richer in detail and the vegetation more delicate and willowy. Here only the central *quadro riportato* is surrounded by a stucco enframement, whereas the cove sections are entirely in fresco, with fictive frames and thrones for the landscapes and sibyls. The elaborate grotesque work of the subsidiary spaces and panels contains the heraldic Sforza lions and quince fruit, giving the ceiling an exuberant quality not present in the more sober *Virgin Immaculate*.

By the time the Barberini acquired Palazzo Sforza, the central section of this fresco had already fallen from its stucco enframement, and the new owners commissioned Giovanni Domenico Marziani ("Il Maltese") to fill the empty space with a depiction of the *Nativity*.[10]

---

[6] Ambrose, Augustine, Jerome, and Gregory. See M. Levi d'Ancona, *The Iconography of the Immaculate Conception in the Middle Ages and Early Renaissance* (New York, 1957), 11, 70.

[7] The scenes of *Jael and Sisera* (Judges 4:12–24) and the *Crushing of the Serpent* illustrate Genesis 3:14–15, where God condemns the serpent for its role in the Fall: "Thou art cursed among all cattle, and beasts of the earth . . . I will put enmities between thee and the woman, and thy seed and her seed: she shall crush thy head, and thou shalt lie in wait for her heel." *Moses and the Burning Bush* (Exodus 3:2–6) symbolizes the Virgin's purity, for the bush burned, yet was not consumed. The *Dream of Nebuchadnezzar* (Daniel 2:31–35) depicts the Babylonian king's vision of a great statue that was crushed by a massive stone cut without hands from a mountain. Daniel's interpretation of the dream (Daniel 2:36–45) foretold the destruction of the Babylonian Empire and its division into many smaller kingdoms, finally to be replaced by the kingdom of God, which would consume all others. The miraculous cutting of the monolith, without human hands, alludes to the Immaculate Conception.

[8] The background scenes of classical ruins recall the type of landscapes with ruins popularized in the 1550s by Hieronymus Cock's engraved views of Rome and might be tentatively ascribed to Lodovico Pozzoserrato (Lodewijck Toeput), who is known to have been working in Rome during the late 1570s. On Toeput, see H. G. Franz, *Niederländische Landschaftsmalerei im Zeitalter des Manierismus* (Graz, 1969), 303–5, pls. 456–57.

[9] Levi d'Ancona, *Iconography of the Immaculate Conception*, 67–68; L. Réau, *Iconographie de l'art chrétien* (Paris, 1955–1959), 2:pt. 2, 84–90.

[10] *Misura e stima* entry of 30 October 1631: "Stanza dov'era cascato la colla del quadro della volta dove sta dipinta la Natività di N.S. del Maltese. Per haver fatto il ponte per li pittori . . . sc. 2.50." BAV, Arch. Barb., Giust. 1726–1792, 115r (Card. Fran.). This document implies that Marziani's fresco was already in place at that time. Payment for unspecified work and a subven-

This replacement painting, too, later suffered collapse, but the new patrons and their artist had chosen a subject for the central rectangle that complemented the existing Sforza scenes. Old Testament kings and prophets in the landscape scenes and the sibyls enthroned in the corners hold tablets inscribed with their prophecies about the birth of the Messiah (Fig. 14). The landscape scene opposite the chapel door, for example, shows Solomon with Jerusalem and the temple in the background (Fig. 13). The inscribed tablet held by the king reads: SAPIENTIA AEDIFICAVIT SIBI DOMVM.[11]

This room served as the antechamber to the adjacent chapel (Fig. 8, PSN C1), and the central panel would originally have been oriented toward the chapel door in the north wall of the room. In both form and content the ceiling represents a departure from the esoteric iconography and relative austerity of the *Virgin Immaculate*. This turn toward extravagance may suggest a different group of artists as well as a different patron. The natal imagery is, moreover, typical of the family chapels of secular patrons concerned with paternity. Cardinal Alessandro's successor, Marchese Paolo Sforza (d. 1597), who inherited the villa upon the cardinal's death in 1581, was possibly the patron here.

Paolo's building activity greatly surpassed that of his predecessor. He added five major rooms (Fig. 8, PSN 1–5; Fig. 9, PST 1–5) to what had been little more than the elongated villa casino of the cardinal and thereby transformed the building into a true suburban palace.[12] Documents from the time when the Barberini acquired the palace indicate that the largest of these new rooms, the sala grande (PSN 1), had a vault with the Sforza coat of arms in the center.[13] The most opulent of the painted ceilings commissioned by Paolo covers the vault of the first antechamber of the new apartment suite (PSN 2). The painted grotesque

tion for a trip may include the *Nativity* as well as other fresco work executed by the artist for Cardinal Francesco on the ground floor of the palace (below, 37, 113–18): "A di 8 detto [maggio 1631] per conto di m.ta pagati come sopra s. Gio. Dom.co Martiali pittore per ricognitione di qnto ha fatto fin ora per S. Em.za e per souventione volont.ria d'un viaggio che gli deve fare sc. . . . 100." SCEP, Quaderno de' Sig.ri Barberini, 1631–1633, 44v (Card. Fran.). Wherever the journey may have taken the artist, he never returned to appear again in Barberini accounts. He also provided a lunette-shaped easel painting of the *Assumption* for the adjacent chapel when the Barberini had it redecorated. BAV, Barb. Lat. 5635, 67v (Card. Fran.) (M. A. Lavin, *Seventeenth-Century Barberini Documents and Inventories of Art* [New York, 1975], 115, no. 496. The only known surviving works by this artist are the *God the Father* and *Musical Angels* in the apse vault at S. Bibiana, 1624–1625 [Fig. 124]. G. Briganti, *Pietro da Cortona . . .* [Florence, 1982], 169–70).

[11] "Wisdom hath built herself a house" (Proverbs 9:11). King David appears in the end cove, holding the tablet IN SOLE POSVIT TABERNACVLVM SVVM, Psalm 18:6 ("He hath set his tabernacle in the sun"). On the opposite cove the Prophet Jeremiah's tablet reads NOVVM FACIET DOMINV[S] SVPER TER[RAM], Jeremiah 31:22 ("The Lord hath made a new thing upon the earth").

Opposite Solomon, the Prophet Isaiah holds an inscription of his chief prophecy, ECCE VIRGO CONCIPIET, ET PAR[IET] FI[LIVM], Isaiah 7:14 ("Behold, a virgin shall conceive, and bear a son"). The sibyls in the corner niches of the cove carry equally prophetic tablets: IN CERT INS VIRGIN[I]S ERIT SALVS GEN[I]TIVM (PERSICA); ECCE VENIET DIVES ET NAS[C]E[T]VR DE PAVPERCVLA ET BESTIE TERRARVM ADORABVNT EVM (SAMIA); DE OLIMPO EXCELSVS VENIET ET ANVNCIABITVR VIRGO IN VALIBVS DISERTOR [Phrigyca]; VIDEBVNT REGES GEN[TI]VM [Libyca]. The Persica's inscription appears corrupted as the result of a restoration. It should read: IN GREMIVM VIRGINIS. . . . X. Barbier de Montault, *Iconographie des sibylles* (Arras, 1874), 21–24; Réau, *Iconographie*, 2:pt. 1, 420–30.

[12] This construction was reported to be in progress in 1583, possibly with the design and direction by Giovanni and Domenico Fontana. M. Guidi, "I Fontana di Melide," *Roma* 6 (1928), 440; Waddy, "Design and Designers," 153–54, nn. 7–8.

[13] 11 October 1626 payment to Simone Lagi, gilder: "per la ramettatura dell'arme nella volta della sala grande nel palazzo alle quattro fontane rifattoci nello scudo l'arme di N.S.re e fuori rifattoci le chiavi con la mitra . . . sc. 15." BAV, Arch. Barb., Giust. 501–625, 262r.

work of this vault typifies sixteenth-century villa decoration as it devolved from the painted and stucco decoration of Raphael's Villa Madama, the landscape scenes decorously echoing the peaceful gardens that surrounded the villa.

The story of Joseph appears in the five narrative scenes, with the coats of arms of four Sforza cardinals in the corners flanked by personified virtues (Figs. 15–20). *Clemency* holds an open book with a page inscribed with the name of Baldassare Croce (Fig. 16),[14] but stylistic examination of the grotesque work, especially the landscape narratives, indicates that Croce was only one of a team of artists who worked here in a collaborative endeavor. The landscape background of the central scene (Fig. 17), particularly, shows the characteristic Flemish two-holed composition, with a central grouping of trees pushed forward near the middle of the composition creating two divergent perspective recessions—a structural device that can be seen in the work of sixteenth-century landscape painters working in the northern tradition.[15] The figures in the Joseph landscapes appear to have been painted by Nicolò Circignani ("Il Pomarancio"). They should be compared with his figures in the landscapes of the Torre dei Venti at the Vatican Belvedere, painted in 1580–1583 just prior to the work at Palazzo Sforza.[16] Many figures, landscape scenes, and details of grotesque work also resemble those in the frescoed vault of the gallery of Palazzo Giustiniani, where a team of artists led by Giovan Battista Ricci da Novara and Ludovico Lanzone worked between 1586 and 1587.[17] Some members of the group may have moved to the Giustiniani Palace from the Sforza project. Given that this part of the Sforza Palace was probably not finished prior to 1584, the Joseph fresco may be tentatively dated ca. 1585. Despite the arms of the cardinals, the crosses of the Order of the Knights of Calatrava, located in the corners of the vertical panels of grotesque work, make Paolo's patronage secure.[18]

Documents of the early Barberini period as well as pre-restoration photographs show that the new owners were content with simply overpainting the Sforza lions with their own heraldic devices (Fig. 18).[19] The shields of Cardinal Antonio Barberini the Elder (with the

[14] Ripa's formulation for *Clemency* (*Nova iconologia*, 83) recommends a female figure holding a legal record and canceling its pages with a pen. Croce changed the court document to an account book with separate entries divided by horizonal lines. The characteristic inverted triangle, the symbol for scudo, appears in the right column of each page. In addition to the artist's name, the words "Bologna"—Croce's native city—and "Palazzo Sforza" can be discerned. The Sforza ceiling is not mentioned by Croce's early biographers. G. Baglione, *Le Vite de' pittori, scultori et architetti* (Rome, 1642), 297–99; C. C. Malvasia, *Felsina pittrice* (Bologna, 1678–1679), 1:527–32; A. Bolognini Amorini, *Vite dei pittori ed artefici bolognesi* (Bologna, 1841–1843), 3:100–4. Croce's role in the Sforza fresco appears to have been limited to the eight personified virtues in the corners.

[15] Franz, *Niederländische Landschaftsmalerei*, 273–76.

[16] The mannered figures of Circignani, bending and swaying not always with evident purpose, appear in *Christ Calming the Storm* (with Paul Brill) in the Sala della Meridiana. The soft beards and compressed facial features characterize the figure style of the artist. P. I.

Stein, "La Sala della Meridiana nella Torre dei Venti in Vaticano," *L'illustrazione vaticana* 9 (1938), 405; F. Mancinelli and G. Casanovas, *La Torre dei Venti in Vaticano* (Vatican City, 1980), 28, figs. 26–27.

[17] F. Borsi, F. Quintero, G. Magnanimi, and C. Cerchiai, *I Palazzi del Senato: Palazzo Cenci, Palazzo Giustiniani* (Rome, 1984), 157–74.

[18] Philip II rewarded Paolo with this distinction for his military service in defense of Spanish interests. N. Ratti, *Della famiglia Sforza* (Rome, 1794), 1:300–2.

[19] 11 October 1626, 8 scudi to Simone Lagi: "Nella prima stanza dopo la sala, dove è la fontana . . . per haver fatto quattro arme da cardinale nelle cantonate. . . ." BAV, Arch. Barb., Giust. 501–625, 262r. This procedure seems to have been followed throughout the building, as indicated by the final total payment to Lagi: "Al detto [21 October 1626] sc. 60 mta in oro come sopra con mt. 949. al do Simone Lagi per un suo conto no. 617 di lavori fatti in mutare diverse armi et imprese nelle volte e stanze di detto [Quattro Fontane] palazzo et altri lavori." BAV, Arch. Barb., Comp. 66, 133r (gior.).

Capuchin crossed arms of Christ and St. Francis) and Cardinal Francesco were painted over the Sforza heraldry. The modern restoration of the fresco resulted in the removal of the seventeenth-century overpaint and revealed the Sforza arms and identifying cartouches below.

Significantly, the appropriateness of the story of Joseph can be understood only in the context of the arms of the Sforza cardinals. It constitutes an Old Testament counterpart to the establishment of the cardinalate and at the same time alludes to the history of the Santa Fiora branch of the Sforza family.

The principal narrative scene at the crown of the vault (Fig. 17) depicts *Joseph Interpreting His Dreams to His Brothers* (Genesis 37:5–10). In the first vision he saw himself with his brothers in the fields binding sheaves of wheat when his sheaf arose and stood alone, while theirs gathered around and bowed down. This scene appears in the left background of the fresco, while Joseph's second dream, in which the sun, moon, and eleven stars shown at once, appears above. A reading of the ceiling beginning from the point of entry into the room provides the observer with the proper viewing sequence (Figs. 15, 19). From this vantage point the central scene commands our attention. Then, beneath this main panel, we see *The Brothers of Joseph Plotting against Him.* Turning to the right, we next study the scene depicting *Joseph Lowered into the Pit.* Now, facing the entrance wall, we encounter *Joseph Sold to the Ishmaelites.* Finally, continuing to turn to the right, we see *Jacob and the Bloody Coat of Joseph* (Fig. 20), the scene directly overhead as we first entered the room.[20] Given the prominent inclusion of the four Sforza cardinals' arms amid these narrative scenes, the moral significance of the biblical story must be connected to the office of the cardinalate.

Pictorial cycles of the story of Joseph enjoyed a degree of popularity in the sixteenth century.[21] Joseph is the prototype of Christ, and his exile, which ultimately proved the salvation of his family, prefigured Christ's incarnation and sacrifice, demonstrating God's providence in his guidance of human affairs.[22] The traditional moral of the story requires the scene of recognition and reconcilation between Joseph and his brothers. Thus the narrative would perhaps have been continued in the now lost frescoes of the subsequent rooms of this suite (PSN 3–4), but it was significant that the narrative segment in this room terminated in the showing of the bloody coat.[23]

---

[20] An inscribed cartouche at the bottom of each cove scene explains the narrative: DECEDE IOSEPHI OCCVRRENTIS FRATRES CONSILIV INHIVNT (Observe: when Joseph comes to meet them, his brothers long for a plan); A FRATRIBVS TADE INVIDIA CORROSIS IOSEPH IN CISTERNA DETRVDITVR (Joseph is thrown into a well by his brothers, who were finally consumed by jealousy); IOSEPH A FRATRIBVS E CISTENA EXTRIS ISMAELITIS VENDITVR (Joseph, taken from the well by his brothers, is sold to the Ishmaelites); IOSEPH VESE DILANIATA ET SANGVINE ASPERSV FALSI FRATRES PATRI DOLENTI AFFERVNT (The lying brothers show the torn cloak of Joseph, sprinkled with blood, to their grieving father).

[21] After Raphael's Joseph scenes in the Vatican Logge, the tapestry cycle designed by Bronzino, Pontormo, and Salviati for the Sala dei Duecento in the Palazzo Vecchio in Florence (1546–1553) was probably the best known of the cycles. B. F. Davidson, *Raphael's Bible: A Study of the Vatican Logge* (University Park-London, 1985), 72–75; G. Smith, "Cosimo I and the Joseph Tapestries for the Palazzo Vecchio," *Renaissance and Reformation* 6 (1982), 183–96.

[22] W. Strabus, *Glossa Ordinaria*, 2 vols. in *Patrologiae Cursus Completus, Series Latina*, ed. J.-P. Migne (Paris, 1879), 113–14, 1: cols. 164–66; Réau, *Iconographie*, 2: pt. 1, 156–62.

[23] These frescoed ceilings of the two successive rooms were destroyed in alterations made by the Barberini ca. 1629–1630: "Pian Nobile dell Palazzo vecchio le 2 stanze fatte di una due che confiano con la Gallarietta. . . . Muro del tramezzo che divide dette camere." ASR, Congregazioni Religiose Maschili, Teatini S. Andrea della Valle, 2200, int. 230, fol. 143 (*misura e stima*, Taddeo).

The central panel establishes the themes of divine election and fraternal betrayal that are spun out in the four cove narratives and lead up to Joseph's ultimate fate of exile (Fig. 19). The viewer, of course, knows that this is all to the good, for Joseph's forced exile is part of God's plan to preserve the family of Jacob (Genesis 45:7). The emphasis here, however, is not on the later salvation of the family by the exiled younger brother; instead, the sequence of narrative scenes unexpectedly concludes with the display of the bloody coat. This provides the key to our understanding of the meaning of the ceiling imagery in its immediate context. Joseph's exile in Egypt and his elevation to the office of chief minister of the pharaoh are seen as the prototype of the churchman who attains high ecclesiastical office. Joseph's dreams show how God elected him to achieve this office.[24] The eight major personified virtues of the ceiling are those deemed most suitable for a cardinal of the Church, just as they are personified in Joseph. Interpreting the life of the Old Testament patriarch as an ethical ideal is a tradition that goes back to the first-century exegete Philo Judaeus, whose life of Joseph was translated into Latin and Italian and published in Venice in 1574–1575.[25] The iconography of the Sforza ceiling belongs to this exegetical tradition.

Taken in the broadest outlines, the story of Joseph also parallels the custom of selecting the younger sons of noble families for ecclesiastical careers and sending them to Rome to look after family interests there. The goal of this process finds fulfillment in the attainment of the cardinal's purple robe, symbolized in the fresco by Joseph's bloody coat (Fig. 20).[26]

The special application of this archetypal story to the history of the Santa Fiora branch of the Sforza becomes evident when we consider the fate of the main Milanese branch. The French invasion of Italy in 1494, instigated by Ludovico Sforza ("Il Moro"), initiated a chain of events resulting not only in his imprisonment and death in exile but, ultimately, in the loss of the duchy of Milan and the permanent expulsion of the Sforza. Just at this time, however, the Sforza di Santa Fiora were dwelling in their feudalities in central Italy, a foreign land, becoming rich and powerful. The succession of Sforza churchmen they established in Rome could be seen as divine election and compensation for the loss of their original homeland in Milan.

The sequence of cardinals' arms conforms to the narrative cycle. Ascanio, the oldest and first of the line of Sforza cardinals, appears directly opposite the line of sight upon entering the room (Fig. 15). Like Joseph, one of the younger brothers, he established a political and economic base in Rome for his Milanese family. Turning to the right, we encounter the arms of each cardinal in chronological sequence: Guido Ascanio,[27] Alessandro, and Francesco.[28] The flanking virtues, personifications, and pagan deities no doubt refer to the

---

[24] A similar use of the Joseph story appears in ivory panels on the sixth-century Throne of Maximian (Archbishop of Ravenna). M. Schapiro, "The Joseph Scenes on the Maximianus Throne in Ravenna," *Gazette des beaux-arts* 40, (1952), 27–38. Smith has noted this meaning in the Joseph cycle of the Casino of Pius IV at the Vatican (Pierleone Genga and Federico Barocci, 1561–1563). G. Smith, *The Casino of Pius IV* (Princeton, 1977), 92–93.

[25] Philo Judaeus, *Iosephi Patriarchae Vitae* . . . , trans. P. F. Zino (Venice, 1574); Philo Judaeus, *Il ritratto del*

vero et perfetto gentilhuomo espresso da Filone Hebreo nella vita di Gioseppe Patriarca, trans. P. F. Zino (Venice, 1575).

[26] I wish to acknowledge the suggestions of Nelson Minnich on the interpretation of the story of Joseph in the context of Sforza family iconography.

[27] Guido Ascanio's arms were quartered with the Farnese because he was the grandson of Paul III and served as papal nephew. Ratti, *Della famiglia Sforza*, 1:234, 240.

[28] Ibid., 308–9.

chief attributes of the cardinals to which they are adjacent—and collectively to the virtues of the Sforza family as a whole. In this history a divine plan is at work; not just an individual but an entire family receives God's favor.

Cardinal Francesco Sforza (1562–1624), the nephew of Guido Ascanio and Alessandro, had achieved the purple in 1583, just before work on the Joseph ceiling commenced.[29] The presence of his arms confirms the continued efficacy of the heavenly sanction in this story.

Marchese Paolo, Francesco's uncle and the patron of the Sforza ceiling, was the youngest of five brothers. He had not been chosen for a position in the Church; instead he followed a military career in the tradition of his *condottiere* ancestor Muzio Attendolo Sforza.[30] Thus it is curious that a secular member of the family should choose to celebrate so elaborately the achievements of his ecclesiastical relatives. The childless Marchese Paolo, however, must have seen the succession of Sforza cardinals as a particularly enduring manifestation of his family's destiny.

The room originally contained a fountain and provided a refreshing place to linger and enjoy the clever allusions of the imagery overhead while contemplating the magnitude of God's providence and Sforza greatness.

Upon the death of Marchese Paolo in 1597, the Sforza Palace became the property of his nephew Alessandro (1572–1631), duke of Segni. Alessandro added to the existing structure a western extension of six vaulted rooms (PSN 7–12) and had them painted with *quadro riportato* scenes from Genesis (Figs. 23–26). In a note of ca. 1625, made in connection with the sale of the property to the Barberini, the Sforza duke stated that he had spent 17,000 scudi on construction at the palace and had paid 1,500 scudi to the painter Antonio Viviani and company for painting done there.[31] Comparison with Viviani's extant work in the Marche shows that two of the ceilings (PSN 11–12, Figs. 25–26) are autograph, whereas two others (PSN 8–9, Figs. 23–24) are probably by assistants working from his designs. To this fresco work should be added a large painted ceiling in room PSN 7, now lost,[32] and two smaller but elaborate stucco and fresco ceilings at the extreme opposite end of the building (not on plan). These last two rooms, forming a private chapel and chapel antechamber, are among the most ornately decorated ceilings in the palace. The antechamber (Fig. 21) contains scenes from the life of the Virgin, with her symbols held by angels in the spandrels.[33] The sacramental space of the small chapel itself (Fig. 22) includes, in the *quadro riportato* at the center, a *Last Supper* with cove scenes of the Passion. The instruments of Christ's suffering appear in the stucco cartouches of the corners.

The building activity of Duke Alessandro and the fresco work contained in the new rooms at the western end of the palace are usually dated ca. 1619–1622,[34] but recent findings

---

[29] Ibid.

[30] Ibid., 300–2.

[31] "Spese fatte nella mia casa alle quattro fontane . . . a Antonio Viviani pittore, e compagni hanno havuto scudi mille cinquecento per pittura." BAV, Arch. Barb., Ind. II, 2813, 73. Published by Hibbard, 1971, 223. G. Magnanimi, *Palazzo Barberini* (Rome, 1983), 91, first connected this document with the extant frescoes in the north wing.

[32] Mentioned in G. Teti, *Aedes Barberinae ad Quirinalem* (Rome, 1642), 109, but without reference to the artist.

[33] The *Assumption* in the roundel at the crown of the vault is not original.

[34] Waddy, "Design and Designers," 153–54, nn. 7–10, with reference to Alò Giovannoli's engraving of 1613–1619 showing the Sforza Palace still without Alessandro's western extension. The engraving is no.

indicate that Viviani died in 1620 in Urbino, six years earlier than had previously been thought. Immediately prior to that he is documented as having been involved with a major fresco project (1618–1620) in the church of S. Pietro in Valle, Fano. The last period during which Viviani is recorded to have been in Rome is 1600–1613; by 1614 he is documented again in Urbino.[35] The Sforza project was of sufficient size—at least seven ceiling paintings and with the considerable payment of 1,500 scudi—to obviate the possibility that Viviani executed it during a hypothetical brief stay in Rome ca. 1619.[36] Since the artist was fully engaged in major fresco projects at the Quirinal and Vatican palaces in 1612–1613,[37] the circumstantial evidence thus provides a terminus ante quem of 1612 for Alessandro's construction and new ceiling paintings on the Quirinal.

The dating of ca. 1612 may also provide the reason for the expansion and redecoration of the Sforza Palace. Alessandro's eldest son, Mario (1594–1658), wedded Renée de Lorraine-Mayenne in 1612. This was an important marital alliance for the Sforza, as the bride was the daughter of Charles de Lorraine duc de Mayenne and niece of the dauphin of the duchy of Lorraine, François de Lorraine II duc de Guise.[38] The imagery of the ceiling paintings in the new rooms provides internal support for the likelihood that Alessandro expanded the palace for the purpose of accommodating the newly enlarged family. Adjoining the usual Sforza lion and quince branch depicted in the elaborate stucco surrounds of the new ceiling frescoes are two new devices not previously seen in the palace imagery—the dolphins and fleurs-de-lis of Renée's family (Figs. 23, 26).[39] This grouping of rooms on the piano nobile provided Renée with a private apartment appropriate to her rank and yet separate from those rooms extending to the east of the sala grande (PSN 1). Following the living arrangement recommended by Alberti and common for noble families,[40] her husband's apartment would have been on the floor below, spiral stairs (PSN S4) discreetly connecting the young couple's private rooms. Appropriately, a sleeping lion in stucco adorns the ceiling of the small chamber leading to the stairs (PSN 10/PBN 12, Fig. 27).[41]

Both the heraldry and the iconography of the biblical scenes in the *quadri riportati* of the ceilings reflect the status and aspirations of the occupants. In order to appreciate the decorum of the vault imagery we must consider the complete cycle within the apartment

34 in a series entitled *Roma antica* (Rome, 1619), and may reflect more the antique substructure (thought to be the Circus of Flora) sanctified by Christian martyrdom than the most recent state of the Sforza Palace. L. Mochi Onori has now redated the Viviani frescoes to ca. 1613–1614. L. Mochi Onori and R. Vodret Adams, *La Galleria Nazionale d'Arte Antica: regesto delle didascalie* (Rome, 1989), 14.

35 A. Costamagna, "Antonio Viviani, detto il Sordo di Urbino," *Annuario dell'Istituto di Storia dell'Arte, Università degli Studi di Roma* 1 (1973–1974), 237, n. 2, 239–240, 281–84.

36 Viviani's work in Fano was completed in October 1620, and he died in December of that year. Ibid.; E. Calzini, "La scuola baroccesca: Antonio Viviani, detto il Sordo," *Rassegna bibliografica dell'arte italiana* 13 (1910), 17.

37 For the payment documents, A. Bertolotti, *Artisti*

urbinati in Roma prima del secolo XVIII: notizie e documenti raccolti negli archivi romani* (Urbino, 1881), 33.

38 Ratti, *Della famiglia Sforza*, 1:330–32.

39 P. Anselme, *Histoire généalogique de la maison royale de France* (Paris, 1728), 3:779–86. Blunt ("Palazzo Barberini," 259) noted that the stucco enframements are similar to those in Palazzo Mattei di Giove. The stucco work on the comparable ceilings at Palazzo Mattei was carried out 1606–1611 under the direction of stuccatore Donato Mazzi. G. Panofsky-Soergel, "Zur Geschichte des Palazzo Mattei di Giove," *Römisches Jahrbuch für Kunstgeschichte* 11 (1967–1968), 111–88, doc. 26; Hibbard, *Carlo Maderno*, 47, 128.

40 L. B. Alberti, *Ten Books on Architecture*, trans. J. Leoni (London, 1955), 84–85.

41 Surrounded by landscape scenes representing the four seasons.

(PSN 7–12), including the lost ceiling fresco in the largest of the rooms (PSN 7). The earliest Barberini documents referring to this ceiling call it the "Creation of the World."[42] We know the subjects of the individual scenes of Viviani's lost work from the list provided by Girolamo Teti: *Creation of the World*, the *Planetary Angels* ("Angelic Rule of the Spheres"), *Garden of Eden* ("Garden of All Delights"), *Creation of Adam and Eve*, the *Expulsion*, *Adam and Eve at Work* ("Mother of All the Living Suffering over Her Multitudinous Offspring"), *Sacrifice of Cain and Abel* ("Acceptable and Unacceptable Sacrifices"), *Cain Slaying Abel* ("Fields Running with Brother's Blood"), and *Building of the Ark*.[43] Teti's enumeration of the scenes—following a logic of narrative sequence and disposition similar to the *Story of Joseph*—permits a hypothetical reconstruction of the iconographic plan of the lost ceiling (Fig. 28). What begins with the creation of the earth and continues with the fall of man and the expulsion from paradise then concludes on a note of hope seen in God's command to Noah to construct the ark.

In the eighteenth century the *Creation of the World* was completely repainted, the compositional format modified, and the number of scenes reduced, but the basic themes of creation and the early generations of man were retained (Figs. 29, 62–63). Following a fire caused by lightning that struck in the room on the floor above, in 1774 the French painter Laurent Pécheux received the commission to replace the central *quadro riportato* of this early eighteenth-century ensemble. He was required to make it an oil on canvas and to paint the subject the same as the damaged original. Pécheux reports in his diary that the original fresco, which he judged to be by Pomarancio, depicted the "division of the elements," as best he could discern from its damaged condition.[44] Pécheux also notes that the "Apparta-

[42] "Camera dov'è dipinto la volta e vi è la Creat.ne del Mondo." ASR, Congregazioni Religiose Maschili, Teatini S. Andrea della Valle, 2200, int. 230, 126, ca. 1638, with reference to work conducted in the room prior to 1632. BAV, Arch. Barb., Ind. II, 2888, 162; Pollak, *Die Kunsttätigkeit*, 1:285; G. Magnanimi, "Palazzo Barberini: i documenti della costruzione," *Antologia di belle arti* 4, nos. 13–14 (1980), 199.

[43] "Mundi Opisicium; Angelicum Spherarum regimen; deliciarum omnium Hortos; Protoplastorum creationem; eorum ex Paradiso eiectionem; omnium viventium Matrem ex multiplici prole laborantem; grata, ingrataque Sacrificia; Fraterno sanguine madida rura; Arcae constructionem." Limiting his discussion to a mere enumeration of scenes, Teti may not even have known who was responsible for these works executed more than twenty-five years earlier. Teti, *Aedes Barberinae* (1642), 109.

[44] "Hav.le s. 270 = mta, di tanti ne va coed.le per la totale mercede della pittura di un quadro ad olio da collocarsi nella volta di una delle stanze dell'appartamento detto della Divina Sapienza, da pagarsi in due rate, la prima di s. 135 alla metà dell'opera, e l'altri s. 135 terminato che farà il detto quadro, che secondo l'apoca doveva finire nel fine di 8bre 1774." BAV, Arch. Barb., Comp. 653, 77 (Quad., Prin. Carlo Maria Barberini). Pécheux's canvas was not lifted into place until

1 August 1775. See no. 72 in the list of his works made by the artist when he was in Rome, 1753–1796 (Bibl. Accad. Scienze, Turin, Miscell. manosc., E, V, 12, fasc. Pécheux). Transcribed in L. C. Bollea, *Lorenzo Pécheux* (Turin, 1936 [1942]), appendix 4, 397–98. Pécheux is silent about the cove scenes, and none of the payments made to various restorers at work in the apartment at that time appears to be connected with them. The florid decorative system of the fresco work suggests an early eighteenth-century date. Their style accords with that of the early work of Niccolò Ricciolini (1687–1772). M. Castrichini and L. Dominici, "Niccolò (e Michelangelo) Ricciolini," in *Verso un museo della città*, eds. M. Bergamini and G. Comez (Todi, 1982), 246, n. 8. In 1764 Niccolò received a commission from Cornelia Costanza Barberini and Giulio Cesare Colonna di Sciarra for two large oil on canvas mural paintings for a room on the secondo piano: *Cardinal Giovanni Colonna, Taken Prisoner by the Turks, Is Delivered by Divine Intercession and Receives the Column of the Flagellation* and *St. Pius V Nominating the Young Ascanio Colonna Prince of Palestrina on 22 February 1571*. See G. Magnanimi, "The Eighteenth-Century Apartments in the Palazzo Barberini," *Apollo* 120 (1984), 254–55. Both Niccolò and his father, Michelangelo Ricciolini (1654–1715), enjoyed the patronage of various members of the Barberini. Blunt's attribution

mento della Divina Sapienza," of which this was a major room, was being prepared for the principessa's (Cornelia Costanza) recently married son, Carlo Maria (1735–1819).[45]

Viviani's surviving frescoes (PSN 8–9, 11–12) continue the story of Genesis introduced in the antechamber to the suite. They should be examined in narrative sequence. The last narrative scene in room PSN 7 depicted, according to Teti, the construction of the ark; thus the vault of room PSN 8 continues the narrative with the *Flood* (Fig. 23), illustrating Genesis 7:23. Here we encounter an insistence on the destruction of all who did not have God's protection in the ark: "And he destroyed all the substance that was upon the earth, from man even to beast, and creeping things and fowls of the air: and they were destroyed from the earth. And Noe [Noah] only remained, and they that were with him in the ark." The Sforza lions and the dolphins of Mario's wife, Renée, appear in opposite corners of the stucco enframement. The two stucco panels at either end of the central fresco contain imprese related to the respective families of the couple. To the right, a Sforza lion attacks a horse, while, on the left, a putto rides through the waves on the back of a dolphin.

The ceiling of the adjacent room (PSN 9, Fig. 24) provides the moral conclusion the viewer is to draw from the *Flood*. God appears to Noah, his sons, and their wives and says to them: "Increase and multiply, and fill the earth" (Genesis 9:1). The rainbow on the right indicates this is the moment when God establishes the covenant with man: "This shall be the sign of the covenant which I have established between me and all flesh upon the earth" (Genesis 9:17). Two dominant themes now begin to emerge: the fruitful generation of man and God's favor and protection of his chosen people.

These themes find confirmation in the two remaining rooms of the suite (PSN 11–12). *God Speaking to Abraham* (Fig. 25) illustrates Genesis 17:3–6: "Abram [Abraham] fell flat on his face. And God said to him: I am, and my covenant is with thee, and thou shalt be a father of many nations. . . . And I will make thee increase, exceedingly, and I will make nations of thee, and kings shall come out of thee." The pendulous swags of fruit, grain, and flowers of the stucco frame seem to reiterate the promise of abundant generations to come. The ceiling of the last room (PSN 12) is even more explicit in its promise of progeny (Fig. 26). There the three angels visit Abraham and announce that Sarah, his wife, shall bear a son (Genesis 18:9–10). The enframement, the most elaborate and delicate of the group, recalls the tasseled canopy of a bed decorated with the combined arms of Mario and Renée.[46] In his suggestions for the decoration of the private rooms of married couples, Alberti was less direct, but recommended beautiful subjects that would have beneficial influence on the conception of children.[47]

The imagery painted on the vaults of the apartment prepared for the newly wed Mario, primogenito of the Sforza di Santa Fiora, represents more than a generic retelling of

of this ceiling to Cortona cannot be credited. A. Blunt, "The Exhibition of Pietro da Cortona," *Burlington Magazine* 98 (1956), 416, n. 2. I would like to thank Ann Sutherland Harris for her suggestions regarding the dating of the repainted ceiling.

[45] Quoted in Bollea, *Lorenzo Pécheux*, 377–78. Carlo Maria, Prince of Palestrina and Duke of Monte Libretti, married Giustina Arese on 4 November 1770.

Pecchiai, *I Barberini*, 260.

[46] This type, known as the "French bed," became popular in Italy in the early years of the seventeenth century. H. Havard, *Dictionnaire de l'ameublement et de la décoration* (Paris, 1894), 3:412–13, fig. 289; ed. V. Del Gaizo, *Grande enciclopedia antiquariato e arredamento* (Rome, 1967), 3:260.

[47] Alberti, *Ten Books on Architecture* 9: chap. IV, 193.

a biblical story. The carefully selected scenes emphasize the fundamental motifs of paternity and divine protection, illustrating what would be a primary concern of every new generation of Sforza. But the story of Genesis would be an appropriate metaphor for the aspirations of any noble family and, as such, appears frequently on the frescoed walls and ceilings of secular palaces.[48] The decorum of the ensemble was still perceived after more than a hundred years, when a later generation of Barberini occupants chose to maintain the narrative integrity of the pictorial cycle in the apartment.

Out of structural necessity the disposition of rooms on the piano terreno of Palazzo Sforza corresponded to the arrangement on the piano nobile. Lions and quince branches in the stucco surrounds of the ceiling *quadri riportati* (Fig. 9, Palazzo Sforza Terreno 2–4, 7–12) confirm that these rooms received decoration under Sforza patronage, but only three ceiling frescoes originally contained within those enframements have survived from the period of Sforza ownership (Fig. 9, PST 2–4; Figs. 30–32).[49] These rooms on the east side of the ground-floor sala grande (PST 1) belong to that part of the palace constructed by Marchese Paolo ca. 1584, but the ducal crowns in the stucco enframement of *Orpheus Charming the Wild Beasts* (PST 3, Fig. 31) demonstrate that Duke Alessandro was reponsible for this embellishment; it therefore appears likely that none of the rooms on the ground floor received their painted and stucco work until the period of Alessandro's occupancy, when the new rooms at the western end of the palace were decorated.

Minerva, Apollo, and the Muses on Mount Helicon (PST 2, Fig. 30) has been ascribed to the Circle of Cesare d'Arpino.[50] The artist found inspiration in the ceiling fresco of the same subject painted by Taddeo Zuccaro in the nearby Casino Bufalo ca. 1559–1560.[51] The figural attenuation and linear drapery folds betray a retardataire stylistic orientation for an artist working in the first decade of the seventeenth century.

Orpheus Charming the Wild Beasts (PST 3, Fig. 31) in the following room must be attributed to Camillo Spallucci[52] on the basis of his fresco work at Palazzo Mattei di Giove (1600–1601), particularly the figures flanking the coat of arms on the ceiling of the ground-floor vestibule.[53] The Sforza lion, clutching a quince branch, listens to Orpheus' song and is joined by, among other animals, a bear and, at the feet of the poet, an eel. These elements allude to the family name and heraldry of Duke Alessandro's wife, Eleonora Orsini.[54] Spallucci must also be given credit for the *Orpheus and Eurydice in the Underworld*, which covers the ceiling of the adjacent room (PST 4, Fig. 32).[55] Both stuccoists and painters seem to have moved from Palazzo Mattei to Palazzo Sforza.

[48] See, for example, the nearly contemporaneous Genesis cycles in Palazzo Mattei di Giove (Panofsky-Soergel, "Palazzo Mattei di Giove," 130–48), which also includes scenes from the story of Joseph, and in Palazzo Patrizi-Clementi (S. Neuburger, "Giovanni da San Giovanni im Palazzo Patrizi-Clementi in Rom," *Mitteilungen des Kunsthistorischen Institutes in Florenz* 23 (1979), 337–46.

[49] Only the two new vaults, which resulted when the Barberini divided the sala grande into two rooms (PBT 5–6), lack the Sforza heraldic devices.

[50] Magnanimi, *Palazzo Barberini*, 96.

[51] The attitudes of some of the figures have been modified, but the nearly identical composition leaves no doubt about the source. For Zuccaro's painting, see J. A. Gere, *Taddeo Zuccaro: His Development Studied in His Drawings* (Chicago, 1969), 187–88, fig. 109.

[52] Thieme and Becker, *Allgemeines Lexikon*, 31:326.

[53] Payment to Spallucci on 23 February 1601 transcribed in Panofsky-Soergel, "Palazzo Mattei di Giove," 173, doc. 13. See Bibliotheca Hertziana, Fototeca Unione no. 7887 (Foto Sansanni).

[54] The roses in the corners of the enframement are also from the Orsini arms. T. Amayden, *La storia delle famiglie romane*, ed. C. A. Bertini (Rome, 1914), 2:117–18 (rpt. Bologna, 1967).

[55] Spallucci borrowed the figural composition from Agostino Carracci's engraving of the same subject (ca.

The three Sforza ceiling frescoes on the piano terreno illustrate the theme of the power of poetry based on Ovidian fables. The *Mount Helicon* derives from the *Metamorphoses* (5:250–68), where the poet describes the visit of Minerva to Mount Helicon, home of the Muses, to see the spring made by the winged horse Pegasus. Apollo's presence in the painted scene indicates an iconographic conflation with the theme of Apollo and the Muses on Mount Parnassus that was common in sixteenth-century painting.[56] *Orpheus Charming the Wild Beasts* is based on *Metamorphoses* 10:86–154, where all of nature, including the forests as well as the animals, attends to the harmonious chords of the poet's *lira da braccio*. *Orpheus and Eurydice in the Underworld* (*Metamorphoses* 10:11–77) shows the ill-fated couple issuing forth from Hades, Orpheus having demonstrated to the gods of the underworld the power of his lyre. In the background the artist has depicted the Gate of Taenarus and, in a conflated scene, Orpheus trying to recross the Styx but being turned away by Charon.

The mythological subjects of these ground-floor frescoes distinguish them from the biblical imagery of the piano nobile and are characteristic of scenes deemed appropriate for the painted decoration of loggias and villas.[57] Mythological scenes inappropriate for the piano nobile could be introduced on the ground floor. The villa-like character of the piano terreno of Palazzo Sforza would have been enhanced by the three-arched loggia opening in the exterior wall of PST 1.[58] Moreover, the predominantly northern exposure of the two apartments on this level (PST 2–6, 7–12) made them ideal for summer habitation. The location of the Sforza Palace on the edge of the city, surrounded by tranquil gardens containing ancient statues of divinities, also suggested a setting suitable for the pastoral poetry alluded to in the fresco work. The association of poetry and villa life with beauty and leisure was natural, and the villa-like piano terreno decoration of the Sforza Palace must have contributed to the atmosphere of contemplative relaxation.[59]

1590–1595). D. DeGrazia Bohlin, *Prints and Related Drawings by the Carracci Family* (Washington, D.C., 1979), no. 178, 293.

[56] On the fusion of Helicon and Parnassus in late Renaissance iconography, see E. Schröter, *Die Ikonographie des Themas Parnass vor Raffael* (Hildesheim-New York, 1977), 241.

[57] Lomazzo, *Arte de la pittura*, 344–46; Armenini, *De' veri precetti*, 197–201. See Magnanimi, *Palazzo Barberini*, 96.

[58] Construction documents of the Barberini period record the closing of these arched openings: "Mo di 2 stracci rimurati nella facciata verso la piazza dove erano gl'archi della loggia ecc." Pollak, *Die Kunsttätigkeit*, 1:305. The original location of this loggia, as part of the Sforza building, has been established by Waddy, *Seventeenth-Century Roman Palaces*, 175.

[59] See, for example, the Sala delle Muse commissioned by Leo X for the papal hunting lodge at La Magliana; the decoration of the Casino of Pius IV in the Vatican gardens, where the Muses dance to the lyre of Apollo; and the contemporaneous (1600–1612) cycle of Apollo and the Muses at Villa Sora Boncompagni near Frascati. Coffin, *The Villa in the Life of Renaissance Rome*, 120–22, 275–78; L. Tarditi, "Villa Sora Boncompagni," in *Villa e paese*, ed. A. Tantillo Mignosi (Rome, 1980), 210–14. This type of painted decoration also reflects garden iconography of the period. E. MacDougall, "Ars Hortulorum: Sixteenth Century Garden Iconography and Literary Theory in Italy," in *The Italian Garden* (Washington, D.C., 1972), 39–59.

PART II

• The Theater of Nepotism: Prince Taddeo's Wing

CHAPTER III

• Arrangement of Apartments and Chronology of Fresco Work (1629–1632)

IN ACCORDANCE with the convention of programmatic unity of rooms en suite, the ceiling paintings of Taddeo's wing are formally and iconographically linked. Even the preexisting Sforza paintings found unified placement within the new cycles. But evaluation of the interconnectedness of the individual ceiling images is possible only with precise identification of the distinct apartment suites and their occupants.

Donna Anna's Piano Nobile Apartment. The decision of the Barberini to rebuild on a grand scale must have been made no later than 1628, for in December of that year a payment document refers to major construction.[1] Although from the beginning Taddeo sought to incorporate the old wing into the new design with minimum adjustments, some modifications to the old palace were necessary. The most radical change took place in the original sala grande (PSN 1), which was divided by a new wall to make two smaller rooms (PBN 5–6), the larger of the two known in the construction documents as a "salotto" and the smaller designated as a "camera."[2] Three new doors were opened in the south wall of the salotto (PBN 5). The opening in the southeast corner served as the main entrance, giving access to the room from two antechambers and the salone[3]; the door near the center of the wall led to the newly created chapel (PBN C1); and a door in the southwest corner led to Anna's private oratory (PBN C1A) adjacent to the chapel.[4] The new door in the southwest corner of the adjacent room (PBN 6) provided additional access to these rooms by means of stairs (PBN S3) from Taddeo's piano terreno apartment below. Thus the principal route of entry into Anna's suite of rooms (PBN 3–12) began at the door in the northwest corner of the salone (PBN 2) and made a ninety-degree turn to the left in the salotto and continued through the camera (PBN 6) to the audience room (PBN 7) and private chambers beyond.

Donna Anna's Garden Apartment. Adjustments were also made in the rooms to the west of the formal piano nobile apartment in order to provide a secluded and less formal group of rooms for the enjoyment of Anna, her children, and her attendants.[5] A wall dividing two rooms of the Sforza Palace (PSN 3–4) was turned ninety degrees (PBN 14 and 18), and an exterior wall was constructed to form a little gallery known in the documents as the "gallarietta"

---

[1] Waddy, *Seventeenth-Century Roman Palaces*, 227; Pollak, *Die Kunsttätigkeit*, 1:264.

[2] Ibid., 284.

[3] Although this main door was later walled up and no sign of it remains in the salotto today, the entire travertine frame and recess are to be seen in PBN 4.

[4] BAV, Arch. Barb., Ind. II, 2888, 201r, 205r–206v, 214v; ASR, Congregazioni Religiose Maschili, Teatini S. Andrea della Valle, 2200, int. 230, 138.

[5] Waddy, *Seventeenth-Century Roman Palaces*, 191–92.

(PBN 15).[6] A door opening in the center of the gallery wall connected it to a salotto (PBN 16), which in turn opened toward the south into an enclosed garden with a fountain. The door to the garden opened directly opposite the gallery door. To this central room were added an old Sforza chapel and its antechamber (PBN C2 and 17) and the newly oriented rooms to the west of the salotto (PBN 14 and 18). In effect, this suite of rooms (PBN 14–18) constituted a miniature villa within the context of a formal palace. Anna had direct access to it through rooms PBN 13–14, or it could be reached from the salone by passing though antechambers PBN 3–4.

Taddeo's Piano Terreno Apartment. The suite of rooms Taddeo had designed for himself on the piano terreno below his wife's main apartment resulted from adjustments similar to those made on the piano nobile. The arches were closed and a dividing wall added to the old Sforza loggia (PST 1) to create two new rooms (PBT 5–6). A chapel was added off the new salotto (PBT C1) with a private oratory attached to the west (PBT C1A). Stairs at PBT S3 led up to Anna's formal rooms and at PBT S5 to the private rooms in the western extension of the palace. Taddeo's apartment thus had an inverted L-shaped configuration (PBT 3–11), corresponding to Anna's suite on the level above.

CHRONOLOGY OF FRESCO WORK

In Donna Anna's apartment, fresco work in the salotto, chapel, and camera began in 1629 and was finished no later than early 1632, since Taddeo and Anna moved into the palace in May of that year—a fact that establishes a firm date ante quem for all fresco work in this wing of the palace (Fig. 4).[7] Taddeo gave the commission for the largest of these rooms, the salotto, to Andrea Sacchi, who painted *Divine Wisdom* (Colorplate I, Fig. 33) on the vault there. The earliest payment (50 scudi) for Sacchi's fresco work in the room dates 22 December 1629, and the final payment (100 scudi), recorded in Taddeo's Libro Mastro A (1623–1630), occurred on 28 November 1630.[8] Giovanni Incisa della Rocchetta hypothesized that subsequent payments must have been recorded in Taddeo's now lost Libro Mastro B.[9] Two additional payments to the artist were made in 1630 amounting to a total of 300 scudi.[10] Denis Mahon argued that, since the first payment (22 December 1629) was made "a conto de' suoi lavori," work on the fresco had not actually begun at that time and that it was not yet finished in December 1630 because the total payment up to that point (300 scudi) would not have been sufficient compensation for a project of such magnitude.[11] Ann Sutherland Harris has accepted the hypothesis that work continued beyond December 1630, but be-

---

[6] Pollak, *Die Kunsttätigkeit*, 1:283–84.

[7] BAV, Arch. Barb., Ind. IV, 13, 13 May 1632.

[8] BAV, Arch. Barb., Comp. 181, 149v/156v and 169v (LM, Taddeo). G. Incisa della Rocchetta, "Notizie inedite su Andrea Sacchi," *L'arte* 27 (1924), 63. In the previous literature all discussion about the dating of Sacchi's *Divine Wisdom* has been made on the basis of Incisa della Rocchetta's original archival research conducted in 1924.

[9] Ibid., 63.

[10] BAV, Arch. Barb., Comp. 181, 166v and 169r–v (26 February for 100 scudi and 13 May for 50 scudi) (LM, Taddeo). D. Mahon, "Poussiniana," *Gazette des beaux-arts* 60 (1962), 64–66. Mahon observes that the entries of 31 December 1630 totaling 300 scudi (169r, 188v, and 193v) must represent a recapitulation of the earlier payments.

[11] Ibid., 65–66. Incisa della Rocchetta ("Notizie su Sacchi," 63) also thought work on the fresco must have continued into 1631.

lieves that the artist was already at work on the project by late summer or early fall of 1629.[12] Other account records now indicate that some fresco work had already been accomplished by the time of the December 1629 payment.[13] Yet another unexamined account book covering the inclusive period 1629–1634 indicates by its wording that the payment of 100 scudi made to the artist on 28 November 1630 was probably the final payment for the completed work; moreover, no further entries concerning Sacchi occur after that date.[14] The *Divine Wisdom* was therefore painted between 1629 and 1630.

The dating of the fresco work by Cortona and assistants in the adjoining chapel is also problematic because the payments are not clearly differentiated from payments made to the same artists for work carried out in the garden apartment of the palace at about the same time. The mural frescoes of the chapel depict scenes from the Infancy and Passion of Christ, and the dome contains angels holding the instruments of the Passion (Figs. 49, 51, 53–58). The payment of 100 scudi made to Cortona 29 October 1631 appears to have covered his work both in the chapel and in the little gallery (PBN 15) of Anna's garden apartment (Figs. 64–65, 67–69), which was almost entirely executed by the assistants.[15] The venal office purchased for Cortona in October 1632 may have served as final compensation for his work in the chapel as well as for initial work on the vault of the salone.[16]

More useful for purposes of dating the fresco work in the chapel are the payments made to Cortona's assistants, Giovanni Francesco Romanelli and Pietro Paolo Baldini ("Modello"). A series of account entries dating from July and November 1631 reflect payments of 25 scudi and 20 scudi and seem to indicate that most fresco work in the chapel was accomplished in 1631.[17] Subsequent payments made to the artists in February 1632 probably refer to the work in the little gallery of the garden apartment, suggesting that activity in the chapel was over by that time.[18] By early 1632 the gilder was already at work in the chapel.[19]

---

[12] A. S. Harris, *Andrea Sacchi* (Princeton, 1977), 58–59.

[13] 22 December 1629: "A maestranze della fabrica del palazzo sc. 50—mta . . . ad Andrea Sacchi pittore a buon conto dell' lavori di pittura fatti e da fare in detto palazzo." BAV, Arch. Barb., Comp. 186, 148v (gior., Taddeo).

[14] 28 November 1630: ". . . sc. cento d'oro pagabile a sig. Andrea Sacchi pittore per recognitione di tutto quello che ha dipinto al nostro palazzo." BAV, Arch. Barb., Ind. IV, 13, at date (mand., Taddeo). This volume, curiously entitled "Diversi mandati della Sig.ra D. Anna" (the spine is labled "Per la fabbrica alle Quattro Fontane"), is a book of payments (*mandati*) made by Taddeo for the palace at Quattro Fontane from 1629 to 1634, listed in chronological order.

[15] BAV, Arch. Barb., Comp. 50, 164r–v (LM, Francesco). The same payment is recorded in Comp. 80, 44v (mand., Francesco) (as cited by Briganti, *Pietro da Cortona*, 198 and O. Verdi, "Le fonti documentarie," in *Il voltone di Pietro da Cortona in Palazzo Barberini, Quaderni di Palazzo Venezia 2* [1983], 95) and SCEP, Quaderno de' Sig.ri Barberini, 1631–1633, 70v.

[16] For the amount and mode of payment to Cortona, see Appendix E.

[17] BAV, Arch. Barb., Comp. 80, 35v, 44r–v (mand., Francesco); SCEP, Quaderno de' Sig.ri Barberini, 1631–1633, 53v, 70v, 71r (Pollak, *Die Kunsttätigkeit*, 1:327, 332).

[18] BAV, Arch. Barb., Comp. 80, 50r, 55r (mand., Francesco); Comp. 67, 166, 175–76 (gior., Francesco); Pollak, *Die Kunsttätigkeit*, 1:332–33. Below, 107–10.

[19] Due to the reorganization of the Barberini Archive it has not been possible to locate and examine the document of 23 January 1632 cited in M. A. Lavin (*Seventeenth-Century Barberini Documents*, 12), which mentions candles issued from the guardarobba to Cortona's assistants for painting in the chapel, but it appears to refer to supplies dispensed on several occasions in the past, "in più volte." Three separate documents indicate that Simone Lagi, the gilder, was already at work in the chapel in January and February 1632. SCEP, Quaderno de' Sig.ri Barberini, 1631–1633, 82v; BAV, Arch. Barb., Comp. 50, 196v (LM, Francesco); Comp. 67, 165 (gior., Francesco). Thus fresco work, of necessity, had to have been completed prior to January 1632.

Andrea Camassei was assigned three ceiling frescoes: the *Creation of the Angels* (PBN 6, Colorplate II, Figs. 59–60) in the camera just beyond the salotto with Sacchi's *Divine Wisdom*, the *Parnassus* in Taddeo's appartment on the piano terreno (PBT 7, Fig. 72), and a small fresco of a *Guardian Angel* for the vault of Taddeo's private oratory (PBT C1A) connected to his chapel (PBT C1). Paper, brushes, and pigments were provided to the artist specifically for work on the *Creation of the Angels* and the *Parnassus* in a payment of 18 scudi recorded in documents of September and October of 1630.[20] A subvention for supplies related to the *Guardian Angel* is dated 2 July 1631.[21] A payment of 200 scudi to Camassei covering all his fresco work at Palazzo Barberini occurred on 28 July 1631.[22]

Romanelli, Baldini, and Giacinto Gimignani, working under the direction of Cortona, painted the vault and overdoors of the little gallery in Anna's garden apartment (PBN 15, Figs. 64–65, 67–69). Payments for this work came in February and June 1632. This painted decoration must have been the last completed in the north wing before Taddeo and Anna moved into the palace in May 1632.[23]

Other than Camassei's *Parnassus* and the small *Guardian Angel* in the oratory, Simone Lagi and Giovanni Domenico Marziani ("Il Maltese") did the fresco work in Taddeo's appartment on the piano terreno (PBT 5–8). Taddeo's painted coat of arms upheld by struggling putti at the crown of the vault in the downstairs salotto (PBT 5, Fig. 71) should be ascribed to Lagi on the basis of the similarity of the putto types to those the same artist painted in the dome of the chapel in Urban's villa at Castelgandolfo, ca. 1626–1627, whereas the *quadratura* balustrade in the same room shows the intervention of Agostino Tassi. Lagi, who was resident gilder at the Vatican and had cleaned the Sistine Ceiling in 1625 at Urban's command, specialized in decorative work such as coats of arms, imprese, friezes, and grotteschi, but he also occasionally painted figural scenes.[24] Already as early as 1626, Lagi was busy at Palazzo

[20] "25 7bre 1630 un mandato di sc. diciotto mta pagabili ad Andrea Camassei che sono per . . . spesi da lui in colori carta penelli et altro per le pitture fatti da lui nella nova fabbrica alle quattro fontane cioè l'opera della creatione degl'angioli e quella del Monte Parnasso . . . sc. 18." BAV, Arch. Barb., Ind. IV, 13, at date (25 September 1630) (mand., Taddeo); Comp. 186, 164r (gior., Taddeo).

[21] ". . . ad Andrea Camassei pittore per . . . d'altri spesi in colori et altro per far dipingere un camerino a chiaroscuro et un angelo custode nel palazzo nostro a capo le case . . . sc. 21.82 1/2." BAV, Arch. Barb., Ind. IV, 13, at date (mand., Taddeo); Comp. 192, 42r (mand., Taddeo); M. A. Lavin, *Seventeenth-Century Barberini Documents*, 9, records a *contramandato* of the same payment; SCEP, Quaderno de' Sig.ri Barberini, 1631–1633, 35 (Pollak, *Die Kunsttätigkeit*, 1:330).

[22] BAV, Arch. Barb., Comp. 192, 50r.

[23] Romanelli and Baldini each received a total of 60 scudi for the gallery frescoes. Gimignani received a lesser amount of 40 scudi. Account entries recording the payments to the individual artists are as follows:

Romanelli—BAV, Arch. Barb., Comp. 80, 50r, 55r (mand., Francesco); Comp. 67, 166, 176 (gior., Francesco); SCEP, Quaderno de' Sig.ri Barberini, 1631–1633, 66 and 67 (Pollak, *Die Kunsttätigkeit*, 1:332), 95v. Baldini—BAV, Arch. Barb., Comp. 80, 50r, 55r (mand., Francesco); Comp. 67, 166, 175 (gior., Francesco); SCEP, Quaderno de' Sig.ri Barberini, 1631–1633, 66 and 76 (Pollak, *Die Kunsttätigkeit*, 1:332), 86v; Gimignani—BAV, Arch. Barb., Comp. 80, 50r, 55r (mand., Francesco); Comp. 67, 166, 176 (gior., Francesco); Comp. 50, 197v, 202r (LM, Francesco); SCEP, Quaderno de' Sig.ri Barberini, 1631–1633, 66 and 76 (Pollak, *Die Kunsttätigkeit*, 1:333), 86v, 95v.

[24] For Lagi at Castelgandolfo, see Bonomelli, *I papi in campagna*, 64–65, nn. 8 and 12; A. Lo Bianco, "Castelgandolfo: il Palazzo e la Villa Barberini," in *Villa e paese*, ed. A. Tantillo Mignosi (Rome, 1980), 265–268, fig. 6. For the Sistine project, E. Steinmann, *Die Sixtinesche Kapelle* (Munich, 1905), 2:783, doc. 7, and B. Nogara, "Restauri degli affreschi di Michelangelo nella Cappella Sistina," *L'arte* 9 (1906), 229. For Tassi, below, 111.

Barberini overpainting Sforza coats of arms and adding new Barberini arms in various rooms.[25] Numerous account documents from 1629–1632 record nonspecific payments as well as those made for work in the piano nobile chapel.[26] Lagi based his design on the Cortonesque concept of the "stemma in arrivo."[27] The inclusion of such an innovative device indicates the artist's knowledge of Cortona's vault fresco for the "gallarietta" of the piano nobile garden apartment then being executed (Fig. 68). Since Lagi was engaged in gilding the piano nobile chapel in the early months of 1632, his work in the piano terreno salotto would have to have been completed during the previous year at the latest.

Marziani's *Hercules at the Crossroads* (PBT 6) and the *Bellerophon Slaying the Chimera* (PBT 8), both mentioned in the *misura e stima* of ca. 1638,[28] have not survived. Five different payments made to the artist between 1628 and 1631, totaling 247 scudi, are nonspecific.[29] Marziani was already on the family roll of Cardinal Francesco in 1626–1627, receiving a monthly stipend of 3.6 scudi,[30] and continued in that capacity until his departure from the scene in late 1631. As a member of the household, Marziani might have been called on for work without generating specific payments. The last major payment made to the artist, 100 scudi on 5 May 1631, must reflect his extended activity in the piano terreno rooms and must also refer to a gift from the cardinal for a trip the artist had to make.[31] This would indicate completion of the artist's work in Taddeo's apartment by at least May 1631. During this same period Marziani also painted the *Nativity* in the central field of the Sforza ceiling in Donna Anna's garden apartment (PBN 17).[32]

No record exists for any fresco activity in the three private rooms at the western end of Taddeo's suite (PBT 9–11), although stucco enframements for *quadri riportati* were already in place from the period of Sforza occupancy.

[25] Above, 16 and n.16.

[26] 21 May 1632: "A Simone Lagi pittore, et indoratore duecento sessantotto scudi 10 giu . . . che importano tutti le lavori fatti da lui per nostro servitio a Monte Rotondo a Roma et altrove per tutto l'anno di 1631 . . . dal nostro Palazzo a Capo le Case . . . sc. 268.10." BAV, Arch. Barb., Comp. 192, at date (mand., Taddeo).

[27] M. Campbell, *Pietro da Cortona at the Pitti Palace* (Princeton, 1977), 125.

[28] ASR, Congregazioni Religiose Maschili, Teatini S. Andrea della Valle, 2200, int. 230, fols. 229, 231; BAV, Arch. Barb., Ind. II, 2888, fols. 245, 247; Pollak, *Die Kunsttätigkeit*, 1:305; Magnanimi, "Documenti della costruzione," 203.

[29] BAV, Arch. Barb., Comp. 49, 175r, 194r, 211v

(LM, Francesco); Comp. 80, 31v (mand., Francesco); SCEP, Quaderno de' Sig.ri Barberini, 1631–1633, 36v, 44v.

[30] BAV, Arch. Barb., Giust. 626–720, 31v, 88v, 134v, 232v; Giust. 721–802, 23v, 82v, 272v (Francesco).

[31] "A di 8 detto [May 1631] per conto di m.ta pagati come sopra a Gio. Dom.co Martiali pittor per recognitione di qnto ha fatto fin ora per S. Em.za e per souventione volont.ria d'un viaggio che gli deve fare sc.— ——100." SCEP, Quaderno de' Sig.ri Barberini, 1631–1633, 44v; BAV, Arch. Barb., Comp. 80, 31v (mand., Francesco).

[32] See the *misura e stima* entry. BAV, Arch. Barb., Giust. 1726–1792, 115r.

CHAPTER IV

• *Domus Sapientiae*: Sacchi's *Divine Wisdom* in the House of the Barberini

SEATED ON A cloud-borne throne, surrounded by her personified virtues, and hovering over a pendulous terrestrial globe, the image of Divine Wisdom on the vault of the salotto of Donna Anna's apartment (PBN 5, Colorplate I, Figs. 33–35) must be judged one of the most unusual creations of the Roman Baroque. Even the format of the work is a novelty. Startled visitors to the palace found themselves confronted with a vault that had been completely painted away to give the effect of an open sky revealing to their eyes an apparition of the mind of God. Not the least remarkable aspect of the ceiling is the heliocentrism suggested by the central placement of the sun (Wisdom) and the eccentric location of the earth—an implicit validation of the Copernican system in the family palace of the pope who permitted the condemnation of Galileo on that point just two years after the completion of this fresco.[1]

Sacchi's exceptional achievement has produced more scholarly discussion than any other ceiling painting in the Barberini Palace.[2] Notwithstanding the fascination commentators have shown for Sacchi's creation, the prevailing assessment has been negative. Incisa della Rocchetta observed that the massive globe of the earth seemed to "tumble awkwardly" along the lower cornice.[3] Ellis Waterhouse found it "a disaster" and simply "terrifying," whereas, for Torgil Magnuson, it elicits from the viewer an "unpleasant feeling" and must have been considered "something of a failure."[4] Most authors have asserted that the artist

[1] Harris, *Andrea Sacchi*, 12; G. S. Lechner, "Tommaso Campanella and Andrea Sacchi's Fresco of 'Divina Sapienza' in the Palazzo Barberini," *Art Bulletin* 58 (1976), 107–8; A. S. Harris, "Letter to the Editor Concerning George S. Lechner's 'Tommaso Campanella and Andrea Sacchi's Fresco of Divina Sapienza in the Palazzo Barberini,' " *Art Bulletin* 59 (1977), 306–7; G. S. Lechner, "Reply to the Editor," *Art Bulletin* 59 (1977), 309; D. Gallavotti Cavallero, "Il programma iconografico per la Divina Sapienza nel Palazzo Barberini: una proposta," in *Studi in onore di Giulio Carlo Argan* (Rome, 1984), 269–90; F. Grillo, *Tommaso Campanella nell'arte di Andrea Sacchi e Nicola Poussin* (Cosenza, 1979), 11–70, esp. 11–44; I. Lavin, "Bernini's Cosmic Eagle," in *Gianlorenzo Bernini: New Aspects of His Art and Thought*, ed. I. Lavin (University Park, Pa., 1985), 212.

[2] The judicious analysis and comprehensive catalogue entry by Harris (*Andrea Sacchi*, 8–13, 57–59) constitute a compendious assessment of all known facts about the fresco and related works, including a complete bibliography up to 1963. Other major studies, listed in chronological order, include: Incisa della Rocchetta, "Notizie su Sacchi," 63–65; H. Posse, *Der römische Maler Andrea Sacchi* (Leipzig, 1925), 37–49; R. Wittkower, *Art and Architecture in Italy, 1600–1750* (Harmondsworth, 1958), 170–71, 3rd ed. (1980), 263; F. Haskell, *Patrons and Painters* (London, 1963), 50–51; Lechner, "Fresco of 'Divina Sapienza,' " 97–108; Harris, *Andrea Sacchi*, 304–7; Lechner, "Reply to the Editor," 106–9; M. M. Byard, "Divine Wisdom-Urania," *Milton Quarterly* 12 (1978), 134–37; F. Grillo, "Tommaso Campanella astrologo e la *Divina Sapienza* di Andrea Sacchi" *Studi Meridionali* 11 (1978), 293–328; idem, *Campanella nell'arte di Sacchi e Poussin*; J. B. Scott, "Allegories of Divine Wisdom in Italian Baroque Art," Ph.D. diss., Rutgers University, 1982, 8–68; Gallavotti Cavallero, "Il programma iconografico," 269–90; A. D'Avossa, *Andrea Sacchi* (Rome, 1985), 61–65; I. Lavin, "Bernini's Cosmic Eagle," 212.

[3] Incisa della Rocchetta, "Notizie su Sacchi," 65.

[4] E. Waterhouse, *Roman Baroque Painting* (Oxford, 1976), 21; Magnuson, *Rome in the Age of Bernini*, 1:342.

cautiously eschewed every element of illusionism, opting instead for an expressive mode of extreme classicism.[5] Such evaluations held the day until the publication of the analysis of Harris, who has established that the *Divine Wisdom* was much more innovative, illusionistic, and successful by contemporary seventeenth-century standards of judgment than many modern observers have allowed.[6]

Sacchi and his patrons seem to have been satisfied with the work. It existed in at least six easel copies, two of which were given by the Barberini as diplomatic gifts to distinguished visitors to Rome,[7] and contemporaries found it worthy of commemoration on the artist's cenotaph in the Lateran:

HIC EST
QUI CUM DIV AETERNITATI PINXERIT
VEL MORTUUS IN HOC TUMULO FAMAE AETERNUM VIVIT
DIVINAE SAPIENTIAE MYSTERIA DIVINIS PENE COLORIBUS
IN BARBERINIS AEDIBUS EXPRESSIT

[Here is a man, who, since he painted with divine immortality, even though now dead in this tomb lives on in the eternity of fame, having depicted the mysteries of divine wisdom in nearly divine hues in the house of the Barberini.][8]

Anachronistic judgments about the merit of the painting may be set aside. Sacchi conceived the *Divine Wisdom* as a mysterious work in conformity with the recondite nature of its subject. The *Divine Wisdom* stands as an anomaly in the history of ceiling painting. At this time it was rare for a formal room of an urban palace to be painted with a scene creating the fiction of an open sky. In the few cases where this was attempted, a *quadratura* armature that fictively continues the vertical of the wall helps to enframe the central image and act as a structured visual transition between the real physical space of the room and the illusionistically open sky above. Such examples can be seen in the ceilings painted by Domenichino and Guercino in Palazzo Costaguti (ex-Patrizi) in Rome, ca. 1622.[9] Even the ceiling paintings

[5] Posse, *Andrea Sacchi*, 41; Haskell, *Patrons and Painters*, 51; Wittkower, *Art and Architecture in Italy*, 263; Waterhouse, *Roman Baroque Painting*, 21; Magnuson, *Rome in the Age of Bernini*, 1:342.

[6] Harris, *Andrea Sacchi*, 9.

[7] Cardinal Richelieu and Prince von Eggenberg, the ambassador of the emperor, were recipients of copies of the work. It was also engraved by Michael Natalis for the *Aedes Barberinae*, 1642, and in several versions by Jean Gerardin (Giovanni Gerardini) in 1662. Harris, *Andrea Sacchi*, 58.

[8] For Sacchi's tomb, see ibid., figs. 1–2. Copies of the *Divine Wisdom* seem to have enjoyed a certain popularity in circles where recherché interests were cultivated. The enthroned, cloud-borne figure of Divine Wisdom appears on the engraved frontispiece of A. Kircher, *Ars Magna Sciendi* (Amsterdam, 1669), with the base of the throne inscribed, in Greek, "Nothing is more beautiful than to know all." This remarkable tome elaborated the universal system of knowledge of the Jesuit polymath. Cardinal Antonio Barberini the Younger, who, after 1634, lived in the company of the *Divine Wisdom* more than any other member of the Barberini family, remained Sacchi's patient and generous patron even during the troubled and unproductive later years of the artist's life. The cardinal's loyalty to the artist can be traced back to 1631, when he first interceded in Sacchi's favor, and must have been based on the Cardinal's favorable assessment of the *Divine Wisdom*. On this point, see Harris, *Andrea Sacchi*, 13, 24.

[9] Domenichino's *Truth Revealed by Time* and Guercino's *Rinaldo and Armida*. Posse, "Das Deckenfresko," 137, figs. 10–11; R. Spear, *Domenichino* (New Haven, 1982), 233–35. Agostino Tassi provided the *quadratura* element for both of the Patrizi-Costaguti ceilings. T. Pugliatti, *Agostino Tassi* (Rome, 1977), 53–54.

of villas and garden casinos, where more daring devices of plein-air illusionism were commonly admitted, employ fictive architectural *quadratura*. Guercino's *Aurora* in the Casino Ludovisi (1621–1623), with *quadratura* enframement by Tassi (Fig. 118), exemplifies this usage. Sacchi's only concession to this transition device is the gilded frieze around the lower edge of the fresco field just above the actual cornice. The Sirens holding up suns in the corners also help to mediate between open sky and the narrow enframement,[10] but the overwhelming impression is one of unmediated contact between viewer and sky.

Captivated by the art and fame of Raphael, Sacchi had as an *idée fixe* the classicizing vision of the human figure as it had been defined by that venerated artist.[11] The aura of repose and ideality that envelops the personified virtues around the central seated figure of Wisdom might have suggested to contemporaries a version of Raphael's *Parnassus* transferred into the clouds. But Sacchi was not merely an imitator of past glories. He had acute knowledge of contemporary achievements in the field of ceiling painting. Sacchi's conception for the figural field of his painting has greater affinity to Lanfranco's *Council of the Gods* (1624–1625) in the Villa Borghese (Fig. 119).[12] The Borghese fresco, like Sacchi's, is meant to be seen from one primary point of view, with the observer's back turned toward the windows. In both works the figures are oriented in one direction, although Lanfranco's massive painted cornice upheld by atlantes puts his Borghese fresco closer to the tradition of *quadratura* ceilings than to the radical approach found in the *Divine Wisdom*.[13]

A moderate *quadratura* device does appear in Taddeo's ground-floor salotto (PBT 5, Fig. 71) directly beneath the Sacchi room, where a painted balustrade serves to harmonize the actual architectural elements of the room with the illusionistically open sky above. Even Cortona's vast trompe l'oeil fresco in the Barberini salone employs a fictive architectural armature to provide structure for the figure groupings. Not until the late 1660s would a Roman artist dare to paint figures in such an open format on the vault of an urban palace without use of any significant *quadratura* element or fictive balustrade as transition device.[14]

Sacchi appears also to have been inspired by the open sky (*cielo aperto*) trompe l'oeil effects of vaults populated with saints and angels seated on ranges of clouds, which he had seen in a number of large-scale fresco cycles in Roman churches.[15] He took note of Lanfranco's dome fresco of the *Assumption* in S. Andrea della Valle (1625–1627) (Fig. 120), completed only two years prior to the Barberini assignment, where figures hover on clouds suspended in the open sky above the viewer's head. There Lanfranco provided compositional structure

[10] The type of work normally assigned to the gilder Simone Lagi, the frieze appears to have been painted *a secco*. The room is square (9.8 × 9.8 meters) and 7.7 meters from floor to center of the vault.

[11] Posse, *Andrea Sacchi*, 46–47.

[12] Gallavotti Cavallero, "Il programma iconografico," 278.

[13] On the Borghese ceiling, see H. Hibbard, "The Date of Lanfranco's Fresco in the Villa Borghese and Other Chronological Problems," in *Miscellanea Bibliothecae Hertzianae* (Munich, 1961), 355–65, esp. 360–62; and M. Winner, "Bernini the Sculptor and the Classical Heritage in His Early Years: Praxiteles', Bernini's, and Lanfranco's *Pluto and Proserpina*," *Römisches Jahrbuch*

für Kunstgeschichte 22 (1985), 197–204.

[14] Francesco Cozza's *Divine Wisdom* in the Pamphili Library (1667–1673). Wittkower, *Art and Architecture in Italy*, 330; L. Trezzani, *Francesco Cozza, 1605–1682* (Rome, 1981), 56; Scott, "Allegories of Divine Wisdom," 146–72.

[15] The major studies on the ceiling paintings in Roman churches are: M. C. Gloton, *Trompe-l'oeil et décor plafonnant dans les églises romains de l'âge baroque* (Rome, 1965); T. Poensgen, *Die Deckenmalerei in italienischen Kirchen* (Berlin, 1969); and a useful bibliography, R. England, *The Baroque Ceiling Paintings in the Churches of Rome 1600–1750: A Bibliography* (Hildesheim-New York, 1979).

by means of figural groupings, cloud formations, and the distribution of light. Sacchi, however, avoided the radical foreshortenings and always maintained the autonomy of the individual figure to a greater degree than did Lanfranco. A venerated masterwork of illusionism such as Melozzo da Forlì's visionary semi-dome fresco of the *Ascension* in the apse of SS. Apostoli (1477–1480)[16] must also have played a role in the formulation of the Baroque artist's innovative conception.

Sacchi perhaps found greater inspiration in religious works because of the sacred nature of his subject and the function of his room as a large antechamber for an adjacent chapel. In the Barberini salotto the viewer becomes the privileged witness to a great mystery, as in the illusionistic dome frescoes of Correggio and Lanfranco. Sacchi's achievement is striking not the least because it draws upon a tradition outside that of secular palace decoration.

The spatial dynamics of the Barberini fresco have been misread. Commentators have been so relentless in comparing the perceived classicism of the *Divine Wisdom* with the High Baroque effusiveness of Cortona's salone fresco—which did not yet exist in 1631—that the anti-classical illusionism of the former has been overlooked. Harris alone has called attention to the spatial workings of the salotto ceiling.[17] Visual evidence negates attempts to see the *Divine Wisdom* "as if it were a *quadro riportato*."[18] Although the artist avoided the extremes of foreshortening, a *di sotto in su* effect is present throughout the work. We see, for example, the base of the throne from a low viewing point, with the sandaled left foot of Wisdom, also seen from below, projecting forward over the convex throne front (Fig. 36). The head of Wisdom is emphatically foreshortened, and the underside of the lion prominent.

But these are mere details, whereas the artist made great effort to provide visual keys to help establish the spatial relationship of the pictorial elements with regard to the position of the viewer. The most obtrusive of these is the terrestrial globe, which the observer sees from its underside.[19] Vast stretches of terra incognita dominate the foreground, whereas Europe and other features in the northern latitudes appear only at the very top of the globe. Dark shadows on the undersides of the clouds at the lower left and upper right show that they occupy the space between the source of light (Wisdom) and the standing position of the viewer, while the pool of light that bathes the northern hemisphere of the earth demonstrates that Wisdom hovers over western Europe, shining down beneficial rays on Italy in particular.

Reliance on photographs taken from improper viewing points has negated the spatial illusionism so carefully calculated by the artist. The readily available archival photographs of the *Divine Wisdom*[20] could easily result in the conclusion that Sacchi painted the ceiling "as if it were a *quadro riportato*," for they are taken—quite unnaturally—from directly beneath the center of the ceiling and consequently flatten all the pictorial elements onto a single surface plane (Fig. 33). The throne of Wisdom, for example, appears to be parallel to the

[16] A. Schiavo, "Melozzo a Roma," *Presenza romagnola* 2 (1977), 89–110.

[17] Harris, *Andrea Sacchi*, 9.

[18] Wittkower, *Art and Architecture in Italy*, 263.

[19] The artist seems to have used an actual three-dimensional globe that could be turned in its housing and copied from beneath. Sacchi's treatment of the terra incognita indicates he employed a globe similar to one

dated 1616 in the possession of Cardinal Francesco. See E. L. Stevenson, *Terrestrial and Celestial Globes* (New Haven, 1921), 1:42, fig. 97.

[20] Virtually all published reproductions of the ceiling are based on ICCD E72393 (Fig. 33) or E72392, which is similar but includes the painted frieze. These photographs have negatively shaped our impression of the ceiling fresco.

picture plane. If, however, we try to reproduce photographically something of the effect gained by the viewer standing in the salotto near the window wall—which is the natural viewing point—looking up at a comfortable angle toward the ceiling, a very different impression of the spatial relationships within the ceiling imagery will be obtained (Colorplate I, Fig. 35). From this experiential vantage point, the throne and surrounding figures seem to tilt upward toward a vertical plane more related to the vertical plane of the south wall of the room.[21] Far from being a *quadro riportato* conceived without concern for the elevated location and architectural context of the work, the three-dimensional composition of the *Divine Wisdom* is predicated on the assumption that the viewer will be standing in the room below, looking up at a moderately inclined angle into the heavens.

A proper understanding of the pictorial function of the terrestrial globe also enables us to perceive the ceiling as originally intended by the artist. The weighty orb that troubled and terrified some observers does not appear so obtrusive when observed from the correct vantage point (Fig. 35) and is even less prominent when seen in situ. Moreover, much of the compositional weight of the orb as it appears in reproductions is countered by the even larger golden orb of the sun, which radiates from around the figure of Wisdom but is scarcely perceptible in black-and-white photographs. The warm tonalities at the center of the ceiling thus balance the cool greens and blues of the earth (Colorplate I).

The subject of Sacchi's ceiling painting is no less novel than the format. Fortunately we know the detailed iconography of that subject from a manuscript folio now preserved in the Barberini Archive in the Vatican Library, written after the completion of the painting but by an individual intimately associated with the creation of the work (Fig. 121).[22] The sheet cannot be called a program for the ceiling in the sense that it served as a prescription for the artist. Instead, like almost all programs of the period, it was penned after the painting had been completed. As a rule, the programs of such large-scale fresco works were not set down until the creation of the pictorial imagery. Allegorical ceiling paintings like Sacchi's emerged from a collaborative process that took place among artist, learned consultant, and patron.[23]

The Barberini Manuscript appears to have been drawn up by Sacchi's iconographic collaborator not long after the completion of the ceiling, perhaps with the intention of having

[21] It must be noted that, due to parallax distortions, even the most carefully thought-out photographs do not reproduce the true spatial relationships of the ceiling within the architectural context of the room. Such photographs as our Fig. 35, however, can provide a closer approximation of the true visual effect than has hitherto been possible.

[22] Appendix B. BAV, Barb. Lat. 6529, misc. V, fol. 52r–v. The document was first published by Incisa della Rocchetta ("Notizie su Sacchi," 64). Harris ("Letter to the Editor," 305) has observed that the manuscript was apparently written by the anonymous author of the ceiling's program.

[23] Charles Hope has scrutinized the role of humanists and patrons in the creation of programmatic works of art of the Renaissance and concluded that the su-

premacy of the artist was rarely contested. C. Hope, "Artists, Patrons, and Advisers in the Italian Renaissance," in *Patronage in the Renaissance*, eds. G. F. Lytle & S. Orgel (Princeton, 1981), 293–343. In general, this conclusion appears to be valid in the seventeenth century as well, but, given the exceptional complexity and iconographic originality of the *Divine Wisdom*, one must conclude that Sacchi needed to rely exceptionally on his consultant. Graphic evidence of the artist's perplexity in dealing with some details of the program appears in the Cooper-Hewitt compositional sketch (Fig. 41), where he found it necessary to label some of the personifications. No work elsewhere in Sacchi's oeuvre begins to approach the programmatic magnitude of the *Divine Wisdom*.

it serve as the basis for a printed pamphlet for visitors to the palace.[24] The handwriting of the sheet (Fig. 121) indicates that a professional scribe copied it from the original, and crease marks suggest that it was folded and sent to someone. Since the page appears bound together with letters addressed to various family members (Urban, Carlo, Francesco, and Taddeo), most of them from 1629–1630, it is easy to imagine that the author sent it to the patron, Taddeo, for approval. But approval was not forthcoming. The patron apparently found the last paragraph objectionable, as he separated it from the main body of the text with a horizontal line and canceled it with an emphatic diagonal stroke of the pen.

The manuscript is succinct and logical in its enumeration of the identities of the figures, their attributes, and the overall meaning of the imagery in the context of the Barberini Palace. It wastes no words and avoids rhetorical circumlocutions. Speaking with authoritative precision, it takes precedence over all other sources of the period, including Teti's ex post facto interpretive official book on the palace.[25] The Barberini Manuscript must be the touchstone for our understanding of Sacchi's painting.

Since Wisdom, in her governance of the world, must be loved and feared, she appears in the act of commanding her heavenly archers, who personify those qualities, to take aim at the earth below. This forceful gesture is accomplished by means of the eye-topped scepter of provident and wise rule (Fig. 36). We learn of the particular Christian nature of Wisdom through her attributes, which are also those of the Virgin: a halo of light ("candor lucis aeternae"), a mirror ("speculum sine macula"), and the sun ("spesiosior soli").[26] The women surrounding Wisdom represent her primary virtues and are identified by means of attributes, which are themselves constellations (Figs. 34, 36). This is appropriate, we are carefully informed, because constellations, being divine things, appear in heaven. Gilded stars mark the attributes.

Then the author of the manuscript, in scholarly fashion, informs us of his biblical source. The personified virtues of Wisdom symbolized by these constellations derive from

[24] Since it formed part of a private apartment, however, the salotto does not seem to have been open to casual visitors to the palace until much later in the century. There was consequently no need for such a factual printed explanation of the *Divine Wisdom*, and the Barberini Manuscript was therefore never published. By the time there was need for such a practical guide, the anonymous late eighteenth-century author of the *Spiegazione* (below, 43, n. 25) had no knowledge of the original program and had to rely instead on Passeri's erroneous interpretation. G. B. Passeri, *Die Künstlerbiographien*, ed. J. Hess (Leipzig-Vienna, 1934), 295–96. The Barberini Manuscript, moreover, implies that the reader is standing in the salotto with the painting overhead.

[25] Teti, *Aedes Barberinae* (1642), 83–96. With its lavish engraved illustrations, Teti's large book, in contrast to the text of the Barberini Manuscript, was meant for the enjoyment of the private library rather than practical on-site use. It represents the principal monument of the Neo-Ciceronianism cultivated by the literary patronage of Urban and his nephews. M. Fumaroli, *L'âge de l'éloquence: rhètorique et "res literaria" de la Renaissance au seuil de l'époque classique* (Geneva, 1980), 205–13. Not a guidebook in the modern sense, the *Aedes* is an interpretive essay. Although Teti wrote more than ten years after the completion of Sacchi's painting, he knew the correct identities of the figures and had some knowledge of the larger meaning of the work; nevertheless, his greatest interest was focused on creative interpretation of the imagery. Later seventeenth-century authors were not privy to even the basic facts about the ceiling and must be read critically. G. P. Bellori, *Le vite de' pittori, scultori e architetti moderni*, ed. E. Borea (Turin, 1976 [Rome, 1672; life of Sacchi written ca. 1685, first pub. 1942: *Le vite inedite del Bellori*, ed. M. Piacentini, Rome, 1942, 50–53]), 544–48; Passeri, *Die Künstlerbiographien*, 295–96; *Spiegazione delle pitture della sala degli eccellentissimi signori principi Barberini coll aggiunta della volta detta della divina sapienza* (Rome, n.d. [probably late 18th cent.]), 15–19.

[26] Wisdom 7:26, 29. For the attributes of the Virgin, see Y. Hirn, *The Sacred Shrine* (Boston, 1957), 435–70.

among those enumerated in the seventh and eighth chapters of the Book of Wisdom. These he lists in order according to their symbolic import and compositional proximity to the central figure of Divine Wisdom:

> Divinity [triangle/Triangulum, Wisdom 7:22]
> Eternity [serpent/Serpens, i.e., Ophiuchus, 8:13/8:17]
> Holiness [altar/Ara, 7:22]
> Purity [swan/Cygnus, 7:24]
> Perspicacity [eagle/Aquila, 7:22/8:8]
> Beauty [tresses of hair/Coma Berenices, 7:29/8:2]
> Suavity [lyre/Lyra, 7:22/8:1]
> Strength [club/Hercules, 7:25/8:7]
> Beneficence [shaft of wheat/Virgo, 7:22]
> Justice [balance/Libra, 8:7]
> Nobility [crown/Corona Borealis, 8:3][27]

Love (7:22) rides the heavenly lion (Leo) and hurls a golden arrow, while Fear (8:15) throws a silver one and is seated on a hare (Lepus).[28]

Up to this point the author of the manuscript has been unusually direct in his discussion of the imagery, limiting himself to the iconographic level of meaning. But in the last paragraph the author shifts to the iconological level of significance and provides us with the broader meaning of the ceiling image:

> Such a painting is appropriate to the majestic edifice of the Barberini family in order that it be understood that since that happy family was born and elected to rule the Church in the place of God it governs with Divine Wisdom, equally loved and revered.[29]

This terse, matter-of-fact statement deserves to be examined with care, for, as we shall see, it contains all that is needed to unlock the meaning of the painting. Curiously this crucial final paragraph is also the one crossed out on the manuscript page.

PREPARATORY DRAWINGS

A brief analysis of Sacchi's preparatory drawings related to the *Divine Wisdom* will provide insight into the genesis of the design and the final realization of the iconographic system.

There are seven sheets of the artist's sketches for the work. A compositional study in the Cooper-Hewitt Museum is the earliest and most informative of the group (Fig. 41).[30] At

[27] Wisdom 7:22–23, 29; 8:3, 7, 13, 17. Eleven of the approximately thirty distinct virtues attributed to Wisdom have been chosen. For the coordination of the attributes with the appropriate constellation, consult Lechner, "Fresco of 'Divina Sapienza'," 100–1, and R. H. Allen, *Star Names: Their Lore and Meaning* (New York, 1963 [1899]).

[28] The love of Wisdom appears as a concept also in the book of Wisdom (7:10; 8:2). The notion of love and

fear of God in relationship to wisdom appears in Psalms (110:10) and in the other sapiential books of Job (28:28), Proverbs (1:7, 15:33), and, especially, Ecclesiasticus, where "The love of God is honourable wisdom" (1:14) and "The fear of the Lord is the beginning of wisdom" (1:16). Also see Ecclesiasticus 1:18, 20, 27.

[29] Appendix B.

[30] Black and red chalk, brown wash, white heightening, with some contours reinforced with pen and

this point in the development of the design the artist had not yet resolved the figure positions and groupings of the virtues. The most prominent difference appears in the area just above the earth. In the drawing, Perspicacity reclines with her back to the viewer in the center left foreground between Strength and Beneficence, whereas Beauty stands in the distance at the extreme right.[31] The lions flanking the throne and serving as the mount of Love in the painting do not yet appear in the drawing, indicating that at this point some aspects of the iconography, too, had not yet been established. Fear, not apparent in photographic reproductions of the drawing, is lightly sketched in with red chalk on the cloud at the upper right.

The artist apparently became dissatisfied with the original position of the head of Wisdom and subsequently redrew it, turning it still more in the direction of Love. This alteration reinforces the powerful diagonal running from upper left to lower right—a feature that remains prominent in the ceiling fresco. The spatial diagonal gains strength from the leaning foreground figure of Perspicacity and from the turn of Wisdom's throne, which, to judge from the throne back, base, and figure of Wisdom, angles dramatically to the right. In the drawing Sacchi sought to balance the thrust of this principal compositional line with a counter diagonal running from the left foreground, where the figures are close to the picture plane, into the depth of the composition toward the extreme right. This secondary spatial dynamic has all but disappeared in the painting.

But the most striking difference between this drawing and the painting lies in the compactness of the composition of the former and the inclusion of only the top portion of the terrestrial globe.[32] All figures are positioned closer to the throne than in the painting, as can be seen, for example, with Divinity. In the drawing the figure obscures the left side of the throne, whereas in the painting ample space appears between the two. Nobility and Justice were also pulled out to the left. Finally, by moving Perspicacity to the right of the globe, Sacchi dispersed what had been the main concentration of figures in the drawing, thereby opening the composition in the center and introducing a gap that attracts the viewer's gaze upward to the foot of Wisdom's throne. The Cooper-Hewitt drawing is surprising for its high-pressure density and energetic clashing of compositional forces. It must be judged more innovative and dynamic than even Cortona's sketches produced at a comparable stage in the design of the Barberini salone fresco (Figs. 41, 96).[33]

So pronounced and thoughtfully considered is the concentrated composition of the

brown ink (31.2 × 33.3 cm.). Cooper-Hewitt Museum of Design, Smithsonian Institution, 1901–39–1714. W. Vitzthum, "Current and Forthcoming Exhibitions: New York," *Burlington Magazine* 101 (1959), 466; F. Stampfle and J. Bean, *Drawings from New York Collections II: The Seventeenth Century in Italy* (New York, 1967), 55–56; J. K. and R. H. Westin, *Carlo Maratti and His Contemporaries* (University Park, Pa., 1975), 87–89; Harris, *Andrea Sacchi*, 9–10, 12, 58; Gallavotti Cavallero, "Il programma iconografico," 279.

[31] The identification of these two figures is based on Harris' observation (*Andrea Sacchi*, 40, n. 59) that the figure at the right holds out the tresses of hair as she does in the final painting and that the other figure must therefore be Perspicacity. Yet it must be allowed that the opposite may be true. The partially nude figure in the center left foreground reclines and rests an outstretched arm upon her raised knee. Although turned in the opposite direction, this posture is nearly identical with that of Beauty in the painting. Moreover, the figure at the right in the drawing appears to be fully clothed, as is the Perspicacity in the painting. The indistinct protrusion at her feet could be the eagle, which otherwise does not appear in the drawing.

[32] As noted by Stampfle and Bean, *Drawings from New York Collections*, 56; Westin and Westin, *Maratti and Contemporaries*, 89; Harris, *Andrea Sacchi*, 9–10.

[33] Below, 145–47. Had Sacchi followed through in the fresco with the dynamic ideas as expressed on this sheet, the *Divine Wisdom* would never have come to exemplify, as it has, Roman Baroque classicism.

drawing that one can hardly imagine an artist as methodical as Sacchi having so misjudged the monumental requirements of his task. The figures on the left in the drawing, for example, form an emphatic vertical against the edge of the composition, the figure of Strength folding neatly into the right angle of the corner. None of these compositional devices could have been of any service to the artist when he turned to the expanse of the vaulted ceiling. This apparent oversight on the part of the artist has so troubled some scholars that they have hypothesized the drawing may have been produced as a preliminary sketch for easel paintings made after the ceiling.[34] Since all the easel versions and engravings are closer to the painted ceiling than to the Cooper-Hewitt sketch, such a hypothesis seems unjustified. Moreover, in the drawing the precise iconography of the composition had not yet been fully formulated, thus indicating the chronological priority of this sketch over all completed versions. These factors lead to the conclusion that the Cooper-Hewitt drawing must have been made prior to the fresco, but that, since it includes only the upper section of the globe, it must have been sketched for the immediate purpose of an easel-format painting to serve as a modello for Taddeo's approval.[35]

Of the three extant easel versions of the *Divine Wisdom*, the most likely candidate for a modello is the canvas, painted with unusually free handling of the brush, that the Barberini sent as a gift to Cardinal Richelieu and which is now in the Hermitage in Leningrad (Fig. 42).[36] Internal evidence lends support to this identification. Here Sacchi began to expand the composition, isolating the throne and introducing greater space around each figure than appears in the Cooper-Hewitt sketch. This adjustment appears especially in the figures of Dignity and Holiness flanking the throne of Wisdom.

Another easel version, in Vienna, is closely related in size to the Leningrad modello and furthers the process of figural expansion (Fig. 43).[37] The head of Perspicacity now appears to the right of the throne lion, and Beauty reclines at a more leisurely angle, resting at a greater distance from the wind-blown drapery of Purity, all the way to the edge of the stretcher.

[34] Westin and Westin, *Maratti and Contemporaries*, 89. For the easel versions, see Harris, *Andrea Sacchi*, 58.

[35] We know that an easel-format version existed as early as April or May 1631, only a few months after the completion of the palace fresco. One is reported in the collection of the dealer Valguarnera. J. Costello, "The Twelve Pictures 'Ordered by Velasquez' and the Trial of Valguarnera," *Journal of the Warburg and Courtauld Institutes* 13 (1950), 273, as cited by Harris, *Andrea Sacchi*, 58.

[36] Teti, *Aedes Barberinae* (1642), 83–84; Posse, *Andrea Sacchi*, 49. Harris (*Andrea Sacchi*, 58) believes that the Richelieu-Hermitage version may be the one once in the Valguarnera group and subsequently reacquired by the Barberini. In the early eighteenth century, when this version was still in the Crozat collection in Paris, it was catalogued as "The Prudentia Divina, a finish'd sketch for the large one in the Palace Barberini." J. Richardson, *An Account of the Statues, Bas-Reliefs, Drawings and Pictures in Italy, France etc.* (London,

1722), 14. As noted by Harris, *Andrea Sacchi*, 58. The Leningrad painting is inventoried in G. F. Waagen, *Die Gemäldesammlungen in der Kaiserlichen Ermitage zu St. Petersburg* (Munich, 1864), no. 209; also the 1958 catalogue, 1:172, no. 132 (83 × 105.5 cm.), as cited in Harris, *Andrea Sacchi*, 58.

[37] Oil on canvas (80 × 102 cm.). Kunsthistorisches Museum, Vienna. Posse, *Andrea Sacchi*, 49. This is the canvas the Barberini gave to the emperor's ambassador, Prince von Eggenberg, in 1639. Harris (*Andrea Sacchi*, 58) considers the forms too flat to be autograph. The more finished treatment and linear contours of the figures indicate that this version must yield priority to the Leningrad version, but, since there appear here details and spatial relationships (especially in the figure of Beauty) that exist in no other version (the jeweled armband, the position of the Coma Berenices, and the strands of hair to the left of her neck), this version may be by the artist himself.

In the fresco the artist continued this compositional shift by moving the figure of Beauty to the extreme right, in a more reclining position and at a still greater distance from Purity. Love and Fear, in the fresco, also occupy more elevated positions in relation to the throne than in sketch or modello. All later versions of the work, both easel and engraved, follow the expanded spatial relationships of the finished fresco. We can see the result, for example, in the much larger and later Chigi version in the Galleria Nazionale d'Arte Antica, Rome (Fig. 44), which appears identical to and is probably based upon the 1642 engraving by Michael Natalis (Fig. 45), except for the obvious addition of the Chigi monti on the throne base.[38]

The evidence of the Cooper-Hewitt sketch also suggests that Sacchi may first have intended to paint a *quadro riportato* with a stucco surround in the center of the vault of the salotto. The logic of this would be indicated by the other ceiling paintings that existed or were being planned for the palace.[39] All of them have just such *quadri riportati*, except for one—the corresponding salotto on the piano terreno in Taddeo's suite of rooms (PBT 5, Fig. 71), which was being painted by Tassi and Lagi at this same time. The open sky ceiling of Taddeo's comparable downstairs salotto leads to the conclusion that the idea of a similar format for the *Divine Wisdom* resulted from a more comprehensive consideration than would have been made by an artist concerned only with his assigned vault. This decision may have been introduced by the patron as a factor in the design process only after Sacchi had already made the preliminary sketch.

Six additional sheets, all studies for individual figures and drapery, have been identified in the Düsseldorf Kunstmuseum.[40] These sketches, related to five of the fourteen figures present in the fresco, postdate the Cooper-Hewitt drawing and demonstrate the meticulous care Sacchi devoted to each figure in the composition. Although other drawings have not been identified, Sacchi must have given as much attention to each of the figures as to those represented by the Düsseldorf group. Harris has estimated that under normal circumstances the artist produced a minimum of five preparatory sketches for each major figure in a work.[41]

The most detailed of the group, a full-length drawing of Wisdom (Fig. 46), reveals an intermediate stage between the early compositional drawing and the completed fresco.[42] The arm and legs of the figure remain bare and the position of the head fixed as in the Cooper-Hewitt drawing, but the figure sits more upright and the throne has been pulled around to a more frontal position as it appears in the fresco. The gesture conveys less emphasis than in the compositional sketch, and the highlighted drapery joins with the mirror to form a counterdiagonal. In the fresco the drapery is pulled down over the legs and the arm to create a more matronly effect, and the positioning of the scepter effectively counters the now-soft-

[38] Oil on canvas (130 × 176 cm.). Harris (ibid., 58) dates this version 1658. It reproduces the smaller head and elongated proportions of the figure of Wisdom seen only in the engraving. According to Passeri (*Die Künstlerbiographien*, 301–2), the version given to Alexander VII was autograph.

[39] Harris, *Andrea Sacchi*, 9.

[40] A. S. Harris and E. Schaar, *Kataloge des Kunstmuseums Düsseldorf, Handzeichnungen: die Handzeichnungen* *von Andrea Sacchi und Carlo Maratta* (Düsseldorf, 1967), 29–30, cat. 18–23, pls. 1, 4, 11–12.

[41] Ibid., 19.

[42] Düsseldorf Kunstmuseum FP 13226 recto: black chalk with white heightening (37.8 × 25.5 cm.). D. Graf, *Master Drawings of the Roman Baroque from the Kunstmuseum Düsseldorf* (London-Edinburgh, 1973), cat. 127; Harris and Schaar, *Kataloge des Kunstmuseums*, 30, cat. 18, pl. 1.

ened diagonal of the drapery. The artist also ultimately decided to cut away the throne back so the head of the figure could be seen against the solar orb. In the fresco Sacchi returned to the *di sotto in su* view first seen in the compositional drawing but abandoned in the intermediate stage of the Düsseldorf drawing.

The verso of the full-length Düsseldorf sketch (Fig. 47) and two additional sheets related to the figure of Wisdom record an intervening stage between the full-length figure study and the figure as it appears in the fresco. In these drawings, each of which contains two studies, the figure appears veiled as in the fresco, but the artist still has not arrived at a solution to the drapery that satisfied him completely.[43] Some variations occur between the Düsseldorf sketches of Eternity, Divinity, and Holiness, and the figures as they appear in the fresco, but these adjustments are mostly in the drapery and concern the relationship of the individual figures to the immediate context.[44] The degree to which Sacchi devoted attention to the particulars of each figure is illustrated by the three studies for the sleeve of Perspicacity, which appear on the verso of the sketch for Eternity.[45]

Sacchi's concentrated attention to each individual figure as a stage in his working procedure significantly affected the final product we see on the vault of the salotto in Palazzo Barberini. The dynamics of the early Cooper-Hewitt drawing were gradually ameliorated in the Düsseldorf figure and drapery studies. This stage of the process is the most restrained. In the executed fresco we encounter a less intense concentration on the individual elements. Although the overall effect is less static than in the intermediate studies, the classicizing repercussions of that intervening stage of the artist's working procedure reappear in the fresco in the relative autonomy of the individual figures and the insistent formal dignity with which they occupy the heavens.

Having seen how fluid was the process by which Sacchi arrived at the final composition for the *Divine Wisdom*, we may now consider the iconographic content and iconological meaning of the work. Four major themes are seen to emerge from the tightly woven program: Divine Wisdom as the Old Testament prefiguration of Christ, the political value of divine election as applied to the papal family and as a theological defense of nepotism, heavenly and earthly love in relation to the secular branch of that family, and astrology as the language of Divine Wisdom and the sign of the divinely ordained destiny of the Barberini.

WISDOM INCARNATE: THE CHRISTOLOGICAL CYCLE OF THE CHAPEL

The subject of Sacchi's Barberini salotto ceiling is unconventional. Never before had it appeared as the main subject of a large-scale ceiling painting in a secular palace.[46] The

[43] Düsseldorf Kunstmuseum, FP 13226 verso (37.8 × 25.5 cm.), FP 13600 (35.5 × 243 cm.), FP 13230 (37 × 33.5 cm.). All three in black chalk with white heightening. Graf, *Master Drawings*, cat. 127; Harris and Schaar, *Kataloge des Kunstmuseums*, 30, cat. 18–20, pl. 4.

[44] Düsseldorf Kunstmuseum, FP 13359 (24.5 × 37.2 cm.), FP 14103 (37.8 × 24.6 cm.), and FP 13858 (38.5 × 24.8 cm.), all in black chalk with white heightening.

Graf, *Master Drawings*, cat. 128–129; Harris and Schaar, *Kataloge des Kunstmuseums*, 30, cat. 21–23, pls. 11–12.

[45] Düsseldorf Kunstmuseum, FP 13359 verso. Ibid., cat. 21.

[46] Following the success and fame of Sacchi's ceiling, the theme of Divine Wisdom appeared in a number of major Roman works, first in commissions sponsored by the Barberini, then in projects completely indepen-

Barberini favored iconographic novelties, and the *Divine Wisdom* characterizes a patronage always in search of something out of the ordinary and attention-getting. The unusual design of the Barberini Palace itself exemplifies the quest for originality generated by the social aspirations of the family.

Sacchi did not draw from the well-established secular humanistic tradition for the representation of Wisdom as "Philosophia"—the love of wisdom.[47] The Barberini *Divine Wisdom* symbolizes the opposite of the humanistic concept of wisdom. It has nothing to do with book learning, human endeavor, or even individual intelligence. The program of Sacchi's ceiling derives instead from the concept of wisdom encountered in the sapiential literature of the Old Testament, especially the Books of Wisdom and Ecclesiasticus. There Wisdom appears as the personification of a quality infused in the individual as a gift of God. For those who possess it, this wisdom signifies divine favor, but only those who search for it in prayer are granted wisdom. Sacchi thus avoided any reference to the humanistic tradition of his subject. He did not even consult Ripa's iconographic handbook, where an overloaded figure of "Sapienza Divina" is explained by means of the text in Ecclesiasticus (Fig. 122),[48] but relied instead entirely upon attributes taken directly from pictorial allusions suggested in the biblical text of the Book of Wisdom.[49]

The only earlier images that appear in any way related to Sacchi's figure are manuscript illuminations of the same Old Testament texts from which the Barberini fresco derives. A thirteenth-century German manuscript Bible in the Beatty Library in Dublin typifies this pictorial tradition (Fig. 123).[50] The illustrated initial "O" of "Omnis sapientia a Domino Deo est" (All wisdom is from the Lord God) (Ecclesiasticus 1:1) depicts the crowned and scepter-holding figure of Wisdom seated on a throne encircled by the initial letter upheld by four angels. The letter forms a celestial band upon which are arranged the sun, moon, and stars. Here Wisdom points upward to remind the viewer of the source of all wisdom as written in the adjoining text. Sacchi's figure gestures downward, bringing that wisdom in the form of love and fear to humankind. The celestial imagery of both Bible illustration and ceiling painting finds justification in the verse from the Book of Wisdom: "For she is more beautiful than the sun, and above all the order of the stars" (Wisdom 7–29).[51]

---

dent of their patronage. By 1644 the subject had already become, for the first time, the main subject of the pictorial cycle of a library. J. B. Scott, "The Counter-Reformation Program of Borromini's Biblioteca Vallicelliana," *Storia dell'arte* 45 (1985), 295–304, esp. 299–300. For the subsequent popularity of the theme, particularly in library cycles, see Scott, "Allegories of Divine Wisdom," 146–266. On the problematic identification of a number of so-called "Wisdom" figures in ceiling paintings by Anselmo Canera (Palazzo Thiene, Vicenza, ca. 1547–1553), Veronese (Villa Barbaro, Maser, 1555–1559), and Titian (Biblioteca Marciana, Venice, 1560–1562), see ibid., 206, n. 47, and I. J. Reist, "*Divine Love* and Veronese's Frescoes at the Villa Barbaro," *Art Bulletin* 67 (1985), 615–27. The interpretations that identify these figures as "Wisdom" do not predate the nineteenth century.

[47] M.-T. D'Alverny, "La sagesse et ses sept filles: recherches sur les allégories de la philosophie et des arts libéraux du IXe au XIIe siècle," in *Mélanges dédiés à la mémoire de Félix Grat* (Paris, 1946), 1:245–78, and "Quelques aspects du symbolisme de la 'sapientia' chez les humanistes," in *Umanesimo e esoterismo*, ed. E. Castelli (Padua, 1960), 321–33; R. Wittkower, "Transformations of Minerva in Renaissance Imagery," in *Allegory and the Migration of Symbols* (London, 1977), 130–42. The humanistic concept of wisdom has been examined by E. F. Rice, *The Renaissance Idea of Wisdom* (Cambridge, Mass., 1958 [rpt. Westport, Conn., 1973]).

[48] C. Ripa, *Nova iconologia* (Padua, 1618), 457–60.

[49] See the attributes of the figure of Wisdom as indicated in the Barberini Manuscript. Appendix B.

[50] E.G. Millar, *The Library of A. Chester Beatty: A Descriptive Catalogue of the Western Manuscripts* (London, 1927), 1: pl. XCVIII(b).

[51] Harris, *Andrea Sacchi*, 11.

The sacred imagery of Sacchi's fresco may seem somewhat out of context until we recall that the salotto served as the antechamber for the adjoining family chapel.[52] The fresco cycle painted on the chapel walls and lunettes in 1631–1632 by Cortona, Romanelli, and Baldini depicts the Infancy and Passion of Christ (PBN C1, Fig. 48).[53] The dove of the Holy Spirit descends from the celestial blue in the fictive oculus of the dome, while angels carrying instruments of the Passion penetrate three of the feigned latticed openings, their wings crossing in front of the painted architectural moldings as they enter into the viewer's space (Fig. 49). A fourth panel, now filled with masonry, may have served as an actual opening that brought natural light into the chapel.[54]

An early sketch for the dome painting (Fig. 50) shows a halved-format decorative scheme.[55] This preliminary design already contains the two most iconographically important instruments of the Passion. The Veil of Veronica and the Column of the Flagellation are both retained in the final work, but otherwise the drawing suggests a radically different distribution of painted panels as well as a differently shaped architectural surface, elliptical rather than circular. At this early point in the design process no indication of the latticework appears, but windows must have been envisioned for the half of the dome not represented. Thus we see depicted in the drawing that portion of the dome opposite the entrance door and the line of sight of the entering beholder.[56] The testimony provided by this graphic evidence indicates that designs for the pictorial imagery of the chapel predate the completion of the architectural context, positing a process in which the design of pictorial and architectural components were under consideration simultaneously.

The *Crucifixion*—the only part of the cycle entirely the product of Cortona's brush—appears above the altar directly opposite the door leading from the salotto (Fig. 51).[57] Passing from the Old Testament personification of Divine Wisdom in the antechamber, the viewer, upon entering the chapel, would immediately encounter the image of Christ, the New Testament embodiment of Wisdom.[58] What is allegorically alluded to in the salotto finds fulfill-

[52] Ibid., 9, alone, has emphasized this fact and its importance for the design of Sacchi's painting.

[53] For a discussion of the attributions of various scenes, see Briganti, *Pietro da Cortona*, 196.

[54] The *misura e stima* of 1638 (BAV, Arch. Barb., Ind. II, no. 2888, 165r–166v) records the construction of the lantern above the chapel and the opening of the window in the vault: "Torretta fatta sopra tetti per dar lume alla Cappella a detto Piano [nobile]. Per haver rotto e fatto la fenestra che da lume alla d.a cappella . . . sc. 3." Pollak, *Die Kunsttätigkeit*, 1:286; Blunt, "Palazzo Barberini," 285; Magnanimi, "Documenti della costruzione," 199; Waddy, *Seventeenth-Century Roman Palaces*, 195, 240, 387, n. 69.

[55] Windsor, Royal Library 4456 (18.7 x 39.7 cm.). Blunt, "Exhibition of Pietro da Cortona," 416; idem, "Palazzo Barberini," 284–85; Blunt and Cooke, *Roman Drawings*, 79, no. 599.

[56] Blunt, "Palazzo Barberini," 284–85.

[57] The lunette above the *Crucifixion* has lost most of its *intonaco* surface, but given the fragment that re-

mains, together with the Dove of the Holy Spirit above and the Christ below, the fresco appears to have depicted God the Father. For the original marble altar, carved with bees by Alessandro Loreto and once located beneath the *Cruxifixion*, see Pollak, *Die Kunsttätigkeit*, 1: 329, and Blunt, "Palazzo Barberini," 285, fig. 30d.

[58] The biblical sources for Christ as Divine Wisdom are Colossians (2:3–4) and I Corinthians (1:23–24, 30). For the crucified Christ as Divine Wisdom: "But we preach Christ crucified, unto the Jews indeed a stumbling-block, and unto the Gentiles foolishness" (I Corinthians 1:23). Strabus, *Glossa Ordinaria*, esp. the gloss on Proverbs (1:20; 8:22), 1:1082, 1091. Also, *Lexikon der Christlichen Ikonographie*, ed. E. Kirschbaum (Freiburg, 1968–1976), 4:41–42; D'Avossa (*Andrea Sacchi*, 72, n. 24) tentatively suggests the possibility of a connection between salotto and chapel on the basis of the Christ = Divine Wisdom equation. On this same point, see Scott, "Allegories of Divine Wisdom," 35–37.

ment in the chapel not only in the image of the altar wall but also in the surrounding scenes showing the process by which God worked his will in the world and by which Wisdom became flesh.[59]

The iconographic linkage between Divine Wisdom and Christ is also reinforced emblematically since the sun symbolizes both.[60] Cortona emphasized this by including a medievalizing iconographic component in the *Crucifixion*. The sun and the moon appear frequently in late medieval representations of the theme, the sun on Christ's right and the moon to his left, but after the late fifteenth century this iconography fell into disuse.[61] Cortona revived the motif, depicting the two celestial bodies in the traditional positions. The sun, which is not seen in photographs, appears to the left of Christ's right hand, dimmed as in the eclipse of the sun alluded to in the account of the Crucifixion given in the synoptic gospels (Matthew 27:45, Mark 15:33, Luke 23:44–45).

But the relationship between Sacchi's fresco and the pictorial cycle of the chapel is more than an abstract theological conceit. The artist made formal adjustments designed to prepare the viewer for the experience of the chapel imagery. Looking at the plan and elevation of the south wall of the salotto (PBN 5; Fig. 52), we note that the chapel door appears offset to the right. This is best seen in relationship to the sun impresa located in the middle of the stucco frieze above the door.[62] The compositional weight of Sacchi's fresco also shifts to the right. Terrestrial orb, throne, and figure of Wisdom all travel off center to the right, as already foreseen in the Cooper-Hewitt preliminary compositional sketch. Moreover, the action of the ceiling imagery moves from upper left to lower right, beginning with the downthrust of Love's arrow, through the arm and scepter of Wisdom, to the eagle and northern edge of the pool of light on the globe.

The desire to orient the ceiling imagery toward the chapel was a consideration of such primacy that one of the chief formal conventions of ceiling painting was not followed here. Viewers entering the salotto from the original door would first have encountered the ceiling painting inverted. As they crossed the room and turned to the left to follow the route of the successive suite of rooms, the heavenly apparition overhead would have gradually become upright, and by the time they had adjusted to this viewing point the chapel door would have been directly opposite.

Still, the effectiveness of this coordination with the chapel entrance becomes clear only when we see the ensemble as it must have been intended to be seen, from the ideal station point (Fig. 52).[63] The great weight of the globe, which has so troubled many observ-

[59] The theological justification for the visual positioning of Divine Wisdom above the Crucifixion also has a tradition in medieval art. G. Schiller, *Ikonographie der Christlichen Kunst* (Gütersloh, 1976), 2:141, cites the example of the twelfth-century St. Godehard Crucifix at Hildesheim, fig. 476.

[60] Malachi 4:2, Wisdom 5:6, and Matthew 17:2 are the common sources for the sun as the symbol of Christ. Ibid., 3:26–27. Without reference to the Christological cycle of the chapel, Gallavotti Cavallero ("Il programma iconografico," 277–79) interprets the figure of Divine Wisdom, with its solar attribute, as a refer-

ence to Christ, the sun being the link between Wisdom, Christ, and the Barberini family.

[61] Schiller, *Ikonographie*, 2:120–21. Raphael's Mond Crucifixion of 1502–1503 (National Gallery, London) is a late example of this iconographic type.

[62] Originally, of course, the main entrance to the salotto was located in the corner to the left of the chapel door.

[63] The necessity of employing a wide-angle lens (24 mm.) to capture something of the true relationships of the ensemble has resulted in some distortions, particularly in the upper area of the photograph. The optical

ers, now has additional purpose. Our eyes are brought down through the commanding gesture of Wisdom to the orb and thence to the open door of the chapel, where originally an aperture in the dome admitted natural light that would have softly bathed Cortona's altar fresco of the *Crucifixion* with miraculous illumination, further inviting the visitor's approach. And as one nears the chapel, progressively more of the figure of the crucified Christ—Divine Wisdom incarnate—becomes revealed to view.

The spatial illusionism of the *Divine Wisdom*, so uncharacteristic of Sacchi's previous work, can now be comprehended in its full operative effect. Wisdom and her host of attendant virtues are to be understood as a heavenly apparition hovering vertically above the chapel and its altar.[64] Even the painted light that emanates from Wisdom carries downward and, transformed into natural light, seems to filter through to the chapel.

For his part, Cortona, too, made adjustments, as a careful examination of the altar fresco will prove. The light originally entering from the opening in the dome has been painted into the fresco in the area around the titulus, descending to illuminate the agonized face of Christ as his upturned glance repeats that of Divine Wisdom (Figs. 36, 51). Prerestoration photographs also show that Cortona made major changes in the altar fresco to enhance its power as seen from the salotto. The standing figures of the Virgin and St. John were originally closer to the cross, as indicated by the outlines of the original *giornate* where they stood. The artist must have subsequently realized that the figure of Christ would possess greater visual impact, as seen from the salotto, if left in isolation. So the secondary figures, with the exception of the kneeling Magdalen, were pushed out to the sides. The viewer instantly perceives the practical result of these alterations, for the gesticulating figures are exactly enframed by the door. Their agitated emotional states and intense upward glances—easily read from the distance of the adjoining room—draw one forward until the full figure of Christ gradually descends into view.

The evidence of the visual linkage between the imagery of the two rooms is all the more noteworthy given the personalities involved. Sacchi and Cortona—two figures modern scholarship has preferred to keep apart—are once again seen to be engaged in a cooperative effort. Sacchi had previously worked under Cortona's direction in the gallery of the Villa Sacchetti at Castelfusano,[65] but no evidence exists of such a hierarchical relationship here, where Sacchi had the largest portion of the immediate assignment. Moreover, nothing approaching the nature of this ensemble appears in the work of Sacchi or Cortona before or after the Barberini enterprise. A third figure may have coordinated the unified program of the salotto and chapel.

The guiding hand of Bernini was surely at work in the creation of this remarkable ensemble. As he was the supervising architect in charge of the overall design and decoration of the palace following the death of Maderno in 1629, his involvement would be difficult to discount.[66] The stonecarver responsible for the chapel altar, Alessandro Loreto, was brought in from St. Peter's, where he was at that time (May 1632) engaged as Bernini's assistant on

---

warping somewhat exaggerates the actual effect of the illusionism, but these distortions at least reveal the visual realities of the ceiling fresco rather than negating them. Fig. 52, taken with a 24 mm. lens, is the closest photographic approximation of the actual visual experience of the salotto-chapel fresco ensemble.

[64] As noted by Harris, *Andrea Sacchi*, 9.

[65] Briganti, *Pietro da Cortona*, 179–80; Harris, *Andrea Sacchi*, 4–5, 54–55.

[66] Bernini's position as supervising architect at Palazzo Barberini is definitively established in the documents generated by a subsequent lawsuit brought by

the reorganization of the crossing piers[67]; his participation in the work in the Barberini chapel thus implies Bernini's supervisory presence. Moreover, the fanciful frieze of Daphne-like figures in the salotto must derive from an inventive design by Bernini (Figs. 37, 39).[68] The fantasy of invention and dynamism displayed in the frieze, where forms appear in the process of metamorphosis, is foreign to Sacchi's style.[69] By contrast, it fits logically in the oeuvre of Bernini.

The Daphne figures who stretch out toward the sun work in the design not only as a Barberini device but would also have reminded contemporaries of the Borghese *Apollo and Daphne* sculpted by Bernini, the base of which carried a moralizing distych composed by Maffeo Barberini. Individual details such as the suns, wings, laurel tendrils, and lizards, as well as the overall novelty of effect, should be compared with similar details on the Baldacchino in St. Peter's, which Bernini—under Urban's patronage—was in the process of designing and executing at this time, and with the frieze of the stylobate he later designed for the Raimondi Chapel in S. Pietro in Montorio (1640–1647). Even the nonclassical compositional structure of the Raimondi frieze, with the flaming heart surrounded by rose branches and fluttering birds, echoes that of the Barberini salotto, with the central sun flanked by spreading vegetable and animal motifs. Moreover, there is a conceptual similarity to both works in that they each reiterate in emblematic form the central themes of the ensembles they adorn.[70] Construction documents record Bernini's involvement with the similar emblematic stucco sculpture of the palace salone, which he coordinated with the iconography of Cortona's ceiling painting.[71] Bernini's participation in the decoration of the salotto and chapel would have been part of his normal duties as supervising architect of all work conducted at the Barberini Palace.

---

the stonemason Nicola Scala in 1641 (BAV, Arch. Barb., Ind. II, 2889, 10), as transcribed by Pollak, *Die Kunsttätigkeit*, 1:262. G. Magnanimi, "Interventi berniniani a Palazzo Barberini," in *Gian Lorenzo Bernini architetto e l'architettura europea del sei-settecento*, eds. G. Spagnesi and M. Fagiolo, (Rome, 1983–1984), 1:167–92, has traced Bernini's intervention in many other parts of the palace.

[67] Pollak, *Die Kunsttätigkeit*, 1:329, 2:436–37; F. Borsi, *Bernini architetto* (Milan, 1980), 271, 295–96, 301.

[68] H. Kauffmann, *Giovanni Lorenzo Bernini: die figürlichen Kompositionen* (Berlin, 1970), 63–64, figs. 37a–c. C. D'Onofrio, *Roma vista da Roma* (Rome, 1967), 303–7.

[69] Sacchi's emblematic frieze for the Chapel of St. Catherine of Siena in S. Maria sopra Minerva (1637–1644) conforms to a more static, conservative vision of classical form. See Harris, *Andrea Sacchi*, 79–80.

[70] For the stylobate frieze, see I. Lavin, *Bernini and the Unity of the Visual Arts* (New York-London, 1980), 49, figs. 24 and 26. On the emblematic meaning of the Barberini frieze, below, 58–59.

[71] "Per haver f.o l'altra porta di mezzo al Salone in testa ch'entra nella stanza ovata 4 mostre di diversi Impresi quali s'è fatte e disfatte d'ord.e del Sr. Principe [Taddeo] e del sr Cavaliere [Bernini], e prima fatto l'agg.o aboz.a e stucc.a una Serena e poi guastata e fatta una testa di medusa con targhe e cochiglia con due cornocopi e pieni di frutti e poi disfatta delli soprad.i lavori se n'è pagato al Favezano Scultore d'ord.e del S. Cav.re Bernino sc. 40. E più robba che ha adoprato e servitù fatta cioè calce stucco Ponti e chiodi sc. 12 e poi fatto come sta al presente ch'è una testa di Medusa con capelli di serpe e due cegni dalle bande si valuta sc. 12, che assieme . . . sc. 64." BAV, Arch. Barb., Ind. II, 2888, 188; transcribed in Pollak, *Die Kunsttätigkeit*, 1:291. Also see F. P. Fiore, "Palazzo Barberini: problemi storiografici e alcuni documenti sulle vicende costruttive," in *Gian Lorenzo Bernini architetto e l'architettura europea del sei-settecento*, eds. G. Spagnesi and M. Fagiolo (Rome, 1983–1984), 1:202–3. Thelen (*Francesco Borromini*, 65, figs. C53, C54) has noted that the sculptural components in Borromini's drawings for the architectural details of the salone were added on Bernini's instructions and possibly in his own hand. The evidence of Bernini's own sheet (ca. 1629, Düsseldorf), with eight studies for the overdoor leading from the salone to the oval room, confirms the artist's involvement with the sculptural details of the palace interior. On this drawing, see A. Harris, *Selected Drawings of Gian Lorenzo Bernini* (New York, 1977), no. 20 (Düssel-

In examining Cortona's preliminary drawing for the chapel dome fresco (Fig. 50), we have seen how the design of the pictorial features of the chapel was already in process before the completion of the architectural matrix. The painter therefore must have had knowledge of preliminary designs for the architectural setting of his scheme. Cortona's sketch thus shows a procedure in which spatial context and pictorial imagery were formulated in tandem.

Bernini would have been responsible for architectural changes made to the original design of the chapel, particularly the window in the dome. He had earlier used a device like that of the Barberini chapel in the vault above the altar aedicula at S. Bibiana (1624–1626), where, as in the chapel, a light source was placed on one side of the vault (Fig. 124). Furthermore, precisely this sort of studied manipulation of illumination became the hallmark of Bernini's designs for the Raimondi and Cornaro chapels. Seen in this sequence of work, the Barberini chapel must be considered the prototype for the controlled source of light Bernini used in the later chapels.[72]

The details of the Barberini chapel design, including the innovative introduction of the window, were doubtless drawn up by Borromini, who functioned as Bernini's amanuensis for work at the palace. Thus an extraordinary constellation of personalities lies behind the genesis and creation of the *Divine Wisdom* and chapel fresco cycle: Bernini, in consultation with Taddeo and an adviser, coming forward with the grand unifying ideas; Borromini assigned the task of seeing to the actual design of the architectural details; and Sacchi and Cortona providing the great pictorial components of the assemblage.

In view of this new understanding of the ensemble, the Barberini salotto and chapel must be seen as one of the earliest testing grounds for two important components of that Berninesque concept known as the *bel composto*—the controlled illumination and scenographic relationship of separate works of art brought into visual proximity.[73] The unity of the visual arts that Bernini would later achieve in the Cornaro Chapel and at St. Peter's was only tentatively realized at Palazzo Barberini, where there was no major sculptural element, but the crucial role such an opportunity for experimentation must have provided for the development of this fundamental ideal of the Roman High Baroque can hardly be overestimated.

TADDEO AND HIS UNCLE

This was no ordinary domestic chapel and antechamber. Even by the inflated standards of Baroque Rome, the opulence and number of rooms in the piano nobile apartment at Palazzo Barberini would have been considered extraordinary. The visitor being received by Donna Anna had to pass through four antechambers (PBN 3–6) before arriving at the

dorf, Kunstmuseum, FP 13764). For the relationship of this sculptural work to the salone ceiling fresco, below, 142, 171, 194.

[72] Citing the precedent of the similar window in the dome of the Chapel of Sts. Sebastian and Anne in S. Andrea, Mantua (painted by Rinaldo Mantovano, 1534), Blunt ("Palazzo Barberini," 284–85, fig. 30b) attributed the idea of the chapel window to Cortona, who subsequently, in 1634, employed a design with controlled lighting for a full-scale model for the apse of

S. Giovanni dei Fiorentini (I. Lavin, *Bernini and the Unity*, 34–35). See ibid., 33–36, 104–6. But Bernini was the supervising architect at Palazzo Barberini, and this feature was an architectural matter requiring the construction of a tower over the chapel. Cortona is not likely at this early date (December, 1629) to have been in a position to make such significant decisions affecting the architectural design. On the design modifications made to the chapel, see above, 50.

[73] Ibid., 6–15, 143–64.

audience room (PBN 7). Rooms comparable to the salotto in other Roman palaces of the period often had significant mural or ceiling imagery,[74] yet the iconography of the rooms would not normally be so purposefully determined by the proximity of the chapel. Such domestic chapel antechambers were usually more modest affairs. Even the old Sforza chapel antechamber (PSN 6/PBN 17, Fig. 13) may have been somewhat extravagant in the context of a secular palace. The pontifical status of the Barberini family perhaps justified a more elaborate facility for ceremonial functions, but there appear to have been quite specific motives behind the design and embellishment of such a grand architectural and pictorial scheme.

The ever-increasing number of honors and offices Urban arranged to have bestowed upon his nephew Taddeo and the social and ceremonial obligations pertaining to them required a domestic theater of appropriate expanse and dignity. In 1626, at the age of twenty-three, Taddeo had been appointed lieutenant general of the Church; in 1627, with his marriage to Anna Colonna, he became linked with one of the great old baronial families of Italy; the purchase of Palestrina in 1629 brought with it the princely title; and upon the death of Taddeo's father, Carlo, in 1630, all of his numerous offices were transferred to the son: general of the Church, governor of the Borgo and Civitavecchia, castellano of Castel Sant'Angelo, captain of the Papal Guards.[75] Many of these, especially the military offices, brought with them considerable financial return.[76]

But the crowning honor came in 1631 with Urban's acquisition of the prefecture of Rome for Taddeo, an achievement long planned by the pope. The office of prefect carried tremendous social prestige, if not actual political power, and—a key attraction for Urban and Taddeo—it was hereditary. For the family it would be a permanent legacy of the Barberini pontificate even after the passing of Urban—an honor that would position his family forever above all other papal houses. The pope's passion for the acquisition of this office was grasped by Pietro Contarini, Venetian ambassador to the Holy See, in a report written already in 1625:

> Signor Don Taddeo, in whom it is hoped to establish the family, a youth of about 23 years of age, of most noble manners, of great innocence, and is greatly loved by all the court. The pope has some plan to make him Prefect of the city after the death of the Duke of Urbino who now enjoys this title. A most dignified office that precedes all others and that lasts in life and also after the death of the pope, he takes his place next to the throne.[77]

Contarini's concluding remark that the prefect stands next to the papal throne indicates the great symbolic value of the office.[78]

Urban had been concerned that every privilege linked with the prefecture throughout

[74] For example, the salotto at Palazzo Farnese, with wall scenes painted by Salviati and Taddeo Zuccaro. Below, 165–66.

[75] *DBI*, 6: 180; Pecchiai, *I Barberini*, 163–64.

[76] Ibid., 168, n. 166.

[77] "Il signor Don Taddeo, nel quale si pensa di stabilire la casa: giovane d'anni 23 in circa, di nobilissime maniere, di grand'ingenuità, et è sommamente amato da tutta la Corte. Qualche disegno vi è nel Pontefice di farlo Prefetto della città, dopo la morte del Duca di Urbino, che hora gode questo titolo. Carico dignissimo che a tutti precede, et dura in vita et dopo la morte anco del Pontefice, tiene luogo nel solio." N. Barozzi and G. Berchet, *Le relazioni della corte di Roma lette al senato dagli ambasciatori veneti nel secolo decimosettimo* (Venice, 1877–1879), 1:215.

[78] On the social importance of the Prefecture for the Barberini, see Reinhard, "Nepotismus," 166, n. 119.

its long history—it proved to be older than the papacy—should be known. He therefore commissioned the Vatican archivist, Felice Contelori, to compile a history of the office.[79] The fruits of this research confirmed the grandest ideas about the office the Barberini could possibly have held. Contelori found that the first prefect had been appointed by Romulus. The antiquity of the office could scarcely be questioned.

Concern over titles expressed itself in the many forms of address Contelori found appropriate to the prefect: "Gloriosissimum" and "Sublimitas Tua," among others.[80] A papal chirograph appeared in August 1632 excusing Taddeo from having to address cardinals with the respectful title of "Eminence" except in cases when he felt like using it.[81] Not surprisingly, the right to precede all ambassadors and other secular princes at the papal court was confirmed, as well as the prefect's standing position on the first step to the right of the papal throne.[82] The prefect, it was claimed, also had traditional jurisdiction over towns and territories held as fiefdoms by the city.[83] An entire chapter treated the evolution of the prefect's vestments, with illustrations of the headgear in particular.[84] Finally, Contelori presented a complete list of all individuals known to have been prefects, from Denter Romulius (Tacitus, 6: 11) to Taddeo Barberini. In order to avoid any mistake about the meaning and purpose of this scholarly endeavor, the book carried a dedication to Taddeo, and the frontispiece engraving depicted him in full regalia (Fig. 125).

The aspirations inculcated in the secular head of the Barberini family by his papal uncle were given expression in the painted imagery of Palazzo Barberini. The personality and political role of Taddeo, and of his wife, Anna, who had some share in these offices and honors, lie behind the program of the *Divine Wisdom*.

The political meaning of the subject of Sacchi's painting derives from the biblical text it illustrates. Traditionally ascribed to Solomon, the text of the Book of Wisdom is written in the first person and presents the Hebrew king as the archetype of the wise ruler. The nature of wisdom, the means of acquiring it, the rewards of those who possess it, and its beneficial participation in the early history of humankind constitute the principal thematic content of the Scripture. Significantly, Solomon addresses himself to kings, magistrates, and princes: "If then your delight be in thrones, and sceptres, O ye kings of the people, love wisdom, that you may reign for ever. Love the light of wisdom, all ye that bear rule over peoples" (6:22–23).[85] In the painting the prominence of the throne and scepter of Divine Wisdom would seem to emphasize this passage and its political meaning.

The core of the philosophical argument emerges in chapters 7–10. The personified

[79] F. Contelori, *De Praefecto Urbis* (Rome, 1631). The book was printed under the auspices of the Apostolic Camera. For Contelori's scholarly endeavors on behalf of the Barberini, see G. B. Beltrani, "Felice Contelori ed i suoi studi negli archivi del Vaticano," *Archivio della Società Romana di Storia Patria* 2 (1879), 262–73.

[80] Contelori, *De Praefecto Urbis*, 21–22.

[81] BAV, Arch. Barb., Ind. I, 341.

[82] "Praefertur oratoribus Caesaris, Regis Franciae, Regis Hispaniarum, Angliae, Poloniae, & Reipublicae Venetae, ac alijs tam intra, quam extra cappellam. . . . Praefectus omnibus proceribus, & dynastis, sive Romanis, sive exteris, quibus in Pontificis sacello cardi-

nalitij subsellij ius non est, tum privatim, tum publice anteferri solet." Contelori, *De Praefecto Urbis*, 27.

[83] Ibid., 19.

[84] Ibid., chap. 2, 3–6. Contelori found that over the centuries the ceremonial helmet of the prefect had taken different forms. Taddeo's is represented in fig. 8 on fol. 15v.

[85] Wittkower (*Art and Architecture in Italy*, 263) thought this was the precise text Sacchi illustrated. The Barberini Manuscript (Appendix B), however, indicates the seventh and eighth chapters as the primary sources.

Wisdom and her virtues are defined in chapters 7–8, whence the attributes and constellations in Sacchi's fresco were taken. Solomon explains that, although born a mortal man, he desired Wisdom, sought her out, and gained from her the knowledge of the true workings of the world (7:1–21). He loved her as a bridegroom loves his bride and through possession of her he became a great warrior and king, having immortality from her:

> Her have I loved, and have sought her out from my youth, and have desired
> to take her for my spouse, and I became a lover of her beauty. Moreover by
> the means of her I shall have immortality: and shall leave behind me an ever-
> lasting memory to them that come after me. Terrible kings hearing shall be
> afraid of me: among the multitude I shall be found good, and valiant in war.
> When I go into my house I shall repose myself with her. (Wisdom 8:2, 13, 15–
> 16)

Recalling the closing words of the Barberini Manuscript, we can understand the political purposefulness of the choice of these biblical passages for illustration on the vault of the salotto: "Such a painting is appropriate to the majestic edifice of the Barberini family in order that it be understood that since that happy family was born and elected to rule the Church in the place of God it governs with Divine Wisdom, equally loved and revered."[86]

The Barberini Manuscript does not, however, elaborate on the means by which wisdom is gained. But the ninth chapter of the Book of Wisdom contains Solomon's prayer asking God that wisdom be given to him: "God of my fathers. . . . Give me wisdom, that sitteth by thy throne" (9:1, 4). Thus the biblical text suggests that this wisdom is acquired through prayer and that its possession translates as political sagacity as much as spiritual knowledge.

Solomon also recounts what Wisdom did to guide and protect great leaders, including Adam, Noah, Abraham, and Joseph (chapter 10). We can only speculate whether the Barberini and their advisers may have been influenced in the choice of biblical texts by the ceiling imagery remaining in the palace from the Sforza period. Solomon had already appeared there in the Sforza chapel antechamber (PSN 6/PBN 17, Fig. 13), carrying a text of some relevance to the wisdom iconography of the salotto ceiling: "Wisdom hath built herself a house" (Proverbs 9:1).[87] And the stories of Adam and Eve, Noah, Abraham, and Joseph illustrating God's way of working in the world and protecting his elect were already in front of the eyes of the Barberini long before Sacchi initiated his work on the *Divine Wisdom*.

The Book of Wisdom could be understood metaphorically, as in the *Glossa Ordinaria*, where Wisdom symbolizes Christ and the love for her is the Christian desire for everlasting life.[88] The image of Wisdom in the salotto thereby leads the visitor to prayer in the nearby chapel, which, in turn, would lead to the acquisition of wisdom.[89] But a more political meaning would perhaps not be out of place in the context of the Barberini Palace. The Book of Wisdom was one of the primary biblical sources mined by Christian political theorists and the authors of guides for the edification of good rulers—works known as *specula principum* (Mirrors of Princes). In his treatise on the proper upbringing of a Christian prince, dedicated

---

[86] Appendix B.
[87] Above, 20–21, Fig. 13.

[88] Strabus, *Glossa Ordinaria*, 1:1167–84.
[89] Harris, *Andrea Sacchi*, 13.

to the future Charles V, Erasmus gave as recommended reading the Books of Proverbs, Ecclesiasticus, and Wisdom.[90]

The ceiling of the Barberini salotto is not only exhortatory but also laudatory, constituting a visual apology for the wealth and power of the nepotic family, so suddenly and recently acquired. The Barberini, it implies, and Taddeo in particular, are lovers of wisdom. They possess her. Their rule represents a just and wise rule, for they have been elected by God to govern the Church.

Sacchi employed Barberini emblems as attributes of Divine Wisdom in order to demonstrate the divine favor and protection bestowed upon that family. The scepter, the sun on her breast, the unspotted mirror, and the great orb of golden light surrounding the figure of Divine Wisdom serve as her chief attributes. This symbolism finds justification in the biblical texts (Wisdom 7:26–29) and in the earlier pictorial tradition in manuscript illumination. The bees on the throne back also have scriptural justification in Ecclesiasticus (24:27), where Wisdom declares: "For my spirit is sweet above honey: and my inheritance above honey and the honeycomb." Cherubim are given placement on the throne arms because they embody the "fulness of knowledge or stream of wisdom."[91] And Solomonic lions flank the throne base: "King Solomon also made a great throne of ivory . . . and there were two hands on either side holding the seat: and two lions stood, one at each hand" (III Kings 10:18–19).[92]

The attributes of Divine Wisdom also carry a more specific meaning. The sun, the lion, and the bee are all Barberini family emblems. Giovanni Ferro lists five sun imprese among Maffeo Barberini's personal emblems and further adds that the sun in the west is the "sign of the Barberini family."[93] A lion impresa also appears in the same grouping of Barberini images,[94] whereas the bees are the heraldic device of the family coat of arms. Contemporary authors writing in praise of Urban and the Barberini often found that the bee and its products, honey and wax, were symbols of Divine Wisdom.[95] By employing attributes of Divine Wisdom that were also closely associated with the Barberini family, Sacchi established a flattering iconographic link between the resident family and the concept of Divine Wisdom. The iconological point would be that the Barberini are beneficiaries of a godlike wisdom descended from above.

Barberini sun imprese appearing at the center of the stucco frieze (Fig. 39) repeat this same notion. The laurel-crowned head of Apollo appears in the center of the two side wall friezes, while plain sun disks are located at the mid-point of the window and chapel wall friezes. Construction documents refer to the female figures in these friezes as "harpies with wings on their feet."[96] The emblematic meaning becomes clear in the section above the

[90] D. Erasmus, *The Education of a Christian Prince*, trans. L. K. Born (New York, 1964), 200. See also Born's important introductory survey of this literary genre, ibid., 1–136. First published as *Institutio Principis Christianus*, 1516, it was published in Leyden as late as 1641.

[91] Pseudo-Dionysius, the Areopagite, *On the Heavenly Hierarchy*, in *The Works of Dionysius the Areopagite*, ed. J. Parker (London, 1897–1898), 24–26, 49 [rpt. New York, 1976].

[92] H. Ost, "Borrominis römische Universitätskirche S. Ivo alla Sapienza," *Zeitschrift für Kunstgeschichte* 30 (1967), 122–23.

[93] G. Ferro, *Teatro d'imprese* (Venice, 1623), 651–54. The sun appeared frequently in Rome as an emblem of Barberini patronage. See J. B. Scott, "S. Ivo alla Sapienza and Borromini's Symbolic Language," *Journal of the Society of Architectural Historians* 41 (1982), 296–97.

[94] VIVIFICAT ET TERRET (He brings to life and terrifies): Ferro, *Teatro d'imprese*, 439.

[95] See, for example F. da Belvedere d'Iesi, *Symboliche conclusioni* (Ancona, 1628), 16–20. For a characteristic instance of the use of the bee as a symbol of Divine Wisdom, consult Scott, "S. Ivo alla Sapienza," 298–301.

[96] *Misura e stima* of 1629–1638: "Per l'aboz.a e stucc.a

chapel door where the harpies' fingers sprout tendrils of laurel as they reach out toward the sun. In this motif we see the two principal Barberini devices of the laurel and sun—symbols of virtue and wisdom—joined to reinforce the idea that the family loves and possesses Divine Wisdom. This emblematic meaning is reversed in the frieze of the side walls (Fig. 40), where now haggish harpies flee the Apollo head in the center. Their locks of hair knotted together, these creatures symbolic of discord and vice—unlike their counterparts in the adjacent frieze—turn downward away from Sacchi's sun of Wisdom in the crown of the vault and look fearfully upward toward it.[97]

These moralizing emblemata based upon Barberini imprese recall Bernini's sculptural group of *Apollo and Daphne* and the distych composed by Urban, which was inscribed into the flayed Borghese dragon-skin cartouche of its pedestal:

QVISQVIS AMANS SEQVITER FVGITIVAE GAVDIA FORMAE,
FRONDE MANVS IMPLET, BACCAS SEV CARPIT AMARAS

[Whoever, loving, pursues the joys of fleeting forms,
Fills his hands with sprays of leaves and seizes bitter fruits.][98]

In that group the laurel chastely flees the sun personified in Apollo, but in the salotto frieze the two are ultimately reconciled as Daphne's laurel embraces the Barberini sun of Wisdom.

In his lengthy discussion of the *Divine Wisdom* Teti, too, emphasizes a more worldly side of the symbolism.[99] He informs the reader that the room painted with the image of Wisdom on the vault served to receive the highest princes. Teti refers especially to the visits of Cardinal Richelieu and Prince von Eggenberg, ambassador of the Holy Roman Emperor Ferdinand III, both of whom, he carefully notes, received as gifts easel copies of the painting.[100] The terrestrial globe reminds him of the diplomatic missions of the Barberini cardinals and of the annexation of the duchy of Urbino to the Papal States, an event crucial to Taddeo's accession to the prefecture.[101] As elsewhere in his interpretive guidebook, Teti puts the emphasis of this discussion on Urban and on Cardinal Antonio the Younger, the author's immediate patron and chief resident of the palace after 1635.[102] Consequently, Taddeo does not have the principal role in Teti's commentary on the *Divine Wisdom*; nevertheless, the learned cicerone confirms the statement of the Barberini Manuscript that the ceiling refers not just to Urban but to the Barberini family:

> Sacchi has introduced these in truth divine images, like very splendid charac-
> ters, in a way speaking, with this purpose in particular, that the descendants

del fregio fatto con arpie con ale ne piedi e conchiglie soli tra detti, f.e di basso relievo ecc.————sc. 90." Pollak, *Die Kunsttätigkeit*, 1:285.

[97] Kauffmann, *Giovanni Lorenzo Bernini*, 63–64, opined that the disks at the center of the side wall friezes might be moons rather than suns. The visual evidence for such an interpretation is inconclusive.

[98] D'Onofrio, *Roma vista*, 303–7, fig. 162.

[99] Teti, *Aedes Barberinae* (1642), 83–96.

[100] Ibid., 83–84; Posse, *Andrea Sacchi*, 48–49; Costello, "Twelve Pictures," 243, n. 3; Harris, *Andrea Sacchi*, 58. Richelieu was in Rome in 1635 and Von Eg-

genberg in 1638–1639.

[101] Teti, *Aedes Barberinae* (1642), 93–94; G. Pisano, "L'ultimo prefetto dell'urbe, Don Taddeo Barberini, e la relazioni tra la corte di Roma e la Repubblica Veneta sotto il pontificato di Urbano VIII," *Roma* 9 (1931), 103–20, 155–64; Pecchiai, *I Barberini*, 167. Only with the death of Francesco della Rovere, Duke of Urbino, could the office of prefect pass to Taddeo.

[102] Teti was a *gentiluomo* in the household of Antonio, who was resident at the palace after 1634. The *Aedes* is dedicated to Antonio.

of the Barberini family continually to be summoned to the administration of the Christian Commonwealth under the governance of Divine Wisdom, might obey this mute address and dispose themselves exactly according to the example of Urban whose wisdom we know to be next to that of divine.[103]

Here the idea of the Barberini family "continually to be summoned" to govern by Divine Wisdom takes on a dynastic tinge and must have been read by critics of the Barberini as a confirmation of their worst suspicions. Taddeo, as head of the secular branch of the family, was the focus of this conceit.

Teti closes his discussion of the *Divine Wisdom* with a rhetorical extravagance. In this well-known passage the author recalls the visit Urban once made to the Barberini Palace, when the pope sat at a table under Sacchi's painting and, "quite by chance," selected for his reading some verses from the Book of Wisdom. At that hallucinatory moment everyone saw Wisdom in three forms: "her Divine and lucid Archetype in the Holy Writ, her prototype in Urban and her representation in the painting."[104] But the uses of Wisdom are seen to be more direct in Teti's final statement and quotation, which come from the Book of Wisdom: "By the means of her I shall have immortality. . . . Among the multitude I shall be found good, and valiant in war" (Wisdom 8:13–15). The meaning here must apply to the nephew—general of the Church—as well as to the uncle.

Sacchi's pictorial essay in theo-political science particularly pertains to Taddeo, for he was head of the secular family. The future generations of the Barberini would be the sons of Taddeo. Nepotism had the greatest need for such ideological bolsters as those provided in the salotto imagery. Urban and his cardinal nephews were relatively immune from attack; Taddeo, however, was compelled to operate for the welfare of the family on the front line of Roman society. The resentments that built up against Urban and Barberini rule of the Papal States fell upon the nephew. They were expressed in matters of precedence.

A revealing controversy over precedence occurred in September 1631, just at the time the decoration of the piano nobile apartment was nearing completion. The incident, although well known, merits repetition because it exemplifies the particular form in which Taddeo's ambitions became manifest and sets the social context in which the imagery of the north wing of Palazzo Barberini was conceived. The mild-mannered youth described in Contarini's early report had been transformed by his position. Contarini's successor, Giovanni Pesaro, made a more cynical evaluation of Taddeo and the intransigence of Urban in pushing for the exaltation of his family despite widespread opposition:

Amid all these controversies and pretensions [Taddeo] Barberini, who at first seemed humble and opposed to pretensions, grew more daring, and the most pretentious of all, and he uttered conceits to everyone, that inasmuch as the

---

[103] "Ipsas vero dias Imagines, veluti splendidissimas personas quodammodo loquentes induxit Sacchius, eo potissimum consilio, ut Barberinae Familiae posteri, Divina gubernante Sapientia ad Rempublicam Christianam administrandam identidem evocandi, mutae huic loquelae pareant seseque accurate componant ad URBANI exemplum, cuius Sapientiam, huic Divinae proximam agnoscimus." Teti, *Aedes Barberinae* (1642), 90.

[104] Ibid., 95. An important analysis of the Neo-Platonic component in this way of seeing the symbolic content of art is to be found in E. H. Gombrich, "Icones Symbolicae: Philosophies of Symbolism and Their Bearing on Art," in *Symbolic Images* (Oxford, 1972), 156.

pope had made his declaration [appointing Taddeo prefect], that it was opportune to assert it in fact, that the cause was that of the Church, that each person is master in his own house, that he who does not consent out of obedience will assent by force: words differently supported but with the same meaning for the ambassadors of the princes, who boldly and opportunely informed the princes.[105]

Among the rights and privileges belonging to the prefect was that of precedence over all other secular members of the papal court. Urban and Taddeo made a point of this issue.

Such matters of etiquette were regarded with the highest degree of seriousness. Taddeo was widely held to be unworthy of this honor bestowed upon him by his uncle:

> The office of the Prefecture conferred on the person of the nephew of the pope gave cause for much disgust among the kings and great princes. Because this being the highest rank of office of Rome, even though Don Taddeo was Prince of Palestrina, General of the Church, and Nephew of the Pope it did not seem to them even with all this that he was a Prince to be compared with the deceased Duke of Urbino, who had this office, and, therefore, not one of the kings and rulers wanted to order that their ambassadors have to give precedence to him.[106]

The ambassadors of France and Venice in particular refused to acknowledge Taddeo as prefect. This insistence upon not recognizing Taddeo's office meant the ambassadors could not give precedence to him, because in so doing it would imply that he held greater rank than the doge or the king of France. Matters became difficult, for in failing to give precedence they would be offending Urban. To avoid difficulty some ambassadors found it more prudent to abstain from appearing at court. Following Taddeo's investiture as prefect, a stressful situation soon became a crisis, since he now demanded that the coaches of all secular persons in Rome not only cede the right-of-way but stop until he passed. Reports at this time, no doubt exaggerated, tell of Taddeo driving around the city with a retinue of sixty or seventy carriages.[107]

The inevitable confrontation occurred less than a month after the investiture when Taddeo's coach became caught in a rut and the carriage of the Venetian ambassador, Giovanni Pesaro, passed without regard for the prefect's rank. Taddeo, enraged, fired his coach-

[105] "Barberino [Taddeo] tra queste controversie e pretensioni, che prima parea humile e contrario di pretensione, accrebbe più ardito, e più pretendente di tutti, e proferiva concetti con tutti, che già che il Papa havea esequito la sua dichiaratione, che conveniva sostenerla in fatta, che la causa era della Chiesa, che ogn'uno è padrone in casa propria, che chi non acconsentirà d'amore, assentirà di forza: discorsi diversamente con equal senso pero tenuti, con gli ambasciatori dei Principi, li quali dell'arditezza avvisarono li Principi et opportunamente." From the ambassador's report to the Venetian Senate. Barozzi and Berchet, *Le relazioni della corte*, 1: 325.

[106] Gigli (*Diario romano*, 122–23), as always, reflects the common opinion on this issue: "La dignità della Prefettura conferita nella persona del Nepote del Papa, diede causa di molto disgusto nelli Re, et Principi grandi: perciocchè essendo questa la maggior dignità di Roma, ancorche D. Taddeo fusse Principe di Pellestrina, e Generale di S. Chiesa, e Nepote del Papa, non pareva con tutto ciò a loro che fosse Principe da compararsi al Duca d'Urbino morto, che haveva questa dignità, e però niuno delli Re et Potentati, voleva ordinare che li loro Ambasciatori gli havessero da dare la Precedenza."

[107] Pecchiai, *I Barberini*, 171.

man and later bribed the driver of the ambassador's coach to rein in his horses the next time the two dignitaries passed. After promising the ambassdor's man a reward and safe haven in a nearby town, Taddeo arranged to be in waiting for Pesaro when he was returning from the Vatican some days later (6 September 1631). As the prefectorial coach drew near, the ambassador's driver pretended to drop his hat and therefore proceeded, on that excuse, to bring the carriage to a halt, but Pesaro, seeing what was transpiring, took the reins himself and drove on without stopping. At Palazzo Venezia the bribed coachman was on the point of being severely abused when rescued by Taddeo's men. According to Gigli, the prefect rewarded the fellow with fifty gold "doppie"; Donna Anna gave him fifty more and a gold embroidered suit besides.[108]

Urban, furious, demanded accountability from the Venetians. Other ambassadors were reported to have locked themselves in their palaces in order to avoid such a calamitous chance meeting with Taddeo. On 20 September, the day Taddeo was officially received at the Campidoglio as prefect, Pesaro departed from Rome in protest, taking with him his entire household. Gigli reports that two months later word arrived from the Colonna feudality of Paliano that the ambassador's coachman had been found murdered there.[109]

The obsession with matters of prestige that resulted in the altercation over precedence also is reflected in the unusual design and decoration of Taddeo's new palace. The strange conceits the visitor sees in the pictorial cycle of the piano nobile apartment had as their impetus bold social aspirations.

LOVE OF WISDOM: THE "GLORIOUS COLONNA"

The prefectess, Anna Colonna, was also an important personage on the stage of Palazzo Barberini. The salotto and chapel were an integral part of her apartment. In her capacity as prefectess and as the highest-ranking woman of Rome (niece of the reigning pope), she had various ceremonial duties.[110] Foreign dignitaries of rank who visited Rome on diplomatic missions, or even as pilgrims, would be received first by the pope and then by Donna Anna. These duties required a suitable ceremonial space such as that provided by the salotto and numerous antechambers in the piano nobile apartment at Palazzo Barberini. It was on such occasions that Anna would have received Cardinal Richelieu and Prince von Eggenberg and presented them with easel versions of the *Divine Wisdom* as politically charged diplomatic gifts.[111]

The heraldry of Anna's family appears prominently on the vault of the salotto in combination with the iconography of Wisdom and the heraldry of her husband. In the Book of Ecclesiasticus, Wisdom herself speaks and reveals her dwelling place: "I dwelt in the high-

[108] Gigli, *Diario romano*, 124.

[109] The accounts vary somewhat according to the source. Ibid., 122–24; BAV, Arch. Barb., Ind. I, 338; Moroni Romano, *Dizionario* 55:115–30; L. Amabile, *Fra Tommaso Campanella ne' castelli di Napoli, in Roma ed in Parigi* (Naples, 1887), 1:404, n. a; Pisano, "L'ultimo prefetto," 113–15; Pecchiai, *I Barberini*, 171–74. For Pesaro's own report to the Venetian Senate, see Barozzi and Berchet, *Le relazioni della corte*, 1:322–27.

[110] The popes traditionally depended on the wives of their nephews or other female relatives to fulfill the functions that would normally be carried out by the wife of a ruling secular prince. Waddy (*Seventeenth-Century Roman Palaces*, 26–27, 353, n.27) has investigated this long-forgotten position of the nephew's wife.

[111] Teti (*Aedes Barberinae* [1642], 85–86) notes that the room was used for the reception of the highest dignitaries.

est places, and my throne is in a *pillar* of a cloud" (24:7). "Pillar" appears in the Vulgate as "columna."[112] Sacchi must have gone to some effort to paint the unusually columnlike cloud that projects from the corner of the ceiling diagonally upward toward the base of Wisdom's bee-topped throne (Fig. 33). The freestanding marble columns at the corners of the wall on the chapel side would have given three-dimensional form to this biblical-heraldic motif. Thus the heraldry of the two families united through the marriage of Taddeo and Anna finds expression in the iconography of Divine Wisdom.

But the heraldic concetto does not stop with this recondite allusion. The Sirens seen in the corners of the vault upholding the Barberini sun allude to an impresa of the Colonna family (Fig. 38). The device was first published as an impresa of Stefano Colonna (d. 1548) (Fig. 126). Swimming over the tempestuous waters between the Pillars of Hercules (columns), the crowned, twin-tailed Siren has the motto: CONTEMNIT TVTA PROCELLAS (She Despises the Storms).[113] The corner Sirens thus combine the two principal imprese of the families joined in the marriage of Taddeo and Anna.

The epithalamic theme announced in this heraldic and emblematic imagery folds neatly into the metaphoric allusions to love and marriage already noted in chapter 8 of the Book of Wisdom, cited by the Barberini Manuscript: "Her have I loved, and have sought her out from my youth, and have desired to take her for my spouse, and I became a lover of her beauty. . . . When I go into my house, I shall repose myself with her" (Wisdom 8:2, 16).

The marriage of Anna and Taddeo, which took place at Castelgandolfo on 24 October 1627 with Urban himself officiating, produced an outpouring of musical compositions and celebratory verse.[114] Anna's father, Filippo Colonna, mounted a musical drama, *La sirena* (by Ottavio Tronsarelli), on the day following the wedding.[115] Poems written by Francesco Bracciolini, Giulio Rospigliosi, Michelangelo Buonarroti, Nicolò Strozzi, and Sforza Pallavicino were collected and published in 1629, the year work on the *Divine Wisdom* began.[116] As could be expected, the imagery of the salotto ceiling does not derive directly from any one poem. Instead, the painting represents an independent congratulatory expression of the nuptials. But the imagery of the ceiling parallels the poetic images encountered in the literary epithalamia, as can be seen in the verses from the poem of one Levinus Hielius:

Gentis amor notus: Syren quo Darana cantu
Mulcet apes: paribus quo Barberina Columnam
Daphnis obit ramis: quo permutata vicissim

[112] "Ego in altissimis habitavi, Et thronus meus in *columna* nubis" (Ecclesiasticus 24:7).

[113] P. Giovio, *Le sententiose imprese . . .* (Lyons, 1562), 98. The lemma beneath the emblem explains its meaning: "Se bene irato & tempestoso e il mare, / Non però la Serena il suo furore / Teme: così l'huom pien d'alto valore / Suol'ogni caso averso superare." Pierre du Prey pointed out to me the relevance of this emblem to the *Divine Wisdom*. P. de la Ruffinière du Prey, "Revisiting the Solomonic Symbolism of Borromini's Church of Sant'Ivo alla Sapienza," *The Rensselaer Polytechnic Institute of Architecture Journal*, "Volume Zero" (1986), 71, n. 32.

[114] A full description of the event appears in volume two of Nicoletti's manuscript life of Urban. BAV, Barb. Lat. 4731, 1437–1442. Bonomelli (*I papi in campagna*, 54–55) contains a synopsis of the event.

[115] M. Murata, *Operas for the Papal Court: 1631–1668* (Ann Arbor, 1981), 13–15, 198, n. 3.

[116] *Componimenti poetici di vari autori nelle nozze delli eccellentissimi signori D. Taddeo Barberini e D. Anna Colonna*, ed. A. Brogiotti (Rome, 1629); *Carmina Diversorium Auctorum in Nuptiis Illustrissimorum DD. Thaddaei Barberini et Annae Columnae*, ed. A. Brogiotti (Rome, 1629).

Gratia proclives animos in mutua cogit
Vincula: & Herculeo nectit constantia nodo.

[The race's well-known love: where the bee soothes the Siren with the Darian song: where on equal branches Daphne traverses the Barberini column: where ever-changed Grace in turn compels ready souls into each other's chains: and constancy binds with a Herculean knot.][117]

The Sirens, bees, columns, and references to Daphne (laurel) had already proliferated in the poems, just as they would in the ceiling painting and frieze of the Barberini salotto.

The tradition of epithalamic ceiling paintings was well established in the imagery of Italian princely palaces. Perhaps the best-known example was to be found in Annibale Carracci's Farnese Gallery, where the allusions to the marriage of Duke Ranuccio Farnese and Margherita Aldobrandini (7 May 1600) and the theme of *omnia vincit amor* decorate vault and walls.[118] Farnese family heraldry and imprese appear there together with Aldobrandini stars in the form of the crown of Ariadne.[119]

One further important parallel in the love imagery of Annibale and Sacchi can be seen in the theme of Eros and Anteros, as it appears in the Farnese fresco, and the Love and Fear of the Barberini work. Eros and Anteros wrestle in the illusionistic corners of the Farnese vault (Fig. 127), but Eros ultimately triumphs.[120] The author of the Barberini Manuscript makes a major point about the perfection of Love as symbolized by his golden-tipped arrow, whereas the silver arrow of Fear is declared to be less perfect. Bellori suggests that this dichotomy refers to the diverse arrows mischievously fired by Cupid at Apollo and Daphne—the golden arrow to enflame with love and the leaden arrow to fill with revulsion.[121] Daphne escapes Apollo only by means of metamorphosis into a laurel tree, but, even so, Apollo wreathed his head, bow, and lyre in laurel as a symbol of his immortal love. Thus Eros and Anteros, transformed into Love and Fear, are symbolically united in the laurel, another Barberini impresa, which appears with Daphne in the stucco frieze of the salotto— where the harpies fear Apollo and the Daphne figures love the sun.[122]

The theme of love would have been even more pronounced had Sacchi followed through in the ceiling fresco with his earliest ideas as expressed in the Cooper-Hewitt drawing of 1629 (Fig. 41). As we have seen, at that stage in the design process the iconographic details had not yet been fully worked out. The figure of Love appears not as in the ceiling riding the lion of the constellation Leo and throwing an arrow, but as a rather straightforward representation of Cupid pulling back on the string of his bow to release the golden arrow toward the earth. Fear, by contrast, was barely sketched in and relegated to the distant right background. Moreover, in both drawing and fresco Wisdom gives her attention to Love, and he occupies the principal compositional diagonal from upper left to lower right.

---

[117] Ibid., 158.

[118] C. Dempsey, " 'Et Nos Cedamus Amori': Observations on the Farnese Gallery," *Art Bulletin* 50 (1968), 363–74.

[119] Other epithalamic ceilings with wedded heraldry, contemporaneous with the *Divine Wisdom*, were painted by Giovanni da San Giovanni. Neuburger, "Giovanni da San Giovanni," 337–46, and, on the salone terreno in Palazzo Pitti, see M. Campbell, "The Original Program of the Salone di Giovanni da San Giovanni," *Antichità viva* 15 (1976), 3–25, esp. 18–20.

[120] J. R. Martin, *The Farnese Gallery* (Princeton, 1965), 86; Dempsey, " 'Et Nos Cedamus,' " 363–65.

[121] Ovid, *Metamorphoses*, 1:453–567; Bellori, *Le vite de' pittori*, 544–45.

[122] Above, 58–59.

At this point Love's attribute would have been the Arrow, constellation Sagitta,[123] rather than the lion.

The changes in the figure of Love that occurred between the Cooper-Hewitt compositional sketch and the fresco may have been motivated by the desire to eliminate pagan imagery from the scene. Sacchi's painting is remarkable in that it makes reference to thirteen constellations without representing a single pagan deity. Cupid would have been the sole exception, and this must have been perceived. Ultimately the figure of Love remains quite curious since the lion is not a common attribute of love. The addition of the lion, however, could be justified on the allegorical and astrological levels of meaning, for, with the change in attributes, Love came to be represented not by the constellation Sagitta but by the significance-laden Barberini constellation of Leo.[124]

Although the love associated with Wisdom must be only that of the chastest variety, an examination of some of the secondary scenes in the chapel will show that the fruits of conjugal love, as suggested by the original Cupid, were also a concern. Notwithstanding the repetition of the Wisdom theme in New Testament form in the chapel frescoes, the domestic function of the chapel was not neglected.

Scenes related to the birth and earthly family of Christ, combined with Colonna columns, dominate the wall and lunette frescoes of the chapel to the point of redundancy: *Annunciation*, *Adoration of the Shepherds*, *Holy Family with St. Anne*, and *Rest on the Flight into Egypt*. As if to emphasize the meaning of the family of Christ as the archetypal young Christian family, Cortona introduced an otherwise extraneous youthful couple into the scene of the *Adoration*. They enter from the left, that is, from the direction of the chapel door, to admire the Christ child (Fig. 53). The *Holy Family* flanked by columns in the lunette above seems to make the point even more personal in its prominent inclusion of the worshipful St. Anne (Anna Colonna), toward whom the Christ child directs his full attention (Fig. 54).

In the opposite lunette the Christ child, standing beneath a canopy of laurel, accepts from Joseph an apple—a symbolic gesture underscoring Christ's redemptive role in overcoming original sin. The column behind Mary has no place in the traditional iconography of the story, but it must once again remind the viewer of the maternal role of Donna Anna, paralleling the trunk of the Barberini laurel tree to the right (Fig. 55). The promise of immortal life symbolized by the child's gesture and the laurel overhead then gains elaboration in the *Ascension* on the wall below (Fig. 56).

As the viewer of this cosmic family epic turns to leave the chapel, he sees the theme of conception, above the door, represented in its purest archetypal form, the *Annunciation* (Fig. 57). And the scene of *San Francesco di Paola Crossing the Sea* (Fig. 58)[125] in the lunette above would have confirmed the basic themes of birth and generation that dominate the chapel. Women traditionally venerated San Francesco di Paola as a great thaumaturge who specialized in human fertility. He was the saint to whom one prayed for a child or in case of any complication arising during childbearing.[126]

[123] Allen, *Star Names*, 349–51, notes that Sagitta was referred to as the "Arrow of Cupid."

[124] Below, 81–84.

[125] The saint is depicted at the moment of his most frequently represented miracle. When he was denied a place on the boat, he simply floated across the Straits of Messina on his cloak. *Bibliotheca Sanctorum*, ed. F. Caraffa (Rome, 1961–1970), 5:1163–82.

[126] P. Regio, *La miracolosa vita di Santo Francesco di Paola* (Naples, 1581), 86r–87v; F. Victon, *Vita, & Mi-*

In the dome panel above the *San Francesco di Paola* lunette Cortona strategically placed the Column of the Flagellation (Fig. 49) to provide the viewer with one final reminder of the family name of the woman to whom the pictorial ensemble alluded. The column depicted by Cortona, with its distinctive flared base, is the jasper relic brought from Jerusalem in 1223 by Donna Anna's ancestor Cardinal Giovanni Colonna and now preserved in the Roman church of S. Prassede (Fig. 128).[127]

The painted frieze of the salotto seems to repeat the theme of Barberini fertility through its imagery of abundance (Figs. 39–40). Bees and snails appear amid palmettes, tendrils, and cornucopia. In the center of each length of the frieze appear the wreathed heads of the Seasons.[128]

Not only is the imagery of the salotto and chapel appropriate to the domestic setting of a secular household but it also reflects the dynastic concerns of the individual patron, reminding the viewer of the purpose of the marriage so elaborately celebrated there. The planning and early stages of execution of the *Divine Wisdom* occurred during the pregnancy of Donna Anna, just when the Barberini were anticipating a *primogenito*. As though in confirmation of the program designed for the salotto and chapel, Anna gave birth auspiciously on 1 January 1630 to a male child, named Carlo after Taddeo's father. Just as this important event had been anticipated in pictorial form, so was it commemorated in literary form:

In si bell'orma il piede
Per lo stadio degli anni a muover prende
Il Barberin TADDEO dal cielo eletto,
Et armato d'amor quanto di fede,
Per superare il tempo, a tempo scende
Nel campo social del casto letto,
Et aggiunta al suo tetto
Da miniera immortal d'Ecclesa Donna
Gloriosa COLONNA,
Erge su'l Tebro un alveario Ibleo
Ove Roma e teatro, egli Aristeo.

[Moving through the stadium of the years / with so beautiful an impression of the foot, / armed with love as much as faith, / the Barberini TADDEO, *by heaven*

---

racula S.P. Francisci a Paula . . ., (Rome, 1625); Réau, *Iconographie*, 3:pt. 1, 536; Kirschbaum, *Lexikon* (1974), 6:cols. 319–21. The history of the household chapel in Italy has yet to be written, but themes of the nativity and early family life of Christ appear frequently in such contexts. The domestic chapel of Palazzo Mattei di Giove, decorated in 1615 by Caspare Celio and known as the "cappella del presepio," contained fresco scenes of the childhood of Christ and an altarpiece of the *Nativity*. Panofsky-Soergel, "Palazzo Mattei di Giove," 141. Perhaps the best-known example, and perhaps the only one more elaborate than the Barberini chapel, is the domestic chapel in Palazzo Medici-Ric-

cardi in Florence. There Benozzo Gozzoli's wall frescoes depict the *Adoration of the Magi* (1459–1460), and Filippo Lippi's *Madonna Adoring Her Child* (late 1450s; now the Dahlem Museum, Berlin) was originally located above the altar.

[127] Moroni Romano, *Dizionario*, 13:9; P. D. Running, "The Flagellation of Christ: A Study in Iconography," Ph.D. diss., University of Iowa, 1951, 78–79; B. Bruni, "La sacra colonna della flagellazione in Santa Prassede," *Capitolium* 35, no. 8 (1960), 15–19; B. M. Apollonj Ghetti, *Santa Prassede* (Rome, 1961), 75–76.

[128] Ripa, *Nova iconologia*, 499–501.

elected, / to time descends so he may conquer time / in the social field of the chaste bed. / And joining to his roof / the immortal treasure of the ecclesiastical woman, / glorious COLONNA, / on the Tiber he establishes a Hyblean beehive / where Rome is theater, and he Aristeus.][129]

Taddeo is here divinely elected to the marriage bed in order, like Aristeus, the beekeeper son of Apollo (*Georgics*, 4:315–558), to cultivate the bees on the banks of the Tiber.

Both the author of the Barberini Manuscript and Teti confirm the dynastic implications of the *Divine Wisdom*. The manuscript refers to the Barberini family as "*born* and elected to rule," and Teti echoes this idea when he observes that Sacchi's figures are there for the purpose of reminding "the descendants of the Barberini," who are "continually to be summoned to the administration of the Christian Commonwealth" to follow the example of Urban's godlike wisdom.[130]

An *avviso* of 11 September 1632 reports on what must have been one of the first major events to take place in the recently finished chapel: "From Rome the eleventh of September 1632: And after lunch on that day [Wednesday] in the chapel of the new palace of Signor Barberini . . . the baptismal ceremony of the baby girl born to His Excellency Signor Prefect of Rome, etc. . . . was conducted by the direction of Monsignor Scannaroli, Bishop of Sidonia."[131] For just such an occasion as this were the chapel and its large antechamber designed and embellished. One can easily imagine the view gained by those invited guests and household members present in the salotto, with Divine Wisdom hovering above the chapel door and radiating downward a beneficent light.

[129] A. Adimari, *Per la nascita dell'eccel.mo D. Carlo figliuolo dell'illustris. & eccellentiss. D. Taddeo Barberini Generale di Santa Chiesa Principe di Palestrina, &c.* (Florence, 1630), Antis. II. "Hyblean beehive" refers to the ancient town and region of Hybla, in Sicily, which was legendary for the purity of its honey.

[130] Teti, *Aedes Barberinae* (1642), 90. Above, 59–60.

[131] "Di Roma li XI Settembre 1632: Et il dopo pranzo di d.o giorno (mercoledì) nella cappella del nuovo palazzo de Sign. Barber. . . . fu per le mani di mons. Scannaroli Vescovo di Sidonia fatta la cerimonia di battezzare la bambina nata all'Ecc.mo Sign. Prefetto di Roma, etc." Pollak, *Die Kunsttätigkeit*, 1:329.

CHAPTER V

• Divine Science: The Barberini and Astrology

THE BARBERINI MANUSCRIPT corroborates the astrological dimension in the program of the *Divine Wisdom* already implicit in the biblical text. Attributes held by the virtues and personifications surrounding Wisdom correspond to constellations, "those being a divine thing," while Wisdom herself appears in association with the sun, "spesiorsior soli" (Fig. 36). The introduction of this astrological element finds justification in the biblical text chosen as the basis for the program of the ceiling:

> For he [God] hath given me [Solomon] the true knowledge of the things that are: to know the disposition of the whole world, and the virtues of the elements, / The beginning, and ending, and midst of the times, the alterations of their courses, and the changes of seasons, / The revolutions of the year, and the dispositions of the stars. (Wisdom 7:17–19)

As we have seen, astral imagery also appears in manuscript illuminations of that text (Fig. 123), but the depiction of celestial bodies is appropriate in the chapel antechamber for another fundamental reason. Since the vault serves as a metaphor of the heavens, it conforms to the convention of decorum and *di sotto in su* iconography. The tradition of chapel ceilings painted as a blue sky with stars can be seen in Giotto's Arena Chapel in Padua and the original vault of the Sistine Chapel by Pier Matteo d'Amelia. The decorative motifs in most of the domes of Christendom make some allusion to the heavenly bodies.[1] Raphael's dome for the Chigi Chapel in S.M. del Popolo, for example, depicts God and the heavenly spheres (Fig. 129).[2] In the reference to astrological imagery the *Divine Wisdom* draws from long-established beliefs. Pagan astrologers and church fathers alike saw in the heavenly bodies and their ordered movement across the sky the supreme visual manifestation of God's providential control of the universe.[3] This ancient tradition links astrology and divine wisdom.

Analysis of the astrological component of Sacchi's painting indicates that the "divine science" is at the core of the program, and that the biblical passage from the Book of Wisdom was chosen as the textual basis for the painting as much for its astrological as for its political-

[1] K. Lehmann, "The Dome of Heaven," *Art Bulletin* 27 (1945), 1–27.

[2] J. Shearman, "The Chigi Chapel in Santa Maria del Popolo," *Journal of the Warburg and Courtauld Institutes* 24 (1961), 138–43; K. Weil-Garris Brandt, "Cosmological Patterns in the Chigi Chapel," in *Raffaello a Roma: il convegno del 1983* (Rome, 1986), 127–57.

[3] J. Firmicus Maternus, *Ancient Astrology Theory and Practice: Matheseos Libri VIII*, trans. J. R. Bram (Park Ridge, N.J., 1975), 17–20. For the justification of astrological practices the most frequently cited passages are in Aquinas, *Summa contra Gentiles* III: lxxxvi, civ-cvi; *Opusculum IX* (*Responsio ad Magistrum Joannem de Vercellis de Articulis xlii*); *Opusculum XXII* (*De Judiciis Astrorum ad Fratrem Reginaldum*). Also see D. P. Walker, *Spiritual and Demonic Magic from Ficino to Campanella* (London, 1958), 214.

allegorical significance. The *Divine Wisdom* ceiling in Palazzo Barberini provides both biblical and astrological proof of God's favor of the resident family.

The tradition of astrological imagery in palace fresco cycles points up the innovative quality of the salotto ceiling. Astrological cycles of the Renaissance period can be grouped into three chief categories. Perhaps the least sophisticated of these are the encyclopedic cycles such as those found in the Quattrocento frescoes of the Palazzo della Ragione in Padua (ca. 1420–1440) and in the Sala dei Mesi in Palazzo Schifanoia at Ferrara (1469–1470).[4] These cycles appear to have devolved from illuminated manuscripts and are characterized by their comprehensiveness, with all planets and zodiacal signs represented in a schematic sequence. They serve as pictograms of the natural cycles of the universe and more frequently than not are mural rather than ceiling paintings. The *Divine Wisdom* fresco in Palazzo Barberini does not conform to this type of astrological cycle. Sacchi's grouping of constellations is selective rather than comprehensive and, for the most part, does not follow any logical astronomical sequence.

A second type comprises painted ceilings that are intended to be accurate star maps. The painted vault of the Sala del Mappamondo at Caprarola (1573–1574) and the similar ceiling of the Sala di Bologna in the Vatican Palace (1575) exemplify this type.[5] The Vatican ceiling (Fig. 130) depicts most of the constellations, with a complete complement of twelve zodiacal constellations and the stars of greatest magnitude superimposed in gilt. The relationship of the stars in each constellation approximates that of the actual stars in the heavens. *Quadratura* scenes occupy the cove sections around the central oval and depict arbored domes under which appear astrologers, both historical and mythical.[6] The Barberini fresco also departs from this type in that the depicted constellations are not in any true astronomical relationship.

Associated with this second category of astrological painted ceilings is a subgroup represented by two similar painted domes in Florence. The vaults above the altars in the Old Sacristy of San Lorenzo (ca. 1439) (Fig. 131) and the Pazzi Chapel at S. Croce (ca. 1459) both depict astrological sky maps representing the hemispherical sky as it would have appeared from Florence on a specific date and time.[7] The date depicted remains in dispute, but the majority of analyses settle on 6 July 1439, the closing day of an important church council

[4] A. Barzon, *I cieli e la loro influenza negli affreschi del Salone in Padova* (Padua, 1924); idem, *Il Palazzo della Ragione di Padova* (Venice, 1964), esp. 47–84; A. Warburg, "Italienische Kunst und internationale Astrologie im Palazzo Schifanoia zu Ferrara," in *Gesammelte Schriften* (Leipzig-Berlin, 1932), 2:459–81; M. Bertozzi, *La tirannia degli astri: Aby Warburg e l'astrologia di Palazzo Schifanoia* (Bologna, 1985).

[5] J. Hess, "On Some Celestial Maps and Globes of the Sixteenth Century," *Journal of the Warburg and Courtauld Institutes* 30 (1967), 406–9. Both ceilings were painted by Giovanni Antonio Vanosino.

[6] Atlas, Isis, Thales, Anaximenes, Aratus, Ptolomy, Manilius, Alfonso X, etc. The figures were painted by Lorenzo Sabbatini with a *quadratura* framework by Ottaviano Mascherino.

[7] A. Warburg, "Eine astronomische Himmelsdarstellung in der alten Sakristei von S. Lorenzo in Florenz," in *Gesammelte Schriften* (Leipzig-Berlin, 1932), 1:169–72, 366–67; P. F. Brown, "*Laetentur Caeli*: The Council of Florence and the Astronomical Fresco in the Old Sacristy," *Journal of the Warburg and Courtauld Institutes* 44 (1981), 176–80; A. Parronchi, "L'emisfero settentrionale della Sagrestia Vecchia," in U. Baldini and B. Nardini, *San Lorenzo: la basilica, le sagrestie, le cappelle, la biblioteca* (Florence, 1984), 72–79; idem, "L'emispero della Sacrestia Vecchia: Giuliano Pesello?" in *Scritti di storia dell'arte in onore di Federico Zeri*, ed. M. Natale (Milan, 1984), 1:134–46; and J. Cox-Rearick, *Dynasty and Destiny in Medici Art: Pontormo, Leo X, and the Two Cosimos* (Princeton, 1984), 166–67.

held in Florence.[8] Unlike the Caprarola and Vatican star maps, the temporal specificity of the San Lorenzo dome is embodied in the positioning of that half of the zodiacal band above the horizon and in the presence of the luminaries, the Sun in Cancer and the Moon in Taurus, with Virgo (barely visible to the left of Leo) on the Ascendant.

The third type of astrological painted ceiling functions as a point of departure for the program of the Sacchi painting. Although not star maps, the horoscopic ceilings of the Villa Farnesina (Peruzzi, 1511) and in the Sala dei Pontefici of the Vatican Palace (Perino del Vaga, 1520–1521) represent important astrological events in the lives of the patrons. The Farnesina painting depicts those planets and constellations prominent in the natal chart of Agostino Chigi,[9] and the imagery of the Sala dei Pontefici features those constellations significant in both the natal and papal election charts of Leo X de' Medici (Figs. 132 and 142).[10] These two themes, birth and election, were also of utmost concern to the Barberini and to the adviser who conceived the *Divine Wisdom*. The concluding statement of the authoritative Barberini Manuscript, it will be recalled, asserted that the presence of Wisdom in the Barberini Palace demonstrated that the family was "*born* and *elected* to rule the Church." This idea appears astrologically in the salotto ceiling.

For Taddeo, Urban, and the Barberini family in general, the Sun embodied the most beneficial astral influence, a fact both ordained by divine providence and planned by careful calculation. The association between Divine Wisdom and the Sun therefore constitutes the primary allegorical and astrological reality of the vault image.

In his book of imprese, dedicated to the then Cardinal Maffeo Barberini, Giovanni Ferro lists five different solar imprese of the future pope.[11] The most important of these is the rising sun: ALIUSQUE ET IDEM (Both different and the same) (Fig. 133).[12] There exists ubiquitous evidence for the fascination with solar imagery. The centrality of the sun as a symbol of the Barberini is announced by the radiant head of Apollo in the center metope under the papal arms and balcony of the west facade of Palazzo Barberini (Fig. 10), by the ancient statue of Apollo in the niche on the landing of the piano nobile at the top of the square staircase (Fig. 134), and in the Apollo head above the fireplace of the salone (Fig. 89).[13] Urban even had a wall in his apartment at the Vatican painted with a shining sun so that each morning he would be greeted by the light of his own impresa.[14] On a less artistic plane, Gigli reports that in June 1640 a hen belonging to an old lady laid an egg marked with a sun and a bee. The chicken immediately dropped dead, but the woman took the egg to

[8] Brown, "*Laetentur Caeli*," 179–80; Parronchi, "L'emisfero settentrionale," 72–79; idem, "L'emipero della Sacrestia Vecchia," 137, maintains that the dome paintings represent the natal horoscopy of Medici and Pazzi *primogeniti*.

[9] F. Saxl, *La fede astrologica di Agostino Chigi* . . . (Rome, 1934); M. Quinlan-McGrath, "The Astrological Vault of the Villa Farnesina: Agostino Chigi's Rising Sign," *Journal of the Warburg and Courtauld Institutes* 47 (1984), 91–105; Cox-Rearick, *Dynasty and Destiny*, 192–94.

[10] C. Rousseau, "Cosimo I de' Medici and Astrology:

The Symbolism of Prophecy," Ph.D. diss., Columbia University, 1983, 162–73; Cox-Rearick, *Dynasty and Destiny*, 188–98.

[11] Ferro, *Teatro d'imprese*, 370, 406, 650–54.

[12] Ibid., 650–52.

[13] On this motif and other manifestations of sun symbolism at Palazzo Barberini, see C. D'Onofrio, *Le Fontane di Roma*, 3rd ed. (Rome, 1986), 371–83.

[14] Painted by Agostino Tassi in 1630. Payment documents in A. Bertolotti, "Agostino Tasso, suoi scolari e compagni pittori in Roma," *Giornale de erudizione artistica* 5 (1876), 217.

cardinal Antonio Barberini the Younger, who rewarded her with ten gold scudi. When the cardinal showed his acquisition to Urban, the pope declared it to be a prodigy of nature.[15]

Solar imagery so pervades Barberini patronage that it appears even in operas created for the theater at Palazzo Barberini. The plot entanglements of *Chi soffre speri* (libretto by Giulio Rospigliosi) find happy resolution in the magic properties of a heliotrope stone.[16] The *intermedio* of the March 1639 Barberini production of the same work included scenography designed by Bernini that represented the rising and setting of the sun.[17] But the solar imagery that appears on so many works of art commissioned by the Barberini family and by Urban, including the Barcaccia Fountain in Piazza di Spagna and the Baldacchino in St. Peter's, is not merely a learned reference to the imprese but also derives ultimately from the primary importance of the Sun in Urban's natal chart. Knowledge of Urban's personal astrology will be essential for a complete understanding of the significance of the solar imagery of the *Divine Wisdom*.

As a young man in Florence and Pisa, Maffeo Barberini developed in a Medicean environment where a profound belief in the efficacy of astrology held sway and where exploitation of astrological imagery for both personal and political expression was commonplace.[18] Proof of Urban's concern with astrological matters appears in his fear of the negative influence of certain astrological events, especially solar eclipses, which he and his advisers deemed potentially fatal. After his election, Urban got into the habit of having nativities calculated for members of the Curia, and, basing his predictions on this information, he went about pronouncing on the dates of their deaths.[19] But the recipients of this attention were not appreciative, and the tables were soon turned. Erecting the pope's own natal chart and predicting the length of his reign and year of his death became something of a rage and quickly developed into a matter of public speculation and rumor mongering.[20] By means of written news items (*avvisi*), word of these dire prognostications spread as far as Madrid and Paris.

Such calculations were based on the complicated formula for astrologically determining the length of life explicated by Ptolemy and further elaborated by the twelfth-century astrologer Abraham ibn Ezra, who applied the procedure specifically to the length of reign of rulers.[21] Urban's obsessive fears became greatly exacerbated by the predictions of astrol-

---

[15] Gigli, *Diario romano*, 193.

[16] The work was first mounted in January 1637. Murata, *Operas for the Papal Court*, 32–34. For a summary of the plot, see 258–59. The heliotrope, or bloodstone is so called because, when placed in water and exposed to the sun's rays, it changes from green to red (Pliny, II: 627).

[17] Dazzled spectators have left accounts of the event: A. Ademollo, *I teatri di Roma nel secolo decimosettimo* (Rome, 1888), 28–30; I. Lavin, *Bernini and the Unity*, 148, n. 8, 151, n. 17; Murata, *Operas for the Papal Court*, 261, n. 10; D'Onofrio, *Le fontana di Roma*, 378, n. 9. Teti (*Aedes Barberinae* [1642], 35) makes special mention of the sun scenery of this production.

[18] On the Medici use of astrological imagery, see Rousseau, "Cosimo I de' Medici," 1–57, 177–207, 279–

396; Cox-Rearick, *Dynasty and Destiny*, 251–91.

[19] Amabile, *Fra Tommaso Campanella*, 1:280–81.

[20] Ibid., 1:298, 311–12, 324, 347; Walker, *Spiritual and Demonic Magic*, 205–6.

[21] Ptolemy (*Tetrabiblos*, III: 10). The procedure for determining the length of reign appears in a mid-twelfth-century Hebrew astrological treatise: A. ibn Ezra, *The Beginning of Wisdom*, ed. R. Levy (Baltimore, 1939), 230–31. The work was published in Latin as *Abrahe Avenaris Judei Astrologi Peritissimi in Re Judiciali Opera*, trans. P. d'Abano (Venice, 1507), and republished in M. Manilius, *Astronomicon*, ed. J. J. Scaliger (Leiden, 1600). Knowledge sufficient for making this calculation would be obtained from the natal chart of the ruler.

ogers concerning his health and the pending solar eclipses of December 1628 and June 1630.[22] Rumors of the pope's imminent demise spread throughout the city and were taken as fact in some circles. The pope himself cannot have been comforted by the news that Spanish cardinals were reported already hastening to Rome so as not to be left out of the coming conclave.[23]

To halt these politically destabilizing activities, Urban initiated a show trial of astrologers. No other event of the Barberini papacy demonstrates how widespread was the practice of astrology. The investigation implicated all ranks of society, from the humble copyists and street purveyors of *avvisi* to members of the papal household and even intimates of the pope himself.[24] The trial, conducted by the Tribunale Criminale del Governatore of Rome, took place in 1630 and focused on the semi-clandestine activities of Orazio Morandi, abbot of S. Prassede, and his circle of aquaintances.[25] Morandi, an avid student of occult subjects, seems to have convened a kind of scholarly colloquium for the purpose of examining Urban's nativity and speculating on his death date. The pope's natal chart is among the large number of genitures of popes and cardinals confiscated from the abbot at the time of his detention.[26] One particularly incriminating document found among Morandi's papers explains what his activities were really about. It carries the title, "XX Genitures of Defunct Supreme Pontiffs with Annotations on the Day of Creation [i.e., election] or Coronation and Death of Those Same Supreme Pontiffs."[27] This comprehensive collection of natal charts of popes from Paul II to Urban VIII, whose death was thought to be pending, must have been compiled with the purpose of discerning a pattern of astrological phenomena that would aid the abbot in predictions about papal deaths and elections. In this regard, Urban's chirograph against Morandi and his associates is explicit:

> They dared to make analyses about the qualities of cardinals *papabili* in order to conjecture and insinuate who ought to or might be our successor the future Pontiff and, with this opportunity, in these [persons] they discovered, or falsely deduced, defects, vices, and abuses of many to the grave dishonor of the Sacred College, and of the Holy Roman Church.[28]

[22] Walker, *Spiritual and Demonic Magic*, 206–7.

[23] Amabile, *Fra Tommaso Campanella*, 2:149, 320, docs. 203d, 346.

[24] Among the well-known names mentioned in the testimony are Francesco Bracciolini, Theodor Amayden, Galileo Galilei, Tommaso Campanella, Niccolò Ridolfi (Master of the Sacred Palace), Niccolò Riccardi (General of the Dominican Order), and Raffaele Visconti (professor of mathematics and Dominican censor of Galileo).

[25] A. Bertolotti, "Giornalisti, astrologi e negromanti in Roma nel secolo XVII," *Rivista europea*, n.s. 5 (1878), 466–514; Amabile, *Fra Tommaso Campanella*, 1:387–98; L. Fiorani, "Astrologi, superstiziosi e devoti nella società romana del seicento," *Ricerche per la storia religiosa di Roma* 2 (1978), 99–112. For transcripts of the proceedings, published in small part by Bertolotti (478–

510), see ASR, Tribunale Criminale del Governatore di Roma, Processi 1630, vol. 251. This documentation also contains material confiscated from Morandi, including numerous natal charts.

[26] Ibid., esp. 11r–14v, 69r–73r, 1007r–1298r.

[27] "Genitura XX Summorum Pontificum defunctorum cum annotatione dierum creationis vel coronationis et obitus eorundem Summorum Pontificum." Ibid., 11r–14v, 69r–73r.

[28] "Ardivano di far discorsi circa le qualità de' cardinali Papabili per congietturare et insinuare che deva o possi essere il futuro Pontefice nostro successore e con tale occasione in quelli discoprivano, o calunniosamente deducevano li defetti, vitj, et vituperij di molti in gravissimo dishonore del Sacro Collegio, et della Santa Romana Chiesa." Ibid., 5. Published by Bertolotti, "Giornalisti, astrologi e negromanti," 479–81.

Morandi's imprisonment was not prolonged. Despite official denial, public opinion held that his death resulted from poisoning.[29]

Morandi maintained that "mere and pure curiosity" motivated his interest in Urban's natal chart,[30] but the stimulus for such "curiosity" emerges with clarity from the pages of testimony taken from the abbot's associates and other witnesses. Nepotism and political intrigue, more than any urge of intellectual speculation, kept the astrologers in business. One of the accused, Francesco Lampone, attempted to defend himself with the observation that all of Rome practiced astrology:

> In Rome one sees that there are many analyses of astrology and it is made almost a special profession and almost everyone has analyses of nativities and prognostications of good fortune. . . . There is not a cardinal nor a prelate nor a prince who does not have his own analyses of birth, with prognostications of good fortune.[31]

In the political culture of seventeenth-century Rome no greater "good fortune" could befall an individual or family than to have an uncle elected pope. The first requirement for such a turn of events is a vacant see, thus the morbid preoccupation with the supposed date of Urban's death. Frequently, discussions of the pope's natal chart were followed by an analysis of charts of the cardinals considered most *papabili* in the next conclave. Lampone confessed that he had erected the chart of Urban, but only at the time of the previous conclave, the one that had elected Urban pope, and that in it he had found only indications of "good fortune."[32] But the witness of his cellmate proved damaging to this testimony, asserting that the astrologer predicted the pope's imminent death, i.e., in 1630, and moreover predicted the next pope would be "il signor Cardinale. . . ."[33] The name, by papal decree, was omitted from the record,[34] but such predictions whetted the venal appetites of potential papal nephews.

A copyist testified to having seen a written analysis about "Cardinali papabili" composed by Abbot Morandi.[35] Following the trial, Tommaso Campanella wrote to Urban, perhaps not without malice, that Niccolò Ridolfi (Master of the Sacred Palace) and Niccolò Riccardi (General of the Dominican Order) had colluded with Morandi in predicting the pope's death, and that the abbot promised the papacy first to one and then to the other in turn.[36]

Precisely because of his fear of their validity and his awareness of the political implications of astrological predictions of this nature, Urban promulgated a bull in 1631 against the practice of judicial astrology that predicted the death or ill health of the pope or any

[29] Gigli, *Diario romano*, 118. For the physician's report, see Bertolotti, "Giornalisti, astrologi e negromanti," 498.

[30] Ibid., 482.

[31] "In Roma si vede che sono fatti molti discorsi di astrologia et se ne fa quasi professione particolare et quasi tutti hanno discorsi di natività con pronostici di buone fortune. . . . Non vi è cardinale ne prelato, ne principe che non abbia i suoi discorsi sopra la nascita con pronostichi di buone fortune." Ibid., 497.

[32] Ibid., 492.

[33] Ibid., 494.

[34] Following Urban's command, the Tribunal omitted from written testimony the names of high officials and papal intimates. Ibid., 480.

[35] Ibid., 484.

[36] Campanella's letter to Urban, dated 9 April 1635. D. Berti, "Lettere inedite di Tommaso Campanella e catalogo dei suoi scritti," *Atti della Reale Accademia dei Lincei, memorie della classe di scienze morali, storiche e filologiche* 2 (1878), 475.

member of his family.[37] But even papal decrees could not affect the menacing astral realities themselves, and Urban therefore enlisted the services of Campanella, the eccentric Dominican friar, philosopher, and astrologer, to perform magical remedies to counter deleterious astronomical events.

Although well known, the nature of the closeted activities of Urban and Campanella are worth recounting because they illustrate the pope's profound belief in astrology.[38] At moments of greatest astrological danger Urban and Campanella, dressed in white robes, locked themselves in a darkened and sealed room decorated with the twelve signs of the zodiac. Music of a gay, suave character associated with the most benefic planets, Jupiter and Venus, was played; herbs (terebinth, laurel, myrtle) with similar properties were burned; and sweet perfumes were released, while Campanella manipulated lamps and candles representing the sun, moon, and planets in configurations corresponding to the most favorable relationships in Urban's natal chart. This artificial universe was to neutralize the deadly astrological influences outside the room. The success of the magical procedure gained Campanella a monthly stipend of 15 scudi.[39]

Although diplomatic reports allude to the general nature of these practices, Urban appears to have ordered that all astrological activities and data related to his person should be kept strictly secret.[40] Prudent self-concern dictated this guardedness. The pope did not wish detailed knowledge of his astrological affairs or of his natal chart to be available for use by others, potentially against him. Justification for this precaution became clear in the Centini affair of 1634 in which rites involving a waxen effigy of the pope and a black Mass were performed with the intent of bringing Urban to a premature end.

Following the astrological prediction that Cardinal Felice Centini would be elected pope at the next conclave, his nephew, Giacinto, sought through witchcraft to hasten the process, sooner to enjoy the fruits of nepotism. The consequences of this enterprise were fatal, not to Urban but to Centini and his co-conspirators.[41] An *avviso* of the same year

[37] "Inscrutabilis" (1 April 1631): Pastor, *History of the Popes*, 29:36–37; Amabile, *Fra Tommaso Campanella*, 1:406. Common opinion held that the true author of the bull was Campanella, who, by banning others from practicing astrology, hoped to remain in the profession alone (*avviso* of 7 September 1631). Ibid., 2:150, doc. 203e.

[38] Ibid., 1:324–27; Walker, *Spiritual and Demonic Magic*, 205–12; Lechner, "Tommaso Campanella," 104–5.

[39] As confirmed in Cardinal Francesco's letter of 14 March 1635 to Giulio Mazarini, the papal nunzio in Paris. A. Bazzoni, *Un nunzio straordinario alla corte di Francia nel secolo XVII* (Florence, 1882), 173–74.

[40] Amabile, *Fra Tommaso Campanella*, 1:326. Campanella found himself in difficulty when the manuscript of his *De Fato Siderali Vitando*, explaining the entire astrological procedure he used with Urban, was obtained and published by his enemies. The work was attached, without Campanella's knowledge, to many copies of his *Astrologicorum Libri VI* (Lyons, 1629). L. Firpo, *Ricerche campanelliane* (Florence, 1947), 155–69; Grillo,

Tommaso Campanella, 44–50. Urban was still concerned to have Campanella remain silent about his relationship with the pope even after 1634 when the friar had left Rome and was living in Paris. Efforts were made "to prevent him revealing anything without special permission from His Holiness as he promised before leaving Rome." Bazzoni, *Un nunzio straordinario*, 172, as cited in Haskell, *Patrons and Painters*, 40, n. 3. In an effort to ensure the friar's compliance, his monthly stipend was continued in Paris, and, hoping to secure the matter, Cardinal Francesco ordered that Campanella be given a bonus of 50 scudi (Mazarini's letter of confirmation, 16 February 1635). Bazzoni, ibid., 173–75. Gallavotti Cavallero ("Il programma iconografico," 271–72) observes that this insistence on secrecy must explain Teti's curious failure to mention any significant astrological element in his discussion of Sacchi's ceiling fresco.

[41] Gigli, *Diario romano*, 145–46, 152–54. Other contemporary accounts are to be found in BAV, Vat. Lat. 7850, 8193, 8891. M. Rosi, "La congiura di Giacinto Centini contro Urbano VIII," *Archivio della Società Ro-*

reported that the pope was jubilant, having calculated from ibn Ezra's formula that any ruler who had the sun in the ninth house, as he had, would be unaffected by evil influences and would, moreover, reign for twenty-four years. Nevertheless, as a further protective measure, Urban arranged to have himself exorcised.[42]

Concern for secrecy perhaps accounts for the paucity of precise astrological data on Urban and other members of the Barberini family. Natal charts were no doubt frequently calculated and consulted, and we know from the Morandi affair that the pope's nativity was a matter of public discussion, but, with the exception of those confiscated from the ill-fated abbot, no charts related to the Barberini have been uncovered, not even among the vast quantity of manuscripts, letters, and personal papers in the Barberini Archive.

An anonymous manuscript volume of ca. 1639 in the Biblioteca Moreniana in Florence contains numerous genitures of popes and other illustrious individuals.[43] Urban's chart appears among them. It alone has been obliterated—and with such obsessive care that the cancellation appears to have been made with the intention of preventing scrutiny of any detail of Urban's natal data (Fig. 135). From the bits of data that can still be discerned, the chart appears to correspond to the nativity preserved in the Morandi documentation.[44] Taking the time of 1:29 P.M. Local Mean Time and combining it with the knowledge that he was born in Florence on 5 April 1568, we can erect the natal chart of Urban VIII (Fig. 136).[45] Confirmation of the accuracy of these data comes from an authoritative source, the personal diary of Urban's father, Antonio di Carlo Barberini:

> This day 5 April 1568 by the grace of God by my wife Camilla a son was born to me at 18 7/8 hours. May God be thanked for it. That same day I baptized him and gave him the name Maffeo Virginio and Romolo.[46]

As was customary in birth and baptismal records, the time is given in clock time (Italian Hours) and must be converted to Local Mean Time, which does in fact compute to approx-

mana di Storia Patria 22 (1899), 347–70; I. Carini, "Attentato di Giacinto Centini contro Urbano VIII," *Il Muratori* 1 (1892), 1–12, published Vat. Lat. 8891; Bertolotti, "Giornalisti, astrologi e negromanti," 510–14. Bernardino da Montalto predicted to Giacinto that his uncle would be the next pope after Urban VIII. This prognostication was based on a reading of the cardinal's nativity. Rosi, "La congiura," 359.

[42] ASM. "4 8bre 1634. Sta dunque allegrissimo [N.ro S.re] e havendo trovato un libro di un certo Abram Ebreo che fu Astrologo di grandissima stima, il quale scrive che chi haverà il Sole nella nona Casa (come ha il Papa) schiferà i tali pericoli, e viverà venti quattro anni nel Prencipato, gli pare di haver assicurata la vita, e di non dover dubbitare di cosa alcuna." Transcribed in Amabile, *Fra Tommaso Campanella*, 1:497, n.a. For ibn Ezra's procedure for calculating length of reign, see ibn Ezra, *Beginning of Wisdom*, 230–31.

[43] BMF, "Oroscopi di illustri personaggi," Bigazzi 235, 36v.

[44] ASR, Tribunale Criminale del Governatore di Roma, Processi 1630, vol. 251, 13r, 1050r. Two of the

four versions of Urban's chart in the Morandi volume (1025r and 1267r) are based on somewhat later times of birth (2:07 P.M. and 1:39 P.M.). The most carefully drawn of the group (13r), indicating a birth time of 1:29 P.M., is the one inserted among the twenty genitures of popes and would seem to represent the astrologer's definitive calculation.

[45] As was customary, the time given in the chart is Mean Solar Time at Florence (i.e., Local Mean Time) rather than the clock time (*ore italiane*) based on the twenty-four hour day beginning at sunset. On the basis of this data the planetary positions have been calculated by Astro Computing Services, San Diego, California.

[46] "Questo di 5 Aprile 1568 come per gra.ia di Dio dalla Cammila mia donna m'è nato il figlio mastio a hore 18 7/8. Iddio ne sia ringratiato. Detto giorno lo battezai, e li posi nome Maffeo Virginio e Romolo." Quoted in S. Pieralisi, *Urbano VIII e Galileo Galilei* (Rome, 1875), 21. Pieralisi, the Barberini librarian, reported that the diary was in the family archive. I have not been able to locate the original. A list of the birth

imately 1:30 P.M., thus corroborating the time given in the Morandi material.[47] Checking the reconstructed chart, we see the glyph for the sun at 25 degrees, 27 minutes in the sign of Aries and this positions the sun in the ninth house of the chart, as several independent sources confirm.[48] (See the table for an explanation of glyphs.)

GLYPHS OF THE PLANETS AND ZODIACAL SIGNS

Planets:		Signs:	
☉	Sun	♈	Aries
☽	Moon	♉	Taurus
☿	Mercury	♊	Gemini
♀	Venus	♋	Cancer
♂	Mars	♌	Leo
♃	Jupiter	♍	Virgo
♄	Saturn	♎	Libra
⊕	Part of Fortune	♏	Scorpio
		♐	Sagittarius
		♑	Capricorn
		♒	Aquarius
		♓	Pisces

An archetypal zodiac (Fig. 137) will show the glyphs of the planets and zodiacal signs and indicate the ideal correspondences of rulerships and houses.[49] The Ascendant, known as the Horoscope in Renaissance astrology, is the degree of the zodiac rising on the eastern horizon at the precise moment and geographic locality of birth. The zodiacal sign at the Ascendant Point constitutes a major factor in any natal chart. Urban VIII's ascending sign,

dates and times of all members of the Barberini family rounds off Urban's time to 19:00 hours ("a hore diciannove"). BAV, Arch. Barb., Ind. I, 1, 392r.

[47] 18:52 in "Italian Hours" is 18 hours and 52 minutes after sunset. With sunset having occurred at 6:38 P.M. on 4 April 1568 (Julian calendar), 18 hours 52 minutes later would be 1:30 P.M. Local Mean Time. The approximate correctness of this calculation can also be verified through the use of the DeLaLande conversion chart. J. J. DeLaLand, *Voyage d'un françois en Italie, fait dans les années 1765 & 1766* (Venice, 1769), I:XXXII–XXXVIII. It should be noted that in using the eighteenth-century DeLaLand chart for dates before ca. 1650, thirty minutes should be added to the "midday" times given in the table. Prior to mid-century the twenty-four-hour clock started precisely at sunset rather than at one-half hour after sunset, as pertained from about 1650 until Napoleonic reforms brought an end to the "Italian Hours" clock. A. Simoni, *Orologi italiani dal cinquecento all'ottocento* (Milan, 1980), 51. For a discussion of "Italian Hours" and the DeLaLand conversion method, see M. Talbot, "'Ore Italiane': The Reckoning of the Time of Day in Pre-Napoleonic Italy," *Italian Studies* 40 (1985), 51–62.

[48] Bertolotti, "Giornalisti, astrologi e negromanti," 492; Amabile, *Fra Tommaso Campanella*, 1:497, n.a. The house division system used here, the Regiomontanus system, is the one commonly employed in the Renaissance.

[49] For ready definitions of astrological terms the reader is referred to J.-L. Brau, H. Weaver, and A. Edmands, *Larousse Encyclopedia of Astrology* (New York, 1980), where the explanation of most astrological concepts corresponds to Renaissance usage. Goold's introduction to Manilius' ancient text on astronomy provides a concise introduction to the classical astrology practiced in the Renaissance. M. Manilius, *Astronomica*, trans. G. P. Goold (Cambridge, Mass.), 1977, xvi–cv. The fundamental modern study of all aspects of classical astrology is A. Bouché-Leclercq, *L'astrologie grècque* (Paris, 1899). Rousseau ("Cosimo I de' Medici," 6–10) and Cox-Rearick (*Dynasty and Destiny*, 161–77) provide accessible analyses of the fundamental concepts for the reading of natal charts and demonstrate, in their discussions of Medicean art and patronage, how astrological concerns were manifested in visual form.

as indicated by the top line of the first house, is Leo, which was 26 degrees, 12 minutes above the astrological horizon at the exact moment of his birth (Fig. 136). Following the system of correspondences established in ancient astrology, each zodiacal sign has a planetary ruler (Fig. 137). The ruler of the sign at the Ascendant becomes the Lord of the Ascendant and is thereby "dignified" or greatly enhanced in power. The ruler of Leo is the Sun; therefore the Sun is the Lord of the Ascendant in Urban's natal chart.[50] A further astrological factor gives extraordinary prominence to the Sun in Urban's nativity. Just as each zodiacal sign has a planetary ruler, so is each planetary body associated with a second sign in which it is said to be "exalted," meaning that its power magnifies when located in that particular sign. The sign of exaltation for the Sun is Aries. Not only is the Sun dignified as the Lord of the Ascendant, its position in Aries results in its exaltation.

The third element in Urban's chart that strengthens the Sun derives from the factor of angular relationships or "aspects" of planetary bodies. Favorable aspecting enhances the power of benefic elements. The Sun is in "Trine" (120 degrees apart) with the Ascendant Point, a position that greatly augments the potency of the solar body. It was this prominent feature of Urban's geniture that Campanella referred to when he noted that the pope "had the Sun in his Horoscope."[51] Not only is the Sun already the Lord of the Ascendant but also the Trine with the Sun at 25 degrees, 27 minutes in Aries aggrandizes that benefic rule.

The fourth solarian feature of Urban's chart is the Sun's position as Prorogator, the "Giver of Life."[52] In Renaissance astrology the Prorogator determines the length of life and, according to Ptolemy, the Sun is always the Prorogator when located in the first, seventh, ninth, tenth, or eleventh house. The Sun in Urban's chart occupies the ninth house and is therefore the Prorogator—the most important element for the determination of his longevity.[53] This was the feature of the pope's personal astrology that was so widely discussed at the time of the Morandi affair and explains his profound fear of solar eclipses, for they constituted the occultation of his Giver of Life.[54]

Urban's solarian geniture accounts for the solar imagery that appears so prominently in his personal iconography and on works of art commissioned under his patronage. The famous Barberini sun, no mere symbol, has its basis in Urban's sun-centered natal astrology.

After the Sun, three other heavenly bodies hold positions of importance in Urban's nativity: Jupiter, Venus, and Moon. Like the solar body, Jupiter and the Moon are both in the signs of their rulerships, Sagittarius and Cancer, and are therefore potent. Jupiter, furthermore, is in conjunction with the *Pars Fortunae* (Part of Fortune).[55] Venus occupies Pisces, the sign of its exaltation. The prominence of Jupiter and Venus is especially significant be-

[50] The Sun is also drawn to the ascending sign by Mars (at 0 degrees, 57 minutes in Leo), with which it is in "mutual reception," as the Sun and Mars each occupy the sign of the other's rulership (Aries and Leo respectively).

[51] Amabile, *Fra Tommaso Campanella*, 2:154, doc. 213. Campanella, like other astrologers of the period, uses the term "Horoscope" in the technical sense, meaning Ascendant Point.

[52] Also known as Apheta or Hyleg. Ptolemy (*Tetrabiblos*, III: 10) formulated this theory. See Bouché-Leclercq, *L'astrologie grècque*, 410–19. The rules for determining the Prorogator were carried forward by

J. Schöner, *Opusculum Astrologicum* (Nuremberg, 1539), pt. 2, unpaginated. See Rousseau, "Cosimo I de' Medici," 491.

[53] I thank Claudia Rousseau for pointing out to me the significance of the Sun as Prorogator in Urban's nativity.

[54] Bertolotti, "Giornalisti, astrologi e negromanti," 483, 492, 507–10.

[55] The *Pars Fortunae* is an imaginary position resulting from a calculation based on the relationship among the Sun, Moon, and Ascendant in a given nativity. Extremely benefic, it signifies wealth and good fortune in general.

cause they are the two most favorable planets, known respectively as the "Greater Benefic" and the "Lesser Benefic."

Taddeo, emulating his uncle, also adopted the sun as a personal impresa. In his biography of Taddeo, Francesco Barberini stated that his younger brother was born in Rome on 16 November 1603, "after midnight, if I remember rightly."[56] "Mezzanotte" carried the literal meaning of halfway through the hours of darkness, which would have been approximately 11:45 P.M. Local Mean Time the previous day, 15 November 1603.[57] Leo was still on the Ascendant (Fig. 138), at 29 degrees, 21 minutes, or less than three minutes in clock time before the first degree of Virgo rose. Thus "after midnight" means that Virgo is Taddeo's Ascendant sign, but, given the imprecise nature of the concept "midnight" and the uncertain nature of Francesco's recollection, the possibility remains that Taddeo, too, may have been born with Leo as his rising sign and with the Sun as the Lord of his Ascendant. The importance of the Sun in Taddeo's chart, however, does not depend on this alone.

The power of the Sun in Taddeo's nativity gains augmentation because of its conjunction with Jupiter and Venus. Conjunction is the strongest of the possible aspects between planets, with Jupiter and Venus being the two most positive of the heavenly bodies. Furthermore, the location of Jupiter in Sagittarius, the sign of its rulership, makes its beneficial relationship to the Sun even more powerful. These astrological factors give importance to the Sun in Taddeo's chart even without consideration of the Ascendant sign, and solar imagery appears with equal prominence in his personal iconography, as can be seen in the sun impresa at the center of the prefect's ceremonial hat (Fig. 139).[58] Solar disks even appear on either side of Taddeo's tomb erected in the church of Santa Rosalia in Palestrina.[59]

The Sun therefore appears not only as family impresa but also as the astrological element of foremost importance in the nativities of both Urban and Taddeo. Some general knowledge of this must be presupposed for seventeenth-century visitors to the Barberini Palace, who saw solar images throughout the building, especially as they looked up and

---

[56] BAV, Arch. Barb., Ind. IV, 1254, unpaginated [2v]. Transcribed in Waddy, *Seventeenth-Century Roman Palaces*, 333.

[57] Taddeo's chart is not among those in the Morandi material (ASR, Tribunale Criminale del Governatore di Roma, Processi 1630, vol. 251). Although the hour of actual birth was sometimes indicated in seventeenth-century baptismal records, this is unfortunately not the case with Taddeo's. AVR, Registro dei Battesimi, S. Giovanni dei Fiorentini, 1600–1616, 61v, 17 November 1603. Nor is the time given in the list of Barberini birth records (BAV, Arch. Barb., Ind. I, 1), which provides the birth times of all other members of the family. In mid-November at the latitude of Rome the sun sets at approximately 4:45 and rises at 6:45. Thus "midnight" would have occurred approximately seven hours after sunset, or 11:45 P.M.

[58] The bust-length portrait, traditionally attributed to Carlo Maratta, is probably the one listed in a Barberini inventory of 1699–1704 (M. A. Lavin, *Documents and Inventories*, 429): "Un Ritratto del S.re D. Taddeo Barberini in habito di Prefetto in Tela da Testa Cornice nera, oro di Carlo Maratta." Mezzetti rejected this attribution on stylistic grounds and instead associated the work with a portrait of Taddeo once in the possession of Maratta's daughter that was said to have been painted by the artist's brother, Bernabeo. A. Mezzetti, "Contributi a Carlo Maratta," *Rivista del Istituto Nazionale d'Archeologia e Storia dell'Arte*, n.s., 4 (1955), 351–52. Harris (*Andrea Sacchi*, 93) observes that the work seems to be based on the engraved portrait of Taddeo in the *Aedes Barberinae*, with the prefect's robe added.

[59] The tomb, erected in 1704, contains a bust of Taddeo wearing the sun-emblazoned prefect's hat. The terra-cotta modello of the bust by Bernardino Cametti is in the Museo di Roma. R. Enggass, *Early Eighteenth-Century Sculpture in Rome* (University Park, Pa., 1976), 154, fig. 148.

beheld the glowing orb of the sun suspended overhead and consuming the center of the salotto vault. The figure of Divine Wisdom—"more beautiful than the sun . . . she is found before it" (Wisdom 7:29)—appears in front of the sun and moreover has a solar disk radiating from her breast, thus establishing a fundamental equation that functions on both the allegorical and astrological levels of the ceiling imagery. As a traditional symbol of the biblical Divine Wisdom, the Sun in the nativities of pope and nephew vouchsafes their possession of God's sapiential favor. The Barberini Manuscript underscores this relationship by asserting the appropriateness of the image of Divine Wisdom to the house of the Barberini because the family was "born" to rule the Church with Divine Wisdom.[60]

With knowledge of the primacy of the Sun in the nativities of Urban and Taddeo, the pictorial cycle of the chapel completes for the viewer the linkage between antechamber and chapel. Just as the eclipse of the sun occurred at Christ's Crucifixion, so are his Resurrection and ultimate Ascension associated with sunrise. The prominent rays emanating from around the head of the risen Christ in the chapel *Ascension* corroborate the equation with the rising sun, thus accounting for the otherwise incongruent inclusion of this scene in the midst of the family scenes of Christ's Infancy (Fig. 56). The astrological Sun in the nativities of the Barberini appears here as the rising sun of Christ ascending into the heavens.[61] Awareness of these astrological and Christological associations gives new and still more profound meaning to Urban's great impresa of the rising sun—ALIUSQUE ET IDEM (Fig. 133).

Given the horoscopic significance of the salotto ceiling, the natal imagery of the narrative wall scenes in the chapel—where Christ is conceived, born, sacrificed, and ascendant as the *sol sapientiae*—can be seen as even more fitting in the context of the overall pictorial ensemble. In view of the domestic function of the chapel for such ceremonies as the baptism of newborn members of the Barberini family, we may wonder if the sign of divine favor was limited to the genitures of Urban and Taddeo alone. The Barberini Manuscript refers to "the

[60] Appendix B. Urban and Taddeo were not the only Barberini to have the Sun prominently in their genitures. Carlo Barberini, Taddeo's father, born in Florence on 28 May 1562 at 20 3/4 hours ("hore venti et tre quarti"), i.e., 4:15 P.M., had in his nativity the Sun in conjunction with Jupiter and Venus, the Greater and Lesser Benefics. We also know that Taddeo's younger brother, the future Cardinal Antonio the Younger, was born during the "hora noctis quarta" (i.e., 11:15 P.M. the previous day) on 4 [3] August 1608. AVR, Registro dei Battesimi, S. Giovanni dei Fiorentini, 1600–1616, 117r, 5 August 1608; and BAV, Arch. Barb., Ind. I, 1, 405r. This puts Taurus on the Ascendant, but the Sun is in Leo, the sign of its rulership. According to Magno Perneo, the dates of Antonio's birth and baptism, 4 and 5 August, portended his uncle's elevation to the papacy, which was to take place on 6 August, fifteen years later. "De Nativitate et Vita Eminent.mi et R.mi Cardinalis Antonii Barberini Junioris Papae Nepotis," BAV, Barb. Lat. 3252, 15r–v. Antonio, too, adopted the sun as his impresa—TRANSIT BENE FACIENDO. P. Le Moyne, *De l'art des devises* (Paris,

1666), 259. For the younger Antonio's biography, *DBI*, 6:166. The nativities of Carlo, Antonio the Elder, Francesco, and Antonio the Younger were calculated by Morandi (ASR, Tribunale Criminale del Governatore di Roma, Processi 1630, vol. 251, 14r, 13v, 69r, 70r.

[61] The association between Christ and the rising and setting suns of Barberini iconography finds confirmation in Romanelli's Life of Christ tapestry cycle later commissioned by Cardinal Francesco (1643–1656). Romanelli, who had worked as Cortona's assistant on the Christological cycle of the chapel, provided the cartoons for the tapestries. The tapestry of the *Crucifixion* (Fig. 110) replicates Cortona's chapel fresco at the explicit request of the cardinal. The top border of the tapestries depicting the *Crucifixion*, the *Last Supper*, and the *Resurrection* contain the Barberini imprese of the rising and setting suns. In all three tapestries Christ's halo, located directly beneath the cartouche containing the suns, explicitly repeats the sunburst of rays in the imprese. Below, 187–88, Fig. 110.

Barberini family" in general, and Teti notes that the *Divine Wisdom* is there to remind the *descendants* of the Barberini family, who are to be *continually* called to the governance of the Church, to follow the example of Urban in honoring Wisdom. Thus the painted ceiling of the salotto also expresses the dynastic hope that future generations of the Barberini will be born under the sun of Divine Wisdom. It must have been taken as proof of the vitality of this idea when, only a few months after Sacchi's completion of the salotto fresco and at the time Cortona was working on the chapel cycle, Donna Anna gave birth on 19 August 1631 to yet another Barberini with a leonine geniture. With the sun in Leo, the sign of its rulership, it was appropriate that the infant, Maffeo, was named in honor of his papal uncle.[62]

The natal horoscopy represented in the *Divine Wisdom* fresco, however, fulfills only half of the declaration made in the Barberini Manuscript, which informs us that the Barberini family was "elected" as well as "born" to rule the Church.[63] The chart erected for the election of Urban VIII confirms this assertion. The conclave that concluded with the elevation of Maffeo Barberini to the papacy was unusually troubled, and it ended with a final counting of the ballots amid considerable turmoil at 8:15 A.M. on 6 August 1623.[64] The election chart shows Virgo on the Ascendant at the moment of the final balloting (Fig. 140), which makes Mercury the Lord of the Ascendant. But because of its neutrality (neither benefic nor malefic), its retrograde movement, and its location in Leo, the sign opposite the sign of its exaltation (Aquarius), Mercury's influence is weakened. The most powerful and significant component of Urban's election is the Stellium of four planets ruled by the Sun in the sign of Leo. The Sun itself is in Leo, the sign of its rulership, and in Sextile aspect (60 degrees) with the Mid-Heaven Point—factors that enhance its astrological potency. Additionally, because it is the only planet to occupy the sign of its rulership, the Sun attains supremacy as the "Sole Dispositor" of the chart.[65] But the conjunction of the Sun with Jupiter, the Greater Benefic, located only two degrees away, represents a second powerful astrological force that would have been interpreted as divine proof of the favorable outcome of the conclave for Urban. At the moment of the election, Jupiter, the most benefic of planets, was in direct relationship to the Sun, the Lord of the Ascendant of Urban's nativity.[66]

Long after the event, Campanella recalled this factor as the chief astrological indication of Urban's election. The heavens were already favorably deployed when the conclave convened:

> Then in the year 1623 there took place in Leo the Great Conjunction precisely on the day the cardinals entered the conclave to make pope Urban VIII, and they did it on the sixth of August, the sun being in the horoscope of the pope.[67]

[62] Pecchiai, *I Barberini*, 213, 217–18.

[63] Appendix B.

[64] Gigli (*Diario romano*, 77) provides the time of the election as 13:00, i.e., 13 hours after sunset the previous evening (which occurred about 7:10 P.M.).

[65] The Dispositor of a planet is the ruler of the sign in which the planet is located.

[66] This overwhelmingly positive astral event was also disadvantageously affected by the simultaneous conjunction with Saturn, the "Greater Malefic." In detriment (i.e., located in the sign opposite its domicile in Aquarius), Saturn's negative potency was actually in-

creased. The procedural complications and the malarial infestation that occurred in the conclave (below, 181–84) would have been read as manifestations of this Saturnine influence.

[67] ". . . Poi l'anno 1623 si fe in Leone le Congiuntione Magna proprio nel giorno ch'intrano i Card.li in conclave a far papa Urbano 8.o e lo fecero a sesto d'Ag.o sendo il sole nell'horoscopo del papa." T. Campanella, "Le monarchie delle nationi finirsi nella romana . . ." (Paris, Bibliothèque de l'Arsénal, cod. Ital. 1083). Transcribed in Amabile, *Fra Tommaso Campanella*, 2:320, doc. 346. The manuscript is dated 1635.

The chart erected for 7:30 P.M.[68] on 19 July 1623, when the cardinals were sealed in the conclave, shows Jupiter and Saturn in conjunction, less than one degree apart, in Leo (Fig. 141).

The term "Great Conjunction" employed by Campanella refers specifically to the proximity of Jupiter and Saturn, which was traditionally held to herald a change in political rulership. This belief found summation in the influential writings of the late fourteenth-century Arab astrologer ibn Khaldun:

> For matters of general importance such as royal authority and dynasties, they [those who interpret conjunctions] use the conjunctions, especially those of the two superior planets . . . Saturn and Jupiter. . . . The great conjunction is the meeting of the two superior planets in the same degree of the firmament, which reoccurs after 960 years. . . . The great conjunction indicates great events, such as a change in royal authority or dynasties, or a transfer of royal authority from one people to another.[69]

At this point, however, the conjoined planets were not yet significant for Maffeo Barberini, since they were more than ten degrees from the Sun located in Cancer at 26 degrees, 31 minutes.[70] Because the Sun had not yet moved into Leo, the two planets were also "out of sign" and therefore not fully potent. The moment of Maffeo's election had not yet arrived astrologically.

On 6 August after the Sun had crossed into Leo, the sign of its rulership, and into conjunction with Jupiter, the Greater Benefic, Urban was elected. Campanella is explicit about the astrological reasons for Urban's elevation to the papacy. The election occurred because the Sun is "in his Horoscope." The author of Urban's obliterated birth chart (Fig. 135) also seems to have recognized the natal astrology as a harbinger of papal election, and labeled the data accordingly: "Papa Urbano VIII Creato Pontefice a di 6 Agosto 1623."[71]

Jupiter also held a prominent position in Urban's natal chart (Fig. 136) because it, like the Sun, occupied the sign of its rulership; thus, after the Sun had moved into Leo, with Jupiter separated from it by a mere two degrees, Urban was elected. The conjunction of Jupiter and the Sun in the sign of the Sun's rulership, which is also the Ascendant of Urban's natal chart, constituted the most favorable of astrological conditions for him precisely at the moment he attained the papal throne.

The three essential astrological influences at the time of Urban's election—the Sun and Jupiter in conjunction in the sign of Leo—not only appear in the Barberini salotto fresco

[68] Gigli (*Diario romano*, 74) reports that the cardinals were locked in the conclave in "the evening at night." The 7:30 P.M. Local Mean Time calculation is only approximate, but a variation of even several hours in either direction would have had little consequence for the relationship between the planets and the sun. This approximate hour is confirmed by F. Petruccelli della Gattina, *Histoire diplomatique des conclaves* (Paris, 1864–1865), 3:56.

[69] Ibn Khaldun, *Prolegomena*, II: 211–13, as cited in E. Garin, *Astrology in the Renaissance*, trans. C. Jackson and J. Allen (London, 1983), 21–22. The significance of the "Great Conjunction" was widely discussed in the West in the fifteenth and sixteenth centuries. See, for example, F. Giuntini, *Speculum Astrologiae* (Lyons, 1573), who was in turn probably following the Arab astrologer Abū Ma'šar Ga'far ibn Muhammad (805–886), *Albumasar de magnis coniunctibus: et annorum revolutionibus: ac eorum profectionibus: octo continens tractatus* (Venice, 1515), with editions at Augsburg (1485, 1488, 1489, 1495) and Venice (1503, 1506). See Rousseau, "Cosimo I de' Medici," 24–28, 85, n. 43.

[70] Conjunction normally requires that the planets be within an orb no greater than ten degrees.

[71] BMF, Bigazzi 235, 36v.

but are also the chief elements positioned on the most powerful compositional line of the painting: the line along which the main narrative action of the work is disposed. Love's downturned arrow leads the viewer's eye from the lion of Leo through the sun of Wisdom to Aquila, the eagle of Jupiter (Fig. 33).[72] The Sun in his natal and election charts demonstrates astrologically that Urban was "born" and "elected" to rule, as asserted in the concluding paragraph of the Barberini Manuscript. The presence of the sun of Divine Wisdom in the Barberini Palace reiterates that divinely ordained fact.[73]

The constellation Aquila represents Jupiter allegorically. It "soars to the heights the bird of mighty Jupiter," says Manilius (*Astronomica*, I:343–45). But Aquila also carries astrological significance as Jupiter because it rises with Sagittarius, which is the sign of Jupiter's rulership.[74] Moreover, Ptolemy, the most venerated of ancient astrological authorities, held that Aquila has influence similar to that of Mars and Jupiter (*Tetrabiblos*, I:9). An important and well-known precedent for this type of astrological ceiling imagery, where extrazodiacal constellations of the *paranatellon* connote planets and zodiacal signs, is to be seen in the Sala dei Pontefici (Perino del Vaga, 1520–1521) of the Vatican Palace (Figs. 132 and 142). Gathered in and around the fictive oculus of the vault are both zodiacal and extrazodiacal constellations. Lyra (in the oculus), Leo, Aquila, and Cygnus are joined to Jupiter and the Sun (Apollo) to represent the chief constellations and planets of the natal chart of Leo X, the patron of the cycle. This same natal configuration also portended elevation to the papacy.[75]

Both the lion and the eagle entered late into the design process of the Barberini *Divine Wisdom*. They do not appear to have been present in the Cooper-Hewitt compositional drawing (Fig. 41). As already noted, at that point Love was to be depicted as a Cupid with his arrow (Sagitta) as the attribute-constellation. The introduction of the lion must reflect a determined desire to bring in an additional astrological component referring to birth and election in the Barberini family. This becomes all the more likely because the lion is forced illogically into the allegorical meaning of the imagery. Cupid with his bow and arrow may have been an unwanted pagan deity among Christian virtues, but his authority as a person-

---

[72] For the constellation Aquila as the eagle of Jupiter, see Hyginus, *Poetica Astronomica*, 2:16, in *The Myths of Hyginus*, trans. M. Grant (Lawrence, Kansas, 1960), 203; Allen, *Star Names*, 56.

[73] Without knowledge of the precise astrological data pertaining to Urban's birth and election, Lechner ("Fresco of 'Divina Sapienza,' " 101, 106) observed the importance of a Sun-Leo relationship in the ceiling and suggested that it referred to the election of Urban. But the interpretation of the central image of Wisdom enthroned between lions as the Sun in its domicile (Leo) and therefore a reference to the election month of August cannot be sustained. The lions on the throne, unlike the lion of Leo ridden by Love, are not marked with stars and consequently do not appear to have astrological significance. They refer instead to the lion throne of Solomon (III Kings 10:18–19). On this particular point, see Harris ("Letter to the Editor," 306). The Barberini Manuscript does not mention the throne lions.

[74] By means of the *paranatellon*—the doctrine that attaches extrazodiacal constellations to the zodiacal signs

with which they rise—the ancients associated Aquila with Aquarius. Manilius (*Astronomica* V:486–503); Hyginus (*Poetica astronomica* II:16); and Firmicus Maternus (*Matheseos* VIII:XVI:1). But Renaissance astrologers put Aquila with Sagittarius, as indicated in Giuntini's discussion of the nativities of Alexander VI and Leo X. Giuntini, *Speculum Astrologiae*, 239r. Also, Allen, *Star Names*, 56.

[75] Rousseau, "Cosimo I de' Medici," 139–42, 164–70; Cox-Rearick, *Dynasty and Destiny*, 196. Like Leo before him, Urban may also have found confirmation of his destiny to rule over Rome and the Papal States in the charts of the founding of the city on 20 April 572 B.C., which, according to a number of sixteenth-century authorities, took place at 12:49 P.M., with Leo on the Ascendant. Ibid., 142–43, fig. 24; L. Gaurico, *Tractatus Astrologicus* (Venice, 1552), bk. 1, 5r. Raphael's celestial sphere on the ceiling of the Stanza della Segnatura may also be a star map of the heavens at the time of Julius II's election to the papacy. See N. Rash-Fabbri, "A Note on the Stanza della Segnatura," *Gazette des beaux-arts* 94 (1979), esp. 98–100.

ification of Love could not be challenged. The lion as an attribute or symbol of love, however, must be considered recherché.[76] One can imagine that the wish to include the astrologically important lion of Leo took precedence over the more straightforward iconography of the original program. Likewise, the eagle of Aquila, apparently not present in the early compositional drawing, was brought in and placed in a position of prominence, rising in the northern latitudes over Italy—as seen on the globe—as was the planet Jupiter at the moment of Urban's election.

A further change that appears to have taken place only during the final execution of the fresco shows how significant was the introduction of the eagle. In the Leningrad modello (Fig. 42) it appears directly beneath the throne, and the scepter of Wisdom points at Perspicacity herself rather than at her attribute, the eagle, as in the ceiling. The head of the eagle in the modello turns as if to look up at Perspicacity. In the fresco, however, not only are the earth and the eagle pulled out to the right, thus positioning the eagle on the compositional diagonal with the lion, but its head turns in the opposite direction as though in response to the gesture of Divine Wisdom. The eagle of Jupiter seems to rise in the northern sky at Wisdom's command, just as the planet Jupiter rose in the north in late July 1623 to meet the Sun in conjunction and bring about Urban's election.

A rarely depicted virtue, Perspicacity may have been chosen from among those listed in the biblical text partly so that the eagle, with its acute vision, could serve as her attribute,[77] but the personification itself is important as an interlocutor for the viewer. Looking directly across the line Leo-Sun-Aquila, she perceives the true relationship of the heavenly bodies on both the allegorical and astrological levels of meaning. The viewer understands that Perspicacity comprehends love (Leo) as the source of the wisdom (Sun) transmitted to the earth and humankind through the pope and his family.

The biblical passage that justifies Perspicacity as a virtue of Wisdom states that she "knoweth things past, and judgeth things to come. . . . She knoweth signs and wonders before they be done, and the events of times and ages" (Wisdom 8:8). Her position in the ceiling and the direction of her glance further imply her understanding that the astrological triad Leo-Sun-Aquila represents the heavenly sign of Urban's divine election. A heavenly astrologer, she foresees events by reading the planets and stars.

The late introduction of the lion and the eagle indicates that from the beginning the Sun was the focus of the astrological significance of the meaning. Only later in the process of creation did the opportunity to bring in these two important astrological components and to establish the astrologically explicit heavenly triad come to be exploited.

Lions and eagles also appear among the personal imprese of Urban published by Ferro. The lion impresa VIVIFICAT ET TERRET (It brings to life and terrifies) depicts a roaring lion and symbolizes, we are told in the text, the raising of Maffeo Barberini to the cardinalate.[78] Sacchi represented the lion of Love also roaring, but here the lion must refer to the elevation to the papacy. Because of the importance of Leo in the natal and election charts of Urban and Taddeo, leonine iconography appears frequently in Barberini imagery. The an-

---

[76] It does appear in emblem literature. D. Meisner, *Thesaurus Philopoliticus* (Frankfurt-am-Main, 1627–1631), 2: pt. 6, no. 10, depicts a Cupid riding on a lion and reining it in, under the motto OMNIA DOMAT AMOR.

[77] I. Lavin, "Bernini's Cosmic Eagle," 209–14, has

examined the emblematic tradition associating eagles and solar imagery as it appears in a Bernini-designed frontispiece engraving (F. Poilly) in N. Zucchi, *Optica Philosophia* (Lyons, 1652–1656).

[78] Ferro, *Teatro d'imprese*, 439.

cient bas-relief of a roaring lion located on the piano nobile level of the square staircase of Palazzo Barberini (Fig. 134) announces the extraordinary importance of Leo in Barberini iconography almost at the threshold of the palace salone; the fireplace in the salone was to have included a stucco lion pelt above the mantel[79]; a roaring lion also greets the visitor from the northeast corner of Cortona's salone vault fresco (Fig. 92);[80] and Rubens' frontispiece for the lavish 1634 Antwerp edition of Urban's Latin poems, alluding to the sweet words of the poet-pope, depicts the biblical story of Samson finding bees and a honeycomb in the mouth of the roaring lion he had slain (Judges 14:5–14): "Out of the strong came forth sweetness" (Fig. 143).[81] A payment for household expenses of 1644 labled "meat given to the lion" indicates that the Barberini carried love of the leonine to a remarkable extreme.[82]

The eagle, too, appears among Urban's personal imprese published by Ferro (Fig. 144) and, as with the leonine device, the eagle impresa refers to Maffeo's well-aspected natal astrology, where the Sun is both Lord of the Ascendant and in Trine with it, and Jupiter is in Sagittarius the sign of its rulership (Fig. 136). Under the motto SUBLIMI SUBLIME (To the heights, from the heights), the eagle and its young, perched high on a mountain peak, gaze upward into the rays of the sun. Ferro explains that the loftier one's birth, the more one aspires to still greater heights. This alludes, the reader is told, to Maffeo's birth in 1568 to noble parents in the most noble city of Florence. But "there were also happy *aspects* in heaven, and he was born not only noble by parents and homeland but also most noble of spirit and character."[83]

Leo, the Sun, and Aquila (as Love, Wisdom, and Perspicacity) hold positions of compositional importance because of their weighty astrological significance, but the other constellations represented in the ceiling also carry meaningful astral power for Urban and Taddeo. The Barberini Manuscript informs us that the virtues of Wisdom are many and that the painting represents only some of the more important attributes (i.e., constellations).[84] Of the more than thirty virtues mentioned in the seventh and eighth chapters of the Book of Wisdom, the author of the program chose only eleven, plus Love and Fear. This selection is based in the astrology of the Barberini, each virtue of Wisdom having been chosen for its appropriateness to a specific attribute-constellation.

Of the fourteen constellations depicted, only three are zodiacal: Leo, Virgo, and Libra. These signs happen to be sequential on the zodiacal band and consequently rise in the heavens successively—first Leo, then Virgo, followed by Libra. The ceiling composition spatially maintains this astrological order, with Leo having risen highest, followed by Virgo and, in succession, Libra, located on a lower cloud and closer to the viewer (Colorplate I, Fig. 35). Returning to the natal and election charts of Urban and Taddeo, we discover why Leo and Virgo have prominence in the ceiling. In both nativities Leo rises on the Ascendant.

[79] Below, 142.

[80] Below, 148.

[81] Urbanus VIII, *Poemata* (Antwerp, 1634). See J. B. Judson and C. van de Velde, *Corpus Rubenianum Ludwig Burchard XXI: Book Illustrations and Title-Pages* (London-Philadelphia, 1978), cat. 68, 283–85. The same biblical text served as the basis for an engraved sheet designed by Pietro da Cortona. M. Fagiolo dell'Arco and S. Carandini, *L'effimero barocco* (Rome, 1977–1978), 2:75, fig.

96. The Rome 1631 edition of Urban's *Poemata* had a Bernini-designed frontispiece illustrating the poet-king David strangling the lion (I Kings 17:34–35). *Bernini in Vaticano* (Rome, 1981), cat. 51, 80–81.

[82] BAV, Arch. Barb., Comp. 224, fol. 464r (gior., Card. Antonio). On the menagerie at Palazzo Barberini, see Teti, *Aedes Barberinae* (1642), 37.

[83] Ferro, *Teatro d'imprese*, 92–93.

[84] Appendix B.

In the election chart Virgo is on the Ascendant. But this explanation still does not account for Libra.

Girolamo Cardano's well-known nativity of Christ shows Libra on the Ascendant Point, 2 degrees, 43 minutes above the astrological horizon (Fig. 145).[85] Christ's chart is literally phenomenal, with a comet exactly at the Ascendant Point. No evidence of this luminous body appears in the Barberini ceiling, but the star Spica (i.e., the shaft of wheat of Virgo emphasizing the Virgin birth) and Jupiter, both in conjunction with the Ascendant and therefore with the comet, are extremely prominent in the fresco composition as well as in the chart. Significantly, Sacchi's Virgo reclines directly under Divinity and opposite the Jovian eagle of Perspicacity. Christ's natal astrology on the salotto vault thereby signifies his physical nativity depicted on the nearby chapel walls.

The enfolding of the natal astrology of Christ with that of mortal humans seems overly bold to the point of impiety until we recall the no less assertive final statement of the Barberini Manuscript, which declares that the Barberini family was "born and elected to rule the Church *in the place of God*." As we have already seen, that idea was in fact too audacious, provoking the censorious pen stroke that canceled the excessively immodest claims of the final paragraph of the written program (Fig. 121). The unorthodox nature of the author's thinking on this point must have shocked even Taddeo.

After Leo, Virgo, and Libra, all other constellations represented in the salotto ceiling are extrazodiacal and, with the exception of two, either rise or set as those three pass through the Ascendant.[86] The exceptions, Ara and Crux, are both held by Holiness, the only figure with more than one attribute-constellation. Ara rises with the first degree of Scorpio, which succeeds the last degree of Libra, and Crux quickly follows.[87] They might therefore be included in the overall scheme on the grounds of their closeness to Libra, but here the allegorical level of signification seems to take precedence over the astrological. The pious author of the ceiling program must have seen the inclusion of these two most Christian of heavenly configurations—the Altar and the Cross—as justifiable for theological reasons alone. Thus they appear in the most direct proximity to Divine Wisdom of all the constellations.

The constellations represented by Sacchi, both zodiacal and extrazodiacal, constitute a selection of the heavenly bodies operative at the most astrologically significant moments in the lives of Urban and Taddeo, coordinated with the virtues of Divine Wisdom as verified in Scripture and with the natal astrology of Christ, who is Divine Wisdom incarnate. The salotto ceiling in Palazzo Barberini thus establishes a cosmic consonance between the birth and election of the resident family and the providential workings of the divine mind as re-

[85] G. Cardano, *In Ptolemaei Librorum de Judiciis Astrorum Libr. IV. Commentaria* (Lyons, 1555), 370–74. For a full discussion of Cardano's natal chart of Christ, see W. Shumaker, *Renaissance Curiosa* (Binghamton, N.Y., 1982), 53–90. Also, for a comparison with earlier nativities of Christ, J. D. North, *Horoscopes and History* (London, 1986), 163–73.

[86] Two ancient astrologers in particular, Aratus and Manilius, discuss which extrazodiacal constellations rise and set with each of the twelve zodiacal constellations. According to Aratus (*Phaenomena*, 589–633), Le-

pus rises and Aquila and Hercules set as Leo rises; Lyra and Cygnus set as Virgo rises. Manilius (*Astronomica*, V: 234–338) adds that Corona rises with Virgo, and Lyra and Aquila with Libra. Neither author mentions Coma Berenices and Triangulum, but, as Coma is located between Leo and Virgo, it must rise with them; and Triangulum must set as Virgo rises, for Aratus (595–601) notes that Pegasus and Eridanus—between which Triangulum is located—set at that time.

[87] Firmicus Maternus, *Ancient Astrology*, 276.

vealed in the disposition of the stars. Divine Wisdom and the astrological destiny of the Barberini are synonymous realities. The power of the astral bodies shining on the vault of the salotto is furthermore illustrated in the Christological cycle of the chapel, where God's self-imposed earthly destiny takes human form.

But the meaning of the *Divine Wisdom* fresco is retrospective as well as prospective in character, portending future events. Under these same potent astral influences new glories would be attained.

The Barberini were concerned not only with natal and judicial astrology—those branches that deal with birth signs and the prediction of political events—they also practiced electional astrology, consulting the movements of the heavenly bodies to determine the most favorable moment for any action or undertaking. Alvise Contarini, Pesaro's successor as Venetian ambassador in Rome (1632–1635), reported to the Venetian Senate on Urban's use of "electional" astrology: "He [Urban] lives by strict rule; he regulates his actions in great part according to the movements of the heavens, about which he is very knowledgeable, even though he has with very great censure prohibited its study to everyone else."[88] The seriousness with which Urban and Taddeo regarded the solarian and leonine nature of their natal astrology can be measured by the pope's concern in choosing the most propitious moment for Taddeo's investiture as prefect. As we have seen, Urban had been planning to acquire this socially prestigious office for his family since at least 1625, and it was viewed by many critics as an honor Taddeo was unworthy of receiving.[89] The pope's intentions in this matter were made official in a consistory of 12 May 1631.[90] The exact hour of the consistory is not known, but, if it convened in the morning, as was customary, then Leo was very likely on the Ascendant, with Jupiter in Trine with the Ascendant Point.[91]

Our knowledge about the public ceremonies and festivities planned by the pope for the actual investiture is more complete.[92] A painting by Agostino Tassi (Fig. 146) preserves the ceremony that took place in the Pauline Chapel of the Quirinal Palace on the morning of 6 August 1631—the eighth anniversary of Urban's election to the papacy.[93] With the Sun in Leo, the sign of its rulership, and in Trine with Jupiter and the Moon, Urban must have felt secure about the success of his action in terms of the future of the Barberini family. The painting depicts the precise moment the pope placed the newly designed, sun-emblazoned

[88] "Vive [Urbano] con gran regola; regola in gran parte le sue attioni con i moti del Cielo, dei quali e molto intelligente, anchorchè con censure grandissime n'habbi proibito lo studio a tutti gli altri." Barozzi and Berchet, *Le relazioni della corte*, 1:366.

[89] Pietro Contarini, the Venetian ambassador in Rome, reported of Taddeo in 1625: "Qualche disegno vi è nel Pontefice di farlo Prefetto della città, dopo la morte del Duca di Urbino che hora gode questo titolo." Ibid., 1:215. On the negative reaction to Taddeo's appointment, see Gigli, *Diario romano*, 122–23.

[90] "Pauli Alaleonis diarium a die 26 februarii 1630 ad diem 31 dicembris 1637," BAV, Barb. Lat. 2819, 58r; Contelori, *De Praefecto Urbis*, 90.

[91] Leo would have been on the Ascendant from approximately 9:45–11:45 A.M.

[92] "Pauli Alaleonis diarium a die 26 februarii 1630 ad diem 31 dicembris 1637," BAV, Barb. Lat. 2819, 67r–70v; Gigli, *Diario romano*, 120–22.

[93] Rome, Museo di Roma (1631–1633). G. Incisa della Rocchetta, "Tre quadri Barberini acquistati dal Museo di Roma," *Bollettino dei Musei Comunali di Roma* 6 (1959), 20–22; Pugliatti, *Agostino Tassi*, 101–2, fig. 152. A sketch for the principal figural group is at the Art Gallery of Ontario, Toronto (no. 69/34, verso). Ibid., 152, fig. 230. Another equally large painting commissioned from Tassi at the same time is the *Entry of Taddeo Barberini at Porta del Popolo* (Rome, Banco di Santo Spirito), depicting Taddeo's triumphal entry on 3 August upon his return from Urbino and just prior to his investiture as prefect. Ibid., 103–4, fig. 154. These works were commissioned by Urban and paid for by the Tesoreria Pontificia. Ibid., 61–62, 101–2.

prefect's hat upon the head of his nephew, also favored by the Sun in his geniture. Thus Taddeo could also be said to have been "elected" under the sun of Divine Wisdom.[94] Through this event we see how both Urban and Taddeo held consistent faith in their Sun-dominated astrological destiny and how it not only reappeared in the imagery of the Barberini Palace but even governed their actions.

Following the investiture, Taddeo, dressed in full prefectorial regalia and in the company of a vast retinue, rode in triumph through the streets of Rome. The Venetian ambassador, Giovanni Pesaro, later noted with disgust and indignation that, instead of the traditional antique helmet, Taddeo wore what was nothing less than "a tiara despoiled of its crowns" (Fig. 139).[95] The ambitiousness of the pictorial project in the piano nobile apartment at Palazzo Barberini paralleled the actual social and political agenda of pope and nephew.

[94] In the parlance of the time, Taddeo's appointment to the prefecture was consistently referred to as an "election." See the report of the Venetian ambassador, Giovanni Pesaro, to the Venetian Senate. Barozzi and Berchet, *Le relazioni della corte*, 1:322–23.

[95] Ibid., 324.

CHAPTER VI

• The Author of the Program

NO SEVENTEENTH-CENTURY document has yet been discovered that lends absolute clarity to the debated issue of who may have served as Sacchi's adviser for the *Divine Wisdom*. In addition to the proposal that Sacchi himself produced the program, the list of proposed advisers now includes Matthias Casimir Sarbiewski, Clemente Merlini, Sforza Pallavicino, Tommaso Campanella, and even Urban VIII.[1] The artist must have participated in the creation of the program, but he is not likely to have been the initiator of the main themes. He does not show much interest in iconographic complexities in his other works, and he reportedly viewed astrology as a waste of time.[2] Sarbiewski's poem on Divine Wisdom, long considered a possible source,[3] is only generically related to the theme as illustrated in the ceiling painting, and, moreover, the Polish Jesuit was not in Rome after 1625, a fact that surely disqualifies him.[4] Merlini and Pallavicino, certainly appropriate advisers to the Barberini on theological matters, have left no record of any particular interest in or knowledge about astrology. Although Urban reviewed a proposal for the subject matter of Cortona's salone ceiling,[5] there is no similar documentation to demonstrate the pope's direct involvement with any of the painted ceilings in the north wing of the palace, where Taddeo held forth as chief patron and overseer. But the lack of positive proof for the intervention of Campanella, the philosopher-astrologer associated with the Barberini who would seem most qualified to produce such a program, also remains a vexing problem.

Campanella is likely to have been the principal intellect behind the creation of the *Divine Wisdom* program and the author of the Barberini Manuscript.[6] The friar's association

[1] Six different individuals have been proposed as authors of the iconographic program of the fresco: Sacchi (Incisa della Rocchetta, "Notizie su Sacchi," 65; D'Avossa, *Andrea Sacchi*, 64–65); Sarbiewski (Pastor, *History of the Popes*, 29:503–4, n. 1; Ost, "Borrominis römische," 122–23; Gallavotti Cavallero, "Il programma iconografico," 271–74); Campanella (Lechner, "Fresco of 'Divina Sapienza,'" 101–3, and "Reply to the Editor," 307–9; Grillo, *Campanella nell'arte di Sacchi e Poussin*, 43–50); Merlini and Pallavicino (Harris, *Andrea Sacchi*, 12–13, and "Letter to the Editor," 304–7); and Urban (Gallavotti Cavallero, "Il programma iconografico," 271–74).

[2] L. Pascoli, *Vite de' pittori, scultori, ed architetti moderni* (Rome, 1730–1736), 2:78, as quoted by Harris, "Letter to the Editor," 306, n. 18.

[3] A poem by the Polish poet M. C. Sarbiewski (1595–1640), "Carmen Saeculare: Divinae Sapientiae, in anno saeculare MDCXXV cum Urbanus VIII Pont. Opt. Max. portam auream aperiret," has been proposed as the inspiration for Sacchi's fresco. Gallavotti

Cavallero, "Il programma iconografico," 272–74, text of poem, 288–90. The poem was first published in M. C. Sarbiewski, *Poemata Omnia* (Antwerp, 1632), 217–24. Its relevance as a source for the ceiling painting had been previously proposed by Pastor, *History of the Popes*, 29:504, n. 1; Ost, "Borrominis römische," 101–42. Harris (*Andrea Sacchi*, 41, n. 76) and Grillo (*Campanella nell'arte di Sacchi e Poussin*, 69, n. 28) reject this notion. The poem and the painting share the biblical Book of Wisdom as a common source, and therefore some correspondence in the imagery of the two works does appear. The authoritative Barberini Manuscript makes no mention of the poem or its author.

[4] A. DeBacker and C. Sommervogel, *BCJ* 7: 627.

[5] Below, 176.

[6] Lechner ("Fresco of 'Divina Sapienza,'" 102–4) first proposed Campanella as the iconographer of the *Divine Wisdom*, seeing Sacchi's fresco as a pictorial representation of Campanella's utopian scheme outlined in his *La città del sole* (written in prison in 1602; first edition, in Latin, Frankfurt, 1623). The imagery of the

with Urban, however, cannot be viewed alone as proof of any role in the decoration of rooms in Taddeo's wing of the family palace. Campanella conducted his astrological rites with Urban in private rooms of the pope's apartments at the Vatican and Quirinal palaces.[7] The pope apparently preferred, when possible, to retire for such activities to the privacy of his villa at Castelgandolfo.[8] Urban had no need to use any of the rooms in the palace of his nephews for these occult practices.

More important for the thematic content of the painted imagery of the piano nobile apartment is Taddeo's association with Campanella. His reasons for employing the services of the astrologer were no less compelling than those of his papal uncle. Because of the correspondences between Taddeo's natal chart and that of his uncle, the astrological predictions with regard to the well-being of the nephew were equally dire, as reports an undoubtedly spurious *avviso* of 18 May 1630:

> Galileo, the famous mathematician and astrologer, is here [in Rome] and he hopes to publish a book in which are impugned many opinions upheld by the Jesuits. He has let it be known that Donna Anna will give birth to a male child, that at the end of June we will have peace in Italy, and that shortly thereafter Don Taddeo and the pope will die.[9]

Another *avviso* of later that same year confirms Taddeo's contact with Campanella, when astral rites were performed to counteract an illness that threatened Taddeo's eldest son.[10] Taddeo thus had relations with Campanella precisely at the time Sacchi was working

temple located at the center of Campanella's city has some resemblance to the Barberini salotto and chapel: "Nothing rests on the altar but a huge celestial globe, upon which all the heavens are described, with a terrestrial globe beside it. On the vault of the dome overhead appear all the larger stars with their names and the influences they each have upon earthly things set down in three verses." T. Campanella, *La città del sole: dialogo poetico / The City of the Sun: A Poetical Dialogue*, trans. D. J. Donno (Berkeley, 1981), 31. Grillo, *Campanella nell'arte di Sacchi e Poussin*, 29–44, 66–70, qualifies Lechner's interpretation as too literal, but see the critical comments of Harris, "Letter to the Editor," 305–6, supported by A. Blunt, "Review of *Andrea Sacchi* by Ann Sutherland Harris," *Apollo* 107 (1978), 349.

[7] Lechner ("Fresco of 'Divina Sapienza,'" 104–6) viewed the salotto with Sacchi's *Divine Wisdom* as the intended location for Urban's astrological practices. For the cogent rebuttal to this argument, see Harris, "Letter to the Editor," 305–6.

[8] An *avviso* of 4 May 1630 reveals that Urban had removed himself from Rome to Castelgandolfo so he could conduct the necessary rites to save himself from the evil influences of an eclipse of the moon. "Si è ritirato a Castelgandolfo a fine di stare in piacere di profumarsi, e di fare tutto quello, che persuade il Campanella nel suo libro." Transcribed in Amabile, *Fra Tommaso Campanella*, 2:149, doc. 203. See also the com-

ments of Harris, "Letter to the Editor," 304, 306. For further discussion of the location where Urban and Campanella closeted themselves, consult L. Amabile, "L'Andata di fra Tommaso Campanella a Roma dopo la lunga prigionia di Napoli," *Atti della Reale Accademia di Scienze Morali e Politiche di Napoli* 20 (1886), 22, who refers to Urban's bedroom at the Quirinal Palace as the location.

[9] "18 maggio 1630. Qua si trova il Galileo, ch'è famoso mattematico, et astrologo, che tenta di stampare un libro, nel quale impugna molte opinioni che sono sostenute dalli Giesuiti. Egli si è lasciato intendere, che D. Anna partorirà un figliuolo maschio, che alla fine di giugno havremo la pace in Italia; e che poco doppo morirà D. Thadeo, et il Papa." Transcribed in ibid., 39. On the reliability of this report, certainly a fabrication of Galileo's enemies, see ibid., 25–26, n. 1, and G. Campori, *Carteggio galileano . . .* (Modena, 1881), 593–94. These drastic predictions for Urban and Taddeo—no doubt intended to discredit Galileo in the eyes of the pope—must have been based on knowledge of the importance of the Sun in the natal charts of the two Barberini in relation to the impending solar eclipse of June 1630.

[10] 21 December 1630: ". . . E dicono ch'ultimamente in casa di questi signori padroni sia stato praticato un certo suo [Campanella's] documento di candele e di torcie, che significano li pianeti, per schivare un influsso,

on the astrological ceiling painting of the new palace. During this time Campanella also enjoyed the confidence of Filippo Colonna,[11] Donna Anna's father, who was a committed believer in the value of astrology and appears to have been solicitous to the pope's requirements for expertise in that discipline. He may even have been responsible for bringing Campanella to the attention of the pope.[12] Taddeo therefore had easy access to Campanella's talents for purposes of astrological operations or advice on any related theological matter. In devising a program for the painted vaults of his new palace that involved recondite astrological knowledge related to the natal and election charts of Urban VIII and himself, with which Campanella was intimately familiar, it would seem curious if Taddeo had not consulted the friar about the project.

Circumstantial factors alone are insufficient to indicate Campanella's participation in the creation of the program, but evidence intrinsic to the fresco also points to Campanella's involvement. Unlike other astrological ceilings of the period, Sacchi's *Divine Wisdom* combines biblical and astrological imagery. Even in the Sala dei Pontefici (Fig. 132) and the Sala di Bologna (Fig. 130) at the Vatican Palace, the imagery is pagan, not Christian. There we see the planets and constellations represented directly as deities from the ancient pantheon. In the Barberini fresco a specifically identified scriptural passage (Wisdom 7–8) served as the basis for an astrological program,[13] and considerable ingenuity was expended to avoid the representation of any pagan god. This synthesis of Scripture and astrology characterizes Campanella's own astrological writings.

His treatise on astrological practice, published in 1629—the year Sacchi began work on the *Divine Wisdom*—displays the same interest in reconciling Holy Scripture and astrology as seen in the Barberini fresco.[14] The full title of the work indicates this concern of the author: *Six Books of Astrological Matters in which Astrology, Purged of All the Superstitions of the Arabs and Jews, Is Treated Physiologically, in Accordance with the Holy Scriptures and the Doctrine of St. Thomas, Albert, and the Greatest Theologians; so that They May, without Suspicion of Evil, Be Read with Profit in the Church of God.*[15]

Campanella cites scriptural and patristic sources throughout the work as proof of the validity of astrology and the orthodoxy of his ideas, but the preface in particular attempts to establish a sound theological basis for what follows in the body of the treatise. In this introductory apology Campanella used one carefully chosen biblical passage to support his argument. Significantly, it is from the same chapter of the Book of Wisdom that, according to

---

che soprastava al figliuolo di D. Taddeo." Quoted in Amabile, *Fra Tommaso Campanella*, 1:398–99, 2:150, doc. 203f. Also see Walker, *Spiritual and Demonic Magic*, 210–11. Given the date, this activity would have been carried out in the Casa Grande in Via de' Giubbonari.

[11] L. Firpo, "Tommaso Campanella e i Colonnesi (con sette lettere inedite)," *Il pensiero politico* 1 (1968), 94.

[12] Amabile, *Fra Tommaso Campanella*, 1:316–18, 2:149, doc. 203c.

[13] As emphasized in the Barberini Manuscript. Appendix B.

[14] Campanella, *Astrologicorum*. The work was written in 1613. The "Astrologicorum Liber Septimus: de Siderali Fato Vitando," detailing the magical procedures Campanella had practiced with Urban, was sent by the friar's Roman enemies to the publisher in Lyons and attached to the volume as Book Seven without the author's knowledge. Firpo, *Ricerche Campanelliane*, 155–69.

[15] *Astrologicorum Libri VI in Quibus Astrologia, Omni Superstitione Arabum, & Iudaeorum Eliminata, Physiologice Tractatur, Secundum S. Scripturas & Doctrinam S. Thomae, & Alberti, & Summorum Theologorum; Ita ut absque Suspicione Mala in Ecclesia Dei Multa cum Utilitate Legi Possint.* See Walker, *Spiritual and Demonic Magic*, 213–23.

[16] Campanella, *Astrologicorum*, 3.

the Barberini Manuscript, had served as the basis for the *Divine Wisdom*. Moreover, Campanella specifically quotes the crucial verse referring to Wisdom's perspicacity: "She [Wisdom] knoweth things past, and judgeth of things to come. . . . She knoweth signs and wonders before they be done, and the events of times and ages" (Wisdom 8:8).[16] This passage was Campanella's main biblical source for confirming the efficacy of the judicial astrology he practiced. Divine Wisdom, the knowledge of things past and things to come, is for Campanella apparent in the stars—in astrology. As he makes clear later in the treatise, Campanella believes that the Divine Wisdom manifested in Scripture indicates that the heavenly bodies provide foreknowledge of mundane events ("natural wisdom"): "Not only may natural wisdom be predicted by the appearance of the sky, but Divine Wisdom incarnate in the New Testament supports this."[17]

As the text chosen to be illustrated on the vault of the Barberini Salotto, the seventh and eighth chapters of Wisdom, where Divine Wisdom is associated with the stars,[18] must have been selected primarily because these passages confirmed what Campanella, Taddeo, and Urban saw as an eternal verity—that the order of the stars and planets contains divine meaning for those who seek it out. The precise astrological details of that image represented a still more specific truth—that the Barberini family was "born and elected" to rule the Church and that this divine favor had been presaged in the disposition of the stars at the moment of Urban's birth. Campanella, as author of the Barberini Manuscript, made this assertion the basis of the *Divine Wisdom* program, as stated baldly in the offending final paragraph of the text. One can only conclude that he went too far in disclosing astrological data about the natal charts of pope and nephew and in paralleling them with the natal astrology of Christ. These excesses must have given offense to Taddeo, even without his being aware of the details of Campanella's thinking, and resulted in the cancellation of the written program's resounding conclusion.

But the excesses of the program of the *Divine Wisdom* are themselves indications of Campanella's authorship. The metaphysical speculations and especially the quasi-messianic vision of astrologically predestined glory for the papal family bear the mark of his thinking. A utopian, Campanella believed that his era was on the verge of a transformation that would culminate in the establishment of a new political and religious order.[19] In return for his insistence on spreading these and other unorthodox views, Campanella received over three decades of imprisonment from the Spanish authorities in Naples. In his early years he had envisioned the Spanish monarchy as the political vehicle for the realization of this better world, but during his time of relative freedom in Rome he saw the Barberini papacy as having potential for fulfilling this role.[20]

A solarian, Campanella held that the great transformation was astrologically manifest

[17] "Prognosticum ex facie coeli non modo naturalis sapientia, sed etiam Dei Sapientia incarnata in Evangelio approbavit." Ibid., 112.

[18] "For he [God] hath given me [Solomon] the true knowledge of the things that are: to know . . . the revolutions of the year, and the disposition of the stars" (Wisdom 7:17–19).

[19] Di Napoli, *Tommaso Campanella*, 127–32; G. Ernst, "Vocazione profetica e astrologica in Tommaso Campanella," in *La città dei segreti: magia, astrologia e cultura esoterica a Roma (XV–XVIII)*, ed. F. Troncarelli (Milan, 1985) 137–55.

[20] For the fullest statement of this belief, see T. Campanella, "Le monarchie delle nationi finirsi nella romana . . ." (Paris, Bibliothèque de l'Arsénal, cod. Ital. 1083, 115–74), published by Amabile, *Fra Tommaso Campanella*, 2:doc. 346.

in the increasing nearness of the sun to the earth as well as in other signs in the heavens, particularly a "great conjunction" of Jupiter and Saturn, which provided proof of imminent political events of universal dimensions.[21] Campanella had taken note of the conjunction of Jupiter and Saturn that occurred on the day the cardinals entered the conclave to elect Maffeo Barberini to the papacy,[22] and he was just the man to promote, even exploit, Urban's already well-developed solar fixation. He made himself indispensable, for a time at least, by providing the pope with an astrological palliative for fears of impending doom.

Acutely interested in the natal astrology of Christ, Campanella found it worthy of discussion in the *Theologicorum* (bk. XIX, chap. 7, art. 4). There he takes exception to those astrologers like Cardano who believe that the stars determined Christ's life, opting instead for the less theologically controversial opinion that the heavenly bodies visible at the time of Christ's birth were determined by God's own will and therefore served as natural signs, not determinants, of his coming into the world.[23] That he dared to relate the astrology of the Barberini to that of Christ was little more than an extension of the analysis he had already made of his own geniture, which—with the Sun in conjunction with the Ascendant—he found to be more extraordinary than Christ's.[24]

Campanella's moment in the sun of papal Rome was made possible by the protective magical rites he administered to the pope, but its most enduring monument appears on the vault of the Barberini salotto. Sacchi's painting of *Divine Wisdom* embodies a pictorial summa of Campanella's speculations on the nature of God and the physical universe. Profoundly stimulated by ontological and epistemological issues, he formulated an idea of wisdom central to both of these areas of concern. This concept receives special attention in the *Metaphysica* (written 1602–1603, 1609–1611) and *Theologicorum* (written 1614–1615), where wisdom is elemental to God's nature and man participates, finitely, in his divine wisdom.[25]

For Campanella, God consists in a unity of three "Primalities"—power, wisdom, and love. He conceived of these qualities as having a mystical three-part oneness corresponding to the triune nature of God. We find the Primalities reflected in the salotto ceiling: Love prominently positioned at the upper left, Wisdom in the center, and Power (i.e., Strength) in the lower left. With her massive club as fulcrum for the entire group of seven virtues on the left side of the pictorial field, Strength forms a compositional triangle with the other two personified Primalities, at the center of which is Divinity holding up her triangle-attribute. Thus Divinity encapsulates the Trinitarian essence of God as expressed in the surrounding Primalities. This compositional idea emerged more clearly in the Cooper-Hewitt sketch than in the final modello and fresco. There, in the lower left corner, Strength anchors the entire

[21] On the approach of the sun, see T. Campanella, *Universalis Philosophiae seu: Metaphysicarum Rerum, Iuxta Propria Dogmata, Partes Tres, Libri 18*, Paris, 1638, pt. III, 70–78. On the Great Conjunction, see the comments of Ernst, "Vocazione profetica," 151–53, based on T. Campanella, *Articuli Prophetales*, ed. G. Ernst (Florence, 1976), 260–95.

[22] Ibid., 320.

[23] T. Campanella, *Origine temporale di Cristo*, trans. R. Amerio (Rome, 1972), 134–43.

[24] Ernst, "Vocazione profetica," 136–55, esp. 143–

50. Campanella's own natal chart is among those in the Morandi collection. ASR, Tribunale Criminale del Governatore di Roma, Processi 1630, vol. 251, 1298r.

[25] I rely here on the analyses in G. Di Napoli, *Tommaso Campanella, filosofo della restaurazione cattolica* (Padua, 1947), 237–43, 316–22; and B. Bonansea, *Tommaso Campanella: Renaissance Pioneer of Modern Thought* (Washington, D.C., 1969), 210–17. I also wish to thank Brian Copenhaver for his useful comments on Campanella's metaphysical speculations.

figural composition, forming a nearly perfect equilateral triangle with Wisdom and Love (Fig. 41). Serving as interlocutor, she directs the attention of the observer toward Wisdom and thence to Love, thus uniting the three Primalities.

Just as Campanella's metaphysical theories are unconventional, so is his natural philosophy distinctive and profoundly anti-Aristotelian. He substituted the usual system of four elements with binary oppositions of heat/cold and sun/earth. The heavenly bodies, the stars and especially the sun, are fire; they represent the divine element, heat, in the world. The earth, in contrast, is cold, constituting the physical element in nature.[26] Without resorting to a purely schematic rendering, Sacchi could hardly have produced a more literal representation of this system of binary oppositions, the warm yellows of the sun engulfing the crown of the vault as the cold greens and blues dominate the corresponding orb of the earth below.

Campanella's letters, manuscripts, and published writings are replete with references to Divine Wisdom and Christ as Divine Wisdom incarnate. God's omnipotent nature and the manner in which he worked his will in the world were commonly referred to as Divine Wisdom, yet Campanella's interest in the astrological manifestations of God's wisdom and will is extreme.

As a solarian, Campanella found the Copernican model of the universe compelling. In his spirited attempt to justify through the use of scriptural passages Galileo's advocacy of the Copernican system, Campanella argued that the physical world we see, including the imperfections on the surface of the moon observed by Galileo, are truthful reflections of God's created universe and that the conclusions to be drawn from these observations are in harmony with Scripture: "Nor does the created book of God's Wisdom contradict the revealed book of his divine wisdom."[27]

Campanella felt that Galileo's researches were justified by Scripture: "that Christ approved rather than condemned knowledge is shown by the passage in 1 Corinthians 3 [1:24], where he is described as the power and the wisdom of God."[28] Here "knowledge" means "natural wisdom" based on the investigation of the physical universe. Most important for our understanding of his usage is that Campanella did not separate the ultimate goal of his own astrological pursuits from Galileo's investigative method. His comprehension of scientific method was entirely bounded by his preoccupation with religious and astrological conceptions. Nevertheless he supported Galileo's procedure of basing philosophical conclusions upon sensory perceptions.[29] Further along in the *Defense*, Campanella observes that the nature of the universe is in constant revelation according to man's attempts to discover new knowledge from it. The physical appearance of God in the form of Christ represents one manifestation of this process; Scripture embodies yet another:

> Christ, the incarnate wisdom of God (as Origen taught), . . . displayed God
> to spiritual men. The world is wisdom in material form, and shows us more
> as we have more capacity. To this end Divine Wisdom wrote Scripture.[30]

[26] Di Napoli, *Tommaso Campanella*, 331–43.

[27] T. Campanella, *The Defense of Galileo*, trans. G. McColley (Northampton, Mass., 1937), 28. Written in prison in Naples 1616. First edition published in Frankfurt, 1622.

[28] Ibid., 29.

[29] L. Blanchet, *Campanella* (Paris, 1920), 241–55.

[30] Ibid., 52.

Given Campanella's use of terms and concepts so close in nature to the juxtaposition of Divine Wisdom, astrological imagery, and Christ in the salotto ceiling and the Christological cycle of the family chapel at Palazzo Barberini, his participation in the project seems certain. For Campanella the relationship among Christ, Divine Wisdom, and astrology was one of the central realities of creation, and he saw it as God's intention that humanity should profit from this association by looking perspicaciously to the stars, as Sacchi's painting advocates.

CHAPTER VII

• Camassei's *Creation of the Angels*:
"Ministers of God's Providence"

IN CONFORMITY WITH the convention of the programmatic unity of rooms en suite, the subject of Camassei's ceiling fresco in the camera (PBN 6, Colorplate II, Figs. 59–60) situated between the salotto and Donna Anna's audience chamber (PBN 7) reinforces the major themes of the *Divine Wisdom* and the Christological cycle of the chapel. Taddeo and his adviser conceived the pictorial imagery of these rooms not as separate entities but as three distinct variations on the same overarching themes of the predestined greatness and divine favor of the Barberini family. As in the *Divine Wisdom*, the subject of this smaller ceiling represents the astrological destiny of the Barberini family to attain pontifical status.

Although more modest in size and conception than the works of Sacchi and Cortona in the preceding rooms, Camassei's painting is no less cosmic in its allusions to the special protection enjoyed by the Barberini as they ruled the Church and the Papal States. The subject, the *Creation of the Angels*, is nearly as unusual as that assigned to Sacchi.[1]

The Church Fathers did not arrive at complete agreement about the exact chronological moment of the creation of the angels,[2] but the great burst of golden light at the center of Camassei's composition allows no question about the patristic source relied upon for the imagery of the Barberini fresco. St. Augustine (*De civitate dei*, XI: ix) held that God created the angels at the same moment, on the first day, when he said, "Let there be light" (Genesis 1:3). Visualizing such an esoteric subject may have been a challenge for Camassei, as it lacks any significant pictorial tradition, but he could turn to creation cycles for some assistance. His source for the dynamic figure of God the Father—the *Creation of the Sun and Moon* from the Sistine ceiling—also confirms the moment being depicted. Significantly this is the first of the Sistine creation narrative scenes to include angels surrounding the figure of God.

Camassei executed the fresco as a *quadro riportato* enclosed in a stucco enframement at the center of the vault (Colorplate II, Fig. 59). God the Father, with commanding outstretched arms, appears in the middle of the composition in an aureole of light and surrounded by the hierarchies of angels whom he has just created. The attribute of each of the nine choirs has been carefully depicted in the fresco, but in reproduction they can be most easily discerned in the engraving made for Teti's volume (Fig. 60).[3]

---

[1] Payment documents issued in 1630 leave no doubt about the subject of the painting: "[18 scudi] ad Andrea Camassei: Pittore spesi da lui in colori, carta, penelli et altro per le pitture della Creatione delli Angioli." BAV, Arch. Barb., Comp. 186, 164r (gior., Taddeo). Also BAV, Arch. Barb., Ind. IV, 13, at date (25 September 1630). The work received only brief mention in the early biographies of the artist: Passeri, *Die Künstlerbiographien*, 169; Pascoli, *Vita de' pittori*, 1:40. Modern literature on this painting remains scant: G. di Domenico Cortese, "La vicenda artistica di Andrea Camassei," *Commentari* 19 (1968), 283–84; A. S. Harris, "A Contribution to Andrea Camassei Studies," *Art Bulletin* 52 (1970), 50, 54. On the iconography of this work, see *Dictionnaire de théologie catholique*, eds. A. Vacant et al. (Paris, 1903–1950), 1:1189–1271.

[2] Ibid., 1193–95.

[3] The drawing in the Uffizi (17229 F, 55.3 x 26 cm.)

The canonical ranking of the angels into three hierarchies each containing three choirs was first accomplished in the *Celestial Hierarchies* of an anonymous late fifth-century writer now known as Pseudo-Dionysius, the Areopagite.[4] In the late sixteenth century the apostolic authority of this text was questioned, but the early decades of the seventeenth century saw increased emphasis in Catholic lands on the devotion properly due to angels.[5] Urban and his nephews gave emphasis to the veneration of the angels and special honor to St. Michael Archangel.[6] Inclusion of the fresco of the *Creation of the Angels* in the Barberini Palace is but one among many manifestations of the cult of angels to appear in Barberini-commissioned works of art.

Since the text of Pseudo-Dionysius is often obscure or lacks adequate descriptions of the angels, Camassei might have relied on Lomazzo's more explicit and accessible discussion for his realization of the scene:[7]

Seraphim (heads with wings of fire)
Cherubim (heads with wings)
Thrones (winged figures without attributes)

Dominations (tiaras)
Virtues (palms and laurel crowns)
Powers (scepters)

Principalities (crowns)
Archangels (various individual attributes)
Angels (no attributes)

The pronouncements of Pseudo-Dionysius on the nature of angels were codified in scholastic theology, where angels are held responsible for conducting relations between God and the

---

is identical to the fresco but not by Camassei himself. Somewhat smaller than the engraving (65 x 29.5 cm.), it is likely a copy after the print. On this issue, consult Harris, "Camassei Studies," 54–55, fig. 15. A. Presenzini, *Vita ed opere del pittore Andrea Camassei* (Assisi, 1880), 57–58, attributes the unsigned engraving to Bloemaert. The much damaged drawing in BAV, Ott. Lat. 3131, 2v–3r, is autograph and exactly the same size as the engraving. Its ruined condition further suggests that it served as model for the engraver. I wish to thank Louise Rice for bringing to my attention this and the similar drawing of the *Parnassus* (below, 115, n. 67).

[4] Pseudo-Dionysius, the Areopagite, *On the Heavenly Hierarchy*, 1–66. On the authenticity of the work, see *The Cambridge History of Later Greek and Early Medieval Philosophy*, ed. A. H. Armstrong (Cambridge, 1967), 457–72.

[5] E. Mâle, *L'art religieux après le Concile de Trente* (Paris, 1932), 297–309. In 1590 a new chapel in Il Gesù was dedicated to the Holy Angels, and a Confraternity of the Guardian Angel was founded in 1614. Fiorani, "Astrologi, superstiziosi," 147–151, esp. 147, n. 112. Two important popular treatises on the proper devotion due to angels appeared during the second decade of the seventeenth century. F. Albertino de Catanzaro, *Trattato del angelo custode . . . con l'offitio dell'angelo custode approvato da N. Signore Papa Paolo Quinto* (Rome, 1612); F. Danieli, *Trattato della divina providenza* (Milan, 1615), esp. 193–95. Also see the extensive commentary on Urban's "Ode Hortatoria ad Virtutem" (Appendix C) made by Magno Perneo, "Magni Pernei Commentarius in Poemata S.D.N. Urbani Papae VIII." BAV, Barb. Lat. 3307, 1008r–1076r. The manuscript dates from the reign of Urban VIII.

[6] See the anonymous poem dedicated to Urban, "De S. Michaele ad Urbanum VIII Carmen." BAV, Barb. Lat., 1772, unpaginated.

[7] Lomazzo, *Trattato dell'arte*, 532–40. Lomazzo (537) specifically notes that he follows the hierarchies according to the Pseudo-Dionysius. There appears to have been no general agreement about the sequence of choirs in the second hierarchy. Danieli (*Divina providenza*, 193–95) reverses the sequence listed by Lomazzo. Nor was there agreement about the functions fulfilled by the choirs in this middle hierarchy.

physical world.[8] Popularly understood to be the "ministers of God's providence"[9] the three angelic hierarchies became the heavenly prototype for the hierarchy of the Church, which was the worldly extension of God's providence.[10] Moreover, like the battalions of a celestial army, each choir of angels possesses unique characteristics and specializes in particular types of divine duties.[11]

The angels of the most exalted of the three hierarchies—Seraphim, Cherubim, and Thrones—are associated with fire and light, which Camassei depicted in the expanding envelope of brightness surrounding God. Seraphim relate to "burning"; Cherubim designate "fulness of knowledge or stream of wisdom"; and Thrones refer to "exaltation."[12] Pseudo-Dionysius' summary of the essential qualities of the first hierarchy confirms the iconographic link between Camassei's angels and Sacchi's *Divine Wisdom*: "The first Order, then, of the holy Angels possesses, more than all, the characteristic of fire, and the streaming distribution of supremely *Divine wisdom*."[13] In his discussion of the painting, Teti observes that some angels are assigned to private individuals, whereas others have more noble duties in the counsel of governing bodies. The ones who carry palms (Virtues), for example, are designated to instill virtue in human minds; and the choir of angels holding scepters (Powers) assists kings and dynasties. Those wearing gold crowns (Principalities) attend to the protection of kingdoms and provinces. All the others help to govern the Christian republic.[14] This notion of the specialized function of each angelic choir had long been fixed in the popular imagination, as can be seen in the discussion in *The Golden Legend*.[15]

In the painting three of the Archangels are singled out for special attention. The helmeted and armored figure of St. Michael, sword in hand, stands in the middle of the composition at the far left. Gabriel, carrying the lily branch, is comparably positioned on the right. Raphael, prince of the Guardian Angels, appears with outspread wings protecting his charge, Tobias, at the lower right of the fresco.[16] All three Archangels direct the attention of Tobias, and the viewer, to God the Father.

Camassei's figure of God the Father (Fig. 60) looks in the direction of those choirs of angels with scepters and crowns (Powers and Principalities) as if commanding them to fulfill their assigned duties of protecting provinces and rulers. The viewer can hardly doubt that this injunction is directed particularly to the protection of the Papal States and to Urban and his nephews who govern the Christian republic.

Notwithstanding the conservative *quadro riportato* format, the immediacy of God's action in the fresco increases when viewed from the point of entry into the room (Fig. 59). Not only does the movement of the figure gain in urgency from this calculated vantage point but the gesture of the right arm appears to penetrate the picture plane emphatically and

[8] *Dictionnaire de théologie catholique*, 1:1228–48.

[9] Danieli, *Divina providenza*, 184.

[10] Pseudo-Dionysius, the Areopagite, *On the Heavenly Hierarchy*, 67–162.

[11] Danieli, *Divina providenza*, 193–95.

[12] Pseudo-Dionysius, the Areopagite, *On the Heavenly Hierarchy*, 24–26, 49.

[13] Ibid., 49.

[14] Teti, *Aedes Barberinae* (1642), 105. Perneo's contemporary commentary on Urban's poetry contains a complete discussion of the hierarchy of angels and the function of each choir with regard to humankind. BAV, Barb. Lat. 3307, 1008r–1076r. See also Presenzini (Andrea Camassei, 51–58), who paraphrases Teti, *Aedes Barberinae* (1642), 102–6; and Haskell, *Patrons and Painters*, 50.

[15] J. de Voragine, *The Golden Legend*, trans. G. Ryan and H. Ripperger (New York, 1969), 580–82.

[16] On the iconography of these princes among the Archangels, see Réau, *Iconographie*, 2:pt. 1, 30–55.

extend down into the room. Just as the command of Sacchi's figure of Wisdom implied beneficial intervention in the Barberini chapel beneath, so does Camassei's figure seem to interpose on behalf of the resident papal family.

Like Sacchi's *Divine Wisdom*, Camassei's *Creation of the Angels* commemorates the attainment of the papal throne by the Barberini. Following his election on 6 August 1623, Urban chose as the day of his official coronation 29 September—the feast of St. Michael and all the angels.[17] In this decision the pope invoked for his reign the protection of the angelic hierarchies. The reverse of a papal medal struck in 1640 confirms this (Fig. 147). A flying St. Michael, arms outstretched with the tiara, prepares to crown the kneeling pope, under the inscription TE MANE TE VESPERE (To you in the Morning, To you in the Evening).[18] The martial and protective presence of St. Michael at Palazzo Barberini appears in his prominent position among the choirs of angels as well as in the stucco frieze of the room, where in the corners, between laurel swags, the Archangel's helmets bridge the angles (Fig. 61).[19]

Urban's devotion to St. Michael is an expression of his Sun-dominated astrological destiny. As we have seen, the Sun holds a prominent position in Urban's natal chart, a fact the pope would have been particularly mindful of following his election, when the efficacy of his solarian astrology had been spectacularly demonstrated. In post-classical astrology each of the seven "planets" is guided by a specific regent angel. St. Michael is the angel of the Sun,[20] a relationship confirmed in the papal commemorative medal, where the Archangel emits solar rays. The inscription reiterates the solar association through allusion to the rising and setting of the Sun—solar images already published among Urban's personal imprese prior to his election.[21]

Given the importance of the Sun in his own geniture, Taddeo also must have been attentive to the devotion due the angel of the Sun. Moreover, because of his recent appointment as general of the Church (February 1630), his devotion to the armed and militant Captain-General of Heaven might be expected. The helmets seen in the stucco frieze would also remind the viewer of Taddeo's military office, as they pertain to the iconography of both Archangel and general. But, as in other matters of personal iconography, the nephew seems to have followed the lead of his uncle. If Taddeo needed encouragement, Urban provided it in the form of a gift—a painting of the Archangel by the Cavaliere d'Arpino, its gold frame

[17] Gigli, *Diario romano*, 79. On the feast of the Archangel as the day when all angels were honored, see Voragine, *Golden Legend*, 585. Not until 1670 were Guardian Angels assigned an independent feast (2 October). *ODCC*, 606.

[18] Ministero delle Finanze, *Relazione della reale zecca*, appendix 3, "Raccolta pontificia" (Rome, 1940), no. 213.

[19] This type of high-crested helmet, known as a morion, was antiquated by the seventeenth century. "Frescio fatto a festoni di fronde di lauro con varie Maschere tra un festone e l'altro e quatro moroni [morioni] nelli Contoni . . . scudi 69.50." From the *misura e stima* of 1629–1638. ASR, Congregazioni Religiose Maschili, Teatini S. Andrea della Valle, 2200, int. 230, 133; BAV, Arch. Barb., Ind. II, 2888, 161. Also Pollak, *Die Kunsttätigkeit*, 1:285.

[20] Bouché-Leclercq, *L'astrologie grècque*, 623, n. 1. Agrippa von Nettesheim linked St. Michael with the sun as well as with the lion of St. Mark, Leo, fire, summer, and other qualities. H. C. Agrippa von Nettesheim, *De Occulta Philosophia Libri Tres* (Venice, 1551), bk. II, f. LIXr.

[21] Urban's ALIUSQUE ET IDEM and PRAESIGNAT AB ORTU imprese both depict the rising sun, while, as Ferro notes, "the sun in the west was always the sign of the Barberini family." Ferro, *Teatro d'imprese*, 651–54.

carved with bees and suns.[22] Such angelic protection and benefaction were to be extended to the papal family as well as to the Barberini pope.

The election and coronation dates of Urban were commemorated in paint at Palazzo Barberini and also annually celebrated there. As early as 1626 the "festa" of Urban's coronation was held at the new residence on the Quirinal.[23] A payment of September 1631—the period just after the final payment to Camassei for his work in the north wing (28 July 1631)—records the lunch provided to the household on the occasion of Urban's visit to the palace, and the candles, lamps, torches, and casks used for the celebration of his election and coronation.[24]

The prominent positioning of the figure of the Archangel Raphael with Tobias[25] in the lower right corner of Camassei's painting reinforces the personal implications of the scene for Taddeo and his family. The fish usually carried by the boy has been omitted; thus the figure can be understood as any Christian soul brought under the protection of its guardian angel into the presence of God.[26] The inclusion of this apotropaic imagery in Donna Anna's apartment suggests its relevance to the young family being raised in those rooms and the divine protection Taddeo held to be so important, for each human soul is assigned its guardian angel at the time of birth.[27] Taddeo's conviction that angels were the mechanism for divine guardianship of the individual also found expression in the image of his personal guardian angel he commissioned Camassei to paint on the ceiling of his private oratory (PBT C1A) in the piano terreno apartment below.[28]

On the day Taddeo and his family moved into their new palace near the Four Fountains, an entry expressing concern for divine benefaction was made in the expense book kept for the construction and decoration of the building:

> On 13 May 1632, with praise to God, the Blessed Virgin Mother Mary, and all their saints and with the protection of our guardian angels I came to live in the new palace at the Four Fountains at about 22:00 [5:45 P.M.] be it with the health of soul and body and peace of everyone.[29]

By the time of the move, Taddeo's own personal hope for the continued protection of his guardian angel had already been permanently expressed in the painted ceilings of his new home.

---

[22] M. A. Lavin, *Documents and Inventories*, 99, no. 2.

[23] See the 26 September 1626 payment of 7.80 scudi for clay lamps ("lumi di creta") for the "festa dell'Incoronat.e di S. S.tà nel Palazzo a Capo le Case." BAV, Arch. Barb., Giust. 501–625, 228r (Card. Fran.).

[24] "Per merinda al Palazzo delle 4 fontane alla famiglia per l'andata di N.S. e per Cand.le per li lumi alli 28 della Creatione di S. B.ne———scudi 10.24 1/2. E per l'allegrezze dell'Incoronat.ne di N.S. per botte, cand.e, fascine, et altro alli 29———[scudi] 3.55." BAV, Arch. Barb., Giust. 1502–1595, 77v (Card. Fran.).

[25] Apocryphal Book of Tobit.

[26] On the belief that all created things are individu-

ally protected by an assigned guardian angel, see Albertino da Catanzaro, *Angelo custode*, 17–25; *Dictionnaire de théologie catholique*, 1:1216–19, 1246–48.

[27] Aquinas, *Summa*, 1a, q. CXIII, a. 5.

[28] 9 July 1631: "Scudi 21 b[aiocchi] 82 ad Andrea Camassei pittore per suo rimborso d'altrettanti spesi in colori et altro per fare dipingere un camerino a chiaro scuro et un angelo custode in detto palazzo." SCEP, Quaderno de' sig.ri Barberini, 1631–1633, 54v (Pollak, *Die Kunsttätigkeit*, 1:330); BAV, Arch. Barb., Comp. 192, 50r (mand., Taddeo); Arch. Barb., Ind. IV, 13, at 2 July 1631 (gior., Taddeo).

[29] "A di 13. Maggio 1632: Con lode d'Iddio B.ma Vergine Madre Maria et di tutti i suoi Santi et con Pro-

As one stepped from the small room with Camassei's fresco into Donna Anna's audience chamber (PBN 7), where Viviani's creation scenes came into view on the vault, the narrative program linking the new Barberini-commissioned frescoes with the Old Testament Sforza cycle would have become apparent. Not only do the older frescoes continue the theme of creation initiated in the preceding room, even the parallel format of *quadri riportati* underscores the thematic unity. Moreover, Taddeo added a stucco frieze beneath the Sforza fresco that, amid the rinceaux scrolls, contains various Barberini and Colonna symbols (Fig. 62)—bees, columns, suns, harpies, crowns, cardinals' hats, Maltese crosses, and the coat of arms of Taddeo's mother, Costanza Magalotti—all denoting the presence of the new occupants.[30]

Because Viviani's creation cycle has been lost, we cannot be certain of the details of its formal arrangement, but Pécheux reports that when he received the commission to repaint the ruined central *quadro riportato*, he tried to follow the subject and form of what remained of the original, which he interpreted as the division of the elements.[31] The canvas now in place in the vault of the room (Fig. 63) must therefore resemble Viviani's original, at least in its general disposition of forms. In the central rectangle of the preceding room the viewer thus encountered God the Father in the process of bringing into being the angels; in the second room God was seen creating the sensible world to which those angels would serve as ministers for the conveyance of his will.

Pécheux's depiction of the active participation of the angels in dividing the elements possibly also derives from Viviani's original. Teti, moreover, referred to another scene (prominently positioned in the center of the cove opposite the entrance) as the "Angelic Rule of the Spheres," implying a representation of the planetary angels (Fig. 28).[32] We can only speculate what such an image would have looked like, but neither Viviani nor Camassei can have been ignorant of the most important rendering of this subject. The dome mosaics of the Chigi Chapel in Santa Maria del Popolo (1513–1516), based on Raphael's design, represent God controlling or, according to some interpretations, creating the angelic regents of the planets located in the eight principal divisions of the cupola (Fig. 129).[33] In each section an angel rises above a pagan deity representing a planet. The eighth section depicts the angel who controls the stars. Significantly the eight drum sections, lower down, contain a painted creation cycle. The scenes of creation and the role of the angels in that process, as depicted in Viviani's frescoes, belong to an iconographic tradition that would have been of considerable use to Camassei and that appears to have been taken into consideration when Taddeo and his advisers determined the subject of the new ceiling painting in the preceding room.

The leitmotif of God's active involvement in the world for the protection of his elect

tettione di nostri Angeli Custodi Venni ad habitare circa le 22 hore nel Palazzo nuovo alle quattro fontane sia con salute d'anima et di corpo et pace di tutti." BAV, Arch. Barb., Ind. IV, 13, at date.

[30] "Per l'aboz.ra e stucc.ra di da. Cornice lo. p. 49 altz. p. 3 con fregio collar.o corsette stampa intag.te gocciolatore modelletto sotto e sei Api tra un modello e l'altro et un fogliame nel fregio l. p. 1 1/2 . . . Scudi 25." ASR, Congregazioni Religiose Maschili, Teatini S. Andrea della Valle, 2200, int. 230, 129. Also Pollak, *Die Kunsttätigkeit*, 1:285. For the Magalotti coat of

arms, see A. Chacón, *Vitae, et Res Gestae Pontificum Romanorum et S.R.E. Cardinalium* (Rome, 1677), 4:537–38, where the arms of Cardinal Lorenzo Magalotti, the brother of Costanza raised to the cardinalate by Urban VIII, is impaled with the Barberini arms.

[31] Bollea, *Lorenzo Pécheux*, 378.

[32] Teti, *Aedes Barberinae* (1642), 109.

[33] Weil-Garris Brandt, "Cosmological Patterns," 127–57, esp. 137–38; Cox-Rearick, *Dynasty and Destiny*, 161–63, fig. 123.

and the working of his plan for humankind runs through all the painted vaults of the piano nobile apartment as one grand overarching theme uniting both Barberini and Sforza frescoes. God, in a variety of manifestations, or his ministers, the angels, appear in all of the piano nobile ceiling paintings. Even the Sforza ceilings of the innermost private rooms of Anna's suite (PBN 8–11) show God and his angels intervening in favor of his chosen people. The largest of these four ceiling paintings, for example, depicts Abraham receiving the three angels who have come to inform him that Sarah will conceive and bear a child (Fig. 26); thus the theme of the angels as God's ministers and as the protectors of humankind enunciated in Camassei's painting finds fulfillment.

Taddeo and his advisers must have given careful thought to these preexisting scenes before judging them to be compatible with the themes they intended to introduce in the preceding rooms. The program of the Barberini frescoes may well have been shaped by the still relevant content of the earlier ceilings. The iconographic novelties and formal innovations of the later works distinguish them from Viviani's traditional Old Testament scenes, but the fundamental preoccupation with divine favor and bountiful progeny remains constant in both cycles. The older works must have served as stimuli for the formulation of the new imagery.

In Fedele Danieli's early seventeenth-century treatise on providence, divine intervention in human affairs and the crucial role of angels in the realization of God's plans for the world are subsumed under the concept of Divine Providence. "By means of them," he writes, "God attends to the preservation of corporeal things."[34] The author outlines all of human history with respect to the action of Providence within it. He explains both pagan and Hebraic antiquity in these terms.[35] Danieli's discussion, however, does not exceed the bounds of what his contemporaries would have held as self-evident commonplaces about the nature and development of history. Likewise, the painted ceilings of the piano nobile apartment of Palazzo Barberini express universally held notions about God's action in the world. The role of the Barberini family within that system, however, embodies a new chapter in the unfolding of the divine scheme.

[34] Danieli, *Divina providenza*, 184.

[35] Ibid., chaps. 3 and 5.

CHAPTER VIII

• Thematic Unity of the Piano Nobile Ceiling Paintings

WHEN TETI sought to execute his assignment to prepare an interpretive guidebook to Palazzo Barberini, he ignored much that was relevant to his task, at least from the viewpoint of the historian. One can only speculate about his reason for failing even to mention the chapel with its important fresco cycle. Completeness is not one of the strong points of the *Aedes Barberinae*, nor, perhaps, was it intended to be. The modern reader of Teti's lavish tome must keep in mind that an objective exegesis of the imagery of Palazzo Barberini cannot be included among the author's goals. Adhering instead to the tradition of classical rhetoric, Teti worked with a very different premise. His interpretations of works of art constitute independent literary exercises by no means limited to the original intentions of artists and patrons, although they may be within the scope of potential meaning suggested by the imagery. Since his purpose is to elucidate the greatness of the Barberini and the divine favor that family enjoys, his interpretations parallel those of the artists, patrons, and other individuals who were responsible for the visual imagery of the palace, but his book cannot be taken as the key to understanding its original intended meaning.[1] Instead, the ceiling paintings provide a starting point for his own interpretations of Barberini iconography, which, occupying a rhetorical middle ground of veracity, are neither wholly true nor entirely fantastic.[2]

Moreover, there are limits to his knowledge about the genesis and creation of the palace imagery. Teti's official position was as "Gentleman" in the household of Cardinal Antonio the Younger, and it was in this capacity that he wrote the book.[3] Cardinal Antonio, however, was not involved in the decoration of the north wing of Palazzo Barberini. Only after Taddeo and his family had abandoned the palace and Cardinal Antonio took up residence there in 1635 did Teti have direct contact with the works of art he came to write about. His friendship with Bracciolini[4] and his presence in the palace during the completion of the *Divine Providence* suggest that his knowledge of that work was perhaps greater. Teti also had knowledge of general Barberini themes and aspirations; he must have had some contact with Sacchi, too, since Cardinal Antonio became that artist's chief patron soon after completion of the work for Taddeo. In consequence, there is much to be gained from Teti's explanations, although they should not be accepted without critical evaluation.[5]

[1] For a contrasting assessment, see the comments of M. Fumaroli, "Cicero Pontifex Romanus: la tradition rhétorique du Collège Romain et les principes inspirateurs du mécénat des Barberini," *Mélanges de l'Ecole Française de Rome: moyen âge temps modernes* 90 (1978), 830–31.

[2] See the discussion of the spectrum of interpretation in J. Montagu, "The Painted Enigma and French Seventeenth-Century Art," *Journal of the Warburg and Courtauld Institutes* 31 (1968), 307–35, esp. 334, n. 125.

[3] The 1642 edition of *Aedes Barberinae* carries a dedication to Cardinal Antonio. The "principe noster" so frequently mentioned in the text is Antonio. Teti is also listed on Antonio's *rolo di famiglia*. BAV, Arch. Barb., Ind. IV, 176 (Antonio, 1642).

[4] G. Teti, "Barberinarum Aedium Brevis Descriptio," BAV, Barb. Lat. 2317, 5v–6r.

[5] See J. Montagu, "Exhortatio ad Virtutem: A Series

Teti's silence is often more puzzling than his elaborate interpretations. He is interested only in the ceilings painted under Barberini patronage. Most of the Sforza ceiling paintings are left unmentioned. Teti also appears uninterested in the formal and thematic links connecting the imagery of rooms en suite. He treats each of the major rooms discretely, each chapter carrying a separate dedication. Finally, his silence about the astrological nature of much of the imagery is particularly noteworthy. He fails to mention even that the symbols held by the personifications in Sacchi's fresco are also constellations. Teti's awareness of this level of meaning is implied in the manuscript version of the *Aedes*.[6] Significantly this major explanatory point does not appear in the much-expanded printed edition. Such an omission must reflect a prudent second thought on the part of the author. The Barberini, as we have seen, did not view astrological matters as appropriate for public consumption, particularly when they related to them personally. Precisely because of the importance of the astrological dimension of the palace imagery, it could therefore not be mentioned.

Although Teti's comments on the meaning of the *Creation of the Angels* are helpful, once again he neglects to mention how the subject relates to the imagery in the preceding room and who might have been responsible for yet another unusual iconographic program. Because of the rarefied nature of the content, we can be sure that the artist did not initiate the theme. There exists, however, sufficient evidence to indicate once again Campanella's participation. In both the *Metaphysica* and the *Theologicorum* he devotes extensive discussion to the nature and function of angels, terming them "executors of divine providence."[7] He enumerates the hierarchies of angels and expounds on the function of each choir, identifying the three hierarchies as corresponding to the three Primalities of Love, Wisdom, and Power.[8] Most important of all, Campanella's angelology has an essential place in his astrology. Angels form the connecting tissue by means of which terrestrial events are affected by the Primalities.[9]

The creation of the angels is the subject of a section of Campanella's *Theologicorum* (bk. V, chap. IV, art. 3). Citing various patristic authorities, Campanella argues that although angels are spiritual beings and therefore immutable, they were created by God in time like the corporeal world. The angels had to have been created because they did not exist *ab aeterno*. This is clear, Campanella points out in paraphrasing Ecclesiasticus (1:4), because Wisdom existed before anything else. The creation of the angels is a significant issue because the mode by which they came into being reflects their nature, which is crucial to Campanella's metaphysics. Basically it reduces to the fact that because angels are spiritual beings operating in a temporal (created) realm, they are able to influence the created world (man) and thereby transmit to us God's will.

Among the individual choirs of particular concern to Campanella are the Virtues, to whom, following St. Gregory, he attributes responsibility for moving the heavenly bodies: "Wherefore when there will be omens in the sun, in the moon and in the stars, the Lord

of Paintings in the Barberini Palace," *Journal of the Warburg and Courtauld Institutes* 34 (1971), 366–72.

[6] G. Teti, "Barberinarum Aedium Brevis Descriptio," BAV, Barb. Lat. 2316, 23v–24v.

[7] *Metaphysica*, pt. III, bks. XII–XIII, XV; *Theologicorum*, bk. V. Book V of the *Theologicorum*, on the na-

ture of angels, has been translated as *Le creature sovrannaturali*, trans. R. Amerio (Rome, 1970).

[8] Ibid., 123–43.

[9] *Metaphysica*, pt. III, bk. XV, chap. II, arts. II–III, 161–62. Di Napoli, *Tommaso Campanella*, 336–37; Walker, *Spiritual and Demonic Magic*, 224–27.

gives the cause for them saying: 'because the virtues of the heavens shall be moved.' "[10] Campanella's concern with the nature of angels appears related to his belief in the efficacy of astrological magic, for the sun and stars are themselves angels. Rejecting the traditional association with St. Michael, Campanella considered the sun to be an angel from the choir of Dominations, the other stars all of the choir of Virtues.[11] As this system of belief took shape on the vaults of Palazzo Barberini, the destiny of that family was depicted in the positioning of the sun and stars, alluding to the nativities of individual family members. These stars, moreover, are nothing less than emblems of God's will as carried out by his angels. In Sacchi's salotto painting we see the stars; in Camassei's painting we encounter the angels who not only guide those stars but, in Campanella's view, are synonymous with them.

With this more complete view of Campanella's metaphysical speculations, we are now better able to see the series of ceiling paintings in the piano nobile apartment as an ensemble to be experienced and comprehended in sequence. The *Divine Wisdom* vault depicts that which existed *ab aeterno*, as manifested in the Primalities of Love, Wisdom, and Power. In the ceiling painting of the following chamber we see that which God first created—the angelic hierarchies representing the behind-the-scenes mechanism by which he communicates the Primalities to the physical world. Then, conveniently, follow Viviani's Creation scenes, including the angels who now govern the heavenly spheres (Fig. 28). Thereafter begins the epic of human history illustrated in Viviani's cove scenes and in the ceilings of the subsequent rooms.

---

[10] "Unde quando erunt signa in sole, luna et stellis, subiungitur causa a Domino: 'quoniam virtutes caelorum movebuntur.' " Campanella, *Le creature sovrannaturali*, 130, based on Matthew 24:29.

[11] Campanella, *Metaphysica*, pt. III, bk. XV, chap. II, art. III, 162. This issue is discussed at length in Walker, *Spiritual and Demonic Magic*, 224–29. Also Lechner, "Fresco of 'Divina Sapienza,' " 103–4.

CHAPTER IX

• The Apartments of Anna and Taddeo

THE FRESCO decoration of Donna Anna's garden apartment (PBN 14–18 and C2) was less opulent than that of the adjacent formal rooms of the main piano nobile apartment. The shift in the pictorial and iconographic mode of the imagery reflects the informal nature of the rooms and the function they fulfilled within the overall ensemble. As the payment documents indicate, all fresco work in this part of the palace was completed by December 1631 or January 1632 at the latest, in time for Taddeo and family to occupy the palace on 13 May 1632.[1]

A large room (PBN 16) served as the nucleus of this subgroup of rooms and opened to the south, directly into the private garden ("giardino segreto") with an inviting fountain and orange trees.[2] The smaller room to the east (PBN 17) served as the antechamber to an old Sforza chapel (PBN C2), now newly redecorated. To the west of the central salotto another room (PBN 18) was also incorporated into the apartment. The small gallery ("gallarietta")[3] to the north (PBN 15), with the central opening in the long wall opposite the windows, functioned as a painted indoor garden balancing the real garden with its fountain on an axis with the garden door and the gallery entrance. Rooms PBN 13 and 14 connected the garden apartment with the main piano nobile apartment, continuing the enfilade of doors from west to east. The central room of the garden apartment could thus be entered either from the gallery or from the room to the west and was therefore readily accessible from Anna's main apartment. These relatively small rooms provided Anna with more intimate and secluded accommodations where she could watch over her children and be attended by her ladies in waiting.[4] The direct access to the garden by means of a door in the center of the south wall of PBN 16 made the apartment like a villa casino within the context of the grand formal rooms of a large urban palace.

A VILLA WITHIN THE PALACE: PASTORAL IMAGERY AND ITS MEANING

The pictorial decoration of the garden apartment also conforms to the more relaxed domestic environment, yet continues—although in a more restrained mode—the themes of abundant progeny and divinely sanctioned dominion so forcefully presented in the main

---

[1] Above, 36.

[2] Waddy (*Seventeenth-Century Roman Palaces*, 191–92) has reconstructed this suite of rooms by means of a careful analysis of all the construction documents and inventories.

[3] As mentioned, for example, in the *misura e stima* of 1634: "Gallarietta acc.to la capella va./Colla fatta per

pittori per dipingere la volta e li muri lo. p. 42 1/2 lar. p. 11 1/2 e più cola simili lo. p. 98 alte. p. 15. p.2. Colle . . . 48.95." ASR, Congregazioni Religiose Maschili, Teatini, S. Andrea della Valle, 2200, int. 229, pt. 2, 70.

[4] Waddy, *Seventeenth-Century Roman Palaces*, 29, 191.

apartment of the piano nobile. Camassei apparently received the commission to paint the vault of the central room (PBN 16), but this was never accomplished, perhaps because the artist's more pressing assignments in the main apartments took longer than expected.[5] The subject of Camassei's projected ceiling painting is not stated in any of the documents, but inventories provide evidence for the less permanent decorations commissioned for the walls and give some suggestion as to what subject might have been considered appropriate for the ceiling.

An inventory of December 1631 indicates that at that early date four gilded leather revetments depicting scenes of gardens and palaces had been prepared for hanging in the room.[6] Similar hangings for the adjacent chapel antechamber (PBN 17) represented a lake, a labyrinth, a river with water displays, a castle "in the Flemish style," and, among other unspecified "gardens and palaces," a view of Castelgandolfo with its Barberini villa.[7] The new wall decoration was conceived to conform to the preexisting vault fresco with its Flemish landscape scenes (Fig. 13), including castles, cities, and ruins in the background.[8] Like the Sforza fresco, the Barberini imagery reflects the decorum of the casino-like character of the garden apartment.

The view of Castelgandolfo, and perhaps other unmentioned localities with Barberini villas and possessions, follows the tradition of villa iconography as seen in the mural and vault decoration of the Villa Farnese at Caprarola and the Villa d'Este at Tivoli, where the occupant is offered the option of a nearby garden or painted views of other villas.[9] The scenes made available to Donna Anna's gaze would have complemented the pleasant, if enclosed, vista of the real garden seen through the windows of the garden apartment rooms.

As previously noted, Marziani added the fresco of the *Nativity* in the central enframement of the chapel antechamber vault (Fig. 13).[10] This intimate scene of the birth of Christ would have tied into the program of the preexisting cove scenes with the Old Testament prophets predicting the coming of the Messiah and would also have presented to the viewer

---

[5] Even the scaffolding had been prepared in the room (PBN 16) for Camassei's anticipated activity, as records the *misura e stima* of December 1634: "Per la fatt.ra del ponte nel salotto dove *dovea* dipingere il Camasei." ASR, Congregazioni Religiose Maschili, Teatini, S. Andrea della Valle, 2200, int. 229, pt. 2, 70; Waddy, *Seventeenth-Century Roman Palaces*, 191, doc. 386, n. 47. In the eighteenth century the coves acquired grotesque work and *quadri riportati* with landscape views, and the central field, still surrounded by the Sforza-period stucco enframement, was painted with a scene of *Apollo in the Chariot of the Sun Preceded by Night and Aurora.*

[6] Painted by Urbinese. BAV, Barb. Lat. 5635, 24. Transcribed in Waddy, *Seventeenth-Century Roman Palaces*, 191.

[7] Ibid., 191–92, 386, n. 49.

[8] Above, 20–21 and Fig. 13.

[9] See the decoration of the Room of Hercules in the Villa Farnese at Caprarola and the dining-room salotto of the Villa d'Este. Both of these earlier examples include depictions of the occupants' other villas and possessions so that, while comfortably dining in one bucolic site, the owner would be further refreshed by visual reminders of other favored retreats. For the Tivoli frescoes, executed in the 1560s by Girolamo Muziano and Federico Zuccaro, see D. R. Coffin, *The Villa d'Este at Tivoli* (Princeton, 1960), 50–54. The comparable room in the Villa Farnese at Caprarola, also a dining room, was executed by Zuccaro in 1566–1572. L. W. Partridge, "The Sala d'Ercole in the Villa Farnese at Caprarola, Part I," *Art Bulletin* 53 (1971), 467–68, and "Part II," *Art Bulletin* 54 (1972,) 50; Coffin, *The Villa in the Life of Renaissance Rome*, 291–95. Subject matter appropriate to villa life continued even in the frescoed ceiling of PBN 14, painted by Giuseppe Bartolomeo Chiari ca. 1695 with a fresco depicting *Apollo in the Chariot of the Sun Surrounded by the Seasons.* See B. Kerber, "Giuseppe Bartolomeo Chiari," *Art Bulletin* 50 (1968), 76–77, fig. 4. According to Pascoli (*Vite de' pittori*, 1:211–12), Bellori provided the program.

[10] This scene, like the one before it, has since fallen from place. Above, 20–21.

the prototype of the maternal function being fulfilled by Donna Anna. The chapel itself was simply refitted with easel paintings in the lunette sections and, presumably, also above the altar.[11]

On occasions when the delights of the garden were not sought, Anna and her ladies could retire to the little gallery (PBN 15), where she could enjoy a surrogate indoor garden with a long narrow barrel vault painted as an ivy pergola (Fig. 64).[12] Romanelli, Baldini, and Giacinto Gimignani executed the vault and mural frescoes of the gallery, following designs provided by Cortona.[13]

In the oval at the center of the vault appears the characteristic Cortonesque device of the Barberini arms, garlanded with laurel, being lifted into place by putti—the motif designated by Malcolm Campbell as the "stemma in arrivo."[14] The fictive pergola terminates at each end with semi-ovals containing shields with Barberini imprese recalling the apiculture imagery of Book Four of Vergil's *Georgics*. At the eastern end is the rustic image of a plough pulled by bees, with the politico-poetic motto TRIA POTIORA (Three Greater Things).[15] The emblem at the opposite end shows a bee on a honeycomb with the motto ΣYN CERA (Pure), seeming to imply that the bees are all together in their comb.

Other decorative motifs and devices in the vault evoke an environment of bucolic antiquity. Four irregularly shaped cove sections separated from one another by the pergola structure contain grisaille acanthus scrollwork with leaping dogs, lions, lionesses, and stags heraldically flanking shields that contain attributes of pagan gods.[16] The heads beneath the shields wear garlands to symbolize the four seasons.[17] The lunettes at the ends of the gallery contain the coats of arms of Cardinal Francesco and Don Taddeo.[18]

The configuration of the vault elements as seen today is the result of a modification that took place in 1677–1678 entailing the removal of the spiral stairs (PBN S5).[19] This led to a lengthening of the vault and the addition of a section of fresco with a third bee impresa— the HIC DOMUS—and two additional sections of grisaille acanthus scrolls, thus destroying the

[12] This standard type of villa decoration can also be seen at Caprarola on the vault of the cortile portico of the piano rialzato painted in the 1560s by a team of artists led by Taddeo and Federico Zuccaro. J. Recupero, *Il Palazzo Farnese di Caprarola* (Florence, 1975), fig. 5; I. Faldi, *Il Palazzo Farnese di Caprarola* (Turin, 1981), 107.

[13] Two preliminary drawings from Cortona's hand record early stages in the evolution of the decorative system of the vault. The earliest of these (Düsseldorf, FP 11033) is a one-eighth section of the vault containing *ignudi*, a dog chasing a stag and a rabbit, and cartouches with a laurel crown and bees. Scroll patterns dominate, and the pergola motif had not yet appeared. A more advanced stage of the design process is embodied in a second drawing (Windsor, 4452). A. Blunt and H. L. Cooke, *The Roman Drawings of the XVII & XVIII Centuries in the Collection of Her Majesty the Queen at Windsor Castle* (London, 1960), 79. Here the pergola is adumbrated in the empty banding and Taddeo's mo-

bile coat of arms appears as in the fresco. Cartouches, shields, and garlanded heads appear along the edge.

[14] Campbell (*Pietro da Cortona*, 124–25), discusses the use of this type of device in the later Sala di Marte at Palazzo Pitti. The Barberini arms were overpainted with those of the Falconieri [Pallavicini] family at a later date. G. Incisa della Rocchetta, "Review of *Pietro da Cortona o della pittura barocca* by Giuliano Briganti," *Archivio della Società Romana di Storia Patria* 89 (1966), 302; Blunt, "Palazzo Barberini," 286, n. 76; Blunt and Cooke, *Roman Drawings*, no. 601.

[15] For the meaning of this impresa, below, 140–41.

[16] The shields are painted with the caduceus of Mercury, a Bacchus herm, the laurel tree of Apollo, and the aegis of Minerva.

[17] Some of the shields are difficult to read because of their poor condition. In photographs the heads are mostly obscured by the stucco cornice.

[18] Cardinal Francesco, it will be recalled, paid for the fresco work of the gallery.

[19] Waddy, *Seventeenth-Century Roman Palaces*, 257–58, 386, n. 51.

original symmetry of Cortona's design.[20] Since the door at the western end of the gallery was pushed outward in that direction, the lunette fresco with Taddeo's arms was lost at that time. The fresco seen in that position today is a replica of the original painted at this later date.[21]

Two narrative scenes appear as overdoors on the wall sections beneath the end lunettes of the vault. Romanelli was apparently responsible for the *Founding of Palestrina* at the western end (Fig. 65), and Gimignani painted the *Sacrifice to Juno* (Fig. 67) at the eastern end.[22] Both scenes were painted as part of a frieze that once extended all around the upper wall of the gallery.[23] The frieze has disappeared except for the two narrative scenes, both in poor condition. The *Sacrifice to Juno* survives as little more than a devastated fragment following its dislocation at the time of the removal of the spiral stairs, and both works have lost imagery on the bottom and the right side, possibly when the doors and surrounding marble enframements were enlarged.[24]

The *Founding of Palestrina* celebrates the recent acquisition of this principality, which had been purchased from Francesco Colonna by Carlo Barberini in 1630 and then inherited by Taddeo a few months later.[25] In the fresco, Caeculus, the mythical founder of Palestrina (Praeneste), offers as proof of his divine lineage the fiery sanction of his father, Vulcan (Fig. 65).[26] This sign of heavenly favor won for Caeculus the numerous followers who had earlier doubted his claims to godly descent but who thereafter became the loyal inhabitants of Palestrina—a significant allusion for the newly arrived Barberini prince.[27] On the hillside in the background rises the famous temple sanctuary of Fortuna Primigenia, which Cortona had reconstructed in a drawing now in the Victoria and Albert Museum.[28] The appearance of this monumental structure in the Barberini fresco carries particular significance because Taddeo was at that time engaged in remodeling his recently acquired palace nestled into the

[20] The break in the *intonaco* where the new section begins can be discerned by the naked eye but cannot be readily seen in photographs.

[21] Waddy (*Seventeenth-Century Roman Palaces*, 386, n. 51) has noted the stylistic divergence of the putti from those in the other sections of the vault fresco.

[22] E. Waterhouse, *Baroque Painting in Rome* (London, 1937), 59, first attributed these works to Cortona and dated them to before 1633. Blunt ("Palazzo Barberini," 286) correctly identified the subjects. Vulcan's hammer and Juno's peacock serve as the identifying attributes. Briganti (*Pietro da Cortona*, 204–5), suggested a date of 1636. W. Vitzthum, "Review of *Pietro da Cortona* by Giuliano Briganti," *Burlington Magazine* 105 (1963), 215, properly associated the works with the campaign in the new chapel and accurately dated them to 1632.

[23] Waddy, *Seventeenth-Century Roman Palaces*, 192, 386, n. 51. The *misura e stima* of 1634, noting the plaster for the frieze 15 palmi high and the painters' scaffolding constructed in two registers, confirms that the upper wall of the gallery was originally conceived with a pictorial component.

[24] The lost areas were repainted at a later date, but these and still later accretions were removed during a recent restoration.

[25] Pecchiai, *I Barberini*, 165–66; *DBI*, 6: 180.

[26] *Paulys Real-Encyclopädie der classischen Altertumswissenschaft*, ed. G. Wissowa (Stuttgart, 1894–), 3: 1244–45, 22: pt. 2, 1551.

[27] M. Servius Honoratus, *In Vergilii carmina commentarii*, eds. G. Thilo and H. Hagen (Leipzig, 1881–1902), 2:181–82.

[28] London, Victoria and Albert Museum, E 306–1937 (57.2 × 116.8 cm.). P. Ward-Jackson, *Victoria and Albert Museum Catalogues: Italian Drawings* (London, 1980), 1:203–4. Three studio drawings at Windsor show the plan, perspective view, and elevation of Cortona's reconstruction. Blunt and Cooke, *Roman Drawings*, nos. 634–36. R. Wittkower, "Pietro da Cortona's Project for Reconstructing the Temple of Palestrina," in *Studies in Italian Baroque Art*, ed. M. Wittkower (Boulder, Col., 1975), 116–24, hypothesized that Cortona made studies of the ancient ruins on site in 1636. Given the certainty that the Palestrina fresco at Palazzo Barberini was completed in December 1631 or January 1632 at the latest, Cortona must have conducted his researches considerably earlier, possibly at the behest of his learned friend Cassiano dal Pozzo, secretary to Cardinal Francesco Barberini.

foundations of the ancient sanctuary.[29] The bipartite arrangement of the apartments in this structure may even have provided Taddeo with the prototype for his design for Palazzo Barberini.[30]

That the fresco alludes to the second founding of the town, now under the aegis of the Barberini, is suggested by the animated building activity represented in the mason's platform projecting above the city gate on the right. But the repainted right edge of the fresco falsifies the original image, which is best seen in Cortona's preparatory drawing at Windsor (Fig. 66).[31] In addition to the scaffold, we now see a half-complete column and, at the lower right, a stonemason carving a heraldic shield to be mounted above the keystone of the arch, such as could be seen on the Porta del Sole, the principal entrance portal to Palestrina, recently rebuilt and renamed by Taddeo to serve as an improved approach to the Barberini villa above the city.[32]

The view of Palestrina would also have had significance for Donna Anna, since the town had belonged to a lateral branch of the Colonna family prior to the sale to her father-in-law. Moreover, like the other views of villas and gardens depicted on the walls of the garden apartment, the *Founding of Palestrina* would have reminded her of the delights of true villa life each time she sought out the quiet pleasures of her own little substitute Palestrina at Palazzo Barberini.

Of all the estates acquired by the Barberini, Palestrina was perhaps the most important for the social agenda of the family, for it brought with it the cachet of a princely title. The ducal crown could now be replaced by the princely crown. This idea is pictorially re-created in the gallery as one enters from the door at the west end (Figs. 68–69). The viewer's eyes first encounter the fresco of the *Founding of Palestrina*, where the prominently crowned figure of Caeculus dominates, but are then drawn upward to the fictive oval opening in the center of the vault, where putti are at that moment lifting Taddeo's coat of arms into place and fitting it with the princely crown. The putto holding the crown at the top of the composition meets the viewer's gaze to confirm the importance of his task. Thus, at the very moment of our arrival into the gallery, we are witness not only to the original founding of Palestrina but also to its refounding under the rule of the Barberini family. Here villa iconography and social aspirations unite.

Cortona had already developed the theme of newly acquired princely dominion at Palestrina in a tapestry panel designed in 1630 just prior to the work in the little gallery. As part of a series of eight tapestries depicting the great castles of Europe—the first major products of the Barberini tapestry manufactory—the *Hic Domus* panel proclaims Palestrina the home of the Barberini (Fig. 70).[33] The heraldic bees appear amid a giant laurel tree dominating the foreground. Above, a banderole contains the Vergilian motto HIC DOMUS

[29] The construction of a central sala uniting two wings of the old Colonna palace took place in 1631–1632. Waddy, *Seventeenth-Century Roman Palaces*, 278–79.

[30] Ibid., 229–30; idem, "Taddeo Barberini as Patron," 195–97.

[31] Windsor, Royal Library 6802 (29.8 × 36 cm.). Blunt, "Palazzo Barberini," fig. 32c; Blunt and Cooke, *Roman Drawings*, 79, no. 600.

[32] As reported in Cardinal Francesco's biography of Taddeo. BAV, Arch. Barb., Ind. IV, 1254, 16v–17r. For the Porta del Sole, see P. Romanelli, *Palestrina* (Naples, 1967), 81, fig. 104.

[33] U. Barberini, "Pietro da Cortona e l'arazzeria Barberini," *Bollettino d'arte* 35 (1950), 43–44; A. S. Cavallo, "Notes on the Barberini Tapestry Manufactory at Rome," *Boston Museum Bulletin* 55 (1957), 22.

(This Is Home) mounted with the princely crown.[34] In the background rises Palestrina with the concave facade of the Barberini villa appearing at the upper edge of the town. Thus the theme of Barberini princely possession at Palestrina seen in the little gallery frescoes was already established in the family iconography.

The theme of the second founding of Palestrina is reiterated in the building activity observed in the *Sacrifice to Juno* (Fig. 67), where a workman carries forward a mortar-laden tray to a mason constructing a wall. The temple depicted on the right must refer to the sanctuary of Juno, the Iunoniarum, thought to have been located at Palestrina.[35] Because of the nature of the sacrifice being made, this scene represents an especially decorous addition to the pictorial imagery of Donna Anna's garden apartment. Young women come forward with geese, the symbol of matronly demureness and modesty appropriate to the cult of Juno Moneta.[36] As the protectress of married women, Juno was associated with human fecundity, and women invoked her particularly for success in childbearing.[37] The urgent and hopeful activities of the nubile women in the fresco represent this function of Juno's cult, and the obtrusive tetrastyle temple positioned frontally and parallel to the picture plane may also be taken as a reminder of Anna's family name.

Anna's role within the Barberini family once again finds confirmation in the imagery of her apartment. Themes of family generation and divine favor that appear in Sacchi's *Divine Wisdom* and Cortona's designs for the Christological cycle in the chapel of the main apartment were therefore already outlined in secular form in the pictorial decoration of the garden apartment.

THE PIANO TERRENO APARTMENT: TADDEO'S IMAGES OF VIRTUE (1629–1631)

Because of the location of his apartment on the piano terreno, Taddeo had to make do with a relatively modest *sala dei palafrenieri* (PBT 3), but an appropriate number of antechambers (PBT 4–6) precedes the audience hall (PBT 7) and the private rooms beyond (PBT 8–11).[38] The three rooms to the east (PBT 12–14) were outside the formal suite but would have been suitable for use as extra rooms during the summer months. The bucolic imagery of Sforza fresco decoration on the vaults of these rooms would have provided decorous adornment for summer rooms (Fig. 6).[39]

Although Taddeo's suite on the piano terreno of the north wing (PBT 3–11) follows the same distribution of rooms as the main piano nobile apartment above (PBN 3–11), the imagery of the painted ceilings is markedly different from the biblical subjects to be seen on the upper floor. The character of the piano terreno frescoes combines the villa-like airiness

---

[34] For the meaning of the HIC DOMUS (*Aeneid* 7:59–67, 122) impresa in Barberini iconography, see Ferro, *Teatro d'imprese*, 72–77.

[35] On the cult of Juno at Praeneste see Pauly-Wissowa, *Real-Encyclopädie*, 2:pt. 2, 604; 22:pt. 2, 1554; W. H. Roscher, *Ausführliches Lexikon der griechischen und römischen Mythologie* (Leipzig, 1884–1937), 2:pt. 2, 604. Ovid (*Fasti*, VI:61–63) refers to an altar there dedicated to Juno.

[36] Pauly-Wissowa, *Real-Encyclopädie*, 2:pt. 2, 593.

[37] Ibid., 578–94.

[38] Waddy (*Seventeenth-Century Roman Palaces*, 180–88) has reconstructed the sequence and function of the rooms in Taddeo's suite as it was constituted in 1632 when he first occupied them. One of these rooms (PBN 10) served as Taddeo's bedroom.

[39] These eastern rooms had no fireplaces. Ibid., 188.

of the vault of the garden apartment gallery with mythological scenes of high moral content. In general the thematic content and formal disposition of the piano terreno painted ceilings are more traditional and less innovative in spirit than the frescoes of the main upstairs apartment.

As in the piano nobile apartment, the first room (PBT 4) was left without fresco work.[40] The second room or salotto (PBT 5), however, comes as a surprise to the visitor who may already have seen its formal counterpart upstairs painted with Sacchi's *Divine Wisdom*. Instead of the somber dignity of that heavenly apparition, one would first have been struck by the playful sound of splashing water coming from the fountain in the center of the floor.[41] On the vault overhead, the heavens appear to open as in the upstairs salotto, but, instead of personifications of divine attributes, a monkey and a goose confront each other on a garden balustrade, and peacocks regard the viewer with suspicion from their lofty position on the parapet (Fig. 71). In the corner opposite the point of entry a crane does battle with a serpent, while ducks and other fowl fly about in the open sky.

The painted coat of arms carried aloft by putti at the crown of the vault proudly announces that this is Taddeo's apartment, the princely crown in place above it declaring the newly acquired status of the possessor. The radiant head of Apollo seen in the central metope of the west facade of the palace reappears here in painted form at the base of the balustrade piers with the peacocks, now complemented by the Colonna Siren in a panel on the face of the pier. But, as indicated by the rays of the sun rising in the east, which produce a sharp line of shadow across the balustrade with the monkey, the painted sun emblem is not the only allusion to Taddeo's solar impresa represented here.

Simone Lagi had already worked for the Barberini both at the Four Fountains and at Castelgandolfo painting coats of arms and other decorative schemes. The *quadratura* element of the balustrade, however, has no precedent in his earlier work. This type of perspectival ceiling painting was a specialized practice, so another artist must have been called in for this component of the work. During the 1620s and 1630s in Rome, Agostino Tassi was the leading practitioner of *quadratura* painting. He painted three large easel canvases for the Barberini in the period 1631–1633, two of which depict Taddeo, so this artist's engagement in the painting of Taddeo's salotto would be credible.[42] *Quadratura* balustrades similar to the one in the Barberini room appear in a number of Tassi's ceilings elsewhere in Rome. His balustrade with pergola painted on the vault of a piano terreno room of Palazzo Lancellotti (1621–1623) is close in conception to the Barberini salotto ceiling, even including monkeys, peacocks, and other birds.[43]

The type of garden imagery painted on the salotto vault traditionally appears in gar-

[40] The first room in the suite (PBT 3) served as the *sala dei palafrenieri*. The range of rooms in the eastern section of the north wing (PBT 12–14), with three ceiling paintings from the Sforza period (Figs. 7, 30–32), are not part of the main suite of Taddeo's apartment.

[41] BAV, Arch. Barb., Ind. II, 2888, 241v. Also the *misura e stima* published in Magnanimi, "Documenti della costruzione," 203. The Swedish artist Nicodemus Tessin noted the fountain when he visited the palace in 1687–1688. O. Sirén, *Nicodemus Tessin D. Y:S Studiere-sor: i Danmark, Tyskland, Holland, Frankrike och Italien* (Stockholm, 1914), 166.

[42] Above, 86–87 and n. 93.

[43] Pugliatti, *Agostino Tassi*, 53–54, fig. 72. A painted balustrade with playing putti in Palazzo Costaguti (1621–1623) is particularly close to that of the Barberini room. I. Mussa, "L'architettura illusionistica nelle decorazioni romane: il 'quadraturismo' dalla scuola di Raffaello alla metà del '600," *Capitolium* 44 (1969), 82, fig. 31.

den loggias, casinos, villas, and, occasionally, in piano terreno rooms of palaces.[44] But the carefree subject matter of the vault is unusual for one of the main rooms of a formal apartment. Construction documents indicate that, prior to the alterations made by the Barberini, this room and the adjacent one (PBT 6) formed a loggia with arched openings facing north.[45] The Sforza fresco that covered this large room was destroyed when the Barberini added a partition wall dividing it into two smaller spaces (PBT 5–6),[46] but the ceiling painted by Lagi may recall the earlier fresco. In any case, the new fresco is similar to decorative schemes typical of loggias.[47] The informal nature of Lagi's fresco and the presence of the fountain, moreover, indicate that this room, together with the other rooms to the east (PBT 12–14), outside the formal suite of rooms, served Taddeo as the downstairs equivalent of his wife's garden apartment and gallery, where, isolated from the actual garden, he could nonetheless enjoy refreshing scenery of an artificial outdoor setting.

A door was opened in the center of the south wall of the salotto to lead to a chapel (PBT C1) and an adjacent oratory where Taddeo could attend Mass in absolute privacy (PBT C1A).[48] Early plans show that this opening had first been conceived as a window to provide natural lighting. The decoration of the chapel must have been simple, for documents do not record any significant fresco and stucco work, thus confirming the more private nature of this chapel as opposed to that on the piano nobile directly above (PBN C1). The oratory, however, referred to as a "camerino" in the documents,[49] did receive a ceiling fresco. Camassei painted the small vault of this subsidiary space in chiaroscuro with the image of Taddeo's guardian angel.[50] The private location indicates the importance of the subject matter to the patron. Scarcely anyone but Taddeo would have had access to this image. Thus a small, intimate echo of the same artist's *Creation of the Angels* (PBN 6) occurs on the piano terreno, reconfirming Taddeo's devotion to the cult of angels, particularly his guardian angel.

A greater understanding of the nature of Taddeo's reverence for his guardian angel can be gained from popular religious tracts of the period, which detail the procedure for communing with one's personal spiritual protector in order to assure the enjoyment of his daily stewardship. The manuals advise the worshiper to meditate on the benefits received from one's guardian angel and to imagine oneself in the presence of God, the angels, and

[44] This can be seen in the pergolated parapet painted by Agostino Ciampelli on the vault of the gallery in the Villa Grazioli (Acquaviva-Montalto) at Frascati (ca. 1606); in a small ground-floor chamber of the Casino Ludovisi (anonymous, ca. 1622) where Cardinal Ludovisi's coat of arms is carried aloft by putti; and in a piano terreno room of Palazzo Lancellotti (Agostino Tassi, 1621–1623), where monkeys, peacocks, and other birds occupy the balustrade and pergola above. *Villa e paese*, ed. A. Tantillo Mignosi (Rome, 1980), 150–51, figs. 17–19; Campbell, *Pietro da Cortona*, fig. 179; Pugliatti, *Agostino Tassi*, 53, fig. 72.

[45] Above, 30, 34

[46] "Camera dov'è Ercole con la virtù e vitio *è stata buttata a basso la pittura*." Pollak, *Die Kunsttätigkeit*, 1:305.

[47] See the frescoes in the loggia at the Palazzo del Quirinale, where a fictive fountain flocked with birds is painted on the wall beneath the pergola of the vault. D. Batorska, "Grimaldi's Frescoes in Palazzo del Quirinale," *Paragone*, no. 387 (May 1982), 3–12, figs. 5–7.

[48] Early in the design process a window was intended instead of the door, but construction documents prove that the opening was executed as a door. "Per haver rotto il muro e fatto la Porta della Cappella." BAV, Arch. Barb., Ind. II, 2888, 241r (Pollak, *Die Kunsttätigkeit*, 1:304); ASR, Congregazioni Religiose (1642), Teatini, S. Andrea della Valle, 2200, int. 229, 120r (Magnanimi, "Documenti della costruzione," 203), int. 230, 219. BAV, Arch. Barb., Ind. II, 2888, 241r.

[49] "Camerino accanto la cappella dove sta il Sr Principe a sentir messa." Pollak, *Die Kunsttätigkeit*, 1:306.

[50] Above, 99 and n. 28.

particularly one's personal protector.[51] The painted image of Taddeo's guardian angel on the vault of his private oratory must have served this devotional function. Furthermore, stairs (PBT S3) connected the piano terreno suite to the piano nobile camera (PBN 6), where Taddeo could enjoy the vision of all the angels in Camassei's *Creation of the Angels*. At a later date, the chapel and oratory were transformed into a corridor, and all trace of decoration has vanished.

Decorum prevents the piano terreno salotto, with its carefree villa imagery, from having the same relationship to the chapel as does the piano nobile salotto to its contiguous chapel. There, as we have seen, the *Divine Wisdom* is oriented toward the chapel door; as a result, the fresco is first encountered upside-down from the point of entry into the room. Taddeo's coat of arms, by contrast, greets the viewer in correct orientation at the point of entry from the first anteroom (PBT 4) and thus does not direct the visitor toward the chapel door. The first anteroom rather than the salotto served as the public access to Taddeo's chapel.

Marziani's *quadro riportato* of *Hercules at the Crossroads* decorated the vault of the next room (PBT 6) in sequence after the salotto. Camassei's *Parnassus*, in similar format, adorned the vault of the following room (PBT 7), which served as the prince's audience chamber. The last in the sequence of rooms with vault imagery (PBT 8) contained another fresco by Marziani, *Bellerophon Slaying the Chimera*. None of the original ceiling paintings in these rooms (PBN 6–8) has survived,[52] but all three are mentioned in the construction documents. The most important of them, the *Parnassus*, is discussed by Teti and was engraved for inclusion in the *Aedes Barberinae* (Fig. 72).[53] In consequence, the iconographic program of the ensemble can be tentatively reconstructed.

The three ceiling paintings that follow in sequence after the salotto contain mythological subject matter and constitute a coherent thematic subgroup, but the full meaning of each painting can be appreciated only in the context of the ensemble. The princely virtue appropriate to the patron and occupant of these rooms and the immortality to be gained from it are the themes of the cycle.

Marziani's *Hercules at the Crossroads* (PBT 6) establishes the principal theme, which is subsequently elaborated in the *Parnassus* and *Bellerophon*. This unified program derives from an ode written by Maffeo Barberini and dedicated to his youthful nephew, the future Cardinal Francesco: "Ode Hortatoria ad Virtutem."[54]

[51] "Meditatione de' beneficii dell'angelo custode: Oratione preparatoria: Te imaginerai stare in presenza di Dio nostro Signore, e de gli suoi Angioli, e particolarmente dell'angelo tuo custode, che sta mirando le tue attioni, e lo pregherai, che t'impetri da Dio gratia di far bene questa mediatione, e di caminar bene in tutto quel giorno." The first point upon which to meditate: "Considera come Iddio particolarmente t'ha assignato un'angelo per tua guida, il quale t'aiutasse si nelle cose temporali, come anco nelle spirituali ti defendesse da tutti i tuoi nemici così visibili come invisibili." Albertino da Catanzaro, *Angelo custode*, 236–37.

[52] Although their subjects would have appealed to his rhetorical sensibility, Teti makes no mention of the two ceilings by Marziani, which suggests that they either were not admired or were perhaps already ruinous by the early 1640s. Presenzini (*Andrea Camassei*, 49–50) noted the precarious condition of the *Parnassus* in 1880, after which no subsequent mention of the work occurs.

[53] Teti, *Aedes Barberinae* (1642), 109–53.

[54] First published in Urbanus VIII, *Poemata* (Paris, 1620), 42–46, the poem was written in 1613–1614 (Appendix C). Francesco made a similarly poetic reply in the form of an elegy using much of the same imagery. The nephew's composition has been published in M. Costanzo, *Critica e poetica del primo seicento* (Rome, 1969), 2:114–18. The dating of the two poems can be deduced from letters of Maffeo and Francesco pub-

Maffeo's exhortatory ode offered moral guidance to his sixteen-year-old nephew, who was then a student at the Collegio Romano.[55] The opening stanza, through allusion to the myth of the "Choice of Hercules," or "Hercules at the Crossroads," expresses the uncle's concern that the young Francesco not choose the "downward road" that "treacherously stretches a path before you with deceitful guidance."[56]

The moral exemplum here is the one invented by Prodicus of Ceos and recounted by Xenophon.[57] When Hercules reached the threshold of manhood, he went out to a secluded place in order to ponder which road of life he should follow. There he encountered two maidens, Virtue and Vice; the latter, with various allurements, beckoned him to choose the easier path, that of sensual pleasures, while the former challenged Hercules to take the arduous higher road to virtue. In Maffeo's poem this higher road leads to Helicon (Parnassus), where Apollo plucks his golden lyre and the Muses sing (Appendix C, lines 13–44). References then follow to four ancient heroes who chose the path of virtue: Theseus, Ulysses, Jason, and Bellerophon (lines 17–44). The poem closes with a more explicit elaboration of the "Choice of Hercules" myth, detailing the fraudulent enticements of pleasure and the strenuous ascent to virtue (lines 53–84). The subjects of the three mythological ceiling paintings in Taddeo's apartment—*Hercules at the Crossroads*, *Parnassus*, and *Bellerophon*—therefore constitute a pictorialization of Maffeo's ode.

Although Marziani's painting of *Hercules at the Crossroads* has disappeared and no drawings by this obscure artist have yet been connected with the project, we may gain some idea of its figural content by examining the tradition for painted representations of this subject. Panofsky's fundamental study of the theme established that Annibale Carracci's redaction of the subject on the ceiling of the Camerino of Palazzo Farnese (1597) embodied a nearly "canonical" version that was to be followed in subsequent works.[58] The learned councillor Fulvio Orsini provided the iconographic program of the Camerino, with careful attention to exemplifying the virtues of the young patron, Cardinal Odoardo Farnese.[59] The cycle of paintings on the vault of the Farnese room parallels in ethical intent the Barberini cycle, and Annibale's central *quadro riportato* image of *Hercules at the Crossroads* (Fig. 148) may therefore serve as a tentative visual guide to the general iconography of Marziani's lost fresco.[60]

---

lished in ibid., 110–13. Montagu ("Exhortatio ad Virtutem," 366–72) has demonstrated that Maffeo's ode served as the basis for the fresco cycle Francesco commissioned in 1678 to replace Marziani's presumably ruined frescoes. Only Camassei's *Parnassus*, which remained intact until the late nineteenth century, was reintegrated into the new scheme. On that later cycle, below, 118–21. For the Latin text of Maffeo's poem and an English translation, see Appendix C.

[55] Costanzo, *Critica e poetica*, 113.

[56] Appendix C, lines 1–4. The "Choice of Hercules" already had a long tradition in post-classical literature and art when Maffeo employed it in his ode to Francesco. The myth appeared, perhaps for the first time since antiquity, in two works by Petrarch. T. H. Mommsen, "Petrarch and the Story of the Choice of Hercules," *Journal of the Warburg and Courtauld Institutes* 16 (1953), 178–92.

[57] Xenophon, *Memorabilia*, 2:1, 21–33.

[58] E. Panofsky, *Hercules am Scheidewege* (Leipzig-Berlin, 1930), 124–38.

[59] Martin, *Franese Gallery*, 38–48.

[60] The Camerino paintings have been the subject of intense analysis: Bellori, *Vite de' pittori*, 47–57; Martin, *Franese Gallery*, 21–48; C. Dempsey, "Annibal Carrache au Palais Farnèse," in *Le Palais Farnèse* (Rome, 1981), 1:272–83; and S. Macchioni, "Annibale Carracci, *Ercole al bivio*. Dalla volta del Camerino Farnese alla Galleria Nazionale di Capodimonte: genesi e interpretazioni," *Storia dell'arte* 42 (1981), 151–70. Annibale's original canvas was removed in 1662 and is now located in the Galleria Nazionale di Capodimonte in Naples. Martin, *Farnese Gallery*, 24, n. 5; Macchioni, "Annibale Carracci," 161–66. The space in the vault of the Camerino now contains a copy of the original.

In his version of *Hercules at the Crossroads* Annibale followed the post-classical tradition of replacing Prodicus' Vice with a personification of Voluptas, or Pleasure.[61] Annibale's Virtue carries as attribute the swordlike *parazonium*, but Marziani could hardly have omitted from the Barberini fresco two still more common attributes of Virtue, the sun and laurel crown.[62] Hercules' lion pelt also must have had a prominent place of since it was a Barberini *impresa* of such importance and, moreover, one that alluded to both strength and poetry. Two other details in Annibale's painting have no counterparts in Prodicus' apologue. The winged horse Pegasus awaits the hero at the top of a mountain, personifying eternal fame achieved through virtue,[63] and a bearded poet, crowned with laurel and holding an open book, reclines at the lower left, promising Hercules "to sing of him eternally if he follows in the path of virtue."[64] We cannot know if Marziani's painting included similar references to immortality and poetic fame through the depiction of Pegasus and the poet, but Camassei's *Parnassus*, the ceiling painting next in sequence, does emphasize these themes.

In the "Ode Hortatoria ad Virtutem" Maffeo associated the mount of virtue with Helicon, the abode of Pegasus and the Muses (lines 9–16).[65] Thus, as the palace visitor leaves the room with Marziani's *Hercules at the Crossroads* and enters the next room, he sees on its ceiling a full-blown depiction of Helicon (Parnassus) (PBT 7).[66] Owing to the engraving published by Teti,[67] we are not in doubt about the imagery once contained within the *quadro riportato* enframement at the center of the vault (Fig. 72).

Crowned with laurel and flanked by laurel trees, Apollo, in the company of the Muses, plays a lyre emblazoned with the mellifluous Barberini bee.[68] The thinly veiled allusion must be to the Barberini poet, Maffeo, who in the frontispiece of Ferro's *Teatro d'imprese* had already appeared on Parnassus attended by Apollo and the Muses (Fig. 149). In the frontispiece engraving, particular emphasis was given to the two Muses on the lower register: on the left, Erato, Muse of lyric poetry, and, on the right, Polyhymnia, Muse of heroic hymns. Maffeo's two most important *imprese*—the ALIUSQUE ET IDEM (the rising sun) and the HIC DOMUS (bees descending into a laurel tree)—appear in cartouches at the bottom of the print.[69] In Camassei's painting, by contrast, the celestial Muse Urania, armillary

[61] Thus following Cicero's abbreviated account of the myth (*De officiis*, I: 32, 118). Dempsey, "Annibal Carrache," 276.

[62] On the function of these two Barberini family *imprese* as symbols of virtue, see Ripa, *Nova iconologia*, 565–66.

[63] The concept appears to have been derived from Fulgentius (*Mythologiae tres libri*, I: 21). Panofsky, *Hercules*, 117.

[64] Bellori, *Vite de' pittori*, 48.

[65] Ovid, *Metamorphoses*, 5: 257–68.

[66] On the conflation of these two localities in post-classical iconography, see above, 30 and n. 56. Although Maffeo's poem refers only to Helicon, the construction documents identify the room as the "Camera d'Apollo" or "Mte Parnaso." BAV, Arch. Barb., Ind. II, 2888, 242, 245–46 (Pollak, *Die Kunsttätigkeit*, 1:304–5); ASR, Congregazioni Religiose Maschili, Teatini S. Andrea della Valle, 2200, int. 230, 223, 229–30 (Ma-

gnanimi, "Documenti della costruzione," 203). Teti (*Aedes Barberinae* [1642], 109, 150–51) designates the scene Parnassus but also alludes to Mount Helicon and the Hippocrene Spring opened there by Pegasus when he struck the rock with his hoof.

[67] Ibid., 106–7; Domenico Cortese, "Andrea Camassei," 283–84. Harris, "Camassei Studies," 54–55. Presenzini (*Andrea Camassei*, 57–58) identified the anonymous engraver as Bloemaert, who probably used as model the now ruined but autograph drawing in BAV, Ott. Lat. 3131, 45v–46, which has the same dimensions as the engraved image.

[68] Two preliminary sketches for the figure of Apollo are at Windsor, 4909: 35.9 × 23 cm., black and white chalk; 4960: 35.9 × 23.7 cm., black and white chalk. Blunt and Cooke, *Roman Drawings*, cat. 94, fig. 10, cat. 95.

[69] The inscription in the central cartouche reads: "Musa sibi ingenium, potuit simulare figuram / Pictor,

sphere in lap, is emphasized in isolation on the right, while Calliope, Thalia, and Euterpe, the Muses of epic poetry, pastoral poetry, and music, sit on the left.

At the extreme lower right the Hippocrene Spring—opened when Pegasus struck the rock with his hoof[70]—flows up and out of the scene. This image would have caused the viewer to recall the fountain in Taddeo's nearby salotto antechamber, the sound of which could perhaps still be heard. In the left background appears the temple of virtue and immortality, presided over by Minerva and crowned with an *ouraborus*, symbol of eternity, surrounding a sun disk. The imagery of the central grouping does not deviate significantly from traditional representations of Parnassus,[71] but on the extreme left and right, figure groupings of four martial heroes and the Fates indicate that the conception for the ceiling comes from Maffeo's ode.[72] Just as the poet promises, Apollo's music soothes the Fates into slumber and thereby saves the heroes from the fiery Underworld (lines 13–20). Jennifer Montagu has identified these four men as Theseus, Ulysses, Jason, and Bellerophon, the classical exemplars mentioned in the poem who chose the difficult path of virtue.[73] Thus the *Parnassus* also shows a parting of the ways comparable to that seen in the preceding room: one road, on the right, leads to the Underworld and perdition, and the other, on the left, leads to immortality.

Bellerophon, with Pegasus on his shield, stands out in front of the other three heroes as they approach the temple of virtue and immortality.[74] The viewer is thus prepared for the third and last in the sequence of mythological ceilings, *Bellerophon Slaying the Chimera*.[75] Although Marziani's fresco has not survived, there can be little doubt about the meaning of this painting. Bellerophon, mounted on Pegasus and destroying the Chimera, is the classical topos for the triumph of virtue over vice. Ripa used this same subject to personify Virtue, noting that the Chimera, with the head of a lion, body of a goat, and tail of a serpent, symbolizes the multiform nature of vice, whereas the etymology of the name Bellerophon means "slaying of the vices."[76] In 1678 Cardinal Francesco had Marziani's ruined fresco re-

virtutes symbola sculpta notant." [The Muse is talent in and of herself, the painter was able to duplicate a figure (together) they record the virtues with a sculpted symbol.] For the Horatian source of the ALIUSQUE ET IDEM, see below 141–42. For the Vergilian allusion of the HIC DOMUS, see below 185.

[70] Ovid, *Metamorphoses*, 5: 256–63.

[71] As analyzed by Schröter, *Ikonographie*, 164–337.

[72] Montagu, "Exhortatio ad Virtutem," 370.

[73] Magno Pereno's contemporary commentary on Maffeo's poem identifies these heroes as symbolizing the four cardinal virtues: Prudence, Temperance, Fortitude, and Justice. "Volens auctor in Ode proposita nepotem pubem et tum eo omnes promovere ad virtutem. . . . Exemplis quatuor Herorum Graecorum scilicet Thesei, Ulyssis, Jasonis, et Bellerophontis, de quibus aucthor hic quatuor virtutes cardinales (puta Prudentiam, Temperantiam, Fortitudinem, et Justitiam, quibus locum in Heliconedatur) significare volunt." BAV, Barb. Lat. 3307, 201v–202v, 690v–691v. The commentary is 1,118 folio pages in length. An earlier draft of the work, BAV, Barb. Lat. 3295, is cited by Montagu ("Exhortatio ad Virtutem," 370–71, n. 22), and Costanzo (*Critica e poetica*, 110). In the Farnese

Camerino the cardinal virtues are also present, but as straightforward personifications. Martin, *Farnese Gallery* 36–38.

[74] Montagu ("Exhortatio ad Virtutem," 369) has exposed the characteristic peculiarities of Teti's interpretation of the scene (*Aedes Barberinae* [1642], 109–13, 150–53). He appears to have had no knowledge of the relevance of Maffeo's poem and even makes statements belied by the visual evidence itself. For him the heroes represent prudence, wisdom, and piety. Nor is he particularly attentive to visual details; thus he reserves special praise for the "Doric order" round temple in the background without noticing the Corinthian capitals.

[75] For the myth of Bellerophon, see Hyginus, *Myths*, 157.

[76] Ripa, *Nova iconologia*, 566–67. Bellerophon also appears in Alciati with the same signification under the heading "Consilio & virtute Chimaeram superari, hoc est, fortiores & deceptores" and the lemma "Bellerophon, ut fortis eques, superare Chimaeram, / Et Lycii potuit sternere monstra soli: / Sic tu Pegaseis victus petis aethera pennis, / Consilioq animi monstra superba domas." A. Alciati, *Emblemata cum Commentariis* (Padua, 1621), 81–85.

placed by one of the same subject painted by Giuseppe Passeri (Fig. 74).[77] This later work may provide some idea of the composition of the original, since both versions had to conform to the vertical *quadro riportato* format of the old Sforza stucco enframement. Passeri, as Marziani before him must have done, closely followed the text of Maffeo's poem:

> This slayer of the triformed / Chimera, Bellerophon is preeminent among these men. The laurel of Phoebus draws Pegasus with its foliage / and Pegasus is nourished by the sweet nectar, / but it is denied to us to know the / power concealed beneath the Aonian honey. / Cynthian Apollo reveals secret senses. / Hear him singing: whom golden / virtue cherishes in her arms, that blessed / victor triumphs after the monsters have been conquered.[78]

In Passeri's fresco, as in the poem, Golden Virtue hovers protectively over the hero, her traditional symbols of sun and laurel serving to remind the viewer of the virtue of Taddeo and the Barberini family.[79]

The mythological cycle of ceiling images on the vaults of Taddeo's apartment, like its iconographic prototype in the Farnese Camerino, not only illustrated the patron's virtues through repeated reference to his imprese but, as in Maffeo's ode, exhorted him to live up to an ideal standard. When the program for the piano terreno cycle was conceived, Taddeo had crossed the threshold of manhood; he was twenty-six in 1629 and had already made the choice of Hercules as posited in Marziani's painting in the first of the three rooms. The imagery of the following ceilings, the *Parnassus* and the *Bellerophon*, allegorically represents Taddeo's prudent decision and also symbolizes the two branches of the path of virtue: the contemplative and the active life.[80] Upon entering the audience room (PBT 7) with its Apollonian subject, the visitor could see that the heroes and Taddeo, rejecting the broad path of sensual pleasure, had chosen the difficult ascent to virtue. But the painting's allusion to poetic endeavor, and the immortal glory achieved thereby, indicates that this is the contemplative side of virtue. The vault imagery celebrates the prince's cultivated side as patron and protector of the Muses.

Only in the private room beyond (PBT 8), where few visitors would have been admitted, do we see active virtue personified in Bellerophon.[81] Taddeo's concern with the political world of human affairs finds expression here.[82] The strident, martial character of this subject would remind the viewer that one of Taddeo's most important offices was that of general of the Church and, as such, he was head of the papal army and fleet of galleys.[83] A

---

[77] Montagu, "Exhortatio ad Virtutem," 368–69; I. Faldi, *Galleria Nazionale d'Arte Antica acquisiti, doni, lasciti, restauri e recuperi, 1962–1970* (Rome, 1970), 80; G. Sestieri, "Giuseppe Passeri pittore," *Commentari* 28 (1977), 115–16.

[78] "Ode Hortatoria ad Virtutem," see Appendix C, lines 35–44.

[79] Montagu, "Exhortatio ad Virtutem," 371.

[80] This division in the path of virtue also appears in the Farnese Camerino, where *Hercules Resting from His Labors* symbolizes the active life and *Hercules Bearing the Globe* represents the contemplative life. Bellori, *Vite de' pittori*, 49–51. Fulgentius (*Mythologiae*, 2: 1) is the antique source for the allegorization of the bipartite na-

ture of the virtuous life. Martin, *Farnese Gallery*, 27–30.

[81] Annibale had originally planned to place a fresco of this subject in one of the lunettes of the Farnese Camerino (drawing in the Louvre, Cabinet des Dessins, no. 7204). In the painted cycle this subject was changed to *Perseus and Medusa*, which carries the same allegorical significance of virtue triumphant over vice. Martin, *Farnese Gallery*, 34, 248–49, no. 40, fig. 138; Dempsey, "Annibal Carrache," 282–83.

[82] According to Perneo's commentary on Maffeo's ode, Bellerophon symbolizes justice. BAV, Barb. Lat. 3307, 691r.

[83] Pecchiai, *I Barberini*, 165–66. As the 1648 inventory of Taddeo's private library demonstrates, he was

later inventory of Taddeo's possessions at the Casa Grande ai Giubbonari refers to a private room containing maps and other objects that might be associated with military activities.[84] One can easily imagine that the room with the *Bellerophon* might have served such a function in Taddeo's apartment in the Barberini Palace at the Four Fountains.[85]

The images of virtue painted on the vaults of the piano terreno apartment embodied an ideal of moral probity and princely demeanor to be held ever present before the eyes of the papal nephew. More than a dry catalogue of moral exempla, the cycle of painted ceilings for the young prince's suite was to inspire his actions as well as to mirror his virtue.

Taddeo may have been well pleased with the majestic palace and its sumptuous painted imagery, but his wife was not. In his biography of Taddeo, Cardinal Francesco states that Donna Anna disliked the quality of the air on the Quirinal.[86] An *avviso* of 14 October 1634 adds detail to this explanation, noting that Taddeo and his family were constrained to move out because of the excessive humidity still encountered in the newly finished building.[87] Cardinal Francesco also provides the candid reason why this bad air provoked such concern. Donna Anna wanted to return to the Casa Grande because she had given birth to two male children there, whereas the child born at the new palace was female. A fourth child was anticipated, and she wished it to be another son.[88] Taddeo apparently found this argument persuasive. In the fall of 1634, after having lived at the palace near the Four Fountains for only two years, Taddeo and his family abandoned the new building to return to their old house on the Via de' Giubbonari.[89] Soon thereafter Cardinal Antonio the Younger took up residence in the north wing of the family palace on the Quirinal.[90]

CARDINAL FRANCESCO'S REDECORATION OF THE PIANO TERRENO APARTMENT (1678)

Long after the deaths of both Taddeo and Anna, Cardinal Francesco, in 1678, redecorated the piano terreno apartment preparatory to making it suitable as a gallery for the display of painting and sculpture (Fig. 7).[91] By that time the *Hercules at the Crossroads* and the *Bellerophon Slaying the Chimera* must already have been in a ruinous state. Thus, retaining only Camassei's *Parnassus*, Francesco commissioned artists to repaint both of the vaults that originally held frescoes by Marziani. In addition, he ordered new works for the previously

---

much given to the study of military affairs. Books of Urban's poetry are listed amid quantities of treatises on engineering, warfare, and fortifications. Three works in particular seem significant, if not surprising: F. Contelori, *De Praefecto Urbis*; F. Bracciolini, *L'elettione di Urbano Papa VIII*; and N. Machiavelli, *Il principe*. BAV, Arch. Barb., Ind. II, 2442, unpaginated.

[84] ASR, Notai del Tribunale del Auditor Camerae, Istromenti, Notaio Jacobus Simoncellus, 6601, 883r–884v. I thank Patricia Waddy for this suggestion and reference.

[85] The only other room in the suite that would have been available for such activities was that at the extreme northwest corner of the wing (PBT 9). The two rooms to the south (PBT 10–11) functioned respec-

tively as bedchamber and small service room. The rooms beyond the *Bellerophon* (PBT 9–11), in any case, must have been devoted to very practical and private affairs because no thought seems to have been given to painting the vaults there.

[86] BAV, Arch. Barb., Ind. IV, 1254, unpaginated.

[87] Ademollo, *Teatri di Roma*, 8.

[88] BAV, Arch. Barb., Ind. IV, 1254, unpaginated.

[89] Ademollo, *Teatri di Roma*, 8.

[90] Beginning 1 February 1635. Waddy, *Seventeenth-Century Roman Palaces*, 244.

[91] Waddy (ibid., 258–60, 265) has identified the alterations in the piano terreno suite made during Cardinal Francesco's activity there in 1678.

undecorated private rooms (PBT 9–11), since these, too, were now to be accessible to visitors. The new program, however, was little more than an elaboration of Taddeo's original cycle, a further spinning out of the details of the ode Maffeo had presented to Francesco more than sixty years earlier.

Montagu's analysis of this cycle includes the publication of the artists' payment documents and an explication of the program in terms of the "Ode Hortatoria ad Virtutem."[92] A certain Giacinto Camassei, a relative or perhaps student of Andrea, replaced the *Hercules at the Crossroads* with *Ulysses and the Sirens* (Fig. 73).[93] The hero, protected by Minerva to his right, outwits the Sirens and escapes the fatal allurement of their seductive song.[94] Inclusion of Minerva in the scene indicates the influence of Annibale's version of the same subject in one of the ancillary scenes of the Farnese Camerino (Fig. 150).[95] In his exegesis of the Farnese painting Giovan Pietro Bellori observes that the presence of Minerva has no basis in Homer but rather is represented by Annibale in order to show the "divine assistance" received by Ulysses.[96] Bellori also notes that Homer used this fable to symbolize that "if man wishes to escape calamity and misfortune he must close his ears to voluptuousness and bind himself to the mast of reason."[97] In his commentary on Maffeo's poem, Magno Perneo states that Ulysses represents temperance, meaning the denial of sensual pleasures,[98] and this may be taken as the essential significance of the Barberini ceiling.

With the elimination of *Hercules at the Crossroads*, a change occurred in the program of the new series of ceiling paintings in the piano terreno apartment. The viewer no longer encounters a choice, but rather sees voluptuousness successfully resisted. Although the composition of *Ulysses and the Sirens* takes inspiration from Annibale's version, the artist made significant adjustments in order to link the image formally and programmatically to the *Parnassus* in the following room. In construction and ornamentation, Camassei's version of Ulysses' ship recalls that of Annibale, but on a more modest scale. Both run parallel to the picture plane, with Ulysses in the center and the Sirens on the left.

The most telling modification introduced in the Barberini painting appears in the relationship between Ulysses and the Sirens. In Annibale's fresco the hero dominates the picture field in the center foreground. Camassei changed this by moving the Sirens from the background to the foreground, thus giving them an emphasis they lacked in the prototype. A twofold purpose lies behind this adjustment. With the emphasis given to the Sirens, the parallel between their song of pleasure and the hymn of virtue sung by the Muses on Parnassus, in the next room, emerges with greater clarity for the viewer's edification. Perhaps this arrangement was also intended to bring to mind the singing contest between the Sirens and the Muses recounted in the *Metamorphoses* (5:294–678), which resulted in the defeat of

[92] Each of the three painters involved in the project received a total of 30 scudi issued in two payments (12 May and 25 June 1678). BAV, Arch. Barb., Comp. 91, 213r, 229r. Montagu, "Exhortatio ad Virtutem," 366–72. To these should be added the *giustificazioni* of the payments: BAV, Arch. Barb., Giust. 12566–12622, 17r, 216v–217r.

[93] Pascoli, *Vite de' pittori*, 1:44; Harris, "Camassei Studies," 66; Montagu, "Exhortatio ad Virtutem," 368–69.

[94] *Odyssey*, 12:155–205.

[95] The Camerino scenes were engraved by Pietro Aquila and published in 1674. Martin, *Farnese Gallery*, 23, n. 3.

[96] Bellori, *Vite de' pittori*, 52–53. The addition of the goddess in the Camerino painting seems to have been the invention of Fulvio Orsini.

[97] Ibid. I use the translation from G. P. Bellori, *The Lives of Annibale & Agostino Carracci*, trans. C. Enggass (University Park, Pa., 1968), 25.

[98] BAV, Barb. Lat. 3307, 691r.

the former and, as just punishment, their transformation into magpies. Secondly, the programmatic continuity of the vault imagery becomes evident when, in the *Parnassus*, the four heroes occupy a position on the left side comparable to that held by the Sirens in the preceding ceiling. Thus vice is replaced by virtue. In the first ceiling Ulysses successfully resists the alluring song of sensuality; in the second, he, together with the other heroes, heeds the elevating chorus of the Muses.[99]

The three other virtuous heroes—Bellerophon, Theseus, and Jason—appear in the smaller private rooms at the extreme western end of the northern wing (PBT 8–10). Marziani's ruined *Bellerophon Slaying the Chimera* (PBT 8) was repainted by Giuseppe Passeri (Fig. 74), as discussed above. This was followed by an entirely new painting on the vault of the succeeding room (PBT 9, Fig. 75), *Theseus and Ariadne by the Labyrinth*, painted by Urbano Romanelli.[100] The scene shows Ariadne providing Theseus with a ball of thread to assist him in finding his way out of the maze after killing the centaur.[101] Here the labyrinth symbolizes worldly pleasure, and Theseus represents prudence.[102] The cupids above the couple seem to show love as the motivation behind Ariadne's crucial assistance.

The last of the four heroes of Maffeo's poem appears on the ceiling of the small chamber (PBT 10) immediately to the south of the room with *Bellerophon*. Painted by Giuseppe Passeri, the *Jason and the Argonauts with the Golden Fleece* represents Jason aboard his ship the *Argo* (Fig. 76).[103] The hero holds his skillfully gained prize, the Golden Fleece, and is supported by Medea, Jason's wife and sorceress, who was responsible for his successes.[104] As a representation of the triumph of virtue over vice, the allegorical meaning of this scene parallels those depicting the other heroes. The dragon slain by Jason, which had guarded the Golden Fleece, embodies vice. Medea, paradoxically, symbolizes the aid of reason in the attainment of virtue (the Golden Fleece).[105] According to Perneo, Jason symbolizes fortitude,[106] making complete the series of the cardinal virtues as represented by the four Greek heroes.

[99] The dichotomy between lascivious pleasures and literary pursuits symbolized by the Sirens and the Muses is expounded in emblematic literature, especially in Alciati's discussion of the emblem depicting Ulysses and the Sirens. Alciati, *Emblemata*, Emblem CXVI, 490–93.

[100] The son of Giovanni Francesco Romanelli. Baldinucci, *Professori del disegno*, 5:435–36; I. Faldi, *Pittori viterbesi di cinque secoli* (Rome, 1970), 72–73. See Montagu, "Exhortatio ad Virtutem," 368 and n. 4. This fresco, which, together with the others of the piano terreno, was restored 1962–1970 (Faldi, *Galleria Nazionale d'Arte Antica*, 84), had already suffered irreparable damage. The entire central portion of the *intonaco* collapsed in 1968, and the shattered pieces could be only partially reassembled. Ariadne's entire right arm and the ball of thread have been lost.

[101] Ovid, *Metamorphoses*, 8:169–74; Plutarch, *Lives*, 1:19.

[102] Picinelli, *Mundus Symbolicus*, 1: 173, 2: 66; Perneo, BAV, Barb. Lat. 3307, 691r.

[103] Faldi, *Galleria Nazionale d'Arte Antica*, 82; Montagu, "Exhortatio ad Virtutem," 368–69. For a discussion of the preparatory drawing in the Kunstmuseum Düsseldorf (FP 2254), see E. Schaar, *Italienische Handzeichnungen des Barock aus den Beständen des Kupferstichkabinetts im Kunstmuseum Düsseldorf* (Düsseldorf, 1964), no. 120; D. Graf, "Der römische Maler Giuseppe Passeri als Zeichner," *Münchner Jahrbuch der bildenden Kunst* 30 (1977), 135–38, fig. 3.

[104] Apollonius Rhodius, *Argonautica*, bk. 3; Ovid, *Metamorphoses*, 7:1–159.

[105] This is the interpretation given by Malvasia (*Felsina pittrice*, 2:368–73) in his discussion of the Carracci frieze of the same subject in Palazzo Fava in Bologna (ca. 1583–1584). D. Posner, *Annibale Carracci* (London, 1971), 2: 9. For a similar interpretation of the story of Jason as an allegory of virtue, with the Fleece signifying honor and glory, see C. Goldstein, "Louis XIV and Jason," *Art Bulletin* 49 (1967), 327–28.

[106] Perneo, BAV, Barb. Lat. 3307, 691r.

At the same time that the other rooms received narrative scenes, a small chamber (PBT 11), formerly a service room adjoining Taddeo's bedroom (PBT 10), was painted by Urbano Romanelli with a modest *quadro riportato* image of a *Putto on Amphora* (Fig. 77).[107] The emblematic image of a putto sailing across the sea on an amphora derives from an antique gem in the collection of Cardinal Francesco.[108] Bellori's engraved illustration of the gem shows that the neck of the urn was to have on it a bee. In the fresco the bee is no longer in evidence, but, as Montagu has demonstrated, this image was an impresa of Cardinal Francesco.[109] The meaning of the impresa remains somewhat obscure, but, in interpreting the gem, Walter Robert-Tornow suggested that the urn is funerary and that the bee symbolizes the resurrection of the ashes contained within. The motto ET ULTRA (And Beyond) alludes to the eternal life embodied in the bee as a symbol of apotheosis.[110] Recapitulating the basic theme of Maffeo's poem and of the entire painted cycle—immortality achieved through virtue—this personal emblem of Francesco served as a fitting conclusion to the new series of vault images. The motto also makes witty allusion to its location as the conclusion of the piano terreno cycle. One can go beyond this point only by ascending the spiral stairs (PBT S5).[111]

The cycle of ceiling paintings commissioned by Cardinal Francesco in 1678 serves as a documented case of how the painted imagery of rooms en suite was programmatically linked. It also demonstrates again how the imagery from an earlier cycle located in the same rooms had considerable impact on a new program.

[107] Faldi, *Galleria Nazionale d'Arte Antica*, 86–87; Montagu, "Exhortatio ad Virtutem," 368–69.

[108] G. P. Bellori, *Notae in Numismata tum Ephesia, tum Aliarum Urbium Apibus Insignita* (Rome, 1658), pl. VII; Montagu, "Exhortatio ad Virtutem," 368–69.

[109] Ibid., 369, esp. n. 13.

[110] W. Robert-Tornow, *De Apium Mellisque apud Ve-teres Significatione et Symbolica et Mythologica* (Berlin, 1893), 134.

[111] Montagu ("Exhortatio ad Virtutem," 368) also publishes a payment for scaffolding, which indicates that even the tiny vault adjacent to these stairs was painted with a bee.

PART III

- # The Salone Fresco: Cortona's *Divine Providence*

CHAPTER X

• Genesis and Execution: "It Took Me Longer Than I Thought"

THE CENTERPIECE of the entire pictorial project at Palazzo Barberini was to be Cortona's fresco on the vault of the palace salone (Colorplates III and IV, Fig. 80). Almost immediately upon its unveiling, contemporaries responded to this monumental work with both acclaim and criticism. Classicizing artists like Poussin faulted it for offensive foreshortenings, inconsistent lighting, and excessive spatial illusionism.[1] Even the program of the painting irritated some observers—individuals perhaps already critical of nepotistic ostentation—because of its apparent secularizing aggrandizement of a reigning pontiff.[2]

Misconceptions about the meaning of the salone fresco have still not been put entirely to rest. In modern scholarship critical assessment has taken a different but no less erroneous form, seeing the expansive pictorial apparatus as little more than an example of rhetorical excess and shameless self-promotion. Although the salone painting may not be totally acquitted of these offenses, this anachronistic approach adds little to our understanding of the meaning of the work. If the original intentions of artist, adviser, and patrons are to be grasped, we must seek to penetrate the barrier of incomprehensibility subsequently erected by the transformation of political and cultural values.

Cortona's fresco must be seen in the context of the traditional papal and nepotic iconography whose culmination it represents. Like Sacchi's *Divine Wisdom* and Camassei's *Creation of the Angels*, Cortona's *Divine Providence* memorializes the election of Urban VIII and the Barberini family to the highest office in Christendom. Early skepticism about the political decorum of the imagery reflects not the failure of artist or poet, nor even the excessive worldly ambitions of Barberini pope and nephews, so much as the passing of an epochal moment in the history of the papacy, after which Europe could turn its back on the political will of the popes.

ARCHITECTURAL MATRIX

The determination to cover the salone (Fig. 78) with a masonry vault was an unusual choice and implied an intention to commission a painted ceiling; it was not common to cover a *sala dei palafrenieri* with such a vast uninterrupted vault structure. Comparable large guard-

---

[1] M. Beal, *A Study of Richard Symonds: His Italian Notebooks and Their Relevance to Seventeenth-Century Painting Techniques* (New York-London, 1984), 45–47.

[2] See the guarded response of Domenichino to news he received in Naples about the salone painting as being more worthy of a secular prince. Appendix G. Francesco Angeloni (ca. 1559–1652), Domenichino's correspondent in Rome, was an antiquarian and art collector. He served as secretary to Cardinal Ippolito Aldobrandini. *DBI*, III, 241–242.

rooms in Roman secular palaces of the sixteenth and early seventeenth centuries display ornately coffered, flat wood-beamed ceilings. Palazzo Farnese provided one of the grandest examples (Fig. 151), one the Barberini would not have overlooked. It represented the culmination of an architectural tradition and a metaphor of the status of the old nepotic family most admired by the inhabitants of the modest Casa Grande on the nearby Via de' Giubbonari. For the Barberini, this was the model to surpass—which they did, by four meters in length.[3]

In two earlier designs for palace saloni of lesser dimensions Maderno had already provided possible solutions. Both the Borghese Garden Palace on the Quirinal (Fig. 152), today the Palazzo Rospigliosi-Pallavicini, and Palazzo Mattei di Giove contain large saloni with masonry vaults.[4] Despite the break with tradition, however, these vaulting systems were interrupted with numerous window embrasures and allowed for only restricted fields of pictorial imagery in the central sections of the vault. The *quadro riportato* stucco enframements of the fresco scenes on these vaults further diminished the impact of the pictorial element and the potential for illusionistic display. In the Barberini salone Maderno eliminated the stucco moldings and lowered the windows to wall level below the cornice, leaving the entire surface of the vault free of interruptions or decorative encrustations. This deviation from tradition provided a vast pictorial field and indicated that unusual plans were in the making.

The model for the vault and painted ceiling of the salone was not to be found in secular palaces but in the Vatican Palace of Sixtus V. The Sala Clementina (1592–1595) is a *sala dei palafrenieri* of approximately the same size as the Barberini salone[5] and has a continuous vaulted ceiling frescoed with papal imagery (Fig. 164).[6] Even the loggia-like superimposed levels of arched windows in the western facade of Palazzo Barberini recall the loggia of the Cortile di San Damaso that abuts the Sala Clementina.[7] Appreciation of this model provides insight into the motivations of the patrons of Palazzo Barberini. The salone was to be unlike that in any other secular residence of the city. Its design and decoration reflect the combined secular and ecclesiastical aspirations of the family. The Barberini were not just another Roman baronial family but one of pontifical rank.

The structure of the vault was closed in September 1630,[8] and the choice of an artist to paint its surface must have been under consideration in the subsequent months. Sacchi,

[3] For a discussion of the traditional form and function of the salone, or *sala dei palafrenieri*, in Roman palaces of the Renaissance, see C. L. Frommel, *Der römische Palastbau der Hochrenaissance* (Tübingen, 1973), 1:66–70. The salone of Palazzo Barberini measures 24.7 × 14.7 meters, as compared with the 20.65 × 14.3 meters of the Farnese salone.

[4] For the salone of the Borghese Garden Palace (19.3 × 13.3 meters) and the heraldic fresco by Bernardo Castelli (1616), see H. Hibbard, "Scipione Borghese's Garden Palace on the Quirinal," *Journal of the Society of Architectural Historians* 23 (1964), 163–92, esp. 184, and Hibbard, *Carlo Maderno*, 192–94. On the salone of Palazzo Mattei (approx. 11 × 13 meters), ibid., 127–29.

[5] The Vatican sala, constructed by Taddeo Landini for Clement VIII, measures 25.5 × 12.5 meters, about

a meter longer and two meters shorter than the Barberini salone. Both rooms were unusually large in comparison with the saloni of other Roman palaces of the fifteenth and sixteenth centuries. On the design and authorship of the Sala Clementina, see J. Wasserman, "The Palazzo Sisto V in the Vatican," *Journal of the Society of Architectural Historians* 21 (1962), esp. 35. For a discussion of the relative sizes of saloni in Roman palaces of the Renaissance, see Frommel, *Römische Palastbau*, 1:67–69.

[6] Below, 161–63.

[7] Waddy, "Design and Designers," 177.

[8] Francesco provided a lunch for the workmen on this occasion. M. A. Lavin, *Documents and Inventories*, 48. Also, BAV, Arch. Barb., Comp. 50, 79r, 31 October 1630.

Camassei, and Cortona were all at work in the north wing by early the following year. The decision must have depended to some degree on the success of those endeavors. Particularly satisfied with Camassei's performance, Taddeo backed him for the salone project. Graphic evidence of the artist's preliminary intentions for a corner of the coved vault appears in a large drawing at Chatsworth (Fig. 79).[9] The impaled coat of arms divided vertically between Barberini bees, faintly indicated on the left, and the Colonna column, on the right, emphasizes Taddeo's patronage, just as the princely crown above the escutcheon and the flanking personifications of Armed Virtue and the Tiber must allude to the patron's titles of prince of Palestrina, general of the Church, and prefect of Rome. Prudence, seated apart on the right, suggests that the full complement of the cardinal virtues was to be present in the ceiling. The terminal figures with linked arms show that Camassei's inspiration came from the Farnese Gallery (Fig. 127), and the putto holding the crown demonstrates knowledge of the Cortonesque *stemma in arrivo* of the small gallery (Fig. 68) and piano terreno salotto (Fig. 71). The absence of any attempt at spatial illusionism may have been perceived by the patrons as less than imaginative, and a disconcerting shift of scale between Prudence and the other figures may also have proven detrimental to Camassei's bid for the salone commission. Passeri reports that Camassei was actually awarded the commission, but, in the end, thanks to the intervention of Giulio Sacchetti, Francesco Barberini, and a certain unnamed Jesuit father, Urban overturned the decision and designated Cortona instead.[10]

Sacchetti's role in this choice indicates his satisfaction with Cortona's work in the vaulted gallery of the cardinal's villa at Castelfusano, where the artist successfully demonstrated his organizational abilities in supervising a group of painters and bringing to completion a large-scale ceiling project.[11] These qualities, essential to the monumental task at hand in the salone, were demonstrably beyond those possessed by Camassei, but the change in commission may equally reflect a rivalry among the Barberini nephews. Cardinal Francesco was sponsoring Cortona's work in the north wing and had become the artist's principal patron at this time. He paid for all of Cortona's work in the palace, including the frescoes in the chapel and garden apartment.[12] Each nephew pushed for his own favorite. But the outcome was perhaps inevitable. Urban's role in the affair was not just as neutral arbiter, however, since Cortona had already been favored with papal commissions.[13] Moreover, the incident confirms the pope's involvement even at the inception of the salone project. Sandrart reports that Urban came frequently from his summer residence, the nearby Palazzo del Quirinale, to observe Cortona at work on the vault.[14]

[9] Chatsworth, no. 653 (29.2 x 40.7 cm.), with extensive application of watercolor in the draperies of the figures. Identified and analyzed by A. S. Harris, "Camassei et Pierre de Cortone au Palais Barberini," *Revue de l'art* 81 (1988), 73–76, who also associates with the salone drawing a figure study of Rome (fig. 3), which was on the art market in New York in 1988. M. Jaffé, *Old Master Drawings from Chatsworth* (Alexandria, Va., 1987–1988), 114, cat. 66, colorplate 10, attributed the drawing to Romanelli.

[10] Passeri, *Die Kunstlerbiographien*, 169–70, 378–79. J. Hess ("Maps and Globes," 379, n. 4) hypothesized that the Jesuit father was Giovanni Domenico Otto-

nelli, who subsequently collaborated with Cortona in the production of a treatise. Below, 159 and n. 152.

[11] On Cortona's work at Castelfusano, consult Briganti, *Pietro da Cortona*, 177–80.

[12] For the amount and exceptional mode of payment to Cortona, see Appendix E.

[13] The fresco cycle in the church of Santa Bibiana (1624–1626) and the *Trinity* altarpiece for the Cappella del Sacramento at St. Peter's (1628–1631). Briganti, *Pietro da Cortona*, 167–70, 187–90.

[14] J. von Sandrart, *Academie der Bau-, Bild- und Mahlerey-Künste*, ed. A. R. Peltzer (Munich, 1925), 287.

CHRONOLOGY OF WORK

Owing to the unusual thoroughness of the records kept by Cardinal Francesco's accountants, the progress of work on the salone ceiling can be traced in detail. The wood for the scaffold was acquired in early fall 1631,[15] and the structure was in place by June of the following year when the carpenter was paid.[16] The design and erection of the scaffold presented a particular problem, not only because of the vastness of the ceiling but because the salone had to be kept open at floor level to allow access to the piano nobile apartment in the north wing.

A general impression of the solution can be gained from the payments for construction and dismantling of the structure. These documents mention three types of structures. A principal platform ("ponte grande") was supported at cornice level by four reinforced wood beams resting on the side cornices at the base of the vault and spanning the width of the room.[17] Holes were made in the crown of the vault so that chains attached to the structural members above could carry the weight of each beam.[18] There were two chains per beam. Wood planks were placed across the beams to provide a platform under that area where the artist and his assistants were working at any given time. This scaffold system left unobstructed the room below. A smaller, probably semi-mobile, scaffold ("sopra ponte") was erected upon this so that the higher areas of the vault could be reached.[19] Two secondary structures ("ponti") supported stairs giving access to the main platform from one of the mezzanine windows above the oval room and from a door opened in the upper wall toward the south, near the spiral stairs.[20] Periodic payments for wood planks indicate that the floor of

[15] BAV, Arch. Barb., Comp. 192, 71r, 25 September 1631 (Taddeo); SCEP, Quaderno de' sig.ri Barberini, 1631–1633, 45, 7 October 1631 (Taddeo). Transcribed in Pollak, *Die Kunsttätigkeit* 1:327.

[16] BAV, Arch. Barb., Ind. IV, 13, 9 June 1632 (Taddeo); Arch. Barb., Comp. 192, 154r, 9 July 1632 (Taddeo); SCEP, Quaderno de' sig.ri Barberini, 1631–1633, 90 (Taddeo). Transcribed in Pollak, *Die Kunsttätigkeit*, 1:327.

[17] "Per spese fatte per farli ponti del salone del Pal. alle 4 fontane, e per levare il ponte grande, et il sopraponte dove dipingeva il S. Pietro." BAV, Arch. Barb., Comp. 70, 115, 31 December 1641 (Francesco). "Per la tirat.ra e mett.ra in opera di no. 4 travi di long.a p. 75 p. fare il ponte alli pittori p. la volta del salone con haver messo li suoi staffoni e paletti e catene che posano s.a la volta sc. 10." ASR, Congregazioni Religiose Maschili, Teatini S. Andrea della Valle, 2200, int. 229, pt. 2, 70. Transcribed in Magnanimi, "Documenti della costruzione," 213.

[18] "Per la tiratura e mettitura in opera di n.o 4 travi messi per fare il ponte per li pittori per dipingere la volta del salone con haverci messo due staffoni per ciascuno trave, e sbugiato la volta e attaccato le catene a detti staffoni per ciascun trave e con suoi paletti sopra detta volta, scudi 10, per aver fatto il ponte per accomodare la scala dove ha da salire il pittore per andare a dipingere, che passa per la finestra del mezzanino in

tutta la sala verso la stanza ovata . . . , scudi 1.60" (prob. May 1632). ASR, Notai del Tribunale del Auditor Camerae, Istromenti, Notaio Dominicus Fonthia, 3175, 1009r. Transcribed in Verdi, "Fonte documentarie," 94–95, doc. 3.

[19] The crown of the vault was approximately 4.5 meters above the platform of the *ponte grande*.

[20] "Per haver fatto il ponte p. fare la scala che salì dalla fenestri del sal.e al ponte grande, scudi 1.60." ASR, Congregazioni Religiose Maschili, Teatini S. Andrea della Valle, 2200, int. 229, 35v. Transcribed in Magnanimi, "Documenti della costruzione," 213. "Per aver fatto una porticella nel muro acciò li pittori potessero andare sopra li ponti per dipingere la volta del salone, scudi 3.20" (prob. March 1635). ASR, Congregazioni Religiose Maschili, Teatini S. Andrea della Valle, 2200, int. 230, 58v. Transcribed in Verdi, "Fonti documentarie," 95, doc. 4. On the location of this little door in the Stanza delle Medaglie near the top of the elliptical staircase, consult Fiore, "Palazzo Barberini," 199. "Per haver fatto le scale per dipingere la volta del salone . . . sc. 2.40." BAV, Arch. Barb., Giust. 2315–2416, 93r, 1 April 1635 (Francesco). The new door and stairs were required only as work on the vault progressed toward the western end of the salone. This would seem to indicate that the fresco was at least half completed by this time.

the main platform was shifted about as work on the fresco progressed.[21] Because of the openness of the structure, and the possibility of shifting the planking, the artist was able to test periodically the visual effectiveness of his work from floor level without having to dismantle the scaffold. The flexibility of the design was demonstrated in early December 1637 when Francesco d'Este visited the palace and Cortona's assistants uncovered the partially completed fresco for his viewing.[22] This visual accessibility constituted an important advantage for Cortona since it enabled him to control such important factors as figure scale and relationships, color intensity, and spatial illusionism, and to adjust his work accordingly as the project proceeded.

The function and security of the scaffold were of concern to the painter, and, as Pozzo's treatise advises,[23] Cortona likely participated in its design and construction. Even with its ingenious design and all precautions taken, disaster was not avoided, as records a document of 6 November 1636 paying for the burial of "a poor mason who fell from the painters' platform in the salone."[24]

Cortona and his assistants, Romanelli, Baldini, and Bottalla,[25] began work on the salone vault in July 1632.[26] Since their work in the north wing was probably not finished

---

[21] 20 December 1632: "Ricordo del . . . numero quatro cento trenta cinque tavole di Castagnio quale forno messe p il palgo nella Sala per depingere la Volta. . . . 435." Transcribed in M. A. Lavin, *Documents and Inventories*, 13. 28 April 1636: "Per far ponti nel salone per li pittori . . . 40 piane d'Ischio capate a b. 15 l'una, [scudi] 6." BAV, Arch. Barb., Giust. 2685–2742, 156r (Francesco). Transcribed in Verdi, "Fonti documentarie," 97, doc. 23.

[22] BAV, Arch. Barb., Comp. 224, 93r (gior., 1636–1644). Published by Verdi, "Fonti documentarie," 97, doc. 27. Below, 131–32 and n. 41, 193 and n. 4.

[23] "Ancorchè il primo, che si deve esporre al pericolo sia il muratore, deve pero nondimeno considerar anche il pittore a che sostegno commette la sua vita; ne perchè quello più arrischiato non teme il precizio, per questo dobbiamo esporci alla ventura; perchè finalmente l'altrui buona sorte non puo assicurarci dalla caduta." A. Pozzo, "Breve istruzione per dipingere a fresco," in *Perspectiva Pictorum et Architectorum* (Rome, 1693–1702), pt. 2, appendix (reprinted in *Il voltone di Pietro da Cortona in Palazzo Barberini*, Quaderni di Palazzo Venezia 2 [1983], 49–52, and Mora et al., *Conservation*, 392–99). Eng. trans. in M. P. Merrifield, *The Art of Fresco Painting as Practised by the Old Italian and Spanish Masters* (London, 1952), 53–60. The travel diary of the English painter Richard Symonds (in Italy 1649–1651) includes an important discussion of fresco technique as practiced by the Roman fresco painter Giovanni Angelo Canini (1609–1666). See Beal, *Richard Symonds*, 163–80.

[24] "Sc. 3.60 al curato di Sta. Susanna per haver fatto sepellire un povere muratore che cascò dalli palezi delli pittori nella sala grande." BAV, Arch. Barb., Comp.

224, 38v, 6 November 1636 (Antonio).

[25] Giovanni Maria Bottalla (Savona 1613–Milan 1644), called "Il Raffaellino," became associated with Cortona through the protection of Cardinal Giulio Sacchetti. *DBI*, 13: 404–5. By 1634 he was on the *rolo di famiglia* of Francesco, together with Romanelli and Baldini. The major study on this short-lived artist is by M. Migliorini, "Gio. Maria Bottalla, un savonese alla scuola di Pietro da Cortona," *Società Savonese di Storia Patria, atti e memorie* 12 (1978), 75–85. For Romanelli and Baldini, see above, 35–36, 50, 107.

[26] Scudi 45.22½ "per un conto di diverse spese fatte et maestranze di muratori e manovali, che hanno lavorato da luglio in qua et per tutto agosto prossimo passato alla sala grande del palazzo nuovo alle 4 Fontane." BAV, Arch. Barb., Comp. 80, 71r, 17 September 1632 (Francesco). Transcribed in Verdi, "Fonti documentarie," 95, doc. 7. It is likely that this payment was for the *arriccio*, the preliminary layer of rough plaster applied to the vault. But some painting activity may have begun as early as late August or early September. Scudi 29 ". . . per giornate date dal muratore in far le colle a Pietro cortonese che *dipinge* la volta grande del palazzo alle 4 fontane; e per far levare l'iscritione e altro dal deposito del Barelai il tutto sino alli 15 del corrente mese." BAV, Arch. Barb., Comp. 80, 77v, 18 November 1632 (Francesco). Transcribed in Verdi, "Fonti documentarie," 95, doc. 8. The removal of the inscription would have been a negligible expense, probably no more than 1 scudo. Thus, if the remainder, 87 scudi, is divided by the daily wage for the *muratore*, 4 giuli or .4 scudi, the payment indicates that the *muratore* had by 15 November already worked seventy days in applying the *intonaco* for Cortona.

until March or April of that year,[27] a hiatus of no more than two or three months existed between the two campaigns. The most important documents for following Cortona's work on the ceiling might at first sight appear the least significant. These are the monthly payments made to the workmen who daily applied the fresh plaster (*intonaco*) to the vault. Since fresco technique requires that pigment be applied while the plaster is still wet, each day Cortona worked directly on the ceiling a *muratore* (mason) was present to apply the plaster to the section of the vault to be painted that day.[28] These workmen were paid on a monthly basis, with the number of days worked indicated on the payment document. Payments to the *muratori* therefore reflect the days Cortona was active in the salone. The table charts the payments by year and month and provides the chronology of Cortona's activity.[29] These financial data, combined with information contained in early biographies of the artist, provide an account of Cortona's struggle with the monumental assignment.

Days of Work Paid to the *Muratori*

	1632	1633	1634	1635	1636	1637	1638
Jan.		0	26	23	22	21	33
Feb.		0	25	25	23	22	23
Mar.		0	26	24	23	23	*
Apr.		25	25	0	25	23	44
May		18	17	25	23	25	22
June		24	24	23	24	20	23
July	*	25	23	16	24	0	23
Aug.	*	20	22	*	21	0	25
Sept.	*	*	25	43	31	0	25
Oct.	*	51	23	26	21	0	21
Nov.	113	26	23	27	22	0	20
Dec.	0	25	22	18	21	0	10

* = payment combined with following month
Total days of work = 1,541
Total days of work after application of *arriccio* (beginning April 1633) = 1,428

The first five months of work (July–November 1632) were taken up with preparing the surface of the vault, making preliminary designs for the painting, and squaring off the pictorial field. Pozzo outlines what was the traditional Roman technique. The first coat of plaster to be applied to the surface is called the *arriccio*, or rough plasterwork.[30] Because of the humidity and noxious odor emitted by wet *arriccio*, it was considered unhealthful to begin applying the second layer, or *intonaco*, until well after the *arriccio* was thoroughly dry.[31] Concern over this procedure may partly explain the break in work on the vault during the damp winter months, from December through March of the following year

---

[27] Above, 34–36.

[28] The technique seems to have varied slightly from region to region according to the quality of locally available materials. Pozzo's treatise provides what must have been the standard practice in Rome throughout the seventeenth century (pt. 2, appendix). For a sum-

mary of fresco procedure as practiced in the Renaissance and Baroque periods, consult Mora et al., *Conservation*, 144–56.

[29] Appendix D for documentation of the table.

[30] Pozzo, "Breve istruzione," pt. 2, appendix.

[31] Ibid.

(1633), but Cortona may also have been absorbed at this time in painting the ceiling of the sacristy at Santa Maria in Vallicella,[32] and in marking into squares the surface of the vault of the salone preparatory to commencing the actual fresco work.[33] Thereafter, however, two years of uninterrupted labor followed. From April 1633 through March 1635 Cortona averaged twenty-four days of work monthly, suspending activity only on Sundays and feast days. The complete cessation of work in April 1635 is mysterious, particularly since it is followed by another two-year period of intense effort (averaging twenty-three days per month).[34] This sudden stoppage corroborates the recent discovery that Cortona painted the ceiling of the Sacchetti Villa del Pigneto in 1635.[35] Likewise, the reduced number of workdays in July of the same year must reflect Cortona's work on Urban's small private chapel at the Vatican, for which he was paid in September.[36]

The last suspension of work appears between July and December 1637 while Cortona was away on a trip to Florence and northern Italy.[37] The documented fact that no actual work was conducted on the ceiling at this time helps to clarify the nature of the conspiracy of Romanelli and Bottalla as recounted by Baldinucci.[38] As Cortona's absence from Rome became extended[39] and Cardinal Francesco grew anxious over the lack of progress on the ceiling, and perhaps concerned over the artist's will and ability to complete it, Cortona's assistants, with the help of the still miffed Taddeo, began to spread word of their desire to finish the fresco according to their own designs. This they sought to accomplish with the aid of certain unspecified "vile rabble," and even by seeking to enlist the support of casual visitors to the palace.[40] Romanelli and Bottalla received a gratuity from Cardinal Francesco for showing the unfinished fresco to one such visitor, Francesco d'Este, who toured the palace

[32] Because the final payment for the sacristy vault was not made to Cortona until 12 January 1634 (Pollak, *Die Kunsttätigkeit*, 1:436), Briganti (*Pietro da Cortona*, 139) opted to date the Vallicella fresco toward the end of 1633, but the final payment is not likely to have been so prompt. The payment for planking for the scaffolding had already occurred on 4 September 1632 (Pollak, *Die Kunsttätigkeit*, 1:433), so that the sacristy vault would have been accessible to Cortona by at least December 1632 just when the break in work at Palazzo Barberini occurred. Cortona therefore must have painted the sacristy vault between December 1632 and March 1633.

[33] For the procedure, called graticulation (*graticolare*), see Pozzo, "Breve istruzione," pt. 2, appendix.

[34] This hiatus must also reflect the shifting of Cortona's efforts to the completion of the fresco and stucco decoration in the Chapel of the Concezione (project completed by midsummer 1635; Pollak, *Die Kunsttätigkeit*, 1:1631) in San Lorenzo in Damaso, Cardinal Francesco's titular church at the Cancelleria, and to the frescoes of Urban's private chapel in the Appartamento Vecchio at the Vatican Palace. Payment made to Cortona 12 September 1635 (ibid., 1:385).

[35] Following a close reading of the early sources, Blunt ("Pietro da Cortona," 416) hypothesized a date

of 1634–1635 for the Pigneto gallery fresco.

[36] Pollak, *Die Kunsttätigkeit*, 1:385; Briganti, *Pietro da Cortona*, 208.

[37] As noted also by Verdi, "Fonti documentarie," 92. For the trip north, below, 154–57.

[38] F. Baldinucci, *Notizie de' professori del disegno . . . ,* ed. F. Ranalli (Florence, 1845–1847), 5: 419.

[39] See Cortona's response of 13 September 1637 to a letter from Cardinal Francesco, which apparently requested that the artist to return to Rome and resume work on the nearly finished salone ceiling. BAV, Barb. Lat. 6458, 96r. Transcribed in Campbell, *Pietro da Cortona*, doc. 3, 224–25.

[40] Baldinucci's son, F. S. Baldinucci, relates an earthier version of troubles between Cortona and his assistants. Bottalla, he reports, urinated in a bucket of plaster, which would have ruined an entire section of the fresco, except that a *muratore* saw him in the act and reported it to Cortona, who then fired all of his assistants. Whether this tale should be associated with the intrigue of 1637 or with some prior altercation is uncertain, but it emphasizes the difficulties Cortona encountered with his assistants. F. S. Baldinucci, *Vite di artisti dei secoli XVII–XVIII*, ed. A. Matteoli (Rome, 1975), 128–29.

in early December.[41] The precise nature of the assertions and deeds of the two assistants remains uncertain, but the lack of payments to the *muratori* proves that their plot had no material success.

Cortona arrived back in Rome on 15 December 1637, but what transpired subsequently is less certain. Some form of confrontation with the conspirators must have occurred. Baldinucci records that Cortona discharged both Romanelli and Bottalla,[42] and it does appear unlikely that Romanelli thereafter had any subsequent role in the salone ceiling. Beginning in the summer of 1637 while Cortona was away, Romanelli had already been commissioned to paint the Sala della Contessa Matilda in the Vatican Palace, and remained involved with that project throughout 1638 and 1639.[43] Bottalla and Baldini, however, seem to have remained with Cortona for the final campaign.

The Venetian painter-poet Marco Boschini makes no mention of Roman difficulties, but does assert that Cortona removed part of the fresco so he could repaint it according to what he had seen in Venice.[44] Ingeniously combining these two reports, Walter Vitzthum has hypothesized that Cortona returned to Rome enraged at the untrustworthy Romanelli and Bottalla and ripped out the part of the ceiling they had painted according to their own designs while he was away.[45] Knowledge of the break in payments to the *muratori* throughout the period Cortona was in the north now makes this explanation untenable. Because Boschini was a polemicist for Venetian art, scholars have been reluctant to accept his version of events,[46] but the available facts make his account plausible.

Boschini knew Cortona personally and served as his guide during the artist's second trip to Venice, in 1643–1644; hence, Cortona's praise of Venetian art as it appears in the poem may not be fairly dismissed as the invention of a fictionalizer distant from the artist. Boschini makes no distinction between the trip of 1637 and the later one, but his knowledge of Cortona was probably based mostly on the contact the two men had in 1643–1644. On that occasion Cortona must have told his guide of the earlier visit to Venice and its Roman aftermath. Far from being a chauvinistic fabrication, Boschini's statement that Cortona tore out what he had done in the Barberini salone upon returning to Rome reflects the artist's own words as he spoke of his admiration for Venetian art while he and his host visited the Doges' Palace and discussed its ensemble of painted ceilings. Furthermore, Cortona was still alive in 1660 when Boschini published the poem, and he was quite capable of refuting gross inaccuracies.

Other evidence is also consistent with Boschini's account. A letter of Giulio Rospigliosi, written from Rome on 5 June 1637, states that the salone fresco was nearly finished and that Cortona intended to complete it within that same month.[47] Rospigliosi may have

[41] BAV, Arch. Barb., Comp. 224, 93r. Transcribed in Verdi, "Fonti documentarie," 97, doc. 27 (12 December 1637).

[42] F. Baldinucci, *Professori del disegno,* 5:418–19.

[43] For work at the Vatican, see Pollak, *Die Kunsttätigkeit,* 1:389–90. Romanelli was away in Naples in late 1638 and early 1639. Pascoli, *Vite de' pittori,* 1:94.

[44] M. Boschini, *La carta del navegar pitoresco,* ed. A. Pallucchini (Venice-Rome, 1966), 521–22. Baldinucci follows Boschini on this point. F. Baldinucci,

Professori del disegno, 5:418–19.

[45] Vitzthum, "Review of *Pietro da Cortona,*" 216.

[46] Briganti, *Pietro da Cortona,* 86–87; T. S. Walmsley, "Evidence and Influence of Venetian Models and Precedents on Pietro da Cortona's Frescoed Decoration of the Gran Salone of the Palazzo Barberini in Rome," M.A. thesis, University of London, 1988, 8–9.

[47] BAV, Vat. Lat. 13362, 268r. Letter to the Balì Camillo, Rospigliosi's brother: "Io dalla Sig.ra Mre fa sapere che ordinai un quadro al Sig.e Pietro da Cortona

been out of touch with Cortona's intentions, for the artist departed for Florence, the ceiling still unfinished, less than two weeks later.[48] The significant point is that the vault was said to be almost finished in June 1637, although, as payments to the *muratori* show, Cortona continued to work intensively on the fresco for a full year after his return.[49] This suggests that Cortona either removed or covered over a sizable section of the ceiling.

Restoration work and technical analysis of the eastern end of the vault around the figure of Minerva conducted in 1981 have produced further evidence in favor of a radical loss of frescoed area. The restorer, Bruno Zanardi, counted 204 physical patches (*giornate*) of *intonaco* in the section of the vault analyzed. On the basis of this count he estimated that there are between 900 and 950 *giornate* in the entire fresco.[50] This compares with the total 1,428 days of work executed by the *muratori* after the *arriccio* had been applied. Even if it is allowed that the *muratori* produced no more than one patch of *intonaco* during a day's work, there is still a deficit of approximately 500 physical *giornate* in the ceiling, about one-third of the total number recorded in the payments.

This crude calculation establishes quantitative evidence of a loss of such large proportions that it cannot be accounted for by normal changes and reworkings; moreover, it is likely that more than one physical *giornata* was produced on many of the days the *muratori* worked. Cortona and individual assistants may have devoted themselves simultaneously to different *giornate*. Stylistic evidence indicates that Bottalla, for example, assisted with the Giants and some of the figures beneath Providence.[51] Possibly as many as four *giornate* were produced on some days, with Cortona working on a crucial figural section and assigning Romanelli, Bottalla, and Baldini to individual sections of the decorative framework or other less important areas of the painting. Such a procedure would mean the 1,428 days of *muratore* work reflect only a small portion of the number of *giornate* actually produced during the seven-and-one-half-year period of the campaign. In this case the difference between the number of *giornate* originally painted and the total present in the fresco would be even greater, indicating a loss much in excess of our original calculation. This line of reasoning adds support to Boschini's claim that Cortona changed the fresco upon his return to Rome, and to the speculations of Briganti and Campbell that much of what we see in the vault today was painted after the northern trip.[52]

The quantitative evidence of payments to the *muratori* suggests that, in effect, Cortona painted the salone ceiling twice.[53] Cortona acknowledges as much: "It took me longer than I thought." Radical loss of fresco surface occurred in 1637 when the artist, dissatisfied with the nearly finished painting, either pulled down or recovered with fresh *intonaco* a large por-

---

molto tempo fa ma perchè egli ha havuto alle mani per più di due anni una grandissima opera che è la volta del salone de' sig.ri Proni alle 4 Fontane non ci si è potuto applicare ma mi ha promesso che una delle prime cose che faccia sarà per me. Nel salone poco più ci resta da fare anzi sperava haverlo a finire per tutto Giugno. Volendo mandar vostra qualche cosa buona ho stimato meglio haver pazienza che per sollecitar troppo havere cosa ordinaria."

[48] Cortona left Rome in the company of Cardinal Giulio Sacchetti and arrived in Florence on 28 June.

[49] Averaging twenty-four days per month, excluding

the final month of December.

[50] B. Zanardi, "Il restauro e le tecniche di esecuzione originali," in *Il voltone di Pietro da Cortona in Palazzo Barberini*, *Quaderni di Palazzo Venezia 2* (Rome, 1983), 36, n. 4 bis.

[51] Migliorini, "Gio. Maria Bottalla," 78–79.

[52] Briganti, *Pietro da Cortona*, 199–200; Campbell, *Pietro da Cortona*, 64.

[53] P. J. Mariette, *Abecedario* (Paris, 1851–1860), 1:122. See Vitzthum, "Review of *Pietro da Cortona*," 216, n. 22.

tion of the ceiling. Cortona's own statement about the excessive time he took to complete the project seems to allude to the many difficulties and setbacks that prolonged the execution of the salone fresco. He observed that in Rome things must be done well, especially in the case of large commissions not frequently received: "I did not want to fail in making that effort of which I was capable."[54] In the treatise Cortona coauthored with the Jesuit father Giovanni Domenico Ottonelli, the artist speaks of his willingness to rework a painting in order to achieve a satisfactory result:

> It is not an unusual or improper thing for a consummate craftsman to put aside or destroy an unfinished work and remake it according to the fullness of his total satisfaction, because this demonstrates not that the work is in itself very defective but how perfect and excellent is the Idea the master has formed in his imagination for realizing the work.[55]

The payment for January 1638 is for thirty-three days of work, indicating that Cortona had already begun to work in late December almost immediately upon his return to Rome.[56] He averaged twenty-two and a half days per month thereafter for the remainder of the year. The last payment, for December 1638, is unusually small, only ten days of work. The final *giornate* of *intonaco* were thus applied before the end of the year. The winter and spring months of 1639 were undoubtedly taken up with a final retouching *a secco*, and no *muratore* work was required.[57]

By late summer Cortona's work was done.[58] In August a payment occurred for transporting the tower required for dismantling the scaffold in the salone.[59] On 24 September Cortona wrote to Michelangelo Buonarroti the Younger that he had begun to remove part of the scaffold and the stucco cornice was being gilded, with the hope that all would be finished within one and a half months.[60] On 3 October Urban visited the palace and inspected the newly exposed ceiling.[61] By 5 December the salone was completely clear for the papal visit

[54] ". . . Mi a portato più tempo che io non credevo, si per essere l'opera grande si anchora per essere in Roma, dove è necesario le cose ridurle bene per essere opere che di questa grandezza non se ne fano ogni giorno, e io non o voluto manchare di farci quella diligenzia che potevo." Letter of 24 September 1639 to Michelangelo Buonarroti the Younger. BLF, Archivio Buonarroti, 43, no. 412. Transcribed by H. Geisenheimer, *Pietro da Cortona e gli affreschi nel Palazzo Pitti* (Florence, 1909), 18, doc. B, and Campbell, *Pietro da Cortona*, 227–28, doc. 11.

[55] "Non è cosa insolita, ne indecente ad un consumato artefice lasciare, o guastare un'opera, non finita, e rifarla secondo la pienezza della sua totale sodisfattione: imperoche questo dimostra non che l'opera sia in se molto difettosa, ma che molto perfetta, e molto eccellente sia l'idea che nell'animo ha formato il maestro per condurla." Ottonelli and Berrettini, *Trattato della pittura*, 210.

[56] Because of the small number of days worked in December, the payment was combined with the work

for January. See Appendix D.

[57] On the necessity of *a secco* retouching, see Pozzo, "Breve istruzione," pt. 2, appendix.

[58] For the amount and mode of payments to Cortona, see Appendix E.

[59] The apparatus was brought from St. Peter's. 31 August 1639: "Sc. 5 m.ta in oro a Girolamo Bottieri pagati per portatura di un Castello per disfare il tavolato dove si dipinge nel Salone del detto Palazzo da S. Pietro a detto loco." BAV, Arch. Barb., Comp. 51, 330v (LM, Card. Fran.). Payment for the return of the tower appears in the same volume (417v) on 31 July 1640: "Sc. 5 per portatura del Castello di legno per disarmare il ponte della sala del Palazzo alle 4 fontane."

[60] BLF, Archivio Buonarroti, 43, no. 412. Transcribed by Geisenheimer, *Pietro da Cortona*, 18, doc. B, and Campbell, *Pietro da Cortona*, 227–28, doc. 11.

[61] ASM, Cancelleria Ducale, Avvisi e notizie dall'estero, 5298, Avvisi di Roma, letter dated 6 October 1639. Cited in M. Del Piazzo, *Pietro da Cortona: mostra documentaria* (Rome, 1969), 18, no. 112.

during which Urban first beheld the totally finished ceiling. His assessment of it was exuberant, and he later declared the work to be the equal of the Vatican Stanze of Raphael.[62]

PICTORIAL SYSTEM AND SPATIAL CONCEIT
OF THE PAINTED ENFRAMEMENT

To provide an organizational armature for the pictorial fields of the salone fresco, Cortona devised an illusionistic structure consisting of fictive entablature and four supporting corner piers, all painted gray in imitation of marble (Colorplate III, Fig. 80).[63] This illusionistic system comprises a bewildering assortment of decorative sculptural and architectural forms: segments of broken pediment, scrolls, masks, cartouches, urns, bucrania, swags, medallions, shells, volutes, and dolphins. At pier level (Figs. 91–94) animated herms painted to imitate stucco sculpture appear in the process of hanging swags of oak leaves. The tritons flanking the imitation gilded-bronze bas-relief medallions, which mask the juncture of the piers and entablature, engage in the similar task of supporting laurel swags. The resultant effect of the trompe l'oeil enframement is to provide a compositional structure of no less liveliness and richness than the five figural fields into which it divides the vault.

Providing structure for the pictorial composition, however, is not the only function of the painted enframement. It operates as the mainspring of the spatial dynamics of the fresco. The scenes transpiring in the two long lateral sections and in the shorter end sections occur in landscape settings (Figs. 85–88), as though the salone were sunk below ground level and the surface of the earth continues just behind the actual stucco cornice of the room. The figures participating in these scenes move both in front of and behind the illusionistic entablature, both inside and outside the actual space of the room as defined by the overall fictive enframement. The smoke rising from Vulcan's forge (Fig. 88), for example, billows forward to obscure the center of the entablature, but also flows behind it into the open sky of the middle section of the vault. The artist spared no detail to demonstrate this spatial conceit. On the entablature above the scene with Venus in the Garden of Love, a Cupid sits unfolding a taffeta cloth (Colorplate III, Fig. 82), his leg curling in front of the architectural member but the drapery falling behind it and reemerging in the scene below. The painted enframement thereby functions as a foil, heightening the illusion by confirming for the beholder that portions of the action transpire within the real volume of the salone.[64]

---

[62] Posse, "Deckenfresko des Cortona," 102, n. 2. ASF, Archivio Mediceo del Principato, Roma-Carteggio Diplomatico, Francesco Niccolini, 1639, 1 January–27 August, 3365.

[63] Posse ("Deckenfresko des Cortona," 155–56) thought the entablature was in imitation of stucco and was followed in this by Pastor (*History of the Popes*, 29:500). Teti (*Aedes Barberinae* [1642], 45), however, states that the architectural enframement imitates marble.

[64] For Cortona's use of the frame as a device for unit-ing image and observer, see I. Lavin, "Pietro da Cortona and the Frame," *Art Quarterly* 19 (1956), 55–59; S. Benedetti, *Architettura come metafora: Pietro da Cortona "stuccatore"* (Bari, 1980), 20–24. The artist may have first developed in temporary works the idea of overlapping with painted elements a fictive architectural enframement. M. S. Weil, "The Devotion of Forty Hours and Roman Baroque Illusions," *Journal of the Warburg and Courtauld Institutes* 37 (1974), 218–48, esp. 230–32.

CHAPTER XI

• Program and Narrative Action of the Scenes: Rosichino the Sweeper

THE ICONOGRAPHY of the ceiling has been the source of much confusion and yet remains to be satisfactorily resolved. Vitzthum traced many errors to Passeri, whose biography of Cortona (ca. 1673) contains a description of the ceiling that was relied upon too uncritically by subsequent authors, including Posse.[1] A rare pamphlet, written by one "Rosichino" and published in 1640 just after the completion of the ceiling, is the definitive source for the iconography of the fresco.[2] Vitzthum first recognized this little work as the earliest printed source for the program of the ceiling,[3] but the identity of the author and the absolute priority of his *Dichiaratione* have yet to be established.

The foreword to the pamphlet, "Rosichino to the spectators," offers much important information about the author and the purpose of his publication.[4] Rosichino states that "duty" keeps him in the salone and that visitors therefore continually come to him asking the meaning of the imagery in the ceiling. In order to make himself knowledgeable about such exalted matters he asked "a poet" to explain to him the significance of the painting. He then had these points printed so he would no longer have to worry about remembering and explaining them to viewers.

Mattia Rosichino's identity emerges only gradually from the household account books of Cardinal Antonio Barberini, the principal occupant of the palace following Taddeo's departure in 1634. Rosichino held the position of "sweeper" (*scopatore*). In October 1638 he received 3.30 scudi for having had the salone and stairs swept during the preceding five-month period.[5] Apparently Rosichino did not do the sweeping himself but was responsible for having it done. He apparently also served as a master of games, since other payments of the same period indicate he provided mallets and walnut balls for the cardinal's billiard game.[6] Still more curious is the sinecure he held with the municipal government of Rome. Capitoline documents refer to him as "Custodis Cisterna" (custodian of the water reservoir?) at the Conservators' Palace.[7] In 1643 and again in 1644 the cardinal paid for Rosichino's new

[1] W. Vitzthum, "A Comment on the Iconography of Pietro da Cortona's Barberini Ceiling," *Burlington Magazine* 103 (1961), 427–29.

[2] M. Rosichino, *Dichiaratione delle pitture della sala de' signori Barberini* (Rome, 1640); Appendix F. Manuscript in BAV, Barb. Lat. 4342, 79–81, and ASR, Cartari Febei 120, 14r–15v.

[3] Vitzthum, "A Comment on the Iconography," 427.

[4] Rosichino, *Dichiaratione* (1640), 3–4; Appendix F.

[5] "Sc. 3.30 a Rosichino per haver fatto scopare la sala, e scale del Palazzo per mesi cinque." BAV, Arch. Barb., Comp. 224, 140v (Gior., Card. Antonio). He also appears on Cardinal Antonio's *rolo di famiglia* of 1 April 1642. BAV, Arch. Barb., Ind. IV, 176. I owe this last reference to Patricia Waddy.

[6] BAV, Arch. Barb., Comp. 224, 11v, 143r, 159v, 189v, 226v, 267v, 312v, 314r (Gior., Card. Antonio, 1636–1641).

[7] ACR, Credenza VI, vol. 37, 185, 8 March 1647, and vol. 40, 210, 4 July 1653.

shoes.[8] By 1670, when the pamphlet was reprinted, Rosichino had been elevated to the position of "private sweeper" (*scopatore secreto*), a position of some responsibility among the servants of a patrician household.[9] He received two new suits each year, one for the winter season and one for the summer, and the cardinal also provided his rent.[10] The picture of Rosichino that emerges is as a kind of doorman-cicerone who was charged with admitting visitors into the salone to view Cortona's masterwork.[11]

That an individual of such modest position would produce the definitive printed program of the Cortona fresco seems remarkable. Rosichino himself makes a disclaimer in the foreword, stating that he is "not too accustomed to retaining [in his head] things so speculative and exalted." But prior to his attachment to the Barberini, Rosichino had been the pupil or perhaps servant of Francesco Bracciolini, the poet credited with having collaborated with Cortona on devising the subject matter of the salone ceiling.[12] Bracciolini is surely the "poet" from whom Rosichino obtained the information he published. Teti, who was a friend of Bracciolini, credits the authorship of the pamphlet to the poet, but, curiously, the relevant passage appears only in the manuscript drafts of the *Aedes Barberinae*. The language is obtuse and couched in poetic conceit. As Teti attempts to describe Cortona's vault painting, he finds that the artist has obscured the painted sky (and its meaning) with clouds:

> I [therefore] obtained a certain means from a friend full of talent, so that it would be possible to see everything as if from some lookout post, I speak of the work [*opus*] of Bracciolini, a very famous man whose outstanding praises it would be superfluous for me to recount to you, and . . . you will receive *his golden little book* [*aureum eius libellum*] packed with all learning, in which you will see such singularly knowledgeable things described that nothing further is able to be considered.[13]

Teti seems to pretend that the meaning of the painting remains hidden from him, too, without the help of Bracciolini, and that, in any case, the reader will receive Bracciolini's pamphlet, so that nothing more need be said about it. In eliminating this informative passage from the printed text,[14] Teti chose to hide his chief source of information about the meaning of the *Divine Providence*. The *Dichiaratione* is not merely another early source for the iconography of the ceiling but the definitive program of the painting as recounted to Rosichino by Bracciolini, an intimate participant in its creation.

For this reason we must distinguish between Rosichino's work and the two other early sources often referred to in analyses of the salone fresco. These are Teti's *Aedes*

[8] BAV, Arch. Barb., Comp. 224, 407v, 464r (Gior., Card. Antonio).

[9] BAV, Arch. Barb., Comp. 229, 281 (Gior., Card. Antonio). The reprinted pamphlet carries the erroneous publication date of 1570. The text is identical to the 1640 edition except that two poems have been added at the end.

[10] BAV, Arch. Barb., Comp. 91, 10v, 30v, 66r, 98v, 138v, 161r, 182v, 226v, 243v, 268r (Mand., Card. Francesco, 1675–1678; BAV, Arch. Barb., Giust. 12799–12830, 27r (Giust., Card. Francesco, 1679).

[11] The opening and closing of the palace door was one of the official duties of the *scopatore*. F. Liberati, *Il perfetto maestro di casa* (Rome, 1658), 103–4. Patricia Waddy called this work to my attention.

[12] See Federico Ubaldini's statement (ca. 1642) that Bracciolini is "Rosichino's master." BAV, Barb. Lat. 4901, 61. Transcribed in Pastor, *History of the Popes*, 29:502.

[13] BAV, Barb. Lat. 2316, 4v–5r; with slight variations in Barb. Lat. 2317, 5v–6r.

[14] Teti, *Aedes Barberinae* (1642), 14–15.

Barberinae[15] and Federico Ubaldini's "Il pellegrino."[16] Teti and Ubaldini were learned gentlemen retained by the Barberini,[17] and they had knowledge of family aspirations and iconography. They both relied on Rosichino's pamphlet when they wrote, but there is no evidence that they had any intimate involvement with the creation of the ceiling. Teti, as we have seen in our examination of the ceiling paintings of the north wing, generally remains within the sphere of the "potentially true" in his interpretations. He even divides his discussion of the salone fresco into two parts. In the first part (1642, 43–58) he closely follows Rosichino and in the second (59–82) he adds his own plausible interpretation of the scene. Ubaldini, by contrast, openly acknowledges his desire to go beyond the intended meaning of the imagery.[18] Rosichino's purpose is to explain to the viewer,[19] who is presumably standing in the salone, pamphlet in hand, the identification of the figures and the general significance of the scenes. Consequently, succinctness is at a premium. By contrast, the works of Teti and Ubaldini are verbose literary exercises meant to be perused by readers lacking immediate access to the salone.[20] They are interpretive rather than factual in intent. For this reason, although still useful, they must be employed with caution, and Rosichino should have priority in cases of conflicting statements. Whereas Ubaldini's view of the salone fresco is fabulous and Teti's potentially true, Rosichino's is manifestly true to the original intent of patrons, learned adviser, and artist.[21]

Rosichino's method of explanation is simple. He identifies the figures, describes their action, and then, usually in a single phrase, states the meaning. He begins with the central section (Figs. 80–81, 83), where the figure of Divine Providence sits high above on a pyramidal grouping of clouds and figures. She rules over the present and the future; therefore Time, in the form of Saturn, and the Fates, who represent the future, appear below. Many other

[15] Ibid.; 2nd ed. (Rome, 1647); Teti had earlier (1640) planned a much smaller guide to the palace: "Barberinarum aedium brevis descriptio," BAV, Barb. Lat. 2316 and 2317.

[16] "Il pellegrino, o vero la dichiaratione delle pitture della sala barberina," BAV, Barb. Lat. 4335, transcribed by S. A. Zurawski, "Peter Paul Rubens and the Barberini, ca. 1625–1640," Ph.D. diss., Brown University, 1979, 272–90; Magnanimi, *Palazzo Barberini*, 262–80; and A. Lo Bianco, "I disegni preparatori," in *Il voltone di Pietro da Cortona in Palazzo Barberini, Quaderni di Palazzo Venezia 2* (Rome, 1983), 99–109. From internal evidence the manuscript seems to date ca. 1640. For Ubaldini, who was secretary to Cardinal Francesco, see G. Vitaletti, "Intorno a Federico Ubaldini e ai suoi manoscritti," in *Miscellanea Francesco Ehrle V: scritti di storia e paleografia*, Studi e testi XLI (Rome, 1924), 5:489–506; A. Vallone, *Aspetti dell'esegese dantesca nei secoli XVI e XVII* (Lecce, 1966), 191–200.

[17] Ubaldini received a monthy stipend from Cardinal Francesco. BAV, Arch. Barb., Giust. 3573–3675, 3r, 72r, 163r (Giust., Card. Francesco, 1640); Teti was also the beneficiary of numerous subventions from Cardinal Antonio. BAV, Arch. Barb., Comp. 224, 102r, 106r (Gior., Card. Antonio, 1637); BAV, Arch.

Barb., Comp. 233, 220v (Mand., Card. Antonio, 1644). He also appears on Cardinal Antonio's *rolo di famiglia* as "prelato et gentiluomo," which indicates that he received a monthly stipend of 3.60 scudi, bread and wine, and probably a room as well. BAV, Arch. Barb., Ind. IV, 176 (Card. Antonio, 1642).

[18] BAV, Barb. Lat. 4335, 6r. See Lo Bianco's comment ("Disegni preparatori" 109) on this point. Ubaldini knew both Rosichino and Bracciolini, mentioning the latter's epic poem on the election of Urban (19v) and alluding to him as "one who having painted much in verse, in the Tuscan idiom, ceded to none" (18r). The cicerone of grave but serene demeanor who meets Ubaldini in the salone (1v) must be Rosichino. He is referred to as an "old servant of the Barberini family" (25v). But Ubaldini's division of the vault fresco into nine parts corresponding to the nine Muses is his own invention and has nothing to do with the original program.

[19] The foreword to the pamphlet is addressed "to the *spectators*." Rosichino, *Dichiaratione* (1640), 3; Appendix F.

[20] Teti's volume includes engravings of the major ceiling paintings in the palace.

[21] See the judicious comments of Montagu, "The Painted Enigma," 334, n. 125.

figures gather around Providence: Justice, Mercy, Eternity, Truth, Purity, Beauty, "and others."[22] Immortality hastens to execute the command of Providence "to crown the arms of Urban VIII Supreme Pontiff." This is the principal action of the ceiling. The three theological virtues enframe the coat of arms with laurel branches, Faith and Hope holding the sides and Charity at the bottom, with the Barberini bees flying in the middle (Colorplate IV). Religion holds the keys, and the personification of Rome crowns the group with the papal tiara. A putto to the left of the tiara holds out another laurel crown, signifier of "poetic worth."[23]

Next our cicerone turns to the short end coves. The scene directly beneath the Providence group depicts Minerva, "representing Wisdom," who overthrows the Giants, crushed by the same mountains they had piled up to challenge Heaven (Fig. 85). This expresses "the defense of ecclesiastical things."[24]

Ovid is the classic source for the story of the Giants, who, at the instigation of Mother Earth, rebelled against the rule of Jupiter.[25] They piled mountains high in order to reach and overthrow the throne of heaven, but Jupiter destroyed them with his thunderbolts, and the insurgents were crushed under the weight of the falling rocks. In the Cortona fresco, however, Minvera appears instead of Jupiter, thus indicating that the source is not Ovid but Claudian's *Gigantomachia*, where Minerva is the chief instrument of the Giants' defeat.[26] In the iconography of the Counter-Reformation the defeat of the Giants was understood as an allegory of the suppression of heresy.[27] The substitution of Minerva for Jupiter finds justification in the tradition of associating her with wisdom and moral virtue as a personification of the Church.[28]

The short cove at the opposite end of the salone represents "the temporal government" (Fig. 86). Authority (with fasces) and Abundance (with cornucopia) enter from the right, while old men, children, and widows await their gifts. Meanwhile, Hercules casts out the Harpies, signifying "the chastisement of kings."[29]

The imagery in this cove features the secular arm of the papacy. Hercules appears here in the role of heroic virtue, and the Harpies personify the avarice that generates "cruelty, deceit, discord, ingratitude, deception and altogether detracts from justice, charity, faith, piety, and every moral and Christian virtue."[30] This ignoble quality is applied to the secular rulers who seek to establish hegemony in Italy at the expense of the Papal States and the prosperity of its citizens, who are represented in the kneeling figures to the right of

[22] There are eleven of these ancillary virtues in the painting. For the sake of legibility, these figures have not been labeled in the iconographic plan (Fig. 81). Rosichino does not mention the figure on the right crowned with laurel. The remaining four figures carry no identifying attributes.

[23] Rosichino, *Dichiaratione* (1640), 5–6; Appendix F.

[24] Ibid., 6–7; Appendix F.

[25] *Metamorphoses* 1:152–58; *Fasti* 5:35–44.

[26] C. Claudianus, *Claudian* (London-New York, 1922), 2:280–91.

[27] For lightning as a weapon in the papal arsenal, see R. Quednau, *Die Sala di Costantino im Vatikanischen Palast* (Hildesheim-New York, 1979), 305–8. For the similar but more secularized political meaning of Giulio Romano's Sala dei Giganti in the Palazzo Te, Mantua, see B. Guthmüller, *Studien zur antiken Mythologie in der italienischen Renaissance* (Weinheim, 1986), 117–41, and C. Tellini Perina, "La Camera dei Giganti: fonti letterarie ed interpretazioni simboliche del mito," in M. Belfanti et al., *I Giganti di Palazzo Te* (Mantua, 1987), 23–41, esp. 40.

[28] H. von Heintze and H. Hager, "Athena-Minerva: Ihr Bild im Wandel der Zeiten," *Jahrbuch der Max-Planck-Gesellschaft zur Förderung der Wissenschaften E.V.* 11, pt. 1 (1961), 36–127, esp. 62.

[29] Rosichino, *Dichiaratione* (1640), 7; Appendix F.

[30] Ripa, *Nova iconologia*, 42, 567–68.

Hercules. The physical violence of Hercules' action makes it clear that he symbolizes the papal army maintained by the pope to keep at bay the avarice of neighboring secular princes. This defense of the territorial integrity of the temporal papacy is assured by Authority, with fasces, who, in turn, guarantees the reign of prosperity personified by Abundance, with the cornucopia. The cartouche at the base of the scene shows Hercules' club sprouting a laurel branch. Rosichino informs us that this is a device of the Barberini family.[31] The club represents fortitude or heroic action,[32] but it is usually said to be made of oak or olive wood. Thus the laurel sprout—another Barberini impresa and symbol of virtue—indicates that the scene alludes to the virtuous heroic action of the Barberini family in defending the territorial possessions of the papacy through the instrument of its temporal arm. Teti sees here the nephews: Hercules is Taddeo in his capacity as general of the Church and prefect of Rome; Authority is Cardinal Francesco as papal vice-chancellor; and Abundance is Cardinal Antonio the Younger as Cardinal Camerlingo.[33] But Rosichino gives no hint of this specificity, implying instead that these three personifications symbolize the political offices held by the nephews rather than the individuals themselves.

The personification in the center of the right lateral cove is Moral Knowledge, being uplifted by Divine Assistance (Fig. 87). Piety tends to a flaming tripod on the right. The mythological scenes on either side of this triad of virtues embody Gluttony and Lasciviousness. On the right the child Bacchus appears in the company of Silenus, fauns, satyrs, and nymphs—personifying "the bad upbringing of youths." On the left, Lasciviousness (Venus), in the form of a reclining woman,[34] seeks to defend herself against Chastity, who, lily in hand, commands a phalanx of blond-headed "Chaste Cupids" to put the swarthy "Lewd Cupids" to the torch.[35] In the background a group of nymphs casually bathe in a fountain, still unaware of their impending chastisement.[36]

The term used by Rosichino to identify the central personification of this cove section is "Scienza." She holds a sacred text and a flaming urn to indicate the exalted nature of the knowledge she seeks. This is not science or knowledge in any modern secular sense, but spiritual or moral knowledge.[37] Given the context between Divine Assistance and Piety, with the allegorical antitypes Lasciviousness and Gluttony in the adjacent scenes, there can be no mistake about the ethical nature of the knowledge personified. The figure's upward striving and the directional stare toward Divine Providence reinforce this impression.

The cartouche at the bottom of the scene presents the moral lesson in emblematic form. It depicts a plough pulled by two bees and guided by a whip-bearing third bee. This extraordinary device, derived from an ancient gem in the collection of Cardinal Francesco,[38] appeared in the frontispiece engraving of the 1631 edition of Urban's Latin poetry with the

---

[31] Rosichino, *Dichiaratione* (1640), 7; Appendix F.

[32] Ripa, *Nova iconologia*, 568.

[33] Teti, *Aedes Barberinae* (1642), 70–78.

[34] Rosichino avoids identifying the figure as Venus in the Garden of Love, as though to do so would be indecorous. For a discussion of the attitudes of Urban, Bracciolini, and Cortona on this matter, see below 176.

[35] Rosichino, *Dichiaratione* (1640), 7–9; Appendix F.

[36] Teti (*Aedes Barberinae* [1642], 70) notes that such public bathing violates Christian modesty. He was per-

haps recalling Urban's edict (issued in 1637) banning nude bathing in the Tiber. Pastor, *History of the Popes*, 29:373, n. 4.

[37] "Scienza e l'ultima perfezione della nostra anima, nella quale sta la nostra ultima felicità. . . . La scienza è perfezione dell'anima" (Dante, *Convivio*, I, I, 1). *Vocabulario degli accademici della crusca* (Venice, 1612), 765.

[38] C.-F. Ménestrier, *Symbolica Dianae Ephesiae Statua a Claudio Menetreio Ceimeliothecae Barberinae Praefecto Exposita* (Rome, 1657), 53–54, 81.

distych "Supremum Regimen, cultae sata iugera terrae / Mellis opus, tria sic tres potiora notant" (Highest rule, sown fields of cultivated land / production of honey, thus the three symbolize these greater things) (Fig. 153).[39] There it refers to the sweet labor of the poet and the moral guidance of the "supreme rule," which are combined in the poetry of Urban, the poet-pope.[40] In his versifying the pope thus combines poetic beauty with moral didacticism. His particular concern about the sins of lust and gluttony led him to compose admonitory sonnets cautioning against the danger of temptations that might result in such vices.[41]

The opposite long cove, on the left, depicts in the center another dominating triad of personifications (Fig. 88). Dignity (*Dignità*) gazes into the mirror held up by Prudence, while Power, dispatched with written orders, departs to lock the door to the Temple of Janus just now being closed by Peace. Fame flies between Power and Peace, while Gentleness ties Furor to a pile of armaments.[42] A torch-bearing Fury collapses beneath Power. On the left side Vulcan makes weapons at his forge. These two scenes allude to the "preparedness which is necessary for the defense of the provinces even in peace time."[43]

Again the central personification is unusual. The Dignity is not that of modern secular usage but refers to "rank of office," particularly in the ecclesiastical hierarchy.[44] Holding the caduceus of peace[45] and the papal key of authority, Dignity undoubtedly personifies the papacy—the "Supreme Dignity."[46] The flanking scenes are Vergilian.[47] The binding of Furor, here a Mars-like figure, and the closing of the Temple of Janus were common allegories for the arrival of peace.[48] The forge of Vulcan, by contrast, symbolizes the preparations for war. A lightning bolt above the scene reminds the viewer that Vulcan provided Jupiter with this deadly weapon.[49] In Counter-Reformation iconography the lightning bolt symbolized the triumph of the Church over her enemies.[50] Rosichino specifies that the "rising" sun in the cartouche is another device of Urban.[51] It appears as such in the compendium of imprese compiled by Giovanni Ferro above the motto ALIUSQUE ET IDEM (Another and yet the same),[52]

[39] Urbanus VIII, *Poemata* (Rome, 1631).

[40] A similar impresa showing two bees pulling the plough was later published in D. de Saavedra Fajardo, *L'idea de un príncipe político christiano* (Munich, 1640), 267–71. Saavedra's motto is Horatian (*Ars poetica*, 343): OMNE TULIT PUNCTUM/qui miscuit utile dulci. [He has won every vote who has blended profit and pleasure.] He explains that the yoke is the Church and that the bees pulling it represent the sweet, cultured rule of the Barberini. The useful and the sweet are combined.

[41] See the "Contro la Lussuria" and "Contro la Gola" in Urbanus VIII, *Poesie toscane del Card. Maffeo Barberini . . .* (Rome, 1637), 13, 15. These poems were written prior to 1623.

[42] This Furor would seem to be Mars, the counterpart to Venus in the opposite cove scene.

[43] Rosichino, *Dichiaratione* (1640), 9–10; Appendix F.

[44] *Vocabulario della crusca*, 264. For the history of the term, particularly in ecclesiastical usage, see *Reallexikon für Antike und Christentum*, ed. T. Klauser (Stuttgart, 1950–), 3:1024–35, esp. 1028–29.

[45] Ripa, *Nova iconologia*, 395.

[46] For this usage, see G. de Novaes, *Introduzione alle vite de' sommi pontefici. . . .* (Rome, 1822), 2:6–7; Barozzi and Berchet, *Le relazioni della corte*, 1:140; Moroni Romano, *Dizionario*, 20:61.

[47] *Aeneid* 1:283–96; 8:416–53.

[48] It appeared on the reverse of a papal medal designed by Benvenuto Cellini for Clement VII in 1534. N. T. Whitman and J. L. Varriano, *Roma Resurgens: Papal Medals from the Age of the Baroque* (Ann Arbor, Mich., 1983), 18–19.

[49] *Aeneid* 8:426–32.

[50] A. Rieth, *Der Blitz in der bildenden Kunst* (Munich, 1953), 28–32. See the poem of Cortona's iconographic consultant, Francesco Bracciolini, entitled "Che la Potestà del Papa è Formidabile," where the pope's possession of the "lightning bolts of God" symbolizes the superiority of his authority over that of mere secular princes ("every scepter of Augustus"). F. Bracciolini, *Delle poesie liriche toscane* (Rome, 1639), 223. See also the papal virtue "Fulminatio" depicted in the Sala di Costantino of the Vatican Palace. Below, 161.

[51] Rosichino, *Dichiaratione* (1640), 10; Appendix F.

[52] Ferro, *Teatro d'imprese*, 650–52.

and comes from the "Centennial Hymn" (*Carmen Saeculare*) of Horace sung to Apollo: "Kind Sun, who in your shining chariot reveal / and then conceal the day, reborn another and yet / the same, may you view nothing greater than / the City of Rome."[53]

The dedication to Apollo is reiterated in the stucco mantelpiece of the fireplace below (Fig. 89), where the head of the sun god appears flanked with laurel swags.[54] Incomplete as seen today, the plinth above the head was designed to support an additional sculptural element, as can be observed in early photographs of the salone when a bust of the emperor Trajan was positioned there. The poetic device thus encapsulates the meaning of the strident imagery in the cove scenes above, where the Rome of Apollo and the Caesars is displaced by the Rome of the popes.

Borromini's finished drawing (1631–1632) for the fireplace[55] shows that originally the sculptural component of the mantel was to have terminated with a stucco lion pelt (Fig. 90). Although the lion was apparently not executed, it did appear above another fireplace mantel in the palace.[56] The original ensemble of sun and lion combines two major Barberini imprese, the juxtaposition creating an ideogram for the colloquial notion of "solleone"—the fiercely hot August sun.[57] The symbolism of the fiery device is appropriate for the fireplace mantel, and further represents the Sun in Leo, which is a key factor in the election chart of Urban and hence the astrological destiny of the Barberini family.[58]

Four octagonal medallions at the corners of the fictive entablature of the vault fresco contain scenes from Roman history depicting the four cardinal virtues, with animals at the bases of the corners symbolizing each corresponding virtue (Figs. 91–94). Scipio represents Temperance, with a unicorn below. Mucius Scaevola personifies Fortitude, together with a lion at cornice level. A hippogriff refers to Justice and the scene of Titus Manlius in the medallion above. The bear is the representative of Prudence together with Fabius Maximus.[59] The animals also relate to the moral lesson represented in each of the narrative scenes in the adjacent coves.

The four scenes from Roman history are reported in Livy, who also used them for the moral lessons they contained. When Cornelius Scipio Africanus returned the captured Saguntine maiden intact to her betrothed (Fig. 91), Livy interpreted it as an act of great generosity.[60] In the ceiling medallion the scene is to be understood as exemplifying temperance in the sense of control over libidinous urges.[61] Thus the unicorn, symbol of chastity,

---

[53] "Alme Sol, curru nitido diem qui / promis et celas aliusque et idem / nasceris, possis nihil urbe Roma visere maius." "Carmen Saeculare," lines 9–12. Q. Horatius Flaccus, *The Complete Odes and Epodes with the Centennial Hymn*, trans. W. G. Shepherd (New York, 1983), 167.

[54] "Per la mettit.a in opera delli conci di travertino scorniciati soglia stipidi architrave fregio cornice e cartelle con le teste d'Apollo in mezzo . . . sc. 3.50." BAV, Arch. Barb., Ind. II, 2888, 188. Transcribed in Pollak, *Die Kunsttätigkeit*, 1:291. The sculpture was probably executed by Domenico Rossi after a design by Bernini. Below, n. 171 and n. 61, 194 and n. 14.

[55] Thelen, *Francesco Borromini*, 61–62, cat. C51.

[56] "Per haver fatto un morione di stucco di tutto punto s.a il Cam.o con una pelle di Leone s.a e con penne doppie il tutto alti p. 5 lar. p. 5 ins. sc. 2." ASR,

Congregazioni Religiose Maschili, Teatini S. Andrea della Valle, 2200, int. 229, 189r (Magnanimi, "Documenti della costruzione," 208); Pollak, *Die Kunsttätigkeit*, 1:320.

[57] *Solleone*: "Il nome deriva dal fatto che in questo periodo il Sole si trova nel segno zodiacale del Leone (vi entra il 23 luglio). *Dizionario enciclopedico italiano* (Rome, 1955–1961), 11:431.

[58] Above, 77–78, 80–82.

[59] Rosichino, *Dichiaratione* (1640), 10–11; Appendix F.

[60] T. Livius, *Ab Urbe Condita*, trans. B. O. Foster (London–New York, 1919), 7:191–95 (26:50).

[61] Scipio was the most common historical representative of temperance in Renaissance art. H. North, *From Myth to Icon: Reflections of Greek Ethical Doctrine in Literature and Art* (Ithaca, N.Y., 1979), 86.

sits in the corner below. Since this creature could be tamed only by a virgin, it shies away from Lasciviousness in the adjacent scene.[62]

Mucius Scaevola represents fortitude (Fig. 92) because, after having failed to kill the Etruscan King Porsenna, he thrust his right hand into a sacrificial fire as a demonstration of Roman determination.[63] The story is one of the topoi of ancient Roman *virtu*. The lion—classic exemplar of fortitude—is the beast below, next to the martial scene with the binding of Furor.[64]

Titus Manlius Torquatus, as consul, condemned his own son to death for having broken Roman military discipline (Fig. 93).[65] The justice of this story is embodied in the hippogriff in the corner as identified by Rosichino. Cortona painted the beast simply as a griffin, with the foreparts of an eagle and the hindparts of a lion rather than a horse, as they should be with a true hippogriff. A griffin, noted for its ferocity,[66] would symbolize the punitive aspects of justice. Nearby putti lift fasces, and a balance rests in the corner. Authority in the end cove scene also carries the consular fasces, showing herself to be the proper agent of justice.

Fabius Maximus, through his delaying tactics, was able to wear down his more powerful enemy Hannibal (Fig. 94).[67] Willingness to bide time until the proper moment for action here represents the virtue of prudence. The bears in the corner reinforce this idea because they give birth to formless cubs that are "with time" gradually sculpted into shape by the mother's tongue.[68] This prudent nurturing contrasts with "the bad upbringing of youths" represented by the child Bacchus in the lap of the adjacent nymph.

The program of the salone fresco is simple, straightforward, and integrally related to its formal design. There are four categories of symbolic imagery in the painting: allegorical personifications and virtues, mythological figures, historical personages, and bestiary animals. Each iconographic type occupies a restricted spatial dimension within the pictorial system. Mythological figures and scenes appear in the fictive space beyond the illusionistic enframement and outside the real space of the room. Personifications and virtues—the most important of the types since they are the most positive and Christianizing in meaning—significantly intervene in the space of the room. The triadic groups crossing in front of the entablature at the center of each lateral cove make this especially clear. The historical figures in the medallions exist as part of the enframement, holding a spatially transitional position, but, as works of fictive sculpture, dwell in a different temporal realm from the other figures. Standing in the corners on top of the real stucco cornice, the animal allegories move obtrusively into the space of the salone.

The exceptions to these spatial categorizations are meaningful. Fame, Peace, and Chastity are personifications who interpose themselves into the mythological scenes, but they do so in order to set things right—to close the door of the Temple of Janus and to rout the minions of Lasciviousness. The pyramidal group with Providence at its apex is the other exception. It reverses the prevailing spatial-iconographic arrangement, thus locating the most

---

[62] Ibid., 244–48.

[63] Livius, 1:255–61 (2:12).

[64] Ripa, *Nova iconologia*, 201–3.

[65] Livius, 4:23–29 (8:7).

[66] T. H. White, *The Bestiary* (New York, 1960), 22–24.

[67] Livius, 5:245–81 (14:23).

[68] White, *The Bestiary*, 45–47. The cornice mostly obscures this detail, but Cortona depicted the bear on the right in the process of licking her shapeless offspring into proper form. For this detail, see the engraving in Teti, *Aedes Barberinae* (1642).

important personification of the ceiling at the illusionistically most elevated point, with the figures of Saturn and the Fates eclipsed beneath at entablature level just within the space of the room.

This arrangement of the figures into basic zones according to type is the iconographic structure of the painting. Within the system there is also a general compositional arrangement determined by considerations of decorum. Just as the palace consists of two groups of apartments—one for the ecclesiastical family members and one for their secular kinsmen— so is the imagery of the ceiling painting divided according to this distinction.[69] Spiritual matters, headed by Moral Knowledge, occupy the lateral cove above the south wing of apartments reserved for the cardinals. The principal subjects of this section are, appropriately, lasciviousness and gluttony. They operate as the antitypes of two essential virtues of pious churchmen, chastity and abstinence. Since this side also faces the garden, the painted scenes are set in gardens with fountains and groves.

Secular concerns, personified in Dignity, appear in the cove above the side with the apartments of Taddeo and Anna. Here the imagery takes on a vigorous military cast, with Vulcan's manufacture of weaponry dominating the scenes, although peace, with the closing of the door to the Temple of Janus, is the goal of this bellicose activity. This alludes to the temporal arm of the papacy, of which Taddeo was an important component. Moreover, the presence of Vulcan, father of Caeculus, the mythic founder of Palestrina, appropriately confirms Taddeo's title as prince of Palestrina.[70]

As prefect of Rome, Taddeo was something of a secular ruler in his own right, at least in theory. The readiness with which terms such as "dignity" and "divine providence" were associated with Taddeo and the prefect's office, as well as with the pope, can be observed in a formulaic letter the nephew wrote, acknowledging an epistolary congratulation he had received after the conferral of the prefecture. In the letter, written to Michelangelo Buonarroti the Younger (30 August 1631), Taddeo notes that his appointment to the "dignity of the prefect" has to do with the success of the Holy Church and that, because of it, praise is due to divine providence.[71]

The fire, smoke, and lightning that rise from Vulcan's forge and from around the temple of Janus have also found decorous placement above that side of the salone with the fireplace.[72]

The opposing scenes in the ends of the vault conform to the same system of bifurcation. Minerva and the Giants, representing the "defense of ecclesiastical matters," and, at the opposite end, Hercules symbolizing the "castigation of kings," with Authority and Abundance signifying the good government of the Papal States, reiterate the ecclesiastical-secular duality.

The biform nature of the vault imagery is a direct reflection of the spiritual-temporal dualism of the papacy itself.[73] Following theo-political notions established as early as the late Middle Ages, the pope held the keys of authority in two distinct realms—"the keys of knowl-

---

[69] See the comments of J. Connors, "Pietro Berrettini da Cortona," in *Macmillan Encyclopedia of Architects*, ed. A. K. Placzek (New York, 1982), 1:457–58.

[70] Above, 108.

[71] BLF, Archivio Buonarroti 42, 281r.

[72] Connors, "Cortona," 457–58.

[73] On this duality, its history, and repercussions, consult P. Prodi, *Il sovrano pontefice* (Bologna, 1982), esp. 43–79 [Eng. trans. *The Papal Prince* (Cambridge, 1987)].

edge and power" ("claves scientiae et potentiae").[74] The Spanish theologian Francisco de Suarez (1548–1617) put it clearly: "The key of knowledge [*scientia*] is in the pontiff for defining truths of faith, the key of power [*potentia*] for ruling the Church."[75] The "keys" are referred to in Matthew (16:19): "And I will give to thee the keys of the kingdom of heaven. And whatsoever thou shalt bind upon earth, it shall be bound also in heaven: and whatsoever thou shalt loose on earth, it shall be loosed also in heaven." The "Scienza" (Moral Knowledge) in the right cove of the fresco therefore refers to the "key of knowledge" and the pope's authority in spiritual matters. The Minerva (Ecclesia) cove is linked to it by this signification. These are the two coves first seen by the visitor entering the room from the square staircase (Fig. 95), whence they are visually and iconographically united. In the opposite long cove scene, on the left, Dignity, with key in hand, dispatches Power ("Potestà") to close the Temple of Janus. This expresses the "key of power," and combines with the Hercules cove to show the full range of peace and prosperity that results from the assertive authority and military preparedness of the papacy in temporal affairs. The combination of the four cove scenes constitutes a *summa* on papal authority.

This symbiotic relationship between the composition of the figural groupings of the ceiling fresco and their iconographic values indicates that the program was not a preconceived literary essay written out by a learned adviser and handed over to the artist to translate into paint. Instead the program resulted from the realization of the artist's pictorial vision of what must have been at most a general outline of appropriate themes agreed upon in consultations among artist, adviser, and patrons. Cortona's preparatory drawings for the project also show that the iconography of the fresco was in constant flux as the artist labored.

PREPARATORY DRAWINGS

Surviving preparatory studies for the salone fresco are few in number[76] but valuable for the evidence they provide of the design process. They form two groups: compositional studies for multi-figured scenes and sketches for important individual figures.

The earliest of the drawings, now in Munich, corresponds to the scene with Hercules and the harpies in the west short end of the ceiling (Fig. 96).[77] As commentators have noted,

[74] "Papa in clave potentia, & scientiae, cuius ususa Deo dependet non nisi per accidens errare potest: sicut per accidens, et naturaliter virtutibus abuti potest: formaliter vero non item." A. Trionfi [Augustinus Triumphus], *Summa de potestate ecclesiastica* (Rome, 1584), 121–26, esp. 125 (bk. 20, art. 6, c.). This work, completed in 1326, was frequently reprinted in the fifteenth and sixteenth centuries, particularly when there was need for asserting the temporal authority of the papacy. See P. B. Ministeri, "De Augustini de Ancona, O.E.S.A. (✝ 1328) Vita et Operibus," *Analecta Augustiniana* 22 (1952), 148–262; M. Wilks, *The Problem of Sovereignty in the Later Middle Ages: The Papal Monarchy with Augustinus Triumphus and the Publicists* (Cambridge, 1963), esp. 254–87.

[75] F. Suarez, *Theologiae R.P. Fr. Suarez . . . Summa . . .* , (Paris, 1877–1878), Diput. 16, Sect. 4. Cited in A. Villalpando, *De Clavium Potestatis Existentia atque Natura* (Washington, D.C., 1921), 40. On the medieval origin of the concept "clavis scientiae et potentiae," see B. Tierney, *Origins of Papal Infallibility, 1150–1350* (Leiden, 1972), 40.

[76] The French painter Laurent Pécheux (1729–1821) reported that in 1775 the Barberini family possessed an album containing the drawings made for the ceiling paintings in the palace. Bollea, *Lorenzo Pécheux*, 397–98. Today no trace of this volume remains. This means that the known drawings are those that by some oversight were not included in the collection, and it accounts for their scarcity, since many more drawings must have been produced during the design and execution of the work.

[77] Munich, Staatliche Graphische Sammlung 12741 (28.4 × 39.9 cm.).

this ink, chalk, and watercolor drawing appears to document an early stage in the development of the artist's concept for the decorative and illusionistic system of the ceiling.[78] The central field consists of a fictive easel painting (*quadro riportato*) held fast by flanking herms, following the Mannerist system used by Annibale Carracci in the Farnese Gallery (Fig. 127). Cortona's illusionism of materials also pays respect to Annibale. The herms with the frame are fleshy beings, while the satyr on the left, the other herm at the extreme right, and the tritons above exist only as feigned stuccoes (*stucchi finti*). The spaces flanking the *quadro riportato* are open to the sky in similar fashion to the corner openings in the Farnese Gallery, but the quadrant of a colonnade appearing beyond the flying putti suggests the Sala Clementina (Fig. 166) as a secondary source. Although the design is more three-dimensional, Cortona follows the same structural system he employed in the gallery of the Villa Sacchetti at Castelfusano (Fig. 154) (1626–1629). The conception is even closer in spirit to Cortona's lost vault painting in the Villa del Pigneto (Fig. 155), also a Sacchetti commission.[79] As at the Pigneto, the Munich drawing shows the corners closed off with decorative structures, while the openings appear just to either side of the *quadri riportati* at each end of the vault. The elaborate detailing of the fictive architecture is unique among the known drawings for the ceiling, suggesting that this drawing must date from an early period when the artist was working on the overall design of the framework.[80] Stylistic evidence also supports a date of no later than 1632. Superimposition of the octagonal medallion and the tail of the triton materially record the artist changing his mind in the search for a satisfactory solution. The drawing even contains the germ of its own demise as a stage in the artist's creative process. Cortona's correction in ink on the left, crossing the frame of the *quadro riportato*, follows the outline of the cove scene as it was ultimately realized (Fig. 86) and charts his first idea for the elimination of the fictive easel painting and the complete opening up of the end cove.[81]

The imagery in the Munich drawing also shows that the program had yet to be fully determined. The *quadro riportato* contains an unfinished representation of Hercules fighting Harpies, as in the final fresco,[82] but the personifications of Authority and Abundance do not

[78] Posse, "Deckenfresko des Cortona," 167–69; P. Helm, B. Degenhart, and W. Wegner, *Hundert Meister-Zeichnungen aus der Staatlichen Graphischen Sammlung Munchen* (Munich, 1958), 65; Lo Bianco, "Disegni preparatori," 83–84; R. Harprath et al., *Zeichnungen aus der Sammlung des Kurfürsten Carl Theodor* (Munich, 1983), 34–35, cat. 26, colorplate 12. L. Kugler, "Ein Beitrag zum Illusionismus im Werke von Pietro (Berrettini) da Cortona," in *De Arte et Libris: Festschrift Erasmus, 1934–1984* (Amsterdam, 1984), 267–68. The medallion at the upper right is a superimposed addition by the same hand. The oil-on-canvas easel version of the salone fresco (Rome, Galleria Nazionale) published by E. Lavagnino, "Il bozzetto di Pietro da Cortona per la volta della sala maggiore del Palazzo Barberini," *Bollettino d'arte* 29 (1935), 82–89, and reintroduced by Kugler (*Studien*, 48–50), is not autograph and had no role in the creation of the ceiling painting. The fidelity of this work to virtually every detail of the fresco indicates that it is a copy made after the original.

[79] Both the building and its decoration are known only from engravings. Briganti, *Pietro da Cortona*, 191–92; Wittkower, *Art and Architecture in Italy*, 232–34, 531–32, nn. 10–13; A. Blunt, *Guide to Baroque Rome* (New York, 1982), 220–22; Blunt, "Pietro da Cortona" (1956), 416; A. Marabottini, L. Bianchi, and L. Berti, *Mostra di Pietro da Cortona* (Rome, 1956), 6, 34–36. Jörg Martin Merz provided the photograph for Fig. 155.

[80] K. Noehles, "Zur 'mostra di Pietro da Cortona' in Rom," *Kunstchronik* 10 (1957), 96, suggests a date of ca. 1631.

[81] Harprath et al., *Zeichnungen des Carl Theodor*, 35.

[82] There is some disagreement about the identification of this scene. See ibid., who interprets it as Hercules killing the Stymphalian birds, and Lo Bianco ("Disegni preparatori," 83), who reads it as Hercules slaying the Lernaean Hydra. Since a Harpy paw appears to the right of Hercules, however, it appears likely that the scene is that of Hercules fighting harpies, as in the fresco. Kugler, "Beitrag," 267, n. 53.

appear. The inclusion of putti carrying aloft a cardinal's hat also indicates a more direct allusion to Cardinal Francesco than occurs in the final design. The medallion contains a combined allegory of Temperance and Water,[83] implying that at this stage the corner medallions were to represent the cardinal virtues through reference to the elements rather than Roman history scenes. The bee-driven plough appears in the cartouche instead of Hercules' club. This sheet is also the only surviving drawing by Cortona for the salone fresco rendered in watercolor and showing that the artist was still concerned with working out a harmonious combination of illusionistic materials.

Notwithstanding major differences in conception, the Munich drawing displays many features linking it with Camassei's abortive design at Chatsworth (Fig. 79).[84] The sheets are approximately the same size (Munich: 28.4 × 39.9 / Chatsworth: 29.2 × 40.7 cm.), and both are touched with watercolor, making them anomalous in the graphic production of the artists. Predictably the Farnese Gallery looms large in each proposal, and high socles, more prominent than in the prototype, serve as platforms for both seated and standing figures. Princely crown and cardinal's hat carried forward by putti refer to the respective patrons, Taddeo for Camassei and Francesco for Cortona. Allegorical elements indicate that inclusion of the cardinal virtues, in some form, was an iconographic requirement. Given these similarities, it is easy to imagine the two drawings as having been submitted simultaneously in early 1632 in direct competition for the salone commission.

Cortona's triumph may have been predetermined by his having the more powerful of the patrons, but the greater opulence of ornamentation and harmony of diverse parts would have given his design an advantage in the eye of a discerning judge. Moreover, unlike his rival and despite the provisional nature of the design, the turn of the heads of the two herms demonstrates that Cortona was already, even at this early stage, concerned with architectural context and with orienting the ceiling imagery to the directional paths of the visitor to the salone. Both figures peer down searchingly in the direction of the entrance from the square staircase—the principal of the two main entrances into the room.

A chalk drawing in the Uffizi represents an intervening stage between the Munich design and the finished fresco (Fig. 97).[85] Although not autograph, the drawing is so Cortonesque in conception it may be a copy after an original design by Cortona. It provides evidence of the major step taken by the artist toward a more illusionistic and unified solution to the design of ceiling paintings. Here the *quadro riportato* has been discarded and the entire cove section behind the painted architectural frame filled with the figural scene. The proportions of the scene are greater on the vertical than they are in the final fresco, so that the head and upturned drapery of Authority would have projected above the painted entablature, as do the heads of Moral Knowledge and Dignity in the lateral cove scenes.[86] The figures offering grapes and shafts of wheat to Authority have yet to be condensed into the single figure

---

[83] The figure above pours water into a wine jar, while a figure with coral and seaweed swims below.

[84] Above, 127.

[85] Florence, Gabinetto Disegni e Stampe 11762 (26 × 62.1 cm.). W. Vitzthum, "Review of *Pietro da Cortona* by Giuliano Briganti," *Burlington Magazine* 105 (1963), 216; Lo Bianco, "Disegni preparatori," 90, cat. 18.

[86] In the drawing the lower edge of the entablature is established by the horizontal line of Hercules' club and the outstretched arm of Authority. This figure appears almost unchanged from the Ceres in Cortona's preparatory drawing (Rome, Private Collection) for the comparable end scene at Castelfusano (Briganti, *Pietro da Cortona*, fig. 79).

of Abundance, but otherwise the iconography is close to the final version, with Hercules on the left and supplicating figures below. Two drawings are known for Authority: a figure study[87] and a finished sketch for the head.[88] The figure study in London depicts the figure in a more upright position than in the fresco. Authority does not yet glide into the scene with such effortlessness to relieve the oppressed indigents below. A small sketch at Stanford is so close to the actual grouping of supplicants that it must have immediately preceded the creation of the full-scale cartoon for the scene.[89]

Early ideas for the lateral cove scenes also appear in surviving drawings. A chalk drawing in Haarlem (Fig. 98) displays major differences from the final design.[90] A crowned figure without identifying attributes leads Dignity (with caduceus), establishing an emphatic left-right progression. On the left, Power, with key in hand, appears amid charging horses and a flying eagle. On the right, bound prisoners are put to the torch. A small sketch for the lion of Fortitude in the corner to the right of this scene is preserved at Windsor.[91] Cortona took inspiration from the open-mouthed lion in the ancient relief acquired by the Barberini in 1635 and placed at the top of the square stairs just to the left of the door leading to the vestibule of the salone (Fig. 134).[92] The head at the bottom of the sketch seems to have been taken directly from the relief.

Another drawing of ca. 1633–1634, now in Ottawa,[93] shows the artist's early idea for the right lateral cove (Fig. 99). Here Moral Knowledge is led forward by Divine Assistance, who takes the form of Minerva instead of the winged figure that appears in the painting. As in the Haarlem drawing, the central figures create a strong directional pull toward the eastern end of the salone, which, in this case, is from right to left. On the right, Piety tends the tripod, but the Bacchic group is differently conceived with a donkey and satyrs rather than Silenus, fauns, and nymphs. Chastity and the fighting cupids are already present, but Lasciviousness, in the guise of Venus, is not yet introduced into the scene.

A drawing in Madrid, perhaps copied after an autograph design, documents a slightly more advanced stage in the evolution of this cove (Fig. 100).[94] Here the winged figure of Divine Assistance emerges in place of Minerva, and a sleeping Venus appears as Lasciviousness under a rustic lean-to. Likewise, on the right, Silenus enters into the Bacchic group as the representative of gluttony. The half-figure at the extreme right is the nymph who holds the infant Bacchus in the fresco.

There are no known compositional drawings for the Minerva end cove or for the

[87] London, British Museum 5211.23 (25 × 28.2 cm.).

[88] Stockholm, Nationalmuseum H 601/1863 (15.2 × 11.5 cm.).

[89] Palo Alto, Stanford University Museum of Art, Mortimer C. Leventritt Fund (11 × 14.9 cm.). B. Davis, "Pietro da Cortona," *Source: Notes in the History of Art* 2, no. 4 (1983), 14–16.

[90] Haarlem, Teylers Museum J 13 (20.1 × 40.9 cm.). Lo Bianco, "Disegni preparatori," 71, cat. 2.

[91] Windsor Castle, Royal Library, 4434 (18.6 × 25.5 cm.). Ibid., 74–77, cat. 6. The sheet is possibly a copy after an autograph drawing.

[92] Ibid.; M. A. Lavin, *Documents and Inventories*, 147, nn. 445–52; and Magnanimi, *Palazzo Barberini*, 127–30,

fig. on p. 129. For the placement of the lion relief: "Per la mett.a in opera del lione di marmo l. p.i 11 1/2 alto 6 1/2 d'aggetto overo rilievo p.i 2, portato dal Giardino . . . sc. 4" (Pollak, *Die Kunsttätigkeit*, 1:296).

[93] The National Gallery of Canada 6134 (27.6 × 41.5 cm.). A. E. Popham and K. M. Fenwick, *European Drawings in the Collection of the National Gallery of Canada* (Toronto, 1965), 56–57; Lo Bianco, "Disegni preparatori," 69–71, cat. 1.

[94] Madrid, Real Academia de San Fernando 319 (21.4 × 57.3 cm.). A. E. Pérez Sánchez, *Real Academia de Bellas Artes de San Fernando: catálogo de los dibujos* (Madrid, 1967), 79–80; idem, *I grandi disegni italiani nelle collezioni di Madrid* (Milan, 1978), cat. 33, colorplate 33.

central opening of the ceiling, but figure studies for Providence and Rome have been preserved. These two drawings are extremely useful, not only because they show two of the three most iconographically significant figures of the ceiling but primarily because they reveal the artist's concern with spatial dynamics and legible dramatic action. The drawing of the upper half of the figure of Rome (Fig. 101), in the Morgan Library, indicates Cortona's interest in conveying a feeling of urgent and purposeful movement.[95] The powerful diagonals of the arms, partially obscuring the face, are conceived to dominate the composition. The head and left arm, particularly, are rendered *di sotto in su*, and the act of crowning gains emphasis by a view up inside the papal tiara about to be placed on the Barberini coat of arms. In the painting Cortona made a telling adjustment. By moving the right hand around to the far side of the tiara rather than having it grasp the lower edge in support, he thereby left the opening completely unobstructed as if in actual preparation for coronation.[96] The theme of papal election and coronation, as we shall see, embraces the entire action of the central section of the salone vault.

The Louvre drawing of Providence (Fig. 102) is a figure and drapery study.[97] The bulk of the draped lower half of the figure dominates the foreshortened torso—an imbalance that Cortona corrected in the painting, where the torso section is enlarged. He made several other noteworthy adjustments in the final fresco figure. The compositional diagonals of the drawing work at cross-purposes, splitting the figure open at the top and lessening its effectiveness as the principal figure and visual terminus of the ceiling imagery. The lower-left to upper-right diagonal established by the positioning of the legs is continued in the outward-turned scepter, whereas the drapery at the lower right initiates a line leading up through the breasts to the extended right arm. In the painting (Fig. 84) the artist resolved this conflict by depressing the bulge of the left knee and turning the scepter to parallel and reinforce the now dominant diagonal leading to the commanding gesture toward Immortality, which is the starting point of the main action of the entire central section of the ceiling. At the same time, since the secondary diagonal beginning with the right foot now terminates at the scepter, the figure of Providence becomes more self-contained and operates as a more effective compositional apex for the group of figures that serves as its pyramidal base.

The necessity of these changes may have become apparent only after Cortona first painted the figure. The *giornata* comprising the head, torso, lower body, and scepter of Providence illogically overlaps the surrounding *giornate*, whereas normal technical procedure would have produced the opposite result (Fig. 84). Having executed the figure the first time, Cortona apparently found it unsatisfactory except for the right arm. Consequently he then removed the unacceptable sections and superimposed a new *giornata* of *intonaco*.[98] A detail of the head of one of the Giants photographed in raking light (Fig. 103) shows a similar instance where Cortona, apparently dissatisfied with the expression, had cut away the original *intonaco*, which included the face and neck, and added a new triangular *giornata*.

---

[95] New York, The Pierpont Morgan Library, 1965.16 (22 × 27.7 cm.). Stampfle and Bean, *Drawings* 47–48, cat. 59; Lo Bianco, "Disegni preparatori," 73–74, cat. 4.

[96] Stampfle and Bean, *Drawings*, 48.

[97] Paris, Louvre, Cabinet des Dessins, 531 (27.6 × 21.4 cm.). J. Bean, *Musée du Louvre: dessins romains du* *XVIIe siècle* (Paris, 1959), 24, cat. 22; Kugler, *Studien*, 39–41.

[98] Magnanimi (*Palazzo Barberini*, 108–9 and n. 25) first noted this *giornata*, with different conclusions. Although not visible to the unaided eye at floor level nor in most photographs, the *giornata* line is perceptible in Magnanimi's colorplate IV.

Although few in number, the surviving drawings record critical stages in the design process and also speak eloquently of the artist's struggle with his daunting commission. They help flesh out the difficulties adumbrated in the payments to the *muratori*. The Munich and Uffizi drawings of the Hercules cove (Figs. 96–97) especially testify to Cortona's willingness to make radical changes when deemed appropriate. The example of the reworked *giornata* in the figure of Providence was not unique,[99] and it demonstrates that the artist often found it necessary to use a trial-and-error approach to the challenging visual problems presented by the size of the vault and the unusually large number of figures and scenes to be coordinated. Cortona was surely alluding to personal experience when he advised artists to keep their unfinished works from public view so that, when necessary, it would be easier to make changes according to the dictates of their own artistic judgment: "The painter paints in seclusion so that he can add and change things as he wants."[100]

The evidence of reworkings provided by documents, early biographers, and technical examination of the fresco surface thus finds confirmation in the painter's graphic production for the project. The image of the artist that emerges from this process is characterized by a heroic persistence in getting the assignment done properly to his own satisfaction, despite all impediments and sparing no effort.

OPTICAL PERSUASION AND THE MEANING OF ILLUSIONISM

No aspect of the salone ceiling has generated greater scholarly attention than its illusionism. Few studies, however, have considered the importance of the points of entry into the room for the functioning of the trompe l'oeil effect. The commercially available photographs used in almost all major analyses of the fresco vitiate the spatial workings of the ceiling because they are taken from a point of view not intended by the artist—from directly beneath the center of the vault and looking straight up.[101]

In these photographs the ceiling is seen as though it were an easel painting conceived to be observed horizontally and two-dimensionally (Fig. 80). This treatment effectively destroys the illusionism of the fresco and substitutes a decorative uniformity for the figures, creating the fiction that all of them possess equal compositional and iconographic value. A photograph taken as the viewer would experience the fresco from the ideal station point (Colorplate III, Fig. 104) reveals that the side sections of the vault curve upward toward the crown of the ceiling. Cortona designed the fresco with the idea of exploiting the curved surface to the advantage of the spatial dynamics of the imagery. The negation of this three-dimensional element in photographs alters the relationship among the figures and skews the compositional devices that give life to the work.

[99] Zanardi, "Restauro e tecniche," 12–13, 36, n. 6. Pozzo ("Breve istruzione," pt. 2, appendix) also allows for the necessity of similar reworkings.

[100] "Il pittore depinge chiuso perchè puo aggiungere e mutare le cose, come vuole." Ottonelli and Berrettini, *Trattato della pittura*, 209.

[101] The most commonly used photographs are Alinari 28565 and ICCD C 11376 & C 11377 (Fig. 80). See, for example, the illustrations in Posse, "Deckenfresko des Cortona," pl. I; H. Voss, *Die Malerei des Barock in Rom* (Berlin, 1924), fig. 243; Briganti, *Pietro da Cortona*, fig. 125; Wittkower, *Art and Architecture in Italy*, fig. 153; J. Held and D. Posner, *Seventeenth & Eighteenth Century Art: Baroque Painting, Sculpture, and Architecture* (New York, 1971), fig. 108; J. R. Martin, *Baroque* (New York, 1977), pl. 111; Magnuson, *Rome in Age of Bernini*, 1:348; Magnanimi, *Palazzo Barberini*, pl. III; Lo Bianco, "Disegni preparatori," fig. 55.

Ill-considered photographs also convey the impression that the ceiling fresco can be visually comprehended in a single view. Actual on-site experience of the ceiling, however, indicates that the viewer perceives only part of the fresco at a time and must move around the room to get optimal views of the various side and end cove sections. The experience is fundamentally a spatial and temporal one. Photographs deny these essential qualities and thereby falsify our perception of the ceiling and its imagery.

The ceiling is best and most comfortably viewed at an oblique angle from the perimeter of the room (Colorplate III, Fig. 104). Ubaldini's fictional cicerone recommends that viewers stand resting their shoulders against the wall as they look upward to study the vault fresco.[102] This advice merits consideration by the modern viewer, too. Photographs taken from the center of the room seem to indicate that all action transpires on the same plane. Looking at the vault at an angle from the perimeter of the room, however, the observer notes a very different relationship among the figures.

A schematized cross section of the vault showing the fictive space of the pictorial composition will aid our understanding of the narrative action and figural relationships (Fig. 105). In the diagram the solid horizontal line marks the top edge of the feigned cornice, which establishes the point at which the arc of the cove terminates and the physical surface of the vault flattens. The figures appearing to be above this line therefore exist illusionistically beyond the actual physical space of the room.[103] The group of virtues around the bees fly upward at a moderate angle. In the fresco this becomes clear in the view of the tiara from underneath and in the dark bands on the abdomens of the bees, whose curvature indicates foreshortening from below (Colorplates III and IV). The figure of Charity, holding the cut ends of the laurel branches, appears to be below the upper edge of the painted cornice and within the space of the room, whereas the figure at the top of this group, Rome, exceeds the level of the cornice. Thus the heraldic group does not fly parallel to the cornice, as it appears when viewed from directly beneath, but ascends gradually in apotheosis—an observation essential to the proper understanding of the meaning.

Turning to Divine Providence, the viewer sees that she appears to be located high above the fictive cornice, situated on a plane perpendicular to that of the floor. For this reason Cortona rendered the figure smaller and more foreshortened than the theological virtues. The figure of Immortality, hastening with her crown of stars to obey the command of Providence, moves at an angle slightly above cornice level toward the heraldic group. Were the action to be continued, as seen from floor level, she would first disappear behind the heraldic group to emerge with Rome at the top of the group. Images of the ceiling photographed from directly below negate these spatial complexities and subvert a correct reading of the action of the central section of the vault.

In designing the composition of the fresco, Cortona followed the conventional wisdom that it should conform to the natural sight lines of the observer upon entering the room.[104] Thus the design depends upon its architectural context, the floor plan of the salone,

[102] BAV, Barb. Lat. 4335, 2v.

[103] The diagrammatic section only approximates the relationships between the individual figures and their visual disposition in space. The artist allowed numerous spatial ambiguities in the final rendering of the figures in an effort to avoid a static composition. This il-

lustrative technique was developed by Enggass in his analysis of Baciccio's nave fresco in Il Gesù. R. Enggass, *The Painting of Baciccio: Giovanni Battista Gaulli, 1639–1709* (University Park, Pa., 1964), fig. 72.

[104] Posse ("Deckenfresko des Cortona," 117–18), followed by Voss (*Barock in Rom*, 537), first made this ob-

and its position in the overall scheme of the piano nobile of the palace (Fig. 3, PBN 2). Since the salone could be entered from either the square staircase on the left or the oval stairs on the right, Cortona organized his design accordingly. If the visitor enters the room from the left, the lateral section with Moral Knowledge comes into view first (Fig. 106). Here the artist linked the figures in a sweeping arc that leads the eye up to the figure of Providence. This compositional device begins at the right foot of the herm figure at the extreme right of the lateral section. It then moves parallel to the cornice through the outstretched arms of the nymph and Silenus up to the figures of Piety and Moral Knowledge toward Providence. Entering from the right (Fig. 107), the viewer's attention is similarly directed toward the central figure. Here the arc begins with the extended arm of the herm, connecting with Vulcan's upraised right arm and sweeping down to the anvil. Along with the billowing smoke, it continues up through Prudence and Dignity to Immortality and, from her flowing sash, to the extended arm of Providence—the starting point for the action of the central section. Through the use of compositional devices Cortona focuses the visitor's attention on the most important figure in the ceiling and leads his or her eye up to the illusionistically highest point in the composition.

The artist thus took into consideration the possible points of entry into the palace. In this way the ceiling reflects the pathways of human traffic in the salone. True perception of the overhead imagery is dependent upon the points of entry and the preplanned routes for visitors. Photographs of the painting that disembody it from the architectural context mask its functioning as an element in the everyday workings of the palace.[105]

Notwithstanding its dramatic spatial illusionism, Cortona eschewed *quadratura* in the salone ceiling, although it was the standard formal system used to expand interior spaces fictively.[106] In true *quadratura* ceilings such as the Sala Clementina (Figs. 164, 166) or Agostino Tassi's painted architecture in the Casino Ludovisi (Fig. 118), the vertical space of the room extends visually beyond the physical surface of the vault by means of fictive architecture that continues the structural lines of the actual walls.[107] Cortona's painted frame depends not on *quadratura* but rather on the trompe l'oeil device of variegated materials.[108] The enframement seems to follow the surface of the actual vault rather than breaking through it. This is characteristic Cortonesque usage. Cortona did not employ illusionistic architectural elements to violate the architectonic integrity of any of the vaults he painted.[109] In the Barberini salone the fictive architectural enframement appears to be tangent with the vault sur-

---

servation. Both authors, however, undermined this important point by not illustrating the ceiling with a photograph taken from the proper angle. Schöne ("Bedeutung der Schrägsicht," 144–72, esp. 154–56, fig. 7) subsequently codified this observation as a universal principle. Kugler ("Beitrag," 257–82, fig. 3, and *Studien*, 58–64, figs. 3, 5, 9) has emphasized the view from the left (square staircase) entrance and demonstrated the importance of the fictive entablature for the effectiveness of the illusionism.

[105] The degree to which we have lost touch with the proper way of seeing the salone ceiling is indicated by the official route for visitors established by the Galleria Nazionale, which currently occupies the salone and

north wing of Palazzo Barberini. The exhibition of paintings has been arranged so that one walks backward through the north wing and enters the salone at the back; as a result, the visit culminates with an inverted view of Cortona's painting.

[106] Notwithstanding the contrary assumption of Wittkower, *Art and Architecture in Italy*, 250.

[107] On this important distinction, see Sjöström, *Quadratura*, 15.

[108] Ibid., 55–56; Magnuson, *Rome in Age of Bernini*, 1:349.

[109] S. Jacob, "Pierre de Cortone et la décoration de la Galerie d'Alexandre VII au Quirinal," *Revue de l'art* 11 (1971), 45–50.

face and thereby actually defines it for the viewer. In so doing, the painted frame provides a spatial reference to enhance the persuasiveness of the fictive space beyond.[110] The painted enframement of the fresco thus serves a threefold illusionistic effect. It simulates marble and gilt bronze, defines figures that cross in front of it as being within the space of the room, and establishes the physical surface of the vault as a plane of reference for figures existing in the fictive space beyond.

Notwithstanding the impression of novelty the salone ceiling conveys to the viewer, the work above all constitutes a synthetic achievement that draws on a variety of modes of illusionistic representation. Cortona, however, did not arrive at this synthesis directly. As we have already seen, the artist first considered a system of *quadri riportati* (Fig. 96) inspired by the Farnese Gallery. Subsequently rejecting this standard Mannerist solution, he then turned to a traditional Roman device of greater simplicity and antiquity—the fictive frame dividing the field of the vault into five sections. This organizational principle echoes in paint the three-dimensional stucco enframement systems used in many Roman ceiling paintings of the late sixteenth and early seventeenth centuries.[111] The *Virgin Immaculate* ceiling in the old Sforza wing of the palace (Fig. 11) typifies the tradition. In the earlier painting, however, no unity of action or space unites the pictorial fields beyond the enframements, whereas in the salone painting a free flow of moving figures occurs in front of, behind, and across the fictive borders.

The artist must have already arrived at this solution by 1635 when he designed a stucco framework for the vault of the Cappella della Concezione in San Lorenzo in Damaso (Fig. 156), in which the open sky appears in the five fields, suggesting a unified space beyond the divisions of the stucco enframement.[112] In the Barberini salone the real stucco frame is transformed into fictive marble. In this sense the Barberini ceiling harks back to the Farnese Gallery and its progeny, such as Lanfranco's painted vault in the gallery of Villa Borghese (Fig. 119), where a feigned marble or stucco enframement contains the main pictorial field.[113] Cortona's salone enframement is architectonic in conception. The same herms that hold up the fictive entablature in the earlier gallery vaults appear in the corner supports of the Barberini fresco. Cortona simply removed Annibale's *quadri riportati* and then reversed the system of the coves, opening the sides and ends to the sky and closing the corners with fictive support elements.[114] The frame, therefore, was the most important component the artist derived from the local Roman tradition of ceiling painting.[115]

It was also the first part to be painted. The recent technical analysis demonstrates that Cortona began with the two medallions and fictive entablature on the eastern end of the vault.[116] In many areas where figures or clouds overlap the fictive architecture, the original painted frame shows through the *a secco* overpaint.[117]

[110] Although he misread it as a *quadratura* element, Wittkower (*Art and Architecture in Italy*, 250–52) correctly noted the importance of the enframement for heightening the overall illusionistic effect.

[111] Benedetti, *Cortona "stuccatore,"* 22–23.

[112] Campbell, *Pietro da Cortona*, 65, 128. The painted sky is not visible in recent photographs, but see Posse, "Deckenfresko des Cortona," 158–59, fig. 159.

[113] Annibale's feigned entablature has its source in the architectural framework of the Sistine ceiling. Martin, *Farnese Gallery*, 73.

[114] The bronze shields of the Farnese Gallery also reappear as the octagonal medallions in the Barberini fresco.

[115] Briganti, *Pietro da Cortona*, 82–84.

[116] Zanardi, "Restauro e tecniche," 11–12.

[117] See, for example, the area of overpaint around the

Cortona was also aware of another important tradition of ceiling painting manifested principally in Lombardy, Emilia, and the Marches. Although he carefully avoided the radical foreshortenings so characteristic of north-central Italian ceiling painting,[118] the idea of placing figures in front of fictively real architecture has sources in the art of Melozzo da Forlì and Correggio. Melozzo's painted dome in the sacristy of San Marco in Loreto (ca. 1484) is one of the most startling examples of this usage (Fig. 157). Prophets sit on a feigned cornice at drum level of the octagonal dome and cross in front of the ribbing, which is painted in imitation of gilt stucco moldings. Trapezoidal panels between the ribs open to the blue sky and provide access to the room for angels holding Instruments of the Passion, who have entered the viewer's space and hover in front of the dome structure much as do the triadic groups in front of Cortona's salone entablature.[119] Cortona had probably already arrived at such a solution before his northern trip in 1637,[120] but its efficacy must have been reinforced when he passed through Loreto on the return to Rome and likely visited the shrine adjacent to Melozzo's sacristy dome.[121]

Melozzo, like Cortona, respected the architectural integrity of the vault and avoided excessive foreshortenings. In his treatise, Cortona displays the highest admiration for Correggio's dome painting in Parma Cathedral. Significantly, however, he makes no comment on the illusionistic extension of space or foreshortening of the figures, which are the prominent features of the main area of the dome. Instead, he is impressed most of all by the trompe l'oeil effect of the fictive parapet in front of which stand exclaiming Apostles (Fig. 158):

> That marvel which is the principal among all the marvels of today was made by him [Correggio] and it is seen in the Cathedral dome of the city of Parma. There he designed a cornice all around with such exquisite artifice that one who lifts his eyes from below to look at it, cannot believe that it is only painted, even if he is told and reassured of this by many. Therefore it follows that, being truly a painting, it tempts everyone to be personally convinced of it with the usual test of touching it with a pole, evidently in order to see and prove if it be relief work and of stucco or else a painted work. Thus, by deceiving the spectator, the power of fictive representation triumphs.[122]

figures of Dignity, Prudence, and Power. Magnanimi, *Palazzo Barberini*, pls. VIII–IX.

[118] Cortona specifically warned against just such violation of the figure: "Avverta anche l'artefice di fuggire certi scorci tanto stravaganti, che hanno alle volte del mostruoso." Ottonelli and Berrettini, *Trattato della pittura*, 178.

[119] R. Buscaroli, *Melozzo e il melozzismo* (Bologna, 1955), 93–94, figs. 25–27; S. Sandström, *Levels of Unreality: Studies in Structure and Construction in Italian Mural Painting During the Renaissance* (Uppsala, 1963), 129–31. Horstmann, *Die Enstehung*, 54–56.

[120] See, for example, the painted dome of the piano nobile chapel (Fig. 44), where angels hover in front of the latticework section of the dome.

[121] On 13 September 1637 Cortona wrote to Cardinal Francesco Barberini from Florence, indicating his intention to travel to northern Italy ("Lombardia") and return to Rome by way of Loreto. BAV, Barb. Lat. 6458, 96r–v. Transcribed in G. Bottari and S. Ticozzi, *Raccolta di lettere sulla pittura, scultura, ed architettura* (Milan, 1822–1825), 5:311–13; and Campbell, *Pietro da Cortona*, 224–25, doc. 3.

[122] "Da lui fu fatta quella maraviglia, che è principalissima tra tutte le maraviglie di hoggidì; e si vede nella Cupola della Cathedrale della Città di Parma: ove egli figurò una cornice intorno intorno con tale, e tanto esquisito artificio, che chi, da basso alzando gli occhi, la rimira non può credere, che sia cosa dipinta; tutto che, esser tale, detto gli venga, e confermato da molti: e quindi segue, che essendo veramente Pittura, porge ad ogn'uno occasione di volersene chiarire presentialmente

Cortona was inspired by the feigned architecture that functioned as a foil for figures and fixed them within the real space of the church. This spatial-architectonic device, rather than the foreshortenings, reappears in the Barberini salone.

Although there is no documentary evidence of a visit to Parma and Mantua, it seems unlikely that any study trip such as Cortona took to "Lombardia" would have excluded these important centers of ceiling painting, and the comments in his treatise seem to indicate a firsthand knowledge of works in these cities.[123] The length of Cortona's trip from the time he left Florence until his return to Rome, which can be calculated as approximately eighty-five days, leaves more than sufficient time for a visit of several days each in Parma and Mantua.[124] Moreover, when Sacchi made a study trip north in 1635–1636 also to look at ceiling painting, his stops included Parma and Mantua as well as Venice.[125]

The lessons of Giulio Romano's experiments in Palazzo Te also seem to have had an impact on Cortona. In the Barberini salone the Minerva cove with the fall of the Giants appears to reflect the artist's knowledge of Giulio's Sala dei Giganti (Fig. 159), where massive figures tumble forward and are crushed beneath boulders and collapsing columns.[126] This is the one area of the salone ceiling in which Cortona allowed foreshortening to play a significant role. Even here, however, only the group of figures on the right (Fig. 85) tumbles headlong and foot-first toward the viewer.

Here also the observer encounters a Giulio-like punning sensibility. The oafish terror of the Giants is the starting point of visual witticisms that run through the entablature, fractured by the force of Minerva's attack, and offer evidence of the imminent collapse of the entire marble framework above the viewer's head. The cascading Giants have not only broken off the cartouche at the base of the scene but spread alarm even to the feigned-stucco herms in the corners, who either become animated and jump aside to avoid the onslaught or find themselves locked in unwelcome embrace as the Giants grasp for stability (Figs. 85, 91–92). Cortona surpassed his model in one respect. Giulio's falling architecture exists only in the fictive realm of the Giants, but the ruptured entablature of the Barberini salone appears to be real, so that the viewer, too, must fear the consequences.

Recent scholarship has tended to discount the importance of Cortona's northern trip for the design of the Barberini ceiling.[127] The mural frescoes of the Sala della Stufa in Palazzo Pitti prove that Cortona had already achieved a neo-Venetian style prior to his visit to Venice. The *Age of Gold* and the *Age of Silver*, painted before continuing the journey to Venice, equal in their sensuous coloring and opulence the post-Venetian scenes of Lasciviousness and Gluttony in the Barberini salone. The development of facility in Venetian colorism did

---

con la solita esperienza di toccarla con un'hasta, per vedere evidentemente, e provare se sia lavoro di rilievo, e di stucco, o pure d'opera dipinta. Così nell'altrui inganno trionfa la forza dell'artificiosa rappresentazione." Ottonelli and Berrettini, *Trattato della pittura*, 23.

[123] Ibid., 23, 121.

[124] He left Florence probably on 20 September 1637 and arrived back in Rome on 15 December of that year. N. Fabbrini, *Vita del cav. Pietro Berrettini da Cortona* (Cortona, 1896), 49, also assumes stops in Modena, Milan, and Verona as well as Parma, Mantua,

and Venice.

[125] He made drawings after Correggio and Veronese in particular. On this trip, see Harris, *Andrea Sacchi*, 17. Sacchi's northern trip is reported by both Passeri (*Die Künstlerbiographien*, 299) and Bellori (*Le vite*, 552).

[126] For the artist's reference to Giulio's tour de force, see Ottonelli and Berrettini, *Trattato della pittura*, 121. The Sala dei Giganti has been the subject of a recent monograph: M. Belfanti et al., *I Giganti di Palazzo Te* (Mantua, 1989).

[127] Briganti, *Pietro da Cortona*, 86–88.

not depend upon a trip to Venice. Titian's Bacchanals were in the Casino Ludovisi in Rome, and Sandrart specifically reports that Cortona studied them.[128] These facts have been used to discredit Boschini's assertion that Cortona returned to Rome and remade the salone ceiling based on what he had learned in Venice.[129] But we have already seen that payments to the muratori and other circumstantial evidence lend support to Boschini's remarks.[130] There is also a certain logic to the report of alterations as the result of a study trip. Cortona's letters indicate his eagerness to see Venetian art in situ, even at the risk of incurring the displeasure of his patron by an extended absence from Rome.[131] Nor did the weather, darkness, and brevity of his stay prevent the artist from seeing the objects of his pilgrimage. Cortona reported ecstatically from Venice, "I have been able to see these works so beautiful."[132]

Cortona had left Rome precipitously in June 1637, leaving the salone ceiling nearly finished[133] and after having earlier, in 1635, declined the opportunity of a similar trip precisely for the reason that he had to work on the ceiling.[134] From the known circumstances it must be concluded that the reason for the trip was compelling and related directly to the ceiling project. Cortona went north in quest of a resolution to technical problems he had encountered with the Barberini fresco. He traveled to Venice specifically to see Venetian art, but not the kind of easel paintings available in Rome and elsewhere in central Italy. He went to see the works that could only be seen in situ in Venice—the painted ceilings of the Doges' Palace.[135]

Boschini's poem makes clear Cortona's primary concern to see the ceiling paintings in the Doges' Palace and the Scuola di San Rocco. For Boschini this desire was only natural since he, too, saw the Venetian solution to problems of ceiling painting as one of the principal achievements of Venetian art. He devoted an entire section of his poem to such issues as how to represent figures in air, difficulties of foreshortening, how to design a "quadro di soffitto," and the proper rendering of light in these paintings.[136] Boschini included Cortona in the poem with the purpose of showing how the head of the Tuscan school had to drink at the fount of Venetian art before he could solve the problems related to the Barberini ceiling. At issue was not just what the artist had learned about Venetian art in general, but what specific Venetian solutions to ceiling painting he had used.

The iconographic language of the Venetian ceilings, with their large numbers of personifications interacting in political and politico-religious allegory, made them a significant model for the Barberini fresco. But it was not their symbolic mode that attracted the artist. This he could have learned from engravings of Rubens' works, such as the Marie de' Medici cycle and ceiling paintings like the *Apotheosis of the Duke of Buckingham*.[137]

[128] Sandrart, *Academie*, 270. Wittkower, *Art and Architecture in Italy*, 534, n. 59.

[129] Briganti, *Pietro da Cortona*, 86–87.

[130] Above, 130–33.

[131] See Campbell, *Pietro da Cortona*, 224–25, doc. 3.

[132] "[H]o potuto vedere queste opere così belle." Ibid., 225–26, doc. 5.

[133] Above, 132–33.

[134] Sandrart, *Academie*, 288.

[135] Zurawski, "Rubens and the Barberini," 151–53. Cortona's sources in Venetian ceiling painting are analyzed by Posse ("Deckenfresko des Cortona," 163–67)

and Walmsley ("Evidence and Influence," esp. 28, 31–42).

[136] Boschini, *Carta del navegar*, 157–220.

[137] For an important analysis of Barberini connections with Rubens and Cortona's response to the impact of the Flemish artist's style and allegorical mode of expression, consult Zurawski, "Rubens and the Barberini," esp. 99–100, 134–55; idem, "Connections between Rubens and the Barberini Legation in Paris, in 1625, and Their Influence on Roman Baroque Art," *Revue belge d'archéologie et d'histoire de l'art* 58 (1989), 23–50.

The formal spatial component of Venetian ceiling paintings drew the artist to them. Veronese's *Triumph of Venice* (Fig. 160), for example, long regarded as an important factor in Cortona's solution, shows the typical Venetian approach to illusionism in ceiling painting.[138] But the precise nature of the lesson Cortona learned from the study of this and other Venetian ceiling paintings of the sixteenth century remains to be clarified.

Prior to Briganti's negative assertion, the accepted reading credited Venetian sources for the entire central field of the Barberini fresco.[139] The part of that rectangle that most directly reflects Venetian spatial solutions, such as in Veronese's *Triumph of Venice*, includes only the pyramidal grouping of figures around Providence, but to this major grouping should also be joined the adjacent figure of Minerva and the cove with the Giants (Figs. 85, 104). These figures appear to be on the same vertical plane much as in the Veronese work. With the logical exception of the falling Giants, Cortona, like the Venetian artist, has also avoided exaggerated foreshortenings. Even the action of Veronese's painting adumbrates the Barberini work. The personified figure of Venice, floating upward on clouds and surrounded by personifications of Peace, Abundance, Felicity, Honor, Security, and Liberty, receives a crown from a victory figure, while Fame flies above.[140] The architecture in Veronese's painting, however, belongs strictly to the fictive realm of the figures and has no logical relationship to the architecture of the room or even the decorative enframements of the ceiling painting. Cortona rejected this disparity in favor of the illusionistically real painted entablature made all the more convincing by Minerva's shattering blow.

Cortona also held Tintoretto in high regard.[141] The central painting in the ceiling of the Sala dei Pregadi or del Senato, Tintoretto's *Venice Receiving the Tribute of the Sea* (ca. 1581–1584/1587),[142] although less persuasive in its spatial illusionism than Veronese's work, seems to have provided Cortona with the most direct and fruitful compositional prototype for his Romanized neo-Venetian solution to the difficulties encountered in the Barberini fresco (Fig. 162). The figure of Venice, with scepter in hand and a gesture of benevolent reception, sits high above, surrounded by pagan gods seated in attitudes of worshipful respect.[143] At the center another circle of figures[144] mediates between Venice and Neptune, Mars, and the

[138] Cortona singled out Veronese and this specific work for praise in his treatise: "Et invero Paolo è stato tanto felice in esprimere alla grande, e maestosamente le cose, che pare chiunque le mira, si senta eccitare a pensieri sublimi, e generosi. E ciò dimostra charo l'opera tra l'altre segnalata dell'ovato, che si vede, e si gode con amore, e maraviglia nella Sala del Gran Consiglio di Venetia." Ottonelli and Berrettini, *Trattato della pittura*, 88–89.

[139] Posse, "Deckenfresko des Cortona," 166; Wittkower, *Art and Architecture in Italy*, 252; J. Schulz, *Venetian Painted Ceilings of the Renaissance* (Berkeley-Los Angeles, 1968), 50.

[140] G. Bardi, *Dichiaratione di tutte le istorie, che si contegono nei quadri posti novamente nelle sale dello Scrutinio, & del Gran Consiglio del Palagio Ducale. . . .* (Venice, 1587), 63–64.

[141] With particular reference to Tintoretto's central rectangular panel in the ceiling of the Sala del Gran Consiglio, *The Doge Receiving Palm and Laurel from Ven-*

ice. Ottonelli and Berrettini, *Trattato della pittura*, 88–89. See Schulz, *Venetian Painted Ceilings*, cat. 42, pl. 104. Boschini (*Carta del navegar*, 128, 243–44) remarks that during his later trip to Venice (1643–1644) Cortona praised Tintoretto's work in the Sala del Gran Consiglio and in the Scuola di San Rocco. Boschini associates Cortona with Tintoretto more than any other Venetian artist.

[142] Schulz, *Venetian Painted Ceilings*, cat. 43, pl. 123; Walmsley, "Evidence and Influence," 38–39. For the iconography of this work, consult A. Kuhn, "Venice, Queen of the Sea," in S. Sinding-Larsen, *Christ in the Council Hall, Institutum Romanum Norvegiae, Acta ad Archaeologiam et Artium Historiam Pertenentia* (Rome, 1974), 5:Appendix I, 263–68.

[143] The deities are Jupiter, Aesculapius, Hercules, Apollo, Mercury, and Saturn.

[144] Possibly alluding to the Venetian Senate that met in the room. Kuhn, "Venice," 263–68.

nereids and tritons bearing upward gifts of the sea. In the Barberini fresco Minerva and the Giants correspond to the plunging figures in the lower half of Tintoretto's painting, and the figure of Venice at the top of the grouping adumbrates Providence.

The manner in which the illusionism of Venetian painted ceilings operated concerned Cortona still more than the allegorical programs they contained. This effect is nowhere apparent in photographs taken directly beneath Venetian ceiling paintings. The illusionism of these works depends upon an oblique angle of view. When seen directly from below, the figures in Veronese's painting appear to be all on the surface plane (Fig. 160); when observed at a more natural angle, however, the figural plane tilts upward, conveying the visual impression that the figures rise perpendicularly to the plane of the floor on which the viewer stands (Fig. 161). This was the principal lesson Cortona learned on site in Venice in 1637, which he brought back to Rome and applied to the eastern end of the salone fresco (Fig. 104), where the Giants, Minerva, Providence and attendant figures rise illusionistically on a vertical plane. Cortona further heightened the illusionism by taking advantage of the actual curvature of the cove, foreshortening the limbs and heads of some of the figures, darkening the undersides of the clouds, and linking Providence with the cove figures and corner herms in a pyramidal configuration.[145] The Roman artist, it should be added, had the advantage over his Venetian mentor. The figures in the cove were already on a physical plane perpendicular to that of the floor and the viewer's line of sight. The problem thereby became a matter of linking the Providence group with the cove figures in a fashion that would make it appear they occupied the same vertical plane. The compositional pyramid affected this linkage.

Technical evidence in the fresco supports a late date for the Providence and Minerva group. The *giornate* comprising the figures of Providence, Saturn, the Fates, Minerva, and the Giants overlap the surrounding areas, suggesting they were late additions.[146] The reworked head of the shrieking Giant to the left of Minerva (Fig. 103) illustrates this procedure. Just to the left and above the inserted triangular *giornata* of the face, the linear indentations[147] in the *intonaco* delineate the shoulder, and bent left arm of the adjacent herm.[148] This entire arm is overpainted with the head and hair of the Giant, showing the latter to be an afterthought that followed at some distance in time. Cortona also overpainted, in tempera *a secco*, the area of the entablature broken by the force of Minerva's lance thrust.[149] The original unbroken entablature beneath the overpaint is visible even to the naked eye. The overlappings and *a secco* application that abound in the eastern end of the fresco reinforce the evidence for a reworking of this part of the fresco following the artist's return from Venice, providing physical proof of the Roman artist's efforts to capitalize on the lessons he had learned there.

The Barberini fresco emerges from the confluence of three distinct traditions of illusionistic ceiling painting: the Roman tradition of fictive entablatures and illusionism of ma-

---

[145] The techniques employed by Cortona to modify what was a basically Venetian system, thereby making more persuasive the vertical extension of space, find precedent in Correggio's fresco in the dome of Parma Cathedral and, closer to home, in Lanfranco's neo-Correggiesque dome in S. Andrea della Valle, Rome (1625–1628); but Cortona never embraced the radical foreshortenings so characteristic of this tradition.

[146] Zanardi, "Restauro e tecniche," 11–12, pls. 1, 3, 5.

[147] Made by pressing a pointed instrument through the cartoon and into the wet plaster.

[148] The underside of the elbow is tangent with the uppermost acute angle of the added *giornata*.

[149] Ibid., 19, pls. on pp. 24–25.

terials, the Lombard-Emilian tradition of figures overlapping feigned architecture, and the Venetian effect of the illusionistic vertical plane of figures. In view of this constellation of formal sources, the principal innovations of Cortona's salone fresco derive from a synthesis of devices rather than any radical new technique. A summation of traditions rather than a departure from the past, the integration of disparate elements is nevertheless so persuasive that a whole new genus of illusionistic ceiling painting resulted.

Cortona designed the salone fresco to delight and instruct the viewer.[150] In so doing, he conformed to a fundamental Counter-Reformation commonplace about the nature and uses of art. He assumed its efficacy in exhorting the viewer to avoid vice and emulate virtue: "visual images have by nature a great power for moving human souls and emotions."[151] This moral-didactic mode of justifying imagery provides the premise for Cortona's treatise and explains the unusual collaboration between artist and theologian.[152] The primary motivation underlying Rosichino's *Dichiaratione* is identical, as he states in the introduction: "because such pleasure does not extend beyond the form and disposition of the colors and figures, the observers, remaining *deprived of the enjoyment of understanding the meaning*, continually turned to me."[153]

The jocular borrowing from Giulio in the Minerva cove serves as a primary case in point. The viewer, first attracted to the spectacle of the avalanche of massive figures, then encounters the impending collapse of the entablature overhead. Having been lured into the scene and having enjoyed it in a purely visceral manner, one is subsequently led to consider the possible symbolic import of the image. Minerva's traditional equation with Wisdom and Ecclesia might follow. Then some recollection of the nature of the Giants' transgression and their deserved punishment would complete the instructive meaning of the scene. Otherwise, Rosichino's pamphlet was at hand, explaining that the Minerva cove expresses "the defense of ecclesiastical things."

Cortona's studied exploitation of illusionism fulfills a key role in this didactic process and exemplifies the convention of optical persuasion. With the exception of the Providence group and the Giants, those figures that most emphatically project into the viewer's space also embody the most positive and desired moral principles, e.g., Minerva, the triadic virtues led by Moral Knowledge and Dignity, the theological virtues, and the animals denoting the cardinal virtues. As we have already seen, this system is reversed in the eastern end of the fresco, but to consistent purpose. The falling Giants lead the eye upward to Providence at the farthest illusionistic point in the ceiling—in proximity to God. Like the biblical Wisdom, Providence personifies an aspect of God's being. The figures interposing in the space of the salone at her command thus represent manifestations of God's benevolent action in the world. Cortona used illusionism not merely as a formal device to startle, but as a metaphor to persuade the viewer of God's intervention in human history for the realization of a providential plan. Illusionism is here the pictorial language of God's providence.

[150] For the afterlife of this Horatian concept in Renaissance art theory, consult R. Lee, *Ut Pictura Poesis* (New York, 1967), 32–34.

[151] "L'immagini vedute hanno dalla natura una gran forza, per muovere gli animi, e gli affetti humani." Ottonelli and Berrettini, *Trattato della pittura*, 51.

[152] On this point see the introductory comments of V. Casale, in ibid., LIII–LXIV. Casale designates this characteristic Catholic Baroque assumption as "iconocracy"—belief in the primacy of images.

[153] Rosichino, *Dichiaratione* (1640), 3; Appendix F.

CHAPTER XII

• The Iconographic Tradition
of Papal Nepotism:
Mirror of Popes and Quest
for Immortality

UNLIKE THE formal prototypes, the iconographic tradition from which the salone fresco derives is entirely Roman in character. One theme in particular finds precedent in Roman fresco cycles of the sixteenth century: the virtues appropriate to the pope and papal family and the means by which these qualities are made effective in spiritual and temporal spheres of papal policy. The quality of secular-ecclesiastical bifurcation that provides structure for the presentation of these virtues in the Barberini fresco also has a tradition in the fresco decoration of papal and nepotic palaces of the previous century. The iconographic prototypes of the salone ceiling have a common theme: the ethical character and political actions of the ideal pope and his family. They reflect the portrait of a perfect papal ruler, presenting to the viewer a "mirror of popes" comparable to the literary genre of princely "mirrors" (*specula*) found in the political theory of the period.[1]

The iconographic sources from which Cortona, his learned consultant, and his patrons drew were the obvious ones according to their intentions for the salone, their conception of Barberini family aspirations, and their own visual experience. The fresco cycles in papal rooms such as the Sala di Costantino and Sala Clementina in the Vatican Palace were the logical and most accessible models. Other precedents are found in the audience chambers of the Farnese family palaces in Rome and at Caprarola. The Farnese, as a successful and long-lived papal family, served as a model to be emulated by the Barberini both in deed and in image.

Vasari's Sala dei Cento Giorni in the Palazzo della Cancelleria represents a synthesis of these two related traditions of papal and familial iconography. This room functioned as a reception chamber for the papal vice-chancellor and is therefore comparable to the Vatican rooms, but it also reflects the concerns of the Farnese cardinal nephew who commissioned the frescoes.

The pictorial cycle in the Vatican Stanze of Raphael provided the most venerable exemplar of the tradition of papal iconography. We have already seen that Urban compared Cortona's *Divine Providence* with the Vatican Stanze—an association that reveals much about how the pope understood the salone fresco.[2] The imagery in the Vatican rooms elaborates the virtues of popes, the obeisance owed to them, and historical instances illustrating mani-

---

[1] On the history of this tradition, see the lengthy introductory essay by L. K. Born in Erasmus, *Education of a Prince*, 1–136.   [2] Above, 135.

festations of these qualities.[3] The most common form of papal exaltation was by allusion to exemplary predecessors, particularly papal namesakes. Thus the deeds of popes named Leo appear prominently in the scenes painted during the reign of Leo X in the Stanza dell'Incendio and the Stanza d'Eliodoro, where the divine sanction of papal authority and the heavenly protection of the papacy as a worldly institution are repeatedly illustrated by historical examples.

The Sala di Costantino (1517–1524) contains the most fully developed fresco cycle belonging to this tradition. The wall scenes contain eight over life-size enthroned figures of popes, each labeled and flanked by personifications of their most outstanding virtues (Fig. 163): Peter (Ecclesia-Aeternitas), Clement I (Moderatio-Comitas), Alexander I (Fides-Religio), Urban I (Justitia-Caritas), Damasus I (Prudentia-Pax), Leo I (Innocentia-Veritas), Silvester I (Fortitudo), and Gregory I (Fulminatio).[4] The major narrative sections, depicted as fictive tapestries, show scenes from the life of Constantine in which the emperor gives appropriate obedience to the Church, for example, the *Donation of Constantine* and the *Baptism of Constantine by Pope Silvester*; two other scenes depict God's intervention in human affairs for the purpose of his providential plan, for example, the *Apparition of the Cross* and the *Battle of the Milvian Bridge*. The historical narratives thereby illustrate the manifestation of the papal virtues and God's action in the world. These scenes were particularly decorous because the Sala di Costantino served as an audience room for ambassadors and secular princes to be received by the pope.[5] Those worldly leaders had only to look at the surrounding wall scenes to understand what was expected of them.

Cortona reserved high praise for Giulio Romano's work in the Sala di Costantino.[6] Artists working for papal patrons frequently mined it for iconographic precedents, and Urban may have had some role in Bernini's borrowing from the *Urban I with Justice and Charity* for his tomb in St. Peter's. Altogether, ten of the fourteen personifications in the Sala di Costantino reappear in the Barberini salone.[7] Moreover, Cardinal Francesco's idea of hanging a cycle of tapestries depicting the life of Constantine (seven by Rubens and five by Cortona) on the salone walls must be owed to his knowledge of the Sala di Costantino and the conceit of fictive tapestries on the walls.[8] Revealingly, when Urban sought to express his satisfaction with Cortona's fresco, he compared it to the Vatican Stanze.[9] The comparison must indicate what Urban had always had in mind for the salone at his family palace.

The extensive ensemble of papal imagery in the Sala Clementina in the adjacent Vatican Palace of Sixtus V, where Urban resided during the winter months, provided another logical point of departure for Cortona (Figs. 164–167). This room, with ceiling and wall scenes by Giovanni and Cherubino Alberti (1596–1600), served as salone or *sala dei palafrenieri* of the papal palace. We have already seen that this room, unique for its size and frescoed vault, provided an architectural model for the Barberini salone and its unusual vaulted ceil-

---

[3] J. Shearman, "The Vatican Stanze: Functions and Decorations," in *Proceedings of the British Academy* 56 (1971), 380–89.

[4] Quednau, *Sala di Costantino*, 157–326.

[5] Ibid., 515.

[6] Ottonelli and Berrettini, *Trattato della pittura*, 122.

[7] Temperance (Moderatio), Justice, Prudence, Fortitude, Faith, Charity, Eternity, Religion, Peace, and Truth.

[8] Zurawski, "Rubens and the Barberini," 166, 184–86.

[9] Posse, "Deckenfresko des Cortona," 202, n. 2. ASF, Archivio Mediceo del Principato, Roma-Carteggio Diplomatico, Francesco Niccolini, 1 January–27 August 1639, f. 3365.

ing. Because of its proximity to the papal apartments, the Sala Clementina cannot be visited easily and until recently has been somewhat neglected in the modern scholarship on Roman ceiling painting.[10] It nevertheless contains the largest frescoed vault painted in Rome between the Sistine Chapel ceiling and that of the Barberini salone. In its use of *quadratura* effects, it stands as a milestone in the development of Roman Baroque ceiling painting.

Ideal papal virtues and namesake glorification are the two principal iconographic modes operative in the Sala Clementina cycle. The wall frescoes depict the theological and cardinal virtues and two history scenes: the *Baptism of St. Clement*[11] and the *Martyrdom of St. Clement*. The scenes with St. Clement allude to Clement VIII Aldobrandini, who commissioned the decoration of the room. In the open sky of the vault, surrounded by a *quadratura* enframement, St. Clement adores the Trinity as angels carry him heavenward (Fig. 165). Personifications of Religion, Justice, Abundance, Charity, Clemency, and Benignity occupy positions on pedestals and pediments in the *quadratura* architecture. All but the last two of these Clementine virtues reappear in the Barberini fresco. Cortona, however, was not inspired by the illusionistic mode of the Alberti, nor by the Correggiesque foreshortenings of many of the angels. Instead he seems to have been most impressed by the freedom of movement given to figures flying about the open space of the sky, and by the playful conceit of the putti who carry papal tiaras and keys and combine them with three-dimensional stars taken from the Aldobrandini coat of arms (Fig. 166). The Alberti produced unusually inventive forms with the heraldic notched bands called "rakes" (*rastrelli*).[12] The heraldic devices in the corners become three-dimensional globes upheld by struggling putti (Fig. 167), but most astonishing of all is the large crenellated crown that seems to have escaped from the heraldic shield and lodged in the corner under the pediment. Yet even this is only to prepare the viewer for the extravaganza transpiring overhead with the circle of foreshortened angels within which appear St. Clement and the Trinity (Fig. 165). The observer understands that the ring of angels creates a living three-dimensional version of the Aldobrandini *rastrello*, now suspended in the heavens above.

The Aldobrandini arms appear crowned with pontifical insignia much as are the bees in the Barberini fresco. The putti flying above Charity in the Sala Clementina crown an Aldobrandini star with the papal tiara, just as Rome in the Barberini salone ceiling crowns the

[10] F. Würtenberger, "Die manieristische Deckenmalerei in Mittelitalien," *Römisches Jahrbuch für Kunstgeschichte* 4 (1940), 100–8; M. C. Abromson, "Painting in Rome during the Papacy of Clement VIII (1592–1602): A Documented Study," Ph.D. diss., Columbia University, 1976, 35–44; idem, "Clement VIII's Patronage of the Brothers Alberti," *Art Bulletin* 60 (1978), 535–39; C.L.C.E Witcombe, "Giovanni and Cherubino Alberti," Ph.D. diss., Bryn Mawr College, 1981, 109–39. See also K. Herrman-Fiore, "Giovanni Albertis Kunst und Wissenschaft der Quadratur, eine Allegorie in der Sala Clementina des Vatikan," *Mitteilungen des Kunsthistorischen Institutes in Florenz* 22 (1978), 61–84. For the recent restoration of the Sala Clementina frescoes, see G. Colalucci and F. Mancinelli, "Mostra dei restauri in Vaticano: apoteosi di San Clemente," *Bollettino dei Monumenti, Musei, e Gallerie Pontificie* 4 (1983),

242–46.

[11] The identification of this scene remains open to dispute. See Abromson ("Clement VIII's Patronage," 1978, 537, n. 32), who, arguing that no tradition exists for the baptism of Clement, identifies the scene as the baptism of Constantine. Earlier sources, however, identify the scene as the baptism of Clement, which would be more appropriate to the iconography of the fresco cycle. G. P. Chattard, *Nuova descrizione del Vaticano o sia della sacrosanta basilica di S. Pietro* (Rome, 1762–1767), 2:154–59.

[12] The precise heraldic term is "bends battled." D. L. Galbreath, *Papal Heraldry*, 2nd ed. (London, 1972), 96. But the idea of forming it into a three-dimensional crown has no place in traditional heraldic imagery.

bees.[13] Cortona's idea of the foreshortened view up inside the tiara appears to have originated here, although, to be sure, the tiara-bearing angel in the Sala dei Pontefici must be the common ancestor. The elements suspended overhead in the Sala Clementina—tiara, pavilion, keys, stars, and crenellated bands—form the papal coat of arms of Clement VIII, thus confirming the convention of the heraldic concetto, particularly in the central scene, where the action is synonymous with the heraldry of the patron. The bees flying across the open sky of the Barberini salone—crowned with tiara, keys, laurel, and the stars—continue the punning use of papal heraldry established at the Vatican Palace. The animal allegories in the corners beneath Benignity and Abundance in the Sala Clementina also reappear in the corners of the Barberini salone.

In Giulio's mural cycle in the Sala di Costantino the virtues appear as qualities appropriate to a good pope. Narrative scenes illustrate the effect of these virtues in the world of deeds, yet the viewer must imagine the ultimate source of the goodness itemized on the wall. The metaphysical origin of all this beneficence and order remains unstated in the Constantinian cycle, which lacks a unifying cosmology that would bring all components together in a meaningful moral and political system. A vault is the logical province of such an intangible concept, and the ceiling fresco of the Sala Clementina provides access, in the representation of the Trinity, to the divine origin of this universal order of which the papacy is agent. Further developing the Clementine project, the Barberini salone ceiling elaborates this ethical structure, but with far greater precision. Cortona shows us the origin, means, and ends of the divine rule of the pope.

Another cycle of papal virtues well known by Cortona and his patrons appears in Vasari's Sala dei Cento Giorni, begun and completed during a lightning campaign from March through October 1546 (Figs. 168–170). In late 1632, just as Cortona commenced work in the salone at Palazzo Barberini, Cardinal Francesco Barberini, newly appointed as papal vice-chancellor, took up residence in the Cancelleria. The Sala dei Cento Giorni thereby became the main audience chamber of Cortona's patron for the salone fresco. Like the rooms at the Vatican, it appears to have been carefully studied by both patron and artist.[14]

In the Cancelleria mural cycle the personifications accompany narrative scenes representing Paul III Farnese conducting various activities appropriate to the virtues he possessed: *Nations Paying Homage to Paul III*, *Paul III Ordering the Rebuilding of St. Peter's*, *Paul III Awarding Benefices*, and *Paul III Blessing the Treaty of Nice*.[15] Among the numerous personified virtues are the requisite cardinal and theological virtues, plus Religion, Fame, Peace, Eternity, Authority, Purity, Providence, and Minerva as Wisdom. These last two virtues are combined above the scene that shows Paul approving the designs for the rebuilding of St. Peter's, as the new structure rises in the background (Fig. 169).[16] The scene illustrates

[13] On this point of influence, see Posse, "Deckenfresko des Cortona," 169.

[14] For Cortona's comments on Vasari's Sala dei Cento Giorni, a work ridiculed by Michelangelo, see Ottonelli and Berrettini, *Trattato della pittura*, 227–28.

[15] The inscriptions, and probably also the iconographic program, were provided by Paolo Giovio. E. Steinmann, "Freskenzyklen der Spätrenaissance in Rom I: die Sala Farnese in der Cancelleria," *Monatshefte*

für Kunstwissenschaft 3 (1910), 45–58; Jacobs, "Patronage and Iconography," 56–88. The major contemporary sources for this cycle are G. Vasari, *Le vite de' più eccellenti pittori scultori ed architettori*, ed. G. Milanesi (Florence, 1906), 7:678–80; and a 1549 letter of Antonio Francesco Doni, see Bottari and Ticozzi, *Raccolta di lettere*, 5:149–62.

[16] The reclining personification of the Vatican, holding tiara, keys, and pavilion, occupies the foreground

the Farnese pope's wisdom in materially providing for the future of the Church;[17] he is both wise and provident in his action. This combination of Wisdom and Providence, unique in the cycles of papal virtues, reappears at Palazzo Barberini, where the two are juxtaposed in the principal personifications of the two main painted ceilings.[18]

As an ideal image of nepotism, the adjacent scene, *Paul III Awarding Benefices* (Fig. 170), depicts the Farnese pope dispensing the wealth of the Church and the Papal States in the form of ecclesiastical offices and benefices. A group of kneeling figures receives cardinals' hats and bishops' miters, while putti assist in the process by distributing medals and upending a cornucopia filled with coins. On the left, portraits of Michelangelo and Antonio da Sangallo, the architects of Palazzo Farnese and St. Peter's, indicate that Paul's munificence extends to both private and public architectural patronage. In theory, the pope accomplishes the distribution of offices and wealth according to the virtue and good works of the recipients, as suggested by the personifications standing on the pedestals to the left and right. Because of Paul's equanimity, the supine figure of Envy chokes on her own venom. Although not depicted here in figural form, Cardinal Alessandro Farnese, the chief beneficiary of Paul's munificence, looms over the entire scene—his personal arms, flanked by Eternity and Fame, rising above in apology for nepotism.[19]

More direct in its praise of the reigning pope than the Barberini fresco and similar cycles at the Vatican, the imagery of the Sala dei Cento Giorni abandons namesake glorification in favor of quasi-historical scenes with portrait images of Paul III and his "nephews," that is, his son and grandson. Although there are historical precedents for this usage,[20] most papal cycles of the period exhibited less specificity. The sycophancy of the Cancelleria frescoes perhaps reflects the nature of the commission, which was nepotic, like the Barberini fresco. Paul's grandson, Cardinal Alessandro Farnese, as vice-chancellor, resided in the Cancelleria and commissioned the decoration.[21] The Cancelleria frescoes thus emphasize the worldly activities of the pope—for example, the theme of Paul as political and architectural patron, universal sovereign, and peacemaker. The concern for peace and prosperity that derives from the proper exercise of papal prerogatives later reappears in Cortona's scenes depicting the closing of the door to the Temple of Janus and the arrival of Authority and Abundance to attend to the needs of the populace (Figs. 86, 88).

steps. Religion and Opulence flank the main scene, while Magnificence and Purity (Sinceritas) occupy niches within the scene itself. Wisdom and Providence flank the coat of arms of Cardinal Raffaele Riario, the nephew of Sixtus IV, who had constructed the palace (1483/85–1511). Fictive antique busts of Numa Pompilius and Marcus Agrippa are historical representatives of the revival of true religion and the building of magnificent temples such as the Pantheon. Jacobs, "Patronage and Iconography," 68–73.

[17] The main inscription beneath the scene is: MAGNIFICENTIAE STUDIUM CUM PRAECLARA PIETATE CONIUNCTUM MORTALES COELUS INFERET (Zeal for magnificence joined with conspicuous piety carries mortals to heaven). Ibid., 72.

[18] For Sacchi's *Divine Wisdom* in Anna's apartment, see above, Chapter IV.

[19] Cardinal Francesco so admired this particular scene that he later chose it as model for a proposed tapestry panel for the Life of Urban series he commissioned. Below, 190, n. 49.

[20] For example, the audience chamber in the Lateran Palace decorated by Callixtus II. Ibid., 57.

[21] The distinction between the less specific Vatican frescoes and the Farnese cycle is reinforced by the nature of the iconography in the Sala del Consiglio (Sala Paolina) in Castel Sant'Angelo (1545–1549). The frescoes painted there by Perino del Vaga, Pellegrino Tibaldi, Girolamo Siciolante, and Marco Pino were a papal commission and celebrate Paul III (Alessandro Farnese) only through his namesakes, St. Paul and Alexander the Great. R. Harprath, *Papst Paul III. als Alexander der Grosse: das Freskenprogramm der Sala Paolina in der Engelsburg* (Berlin-New York, 1978); and Jacobs "Patronage and Iconography," 90–210.

The Sala dei Cento Giorni represents but the first of three major fresco cycles celebrating Farnese family history and its support of the Church, which culminated in the pontificate of Paul III. These cycles, among the principal pictorial expressions of sixteenth-century nepotism, provided useful iconographic prototypes for the Barberini salone ceiling. During the period of Paul III's papacy, the Farnese were able to lay the foundation for a permanent political and economic base in the duchy of Parma and Piacenza, as well as in the ill-fated duchy of Castro and Ronciglione.[22] This achievement, much admired by Urban, explains the extent of the Barberini pope's generosity toward his nephews, particularly Taddeo, upon whom the continuance of the Barberini family physically depended.

The two later rooms also served as audience chambers and are both known as the Sala dei Fasti Farnesiani, or Hall of the Farnese Deeds. Francesco Salviati and Taddeo Zuccaro painted the first of these rooms in Palazzo Farnese (1552–1553, 1564),[23] whereas Zuccaro and assistants painted the second cycle in the Villa Farnese at Caprarola (1562–1563).[24] Cardinal Ranuccio Farnese commissioned the cycle in Rome, and Cardinal Alessandro again appeared as the patron at Caprarola.[25]

Like the Barberini Palace and the imagery of the salone vault, Salviati's wall scenes in Palazzo Farnese are divided into secular and ecclesiastical spheres. On the wall dominated by the enthroned figure of Paul III, the history scenes and personified virtues illustrate the achievements of the Farnese pontificate (Fig. 171). On the opposite wall Aeneas sits in the central position, and the flanking scenes depict the military prowess of secular members of the family in defense of the Church (Fig. 172).[26] This bifurcation constitutes a paradigm of the aspirations of any papal family—Farnese or Barberini—divided into secular and ecclesiastical branches. Two personifications, Temporal Sovereignty and Spiritual Sovereignty, illustrate this dichotomy in the ceiling of the audience room at Caprarola.[27] More than a merely intellectual construction, such a division reflects the dual nature of the papacy and the inner dynamics of nepotism.

Many details of the Salviati frescoes reappear at Palazzo Barberini. The wall with Paul III, like the cycle as a whole, is divided according to the temporal and spiritual concerns of the papacy (Fig. 171). Peace stands to the left of the pope, triumphing over a Turk bound at her feet. With the torch in her right hand she ignites a pile of arms, as flames rise up in front of the round Temple of Janus, from which Fury unsuccessfully struggles to escape. The temple serves as backdrop for the scene representing the Peace Treaty of Nice between Charles V and Francis I, a reconciliation in which Paul's diplomatic initiatives were instrumental. The binding of Furor and the closing of the door to the Temple of Janus in the Barberini work repeat this action. A further indication of the importance of the Farnese cycle as precedent for the Barberini appears in the personification of Religion to the right of Paul, with Heresy kneeling on a pile of crushed books at her feet. The adjacent narrative scene

[22] Pastor, *History of the Popes*, 12:229–34.

[23] R. Broglie, *Le Palais Farnèse* (Paris, 1953), 109–15; I. H. Cheney, "Francesco Salviati (1510–1563)," Ph.D. diss., New York University, 1963, 252–64, 393–401; idem, "Les premières décorations: Daniele da Volterra, Salviati et les frères Zuccari," in *Le Palais Farnèse* (Rome, 1981), 1:253–67; and C. Dempsey, "Mythic Inventions in Counter-Reformation Painting," in *Rome in the Renaissance: The City and the Myth*,

ed. P. A. Ramsey (Binghamton, N.Y., 1982), 60–64.

[24] L. W. Partridge, "Divinity and Dynasty at Caprarola: Perfect History in the Room of Farnese Deeds," *Art Bulletin* 60 (1978), 494–530.

[25] Cheney, "Francesco Salviati," 254; Partridge, "Divinity and Dynasty," 494.

[26] Cheney, "Francesco Salviati," 395–98.

[27] Partridge, "Divinity and Dynasty," 495, 498, 524–28.

depicts the Colloquy of Ratisbon, the meeting arranged by Paul in a last attempt to reconcile the Lutherans with the Church. Collapse of the talks in 1541 led to the war against the Lutheran Schmalkaldic League, as depicted in the background. The scene demonstrates the doctrinal watchfulness of the Farnese papacy. In the Barberini salone, this becomes Minerva destroying the Giants, that is, Wisdom defeating heresy. The two figures at the extreme ends of the wall are Fame and Rome, two personifications also prominently positioned in the Barberini salone.

On the opposite wall (Fig. 172), Aeneas, a seated warrior with lance in hand, exemplifies the military achievements of the secular Farnese. The fictive tapestry above shows the forge of Vulcan, with Venus handing weapons down to the Farnese warrior.[28] The narrative scenes contain depictions of the heroic military accomplishments of the Farnese: *Ranuccio Farnese Appointed General of the Church by Eugene IV (1435)* and *Pietro Farnese Leading the Florentines in Battle Against the Pisans (1363)*. These specific historical personages and deeds depicted in the Farnese frescoes become abstract allegories in the Barberini vault.[29] The forge of Vulcan and the Temple of Janus, together with their appropriate personifications, serve indirectly to convey the effectiveness of the Barberini papacy in the temporal sphere and the important supporting role fulfilled by secular members of the family. The virtue of the abstractness of the Barberini imagery was born of necessity. Unlike the Farnese, the Barberini did not have such a long and glorious past to recount.[30]

The array of virtues essential for the good pope appears in purest form on papal catafalques. Statues personifying the ideal qualities of the deceased pope were placed in proximity to his effigy. The catafalque of Sixtus V, for example, erected in S. M. Maggiore in 1591, contained images of Papal Authority, Religion, Justice, Magnificence, Providence, Faith, and a separate group representing the cardinal virtues.[31] The catafalque of Paul V (S. M. Maggiore, 1622), with sculptures by Bernini, supported a plethora of personifications: Magnificence, Magnanimity, Wisdom, Purity, Majesty, Religion, Providence, Tranquillity, Prosperity (Annona), Gentleness, Alms-Giving, Clemency, Truth, Justice, Mercy, and Peace.[32] Funeral orations delivered at the papal court reiterate many of these same virtues.[33] The virtues and personifications in the Barberini salone ceiling come directly from the tradition of papal virtues.

In the enumeration of these ideal virtues the sixteenth-century cycles in the Vatican, Cancelleria, and Farnese palaces, and those represented on catafalques, derive from the tra-

[28] Cheney ("Francesco Salviati," 262–64) observes that the ease with which figures move from one fictive space into another, such as the Venus or the Fame who sounds the call to battle for an adjacent scene, are precursors of the figures in the Barberini ceiling that move from inside the room into the exterior scenes. See also E. K. Waterhouse, "Tasso and the Visual Arts," *Italian Studies* 2 (1947–1948), 146–62.

[29] On this transformation consult F. Baumgart, "La Caprarola di Ameto Orti," *Studi Romanzi* 25 (1935), 89–90; and Dempsey ("Mythic Inventions," 71–72), who observes that the more abstract ahistorical epic mode began with Annibale Carracci's images of virtue in the Camerino Farnese (Figs. 148, 150), where the subject

of the scenes, Cardinal Odoardo Farnese, is nowhere to be seen. This abstracted approach to epic allegory became the dominant means of expression at Palazzo Barberini.

[30] Posse, "Deckenfresko des Cortona," 106.

[31] O. Berendsen, "The Italian Sixteenth and Seventeenth Century Catafalques," Ph.D. diss., New York University, 1961, 166–67.

[32] Ibid., 196–98; O. Paris-Berendsen, "A Note on Bernini's Sculptures for the Catafalque of Pope Paul V," *Marsyas* 8 (1957–1959), 67–69.

[33] J. M. McManamon, "The Ideal Renaissance Pope: Funeral Oratory from the Papal Court," *Archivum Historiae Pontificiae* 14 (1976), 9–70.

dition of princely *specula*. The salone ceiling proclaims that the pope must be both wise and virtuous, his wisdom and political effectiveness deriving from his personal virtue. The Christianized *specula* of Erasmus and the Spanish Jesuits, Pedro de Rivadeneyra and Diego de Saavedra Fajardo, established the background for the political theory of the cycles of papal virtues that culminates in the Barberini salone ceiling.[34] These treatises, however, were conceived for secular princes. A succinct categorization of the virtues considered ideal specifically for a pope appears in a *speculum* authored by Principio Fabrici, published in memory of Gregory XIII in 1588.[35] The first virtue or characteristic mentioned is the pope's "Religion." Subsequent chapters elaborate on his possession of the theological virtues, grouped together with Wisdom, and the cardinal virtues. The more mundane virtues of Vigilance, Peace, and Abundance follow toward the end of the enumeration. The concluding chapter elucidates the pope's rulership, personal life, and eternal memory gained by means of his virtues.[36] In the Barberini salone fresco, as in Fabrici's treatise, we find a "mirror of popes" in which wisdom and virtue are the predominant qualities.[37]

Each theorist had his own ideas about the precise set of virtues required for the ideal ruler, but most of them are incorporated in the theological and cardinal virtues. Significantly, Faith, Hope, and Charity crown Urban's coat of arms in the salone ceiling, and the four scenes located in the octagonal medallions exemplify the cardinal virtues. A complete set of the seven virtues considered essential for the good ruler thus appears in the Barberini fresco, with emphasis given to the theological virtues in the central section of the vault. In the cove scenes, the virtues and actions of the ideal supreme prince of the Roman Church further unfold before the viewer's gaze.

The most important cove—the one given the most violent and sensational dramatic action—grips the viewer's attention from the opposite end of the vault from the salone entrance (Fig. 85). There Minerva personifies the pope's wisdom in ecclesiastical matters as she defeats the Giants, the mythic precursors of heretics. The goddess's action illustrates the strict care the pope must take in doctrinal matters and in preserving orthodoxy.

At the opposite end of the room Hercules, as heroic virtue vanquishing the Harpies,[38] refers to the castigation of secular princes who challenge the temporal authority of the pope and thereby threaten the prosperity of the Papal States (Fig. 86). It emphasizes the importance of keeping in check those secular rulers who, however Catholic and orthodox in their profession of faith, still seek to increase their political power at the expense of the Church. Guarding against this ever-present threat ensures the preservation of the pontiff's temporal authority in the states under his princely dominion and guarantees the prosperity of his subjects, who, in the fresco, reach up to receive the fruits of this policy from the hands of

[34] Erasmus, *Education of a Prince* [1516]; P. de Rivadeneyra, *El príncipe cristiano* (Madrid, 1595); Saavedra Fajardo, *Príncipe político*.

[35] P. Fabrici, *Delle allusioni, imprese, et emblemi . . . sopra la vita, opere, et ationi di Gregorio XIII . . .* (Rome, 1588). Each of the 231 engraved emblems, or imprese demonstrating a virtue of the deceased Buoncompagni pope consists of a dragon, from the family arms, in some significant action denoting that particular virtue.

[36] If Fabrici's Vigilance can be equated with Rosichino's Preparedness (Vulcan's Forge), all twelve of the principal Buoncompagni virtues appear in the Barberini fresco.

[37] A parallel system of papal virtues, with comparable emphasis on virtue and wisdom, also appears in the orations of preachers given at the papal court. The funeral orations, in particular, seem to have been considered opportune for elaborating on the virtues of the ideal pope. McManamon, "Funeral Oratory," 35–42.

[38] For Hercules as heroic or physical virtue, see Ripa, *Nova iconologia*, 567–68.

Abundance. Hercules' heroic action in the scene preserves the temporal branch of the papacy, as represented by Authority entering the scene at the top. In conformity to the teachings of political theorists and orators, the imagery of the end coves establishes that the pope must possess both the wisdom of Minerva and the virtue of Hercules.

The long cove with the scenes of Bacchus and Venus show how the pope, through his possession of Moral Knowledge gained with the aid of Divine Assistance, overcomes the worldly vices of lasciviousness and gluttony. This illustrates the pope's knowledge of spiritual matters, which restrains the temptations of sensual delight. The perfect pope must be the model of moral probity for the Curia and secular subjects as well.

The opposite long section indicates that the door to the Temple of Janus can be closed and peace attained only through the preparedness of the papal army to defend the temporal power of the papacy. Ever present was the specter of the Sack of Rome. The scene therefore symbolizes the pope's preparations for war that preserve peace and safeguard the city of Rome against external aggression.[39]

Urban was the last of the bellicose popes, but his thinking on this matter had a long history rooted in the realities of politics. He believed that a pope could maintain the independence of his spiritual authority, even in doctrinal matters, only so long as he commanded respect in the temporal realm and remained free from the undue influence of any secular power.[40] Thus, in the center of the cove section, we see Prudence holding up a mirror to the face of Dignity, who thereby perceives the necessity for military preparedness and accedes to Vulcan to continue forging weapons (Fig. 88).

The Barberini fresco illustrates the ideal papal virtues operative under Urban's reign and confirms for the viewer that these same virtues make the Barberini pope worthy of election and guarantee his immortality. This grandiose personal conceit provides the main action of the central opening, where Providence commands Immortality to crown Urban's coat of arms. The source and nature of this eternity cannot be misunderstood. The incorruptibility of the Christian soul is not the theme here, but rather the immortal fame or worldly glory acquired through virtue.

The cult of worldly fame is not the least of the human impulses underlying the iconographic program of the salone ceiling, as confirmed by numerous contemporary sources attesting to the pope's avid quest for personal glory. According to the mordant assessment of the Venetian ambassadors to the papal court, Urban's character was flawed by an inordinate desire for worldly glory and an exalted place in human history:

> Avidity for glory, the passion of great men, excessively agitates him and he is always intent on those things that can aggrandize his personal image in the eyes of men and of history.[41]

Even if we allow for the expected prejudices of a Venetian official, the painted ceiling of the Barberini salone alone amply corroborates this evaluation.

---

[39] Urban had, in fact, opened a public foundry for just such purposes in 1634, as commemorated in a papal medal struck on the occasion. F. Buonanni, *Numismata Pontificum Romanorum. . . .* (Rome, 1706), 2:595.

[40] C. C. Eckardt, *The Papacy and World Affairs as Reflected in the Secularization of Politics* (Chicago, 1937), 76.

[41] Barozzi and Berchet, *Corte di Roma*, 1:226. The report was delivered to the Venetian Senate in 1626 by the "Ambasciatori Straordinari" Girolamo Corner, Girolamo Soranzo, Francesco Erizzo, and Renier Zeno.

The stellar crown being carried forward by Immortality represents the crown of Ariadne, symbolizing "immortal virtue."[42] Honor, glory, and immortality are the positive rewards promised to the virtuous ruler by the authors of the princely "mirrors."[43] The virtue and political acumen of the ruler find reward in the "glory" or immortal fame thus attained. Early interpreters of the salone ceiling understood the main action of the fresco in these terms. Ubaldini identified the figure of Immortality as "Glory," who with Ariadne's crown seeks to carry out the command of Providence and confer laurels on the bees, who fear neither time nor death.[44] In the salone fresco Saturn (Time) and the Fates (Death) are eclipsed by the reign of the virtues established by Divine Providence. Baglione and Titi continued the equation between the figure of Immortality and the concept of glory, calling the entire ceiling the "Triumph of Glory."[45] Although the identification of the winged figure with the stellar crown as "Glory" does not conform to Rosichino's designation, the term remains consistent with the actual meaning of the scene and of the ceiling in its totality. The subject of the fresco is the attainment of glory, that is, eternal fame and immortality, through virtue and wisdom. The artist himself interpreted the work in these general terms when he commented that he had painted it "for the glory of a reigning pontiff and for the honor of his government and family."[46]

Temporary decorations erected on the Capitoline Hill for Urban's *possesso* on 19 November 1623 had already represented the theme of glory and immortality achieved through virtue.[47] The sequence of five pairs of allegorical statues on the balustrade leading up to the Campidoglio concluded at the top of the steps with personifications of Fame and Glory.[48] In his learned exegesis of these images, the rhetorician Agostino Mascardi stated that fame and glory follow virtue, and that they produce the eternal memory or immortality of the hero, Urban.[49] Matthäus Greuter's engraved frontispiece for Mascardi's published description of

[42] Picinelli, *Mundus Symbolicus*, 1:57 (bk. 1, no. 396).

[43] A. H. Gilbert, *Machiavelli's "Prince" and Its Forerunners* (New York, 1938), 228–30; Fabrici (*Delle allusioni*, unpaginated dedication) observes that the virtuous lives of great men (such as Gregory XIII) serve as examples for us to emulate and achieve a still higher level of honor and glory, and that this is the only means of conquering time and death. According to a typical *speculum* of the period, virtue brings honor and, hence, the glory or fame that leads to immortality. R. Silvestri, *Il principe infante* (Frankfurt-Macerata, 1620), 33–51. The connection between virtue, glory, and immortality had been made by the ancients. For the definitions of glory according to classical authors, see F. Biondo, *Roma trionfante*, trans. L. Fauno (Venice, 1544), 194r–195v.

[44] "Vedete quella figura che in sembianza giovanile solleva una corona di stelle, simile a quella, che d'Ariana, si favoleggia, e questa vuol dinotare la Gloria, che al cenno della Providenza spiega l'ali, a circondar de stelle le Barberinie pecchie, et ad adornar, e confermar i lauri, che non paventino, ne la morte, ne il tempo, e verdeggino sempre vivacissimi d'ogni staggione." BAV, Barb. Lat. 4335. Transcribed in Lo

Bianco, "Disegni preparatori," 100.

[45] Baglione, *Vite de' pittori*, 182; F. Titi, *Ammaestramento utile e curioso di pittura* (Rome, 1686), 302.

[46] Cortona refers to the event in the third person: "Un famoso pittore del nostro tempo doveva condurre un'opera grande nella sala d'un nobilissimo palazzo, per gloria d'un Pontefice regnante, e per honore del suo governo e casato." Ottonelli and Berrettini, *Trattato della pittura*, 84. See the index of the treatise, 413, for confirmation that the passage refers to the Barberini salone fresco.

[47] On the history of the ceremonial procession of the *possesso*, see F. Cancellieri, *Storia de' solenni possessi de' sommi pontefici da Leone III a Pio VII* (Rome, 1802); R. J. Ingersoll, "The Ritual Use of Public Space in Renaissance Rome," Ph.D. diss., University of California, Berkeley, 1985, 171–223.

[48] The preceding statues were of Poesia Sagra, Facondia Greca, Disciplina Legale, Teologia, Humanità/Gentilezza, Fortuna, Abbondanza, and Publica Felicità.

[49] A. Mascardi, *Le pompe del Campidoglio per la Santità di Nostro Signore Urbano VIII quando pigliò il possesso* (Rome, 1624), 19–20. Mascardi was probably the au-

the *possesso* (Fig. 173) shows Fame, her wings covered with eyes and ears, flying above the Campidoglio, where the temporary triumphal arch (designed by Antonio de Battista) and allegorical statues are standing in place. Urban's immortal glory found literal expression on the vault of the triumphal arch in the center of the piazza. There, in the traditional position of Roman imperial apotheoses, appeared a "king" bee surrounded by many other bees, like stars. The inscriptions placed around the bees derived from Vergil's *Georgics* (4:219–27), where the poet discusses the nature and cultivation of bees. According to the poet, bees partake of the divine mind (ESSE ILLIS PARTEM DIVINAE MENTIS) and are immortal (NEC MORTI ESSE LOCVM). Mascardi explicates the inscriptions by quoting the full passage:

> Nec morti esse locum, sed viva volare
> Sideris in numerum, atque alto succedere caelo.
>
> [There is no room for death: alive they fly
> To join the stars and mount aloft to Heaven.][50]

The bees in the vault of the Capitoline arch are in apotheosis. The bees in the Barberini salone ceiling, flying heavenward to receive the reward of immortality and "join the stars," repeat this humanistic theme in more animated and illusionistic form.

The theme of immortality as the reward merited by the virtues and noble deeds of the ruler has its origin in the iconography of the Roman imperium.[51] This notion of political theory found expression on Roman coinage with the inscriptions AETERNITAS or MEMORIA AETERNA and referred also to the eternity of the empire and the imperial house.[52] As a virtue, "Aeternitas" was also associated with "Providentia," for the emperor's providence assured the eternity of Rome and his own apotheosis.[53]

The political theory forming the foundation for the iconography of the salone fresco is linked to a continuous tradition extending back to antiquity, which provided the artist with a stockpile of images. Cardinal Francesco's collection of ancient Roman coins, housed in a room near the library at Palazzo Barberini, contained numerous examples of imperial coinage with PROVIDENTIA DEORUM and AETERNITAS inscriptions.[54] On the coins *Providentia* most commonly appears with a staff or scepter, and *Aeternitas* carries a stellar attribute, as do Providence and Immortality in the fresco. But Cortona avoided any direct copying of the personifications from numismatic sources.[55]

An inventory lists one of the coins as a Marcus Aurelius "con la Providenza S[anta]."[56]

thor of the program for the decoration. *Le Pompe* appeared in five editions during the reign of Urban, the last in Rome in 1640. F. L. Mannucci, *La vita e le opere di Agostino Mascardi* (Genoa, 1908), 133–35.

[50] Mascardi, *Pompe del Campidoglio*, 35–37.

[51] H. Mattingly, "The Roman 'Virtues,'" *The Harvard Theological Review* 30 (1937), 112.

[52] F. Cumont, "L'éternité des empereurs romains," *Revue d'histoire et de littérature religieuses* 1 (1896), 439.

[53] M. P. Charlesworth, "Providentia and Aeterni-

tas," *The Harvard Theological Review* 29 (1936), 110, 122, 130.

[54] For an inventory of the collection, see BAV, Arch. Barb., Ind. II, 320a–b, where numerous coins "con la providenza" are mentioned.

[55] For illustrated examples of these types, see H. Mattingly, *Coins of the Roman Empire in the British Museum* (London, 1923–1950), 5:248 (Aeternitas), 582–84 (Jupiter).

[56] BAV, Arch. Barb., Ind. II, 320a–b, unpaginated.

Belief in Divine Providence was associated particularly with Marcus Aurelius because of his Stoicism. One of the primary tenets of this ethical system asserted God's beneficent control over the universe—a concept termed "Pronoia" or "Providence."[57] "Full of Providence are the works of the Gods," wrote the emperor in his venerated *Meditations*,[58] a work widely read in the sixteenth and seventeenth centuries as a manifesto of early modern Stoicism. Cardinal Francesco's sympathy for contemporary neo-Stoicism and the quasi-Christian sentiments expressed in the melancholic emperor's brooding writings found expression in his own Italian translation of the *Meditations*.[59] Embodying in his person all the necessary virtues, Marcus Aurelius represented the best of the Roman emperors and the personification of the ideal ruler.[60] Appropriately, a bust of that perfect emperor, located in a niche above the door on the opposite side of the room, greets the visitor entering the Barberini salone from the square staircase (Fig. 108).[61] It establishes the theme of ideal virtuous rulership under divine guidance continued in the frescoed vault overhead.

The iconography of the Barberini fresco derives from the literary and pictorial tradition of the "mirror of popes," as manifested in the orations, treatises, and painted and sculpted cycles of papal virtues. It nevertheless surpasses these prototypes in the degree to which it depicts the origin, means, and ends of those virtues. Paradoxically this is accomplished without direct representation of Urban, his nephews, or any historical event. We see the source of papal goodness in heaven and its action in the world as allegorically depicted by the intervention of the personified virtues in the mythological cove scenes. Finally, the well-deserved result of the pope's moral probity and political sagacity finds confirmation in his attainment of immortal glory. Yet, far from being only a narrow glorification of one papal ruler and his family, the Barberini fresco depicts everything any good pope would strive to attain. It constitutes a compendium of the requirements for every pope and represents an ideal that remained valid until the nineteenth century, when, with the establishment of the modern Italian state, the papacy was divested of its territorial possessions and the pontiff shorn of temporal rights.

[57] On the term "providence" in antiquity in general, see Pauly-Wissowa, *Real-Encyclopädie*, sup. XIV, 562–65.

[58] "Full of Providence are the works of the Gods, nor are Fortune's works independent of Nature or of the woven texture and interlacement of all that is under the control of Providence." M. A. Antoninus, *The Communings with Himself of Marcus Aurelius Antoninus Emperor of Rome*, trans. C. R. Haines (Cambridge, Mass., 1970), bk. 2, par. 3.

[59] M. A. Antoninus, *I dodici libri di Marco Aurelio Antonino imperadore di se stesso, ed a se stesso*, trans. F. Barberini (Rome, 1675). This was the first Italian translation of the *Meditations*. On the identity of the translator, see Costanzo, *Critica e poetica* 2:120; F. Petrucci Nardelli, "Il Card. Francesco Barberini Senior e la stampa a Roma," *Archivio della Società Romana di Storia Patria* 108 (1985), 184–85. The manuscript of the translation is BAV, Barb. Lat. 3896–3899.

[60] M. P. Mezzatesta, "Marcus Aurelius, Fray Anto-nio de Guevara, and the Ideal of the Perfect Prince in the Sixteenth Century," *Art Bulletin* 66 (1984), 620–33.

[61] This is the door that leads into the salone from the spiral stairs. "Per il busto la testa di m. Aurelio Imperatore fatto di stucco in mezzo del tondo sopra la Porta che va alla lumaca . . . sc. 6." BAV, Arch. Barb., Ind. II, 2888, 188. Transcribed in Pollak, *Die Kunsttätigkeit*, 1:291. The sculptor was probably Domenico Rossi da Fivizzano, who is mentioned in the same document in connection with some of the other sculptural elements in the salone. He worked under the direction of Bernini. I would like to thank Irving Lavin for identifying this sculptor, who appears in the documents as "Favezano." In 1639–1643 Rossi again worked as executor of a Bernini design in the apse of Santa Maria in Via Lata. I. Lavin, *Bernini and the Unity*, 171. According to Teti (*Aedes Barberinae* [1642], 178 and pl. G), an ancient bust of Marcus Aurelius could be seen in the oval room. For Teti's poem about Marcus Aurelius, emperor and philosopher, see ibid., 145–46.

THE EPIC TRADITION AND
FRANCESCO BRACCIOLINI

The variety of Cortona's iconographic sources, as well as the synthesis of traditional types of ceiling painting employed to realize a convincing visual unity of numerous scenes, indicates the breadth of the artist's search for effective means of pictorial expression. Cortona also drew significantly from a third and purely literary genre, that of the epic poem. He seems to have been influenced in this by Francesco Bracciolini, who, although little regarded by modern critics, was esteemed by his contemporaries as the greatest epic poet since Tasso.[62]

Early statements about Bracciolini's involvement with the salone ceiling are scant. The first suggestion that the iconography of the fresco derived from his ideas came in the form of an aside made by Domenichino in a letter of 1640.[63] Ample evidence exists, however, to confirm the poet's participation in the genesis and realization of the program embodied in the painting.

Bracciolini had served as Maffeo Barberini's secretary from 1601 to 1605, but subsequently returned to his native Pistoia to devote himself entirely to literary studies.[64] Upon the elevation of Maffeo in 1623, Bracciolini wrote asking only that he be permitted to come to Rome and die at the feet of his former patron.[65] He also found poetic inspiration in Urban's election and initiated work on an epic poem based on that theme.[66] The manuscript found favor in Rome, and Bracciolini received the desired papal summons. But, appointed secretary to the pope's ascetic brother, the Capuchin Cardinal Antonio Barberini the Elder, also known as "Sant'Onofrio" after his titular church, Bracciolini never regained his intimate relationship with the pope. Still, other favors soon followed, notably a papal brief of 1 June 1625 by which the poet and his family were granted Roman citizenship and the privilege of charging their arms with the Barberini bees. Thereafter Bracciolini was to be known as "Bracciolini dell'Api"—"Bracciolini of the Bees."[67]

Written in twenty-three cantos of *ottava rima*, *L'elettione di Urbano Papa VIII* found its inspiration in Tasso's *Gerusalemme liberata*, the most highly regarded Christian epic of the

[62] F. Ferrari, "Vita del cavalier Gio. Battista Marino," in *La strage degli innocenti del Cavalier Marino* (Venice, 1633), 85. See also the important entries in L. Allacci, *Apes Urbanae, sive de Viris Illustribus* (Rome, 1633), 104–6; and I. N. Erythraeus [G. V. Rossi], *Pinacotheca Imaginum Illustrium Doctrinae vel Ingenii Laude Virorum qui Auctore Superstite Diem Suum Obierunt* (Cologne, 1645–1648), 3:174–78.

[63] "Il capriccio sia del Bracciolini sopra le lodi del papa." Bellori, *Vite de' pittori* [1672], 370. Appendix G. Passeri confirms the inference: "Fu conchiuso che Pietro dovesse dipingerla il quale imediatamente con la poetica fantasia di Francesco Bracciolini da Pistoja celebre poeta di quel tempo in ogni genere di poesia assai caro al Pontefice." Passeri, *Die Künstlerbiographien* 379. See also Passeri's remark that first Andrea Camassei had been chosen to paint the ceiling with "alcuni concetti poetichi, con allusioni alle imprese, et heroiche azioni del Pontefice Urbano, espressi con la penna glo-

riosa del Signor Francesco Bracciolini dell'Api." Ibid., 169–70. Curiously Teti mentions him in connection with the salone ceiling in the manuscript of the *Aedes* (BAV, Barb. Lat. 2316, 4v–5r) but drops the passage in the printed edition, although he does mention Bracciolini in other contexts (*Aedes Barberinae* [1642], 119–22, 174–75).

[64] The major biography remains M. Barbi, *Notizia della vita e delle opere di Francesco Bracciolini* (Florence, 1897); see also Posse, "Deckenfresko des Cortona," 104–8, and Pastor, *History of the Popes*, 29:423–24, but for more recent and synthetic assessments see C. Jannaco, *Il seicento*, 2nd ed. (Milan, 1966), 420–28; and *DBI*, 13:634–36.

[65] Barbi, *Francesco Bracciolini*, 95.

[66] F. Bracciolini, *L'elettione di Urbano Papa VIII* (Rome, 1628). Later republished as *Conclave di Urbano papa ottavo* (Rome, 1640).

[67] Barbi, *Francesco Bracciolini*, 97–98.

sixteenth century. The guiding principle of the tradition of epic poetry, exemplified by *Gerusalemme*, was to combine the ideal poetic form of the *Aeneid* with Christian moral content. Bracciolini accomplished this by means of a tortuous narrative acted out by personifications of vices, virtues, and other abstract principles as well as various mythological and historical characters.

Bracciolini's poem has met with little critical favor among modern scholars of Italian Baroque literature. The observations of the early twentieth-century critic Giorgio Rossi typify the harsh assessment:

> *L'elezione di Urbano VIII* is a poem of scarce poetic worth. In this poem of his
> Bracciolini too often falls into the artificial conceits, clichéd metaphors, [and]
> confused and convoluted turns of thought worthy of the worst among those
> . . . too parrot-like ignoramuses with which the seicento was delirious.[68]

Notwithstanding the collapse of Bracciolini's reputation, a more objective look at his poem and a brief synopsis of the narrative will be useful for our analysis.

Anxious over the possible election of Maffeo Barberini to the papacy, the vices, with Falsity as their leader, form themselves into seven groups and occupy the seven hills of Rome, while Truth and the other virtues repair to Castelgandolfo. After an initial setback, the vices rally and Fury wounds Justice with an arrow. Self-Interest challenges each of the virtues to a duel, and, as the vices gain the upper hand, Justice suggests that the virtues abandon the earth and return to heaven. Charity and Justice then climb up to heaven in search of help. At the threshold of paradise they encounter Divine Providence, who ensures them that God will provide for the proper resolution of the conflict. Then word arrives that the life of Self-Interest is in danger because of excessive drinking. Charity descends, out of pity, to aid the stricken vice. Meanwhile, Ecclesia, in supplication at the foot of the throne of the Eternal, receives assurance that the current crisis will be resolved by the election of Maffeo Barberini to the papacy. Astrea descends in order to learn about the new pontiff from the virtues and hears from Memory and Urania about the origin of the Barberini family. Reason of State opposes the election of Maffeo, using the now revived Self-Interest to spread discord among the cardinals. Religion slays Self-Interest, but then Sickness is dispatched against the cardinals. Maffeo's guardian angel predicts that he will be elected. Making a final stand, Pluto himself sends Envy and Error into the conclave. Maffeo immediately vanquishes Envy, but Error manages to carry off one of the ballots. As Maffeo calls for another vote, a Virgin enters the conclave and banishes Error. Maffeo is elected by unanimous vote.[69]

Although Bracciolini's narrative of the events surrounding the conclave of 1623 is poetic fantasy, the allegorization has a foundation in historical fact. We shall see that self-interest, envy, sickness, and error ran rampant in the conclave that elected Urban VIII.

[68] G. Rossi, "Le postille inedite del Tassoni a *L'elezione di Urbano VIII*," in *Studi e ricerche tassoniane* (Bologna, 1904), 209–10. "A heavy and complicated medieval apparatus remade according to Baroque taste," said A. Belloni, *Il seicento* (Milan, 1929), 212. By contrast, Giulio Rospigliosi, Bracciolini's friend, considered the poem praiseworthy because of its thematic originality and the great difficulty involved in bringing the poetic task to successful conclusion. G. Rospigliosi, "Discorso del sig. Giulio Rospigliosi sopra *L'elettione di Urbano VIII* poema del sig. Francesco Bracciolini dell'Api," in Bracciolini, *L'elettione di Urbano*, 486–91.

[69] See the synopsis in Barbi, *Francesco Bracciolini*, 109–10.

As a work of art celebrating the election of a pope, Bracciolini's epic was no novelty. Panegyrical poems on this theme constituted a traditional literary genre in Rome.[70] As Urban was himself a poet and known advocate of poetic endeavors, his assumption to the papal throne brought forth an unusually abundant crop of such works.[71] Bracciolini's poem stands out not because of its theme but because of its epic form.

Briganti thought it remarkable that Cortona was able to extract anything worthy of consideration from a source so "prolix" and "illegible" as Bracciolini's poem.[72] Yet it remains to be determined just what relationship exists between poem and painting. The narrative scenes in the fresco and those in the epic have no obvious point of connection; still, there are some common formal and iconographic elements. The great variety of allegorical figures—a novel feature of the painting—also characterizes the poem. Moreover, virtues, vices, and other personifications intervene in the narrative scenes of both works. This conglomeration of iconographic types had not been so completely realized in fresco cycles prior to the salone painting, and it appears likely that Cortona's painting here reflects Bracciolini's poem.

Scholars have hypothesized that Bracciolini provided the artist with a written program for the ceiling.[73] Such an assumption implies a relationship between artist and poet inconsistent with the evidence and with what we know about common procedure in such circumstances. The implication that the painter was simply handed a diagram, poem, or prose outline of the program preconceived by the iconographic adviser cannot be sustained. If we had such a written iconographic directive from Bracciolini to Cortona, it would be a rare document for the study of Roman Baroque art.[74] The few written programs that do exist are almost invariably ex post facto, such as those of Campanella and Rosichino.[75] Rather than

[70] See, for example: G. M. Verdizotti, *In Clementis VIII P.O.M. Coronationem Carmen* (Venice, 1592); I. Fraserius, *Carmen in Pauli V Inauguratione* (Paris, 1605); P. Rocco, *Laetitia Orbis in Creationem Gregorii XV, Poemata* (Rome, 1621); O. Ponziani, *Poesie nella elezione e coronazione di pp. Urbano VIII, con un parallelo tra Alessandro Magno e la Santità Sua, della colomba e delle api* (Rome, 1623). For bibliographical listings of similar works, consult F. Cerroti, *Bibliografia di Roma medievale e moderna* (Rome, 1893), 1:220–23, 318, 408–11, 508–15.

[71] Ibid., 508–15.

[72] Briganti, *Pietro da Cortona*, 85.

[73] Posse, "Deckenfresko des Cortona," 108; Wittkower, *Art and Architecture in Italy*, 252; Magnuson, *Age of Bernini*, 1:347.

[74] They are nearly as scarce in the Renaissance. On the question of the respective roles of artists, patrons, and humanist advisers in the creation of the programs of Renaissance art, see C. Gilbert, ed. *Italian Art 1400–1500: Sources and Documents* (Englewood Cliffs, N.J., 1980), xviii–xxvii; and Hope, "Artists, Patrons, and Advisers," 293–343.

[75] See the anonymous manuscript program for the Pamphili Gallery in Piazza Navona: "Breve narratione dell'istorie dipinte dall'eccelente penello di Pietro da Cortona corona de pittori nella galleria del Pal. in Piazza Navona dell'eccmo pnpe Pamphilio," ADP, scaff. 88, n. 35, int. 3. Transcribed in J. Garms, *Quellen aus dem Archiv Doria-Pamphilj zur Kunsttätigkeit in Rom unter Innocenz X.* (Rome–Vienna, 1972), 102–5. Also the anonymous written program of Mariano Rossi's vast Cortonesque *Triumph of Camillus* fresco (1775–1779) in the salone of Villa Borghese: *Descrizione della pittura fatta nella volta della Sala di Villa Pinciana* (Rome, 1779). This inexplicably ignored painting and its learned program now have a complete study: C. Paul, "The Redecoration of Villa Borghese and the Patronage of Prince Marcantonio IV," Ph.D. diss., University of Pennsylvania, 1989, 87–100, 108–28. For a transcription of the published program, see ibid., appendix C, 415–17. The program was first issued as a pamphlet comparable in character and use to that of Rosichino. For an attempt to define "program" as a component of allegorical ceiling paintings of the eighteenth century, see K. L. Schwarz, "Zum ästhetischen Problem des 'Programms' und der Symbolik und Allegorik in der barocken Malerei," *Wiener Jahrbuch für Kunstgeschichte* 11 (1937), 79–88, esp. 85–86, who concludes that the "program" is neither a description nor an explanation but an integral and permanent part of the work of art itself. Also still useful on this issue is H. Tietze, "Programme und Entwürfe zu den grossen österreichischen Deckenfresken," *Jahrbuch der Kunstsammlungen des allerhöchsten Kaiserhäuses* 30 (1911–1912), 1–28.

iconographic prescriptions, they are informed descriptions of the completed work of art. In general, the program does not exist until realized in the finished image. Cortona's preparatory drawings for the salone fresco indicate that not only the formal aspects of the painting but also its iconographic components were subject to change as the work progressed.

In the case of the Barberini salone, the patrons, principally Urban,[76] must have determined that the pope's role as an agent of Divine Providence—so recently explored in Bracciolini's epic—would be the principal subject of the vault fresco.[77] That decision would have secured Bracciolini's participation in the project, but his role would have been consultative and collaborative rather than prescriptive in nature. The visual form in which the iconography was to be realized remained subordinate to the aesthetic judgment of the artist. Bracciolini resided in Rome throughout the period Cortona worked in the salone, so that verbal consultation would have taken place even as the artist gave visual form to the subject.[78] The dominant position of the artist, however, finds resounding confirmation in the near silence of contemporary sources about the contribution of the poet. Bracciolini himself left no reference to his role in the creation of the salone fresco.

Notwithstanding the poet's secondary role, he had an important influence on the artist. His intellect emerges, for example, in the unusual nature of some of the personifications in the painting. Divine Assistance is not a common allegorical figure lifted from the overused pages of Ripa. It does, however, appear in another of Bracciolini's epics, *Roccella espugnata* (1630), which celebrates the fall of the Huguenot stronghold at La Rochelle to the army of Cardinal Richelieu.[79] Lasciviousness and Gluttony, who dominate the mythological scenes of the long cove section on the right, also figure prominently as two of the principal vices in canto I of *L'elettione* (stanzas 43–44).

But the most telling reflection of Bracciolini's influence on the program of the ceiling is the unusual attitude toward the mythological figures portrayed there. For the most part Cortona depicted the pagan gods in a satirical and unflattering fashion, illustrating the antitypes of virtuous behavior. We can see this treatment in the discomfiture of Venus, the stumbling train of Bacchus, the uncontrolled fright of the Giants, the helpless struggle of Mars (as Furor bound to the burning weapons), and even in the sweaty exertions of Vulcan and the Cyclopes.[80] In Cortona's fresco the mythological figures, with the exception of Minerva and Hercules, personify the vices. This is precisely the conceit behind one of Bracciolini's most original literary contributions, *Lo scherno degli dei* (The Mockery of the Gods).

[76] Urban's intervention to change the plan for the central figure (below, 176) demonstrates how actively involved he was, even from a distance, in the design of the fresco. He must have had an equally prominent role in its genesis.

[77] Cortona once insisted that he had never chosen the subject of a painting, nor would he do so if requested: "Ma primo patto apposto dal Cortona era ch'egli non voleva indursi a far veruna proposta, allegando che non avevane mai fatta alcuna in tutta la vita." ["But the first condition set by Cortona was that he did not want to be led into making any proposal [for a subject], giving as reason the fact he had never made any in his entire life."] Reported in a 1666 letter of Onorato Gini, the Savoy agent in Rome. G. Claretta,

"Relazioni d'insigni artisti e virtuosi in Roma col Duca Carlo Emanuele II di Savoia studiate sul carteggio diplomatico," *Archivio della Società Romana di Storia Patria* 8 (1885), 516.

[78] V. Capponi, *Biografia pistoiese* (Pistoia, 1874), 62.

[79] For this remarkable manifestation of the Counter-Reformation mentality, see Barbi, *Francesco Bracciolini*, 123–30; and A. Belloni, *Gli epigoni della Gerusalemme liberata* (Padua, 1893), 253–59. "Divino aiuto" is also a concept that appears in the poetry of Urban. See Urbanus VIII, *Poesie toscane*, 24, 35, 61.

[80] Only Minerva and Hercules, with their long-sanctioned Christian traditions as representatives of Ecclesia and Heroic Virtue, escape this parodizing treatment.

Historians of Italian literature consider this work to be one of the earliest examples of a genre termed the "mock-heroic epic."[81] Bracciolini himself designated the work a "humorous poem" ("poema giocosa") in which he intentionally exposed the pagan gods to the ridicule they deserved. The poet exploited the absurd simile as a means of disparaging his pagan characters. The infuriated eyes of Mars appear as:

> Due gran' fanali, di due galeoni,
>   E per l'incendio lor', che 'l Cielo scotta,
>   La via di latte, diventò ricotta.

[Two great lamps of two large galleys / and because of their fire, which scorched the heavens, / the Milky Way turned to ricotta.][82]

In the introduction the author has Thalia state that such treatment of the false gods contributes to the triumph of true religion.[83] The love triangle formed by Venus, Mars, and Vulcan provides the focus of the poem, which has the characteristics of a domestic farce and concludes with a clamorous and undignified routing of all the pagan divinities from Mount Olympus.

The transferral of this parodizing treatment of the classical gods to the salone fresco was one of Bracciolini's most significant contributions to the project. It also conformed to Urban's official attitude toward the use of "false gods" in poetry. The poet-pope maintained that to show the pagan gods in a good light might lead the guileless reader into error. Instead, poetry should be directed toward positive Christian ends by means of pious imagery untainted by the lascivious or profane.[84] The pope apparently found it acceptable to employ the pagan gods when introduced into a work as negative allegories. Cortona himself documented how firmly Urban held to this moral-aesthetic principle. The artist reports that the original idea for the central figure of the ceiling had been "a majestic Jupiter, to indicate by that image the majesty and felicity of the reigning pontiff." Urban objected, noting that "Jupiter is the chief of the pagan gods and we do not approve that his image be painted or seen in that place." Cortona, using the third person to distance himself from the event, later observed that this objection "was considered prudent, and the advised painter changed his thought."[85] Since, for the most part, the cove scenes represented the pagan deities in a negative light—as allegories of vice—Urban did not object to them.

[81] Jannaco, *Il seicento*, 421–23; *Storia della letteratura italiana*, ed. G. Cusatelli (Milan, 1967), 5:854–60.

[82] F. Bracciolini, *Dello scherno de gli dei, poema piacevole* (Florence, 1618), 4 (canto I, stanza XIII). The intention was also to cast ridicule on poets like Marino, who sought, especially in *L'Adone* (1623), to use the pagan gods for serious poetic expression. Marino, whose works were also tainted with lasciviousness, found little favor in the Rome of Urban VIII. Pastor, *History of the Popes*, 29:411, n. 1.

[83] Bracciolini, *Dello scherno*, unpaginated dialogue between Thalia and Urania.

[84] Urbanus VIII, *Poemata* (Paris, 1642), 1–5. This theoretical introduction is entitled "Poesis probis et piis

ornata documentis primaevo decori restituenda." In a similar vein, "Grave error de' poeti, ch'intraprendono a cantar d'amore impudichi." Sonnet I, 299. See also Pastor, *History of the Popes*, 29:410–11, 418–19.

[85] Ottonelli and Berrettini, *Trattato della pittura* 84. See Casale's analysis in the introduction, xlv–xlvi, for verification that the passage refers to the Barberini fresco. The substitution of the personification of Divine Providence for the figure of Jupiter did not represent a change in the subject of the ceiling, but only a modification in the visual form by means of which that theme was to be expressed. The Stoic philosophers of antiquity saw in Zeus/Jupiter the embodiment of providence. Evidence of the original program's pagan cen-

Bracciolini may also have contributed an important factor to Cortona's innovative formal devices for integrating the secondary narrative scenes with the central section of the fresco. The extraordinary scale of the project demanded novel solutions to the problem of the organization and unity of the numerous components of the pictorial field. In response, Cortona turned to unifying devices of unusual scope. He introduced sweeping compositional arcs that reach the entire length and breadth of the vault and bind the cove scenes with the central figure of Providence. As we shall see, the theoretical principles upon which the artist relied in order to resolve the formal difficulties presented by the size of the vault are remarkably similar to Bracciolini's theory of epic poetry.

In 1636, while he was *principe* of the Accademia di San Luca (1634–1638), Cortona and his protégés engaged in an elevated theoretical discussion with Sacchi and his followers on the proper nature of painting, particularly with regard to the appropriate form of large works.[86] Unfortunately the original record of the discussion appears to have been lost, and a paraphrase of it is all that remains, but even this outlines the nature of the event in convincing detail.[87] Both sides bolstered their arguments with references to the terminology of literary criticism. In both word and deed Cortona upheld the validity of large-scale works. The followers of Sacchi responded that the eye tires and the mind becomes distracted before the excesses of vast works filled with a superfluity of elements. A painting, they observed, should be unified and simple like a tragedy, avoiding the uselessness and confusion of a multiplicity of figures. It should thus conform to the Aristotelian unities of place, time, and action, as does Sacchi's salotto ceiling in Palazzo Barberini. The defenders of large-scale works maintained that just as a painting can be compared to a tragedy, so can it be like an epic poem:

> In the case of the subject being vast, so ought the expression be proportionate to it. There needs to be introduced charming episodes which link with the principal theme. These become necessary as long as they contribute to the subject the richness suitable to it and tie together the groups and differentiate the areas of light and dark.[88]

Cortona and his group argued that when a work has a subject that is epic in proportions, the painter should cast it in epic form. For the sake of variety and magnificence, it would be necessary to introduce secondary scenes that, while distinct from the main subject, are still unified with it. They sought to achieve variety through unified multiplicity.

At the time of the academic discussion, Cortona was struggling to arrive at just such

tral figure abounds in the Jovian attributes and scenes surrounding Divine Providence in the fresco as completed. The lightning bolt, the crown of stars (cf. the star-crowned central figure of Jupiter in Lanfranco's Villa Borghese fresco, Fig. 119), the Fall of the Giants, and the entire assemblage of pagan deities gathered in the cove sections all echo the intended presence of Jupiter Optimus Maximus.

[86] M. Missirini, *Memorie per servire alla storia della romana accademia di S. Luca* (Rome, 1832), 111–13; Wittkower, *Art and Architecture in Italy*, 263–65; Harris, *Andrea Sacchi*, 33–35; and M. Poirier, "Pietro da Cortona e il dibattito disegno-colore," *Prospettiva* 16 (Jan. 1979), 28–29.

[87] Missirini, *Memorie per servire* 111–13.

[88] "E che allora vasto essendo il concetto debbe essere l'espressione in proporzione di quello: e volervisi leggiadri episodi introdurre, che si incatenino col principale argomento; li quali già si rendono necessari quante volte concorrono a dare all'ogetto quella richezza che gli conviene, e legano i gruppi, e distinguono le masse de' lumi, e dell'ombre." Ibid., 112–13.

a solution of unity within diversity in the Barberini fresco. There the mythological scenes in the coves correspond to the episodes in epic poetry. The artist strove to unite them with the principal theme by means of the sweeping compositional arcs of the lateral sections and the movement of the personifications both in the space of the room and into the fictive outside space of the narrative cove scenes.

Cortona's defense of his theoretical position and the realization of that theory in the *Divine Providence* parallel Bracciolini's theoretical concerns regarding the unitary nature of the episodic plot in epic poetry. A group of the poet's letters provides evidence for this relationship.[89] In two letters of about 1620 addressed to his youthful nephew, Giuliano, the poet expounded on his conception of the nature of epic poetry. He maintained that, despite Aristotle's condemnation of the episodic in poetry, supplementary yet subordinate scenes lend pleasing variety to the plot: "If variety brings with it delight, let us put as much of it as possible within the unity of our plot; let us help it with the dependence of the episodes and with the other means taught to us by art."[90] The need for episodes to enliven the narrative was particularly acute in Bracciolini's Christian epics because of the preordained beneficial outcome of events. He argued, by way of justification, that the presence of episodes in itself does not make a plot episodic in the sense Aristotle had condemned. A truly episodic and therefore censurable quality results only when the episodes are badly arranged and not operative in the larger central story.[91] Bracciolini's particular concern about the integration of episodes within the plot issued from the accusation that he had been episodic in his first epic poem, *La croce racquistata* (Paris, 1605).[92] His critic, however, was an Aristotelian literalist. Although the main plot of that work contains episodes, the whole consists of carefully constructed connections between these subplots and the main theme.[93] Thus the poet could reply that although he had violated the letter of Aristotelian law, he had respected the spirit of unity within the plot.[94]

Bracciolini's concern for formal unity in his epics reappears in Cortona's unifying devices in the cove scenes or episodes of the Barberini fresco. The art theory underlying the Sacchi-Cortona discussion in the Accademia di San Luca was couched within a framework of literary criticism. Sacchi's attack on Cortona took Aristotelian form, accusing him of violating the "unities" and, in effect, of being episodic. Cortona organized his defense along the same lines Bracciolini used to justify himself against accusations of episodicity. The painter's thinking on this point need not have been exclusively determined by Bracciolini, but the precision with which Cortona's defense follows the poet's ideas cannot be disassociated from their joint activity in the Barberini salone. At the time of the discussion, Cortona was giving visual form to an epic subject conceived by Bracciolini and engaged in consultation with the poet as the execution of the fresco and the realization of the iconographic program progressed.

Because of the nature of the informal working relationship between artist and poet, we cannot definitively establish that Bracciolini's poetic theory determined the formal unities

[89] F. Bracciolini, *Lettere sulla poesia*, ed. G. Baldassarri (Rome, 1979).

[90] Ibid., 36–37.

[91] Ibid., 36–37, 78–79.

[92] See Lodovico Norisio's letter of 5 September 1611. Ibid., 70.

[93] A. Belloni, *Poema epico e mitologico* . . . (Milan, 1908), 268.

[94] Bracciolini, *Lettere sulla poesia*, 78–79.

centered in the episodic scenes of the Barberini ceiling. But it is possible to observe that the fluid grouping of the figure masses, the interlocking of forms, and the violation of the formal architectonic barriers—outstanding unifying features of the salone fresco—have no precedent in Cortona's work prior to his collaboration with Bracciolini, nor do these qualities appear with equal effect in any of his subsequent paintings.[95]

In 1640, in conjunction with the completion of the salone fresco and the appearance of Rosichino's explanatory pamphlet, Bracciolini's epic on the election of Urban was reissued as *Conclave di Urbano papa ottavo*, as part of the ongoing literary project to elucidate and disseminate the message of Barberini imagery. The connection between the epics of poet and painter was thus tacitly acknowledged.

[95] See the comments of D. Posner, "Review of *Pietro da Cortona o della pittura barocca* by Giuliano Briganti," *Art Bulletin* 46 (1964), 415.

CHAPTER XIII

• "A Swarm Came from Tuscany": Providence in Historical Context

ALTHOUGH THE extent of the influence of Bracciolini's theories on Cortona's fresco must remain speculative, his contribution in one area remains irrefutable. He introduced the theme of Divine Providence into Barberini iconography. In the preface to *L'elettione* the publisher Andrea Brogiotti informs the reader that the author had originally intended to entitle the poem simply "La Divina Providenza," but after realizing that this was too general, he considered an alternative, "La Divina Providenza nell'elettione di Urban VIII." Ultimately even this had to be rejected for being too complicated. The abbreviated title finally chosen, asserts Brogiotti, recognizes all the more that "Divine Providence had been the motivating cause and ordainer of the means of Urban's election."[1]

Bracciolini did not originate the idea of connecting the action of Divine Providence in the world with papal election. That God intervened in the conclaves to ensure the election of his chosen one and thereby provide for the fulfillment of his plan for the Church and humankind was accepted as a theological commonplace. The notion is even embodied in the standard formula placed after the papal signature—"Divina Providentia Pontifex Maximus" (Supreme Pontiff by Divine Providence).[2]

The sermons delivered at the papal court indicate the pervasive belief in Providence.[3] God's active involvement in the world occurred particularly in times of crisis such as the "Vacant See" following the death of a reigning pope.[4] Orations delivered to the assembled cardinals immediately prior to their entry into the conclave ("orationes de eligendo") commonly invoked Providence in the form of the Holy Spirit.[5] Uncertainty remains as to when divine action in the conclaves was first concretized as specifically "providential" in nature, but there is no question about the ultimate source of this concept in Stoic philosophy and Roman imperial iconography.[6] Providence, the belief in the beneficent intervention of the

[1] Bracciolini, *L'elettione di Urbano*, unpaginated preface.

[2] The formula appears to have evolved from Roman imperial usage. Panegyricists addressed the emperor as "Divinae Providentiae Imperator." J. Ferguson, *Moral Values in the Ancient World* (London, 1958), 197. It now seems probable that the title "Pontifex Maximus" was revived for papal use only in the early fifteenth century. I. Kajanto, " 'Pontifex Maximus' as the Title of the Pope," *Arctos* 15 (1981), 46–47. Revival of the "Divina Providentia" and other exalted Latinate conceptions may also have occurred at that time.

[3] J. W. O'Malley, *Praise and Blame in Renaissance Rome: Rhetoric, Doctrine, and Reform in the Sacred Orators of the Papal Court, c. 1450–1521* (Durham, N.C., 1979),

126.

[4] Charlesworth, "Providentia and Aeternitas," 121. On the "Vacant See" as a period of crisis, see L. Nussdorfer, "The Vacant See: Ritual and Protest in Early Modern Rome," *The Sixteenth Century Journal* 18 (1987), 173–89.

[5] At the conclusion of the oration the cardinals file into the conclave as the choir sings "Veni Creator Spiritus." *Caeremoniale Continens Ritus Electionis Romani Pontificis Gregorii Papae XV Iussu Editum . . .* (Rome, 1622), 97; Moroni Romano, *Dizionario*, 49:47–53.

[6] J. R. Fears, *'Princeps a Diis Electus': The Divine Election of the Emperor as a Political Concept at Rome* (Rome, 1977), 277, 324.

gods in human affairs, represented a cardinal doctrine of Stoicism. The concept also appears in the coinage of the Roman imperium, as *Providentia Augusti* or *Providentia Deorum*, to legitimate the often tenuous process of succession.[7] In the elective system of papal succession, which by nature invited dissention, the idea developed that an unseen hand worked the will of God even in cases of acrimonious disputation and confusion, as often occurred in the conclaves. Churchmen held that "God regulates the realms of Christianity with particular providence and, with the assistance of the Holy Spirit, participates in the election of popes."[8]

The connection Bracciolini made between Providence and papal election therefore belonged to accepted usage. Yet this tradition acquired special relevance in the conclave of 1623 from which Urban emerged as pope. The almost totally unanticipated election of Maffeo Barberini occurred under unusually disordered circumstances. Historically the divine action in conclaves was emphasized when elections proved particularly difficult or produced unexpected results.[9] Unforeseen compromise candidates like Urban had special need of ideological bolsters and made full use of the divine-election concept. Precisely because of the unexpected complexities, contemporaries held that Urban's election exemplified the action of Divine Providence in papal conclaves. The difficulties that culminated in his election were fourfold: the institution of a new election procedure, the deadlock of the opposing factions, the outbreak of malaria among the cardinals, and the mysterious disappearance of one of the ballots in the final tabulation of votes.

The traditional process by which popes ascended the throne of St. Peter had been subject to much abuse.[10] Standard practice allowed powerful secular princes to seek to control the elections according to their own narrow interests. The machinations of the cardinals themselves, moreover, had become so blatant and worldly in motivation that many pious observers feared that the operation of God's will in the conclaves had been placed in jeopardy. Urban's predecessor, Gregory XV, issued two bulls reforming the election process: "Aeterni Patris" (1621) and "Decet Romanum Pontificem" (1622).[11]

Reform-minded prelates identified the means of casting votes as the most problematic issue. Traditionally popes were chosen by the process known as "inspiration," "acclamation," or "adulation." The powerful cardinals would bring their candidate before the assembly and say the words "ego eligo," with the idea that the others would join in the proclamation. This could be done suddenly without warning and at any time of day or night, without due reflection on the part of the majority of cardinals, and could create a panic in which many of them would join in acclaiming one of their number simply from fear of being left

[7] J.-P. Martin, *Providentia Deorum: recherches sur certains aspects religieux du pouvoir imperial romain* (Rome, 1982), passim. Pauly-Wissowa, sup. 14:562–65. For the numerous "Providentia" coins in Cardinal Francesco's collection, see BAV, Arch. Barb., Ind. II, 320a–b, unpaginated.

[8] "Che dalla providenza divina procedono tutte le cose . . . ," BAV, Barb. Lat. 2032, 307r. The manuscript (ca. 1622) is gathered with letters and material related to the drafting of the bulls on election reform. It appears to have been an apology for the traditional election process, demonstrating that God works his

will no matter how troubled the circumstances.

[9] C. L. Stinger, *The Renaissance in Rome* (Bloomington, Ind., 1985), 90–91.

[10] The use of simony and intrigue by the Spanish faction to elect Alexander VI Borgia was only the most outstanding of many examples in which the successor to St. Peter gained office by less than pious means. Pastor, *History of the Popes*, 5:382–85.

[11] *Caeremoniale Continens Ritus Electionis*; *Magnum Bullarium Romanum*, eds. L. and A. M. Cherubini (Luxembourg, 1727–1758), 3:444–65; G. Berthelet, *La elezione del papa* (Rome, 1891), 73–90.

out of the election and losing the favor of the new pope. The openness of the old procedure left it vulnerable to abuses that in effect deprived the cardinals of their freedom of choice in the matter of voting. To many observers this seemed a potential impediment to the working of the divine will in the conclave. Without totally disallowing the traditional means, Gregory's bull established that henceforth a carefully outlined system of secret balloting should be followed, thereby guaranteeing the freedom of conscience of the cardinals and facilitating the election of God's choice in the matter.[12] Urban VIII was the first pope elected by this new procedure.[13]

The reformed voting system first took effect under dramatic circumstances. The conclave convened on 19 July in extraordinary heat and amid considerable apprehension about the viability of the new procedure. It emerged almost immediately that the two main factions—one headed by the deceased pope's nephew, Cardinal Ludovico Ludovisi, and the other led by the nephew of Paul V, Cardinal Scipione Borghese—fielded forces so evenly matched that neither could impose its will upon the conclave. Nor could they agree on a compromise candidate among those considered *papabile*. The openness of the old voting system had the advantage of strengthening the hands of the pope-makers, but now it seemed the new system had neutralized their action in the proceedings to the degree that it became impossible to arrive at a conclusion. Fears about the workability of Gregory's electoral reforms appeared confirmed.[14]

Only at this point of impasse, after ten days of fruitless negotiations, did the name of Maffeo Barberini enter the list of compromise candidates. Many of the older cardinals immediately objected because of Barberini's youth (he was only fifty-six), and he withdrew his name when it became clear that the two-thirds majority necessary for election remained beyond reach.[15] At this juncture malaria broke out in the conclave and, by 3 August, had afflicted ten of the fifty-four cardinals present. By the 5th many of the cardinals' secretaries (conclavists) and servants had fallen ill and had to leave the conclave. As the situation grew more desperate, it became clear that a stalemate existed in which nothing less than divine intervention would be effective.[16]

Amid this confusion Barberini began to emerge as a more viable compromise candidate, but Borghese remained intransigent in his opposition. The negotiations became embittered, and there were those in the conclave who hoped that Borghese's fever would increase—he, too, had been afflicted—and that he would be constrained to leave the conclave.[17] Finally on the evening of the 5th it became apparent that an end to the conclave had to be

[12] L. Lector [J. Güthlin], *Le conclave, origines, histoire, organisation, législation ancienne et moderne* (Paris, 1894), 581–632, esp. 607–19; Pastor, *History of the Popes*, 27:110–19. Also see BAV, Barb. Lat. 2032, 307r–24r.

[13] Gigli's discussion (*Diario romano*, 75–76) of the Gregorian bull indicates how widespread was the interest in electorial reform.

[14] A group of cardinals resolved to undo Gregory's bulls. R. Quazza, "L'elezione di Urbano VIII nelle relazioni dei diplomatici mantovani," *Archivio della Società Romana di Storia Patria* 46 (1922), 33–44.

[15] The prolongation of the conclave gave opportunity for increased civil unrest, always a danger during the period of the "Vacant See," and numerous rapes, robberies, and murders were reported throughout the city. Gigli (*Diario romano*, 77) reported the discovery of great numbers of headless cadavers in the streets and floating in the Tiber.

[16] Quazza, *L'elezione di Urbano*, 33. The general opinion was that the disease resulted from the spoilage of excess amounts of food brought into the conclave. I. Carini, ed., "Il conclave di Urbano VIII," in *Spicilegio vaticano* 1 (1890), 359; Petruccelli della Gattina, *Histoire diplomatique*, 3:83; Quazza, "L'elezione di Urbano," 29, n. 6.

[17] Pastor, *History of the Popes*, 28:19.

reached quickly and that Barberini represented the only possibility for a speedy conclusion. Borghese dropped his opposition and during the morning balloting on 6 August Barberini received forty-nine votes, well above the required two-thirds majority. Many of the cardinals exulted in the election, but, in counting the total number of ballots cast, scrutineers discovered that one had disappeared.[18] Some of Barberini's opponents immediately called his election into question, and confusion reigned in the conclave. The procedural complication was compounded by the fact that word of the election had already spread to the city. In the middle of the ensuing general consternation and indecision, some of the cardinals began to fear the threat of schism that might result from a contested election. In order to dispel any doubt about his election, Barberini himself called for a recount. The missing ballot was retrieved in the count retaken.[19] Bracciolini versified Urban's heroic deed in the following lines:

> E dove ogni Pontefice già fue
> Solo una volta eletto, è questo due.

> [And whereas every other pontiff was elected / only once, this one was twice.][20]

Urban's supporters deemed his action one of lofty selflessness. Later the deed was immortalized in a bronze medallion.[21]

But the toll of the conclave was horrible. Eight cardinals and forty conclavists died. Urban himself soon fell ill and may have escaped death only because of his unusual robustness.[22] Of all the extraordinary aspects of the conclave, however, the most unusual was the unanticipated election of such a modest and youthful candidate as Barberini. That he had triumphed in the face of so many difficulties seemed to indicate God's providential participation in the conclave. As a contemporary commentator noted:

> The election could with reason be called surprising not only because of the circumstance of Gregory's new bull, but also because of the great number of old and meritorious cardinals and the disunion of the two heads of the opposed factions. No less worthy of admiration is the Divine Providence, which, after

[18] Ibid., 20–24. It was reported that Cardinal Scaglia, who was one of the three officiating scrutineers and unsympathetic to Barberini's candidacy, furtively slipped the ballot into his sleeve. "Conclave dell'anno 1623 nel quale messa la prima volta in uso la bolla della elettione publicata da Gregorio XV," BAV, Barb. Lat. 4724; A. Nicoletti, "Della vita di Papa Urbano Ottavo e istoria del suo pontificato," BAV, Barb. Lat. 4730, 669–70.

[19] Barberini addressed the conclave as follows: "Ill.mi Sig.ri non ha da succedere se non quello che Dio vole, fermiamo il punto, che lo scrutinio sia andato bene, ma giacché manca una Cedola nell'accesso, con tutto che senza quella il numero dei due terzi de' Voti e compito, che sono necessarj per questa elezione, nulla di meno acciò sia quello, che Dio vuole, deveniamo al nuovo accesso." From an anonymous contemporary bi-ography of Urban. "Sincero racconto della vita del già pontefice Urbano VIII, dalla sua puerizia all'assunzione al ponteficato" (BAV, Vat. Lat. 8891), transcribed in Carini, "Il conclave di Urbano VIII," 370. Pastor, History of the Popes, 28:23–24.

[20] Bracciolini, L'elettione di Urbano, canto 22, stanza 77, lines 7–8.

[21] Described in a Barberini inventory as depicting "the creation of Pope Urban by the balloting of the cardinals in which, because of the lack of a ballot, he declined the papacy without a new vote." BAV, Arch. Barb., Ind. II, 318, unpaginated.

[22] Pastor, History of the Popes, 28:25, n. 4. A. Celli, The History of Malaria in the Roman Campagna, ed. A. Celli-Fraentzel (London, 1933), 130. Gigli (Diario romano, 79) reports that Urban insisted he had been poisoned by a bouquet of flowers.

having restored to the electors their freedom of choice by means of the secret voting, with no less gentleness made them know how to conduct themselves in this election so that the majority of them confessed to not being able in this conclave to elect as pope anyone other than Cardinal Barberini.[23]

Urban felt that Gregory's reforms had been vindicated in the outcome of the election. Despite seemingly insurmountable difficulties, the conclave had been brought to a felicitous conclusion and the operation of Divine Providence in the proceedings assured. As one of his first major acts as pontiff, Urban confirmed the reforming bulls of Gregory with a bull of his own: "Ad Romani Pontificis Providentiam" (1625).[24]

Contemporary accounts record the appearance of a physical manifestation of the heavenly approbation shown in the election. On 4 August, during the most desperate moments of the conclave, a swarm of bees descended from the direction of Tuscany and, according to some accounts, took the form of a papal tiara, then settled on the wall outside the room that contained Barberini's cell.[25] This augury became codified in Urban's official biography commissioned from Andrea Nicoletti by Cardinal Francesco. It thus entered Barberini family mythology:

A few days before this election a great group of bees entered the Vatican Palace from that part facing the meadows that look out toward Tuscany, and the swarm rested on the wall of the room in which was the cell of Barberini. If this happened by chance, it can be said a remarkable encounter that a little before the assumption to the papal throne of a Tuscan, whose coat-of-arms is made up of bees, a swarm came from Tuscany and settled over his cell in the conclave. If it happens by particular disposition of Divine Providence that nat-

[23] "Conclave dell'anno 1623 nel quale messa la prima volta in uso la bolla della elettione publicata da Gregorio XV," BAV, Barb. Lat. 4724, 69v–70r. This anonymous manuscript appears to date from shortly after Urban's election and was later expropriated by G. Leti, *Conclavi dei pontefici romani* (Geneva, 1667), 449–50. A manuscript commentary by Magno Perneo (b. 1560), written in September 1623 immediately following the election, corroborates the participation of Divine Providence in the conclave, particularly in the method of election: "Praeordinarius autem prudentissimus Deus non solum hanc electionem, sed modum eligendi et media—tum prima tum remota—per quae itur ad illam ut certo et infallibilitur a usque coactione necessitate sive violentia, sequatur effectus. Qua ratione divina providentia habet ut cuncta comodo eveniant quomodo ipse praevidit ventura intra ordinem sua providentia, necessario sive contingentur secundum conditionem causarum quas ordinavit ad effectum assequendum." [God, however, preordaining and most wise, foresaw not only this election but also the method of electing and the means—both primary and remote—through which the election was arrived at, so that the effect would follow certainly and infallibly, whether by necessity or by violence. For which reason,

divine providence provides that everything shall come about fittingly in the way God himself foresaw what will be through his own providence, in order, either necessarily or contingently, according to the condition of the causes which he has ordered to attain the effect.] M. Perneo, "Canticum super electione Urbani Octavi Pont. Opt. Max.," BAV, Barb. Lat. 3261, 60 r–v.

[24] *S.D.N.D. Urbani Divina Providentia Papae VIII. Confirmatio Bullae Gregorii XV. de Electione Romani Pontificis, & Caeremonialis Continentis illius Ritus* (Rome, 1626). *Magnum Bullarium Romanum*, 4:95–96; Berthelet, *La elezione del papa*, 123–125.

[25] The report of Perneo (BAV, Arch. Barb. 3261, 135r–136v) is the earliest known account of the miracle of the bees. In fulfilling his duty as "Camerlengo del Clero," Perneo was required to be present daily immediately outside the chambers of the conclave to await the results of the voting. See Moroni Romano, *Dizionario*, 7:89–90. Subsequent reports indicate the dissemination of this extraordinary event throughout Rome and to all of Europe: Gigli, *Diario romano*, 77–78; G. Ferro, *Ombre apparenti nel teatro d'imprese* (Venice, 1629), unpaginated dedication; H. Conring, *De Electione Urbani IIX & Innocenti X*, in *Opera* (Braunschweig, 1730 [1651]), 692; Leti, *Conclavi*, 450–51.

ural events in themselves insignificant are sometimes used to announce some other event, it can be said that this sign had been sent by God to demonstrate his will with regard to the person who ought to be elected and to enlighten the electors in the midst of such darkness of private interests and dissension.[26]

Contemporary sources not only demonstrate the association between divine election and Urban's rise to the papal throne but also show how the appearance of a swarm of bees embodied that providential event. This provides a specific historical context for understanding the action of the central section of Cortona's fresco, where the bees fly overhead as Divine Providence commands Immortality "to crown the arms of Urban VIII Supreme Pontiff"—an action reiterated by Rome, who crowns the bees with the papal tiara (Colorplate III, Fig. 83).[27]

Re-creating the events of the conclave in allegorical form, the salone ceiling depicts the portentous appearance of the bees and the decisive intervention of Divine Providence in Urban's election. Emblematically, it also represents HIC DOMUS (This Is Home), the principal Barberini family impresa, with bees landing in laurel (Fig. 70). The Vergilian passage alluded to in the impresa, significantly, tells of the auspicious swarm that heralded Aeneas's arrival in Latium and the establishment of a new ruling dynasty (Aeneid 7:59–69, 122).[28]

Immortality fulfills an important role in this allegorization of historical events. Divine Providence made Urban immortal by electing him to be pope, but his virtuous action had made him worthy of that immortality. Urban's personal conduct during the conclave was deemed virtuous in the degree of heroic self-abnegation he showed for the general welfare of the Church. His response to the complication of the missing ballot indicated, according to Nicoletti, the depth of his virtue and magnanimity:

> It was a truly memorable deed that will render his name forever most glorified because, seeing himself at one point pope and then not pope, with great courage and with such a magnanimous heart he decided to let the welfare of the universal Church prevail over his own desire for the supreme principate. Wherefore amongst his other signal faculties and spiritual qualities are the constancy, magnanimity, and generosity he demonstrated in his heroic act, it will be sufficient to render his fame immortal and celebrate to the world the manner in which he assumed the papacy.[29]

---

[26] Nicoletti, BAV, Barb. Lat. 4730, 671–72; repeated in Conring, De Electione Urbani IIX, 692.

[27] Rosichino, Dichiaratione (1640), 6; Appendix F. C. Witcombe has outlined the tradition of the theme of coronation in papal ceiling paintings of the sixteenth century, interpreting the motif as a symbol of divine sanction. C.L.C.E. Witcombe, "An Illusionistic Oculus by the Alberti Brothers in the Scala Santa," Gazette des beaux-arts 110 (1987), 69–70. A modest precedent for the mid-air coronation of the Barberini bees appears in a small ceiling fresco attributed to Giovanni da San Giovani (ca. 1624) in the Sala delle Dame of the Quirinal Palace. See I. Roveri, "Scoperto nel Palazzo del Quirinale: un affresco del seicento," Costume 9 (Feb. 1964), 55–57; A. Negro, Guide rionali di Roma: rione

II—Trevi, pt. 2 (Rome, 1985) 189.

[28] Above, 109–10 and n. 34. Ubaldini (BAV, Barb. Lat. 4335), as transcribed in Lo Bianco ("Disegni preparatori," 100), observed that, for him, the bees were those that appeared in a laurel tree and presaged a change in rulership. I would like to thank Irving Lavin, who first suggested to me a connection between the miracle of the bees, the election of Urban, and the Cortona fresco.

[29] Guercino's Allegory of Fame (1621) in the Casino Ludovisi, which also employs family heraldry in the celebration of a papal election (Gregory XV), may have served as a precedent for Cortona. See C. H. Wood, "Visual Panegyric in Guercino's Casino Ludovisi Frescoes," Storia dell'arte 58 (1986), esp. 225–28. "Attione in

Like the Barberini salone ceiling, Nicoletti's encomium on Urban's exemplary behavior in the conclave focuses on the theme of immortal glory acquired through virtue. The apotheosis of the bees that takes place in the fresco thus symbolizes Urban's election by Divine Providence because of his virtue.

TAPESTRY CYCLES: THREE HISTORICAL INSTANCES OF PROVIDENTIAL ACTION AND DIVINE ELECTION

Francesco Barberini commissioned three major tapestry cycles that complement the program of the *Divine Providence*. The cardinal's interest in tapestries began with seven scenes from the life of Constantine by Rubens (1623–1625), received as a diplomatic gift from Louis XIII in 1625.[30] The cardinal subsequently established his own tapestry works in Rome, with Jacomo della Riviera (Jacob van den Vliete) as master weaver, and commissioned six additional designs from Cortona (woven 1630–1641) to complete the set of narrative scenes of the first Christian emperor's life.[31] A second major cycle followed in 1643–1656, depicting twelve scenes from the life of Christ based on cartoons by Romanelli and his assistant Paolo Spagna.[32] The third large-scale tapestry cycle comprised ten panels with scenes from the life of Urban VIII (woven 1663–1683) after cartoons by Antonio Gherardi, Fabio Cristofani, Pietro Lucatelli, Giacinto Camassei, and Giuseppe Belloni.[33] All three cycles appear to have been conceived for occasional display in the salone.[34]

vero memorabile, che renderà per sempre gloriossimo il suo nome, perchè vistosi in un punto Papa, e non papa seppe con tanta intrepidezza, e con si magnanimo cuore far prevalere il bene della Chiesa universale alla cupidità propria del supremo principato; onde fra l'altre sue segnalate prerogative, e doti dell'animo, la costanza, la magnanimità e la generosità che egli mostrò in quest'atto eroico basterà per rendere immortale la fama di lui, e celebre al mondo la maniera, con la quale fu assunto al Pontificato." Nicoletti, BAV, Barb. Lat. 4730, 664.

[30] D. DuBon, *Tapestries from the Samuel H. Kress Collection at the Philadelphia Museum of Art: The History of Constantine the Great Designed by Peter Paul Rubens and Pietro da Cortona* (London, 1964), 11–14; W. Vitzthum, "Review of *Tapestries from the Samuel H. Kress Collection at the Philadelphia Museum of Art: The History of Constantine the Great Designed by Peter Paul Rubens and Pietro da Cortona* by David DuBon," *Burlington Magazine* 107 (1965), 262–63. Zurawski, "Rubens and the Barberini," 48–50.

[31] Cavallo, "Notes on the Barberini Tapestry Manufactory," 17–26; Barberini, "Pietro da Cortona," 145–52. All thirteen panels of the Constantine series are now located in the Philadelphia Museum of Art.

[32] Ibid., 150–51; Faldi, *Galleria Nazionale d'Arte Antica*, 69; O. Ferrari, *Arazzi italiani* (Milan, 1982), 18. Gasparo Rocci executed the cartoon for the *Crucifixion* panel based on Cortona's fresco in the chapel. DuBon,

Tapestries, 144. All of the tapestries in this cycle are preserved in the Church of St. John the Divine, New York. Eleven cartoons are in the Galleria Nazionale, Rome.

[33] H. Göbel, "Das Leben Urbans VIII.: Die Pfeilerteppichserie aus der römischen Manufaktur des Kardinals Francesco Barberini," *Der Cicerone* 21 (1929), 305–11; M. Calberg, "Hommage au pape Urbain VIII, tapisserie de la manufacture Barberini à Rome," *Bulletin des Musées Royaux d'Art et d'Histoire*, 4th ser., 31 (1959), 99–110; I. Faldi, *I cartoni per gli arazzi Barberini della serie di Urbano VIII* (Rome, 1967); U. Barberini, "Gli arazzi e i cartoni della serie 'Vita di Urbano VIII' della arazzeria Barberini," *Bollettino d'arte* 53 (1968), 92–100; Ferrari, *Arazzi italiani*, 19. All ten panels are in the possession of the Vatican Museums. The Galleria Nazionale, Rome, possesses all ten of the original cartoons. In addition to the ten executed panels, four other scenes were projected. "Memoria delli altri quattro pezzi d'arazzi che restano da farsi della vita di Papa Urbano VIII," BAV, Arch. Barb., Ind. II, 2693.

[34] For the Constantine series, see Barberini, "Pietro da Cortona," 45; DuBon, *Tapestries*, 16; and especially Zurawski ("Rubens and the Barberini," 166–187), who first pointed to the integrated program of fresco and tapestries, including a reconstructed plan of the disposition for the series as it would have been arranged in the salone. F. Baldinucci (*Vite di artisti*, 5:423) reports that the Life of Christ cycle was to hang on the salone

Each of the tapestry cycles illustrates the principal theme of the salone vault fresco by means of specific historical example. The Constantine cycle provides the most venerable secular exemplum of God's providential intervention in human affairs to establish and safeguard the Church in its worldly and spiritual mission. This notion is emblematically stated in the cartouche of the top border of each tapestry panel, where the CHI-RHO appears as symbol of God's guiding presence behind the narrative event. In illustrating the divine favor shown to Constantine and, in turn, the emperor's benevolent protection of the Church, the series also legitimated the temporal prerogatives of the popes as the modern successors to the emperors of Roman antiquity.

Six panels designed by Cortona complement those by Rubens in a fashion that emphasizes this continuity.[35] The *Apparition of the Cross*, for example, depicts God's promise to Constantine that under that sign he would defeat his enemy Maxentius. *Constantine Burning the Memorials* shows the emperor's piety and concern for the welfare of the Church in his destruction of decrees that favored pagan religion and held the Church under oppressive taxation.[36] Likewise, *Constantine Destroying the Idols* illustrates his defense of true religion. The panel representing the *Statue of Constantine*—a gilt bronze figure on an inscribed pedestal—refers to a monument of the victorious emperor erected by the Senate and people of Rome,[37] and, by allusion, to the statue of Urban recently commissioned from Bernini by the city government of Rome for the Conservators' Palace on the Campidoglio.[38]

The iconographic association between the Constantine series and the salone fresco must also have been reinforced by their common formal and thematic sources in the Vatican Sala di Costantino, where feigned tapestries decorate the frescoed walls with scenes from the life of Constantine, and the popes enthroned nearby demonstrate the continuum linking the Christian emperor to the successors to St. Peter.[39]

No sooner was the salone fresco finished and the Constantine cycle completed than Cardinal Francesco initiated a new series of tapestry panels illustrating the life and Passion of Christ.[40] This series elaborated God's most significant act of providence, showing the incarnation, life, and Passion of Christ, and illustrated how the divine plan for the salvation of humankind first came into being. Each scene depicts either a crucial moment of God's

---

walls. In January 1677 Cardinal Francesco paid for the recent hanging of the Life of Urban series in the salone. BAV, Arch. Barb., Comp. 91, 106r. Cardinal Carlo Barberini, Taddeo's son, had the tapestries displayed on the facade of the Casa Grande ai Giubbonari in 1683 on the occasion of the procession of San Lorenzo in Damaso. G. Campori, *L'arazzeria estense* (Modena, 1876), 74–75. In the winter months tapestries were also used for comfort as well as display and were hung in the living quarters of the apartments.

[35] Zurawski, "Rubens and the Barberini," 104–9. The scenes are: *Constantine Fighting the Lion* (Cortona), the *Double Marriage of Constantine and Licinius* (Rubens), the *Apparition of the Cross* (Cortona), the *Battle of the Milvian Bridge* (Cortona), the *Triumphal Entry into Rome* (Rubens), the *Statue of Constantine* (Cortona), the *Baptism of Constantine* (Rubens), the *Campaign against Licin-*

ius, *Sea Battle* (Cortona), *Constantine Burning the Memorials* (Cortona), *Constantine Destroying the Idols* (Cortona), *St. Helena Finding the True Cross* (Rubens), the *Building of Constantinople* (Rubens), and the *Death of Constantine* (Rubens).

[36] Ibid., 115–16.

[37] Ibid., 113–14.

[38] This honor was first discussed by city officials as early as 1635. Pollak, *Die Kunsttätigkeit*, 1:338–39, docs. 978–79.

[39] Zurawski, "Rubens and the Barberini," 183–85.

[40] The following scenes are included in the cycle: the *Annunciation*, *Rest on the Flight into Egypt*, the *Adoration of the Shepherds*, the *Adoration of the Magi*, the *Baptism of Christ*, *Christ's Charge to Peter*, the *Last Supper*, the *Agony in the Garden*, the *Crucifixion*, the *Resurrection*, and a *Map of the Holy Land*.

intervention in the narrative or human recognition of his guiding involvement in the progress of events. In the *Rest on the Flight into Egypt*, for example, as the Virgin nurses the Christ child, an angel appears to the sleeping Joseph and warns him to flee into Egypt for the protection of the child (Matthew 2:13). A cross in the background of the *Baptism of Christ* foretells the purpose of Christ's mission on earth.

As in the Constantine cycle, symbols in the border cartouches at the top of each scene emblematically recapitulate the primary moral principles of the narrative cycle. The panels representing the birth and teaching cycle of Christ have above them Urban's device of the plough guided by bees, as seen in the cartouche beneath Moral Knowledge in the south cove of the salone vault (Fig. 87). There, as we have observed, it referred to divine guidance ("Supremum Regimen") of the human soul, particularly to the corresponding moral guidance of Urban's pontificate.[41] Transferred to the tapestry cycle, this device now demonstrates God's prescience and omnipotence in the narrative transpiring in the scenes below. At no point in the cycle of scenes does this meaning become clearer than in the *Charge to Peter* (Fig. 109),[42] for here Christ hands over to St. Peter the keys to the kingdom of heaven ("the keys of knowledge and power"), thereby providing for the establishment of the Church as a worldly and spiritual institution. In the right background rises a domed temple suggestive of St. Peter's Basilica. This panel constitutes the chronological midpoint of the cycle and must have occupied a prominent position when the complete series hung in sequence. Such emphasis conforms to the iconographic theme of the salone fresco, since the *Charge to Peter* represents one of the primary scriptural events for the legitimization of the papacy.

Just as the Sala di Costantino had served as an important model for the Constantine series, the Life of Christ tapestries find their ultimate source of inspiration in the quattrocento mural scenes and Raphael's tapestry cycle for the Sistine Chapel.[43] The point of comparison rests not so much in the details of the two groups of tapestries but in their relationship to the frescoed scenes. Raphael's Acts of the Apostles series continues the narrative initiated in Michelangelo's creation scenes on the ceiling. The quattrocento wall frescoes depicting the lives of Moses and Christ, located above the first cornice, bridge the physical space and narrative time between the creation scenes on the ceiling and the apostolic era appearing in the tapestries on the lower wall. The *Last Judgment* above the altar concludes this narrative of events at the end of time. Significantly the salient issue in the Acts of the Apostles is the notion of apostolic succession, sanctioning the authority of the popes, the Vicars of Christ. The same theme dominates the Barberini tapestries, where the *Charge to Peter* fulfills a pivotal role corresponding to Perugino's *Charge to Peter* on the Sistine wall and the *Pasce Oves Meas* of the Sistine tapestry cycle.

The cartouches above the Passion scenes of Romanelli's tapestries contain the rising sun.[44] As we have seen, this is yet another Barberini device—one that appears in the car-

---

[41] Above, 140–41. The other cartouches of the tapestry borders contain the theological virtues.

[42] "And I will give to thee the keys of the kingdom of heaven. And whatsoever thou shalt bind upon earth, it shall be bound also in heaven: and whatsoever thou shalt loose on earth, it shall be loosed also in heaven." Matthew 16:19

[43] Vitzthum, "Review of *Tapestries*" 262. On the Sis-

tine wall frescoes, see L. D. Ettlinger, *The Sistine Chapel before Michelangelo* (Oxford, 1956). For Raphael's tapestries, see J. Shearman, *Raphael's Cartoons in the Coll. of Her Majesty the Queen and the Tapestries for the Sistine Chapel* (London, 1972), 45–90.

[44] The *Agony in the Garden*, which again has the plough, is an anomalous unit in this scheme.

touche beneath Dignity in the salone (Fig. 88), where it refers to the eternity of the Roman papacy.[45] In the context of the Passion scenes the impresa also prefigures Christ's resurrection and the promise of eternal life brought to humankind.

Cortona's fresco in the piano nobile chapel (Fig. 51) provided the model for the *Crucifixion* panel of this group (Fig. 110), and the *Annunciation* and *Adoration* panels also reflect—although less literally—the comparable scenes there, where Romanelli had assisted Cortona. As in the tapestry series, Christ's life and Passion are the principal subjects of the chapel frescoes. The ensemble of tapestries would have appeared like the chapel fresco cycle magnified and unfolded on the walls of the salone.[46] But, whereas the chapel frescoes emphasize Christ's childhood, the tapestry scenes expand on Christ's teaching mission on earth and the final events of his life. In the chapel we see more of the beginnings of God's providence; in the salone hung with the tapestries, we see more of the purpose of his intervention in human affairs.

The Life of Urban VIII tapestries complete the trilogy, illustrating in fabric the historical instances of God's guidance of worldly events. Although this cycle was late in its actual realization, it evolved from a fresco scheme proposed by Federico Ubaldini for the salone walls ca. 1643–1644 and is therefore in its conception contemporaneous with the Life of Christ cycle.[47] Ubaldini intended to show only scenes of Urban's reign, beginning with his election.[48] Apparently the first four scenes would have appeared on the south wall of the salone, in chronological order from right to left, and the last two on the north wall, separated by the fireplace. This means that the first wall fresco to greet the visitor entering from the square staircase would have been the election scene. Hence it would have established election as the principal theme of the entire pictorial cycle, as does the central section of the vault fresco above.

As completed, the series of the Life of Urban consists of ten narrative panels and various accessory pieces.[49] The tapestry representing the election of Urban closely follows the instructions of Ubaldini (Fig. 111):

[45] Above, 141–42.

[46] Four of the eight chapel scenes reappear in the tapestries: the *Annunciation*, the *Adoration*, the *Rest on the Flight*, and the *Crucifixion*.

[47] "Abbozzo per le pitture alle parieti della Sala Barberina. Le attioni principali di Papa Urbano ottavo distinte in sei quadri," BAV, Barb. Lat. 4901, 61. Transcribed in Pastor, *History of the Popes*, 29:502, n. 1. The scenes proposed by Ubaldini were "La creatione di esso Papa Urbano," "L'aprimento della Porta Santa," "La correttione dei riti e de' libri ecclesiastici," "L'acquisto dello stato di Urbino," "Il tener lontano la peste, la fame e la guerra dallo Stato ecclesiastico," and "La difesa dello Stato della Chiesa." The fresco series was divided into three scenes related to ecclesiastical matters and three concerned with temporal affairs. Only three of Ubaldini's proposed scenes were ultimately used in the tapestry series, and even these were much modified. Ubaldini was Cardinal Francesco's secretary. Vitaletti, "Intorno a Ubaldini," 489, n. 3.

[48] Ubaldini had been commissioned by Cardinal Francesco to write the history of Urban's pontificate. "Istoria del pontificato di PP. Urbano VIII," BAV, Barb. Lat. 4728. The manuscript is dated 1640.

[49] There appears to be some discrepancy between the imagery of the tapestry panels and the titles mentioned in payment documents and inventories. The following are descriptive titles based on the scenes represented in the panels: *Maffeo Receiving the Doctorate in Pisa* (Antonio Gherardi), *Maffeo Presides over the Works at Lake Trasimeno* (Antonio Gherardi), *Maffeo Created Cardinal by Paul V* (Antonio Gherardi), *Ballot for the Election of Urban* (Fabio Cristofani), *Urban Recognized Pope by the Catholic Powers* (Pietro Lucatelli), *Urban Invokes Saints Peter and Paul for the Defense of the Coast of Lazio against Pirates* (Giacinto Camassei), *Urban Consecrates St. Peter's Basilica* (Fabio Cristofani), the *Annexation of Urbino* (Pietro Lucatelli), *Urban and the Countess Matilda: The Acquisition of the Papal States* (Giuseppe Belloni), and the *Fortification of Rome* (Pietro Lucatelli).

The creation of the said Pope Urban, with the representation of the repetition of the balloting. For this, one can have recourse to the poem of Bracciolini, Rosichino's master, in the place where he deals with this, in order to represent there figures in the air denoting the virtues that participated in an event so heroic.[50]

The tapestry shows a conflated version of the historical events of the conclave. The scene is set in the Sistine Chapel, where the final voting took place. On the right, three cardinal scrutineers in charge of the balloting conduct a frantic search for the missing ballot. While one of the officials in the background examines the chalice that had served as container for the voting slips, another physically calculates the votes. Maffeo gestures for the count to be retaken, while Cardinal Ludovico Ludovisi, behind him, and Cardinal Scipione Borghese, seated in front, avidly follow the proceedings. Two older cardinals, perhaps enemies of Maffeo, seem to calumniate in the background. At that moment the missing ballot is discovered and held aloft by the scrutineer in the foreground. Two virtues, Modesty and Magnanimity,[51] enter the conclave, gesturing toward Maffeo as a kneeling conclavist offers the papal tiara to him. An open window in the left background reveals the parting clouds.

In 1677 two additional tapestry pieces were woven to accompany the Life of Urban cycle: a *Transfiguration* and an *Archangel Michael*.[52] These images would have further strengthened the theme of Urban's election embodied in the series, for he was elected on the Feast of the Transfiguration (6 August) and, as we have seen, chose to have his coronation on the Feast of St. Michael Archangel (29 September), his special patron.[53]

Although the Life of Urban narrative panels refer to historical events, only three of them can be said to depict in any accurate detail an actual historical occurrence.[54] The allegorical element dominates the action of all ten scenes. For example, the tapestry representing *Urban and the Countess Matilda: Acquisition of the Papal States* (Fig. 112) betokens the sovereignty of the papacy over its temporal possessions. The Tuscan countess acted as a secular protectress of the papacy in disputes with the empire and, at her death in 1115, willed her

---

See Barberini, "Arazzi e cartoni," 92–100. An anonymous, undated manuscript from the Barberini Archive indicates that four additional panels were planned. "Memoria delli altri quattro pezzi d'arazzi che restano da farsi della vita di Papa Urbano VIII," BAV, Arch. Barb., Ind. II, 2693. These were to depict the following deeds of Urban's reign: "Vittorie navale ottenuta dalle galere ponificie in tempo del suo pontificato," "Premio de virtuosi che fiorirono in suo tempo espresso ad imitatione della pittura che'e nel Palazzo della Cancelleria di mano di Giorgio Vasari; alludendosi anche alle promotioni al cardinalato di soggetti riguardevoli," "Virtù singolari di sua St.à e Roma che per special dilettatione sua fiorina anche di moltissimi arti liberali quali se non fosse stato il suo pontificato, si sarebbero perdute. Erettione della lettura di rettorica in Sapienza et acquisto della Biblioteca Palatina fatta portare in Roma," and "Pietà di esso si nel istitutione di diverse colleggii; cioè quello de Schiavoni in Loreto uno in Portogallo; beatificatione di Andrea Avellino, Giacomo della Marca, Francesco Borgia, Felice da Cantalice, Maria Madelena de Pazzi, tre martiri Giesuiti de Giappone e ventitrè Franciscani; Andrea Corsini, Gaetano Tieno e Gio. di Dio."

[50] Ubaldini, BAV, Barb. Lat. 4901; transcribed in Pastor, *History of the Popes*, 29:502, n. 1.

[51] Ripa, *Nova iconologia*, 316–17, 346–47. C. Johnston, G. V. Shepherd, and M. Worsdale, *Vatican Splendor: Masterpieces of Baroque Art* (Ottawa, 1986), 134–35. Nicoletti, it will be remembered, designated Urban's gesture of calling for a new vote as indicative of his "magnanimity." BAV, Barb. Lat. 4730, 664. Above, 185.

[52] BAV, Arch. Barb., Comp. 91, 166r.

[53] Gigli, *Diario romano*, 77, 79. On Urban's particular devotion to St. Michael, see Nicoletti, BAV, Barb. Lat. 4731, 10–15, 833, and above, 98.

[54] *Maffeo Created Cardinal*, the *Ballot*, and the *Consecration of St. Peter's*.

lands in central and northern Italy to the Apostolic See—a donation that was fundamental to subsequent papal claims to temporal power.[55] In the tapestry she offers Urban a pomegranate, symbol of her custodianship of the Papal States, as the pope sits flanked by Carlo Barberini (in armor as general of the Church) and Taddeo (in the prefect's vestments, assisted by a personification of the Church). Personifications of the cities and rivers of Matilda's lands offer themselves to Urban as Fame flies above, holding a banderole with the motto of the countess—UNIT ET TUETUR.[56] Similar allegorical figures and personifications participate in all of the tapestry scenes, showing, as in the salone fresco, the providential will being worked out in the various narrative events.[57]

As in the Life of Constantine and Life of Christ tapestry cycles, the Life of Urban series makes manifest the workings of Divine Providence in historical events. In the first two cycles, however, the theme of providential election was only implicit—the *Apparition of the Cross to Constantine* and the *Charge to Peter*. But in the Urban tapestries it is literally depicted. The predominance of the theme of election seems to have prompted display of the series for celebrations of subsequent papal elections. A payment document for the workman who hung the Urban tapestries in the salone in 1676 also authorizes payment for work on Cardinal Francesco's cell for the papal conclave of that year. The election of Innocent XI and the customary festivities provided an ideal occasion for showing the panels.[58]

The relevance of the Barberini tapestry cycles for the salone fresco does not depend on their mere physical proximity to it, however appropriate such an arrangement would have been. A common underlying moral philosophy—the belief in divine election, present in the iconography of both fresco and tapestries—validates the relationship between the painted and woven imagery. The tapestries lend historical specificity to the moral abstractions of the salone vault and thereby confirm its truths.[59]

[55] Urban was especially devoted to the memory of the countess, whom he considered the ideal secular ruler in her relations with the papacy. He composed an ode in her praise, had her remains brought from Mantua to Rome, and commissioned Bernini to erect a tomb for her in St. Peter's. E. Lubowski, *Gio. Lorenzo Bernini als Architekt und Dekorator unter Papst Urban VIII* (Berlin, 1919), 41–43; Pastor, *History of the Popes*, 29:476–78; J. B. Scott, "Papal Patronage in the Seventeenth Century: Urban VIII, Bernini, and the Countess Matilda," in *L'âge d'or du mécénat (1598–1661)*, eds. R. Mousnier and J. Mesnard (Paris, 1985), 119–27. Ubaldini had already referred to Matilda's tomb in his proposal for wall frescoes for the salone—"La diffesa dello Stato delle Chiesa." Transcribed in Pastor, *History of the Popes*, 29:502, n. 1, no. 6.

[56] "It unifies and protects."

[57] Vitzthum hypothesized that the Life of Urban series might have been hung on the lower walls of the salone, with the Life of Christ cycle in the register above: "Two spheres are separated: situated no doubt below, the life of the Vicar of Christ, and, above, that of Christ himself with the connecting link, Christ's *Charge to Peter*, significantly mentioned last in the Bar-

berini inventory. And above both, represented on the ceiling by Pietro da Cortona, the ultimate sphere: *Divine Providence* . . . a baroque analogy to the walls and ceiling of the Sistine Chapel." Vitzthum, "Review of Tapestries," 262–63. Even the walls of the Barberini salone were not sufficiently vast to hold the full complement of both tapestry cycles simultaneously.

[58] See the *mandato* of Cardinal Francesco: "A Matteo Muzzi festarolo . . . 2 sc. per haver apparato, e sparato la metà del salone nel Pal.o alle quattro fontane con l'arazzi rappresentanti l'istoria della St.a mem. di Papa Urbano 8°; e sc. 2 per la nostra stanza del conclave passato . . . li 18 gen. 1677." BAV, Arch. Barb., Comp. 91, 106r.

[59] The four cartoons of Doctors of the Church, which now hang mounted on the upper wall of the salone (Fig. 78), were first positioned there at least as early as 1644. See the inventory of Cardinal Antonio's possessions transcribed by M. A. Lavin, *Documents and Inventories*, 158. They are the result of commissions for the embellishment of St. Peter's Basilica made during Urban's pontificate. The *Thomas Aquinas* (Sacchi, 1632) and *Bonaventure* (Lanfranco, 1629–1630) were made for two of the four pendentive mosaics in the Chapel of the

Madonna della Colonna. The *Leo the Great* (Sacchi, 1638–1639) and *Bernard of Clairvaux* (Carlo Pellegrini, 1637) were made for the pendentive mosaics in the Chapel of St. Michael Archangel. See Harris, *Andrea Sacchi*, 60–61; F. DiFederico, *The Mosaics of Saint Peter's* (University Park, Pa., 1983), 63–64, 66–67. Of the large number of cartoons that must have been available from the vast decorative project at St. Peter's, these four were chosen because of their relevance to Barberini family iconography. Aside from the general appropriateness of Church Doctors associated with the Archangel St. Michael and the Virgin (della Colonna), they seem also to have even more direct relationship to Barberini imprese. Aquinas, the Angelic Doctor, is crowned with stars and has the sun emblazoned on his breast; Bonaventure, known as the Seraphic Doctor, has the cardinal's hat as his attribute; Leo the Great, depicted with his tiara attribute, was a Tuscan defender of Rome and the primacy of the papacy; and Bernard, the Doctor Mellifluous, is accompanied by angels holding the cross and a piece of honeycomb, attribute of the saint's eloquence.

CHAPTER XIV

• The Audience of the Salone Fresco and the Issue of Intelligibility

ONE OF THE most vexing questions related to an accurate appreciation of the meaning and function of the Barberini salone fresco pertains to the nature of the audience for whom it was intended. The degree to which the salone was accessible to the general public has not been considered. Nor has there been a scholarly effort to determine how and in what depth contemporaries understood the imagery they encountered on the vault. Fortunately, substantial evidence exists to identify the status of its audience and to clarify the level of understanding seventeenth-century viewers gained of the images they saw.

Rosichino's statements and the very existence of his little guidebook indicate that the salone was open to any person who could make a presentable appearance at the palace gate during appropriate hours. His garrulous remark that the observers "continually" turned to him for explanation of the painting indicates that by 1640, less than one year after the unveiling of the ceiling, visitors were arriving in sufficient numbers to disturb him and warrant the publication of a printed guide.[1] This supposition finds further support in the early entry of the salone into general guidebooks printed for use by pilgrims and other visitors to Rome interested in seeing the modern as well as the ancient monuments of the Eternal City.[2] The English traveler John Evelyn visited the palace on 7 November 1644 and saw the "volto . . . newly painted a fresca by that rare hand of Pietro Berettieri il Cortone."[3] This general accessibility is consistent with the function of the salone as an open, sparsely furnished, semi-public room guarded by *palafrenieri*. The coming and going of casual visitors would in no way have interfered with domestic activities in the closed private apartments beyond the salone. On the contrary, just as literati like Bracciolini, Teti, and Ubaldini served as ornaments for the cardinal households they attended, the number of curious visitors coming to see the salone fresco would add luster to the patrons' name and spread word of the spiritual and worldly status of Urban and his nephews so grandiosely proclaimed in Cortona's work.

Visitors of rank gained special access. Duke Francesco d'Este obtained a preview showing of the still unfinished fresco in early December 1637 while Cortona was away from Rome. On that occasion Romanelli and Bottalla pulled back the cloth covering to reveal to the distinguished visitor the painting as seen up through the openwork of the scaffolding.[4] Even

---

[1] Rosichino, *Dichiaratione* (1640), 3; Appendix F.

[2] F. de Rossi, *Ritratto di Roma moderna* (Rome, 1645), 272–73.

[3] J. Evelyn, *The Diary of John Evelyn*, ed. E. S. de Beer (Oxford, 1955), 1:228–29.

[4] Romanelli and Bottalla received a tip from Cardinal Francesco for showing the fresco to the duke. Five scudi "per donare d'ordine di sua eminenza a quelli del Cortona pittore che scoprino la volta della sala al principe d'Este." BAV, Arch. Barb., Comp. 224, 93r. Transcribed in Verdi, "Fonti documentarie," 97, doc. 27 (12 December 1637).

Odoardo Farnese, the archenemy of the Barberini, saw the salone fresco after the banquet held in his honor and hosted by Cardinal Antonio on 5 December 1639.[5] At this time the Barberini still hoped to arrange a socially and territorially beneficial marriage alliance with the duke.[6] Urban himself arrived at the conclusion of the meal to show the painted vault to Farnese, who, feigning delight, found it "extremely charming."[7] For his part, the duke despised the Barberini as *parvenus* unworthy of the positions of wealth and power into which they had so suddenly been catapulted by Urban's election.[8] Farnese was particularly adamant in his refusal to acknowledge Prince Taddeo, much less cede to him the right of precedence required by his prefectorial rank. Taddeo had to absent himself from Rome before the duke would enter the city. Farnese used his visit to Rome mainly for the purpose of casting grievous social insults on the pope and his family. He unaccountably failed to appear at the customary audience with the prefectess, leaving Donna Anna waiting with the group of aristocratic women she had gathered about her for the reception.[9] As he prepared to leave the city, the duke, dressed in armor, stormed unannounced into the Vatican Palace, brushed aside the papal guards, and strode directly into Urban's private chamber to berate the still reclining pope for the perceived insolence of his nephews.[10] The message of the ceiling, in this instance, was ineffective.

The oval room at the far end of the salone points to yet another type of individual who had the opportunity to see the Cortona fresco. According to Teti, this elliptical chamber served as a kind of informal academy where cultured men convened for "literary exercises" held under the patronage of Cardinal Antonio.[11] Statues of emperors, philosophers, and orators filled the niches, inspiring to classical eloquence those men who gathered in the room.[12] Lucas Holstein, Lelio Guidiccioni, and Francesco Bracciolini belonged to this group of cultivated and accomplished individuals, but the majority of the participants were cardinals; for this reason they became known as the "Purple Swans" (*Purpurei Cycni*).[13] These learned men dedicated themselves to Minerva, "Mother of the Muses," and to Apollo, "God of Poetry."

The stucco sculpture in the pediment above the door leading from the salone into the oval room announces this exalted literary dedication (Fig. 113). Two swans, the birds sacred to Apollo, support the Medusa-head shield of Minerva.[14] The cove scene above the pediment depicts the goddess herself in full flight (Fig. 78). This imagery was not only relevant to the

[5] Teti, *Aedes Barberinae* (1642), 44; F. de Navenne, *Rome et le Palais Farnèse* (Paris, 1923), 1:172–73.

[6] DeMaria, "La Guerra di Castro," 198; Nussdorfer, *City Politics*, 243.

[7] ASF, Archivio Mediceo del Principato, Roma-Carteggio Diplomatico, F. Niccolini, 5 December 1639. Transcribed in Posse, "Deckenfresko des Cortona," 102, n. 2.

[8] Pastor, *History of the Popes*, 29:384–85; DeMaria, "La Guerra di Castro," 198.

[9] Pastor, *History of the Popes*, 29:383–85; Borri, *Odoardo Farnese*, 20.

[10] Grottanelli, "Il Ducato di Castro," 558.

[11] Teti, *Aedes Barberinae* (1642), 15. Although no written record exists of the meetings that took place in the oval room, it was ready to house such events by 1632, with statues installed by 1633, so that the "exer-cises" could have been held during the time Cortona and Bracciolini were planning and executing the vault fresco.

[12] Documents of 1633, 1636, and 1640 refer to heads of a Muse and Cicero for the ovals above the niches. See Pollak, *Die Kunsttätigkeit*, 1:328–29.

[13] Teti, *Aedes Barberinae* (1642), 171–75. A special appendix added to many copies of *Aedes Barberinae* contains engraved portraits of the "Purple Swans" as sculpted monuments in the Temple of Immortality.

[14] "E poi fatto come sta al presente ch'è una testa di Medusa con capelli di serpe e due cegni dalle bande si valuta sc. 12." BAV, Arch. Barb., Ind. II, 2888, 188. Transcribed in Pollak, *Die Kunsttätigkeit*, 1:291. The sculpture was executed by Domenico Rossi after a design by Bernini. Above, n. 171, n. 61.

learned activities of the "Purple Swans" but also represented a symbolic mode of thinking that accorded well with the literary and poetic allusions that filled their discourse. These men were perhaps the most intellectually sophisticated of the individuals who had regular access to the salone. One among their number had even consulted with the artist on the iconography of the vault fresco. Little of its meaning or its potential for interpretation would have escaped them.

Such was not the case with the average curious visitor. Rosichino makes it clear that many of the people who came to see the salone fresco could not understand its imagery to their satisfaction and therefore turned to him for explanation. They could enjoy the beauty of the painting, "but because such pleasure does not extend beyond the form and disposition of the colors and figures, the observers, remaining deprived of the enjoyment of understanding the meaning, continually turned to me . . . and summoned me again to explain the paintings to them."[15] The existence of Rosichino's pamphlet testifies to the difficulty many contemporaries had in understanding the full meaning of at least some passages in the Cortona fresco. Even Domenichino, living in Naples at the time of the work's unveiling, wrote of his interest in knowing about the program and how Cortona realized it in paint.[16]

The eagerness of palace visitors to obtain knowledge of the meaning of the imagery was assuaged by the Barberini, who were solicitous in providing the means to gain that understanding. Rosichino's work, meant for the average visitor, first manifested this concern; Teti's volume, intended for the most high-ranking and noble of visitors, followed.[17]

The unbound pamphlet published by Rosichino must have been available for a gratuity. Teti's folio-sized book, by contrast, was an opulent production. Most of the extant copies have full red morocco bindings with tooled gold borders and the armorial bearings of the individual who received the book.[18] These copies were apparently given to distinguished visitors to the palace. Moreover, unlike Rosichino's little guide, the larger work included lavish illustrations with fold-out engravings of the major painted and sculptural decorations of the palace.[19] Its usefulness remained independent of a personal visit to the edifice. The 1647 edition of *Aedes Barberinae* bore a dedication to Cardinal Mazarin. These aspects of the publication indicate an interest in the propagandistic dissemination of the palace imagery.

In his commentary on *L'elettione*, Rospigliosi also concerned himself with the issue of audience. He placed potential readers into three categories: the vulgar common person, the noble gentleman, and the literato. Bracciolini, he says, knows how to write for every sort of person: "The vulgar are plebeians, who for the most part are not educated; the noble gentle-

---

[15] Rosichino, *Dichiaratione* (1640), 3; Appendix F.

[16] Appendix G.

[17] A second edition of the *Dichiaratione* appeared in 1670 (with the erroneous publication date of 1570). M. Rosichino, *Dichiaratione delle pitture della sala de' signori Barberini* (Rome, 1570 [1670]). D. E. Rhodes, "Rosichino and Pietro da Cortona: A Correction with Notes on the Printer Fabio de Falco," in *Studies in Early Italian Printing* (London, 1982), 333–34. Even more rare than the original edition, copies of the 1670 reprint are preserved in the Vatican Library (Ferraioli IV, 8893, int. 1), and the British Museum. Cardinal Francesco ordered another printing of 500 copies just prior

to his death in 1679. On the publication history of Rosichino's *Dichiaratione*, see ibid., 188 and n. 335.

[18] See, for example, the copies with the arms Fabio Chigi (BAV) and Giulio Sacchetti (Library Company of Philadelphia). A copy now in the British Museum had been given to the grand dauphin, the son of Louis XIV.

[19] As late as 1670 Cardinal Francesco ordered two additional copies of the 1647 edition of the *Aedes Barberinae*, one of which was to be given to the Spanish ambassador. Petrucci Nardelli, "Il Card. Francesco Barberini," 162.

men, who, held back by their comfortable circumstances, do not immerse themselves in study and who tend to be moderately literate; and the literati, who spend their years over books."[20] Since their tastes are diverse, continues Rospigliosi, it is impossible to please these groups equally. Aristotle advised poets to write for the gentlemen, for at this level all three groups can gain understanding and enjoyment from the work. But rather than write always for mediocre gentlemen, Bracciolini modified his style according to the subject of his work and the audience he had in mind. Thus *Lo scherno degli dei* appeals to the vulgar and is appropriately filled with pleasant laughs; *La croce racquistata* aims at the moderately educated, but he composed *L'elettione* "to please much more those who know a lot."[21]

The inclusion of Rospigliosi's essay as an afterword to *L'elettione* indicates Bracciolini's tacit approval of the sentiments expressed in it, but the poet himself had also earlier commented on this issue in a letter written to his nephew. With regard to the readership toward which the epic poet should direct his efforts, Bracciolini, agreeing with Aristotle, offered the following advice:

> You ought not to worry about writing only for intellectuals, because these are so rare that your compositions would gain little attention. I do not say, however, that you aim to write to please the ignorant, because nothing is pleasing to them but stupidities; you, a poet, would become a fool on this account. But you ought to make it your goal to write for gentlemen who are usually moderately educated. And by pleasing gentlemen, the literati will derive from you the entire delight of profound knowledge, by realizing you have written well, for this is the true pleasure that is to be expected from the poet, whereas the other pleasures must come from elsewhere. The ignorant, partially content and partially amazed without knowing why, will be carried by the tide and will go on their way like a herd of sheep.[22]

The Barberini ceiling is directed to this middle-brow audience, combining elements appropriate to the entire spectrum of potential viewers. Enticing low-brow amusements such as the falling Giants, the startled Venus, and drunken Silenus coexist with abstruse personifications like Moral Knowledge, Divine Assistance, and Dignity. Even without the aid of Rosichino's guide, each observer could appreciate the form and meaning of the salone fresco according to individual levels of sophistication. The fullest meaning of the vault imagery could be grasped only by those few individuals "who know a lot," but the majority of visitors, although not understanding every detail, could appreciate something of the moral sig-

---

[20] Rospigliosi, "Discorso."
[21] Ibid.
[22] "Non dovete mettervi in pensiero di scriver solamente agli scienziali, perchè questi son sì rari che poco grido consequirebberro i componimenti vostri. Non dico pero già che voi intendiate di scrivere e piacere agli ignoranti, perchè, non piacendo a loro se non le sciocchezze, voi, di poeta in vece, sciocco ne diverreste; ma vi dovete prender per oggetto di scrivere a gentiluomini, che per lo più mezzanamente letterati sogliono essere: e a questi piacendo, i letterati l'intero diletto della profondità delle scienze, da voi il trarranno dalla considerazione d'aver voi bene imitato che questo e'l proprio diletto che ha da venire dal poeta, e gli altri d'altronde hanno a venire. E gli ignoranti, parte contenti e parte stupiti senza saperne il perchè, portati saranno dalla piena, e se ne andranno in branco come le pecore." Bracciolini, *Lettere sulla poesia*, 40. The letter was written ca. 1640.

nificance of the scenes and the central reference to divine election and immortality gained through virtue. Everyone, moreover, could identify the entertaining mythological scenes and comprehend the basic message of patronage and power that had provided the impetus for the entire pictorial project at Palazzo Barberini.

Interest in the meaning of the salone fresco continued long after the deaths of both Urban and Bracciolini. Demand for knowledge about the ceiling warranted a reissuing of Rosichino's *Dichiaratione* in 1670, thirty years after the original publication. The text of the pamphlet remained unchanged, but a significant emblematic addition appears in the new printing. The cover carries the woodcut image of a bee with the lyre of Apollo fastened at its neck, the "honeyed lyre" (Fig. 174).[23] Superimposed stars form a constellation indicating that this is the celestial lyre (Lyra), with its chief star, Vega, located at the mandible.

The idea of immortality gained through poetic virtue received its final expression here. This concept, repeatedly explored in Urban's lifetime,[24] constitutes a fundamental element for understanding the innovative nature of Barberini iconography as represented in the painted ceilings of the palace. Nor can there be doubt about the meaning of its appearance on the final official document related to the salone ceiling. It embodies emblematically the Vergilian lines earlier inscribed on the triumphal arch erected on the Campidoglio for Urban's *possesso*, where bees were seen in apotheosis:

> There is no room for death: alive they fly
> To join the stars and mount aloft to heaven.[25]

The mellifluous bee is the Barberini poet-pope, Urban himself, his eternal memory confirmed by the lyre in the heavens.

---

[23] Leone Allacci, author of the *Apes Urbanae*, invented the "honeyed lyre" to refer to Barberini patronage of poetry. L. Allacci, *Melissolyra de Laudibus Dionysii Petavii* (Rome, 1653), 3–4. Allacci had become Cardinal Francesco's librarian in 1638. *DBI* 2:467–71.

[24] Ferro, *Teatro d'imprese*, 2:185–86; F. Macedo, *Panegyricus Urbano VIII. Apes Barberinae. Lyra Barberina* (Rome, 1642).

[25] Georgics 4:226–27. Above, 170.

EPILOGUE

THE MEANING OF the painted ceilings of Palazzo Barberini can now be fully and precisely grasped. All three of the major piano nobile frescoes commissioned by the papal nephews—Sacchi's *Divine Wisdom*, Camassei's *Creation of the Angels*, and Cortona's *Divine Providence*—assert the divine election of the Barberini family to rule the Church and the Papal States. But the unprecedented magnitude of the social, political, and artistic endeavor behind the realization of this pictorial ensemble perhaps expresses the tensions and doubts as much as the ambitions of a family newly arrived in an arena where the rules of engagement had already begun to change.

With the signing of the Peace of Venice (31 March 1644), the War of Castro came to an ignominious close for the pope and his nephews. By terms of the agreement, the papal edict of excommunication against Odoardo Farnese was to be lifted and Castro and all other confiscated properties returned to the duke. When Odoardo retook possession of his territory on 28 July 1644, Urban was already on his deathbed. He died embittered by his treatment at the hands of the Italian princes and disappointed by the poor showing of his nephews in the affair.[1]

The beginning of a new pontificate was always a difficult time for the relatives of the preceding pope, but the Barberini nephews found the early years of the reign of Innocent X Pamphili to be exceedingly troublesome. Questions quickly arose about monetary improprieties and mismanagement of funds expended on the recent war.[2] Like the Farnese duke and the league of Italian princes, many Romans tended to see the war as having been generated more by the narrow interests of the Barberini than by concern for the Church and the Papal States. Long-festering resentments had burst into the open as tax was added to tax to pay for the ill-fated military exploits of the war, conducted by Taddeo and Antonio the Younger. Even the levelheaded Gigli had to complain, perhaps exaggeratedly, about the sixty-three different taxes Urban had imposed on his subjects to pay for the wartime expenditures.[3] The infelicities of the closing years of Urban's reign only made more violent the reaction against two decades of extraordinary nepotism.

Official investigations into the reputed financial irregularities were already being spoken of when the Barberini nephews prudently departed from Rome, seeking the protection of their former agent in Paris, Mazarin. Cardinal Antonio the Younger was the first to flee, on 28 September 1645, by river boat at night and disguised as a charcoal seller.[4] Cardinal Francesco and Taddeo, dressed, it was said, as humble priest and huntsman, followed in January 1646 and, after narrowly escaping shipwreck at sea, joined Antonio in exile in France.[5]

---

[1] Pastor, *History of the Popes*, 29:399–404.

[2] Ibid., 30:51–52, 56; E. Chinazzi, *Sede vacante per la morte del papa Urbano VIII Barberini e conclave di Innocenzo X Pamfili* (Rome, 1904), 9–17.

[3] Gigli, *Diario romano*, 253; Nussdorfer, "City Politics," 215.

[4] E. Rossi, "La fuga del Cardinale Antonio Barberini," *Archivio della Società Romana di Storia Patria* 59 (1936), 303–27.

[5] Gigli, *Diario romano*, 274–75.

Donna Anna followed in April.[6] The Camera Apostolica confiscated all Barberini benefices and properties.[7] Innocent was so enraged by the departure of the Barberini that he threatened to raze their palace, calling it the La Rochelle of Rome.[8] Cardinal Antonio, however, having anticipated just such a reaction, had already consigned Palazzo Barberini to the king of France, and it was quickly hung with the arms of Louis XIV, made the residence of the French ambassador, and filled with French soldiers.[9] The ascetic Cardinal Antonio the Elder, ever detached from family affairs, remained in Rome, where he died in December of the same year. The nameless epitaph he had placed on his tomb in the Capuchin monastery of S. M. della Concezione exemplified his unworldly attitude: "Here rest dust, ashes and nothing."[10] From France word arrived in Rome in December 1647 that Taddeo had died there.[11]

As early as February 1648 Cardinal Francesco was able to return to Rome, albeit under the protection of the French king. Negotiations for the return of Cardinal Antonio were more difficult and protracted, but he, too, finally reentered the Eternal City in July 1653, reportedly to the cheers of the populace as he reclaimed his palace on the Quirinal[12] His way had been paved by a marriage alliance, arranged to seal the reconciliation of feuding papal families, between Taddeo's son, Maffeo, and Olimpia Giustiniani, the niece of Innocent. Under the watchful eye of the pope's sister-in-law, Donna Olimpia Maidalchini, the young couple took up residence in the newly aggrandized Pamphili Palace in Piazza Navona, where Pietro da Cortona was already at work on a vast ceiling painting.

As the political vitality of the papacy waned, so did the efficacy of that institution as a vehicle for nepotistic promotion. For that reason, the Barberini occupied a noteworthy moment of transition in the history of early modern Europe. An old political culture based on familial relationships reached its apogee at Palazzo Barberini just as a new one was rising in France. One could argue that the Barberini and their image consultants failed, but, if so, they nevertheless created a useful model of patronage and propaganda for the weaker and less inspired papal families who succeeded them, and, most of all, for the power brokers of European monarchical absolutism already on the road to Versailles.

[6] Ibid., 278.

[7] Pastor, *History of the Popes*, 30:56.

[8] P. Linage de Vauciennes, *Le differend des Barberins avec le pape Innocent X* (Paris, 1678), 199–200.

[9] Gigli, *Diario romano*, 281; Pastor, *History of the Popes*, 30:53.

[10] HIC IACET PVLVIS, CINIS ET NIHIL. Ibid., 28:43.

[11] Taddeo died in Paris on 24 November 1647.

[12] Gigli, *Diario romano*, 419–22; Linage de Vauciennes, *Le differend des Barberins*, 163–425; D. Chiomenti Vassalli, *Donna Olimpia o del nepotismo nel seicento* (Milan, 1979), 194–204.

• Measurements and Monetary Values in Seventeenth-Century Rome

1 palmo romano = 0.223 meters.
1 scudo (silver) = 10 giuli (silver) = 100 baiocchi (copper).

In addition to the common scudo ("scudo di moneta corrente"), the papal currency often used in official transactions was the "scudo d'oro pontificio." Its value relative to the "scudo di moneta" fluctuated, but in 1640 was worth 1.465 common scudi. F. Piola Caselli, "Aspetti del debito pubblico nello stato pontificio: gli uffici vacabili," *Annali della Facoltà di Scienze Politiche, Università degli Studi di Perugia*, n.s. 1 (1970–1972), 33, n. 4, 73.

Payment documents designate gold scudi as such. When no such designation occurs, the currency is assumed to be the less valuable common, that is, silver, scudo.

Something of the real value of these denominations can be obtained from the state-controlled price of bread. One loaf cost one baiocco. The size and weight of the loaf varied according to the price of grain. Nussdorfer, "City Politics," 286, n. 35.

As a ready source for useful technical information regarding many aspects of life in seventeenth-century Rome, for example, papal government, bookkeeping, finance, mail, archives, and heraldry, see F. Hammond, *Girolamo Frescobaldi: A Guide to Research* (New York-London, 1988), 55–87, with excellent bibliography.

• The Program of Sacchi's
Divine Wisdom

(BAV, Barb. Lat. 6529, Miscellanea V, fol. 52)

Perchè l'increata Sapienza, nel governo ammirabile del mondo deve esser'amata, et temuta, perciò dalla Pittura si rappresenta in atto di commandare all'Amore et al Timore, suoi diversi Arcieri, che tirino di mira al bersaglio del Mondo, per saettare et ferire salutevolm.te gli animi degli homini. Si dipinge assisa in real'trono celeste, è coronata come Regina, e moderatrice dell'Universo, è vestita di bianco, è circondata di luci, essendo essa candor lucis aeternae. Tiene uno specchio terso e chiaro, chiamandosi speculum sine macula. Ha il sole in petto, acciò che apparisca spesiosior soli. Regge con la destra uno scettro o chiuso, per segno del provido et saggio reggimento.

Le altre donne, che a torno stanno, rappresentano gli attributi della Sapienza, convenientemente divisati, con simboli di varie costellationi, essendo quelli cosa divina e rappresentandosi in cielo. Sono d.ti attributi in gran numero, chiaram.te espressi, nel settimo et ottavo capo del libro della Sapienza, de'quali alcuni più principali ha scelto et rappresentato la Pittura.

La Divinità col triangolo, chiaro simbolo dell'unità dell'essenza et trinità delle Persone.

L'Eternità col serpe, segno di essa da tutti conosciuto.
La Santità con l'altare.
La Schiettezza, o Purità, col cigno candidissimo.
La Perspicacità con l'Aquila.
La Bellezza con la chioma di Berenice.
La Suavità con la lira.
La Fortezza con la clava.
La Beneficenza con la spiga.
La Giustizia con la bilancia.
La Nobiltà con la corona d'Arianna.

L'Amore, giovinetto generoso e di color vivace, cavalcando il leone celeste, della sua generosità proportionato geroglifico, avventa una frezza d'oro, tra metalli perfettissimo, per avviso della perfettione et eccellenza dell'Amore.

Il Timore, meno perfetto, ne lancia uno d'argento, e, per esprimerlo con i suoi controsegni, si dipinge pallido, et a sedere sopra la costellatione del lepre.

Conveniva tal Pittura al maestoso Edefitio della Casa Barberina, acciò che s'intendesse che, si come si felice fameglia è nata et eletta in luogo d'Iddio, per li primi governi della Chiesa, così, con divina Sapienza, parimenti amata e riverita, la governa.

[Because uncreated Wisdom, in the admirable governance of the world, ought to be loved and feared, for the purpose of the painting she is represented in the act of commanding Love and Fear, her divine archers, who take aim at the target of the world, to shoot and wound beneficially the souls of men. She is painted seated on a heavenly throne, crowned as Queen and arbitrator of the Universe, dressed in white, surrounded by light, being *candor lucis aeternae*. She has a bright clear mirror, calling herself *speculum sine macula*. She has the sun on her breast in order that she might appear *spesiosior soli*. She holds out with her right hand a scepter or baton as sign of providence and wise rule.

The other women, who are round about, represent the attributes of Wisdom, conveniently distinguished with symbols of the various constellations, those being a divine thing and being represented in the heavens. The said attributes are great in number, clearly expressed, in the seventh and eighth chapters of the Book of Wisdom, some of the more important of which the painting has selected and represented.

Divinity with triangle, clear symbol of the unity of the essence and trinity of the Persons.

Eternity with the serpent, sign of this known by everyone.
Sanctity with the altar.
Sincerity or Purity with the pure white swan.
Perspicacity with the eagle.
Beauty with the coma berenices.
Gentleness with the lyre.
Strength with the club.
Beneficence with the shaft of grain.
Justice with the balance.
Nobility with the crown of Ariadne.

Love, a high-spirited youth with vivid complexion, riding the heavenly lion, hieroglyph proportionate to his high-spiritedness, hurls a golden arrow, most perfect among metals, as indication of the perfection and excellence of Love.

Fear, less perfect, throws one of silver, and, in order to express him with his countersigns, he is painted pale, and is seated upon the constellation of the rabbit.

Such a painting is appropriate to the majestic edifice of the Barberini family in order that it be understood that since that happy family was born and elected to rule the Church in the place of God it governs with Divine Wisdom, equally loved and revered.]

• "Ode Hortatoria Ad Virtutem" by Maffeo Barberini

(Urbanus VIII, *Poemata*, Paris, 1620, 42–46)

Ingresse pubis limina lubricis
   Calcando plantis se tibi semita
   Decliuis offert, et doloso
   Pandit iter malefida ductu,
Francisce fratris germen amabile,
   Ob quem sub imo condita pectore
   Me cura mordet, detinetque
   Sollicitum genitoris instar:
Subsiste mecum, nec grave duxeris,
   Hinc ex amoena, quae patet orbita   10
   Ductore me flectens adire
   Per salebras Eliconis Antrum;
Huch nate gressus: is licet aureo
   Phoebi cientis pectine musicas
   Audire chordas, dum canentes
   Dulce melos sociant camoenae.
Hic multiformi carmine barbitos
   Eburna Parcas sopit, et eripit
   Heroas Orco, quos perenni
   Fonte beat comitata virtus.   20
Huic obsecutum conspicis inclytum
   In collis almo vertice Thesea,
   Quem flexuosis non fefellit
   Tramitibus fabricatus error.
Sic vectus altum, per mare subdolos
   Cantus Vlysses dicitur integer
   Audisse sic vitasse Circes
   Pocula, lethiferas, et herbas:
Spectandus hic contemptor anhelitus
   Spirantis ignem divite velleris   30
   Praeda coruscat, Iuctuosus
   Messor agri gravis aere, et hastis:
Conficta Proeto crimina deferens
   Coniux necari, quem petit innocens
   Hos inter excellit triformis
   Bellerophon domitor Chimoerae
Phoebea laurus frondibus allicit,

Dulcique pascit nectare Pegasus,
   At nosse vim nobis negatur
   Melle sub Aonio latentem.   40
Sensus recludet Cynthius abditos
   Audi canentem: Quem fovet aurea
   Virtus in vlnis, ille monstris
   Victor ovat domitis beatus.
Non hunc voluptas mollit, et impetus
   Non vincit irae, quae violentius
   Succis, et herbis in ferarum
   Terga viros, et in ora vertunt.
Vt ecce plaudit Castalidum chorus,
   Phoebique concors carmina concinit?   50
   Hic siste rursum me petente
   Sacra refert tibi verba Chiron.
Incompta quondam, claraque simiplici
   Nitore formae talibus Herculem est
   Affata virtus, dum procaci
   Blanda sono loquitur voluptas:
Haec sumptuoso tegmine turgida,
   Pexoque mollis crine, micantibus
   Ornata gemmis, appetenda
   Sub specie male caute pubes,   60
Edocta fraudes nectere fraudibus
   Te ducit, atris, qua scatet anguibus,
   Dum flore vernans se terendam
   Perfacili via prona gressu,
Ostentat, vmbras frondibus explicat
   Hic arbor, ales dum canit; ah fuge,
   Ouae poma pendent, quosque vitis
   Fert gravidis latices racemis:
Haec pulchra visu poma necem ferunt,
   Haec quae renidet lumina decipit,   70
   Lethale nam laruata virus
   Purpureo tegit uva succo
Si me sequeris per loca sentibus
   Infesta, tesquis horrida, per nives,

Per saxa, per montis cacumen,
    Sternet iter tibi ferrum, et ignis:
Ureris aestu pulvere sordidus
    Pulchro, madebis tempora nobili
    Sudore non fractus labore, et

Magnanimo generosus ausu.   80
Evectus alis hisce per Aethera
    Tranabis ignem, et lactis iter pede
    Premens coruscanti micabis
    Luce novum decus inter astra.

[O you who have entered upon the doorway of youth with
    uncertain steps, a path which must be trod by you offers
    itself sloping downwards, and with deceitful encouragement
    this faithless road stretches forth,
O Franciscus, beloved offspring of my brother
    on account of whom care, buried deep under
    my heart, gnaws at me and anxiety, just
    like a father's, overwhelms me:
Stay with me and you will not have strayed seriously
    from here, from this charming worn rut which is   10
    revealed, turning to approach the Cave through
    the wilds of Helicon, with me as your guide;
O son you have come to this place: here it is possible
    to hear the musical chords from the golden quill
    of Phoebus' plucking, while the muses, singing
    a sweet song, throng together.
Here the ivory lyre with her variegated song
    lulls the Fates to sleep and snatches from
    underground Orcus the heroes whom accompanying
    virtue blesses with her eternal fountain.   20
You see famous Theseus here on the kind
    summit of this hill, yielding to the lyre,
    Theseus whom calculated error did not
    deceive with its crooked, winding paths.
Thus carried across the deep, through the seas,
    Ulysses is said to have heard the beguiling songs
    unharmed and thus to have avoided Circe's
    potions and the death-bringing herbs:
Here the despiser of the fire-breathing dragon
    must be seen, the one who, with a shake, causes   30
    the prize to shine by the richness of its fleece, this
    sorrowful reaper of the field heavy with bronze and spears:
Turning aside the alleged crimes against Proteus,
    the husband who was to be murdered, whom Bellerophon
    once innocently sought out, this slayer of the triformed
    Chimera, Bellerophon is preeminent among these men.
The laurel of Phoebus draws Pegasus with its foliage
    and Pegasus is nourished by the sweet nectar,
    but it is denied to us to know the
    power concealed beneath the Aonian honey.   40

Cynthian Apollo reveals secret senses
   Hear him singing: whom golden
   virtue cherishes in her arms, that blessed
   victor triumphs after the monsters have been conquered.
Pleasure does not soften this one and the rush
   of anger does not overcome him, emotions which
   more violently than potions or herbs turn men
   into the bodies and countenances of wild animals.
Behold, as the Castalian chorus claps,
   does the harmony of Phoebus also celebrate songs?   50
   Stop here, while I go in search again, and
   Chiron also relates sacred words to you.
Virtue, once unkempt, now shines with the
   simple splendor of her form, addressed Hercules
   with such words while charming pleasure
   speaks with a shameless voice:
This one swollen with expensive finery,
   soft with combed hair and adorned with sparkling
   gems, a youth under evil pretext that
   must be sought most cautiously,   60
Having been taught to weave frauds with frauds,
   she leads you where the path teems with black snakes,
   while the steep path, blooming with flowers, shows
   that it must be trod with a very easy step,
Here a tree spreads out shade with its leaves
   while a bird sings; oh flee the apples
   which hang here and the juices which the
   vine bears with its weighty clusters of grapes:
These apples, beautiful to look at, bring death,
   this bunch of grapes which shines deceives the eyes   70
   for by a magic spell, it conceals a
   fatal poison in its purple juice
If you will follow me through these places beset with
   thorns and rough with desert places, if you will
   follow me through snows and rocks to the top of the
   mountain, fire and sword will overcome the journey for you:
Covered with fine dust you will burn with
   heat; not broken by this labor your temples will
   drip with noble sweat and you will become
   magnanimous with your great-hearted daring.   80
Carried by these wings through the heavens
   you will pass through fire, and treading this
   path with a milk white foot you will shine with
   a gleaming light, a new glory among the stars.]

• Documentation of *Muratori* Payments for the Salone Fresco

A COMPREHENSIVE compilation of the *muratori* payments has been hampered because the documents are scattered through the household account books amid a vast quantity of miscellaneous payments and receipts. Much time is expended in locating and identifying the relevant items, but this is only the initial impediment to effective use. Many of the documents appear to have been written hastily; in consequence, the reading of numerical values is especially problematic, and since each payment can produce as many as five documents, confusion of the dates and numbers can result in crediting a payment where none originally existed. Moreover, the information included in an indvidual document is often neither uniform nor complete. One document may be undated, another without indication of a specific number of days worked.

Some of the *muratori* payments have been previously published. Pollak (*Die Kunsttätigkeit*) partially transcribed eight. M. A. Lavin (*Documents and Inventories*) added to this body of material. The contribution of O. Verdi ("Fonti documentarie") is the most important and comprehensive publication of the documents to date. But all of these published sources add up to no more than one-fourth of the total number of payments made. The organizational difficulties encountered in compiling a comprehenisve listing are daunting; yet only a complete, analytical accounting of the *muratori* payments can provide a useful outline of Cortona's activity in the Barberini salone.

The following compilation of data has resulted from a thorough search of the Barberini account volumes from 1627 to 1642. The findings have been organized by document date, using a data-processing program. This has facilitated the grouping of documents that were generated by the same payment and has allowed for a printout of a complete chronological listing. The grouping of documents yielded maximum information about a given payment and permitted internal verification of the quantitative data.

Muratori paid .4 scudi = 4 giuli per day.

Interpolated data are enclosed in brackets.

Paradigm: Year of work
         Month of work: days of work, payment amount
         Document date, document type, location (previous publication)

1632

Jul–Nov: [113] days, [45.20] sc.
    9/17, Mand., BAV, Arch. Barb., Comp. 80, 71r
      (Verdi, 95, doc. 7).
    11/17, Giust., BAV, Arch. Barb., Giust. 1624–

1725, 143r (M. A. Lavin, 48) (Oct–Nov).
  11/18, Mand., BAV, Arch. Barb., Comp. 80, 77v
    (Verdi, 95, doc. 8) (Jul–Nov).
  2/14/1633, Gior., BAV, Arch. Barb., Comp. 67,
    268 (M. A. Lavin, 13) (Jul–Nov).
  2/15, LM, BAV, Comp. 50, 266 (Jul–Nov).

2/15, Quad., SCEP, Quad. Barb., 1633–1636, 18v
(Pollak, 1:327, doc. 917).

Dec: 0 days

1633

Jan: 0 days
Feb: 0 days
Mar: 0 days
Apr: 25 days, 10 sc.
  5/–, Giust., BAV, Arch. Barb., Giust. 1726–1792,
    263r (Verdi, 95, doc. 11).
  5/4, Mand., BAV, Comp. 80, 100v (Verdi, 95, doc.
    10).
  5/14, Gior., BAV, Arch. Barb. 67, 299.
  5/16, Quad., SCEP, Quad. Barb., 1633–1636, 41v.

May: 18 days, 7.20 sc.
  5/–, Giust., BAV, Arch. Barb., Giust. 1726–1792,
    63v (Verdi, 95, doc. 9).
  5/30, Gior., BAV, Arch. Barb., Comp. 67, 304.

Jun: 24 days, 9.60 sc.
  7/1, Gior., BAV, Arch. Barb. 67, 321.
  7/1, Quad., SCEP, Quad. Barb., 1633–1636, 48v
    (Pollak, 1:327, doc. 918).
  7/4, LM, BAV, Arch. Barb. 50, 293v.
  7/4, Mand., BAV, Arch. Barb., Comp. 80, 160r
    (Verdi, 96, doc. 14).

Jul: 25 days, 10 sc.
  8/–, Giust., BAV, Arch. Barb., Giust. 1793–1886,
    9r (Verdi, 96, doc. 12).
  8/17, Gior., BAV, Arch. Barb., Comp. 67, 335.
  8/17, LM, BAV, Arch. Barb., Comp. 50, 293v.
  8/17, Quad., SCEP, Quad. Barb., 1633–1636, 61r
    (Pollak, 1:327, doc. 919).

Aug: 20 days, 8 sc.
  9/8, Giust., BAV, Arch. Barb., Giust. 1793–1886,
    41r.
  9/9, Quad., SCEP, Quad. Barb., 1633–1636, 65v
    (Pollak, 1:327, doc. 920).
  9/9, Gior., BAV, Arch. Barb., Comp. 67, 341.
  9/9, LM, BAV, Arch. Barb., Comp. 50, 293v.

Sep–Oct: 51 days, 20.75 sc.
  11/9, Quad., SCEP, Quad. Barb., 1633–1636, 75
    (Pollak, 1:327, doc. 920).
  11/9, LM, BAV, Arch. Barb., Comp. 50, 293v.

Nov: 26 days, 10.40 sc.
  12/–, Giust., BAV, Arch. Barb., Giust. 1793–1886,
    189r.
  12/16, Gior., BAV, Arch. Barb., Comp. 67, 357.
  12/16, LM, BAV, Arch. Barb., Comp. 50, 336v.
  12/16, Quad., SCEP, Quad. Barb., 1633–1636, 80v
    (Pollak, 1:327, doc. 920).

Dec: 25 days, 10 sc.
  1/–/1634, Giust., BAV, Arch. Barb., Giust. 1793–
    1886, 217r.

1/8, LM, BAV, Arch. Barb., Comp. 50, 336v.
1/8, Quad., SCEP, Quad. Barb., 1633–1636, 88r
  (Pollak, 1:327, doc. 921).
1/8, Gior., BAV, Arch. Barb., Comp. 67, 386.

1634

Jan: 26 days, 10.40 sc.
  2/–, Giust., BAV, Arch. Barb., Giust. 1793–1886,
    245r.
  2/4, Gior., BAV, Arch. Barb., Comp. 67, 342.
  2/4, LM, BAV, Arch. Barb., Comp. 50, 336v.
  2/6, Quad., SCEP, Quad. Barb., 1633–1636, 97v
    (Pollak, 1:327, doc. 921).

Feb: 25 days, 10 sc.
  3/10, LM, BAV, Arch. Barb., Comp. 50, 336v.
  3/10, Quad., SCEP, Quad. Barb., 1633–1636,
    103v.

Mar: 26 days, 10.40 sc.
  4/–, Giust., BAV, Arch. Barb., Giust. 1887–1975,
    86r.
  4/8, Gior., BAV, Arch. Barb., Comp. 67, 410.
  4/8, LM, BAV, Arch. Barb., Comp. 50, 336v.
  4/8, Quad., SCEP, Quad. Barb., 1633–1636, 111v.

Apr: 25 days, 10 sc.
  5/–, Giust., BAV, Arch. Barb., Giust. 1976–2074,
    41r.
  6/6, Mand., BAV, Arch. Barb., Comp. 80, 150v.

May: 17 days, 6.80 sc.
  5/–, Giust., BAV, Arch. Barb., Giust. 1976–2074,
    41r.
  6/6, Mand., BAV, Arch. Barb., Comp. 80, 150v.
  7/20, Quad., SCEP, Quad. Barb., 1633–1636, 128r
    (Apr–May).

Jun: 24 days, 9.60 sc.
  7/–, Giust., BAV, Arch. Barb., Giust. 1976–2074,
    67r.
  7/20, LM, BAV, Arch. Barb., Comp. 50, 336v.
  7/20, Gior., BAV, Arch. Barb., Comp. 67, 437.
  7/24, Mand., BAV, Arch. Barb., Comp. 80, 160r
    (Verdi, 96, doc. 14).
  7/28, LM, BAV, Arch. Barb., Comp. 50, 336v.
  7/28, Gior., BAV, Arch. Barb., Comp. 67, 434.
  7/28, Quad., SCEP, Quad. Barb., 1633–1636,
    131v.

Jul: 23 days, 9.20 sc.
  8/–, Giust., BAV, Arch. Barb., Giust. 1976–2074,
    122r.
  8/8, Mand., BAV, Arch. Barb., Comp. 80, 162v.
  8/11, LM, BAV, Arch. Barb., Comp. 50, 336v.
  8/11, Quad., SCEP, Quad. Barb., 1633–1636,
    137v.

Aug: 22 days, 8.80 sc.
  9/–, Giust., BAV, Arch. Barb., Giust. 1976–2074,
    232r.

9/19, Gior., BAV, Arch. Barb., Comp. 67, 454.

9/19, LM, BAV, Arch. Barb., Comp. 50, 336v.

9/20, Quad., SCEP, Quad. Barb., 1633–1636, 165v.

Sep: 25 days, 10 sc.

10/–, Giust., BAV, Arch. Barb., Giust. 2075–2147, 156r.

Oct: 23 days, 9.20 sc.

11/–, Giust., BAV, Arch. Barb., Giust. 2075–2147, 157v.

11/9, Mand., BAV, Arch. Barb., Comp. 80, 179v.

11/15, Gior., BAV, Arch. Barb., Comp. 67, 469.

11/15, LM, BAV, Arch. Barb., Comp. 50, 336v.

11/15, Quad., SCEP, Quad. Barb., 1633–1636, 153r (Sep–Oct).

Nov: 23 days, 9.20 sc.

12/19, Giust., BAV, Arch. Barb., Giust. 2148–2240, 8r.

12/19, Mand., BAV, Arch. Barb., Comp. 80, 187r.

Dec: 22 days, 8.80 sc.

1/–/1635, Giust., BAV, Arch. Barb., Giust. 2241–2314, 121r.

5/22, Gior., BAV, Arch. Barb., Comp. 68, 34 (Verdi, 96, doc. 15).

5/22, LM, BAV, Arch. Barb., Comp. 51, 77v.

5/22, Istr., BAV, Arch. Barb., Comp. 41, 571v–573r.

1635

Jan: 23 days, 9.20 sc.

2/–, Giust., BAV, Arch. Barb., Giust. 2241–2314, 120r.

2/25, Gior., BAV, Arch. Barb., Comp. 68, 15.

5/22, Istr., BAV, Arch. Barb., Comp. 41, 571v–573r.

6/25, LM, BAV, Arch. Barb., Comp. 51, date.

Feb: 25 days, 10 sc.

3/–, Giust., BAV, Arch. Barb., Giust. 2241–2314, 125r.

6/22, LM, BAV, Arch. Barb., Comp. 51, 77v.

Mar: 24 days, 9.60 sc.

4/–, Giust., BAV, Arch. Barb., Giust. 2241–2314, 124r.

5/19, Mand., BAV, Arch. Barb., Comp. 80, 210r.

6/22, LM, BAV, Arch. Barb., Comp. 51, 77v.

Apr: 0 days

May: 25 days

5/19, Mand., BAV, Arch. Barb., Comp. 80, 210r.

Jun: 23 days, 9.20 sc.

7/6, Giust., BAV, Arch. Barb., Giust. 2315–2416, 101r.

Jul: [16] days, [6.40 sc.]

8/12, Mand., BAV, Arch. Barb., Comp. 80, 224r (Verdi, 96, doc. 16) (Jun–Jul).

8/17, LM, BAV, Arch. Barb., Comp. 51, 77v (Jun–Jul).

8/17, Gior., Arch. Barb., Comp. 68, 58 (Jun–Jul).

Aug–Sep: 43 days, 17.20 sc.

10/31, LM, BAV, Arch. Barb., Comp. 51, 77v.

10/31, Gior., BAV, Arch. Barb., Comp. 68, 77 (Verdi, 96, doc. 18).

Oct: 26 days, 10.40 sc.

11/5, EU, BAV, Arch. Barb., Comp. 93, 83r.

11/30, LM, BAV, Arch. Barb., Comp. 51, 77v.

11/30, Gior., BAV, Arch. Barb., Comp. 68, 82.

Nov: 27 days, 10.80 sc.

12/17, Giust., BAV, Arch. Barb., Giust. 2418–2488, 24r.

12/31, LM, Arch. Barb., Comp. 51, 77v.

Dec: 18 days, 7.20 sc.

1/11/1636, Giust., BAV, Arch. Barb., Giust. 2418–2488, 136r.

1/31, Gior., BAV, Arch. Barb., Comp. 68, 105 (Verdi, 96, doc. 19).

1/31, LM, BAV, Arch. Barb., Comp. 51, 77v.

1636

Jan: [22 days], [8.80 sc.]

2/20, Giust., BAV, Arch. Barb., Giust. 2418–2488, 214v (Dec–Jan).

2/28, Gior., BAV, Arch. Barb., Comp. 68, 114 (Dec–Jan).

2/28, LM, BAV, Arch. Barb., Comp. 51, 167v (Dec–Jan).

Feb: 23 days, 9.20 sc.

3/12, Giust., BAV, Arch. Barb., Giust. 2418–2488, 230v.

3/12, EU, BAV, Arch. Barb., Comp. 93, 97v.

3/30, Gior., Arch. Barb., Comp. 68, 120.

3/31, LM, Arch. Barb., Comp. 51, 167v.

Mar: 23 days, 9.20 sc.

4/–, Giust., BAV, Arch. Barb., Giust. 2489–2567, 29v (Verdi, 96, doc. 20).

4/16, Giust., BAV, Arch. Barb., Giust. 2489–2567, 34r (Verdi, 96, doc. 20).

4/16, EU, BAV, Arch. Barb., Comp. 93, 101r.

4/30, Gior., BAV, Arch. Barb., Comp. 68, 127.

4/30, LM, BAV, Arch. Barb., Comp. 51, 167v.

Apr: 25 days, 10 sc.

5/16, EU, BAV, Arch. Barb., Comp. 93, 106r.

5/16, Giust., BAV, Arch. Barb., Giust. 2489–2567, 123v.

5/31, Gior., BAV, Arch. Barb., Comp. 68, 138.

May: 23 days, 9.20 sc.

6/30, Giust., BAV, Arch. Barb., Giust. 2489–2567, 170r.

6/30, Gior., BAV, Arch. Barb., Comp. 68, 149.

6/30, LM, BAV, Arch. Barb., Comp. 51, 167v.

Jun: 24 days, 9.60 sc.

7/–, Giust., BAV, Arch. Barb., Giust. 2489–2567, 190v, 192v, 196r (Verdi, 96, doc. 21).

7/31, LM, BAV, Arch. Barb., Comp. 51, 167v.

7/31, Gior., BAV, Arch. Barb., Comp. 68, 156.

Jul: 24 days, 9.60 sc.

9/6, Giust., BAV, Arch. Barb., Giust. 2568–2634, 145r.

Aug: 21 days, 8.40 sc.

9/–, Giust., BAV, Arch. Barb., Giust. 2568–2634, 141v (Jul–Aug).

9/6, EU, BAV, Arch. Barb., Comp. 93, 121v.

9/6, Giust., BAV, Arch. Barb., Giust. 2568–2634, 145r.

9/30, LM, BAV, Arch. Barb., Comp. 51, 167v (Jul–Aug).

Sep: 31 days, 12.23 sc.

10/18, Giust., BAV, Arch. Barb., Giust. 2568–2634, 184r.

10/31, Gior., BAV, Arch. Barb., Comp. 68, 180.

10/31, LM, BAV, Arch. Barb., Comp. 51, 167v.

Oct: 21 days, 12.10 sc.

11/7, Giust., BAV, Arch. Barb., Giust. 2568–2634, 226r.

11/7, EU, BAV, Arch. Barb., Comp. 93, 127r.

11/30, Gior., Arch. Barb., Comp. 68, 186.

11/30, LM, Arch. Barb., Comp. 51, 167v.

Nov: 22 days, 8.80 sc.

12/8, EU, BAV, Arch. Barb., Comp. 93, 130v.

12/10, Giust., Arch. Barb., Giust. 2635–2684, 5v.

Dec: 21 days, 8.40 sc.

12/–, Giust., BAV, Arch. Barb., Giust. 2635–2684, 1v (Verdi, 96, doc. 21) (Nov–Dec).

12/31, Giust., BAV, Arch. Barb., Giust. 2635–2684, 10r (Verdi, 96, doc. 21).

12/31, Gior., BAV, Arch. Barb., Comp. 68, 195 (Nov–Dec).

12/31, LM, BAV, Arch. Barb., Comp. 51, 167v (Nov–Dec).

1637

Jan: 21 days, 8.40 sc.

2/10, EU, BAV, Arch. Barb., Comp. 93, 138r.

2/10, Giust., BAV, Arch. Barb., Giust. 2635–2684, 239v.

2/28, Gior., BAV, Arch. Barb., Comp. 68, 223.

2/29, LM, BAV, Arch. Barb., Comp. 51, 236v.

Feb: 22 days, 8.80 sc.

3/14, EU, BAV, Arch. Barb., Comp. 93, 144v.

3/14, Giust., BAV, Arch. Barb., Giust. 2685–2742, 48r.

3/31, Gior., BAV, Arch. Barb., Comp. 68, 229.

3/31, LM, BAV, Arch. Barb., Comp. 51, 236v.

Mar: 23 days, 9.20 sc.

5/6, EU, BAV, Arch. Barb., Comp. 93, 155r.

5/6, Giust., BAV, Arch. Barb., Giust. 2743–2816, 18r (Verdi, 97, doc. 25).

Apr: 23 days, 9.20 sc.

5/6, Giust., BAV, Arch. Barb., Giust. 2743–2816, 18r (Verdi, 97, doc. 25).

5/6, EU, BAV, Arch. Barb., Comp. 93, 155r.

5/30, LM, BAV, Arch. Barb., Comp. 51, 236v (Mar–Apr).

May: 25 days, 10 sc.

6/–, Giust., BAV, Arch. Barb., Giust. 2743–2816, 60v (Verdi, 97, doc. 26).

6/5, Giust., BAV, Arch. Barb., Giust. 2743–2816, 63v (Verdi, 97, doc. 26).

6/20, LM, BAV, Arch. Barb., Comp. 51, 236v.

6/30, Gior., BAV, Arch. Barb., Comp. 68, 259.

Jun: 20 days, 8 sc.

6/31, Gior., BAV, Arch. Barb., Comp. 68, 271.

7/7, Giust., BAV, Arch. Barb., Giust. 2743–2816, 169v (Verdi, 97, doc. 26).

7/31, LM, BAV, Arch. Barb., Comp. 51, 236v.

Jul: 0 days
Aug: 0 days
Sep: 0 days
Oct: 0 days
Nov: 0 days
Dec: 0 days

1638

Jan: 33 days, 13.20 sc.

2/17, Giust., BAV, Arch. Barb., Giust. 2871–2950, 43r (Verdi, 97, doc. 26).

2/29, LM, BAV, Arch. Barb., Comp. 51, 236v.

Feb: 23 days, 9.20 sc.

3/14, Giust., BAV, Arch. Barb., Giust. 2871–2950, 150r (Verdi, 97, doc. 28) (8 Feb–8 Mar).

3/31, LM, BAV, Arch. Barb., Comp. 51, 236v (8 Feb–8 Mar)

Mar–Apr: 44 days, 17.60 sc.

5/–, Giust., BAV, Arch. Barb., Giust. 2871–2950, 241v (Verdi, 97, doc. 29).

5/31, LM, BAV, Arch. Barb., Comp. 51, 236v.

May: 22 days, 8.80 sc.

6/–, Giust., BAV, Arch. Barb., Giust. 2871–2950, 285v (Verdi, 97, doc. 29).

6/16, Gior., BAV, Arch. Barb., Comp. 68, 371.

6/16, LM, BAV, Arch. Barb., Comp. 51, 236v.

Jun: 23 days, 9.20 sc.

7/31, Gior., BAV, Arch. Barb., Comp. 68, 381.

7/31, LM, BAV, Arch. Barb., Comp. 51, 236r.

Jul: 23 days, 9.20 sc.

8/–, Giust., BAV, Arch. Barb., Giust. 2994–3081,

35v (Verdi, 98, doc. 30).

8/31, LM, BAV, Arch. Barb., Comp. 51, 236r.

8/31, Gior., BAV, Arch. Barb., Comp. 68, 390.

Aug: 25 days, 10 sc.

9/–, Giust., BAV, Arch. Barb., Giust. 2994–3081, 118v (Verdi, 98, doc. 30).

9/4, Giust., BAV, Arch. Barb., Giust. 2994–3081, 122r (Verdi, 98, doc. 30).

9/30, LM, BAV, Arch. Barb., Comp. 51, 236r.

9/30, Gior., BAV, Arch. Barb., Comp. 68, 396.

Sep: 25 days, 10 sc.

10/–, Giust., BAV, Arch. Barb., Giust. 2994–3081, 226r (Verdi, 98, doc. 30).

Oct: 21 days, 8.40 sc.

10/–, Giust., BAV, Arch. Barb., Giust. 2994–3081, 221v (Verdi, 98, doc. 30) (Sep–Oct).

11/12, Giust., BAV, Arch. Barb., Giust. 2994–3081, 226r (Verdi, 98, doc. 30).

11/30, LM, BAV, Arch. Barb., Comp. 51, 236r (Sep–Oct).

Nov: 20 days, 8 sc.

11/30, Gior., BAV, Arch. Barb., Comp. 68, 411 (Oct–Nov).

Dec: 10 days, 4 sc.

12/31, LM, BAV, Arch. Barb., Comp. 51, 236r (Nov–Dec).

• Amount and Mode of Payments
to Cortona

THE FINANCIAL reimbursement Cortona received for his eight years of work at Palazzo Barberini was exceptional, yet the method of payment and its significance for the rank of the patron and status of the artist have not been examined.[1]

Unlike his assistants, Romanelli, Bottalla, and Baldini, who were on the family roll of Cardinal Francesco and received ten scudi (silver) each per month during the years they worked at the palace,[2] Cortona did not receive regular direct payments from the patron. He benefited from only two payments from Cardinal Francesco. The first, 100 scudi, is recorded in three documents dating from October to November 1631 and appears to be related to the initial work in the little gallery and chapel on the piano nobile of the north wing, as well as to work on the scaffold of the salone.[3] The next direct payment did not occur until more than eight years later when, on 28 February 1640, a *mandato* was issued for 2,000 scudi d'oro as final payment for the salone vault and all other work Cortona had done in the palace.[4]

Cortona had worked on, and was paid for, other fresco projects and easel paintings—for the Barberini and other patrons—during the time that elapsed between these two payments, but it is unlikely that he would have been responsible for the undoubtedly sizable expenses related to work in the salone over these eight years. Although the precise nature of the financial arrangement has not been known, Cardinal Francesco did provide Cortona with a steady income while he was engaged at the Barberini Palace.

Three documents of October 1632 indicate that the cardinal purchased a venal office known as a *Cavalierato Pio* for Cortona at a cost of 400 scudi d'oro.[5] The *Cavalierato Pio* was

---

[1] A modified version of the discussion in Appendix E has been published. J. B. Scott, "Pietro da Cortona's Payments for the Barberini Salone," *Burlington Magazine* 131 (1989), 416–18.

[2] Lo Bianco, "Disegni preparatori," 58, 60, n. 16. For seventeenth-century Roman monetary denominations, see Appendix A.

[3] "Diversi lavori di pittura da lui fatte al detto palazzo e voltone cioè fatti e da farsi." BAV, Arch. Barb., Comp. 50, 164r–v (29 October 1631, LM, Card. Fran.). "Per spese da farsi." BAV, Arch. Barb., Comp. 80, 38r (13 November 1631, mand., Card. Fran.). See Briganti, *Pietro da Cortona*, 198; Verdi, "Fonti documentarie," 95, doc. 6. "Per spese da farsi." SCEP, Quaderno de' sig.ri Barberini, 1631–1633, 70v (17 November 1631, quad., Card. Fran.).

[4] "Sono per resto, et intiero pagamento tanto dell'opera del Voltone del Palazzo alle 4 fontane, quanto per ogn'altra cosa fatta sino al presente giorno . . . 28 Feb.r 1640." BAV, Arch. Barb., Comp. 81,

144v. See M. Del Piazzo, *Pietro da Cortona: mostra documentaria* (Rome, 1969), 18, doc. 114; and M. A. Lavin, *Documents and Inventories*, 14, doc. 106. The same payment also appears in BAV, Arch. Barb., Comp. 51, 144 (4 April 1640, LM, Card. Fran.).

[5] "A Pietro Berrettino Cortonese Pittore scudi quattrocento doro stampe in nostro a Siri pagat.li con mand.o 2842 alla Dateria di N.S. per il prezzo di un Cavalierato Pio resegnata a favore del med.o Pietro Cortonese con li frutti dal p.mo di Nov.bre pross.mo avvenir 1632 come per fede del Causeo ricettore di Detta Dateria come al rin.o 40. Sc. 400." BAV, Arch. Barb., Comp. 67, 228 (29 October 1632, gior., Card. Fran.). Also, BAV, Arch. Barb., Comp. 80, 73r (19 October 1632, mand., Card. Fran.); and BAV, Arch. Barb., Comp. 50, 237r (29 October 1632, LM, Card. Fran.). The interest was paid in the less valuable common scudo (silver). E. Stumpo, *Il capitali finanziario a Roma fra cinque e seicento* (Milan, 1985), 36.

the second of two categories of nonecclesiastical offices issued through the Cancelleria. The office carried the official duty of guardianship of the pope and the papal family, although its holders had no genuine function to fulfill beyond collecting the annual seven percent return on the principal.[6]

A third document, dated 19 August 1635, has been interpreted as a direct payment of 1,810 scudi d'oro to Cortona,[7] but it in fact represents the purchase price of another venal office, as two later records indicate. A document of 30 October 1635 specifies that the 1,810 scudi d'oro were the price of a Janissary office given to Cortona by Cardinal Francesco in return for work on the vault.[8] As the purchase price indicates, this was a more substantial office, which brought its holder a 7.2 percent return on the principal and carried a certain prestige.[9] The Janissary was the higher of the two categories of nonecclesiastical venal offices administered by the Cancelleria. Holders of this office were limited to one hundred and served as intermediaries between petitioners and the Curia. They apparently received additional payments from the supplicants whose petitions they presented, which varied according to the importance and success of the petition.[10]

By means of these two offices Cardinal Francesco provided Cortona with a steady remuneration, beginning with 28 scudi per annum in November 1632 when work on the salone's vault was being initiated; an additional 130.2 scudi per annum were given in October 1635 when the vault must have been at least half completed. Over the period Cortona worked at the palace his receipts from these sources would have come to 719.2 scudi, and to this should be added the sum of the two direct payments (100 and 2,000). Because the final direct payment of 2,000 was made in the more valuable scudi d'oro, that sum should be converted at the rate current in 1640 (1 scudo d'oro = 1.465 scudi di moneta), which equals 2,930 scudi.[11] Thus the total remuneration would have been 3,749.2 scudi di moneta. Of course the annual return from the venal offices was to continue for the rest of the artist's life, or until he sold them at market value (usually much in excess of the purchase price). In this respect they were even more valuable than the final direct payment of 2,000 scudi d'oro.

The payment made by the time of the vault's completion, 3,749.2 scudi, compares favorably with the direct payment of 3,050 scudi made by Clement VIII to the Alberti brothers for their comparable fresco project in the Sala Clementina of the Vatican Palace.[12]

---

[6] As the post could not be inherited, it therefore returned to the Cancelleria Apostolica for resale upon the death of a holder. Beyond the right of the holder to use the title "cavaliere," the *Cavalierato Pio* cannot have carried great prestige as there were 671 such knights. For venal offices, see Piola Caselli, "Aspetti del debito," 12–13, 22–31.

[7] Verdi, "Fonti documentarie," 92, 96, doc. 17. BAV, Arch. Barb., Comp. 80, 227 (19 August 1635, mand., Card. Fran.).

[8] "Pietro Berrettini da Cortona Pittore deve dare scudi 1810 di mta. in oro a Canc.ria Ap.ca sono per il prezzo di un Giannizzerato vacato per morte di Mons.re Giustiniano datoli da noi a buon conto dell'operi fatte e da fare tanto al voltone grande del Palazzo alle 4 fontane quanto in altri luoghi conf.e al ord.e soscritto sotto li 30 ord.e 1635 da Mons.re ill.mo

Scanaroli Maggiord.mo." BAV, Arch. Barb., Comp. 51, 144v (30 October 1635, LM, Card. Fran.), and 28r (5 October 1635, LM, Card. Fran.).

[9] Piola Caselli, "Aspetti del debito," 40.

[10] Ibid., 24–26, 42, n. 5; and Moroni Romano, *Dizionario*, 67:172–73.

[11] Piola Caselli, "Aspetti del debito," 73.

[12] For the payment to the Alberti, see M. A. Gualandi *Memorie originali italiane risguardanti le belle arti* (Bologna, 1840–1845), 6:72; Witcombe, "Giovanni and Cherubino Alberti," 331; Abromson, "Clement VIII's Patronage," 536, n. 26, and 545–46 for transcriptions of the contract and payment documents. Even allowing for the mural frescoes in the Sala Clementina, the total painted surface is no greater than at the Barberini salone.

Significantly, however, the Alberti were bound by a contract that obliged them to provide all the necessary materials,[13] whereas Cortona appears to have had no legal obligation to his patron. These circumstances also appear favorable compared with those endured by Annibale Carracci at Palazzo Farnese, where he was retained in the household of Cardinal Odoardo Farnese virtually as a servant, receiving ten scudi per month plus room and board for the nine years he lived and worked there (1595–1604).[14] The notorious insult of Annibale's final payment of 500 scudi—delivered in a saucer—for his work in the Camerino and gallery was only one manifestation of the low esteem he suffered under an antiquated system of patronage.[15]

The total payment to Cortona for his eight years' work at Palazzo Barberini—at 468.65 scudi per year—can also be seen in perspective by comparing other wages and salaries of the period. During the construction of Bernini's colonnades for St. Peter's Square (1656–1667), the manual laborers (*manuali*) made from 5 to 65 baiocchi per day (100 baiocchi = 1 scudo), depending upon their skill and experience.[16] The 40 baiocchi (i.e., 4 giuli) daily wage earned by the *muratori* who worked with Cortona on the vault of the salone would have been a moderate amount for skilled labor of the period.[17] Since the *muratori* worked an average of twenty-eight days per month over the seven-and-one-half-year period, each might, in theory at least, hope to earn approximately 110.4 scudi per year. Cardinal Francesco's coachman, perhaps somewhat exceptional for his position, received a salary of 3.5 scudi per month (42 scudi per annum) plus room and board (*companatici*).[18] As members of the cardinal's *famiglia*, Cortona's assistants received 120 scudi each per annum, but without *companatici*. At the other end of the scale, a cardinal whose annual income fell below 5,500 scudi was considered poor.[19] Moreover, Cortona's total remuneration was not enormous by the standards of some papal extravagances of an occasional nature. For the funeral of Carlo Barberini, father of the nephews and brother of Urban, which was held on 3 August 1630, the pope was said to have provided 12,000 scudi.[20]

The way in which Cortona's payments were transacted also has implications for his standing. Cortona's assistants and the lesser artists at Palazzo Barberini received a monthly stipend as well as occasional payments for specific work. They were listed on the roll of Cardinal Francesco's *famiglia*, together with grooms, coachmen, and other servants. By contrast, artists such as Sacchi and Camassei, who were esteemed by individual Barberini patrons, had no stipends but consistently received direct payments for their work.[21] On purely

[13] The artists were contractually obligated to complete work within a specified period and to provide at their own expense "colors, paper, brushes, palettes and whatever will be needed." Ibid.

[14] Bellori, *Vite de' pittori*, 43.

[15] Ibid., 77–79, gives the fullest account. See also Posner, *Annibale Carracci*, 1:146–47; and Dempsey, "Annibal Carrache," 310–11.

[16] P.J.A.N. Rietbergen, *Pausen, Prelaten, Bureaucraten* (Nijmegen, 1983), 349–50.

[17] BAV, Arch. Barb., Giust. 1726–1792, 263r (Verdi, "Fonti documentarie," 95, doc. 11).

[18] BAV, Arch. Barb., Comp. 142. This computa-tion, based on data supplied by Patricia Waddy, covers the period 1637–1642.

[19] Rietbergen, *Pausen*, 350–51.

[20] Gigli, *Diario romano*, 116; C. Pietrangeli, "La Sala dei Capitani," *Capitolium* 37 (1962), 640–48; Nussdorfer, "City Politics," 236–37.

[21] For payments to Sacchi, see BAV, Arch. Barb., Comp. 181, 149v/156v and 169v (LM, Taddeo) (Incisa della Rocchetta, "Notizie su Sacchi," 63); BAV, Arch. Barb., Comp. 181, 166v and 169r-v (LM, Taddeo) (Mahon, "Poussiniana," 64–66). For Camassei, BAV, Arch. Barb., Ind. IV, 13, at date (25 September 1630, mand., Taddeo); BAV, Arch. Barb., Comp. 186, 164r

financial grounds this method may have been preferable, even for Cortona, but the conferral of the venal offices in place of stipends or periodic cash payments bore the mark of rank and exalted patronage. This mode of payment, moreover, contrasts favorably with those under which artists of an earlier generation had worked on large projects involving fresco. The contract between Clement VIII and the Alberti brothers implied a craftsman-like status of workers hired to do piecework and paid at regular monthly intervals. The humiliating circumstances of Annibale's relationship to his patron even carried the suggestion of servitude. Cortona avoided both these indignities, and the offices of Knight and Janissary must also have conveyed to the public the high regard in which he was held by pope and cardinal nephew.

(gior., Taddeo); BAV, Arch. Barb., Comp. 192, 42r (mand., Taddeo); SCEP, Quaderno de' sig.ri Barberini, 1631–1633, 35 (Pollak, *Die Kunsttätigkeit*, 1:330); BAV, Arch. Barb., Comp. 192, 50r (mand., Taddeo).

• The *Dichiaratione* of Mattia Rosichino (1640)

Dichiaratione delle pitture della sala de' signori Barberini,
Roma, MDCXXXX

Rosichino agli spettatori: Come l'huomo mira le pitture fatte dal Signor Pietro Berettini da Cortona nella volta della sala de' Signori Barberini; così comprende ch'elle sono quelle cose, che sopra tutte le altre dilettano gli occhi de' mortali. Ma perchè tal diletto non si dilata, se non alla forma, e alla dispositione de' colori, e delle figure; i riguardanti rimanendo privi del godimento d'intenderne il significato, tutto il giorno si volgevano a me, che di continuo (così portando il mio carico) dimoro qui, e richiedevanmi che io gliel dichiarasi: Credevan forse ch'io col praticar sempre dove queste pitture sono, anche intrinsecamente le conoscessi. Sforzato dunque da questi curiosi me n'andai da uno, il quale o è poeta, o filosofo almeno, e dettogli il bisogno che havevo per l'altrui curiosità della sua dottrina, egli per compassione [3] me ne prestò alquanto; e resemi dotto della dichiaratione ch'io cercavo. Ma temendo io del difetto della memoria non troppo avvezza a ritener cose cosi speculative et alte; deliberai di farle stampare, e di presentarle a voi spettatori, per liberar me da quella noia, e per sodisfare alle vostre dimande. Vi prego solo che s'io non dicessi tanto puntualmente le cose quanto mi sono state insegnate, che scusiate la mia non buona memoria, e la recompensiate con la buona volontà che ho havuto, et ho di servirvi. [4]

Divisa e dipinta la volta della gran sala Barberina in cinque parti. In quella di mezzo è la divina Providenza, che siede sopra una nuvola, ornata di splendori con lo scettro in atto di commandare al presente, & al futuro; e perciò il tempo, che in forma di Saturno divora i proprii figliuoli, si tien sotto di se, e le Parche. Vi stanno attorno la Giustitia, la Misericordia, l'Eternità, la Verità, la Purità, la Bellezza, & altre, [5] che pare che habbino desiderio d'obbedirla: ma tra tutte dimostra l'Immortalità d'esseguire i comandamenti, movendosi con la corona di stelle ad incoronare l'insegna di Urbano Ottavo Sommo Pontefice; questa è circondata da due gran rami di lauro, che insieme arrendendosi, fanno la simiglianza di uno scudo, sostenuto dalla Fede, e dalla Speranza da i lati, e da piedi dalla Carità, volandovi dentro le tre Api. Stannovi di sopra la Religione con le Chiavi, e Roma col Regno Papale: & un bambino con la ghirlanda pur di lauro, segno del valor poetico, che va quivi presso scherzando.

Nella seconda parte; cioè nella fronte della sala verso il giardino sta l'imagine di Pallade dinotante la Sapienza, che abbatte con l'asta i Giganti, i quali veggionsi precipitati & [6] oppressi da quei monti, ch'essi medesimi havevano ammassati per contrastar col Cielo. E qui s'esprime la diffesa delle cose Ecclesiastiche.

Di contro, la terza parte rappresenta il governo temporale, e quelle due giovani, che mostrano di venire da alto, significano l'una l'Autorità col fascio consolare, e l'altra col cornucopia l'Abbondanza; sono avanti di queste inginocchiati ogni sorte di persone, come vecchi, fanciulli, vedove, & altri molti, che da esse aspettano de' suoi doni. Nell'Hercole poi, che scaccia l'arpie, s'intende il castigo de' rei. Di sotto questa parte nell'ornamento finto di basso rilievo è una mazza dell'istesso Hercole, che germoglia: una dell'imprese della Casa Barberina.

Dalla man dritta nell'entrare è la quarta parte; e vi si scorge la Scienza [7] sollevata dall'Aiuto divino, che si dinota nel giovane che è si destro su l'ali: tiene detta Scienza il libro dall'una mano per la cognitione delle cose, e dall'altra la fiamma a significare, ch'egli è suo proprio l'ergersi in alto: sta parimente accompagnata dalla Pietà verso Dio espressa nella matrona d'habito honesta, e veneranda, che ha il tripode, e dentrovi il fuoco apparecchiato per lo sacrifitio. Sotto la detta Scienza sono la gola, e la lascivia: la prima si dimostra in Sileno, a cui da Fauni, e Satiri si mesce il vino nella gran tazza, ch'ei tiene in mano. E vedendosi le Baccanti con Bacco fanciullo in grembo, che avidamente da di piglio all'uva, ci s'appresenta la rea educatione de' figliuoli. Vien figurata la lascivia in una femmina prostrata, appresso la quale si discernono alcuni [8] Amori pudichi, e lascivi; ma i pudichi animati dalla Castità figurata nella donna vestita di bianco, col giglio in mano, discacciano con le faci gli impudichi, si che colei che giace ne sta come spaurita. E di qui poco lontano è dipinta una fonte con femmine d'intorno, una delle quali sta adornandosi, per dinotarci quali siano le vane delitie mondane. L'impresa che qui si scorge è l'aratro tirato da due api con una che è al governo di esse, che con la sferza le va guidando.

A fronte di questa si mira l'ultima parte; ed è in essa la Dignità, la quale ha nella destra il caduceo, e nella sinistra una chiave. La Prudenza riverente le presenta lo specchio; e la Potestà delegata con una chiave, e con un foglio scritto le sta vicina, ma in atto di partire. Quivi presso è la Fama; e la Pace con l'olivo [9] serra la porta del tempio di Giano, fuori della quale si vede il Furore, con sue fiaccole sopra molti armamenti legato, che in vista par che si scuota, senonchè la Mansuetudine con un laccio il tien fermato. Havvi ancora alcuna Furia con la sua facella, che atterrata, appare priva di vigore. Non molto da lungi è la fucina di Vulcano, dove diversi Ciclopi s'affaticano a fabbricar'armi, alludendo al provedimento, che anche nel tempo pacifico si deve havere per la difesa delle Provincie. E qui è il sole oriente per impresa.

Oltre a ciò sono nelle quattro cantonate di questa volta quattro medaglioni, ne'quali si esprimono le quattro virtù, Temperanza, Fortezza, Giustitia, e Prudenza. La Temperanza, quando Scipione il giovane rimandò intatta la giovanetta donna sua preda [10] allo sposo Saguntino. La Fortezza con Mutio Scevola, quando abrugiò la sua destra, ch'errando uccise un privato, in vece del Re Porsenna. La Giustitia con Tito Mallio, quando fece tagliar la testa al figliuolo trasgressore, ancorchè felicemente, del suo divieto. La Prudenza con l'historia di Fabio Massimo, quando egli contenendosi negli alloggiamenti tenne a bada Annibale. Sotto le medaglie si mirano effigiati per dimostrar la Temperanza l'Alicorno: per la Fortezza il Leone: l'Hippogrifo per la Giustitia: e per la Prudenza alcuni Orsi, perchè col tempo perfettionano i parti loro.

[*Declaration on the Paintings of the Hall of the Signori Barberini*,
Rome, 1640

Rosichino to the Spectators: As one gazes at the paintings made by Signor Pietro Berrettini da Cortona on the vault of the hall of the Signori Barberini, he understands that they are among those things that above all others delight the eyes of mortals. But because such pleasure extends only to the form and disposition of the colors and figures, the observers, remaining deprived of the enjoyment of understanding the meaning, continually turned to me, since I am always around here (as required by my position), and asked me to explain the paintings to them. They perhaps thought that because I am always present where these paintings are located that I even knew them intrinsically. Forced therefore by these curious people, I went on this matter to someone who is a poet, or at least a philosopher, and told him of the need I had of his erudition because of the curiosity of others. Out of compassion he shared it with me and made me knowledgeable of the explanation I sought. But fearing the defect of a memory not too accustomed to retaining things so speculative and exalted, I decided to have them printed and to present them to you spectators in order to free myself from that nuisance and satisfy your questions. I beg of you only that, if I do not tell those matters exactly as they were taught to me, you excuse my poor memory and accept in compensation the good will I have had and have to serve you.

Declaration on the Paintings: The vault of the great hall of the Barberini is divided and painted in five parts. In the center part is Divine Providence, who sits on a cloud, ornamented with splendors, with a scepter, and in the act of commanding the present and the future. And therefore Time, who in the form of Saturn devours his own children, is held with the Fates under her. Around her are Justice, Mercy, Eternity, Truth, Purity, Beauty, and others who seem to want to obey her. But above all others Immortality appears to execute the commands, moving with the crown of stars to crown the arms of Urban VIII Supreme Pontiff. The papal arms are surrounded by two great branches of laurel, which rendered together create the image of a shield supported by Faith and Hope at the sides and by Charity at the bottom, with the three bees flying inside these. Above are Religion with the keys and Rome with the Papal Tiara, and a child with a garland also of laurel—sign of poetic excellence—is playing there nearby.

In the second part, that is, in the front of the hall toward the garden, is the image of Minerva, denoting Wisdom, who overthrows with her lance the Giants who are seen hurled down and weighed down by those mountains they themselves had amassed in order to challenge Heaven. Here is expressed the defense of ecclesiastical things.

Opposite, the third part represents the temporal government. Those two youths who seem to be coming from above signify, first, Authority with the consular fasces, and, second, Abundance with the cornucopia. Kneeling in front of these are all kinds of people, such as old men, children, and widows, and many others who expect gifts from them. There, by Hercules, who casts out the Harpies, is meant the chastisement of kings. Beneath this part, in the feigned bas-relief ornament is the club of this same Hercules, which sprouts—a device of the Barberini family.

On the right as you enter is the fourth part; here one sees Knowledge uplifted by Divine Assistance, who is denoted in the young man who is agile with his wings. Knowledge holds a book in one hand for the knowledge of things and, in the other, a flame to symbolize that it is her nature to uplift herself. She is also accompanied by Piety toward God, expressed in the modestly dressed and venerable woman who has a tripod with fire inside ready for the sacrifice. Beneath Knowledge are gluttony and lasciviousness. The first is represented by Silenus, for whom fauns and satyrs pour wine in the great cup he holds in his hand. Bacchantes, with young Bacchus in their lap avidly devouring a bunch of grapes, represent the bad upbringing of youths. Lasciviousness is embodied in a reclining woman next to whom are discerned some chaste and lewd cupids. But the chaste ones, urged on by Chastity, personified by the woman dressed in white with the lily in hand, drive away the lewd ones with torches so that she who is lying seems frightened by them. Not far from here there is painted a fountain with women around it, one of whom is adorning herself in order to denote the vanity of worldly pleasures. The device perceived here is the plough pulled by two bees with a third who steers it and is guiding them with a whip.

Opposite this, ones sees the last section. In this, Dignity holds in the right hand the caduceus and in the left a key. Prudence reverently holds up a mirror to her, and Power, delegated with a key and a written sheet, is nearby but in the act of departing. Then next is Fame. And Peace with the olive branch closes the door to the Temple of Janus, outside of which one sees Furor tied with his torches on top of many armaments. He seems in appearance to struggle, except that Gentleness holds him still with a noose. There is also Fury with her torch who, thrown down, appears deprived of strength. Not far away is the forge of Vulcan where several cyclopes exert themselves to make weapons, alluding to the preparedness which is necessary for the defense of the provinces even in peace time. Here the rising sun is the device.

Besides this there are four medallions in the four corners of this vault. In these are expressed the four virtues—Temperance, Fortitude, Justice, and Prudence. Temperance: when Scipio the Younger sent back untarnished to her Saguntine spouse the young maid he had captured as his booty. Fortitude: with Mucius Scaevola when he burned his right hand, having erred killing a civilian instead of King Porsenna. Justice: with Titus Manlius when he even happily had beheaded his son who had violated his prohibition. Prudence: with the story of Fabius Maximus when restraining himself in his quarters held Hannibal in check. Under the medallions one sees portrayed a unicorn to represent Temperance, a lion for Fortitude, a hippogriff for Justice, and some bears for Prudence because they develop their offspring slowly with time.]

• Domenichino's Letter to Francesco Angeloni (1640)

Al sig. Francesco Angeloni, Roma.

Ho avuto caro della nuova pittura del Cortona scoperta: il mondo fu sempre indifferente del suo parere, ma il vero parere è quello d'uno più intendente che dica il vero; e chi sa le fatiche di se stesso sarà meno scarso a censurare l'opere d'altri. A me sarebbe curioso solo il sapere l'ordine tenuto sopra tutta l'invenzione dell'istorie applicate: parmi avere inteso il capriccio sia del Bracciolino sopra le lodi del papa. Secondo quel poco che m'è stato significato, dubito che manchi, e che converrebbe più tosto a principe secolare; non so che mi dica, ed io che non m'intendo di qui principierei a giudicare: però mi rimetto, mentre le bacio le mani.

Di Napoli il primo di settembre 1640.

[To sig. Francesco Angeloni, Rome.

I have been delighted in learning about the newly unveiled painting by Cortona. The opinion of the general public is unimportant, but the true judgment is that of someone more informed who speaks the truth; one who knows how he himself has had to labor will be less likely to censure the works of others. I would be curious only to know the means of invention of the stories represented; it seems I have heard that it is a fantasy of Bracciolini's on the praises of the pope. According to the little information given to me, I doubt that it is wanting, and it would appear to be more suitable for a secular prince. And not being fully informed, I would not want to begin passing judgment from here. Therefore, I leave it to you, while kissing your hands.

From Naples the first day of September 1640]

BIBLIOGRAPHY

MANUSCRIPT AND DOCUMENTARY SOURCES

ACR
  Archivio della Camera Capitolina, Credenza VI,
    vol. 37
  Archivio della Camera Capitolina, Credenza VI,
    vol. 40
ADP
  Scaffale 88, busta 35, int. 3, "Breve narratione
    dell'istorie dipinte dall'eccelente penello di Pie-
    tro da Cortona corona de' pittori nella galleria
    del pal. in Piazza Navona dell'eccmo pnpe Pam-
    philio."
ASF
  Archivio Mediceo del Principato, Roma-Carteggio
    Diplomatico, Francesco Niccolini, 1639, 1 Jan—
    27 Aug.
ASM
  Cancelleria Ducale, Avvisi e notizie dall'estero,
    5298, Avvisi di Roma.
ASR
  Cartari Febei 120, 14r–15v ("Dichiaratione delle
    pitture della sala de' sig.ri Barberini. L'anno
    1640").
  Congregazioni Religiose Maschili, Teatini S. An-
    drea della Valle, 2200, int. 229 (misura e stima,
    1634).
  Congregazioni Religiose Maschili, Teatini S. An-
    drea della Valle, 2200, int. 230 (misura e stima,
    1638).
  Notai del Tribunale del Auditor Camerae, Istro-
    menti, Notaio Dominicus Fonthia, 3175, 931r–
    1062v ["Conto del palazzo alle 4 fontane p serv.o
    dell'em.mo sig.r card.le prone" (misura e stima,
    1641)].
  Notai del Tribunale del Auditor Camerae, Istro-
    menti, Notaio Jacobus Simoncellus, 6601 [In-
    ventory of the estate of Taddeo Barberini,
    1648].
  Tribunale Criminale del Governatore di Roma,
    Processi 1630, vol. 251.
AVR
  Registro dei Battesimi, S. Giovanni dei Fiorentini,
    1600–1616.
BAV, Arch. Barb.
  Ind. I, 1–3, "Libro d'instrumenti publici spettanti
    all'ecc.ma fameglia Barberina."
  Ind. I, 338, "Scritture concernenti il fatto seguito
    tra il sig.e prenc.e d. Taddeo Barberini prefetto

di Roma e l'ecmo Gio. Pesaro ambasc.re di Ve-
    netia li 8 agosto 1632 [sic] per causa dell'incontro
    delle carrozze di ambedue nella strada della do-
    gana. . . ."
  Ind. I, 341, "Chirografo nel quale la S.tà di N.
    S.re esenta l'ecc.mo s.d. Taddeo Barberini
    pref.o di Roma dal dare titolo d'eminenza alli
    cardinali di S. Chiesa et al Gran Mro Malta, se
    non quando parera bene a se di farlo. Dato li 2
    Agosto."
  Ind. II, 318, "Annotazioni delle medaglie di Papa
    Urbano VIII."
  Ind. II, 320a–b, "Stima de' camei, corniole, me-
    daglie, e monete antiche che si conservano nel
    museo dell'eccma casa Barberini, fatta da Fran-
    cesco Ticoroni Antiquario."
  Ind. II, 2442, "Inventari diversi. Inventario fatto
    dalla principessa d.a Anna dopo la morte del
    principe d. Taddeo Barberini, 1648."
  Ind. II, 2693, "Memoria delli altri quattro pezzi
    d'arazzi che restano da farsi della vita di Papa
    Urbano VIII."
  Ind. II, 2813, "Iura Diversa super Palatio ad
    Quattuor Fontes dal 1505 al 1593."
  Ind. II, 2888, "Libro contenente le misure e stima
    de' lavori del Palazzo alle Quattre Fontane da
    aprile 1629 a tutto dicembre 1638."
  Ind. II, 2889, "Nota delli denari pagati alli mura-
    tori, falegnami, ferraro, ed altri per li lavori
    della nuova fabrica al Palazzo delle Quattro Fon-
    tane . . . 1631–1640."
  Ind. IV, 13, "Diversi mandati della sig.ra d.
    Anna" ("Per la fabbrica alle Quattro Fontane").
  Ind. IV, 176, "Ruollo della famiglia . . . Antonio
    Barberini . . . 1642."
  Ind. IV, 1254, "Descrittione della vita del sig.e d.
    Taddeo Barberini."
  Comp. 41, I, 1631–1635, Card. Fran.
  Comp. 49, LM, 1623–1629, Card. Fran.
  Comp. 50, LM, 1630–1634, Card. Fran.
  Comp. 51, LM, 1635–1640, Card. Fran.
  Comp. 66, gior., 1624–1629, Card. Fran.
  Comp. 67, gior., 1630–1634, Card. Fran.
  Comp. 68, gior., 1635–1640, Card. Fran.
  Comp. 70, gior., 1641–1648, Card. Fran.
  Comp. 80, mand., 1630–1636, Card. Fran.
  Comp. 81, mand., 1637–1641, Card. Fran.
  Comp. 91, mand., 1675–1678, Card. Fran.
  Comp. 93, EU, 1634–1637, Card. Fran.

Comp. 142, SC, 1637–1643, Card. Fran.

Comp. 181, LM, 1623–1630, Prin. Taddeo

Comp. 186, gior., 1623–1630, Prin. Taddeo

Comp. 192, mand., 1630–1633, Prin. Taddeo

Comp. 224, gior., 1636–1644, Card. Ant. the Younger

Comp. 229, gior., 1664–1667, Card. Ant. the Younger.

Comp. 233, mand., 1636–1644, Card. Ant. the Younger

Comp. 653, quad., 1774–1777, Prin. Carlo Maria

Giust. 501–625, 1626, Card. Fran.

Giust. 626–720, 1626–1627, Card. Fran.

Giust. 721–802, 1627, Card. Fran.

Giust. 1502–1595, 1630–1632, Card. Fran.

Giust. 1624–1725, 1632, Card. Fran.

Giust. 1726–1792, 1632–1633, Card. Fran.

Giust. 1793–1886, 1633, Card. Fran.

Giust. 1887–1975, 1633–1634, Card. Fran.

Giust. 1976–2074, 1634, Card. Fran.

Giust. 2075–2147, 1633–1634, Card. Fran.

Giust. 2148–2240, 1634–1635, Card. Fran.

Giust. 2241–2314, 1635, Card. Fran.

Giust. 2315–2416, 1634–1635, Card. Fran.

Giust. 2418–2488, 1635–1636, Card. Fran.

Giust. 2489–2567, 1636, Card. Fran.

Giust. 2568–2634, 1636, Card. Fran.

Giust. 2635–2684, 1636–1637, Card. Fran.

Giust. 2685–2742, 1635–1637, Card. Fran.

Giust. 2743–2816, 1637, Card. Fran.

Giust. 2871–2950, 1638, Card. Fran.

Giust. 2994–3081, 1638, Card. Fran.

Giust. 3573–3675, 1640, Card. Fran.

Giust. 12566–12622, 1677–1678, Card. Fran.

Giust. 12799–12830, 1678–1679, Card. Fran.

BAV, Barb. Lat.

1772, "De S. Michaele ad Urbanum VIII Carmen."

2032, [Ludovisi mss. pertaining to papal election reform].

2316, G. Teti, "Barberinarum Aedium Brevis Descriptio."

2317, G. Teti, "Barberinarum Aedium Brevis Descriptio" (fols. 1–16 of Barb. Lat. 2316).

2819, "Pauli Alaleonis Diarium a Die 26 Februarii 1630 ad Diem 31 Dicembris 1637."

3252, M. Perneo, "De Nativitate et Vita Eminent.mi et R.mi Cardinalis Antonii Barberini Junioris Papae Nepotis."

3261, M. Perneo, "Canticum Super Electione Urbani Octavi Pont. Opt. Max."

3295, M. Perneo, "Commentarius in Poemata S.D.N. Urbani Papae VIII," (draft of Barb. Lat. 3307).

3307, M. Perneo, "Magni Pernei Commentarius in Poemata S.D.N. Urbani Papae VIII."

3896–3899, [F. Barberini], "I dodici libri di Marco Aurelio Antonino Imperatore di se stesso, ed a se stesso. . . ."

4335, [F. Ubaldini], "Il pellegrino, o vero la dichiaratione delle pitture della sala barberina."

4342, [M. Rosichino], "Dichiaratione delle pitture della sala de' sig.ri Barberini," 83–86.

4724, "Conclave dell'anno 1623 nel quale messa la prima volta in uso la bolla della elettione publicata da Gregorio XV. Fu creato pontefice il Card. Maffeo Barberino detto Urbano VIII."

4728, F. Ubaldini, "Istoria del pontificato di PP. Urbano VIII."

4730–4739, A. Nicoletti, "Della vita di Papa Urbano Ottavo e istoria del suo pontificato" (Nicoletti's notes are contained in Barb. Lat. 4740–4748).

4901, F. Ubaldini, "Abbozzo per le pitture alle parieti della sala barberina."

5635, "Inventario della guardarobba" (Card. Fran., 1631–1636).

6458, [Letters to Urban VIII and Cardinal Francesco Barberini].

6529, "Camera della Divina Sapienza, Palazzo Barberini," misc. V, f. 52.

BAV, Ott. Lat.

3131, "Raccolta di disegni del Museo Vaticano di Carpegna."

BAV, Vat. Lat.

13362, [Letters of Giulio Rospigliosi (Clement IX), 1630–1637].

BMF

Bigazzi 235, "Oroscopi di illustri personaggi."

SCEP

Quaderno de' sig.ri Barberini, 1631–1633.

Quaderno de' sig.ri Barberini, 1633–1636.

PRINTED SOURCES

Abromson, M. C., "Painting in Rome During the Papacy of Clement VIII (1592–1605): A Documented Study," Ph.D. diss., Columbia University, 1976.

———. "Clement VIII's Patronage of the Brothers Alberti." *Art Bulletin* 60 (1978): 531–47.

Abū Ma'šar Ga'far ibn Muhammad. *Albumasar de magnis convictibus: et annorum revolutionibus: ac eorum profectionibus: octo continens tractatus.* Venice, 1515.

Ademollo, A. *Giacinto Gigli ed i suoi diarii del secolo XVII.* Florence, 1877.

———. *I teatri di Roma nel secolo decimosettimo.* Rome, 1888.

Adimari, A. *Per la nascita dell'eccel.mo D. Carlo figliuolo dell'illustris. & eccellentiss. D. Taddeo Barberini Gene-*

rale di Santa Chiesa Principe di Palestrina, &c. Florence, 1630.

Agrippa von Nettesheim, H. C. *De Occulta Philosophia Libri Tres.* Venice, 1551.

Alberti, L. B. *Ten Books on Architecture.* Trans. J. Leoni. London, 1955.

———. *On Painting and On Sculpture.* Trans. C. Grayson. London, 1972.

Albertino da Catanzaro, F. *Trattato del angelo custode . . . con l'offitio dell'angelo custode approvato da N. Signore Papa Paolo Quinto.* Rome, 1612.

Alciati, A. *Emblemata cum Commentariis.* Padua, 1621.

Allacci, L. *Apes Urbanae, sive de Viris Illustribus.* Rome, 1633.

———. *Melissolyra de Laudibus Dionysii Petavii. . . .* Rome, 1653.

Allen, R. H. *Star Names: Their Lore and Meaning.* New York, 1963 [1899].

d'Alverny, M.-T. "La sagesse et ses sept filles: recherches sur les allégories de la philosophie et des arts libéraux du IXe au XIIe siècle." In *Mélanges dédiés à la memoire de Félix Grat.* Paris, 1946, 1:245–78.

———. "Quelques aspects du symbolisme de la 'sapientia' chez les humanistes." In *Umanesimo e esoterismo.* Ed. E. Castelli. Padua, 1960, 321–33.

Amabile, L. "L'Andata di fra Tommaso Campanella a Roma dopo la lunga prigionia di Napoli," *Atti della Reale Accademia di Scienze Morali e Politiche di Napoli* 20 (1886): 1–51.

———. *Fra Tommaso Campanella ne' castelli di Napoli, in Roma ed in Parigi.* 2 vols. Naples, 1887.

Amayden, T. *La storia delle famiglie romane.* Ed. C. A. Bertini. 2 vols. Rome, 1914.

Anselme, P. *Histoire généalogique de la maison royale de France.* 8 vols. Paris, 1726–1733.

Antoninus, M. A. *I dodici libri di Marco Aurelio Antonio imperadore di se stesso, ed a se stesso.* Trans. F. Barberini. Rome, 1675.

———. *The Communings with Himself of Marcus Aurelius Antoninus Emperor of Rome.* Trans. C. R. Haines. Cambridge, Mass., 1970.

Apolloni Ghetti, B. M. *Santa Prassede.* Rome, 1961.

Armenini, G. B. *De' veri precetti della pittura.* Ravenna, 1587.

Armstrong, A. H., ed., *The Cambridge History of Later Greek and Early Medieval Philosophy.* Cambridge, 1967.

D'Avossa, A. *Andrea Sacchi.* Rome, 1985.

Baglione, G. *Le vite de' pittori, scultori et architetti.* Rome, 1642.

Baldinucci, F. *Notizie de' professori del disegno. . . :* Ed. F. Ranalli. 7 vols. Florence, 1845–1847.

Baldinucci, F. S. *Vite di artisti dei secoli XVII–XVIII.* Ed. A. Matteoli. Rome, 1975.

Barberini, M. [See Urbanus VIII.]

Barberini, U. "Pietro da Cortona e l'arazzeria Barberini." *Bollettino d'arte* 35 (1950): 43–51, 145–52.

———. "Gli arazzi e i cartoni della serie 'Vita di Urbano VIII' della arazzeria Barberini." *Bollettino d'arte* 53 (1968): 92–100.

Barbi, M. *Notizia della vita e delle opere di Francesco Bracciolini.* Florence, 1897.

Barbier de Montault, X. *Iconographie des sibylles.* Arras, 1874.

Barcia, F. *Bibliografia delle opere di Gregorio Leti.* Milan, 1981.

Bardi, G. *Dichiaratione di tutte le istorie, che si contegono nei quadri posti novamente nelle sale dello Scrutinio, & del Gran Consiglio del Palagio Ducale. . . .* Venice, 1587.

Barozzi, N. and G. Berchet. *Le relazioni della corte di Roma lette al senato dagli ambasciatori veneti nel secolo decimosettimo.* 2 vols. Venice, 1877 and 1879.

Barzon, A. *I cieli e la loro influenza negli affreschi del Salone in Padova.* Padua, 1924.

———. *Il Palazzo della Ragione di Padova.* Venice, 1964.

Batorska, D. "Grimaldi's Frescoes in Palazzo del Quirinale." *Paragone* 33 (1982): 3–12.

Baumgart, F. "La Caprarola di Ameto Orti." *Studi Romanzi* 25 (1935): 77–179.

Bazzoni, A. *Un nunzio straordinario alla corte di Francia nel secolo XVII.* Florence, 1882.

Beal, M. *A Study of Richard Symonds: His Italian Notebooks and Their Relevance to Seventeenth-Century Painting Techniques.* New York–London, 1984.

Bean, J. *Musée du Louvre: dessins romains du XVIIe siècle.* Paris, 1959.

Belfanti, M. et al. *I Giganti di Palazzo Te.* Mantua, 1989.

Belloni, A. *Gli epigoni della Gerusalemme liberata.* Padua, 1893.

———. *Poema epico e mitologico. . . .* Milan, 1908.

———. *Il seicento.* Milan, 1929.

Bellori, G. P. *Notae in Numismata tum Ephesia, tum Aliarum Urbium Apibus Insignita.* Rome, 1658.

———. *The Lives of Annibale & Agostino Carracci.* Trans. C. Enggass. University Park, Pa., 1968.

———. *Le vite de' pittori, scultori e architetti moderni.* Ed. E. Borea. Turin, 1976.

Beltrani, G. B. "Felice Contelori ed i suoi studi negli archivi del Vaticano." *Archivio della Società Romana di Storia Patria* 2 (1879): 165–208, 257–79.

Belvedere d'Iesi, F. da. *Symboliche conclusioni.* Ancona, 1628.

Benedetti, S. *Architettura come metafora: Pietro da Cortona "stuccatore."* Bari, 1980.

Berendsen, O. "The Italian Sixteenth and Seventeenth Century Catafalques," Ph.D. diss., New York University, 1961.

[Paris-Berendsen]. "A Note on Bernini's Sculptures for the Catafalque of Pope Paul V." *Marsyas* 8 (1957–1959): 67–69.

Bernini in Vaticano. Rome, 1981.

Berrettini, P. [See Ottonelli, G. D.]

Berthelet, G. *La elezione del papa*. Rome, 1891.

Berti, D. "Lettere inedite di Tommaso Campanella e catalogo dei suoi scritti." *Atti della Reale Accademia dei Lincei, memorie della classe di scienze morali, storiche e filologiche* 2 (1878): 439–519.

Bertolotti, A. "Agostino Tasso, suoi scolari e compagni pittori in Roma." *Giornale di erudizione artistica* 5 (1876): 193–223.

———. "Giornalisti, astrologi e negromanti in Roma nel secolo XVII." *Rivista europea*, n.s. 5 (1878): 466–516.

———. *Artisti urbinati in Roma prima del secolo XVIII: notizie e documenti raccolti negli archivi romani*. Urbino, 1881.

Bertozzi, M. *La tirannia degli astri: Aby Warburg e l'astrologia di Palazzo Schifanoia*. Bologna, 1985.

Bibliotheca Sanctorum. Ed. F. Caraffa. 13 vols. Rome, 1961–1970.

Biondo, F. *Roma trionfante*. Trans. L. Fauno. Venice, 1544.

Blanchet, F. *Campanella*. Paris, 1920.

Blunt, A. "The Exhibition of Pietro da Cortona," *Burlington Magazine* 98 (1956): 415–17.

———. "The Palazzo Barberini: The Contributions of Maderno, Bernini, and Pietro da Cortona." *Journal of the Warburg and Courtauld Institutes* 21 (1958): 256–87.

———. "Review of *Andrea Sacchi* by Ann Sutherland Harris." *Apollo* 107 (1978): 349.

———. *Guide to Baroque Rome*. New York, 1982.

———. and H. L. Cooke. *The Roman Drawings of the XVII & XVIII Centuries in the Collection of Her Majesty the Queen at Windsor Castle*. London, 1960.

Bollea, L. C. *Lorenzo Pécheux*. Turin, 1936.

Bolognini Amorini, A. *Vite dei pittori ed artefici bolognesi*. 5 vols. Bologna, 1841–1843.

Bonansea, B. *Tommaso Campanella: Renaissance Pioneer of Modern Thought*. Washington, D.C., 1969.

Bonomelli, E. *I papi in campagna*. Rome, 1953.

Borri, F. *Odoardo Farnese e i Barberini nella Guerra di Castro*. Parma, 1933.

Borsi, F. *Bernini architetto*. Milan, 1980.

Borsi, F., F. Quinterio, G. Magnanimi, and C. Cerchiai. *I Palazzi del Senato: Palazzo Cenci, Palazzo Giustiniani*. Rome, 1984.

Boschini, M. *La carta del navegar pitoresco*. Ed. A. Pallucchini. Venice–Rome, 1966.

Bottari, M. G. and S. Ticozzi. *Raccolta di lettere sulla pittura, scultura ed architettura*. . . . 8 vols. Milan, 1822–1825.

Bouché-Leclercq, A. *L'astrologie grècque*. Paris, 1899.

Bracciolini, F. *Dello scherno de gli dei, poema piacevole*. Florence, 1618.

———. *L'elettione di Urbano Papa VIII*. Rome, 1628.

———. *Delle poesie liriche toscane*. Rome, 1639.

———. *Conclave di Urbano papa ottavo*. Rome, 1640.

———. *Lettere sulla poesia*. Ed. G. Baldassarri. Rome, 1979.

Brau, J.-L., H. Weaver and A. Edmands. *Larousse Encyclopedia of Astrology*. New York, 1980.

Brayda di Soleto, P. "Il titolo di eminenza ai cardinali ed i Duchi di Savoia (tre documenti inediti del 1630)." *Bollettino storico-bibliografico subalpino* 24 (1922): 230–50.

Briganti, G. *Pietro da Cortona*. . . . Florence, 1982.

Brogiotti, A., ed., *Carmina Diversorium Auctorum in Nuptiis Illustrissimorum DD. Thaddaei Barberini et Annae Columnae*. Rome, 1629.

———. *Componimenti poetici di vari autori nelle nozze delli eccellentissimi signori D. Taddeo Barberini e D. Anna Colonna*. Rome, 1629.

Broglie, R. *Le Palais Farnèse*. Paris, 1953.

Brown, P. F. "*Laetentur Caeli*: The Council of Florence and the Astronomical Fresco in the Old Sacristy." *Journal of the Warburg and Courtauld Institutes* 44 (1981): 176–80.

Bruni, B. "La sacra colonna della flagellazione in Santa Prassede." *Capitolium* 35, no. 8 (1960): 15–19.

Buonanni, F. *Numismata Pontificum Romanorum*. . . . 2 vols. Rome, 1706.

Buscaroli, R. *Melozzo e il melozzismo*. Bologna, 1955.

Byard, M. M. "Divine Wisdom-Urania." *Milton Quarterly* 12 (1978): 134–37.

Caeremoniale Continens Ritus Electionis Romani Pontificis Gregorii Pape XV Iussu Editum. . . . Rome, 1622.

Calberg, M. "Hommage au pape Urbain VIII, tapisserie de la manufacture Barberini à Rome." *Bulletin des Musées Royaux d'Art et d'Histoire*, 4th ser., 31 (1959): 99–110.

Calzini, E. "La scuola baroccesca: Antonio Viviani, detto il Sordo." *Rassegna bibliografica dell'arte italiana* 13 (1910): 8–17, 92–101.

Campanella, T. *Astrologicorum Libri VI*. . . . Lyons, 1629.

———. *Universalis Philosophiae seu: Metaphysicarum, Iuxta Propria Dogmata, Partes Tres, Libri 18*. Paris, 1638.

———. *The Defense of Galileo*. . . . Trans. G. McColley. Northampton, Mass., 1937.

———. *Le creature sovrannaturali*. Trans. R. Amerio. Rome, 1970.

———. *Origine temporale di Cristo*. Trans. R. Amerio. Rome, 1972.

———. *Articuli Prophetales*. Ed. G. Ernst. Florence, 1976.

———. *La città del sole: dialogo poetico / The City of the Sun: A Poetical Dialogue.* Trans. D. J. Donno. Berkeley, 1981.

Campbell, M. "The Original Program of the Salone di Giovanni da San Giovanni." *Antichità viva* 15 (1976): 3–25.

———. *Pietro da Cortona at the Pitti Palace.* Princeton, 1977.

Campori, G. *L'arazzeria estense.* Modena, 1876.

———. *Carteggio galileano. . . .* Modena, 1881.

Cancellieri, F. *Storia de' solenni possessi de' sommi pontefici da Leone III a Pio VII.* Rome, 1802.

Capponi, V. *Biografia pistoiese.* Pistoia, 1874.

Cardano, G. *In Ptolemaei Librorum de Judiciis Astrorum Libr. IV Commentaria.* Lyons, 1555.

———. *Opera Omnia.* 10 vols. Lyons, 1662; rpt. New York–London, 1967.

Carini, I. "Attentato di Giacinto Centini contro Urbano VIII." *Il Muratori* 1 (1892): 1–12.

———, ed. "Il conclave di Urbano VIII." In *Spicilegio vaticano* 1 (1890): 333–75.

Castrichini, M. and L. Dominici, "Niccolò (e Michelangelo) Ricciolini." In *Verso un museo della città.* Eds. M. Bergamini and G. Comez. Todi, 1982, 242–52.

Cavallo, A. S. "Notes on the Barberini Tapestry Manufactory at Rome." *Boston Museum Bulletin* 55 (1957): 17–26.

Celli, A. *The History of Malaria in the Roman Campagna.* Ed. A. Celli-Fraentzel. London, 1833.

Cerroti, F. *Bibliografia di Roma medievale e moderna.* Rome, 1893.

Chacón, A. *Vitae, et Res Gestae Pontificum Romanorum et S.R.E. Cardinalium. . . .* 4 vols. Rome, 1677.

Charlesworth, M. P. "Providentia and Aeternitas." *The Harvard Theological Review* 29 (1936): 107–32.

Chattard, G. P. *Nuova descrizione del Vaticano o sia della sacrosanta basilica di S. Pietro.* Rome, 1762–1767.

Cheney, I. H. "Francesco Salviati (1510–1563)." 4 vols. Ph.D. diss., New York University, 1963.

———. "Les premières décorations: Daniele da Volterra, Salviati et les frères Zuccari." In *Le Palais Farnèse,* vol. I. Rome, 1981, 243–67.

Chinazzi, E. *Sede vacante per la morte del papa Urbano VIII. Barberini e conclave di Innocenzo X Pamfili.* Rome, 1904.

Chiomenti Vassalli, D. *Donna Olimpia o del nepotismo nel seicento.* Milan, 1979.

Claretta, G. "Relazioni d'insigni artisti e virtuosi in Roma col Duca Carlo Emanuele II di Savoia studiate sul carteggio diplomatico." *Archivio della Società Romana di Storia Patria* 8 (1885): 511–54.

Coffin, D. R. *The Villa d'Este at Tivoli.* Princeton, 1960.

———. *The Villa in the Life of Renaissance Rome.* Princeton, 1979.

Colalucci, G. and F. Mancinelli. "Mostra dei restauri in Vaticano: apoteosi di San Clemente." *Bollettino dei Monumenti, Musei, e Gallerie Pontificie* 4 (1983): 242–46.

Connors, J. "Pietro Berrettini da Cortona." In *Macmillan Encyclopedia of Architects.* Ed. A. K. Placzek. 4 vols. New York, 1982. 1:455–66.

Conring, H. *De Electione Urbani IIX & Innocenti X.* In *Opera.* Braunschweig, 1730 [1651], 664–704.

Contelori, F. *De Praefecto Urbis.* Rome, 1631.

Cortona, P. da. [See Ottonelli, G. D. and P. Berrettini.]

Costamagna, A. "Antonio Viviani, detto il Sordo di Urbino." *Annuario dell'Istituto di Storia dell'Arte, Università degli Studi di Roma* 1 (1973–1974): 237–303.

Costanzo, M. *Critica e poetica del primo seicento.* 2 vols. Rome, 1969.

Costello, J. "The Twelve Pictures 'Ordered by Velasquez' and the Trial of Valguarnera." *Journal of the Warburg and Courtauld Institutes* 13 (1950): 237–84.

Cox-Rearick, J. *Dynasty and Destiny in Medici Art: Pontormo, Leo X, and the Two Cosimos.* Princeton, 1984.

Cumont, F. "L'eternité des empereurs romains." *Revue d'histoire et de littérature religieuses* 1 (1896): 435–52.

Cusatelli, G., ed. *Storia della letteratura italiana.* 9 vols. Milan, 1965–1969.

Danieli, F. *Trattato della divina providenza.* Milan, 1615.

Davidson, B. F. *Raphael's Bible: A Study of the Vatican Logge.* University Park, Pa.–London, 1985.

Davis, B. "Pietro da Cortona." *Source: Notes in the History of Art* 2, no. 4 (1983): 14–16.

DeGrazia Bohlin, D. *Prints and Related Drawings by the Carracci Family.* Washington, D.C., 1979.

DeLaLande, J. J. *Voyage d'un françois en Italie, fait dans les années 1765 & 1766.* 8 vols. Venice, 1769.

Del Gaizo, V., ed. *Grande enciclopedia antiquariato e arredamento.* 5 vols. Rome, 1967.

Del Piazzo, M. *Pietro da Cortona: mostra documentaria.* Rome, 1969.

DeMaria, G. "La Guerra di Castro e la spedizione de' presidii." *Miscellanea di storia patria* 4 (1898): 193–256.

Dempsey, C. " 'Et Nos Cedamus Amori': Observations on the Farnese Gallery." *Art Bulletin* 50 (1968): 363–74.

———. "Annibal Carrache au Palais Farnèse." In *Le Palais Farnèse,* Vol. I. Rome, 1981, 269–311.

———. "Mythic Inventions in Counter-Reformation Painting." In *Rome in the Renaissance: The City and the Myth.* Ed. P. A. Ramsey. Binghamton, N.Y., 1982, 55–75.

Descrizione della pittura fatta nella volta della sala di Villa Pinciana. Rome, 1779.

Dictionnaire de théologie catholique. Eds. A. Vacant et al. 15 vols. Paris, 1903–1950.

DiFederico, F. *The Mosaics of Saint Peter's*. University Park, Pa., 1983.

Di Napoli, G. *Tommaso Campanella, filosofo della restaurazione cattolica*. Padua, 1947.

Pseudo-Dionysius, the Areopagite. *On the Heavenly Hierarchy*. In *The Works of Dionysius the Areopagite*. Ed. J. Parker. London, 1897–1898 [rpt. New York, 1976].

Dizionario biografico degli Italiani. Rome, 1960–. [*DBI*]

Dizionario enciclopedico italiano. 12 vols. Rome, 1955–1961.

Domenico Cortese, G. di. "La vicenda artistica di Andrea Camassei." *Commentari* 19 (1968): 283–84.

DuBon, D. *Tapestries from the Samuel H. Kress Collection at the Philadelphia Museum of Art: The History of the Constantine the Great Designed by Peter Paul Rubens and Pietro da Cortona*. London, 1964.

Eckardt, C. C. *The Papacy and World Affairs as Reflected in the Secularization of Politics*. Chicago, 1937.

Eiche, S. "Cardinal Giulio della Rovere and the Villa Carpi." *Journal of the Society of Architectural Historians* 45 (1986): 115–33.

Enggass, R. *The Painting of Baciccio: Giovanni Battista Gaulli, 1639–1709*. University Park, Pa., 1964.

———. *Early Eighteenth-Century Sculpture in Rome*. University Park, Pa., 1976.

England, R. *The Baroque Ceiling Paintings in the Churches of Rome 1600–1750: A Bibliography*. Hildesheim–New York, 1979.

Erasmus, D. *The Education of a Christian Prince*. Trans. L. K. Born. New York, 1964 [1516].

Ernst, G. "Vocazione profetica e astrologica in Tommaso Campanella." In *La città dei segreti: magia, astrologia e cultura esoterica a Roma (XV–XVIII)*. Ed. F. Troncarelli. Milan, 1985.

Erythraeus, I. N. [G. V. Rossi], *Pinacotheca Imaginum Illustrium Doctrinae vel Ingenii Laude Virorum qui Auctore Superstite Diem Suum Obierunt*. Cologne, 1645–1648.

Ettlinger, L. D. *The Sistine Chapel before Michelangelo*. Oxford, 1956.

Evelyn, J. *The Diary of John Evelyn*. Ed. E. S. de Beer. 6 vols. Oxford, 1955.

Fabbrini, N. *Vita del cav. Pietro Berrettini da Cortona*. Cortona, 1896.

Fabrici, P. *Delle allusioni, imprese, et emblemi . . . sopra la vita, opere, et ationi di Gregorio XIII. . . .* Rome, 1588.

Fagiolo dell'Arco, M. and S. Carandini. *L'effimero barocco*. 2 vols. Rome, 1977–1978.

Faldi, I. *I cartoni per gli arazzi Barberini della serie di Urbano VIII*. Rome, 1967.

———. *Galleria Nazionale d'Arte Antica, acquisiti, doni, lasciti, restauri e recuperi, 1962–1970*. Rome, 1970.

———. *Pittori viterbesi di cinque secoli*. Rome, 1970.

———. *Il Palazzo Farnese di Caprarola*. Turin, 1981.

Fears, J. R. *'Princeps a Diis Electus': The Divine Election of the Emperor as a Political Concept at Rome*. Papers and Monographs of the American Academy in Rome, 26. Rome, 1977.

Felten, W. "Nepotismus." In *Wetzer und Welte's Kirchenlexikon*. Freiburg-im-Breisgau, 1882–1901, 9:101–54.

Ferguson, J. *Moral Values in the Ancient World*. London, 1958.

Ferrari, F. "Vita del cavalier Gio. Battista Marino." In *La strage degli innocenti del Cavalier Marino*. Venice, 1633, 65–93.

Ferrari, O. *Arazzi italiani*. Milan, 1982.

Ferro, G. *Teatro d'imprese*. Venice, 1623.

———. *Ombre apparenti nel teatro d'imprese*. Venice, 1629.

Fiorani, L. "Astrologi, superstiziosi e devoti nella società romana del seicento." *Ricerche per la storia religiosa di Roma* 2 (1978): 97–162.

Fiore, F. P. "Palazzo Barberini: problemi storiografici e alcuni documenti sulle vicende costruttive." In *Gian Lorenzo Bernini architetto e l'architettura europea del sei-settecento*. Eds. G. Spagnesi and M. Fagiolo. 2 vols. Rome, 1983–1984, 1:193–209.

Firmicus Maternus, J. *Ancient Astrology Theory and Practice: Matheseos Libri VIII*. Trans. J. R. Bram. Park Ridge, N.J., 1975.

Firpo, L. *Ricerche campanelliane*. Florence, 1947.

———. "Tommaso Campanella e i Colonnesi (con sette lettere inedite)." *Il pensiero politico* 1 (1968): 93–116.

Franz, H. G. *Niederländische Landschaftsmalerei im Zeitalter des Manierismus*. Graz, 1969.

Fraserius, I. *Carmen in Pauli V Inauguratione*. Paris, 1605.

Frommel, C. L. *Der römische Palastbau der Hochrenaissance*. 3 vols. Tübingen, 1973.

Fumaroli, M. "Cicero Pontifex Romanus: la tradition rhétorique du Collège Romain et les principes inspirateurs du mécénat des Barberini." *Mélanges de l'Ecole Française de Rome: moyen âge temps modernes*. 90 (1978): 797–835.

———. *L'âge de l'éloquence: rhétorique et "res literaria" de la Renaissance au seuil de l'époque classique*. Geneva, 1980.

Galbreath, D. L. *Papal Heraldry*, 2nd ed. London, 1972.

Gallavotti Cavallero, D. "Il programma iconografico per la Divina Sapienza nel Palazzo Barberini: una proposta." In *Studi in onore di Giulio Carlo Argan*. Rome, 1984, 1:269–90.

Garin, E. *Astrology in the Renaissance*. Trans. C. Jackson and J. Allen. London, 1983.

Garms, J. *Quellen aus dem Archiv Doria-Pamphilj zur Kunsttätigkeit in Rom unter Innocenz X*. Rome–Vienna, 1972.

Gaurico, L. *Tractatus Astrologicus*. . . . Venice, 1552.

Geisenheimer, H. *Pietro da Cortona e gli affreschi nel Palazzo Pitti*. Florence, 1909.

Gere, J. A. *Taddeo Zuccaro: His Development Studied in His Drawings*. Chicago, 1969.

Gigli, G. *Diario romano, (1608–1670)*. Ed. G. Ricciotti. Rome, 1958.

Gilbert, A. H. *Machiavelli's 'Prince' and Its Forerunners*. New York, 1938.

Gilbert, C. E., ed. *Italian Art 1400–1500: Sources and Documents*. Englewood Cliffs, N.J., 1980.

Giovannoli, A. *Roma antica*. Rome, 1619.

Giovio, P. *Le sententiose imprese*. . . . Lyons, 1562.

Giuntini, F. *Speculum Astrologiae*. Lyons, 1573.

———. *Speculum Astrologiae*. . . . 2 vols. Lyons, 1581.

Gloton, M. C. *Trompe-l'oeil et décor plafonnant dans les églises romains de l'âge baroque*. Rome, 1965.

Göbel, H. "Das Leben Urbans VIII.: Die Pfeilerteppichserie aus der römischen Manufaktur des Kardinals Francesco Barberini." *Der Cicerone* 21 (1929): 305–11.

Goldstein, C. "Louis XIV and Jason." *Art Bulletin* 49 (1967): 327–29.

Gombrich, E. H. "Aims and Limits of Iconology." In *Symbolic Images*. Oxford, 1972, 1–25.

———. "Icones Symbolicae: Philosophies of Symbolism and Their Bearing on Art." In *Symbolic Images*. Oxford, 1972, 123–95.

———. *Means and Ends: Reflections on the History of Fresco Painting*. London, 1976.

Graf, D. *Master Drawings of the Roman Baroque from the Kunstmuseum Düsseldorf*. London-Edinburgh, 1973.

———. "Der römische Maler Giuseppe Passeri als Zeichner." *Münchner Jahrbuch der bildenden Kunst* 30 (1977): 131–58.

Grillo, F. "Tommaso Campanella astrologo e la *Divina Sapienza* di Andrea Sacchi." *Studi Meridionali* 11 (1978): 293–328.

———. *Tommaso Campanella nell'arte di Andrea Sacchi e Nicola Poussin*. Cosenza, 1979.

Grisar, J. "Päpstliche Finanzen, Nepotismus und Kirchenrecht unter Urban VIII." *Miscellanea Historiae Pontificiae*. Vol. 7. Rome, 1943, 207–366.

Grottanelli, L. "Il Ducato di Castro: i Farnesi ed i Barberini." *La rassegna nazionale* 56 (1890): 476–504, 824–38; 57 (1891): 58–75, 554–85.

Gualandi, M. A. *Memorie originali italiane risguardanti le belle arti*. 6 vols. Bologna, 1840–1845.

Guidi, M. "I Fontana di Melide." *Roma* 6 (1928): 433–46, 481–94.

Guldan, E. *Die jochverschleifende Gewölbedekoration von Michelangelo bis Pozzo*. . . . Göttingen, 1954.

Güthmüller, B. *Studien zur antiken Mythologie in der italienischen Renaissance*. Weinheim, 1986.

Hallman, B. M. *Italian Cardinals, Reform, and the Church as Property*. Berkeley, 1985.

Hammond, F. "Girolamo Frescobaldi and a Decade of Music in Casa Barberini: 1634–1643." *Analecta Musicologica* 19 (1980): 94–124.

———. *Girolamo Frescobaldi: A Guide to Research*. New York–London, 1988.

Harprath, R. *Papst Paul III. als Alexander der Grosse: das Freskenprogramm der Sala Paolina in der Engelsburg*. Berlin–New York, 1978.

——— et al. *Zeichnungen aus der Sammlung des Kurfürsten Carl Theodor*. Munich, 1983.

Harris, A. S. "A Contribution to Andrea Camassei Studies." *Art Bulletin* 52 (1970): 49–70.

———. *Andrea Sacchi*. Princeton, 1977.

———. "Letter to the Editor Concerning George S. Lechner's 'Tommaso Campanella and Andrea Sacchi's Fresco of Divina Sapienza in the Palazzo Barberini.' " *Art Bulletin* 59 (1977): 304–7.

———. *Selected Drawings of Gian Lorenzo Bernini*. New York, 1977.

———. "Camassei et Pierre de Cortone au Palais Barberini." *Revue de l'art* 81 (1988): 73–76.

——— and E. Schaar. *Kataloge des Kunstmuseums Düsseldorf, Handzeichnungen: die Handzeichnungen von Andrea Sacchi und Carlo Maratta*. Düsseldorf, 1967.

Haskell, F. *Patrons and Painters*. London, 1963.

Havard, H. *Dictionnaire de l'ameublement et de la décoration*. 4 vols. Paris, 1894.

Heintze, H. v. and H. Hager. "Athene-Minerva: Ihr Bild im Wandel der Zeiten." *Jahrbuch der Max-Planck-Gesellschaft zur Förderung der Wissenschaften E.V.* 11, pt. 1 (1961): 36–127.

Held, J. and D. Posner. *Seventeenth & Eighteenth Century Art: Baroque Painting, Sculpture, and Architecture*. New York, 1971.

Helm, P., B. Degenhart, and W. Wegner, *Hundert Meister-Zeichnungen aus der Staatlichen Grapischen Sammlung München*. Munich, 1958.

Herrman-Fiore, K., "Giovanni Albertis Kunst und Wissenschaft der Quadratur, eine Allegorie in der Sala Clementina des Vatikan." *Mitteilungen des Kunsthistorischen Institutes in Florenz* 22 (1978): 61–84.

Hess, J. "On Some Celestial Maps and Globes of the Sixteenth Century." *Journal of the Warburg and Courtauld Institutes* 30 (1967): 406–9.

Hibbard, H. "The Date of Lanfranco's Fresco in the Villa Borghese and Other Chronological Problems." In *Miscellanea Bibliothecae Hertzianae*. Munich, 1961, 355–65.

Hibbard, H. "Scipione Borghese's Garden Palace on the Quirinal." *Journal of the Society of Architectural Historians* 23 (1964): 163–92.

———. *Carlo Maderno and Roman Architecture, 1580–1630.* London, 1971.

Hirn, Y. *The Sacred Shrine.* Boston, 1957.

Hope, C. "Artists, Patrons, and Advisers in the Italian Renaissance." In *Patronage in the Renaissance.* Eds. G. F. Lytle and S. Orgel. Princeton, 1981, 293–343.

Horatius Flaccus, Q. *The Complete Odes and Epodes with the Centennial Hymn.* Trans. W. G. Shepherd. New York, 1983.

Horstmann, R. *Die Entstehung der perspektivischen Deckenmalerei.* Munich, 1965.

Hülsen, C. *Römische Antikengärten des XVI. Jahrhunderts.* Heidelberg, 1917.

Hyginus. *The Myths of Hyginus.* Trans. M. Grant. Lawrence, Kan., 1960.

ibn Ezra, A. *The Beginning of Wisdom.* Ed. R. Levy. Baltimore, 1939.

Incisa della Rocchetta, G. "Notizie inedite su Andrea Sacchi." *L'arte* 27 (1924): 60–76.

———. "Tre quadri Barberini acquistati dal Museo di Roma." *Bollettino dei Musei Comunali di Roma* 6 (1959): 20–37.

———. "Review of *Pietro da Cortona o della pittura barocca* by Giuliano Briganti." *Archivio della Società Romana di Storia Patria* 89 (1966): 300–3.

Ingersoll, R. J. "The Ritual Use of Public Space in Renaissance Rome." Ph.D. diss., University of California, Berkeley, 1985.

Iodice, M. G. "Il Cardinale Francesco Barberini." Thesis, Università degli Studi di Roma, 1964–1965.

Jacob, S. "Pierre de Cortone et la décoration de la Galerie d'Alexandre VII au Quirinal." *Revue de l'art* 11 (1971): 42–54.

Jacobs, F. H. "Studies in the Patronage and Iconography of Pope Paul III (1534–1549)." Ph.D. diss., University of Virginia, 1979.

Jaffé, M. *Old Master Drawings from Chatsworth.* Alexandria, Va., 1987–1988.

Jannaco, C. *Il seicento,* 2nd ed. Milan, 1966.

Johnston, C., G. V. Shepherd, and M. Worsdale. *Vatican Splendor: Masterpieces of Baroque Art.* Ottawa, 1986.

Judson, J. B. and C. van de Velde. *Corpus Rubenianum Ludwig Burchard: Book Illustrations and Title-Pages.* 2 vols. London–Philadelphia, 1978.

Kajanto, I. " 'Pontifex Maximus' as the Title of the Pope." *Arctos* 15 (1981): 37–52.

Kauffmann, H. *Giovanni Lorenzo Bernini, die figürlichen Kompositionen.* Berlin, 1970.

Kerber, B. "Giuseppe Bartolomeo Chiari." *Art Bulletin* 50 (1968): 75–86.

———. *Andrea Pozzo.* Berlin, 1971.

Kircher, A. *Ars Magna Sciendi.* Amsterdam, 1669.

Kirschbaum, E. *Lexikon der christlichen Ikonographie.* 8 vols. Freiburg-im-Breisgau, 1968–1976.

Kraus, A. "Amt und Stellung des Kardinalnepoten zur Zeit Urbans VIII. (1623)." *Römische Quartalschrift* 53 (1958): 238–43.

———. "Der Kardinal-Nepote Francesco Barberini und das Staatssekretariat Urbans VIII." *Römische Quartalschrift* 64 (1969): 191–208.

Kugler, L. "Ein Beitrag zum Illusionismus im Werke von Pietro (Berrettini) da Cortona." In *De Arte et Libris, Festschrift Erasmus, 1934–1984,* Amsterdam, 1984, 257–82.

———. *Studien zur Malerei und Architektur von Pietro Berrettini da Cortona: Versuch einer gattungsübergreifenden Analyse zum Illusionismus im römischen Barock.* Essen, 1985.

———. "Zum Verhältnis von Malerei und Architektur in den Deckenfresken von Pietro (Berrettini) da Cortona." In *Studien zu Renaissance und Barock: Manfred Wundram zum 60. Geburtstag.* Eds. M. Hesse and M. Imdahl. Frankfurt, 1986, 149–76.

Kuhn, A. "Venice, Queen of the Sea." In S. Sinding-Larsen, *Christ in the Council Hall, Institutum Romanum Norvegiae, Acta ad Archaeologiam et Artium Historiam Pertenentia.* Vol. 5. Rome, 1974, appendix, 263–68.

Laurain-Portemer, M. "Absolutisme et népotisme: la surintendance de l'état ecclésiastique." *Bibliothèque de l'Ecole des Chartes* 131 (1973): 487–568.

Lavagnino, E. "Il bozzetto di Pietro da Cortona per la volta della sala maggiore del Palazzo Barberini." *Bollettino d'arte* 29 (1935): 82–89.

Lavin, I. "Pietro da Cortona and the Frame." *Art Quarterly* 19 (1956): 55–59.

———. *Bernini and the Unity of the Visual Arts.* New York–London, 1980.

———. "Bernini's Cosmic Eagle." In *Gianlorenzo Bernini: New Aspects of His Art and Thought.* Ed. I. Lavin. University Park, Pa., 1985, 209–14.

Lavin, M. A. *Seventeenth-Century Barberini Documents and Inventories of Art.* New York, 1975.

Lechner, G. S. "Tommaso Campanella and Andrea Sacchi's Fresco of 'Divina Sapienza' in the Palazzo Barberini." *Art Bulletin* 58 (1976): 97–108.

———. "Reply to the Editor." *Art Bulletin* 59 (1977): 307–9.

Lector, L. [J. Güthlin]. *Le conclave, origines, histoire, organisation, législation ancienne et moderne.* Paris, 1894.

Lee, R. *Ut Pictura Poesis.* New York, 1967.

Lehmann, K. "The Dome of Heaven." *Art Bulletin* 27 (1945): 1–27.

Le Moyne, P. *De l'art des devises.* Paris, 1666.

Leonardo da Vinci. *Treatise on Painting*. Ed. A. P. McMahon. Princeton, 1956.

Letarouilly, P. *Edifices de Rome moderne*. Paris, 1860.

Leti, G. *Il nipotismo di Roma, o vero relatione delle raggioni che muovono i pontefici all'aggrandimento de' nipoti*. 2 vols. Amsterdam, 1667.

———. *Conclavi dei pontefici romani*. Geneva, 1667.

Levi d'Ancona, M. *The Iconography of the Immaculate Conception in the Middle Ages and Early Renaissance*. New York, 1957.

Lexikon für Theologie und Kirche. 10 vols. Freiburg, 1957–1965.

Liberati, F. *Il perfetto maestro di casa*. Rome, 1658.

Linage de Vauciennes, P. *Le differend des Barberins avec le pape Innocent X*. Paris, 1678.

Livius, T. *Ab urbe condita*. Trans. B. O. Foster. London–New York, 1919.

Lo Bianco, A. "Castelgandolfo: il Palazzo e la Villa Barberini." In *Villa e paese*. Ed. A. Tantillo Mignosi. Rome, 1980, 262–73.

———. "I Disegni preparatori." In *Il voltone di Pietro da Cortona in Palazzo Barberini, Quaderni di Palazzo Venezia 2*. Rome, 1983, 53–90; appendix, 99–110.

Lomazzo, G. P. *Trattato dell'arte de la pittura*. Milan, 1584.

Lubowski, E. *Gio. Lorenzo Bernini als Architekt und Dekorator unter Papst Urban VIII*. Berlin, 1919.

Macchioni, S. "Annibale Carracci, *Ercole al bivio*. Dalla volta del Camerino Farnese alla Galleria Nazionale di Capodimonte: genesi e interpretazioni." *Storia dell'arte* 42 (1981): 151–70.

MacDougall, E. "Ars Hortulorum: Sixteenth Century Garden Iconography and Literary Theory in Italy." In *The Italian Garden*. Washington, D.C., 1972, 39–59.

Macedo, F. *Panegyricus Urbano VIII. Apes Barberinae. Lyra Barberina*. Rome, 1642.

McManamon, J. M. "The Ideal Renaissance Pope: Funeral Oratory from the Papal Court." *Archivum Historiae Pontificiae* 14 (1976): 9–70.

De' Maffei, F. "Perspectivists." In *Encyclopedia of World Art*, New York, 1966, 11:221–243.

Magnanimi, G. "Palazzo Barberini: i documenti della costruzione." *Antologia di belle arti* 4, nos. 13–14 (1980): 194–214.

———. *Palazzo Barberini*. Rome, 1983.

———. "Interventi berniniani a Palazzo Barberini." In *Gian Lorenzo Bernini architetto e l'architettura europea del sei-settecento*. Eds. G. Spagnesi and M. Fagiolo. 2 vols. Rome, 1983–1984, 1:167–92.

———. "The Eighteenth-Century Apartments in the Palazzo Barberini." *Apollo* 120 (1984): 252–61.

Magnum Bullarium Romanum. Eds. L. and A. M. Cherubini. 19 vols. Luxembourg, 1727–1758.

Magnuson, T. *Rome in the Age of Bernini*. 2 vols. Stockholm, 1982 and 1986.

Mahon, D. "Poussiniana." *Gazette des beaux-arts* 60 (1962): 1–138.

Mâle, E. *L'art religieux après le Concile de Trente*. Paris, 1932.

Malvasia, C. C. *Felsina pittrice*. 3 vols. Bologna, 1678–1679.

Mancinelli, F. and G. Casanovas. *La Torre dei Venti in Vaticano*. Vatican City, 1980.

Manilius, M. *Astronomica*. Trans. G. P. Goold. Cambridge, Mass., 1977.

———. *Astronomicon*. Ed. J. J. Scaliger. Leiden, 1600.

Mannucci, F. L. *La vita e le opere di Agostino Mascardi*. Genoa, 1908.

Marabottini, A., L. Bianchi, and L. Berti. *Mostra di Pietro da Cortona*. Rome, 1956.

Mariette, P. J. *Abecedario*. 6 vols. Paris, 1851–1860.

Martin, J.-P. *Providentia Deorum: recherches sur certains aspects religieux du pouvoir imperial romain*. Rome, 1982.

Martin, J. R. *The Farnese Gallery*. Princeton, 1965.

———. *Baroque*. New York, 1977.

Mascardi, A. *Le pompe del Campidoglio per la Santità di Nostro Signore Urbano VIII quando pigliò il possesso*. Rome, 1624.

Mattingly, H. *Coins of the Roman Empire in the British Museum*. 5 vols. London, 1923–1950.

———. "The Roman 'Virtues.'" *The Harvard Theological Review* 30 (1937): 103–17.

Meisner, D. *Thesaurus Philopoliticus*. 2 vols. Frankfurt-am-Main, 1627–1631.

Ménestrier, C. *Symbolica Dianae Ephesiae Statua a Claudio Menetreio Ceimeliothecae Barberinae Praefecto Exposita*. Rome, 1657.

Merrifield, M. P. *The Art of Fresco Painting as Practised by the Old Italian and Spanish Masters*. London, 1952.

Mezzatesta, M. P. "Marcus Aurelius, Fray Antonio de Guevara, and the Ideal of the Perfect Prince in the Sixteenth Century." *Art Bulletin* 66 (1984): 620–33.

Mezzetti, A. "Contributi a Carlo Maratta." *Rivista del Istituto Nazionale d'Archeologia e Storia dell'Arte* 4 (1955): 253–354.

Migliorini, M. "Gio. Maria Bottalla, un savonese alla scuola di Pietro da Cortona." *Società Savonese di Storia Patria, atti e memorie* 12 (1978): 75–85.

Millar, E. G. *The Library of A. Chester Beatty: A Descriptive Catalogue of the Western Manuscripts*. 2 vols. London, 1927 and 1930.

Ministeri, P. B. "De Augustini de Ancona, O.E.S.A. (✠ 1328) Vita et Operibus." *Analecta Augustiniana* 22 (1952): 148–262.

Missirini, M. *Memorie per servire alla storia della romana accademia di S. Luca*. Rome, 1823.

Mochi Onori, L. and R. Vodret Adamo. *La Galleria Nazionale d'Arte Antica: regesto delle didascalie*. Rome, 1989.

Mommsen, T. H. "Petrarch and the Story of the Choice of Hercules." *Journal of the Warburg and Courtauld Institutes* 16 (1953): 178–92.

Montagu, J. "The Painted Enigma and French Seventeenth-Century Art." *Journal of the Warburg and Courtauld Institutes* 31 (1968): 307–35.

———. "Exhortatio ad Virtutem: A Series of Paintings in the Barberini Palace." *Journal of the Warburg and Courtauld Institutes* 34 (1971): 366–72.

Mora, P., L. Mora, and P. Philippot. *Conservation of Wall Paintings*. London, 1984.

Moroni Romano, G. *Dizionario di erudizione storico-ecclesiastica*. 103 vols. Venice, 1840–1861.

Mrazek, W. "Ikonologie der barocken Deckenmalerei." *Österreichische Akademie der Wissenschaften, philosophisch-historische Klasse, Sitzungsberichte* 228, no. 3 (1953): 1–88.

Murata, M. *Operas for the Papal Court: 1631–1668*. Ann Arbor, Mich., 1981.

Mussa, I. "L'architettura illusionistica nelle decorazioni romane: il 'quadraturismo' dalla scuola di Raffaello alla metà del '600." *Capitolium* 44 (1969).

Navenne, F. de. *Rome et le Palais Farnèse.* . . . 2 vols. Paris, 1923.

Negro, A. *Guide rionali di Roma: rione II—Trevi*, pt. 2. Rome, 1985.

Neuburger, S. "Giovanni da San Giovanni im Palazzo Patrizi-Clementi in Rom." *Mitteilungen des Kunsthistorischen Institutes in Florenz* 23 (1979): 337–46.

Noehles, K. "Zur 'mostra di Pietro da Cortona' in Rom." *Kunstchronik* 10 (1957): 94–97.

Nogara, B. "Restauri degli affreschi di Michelangelo nella cappella Sistina." *L'arte* 9 (1906): 229–31.

North, H. *From Myth to Icon, Reflections of Greek Ethical Doctrine in Literature and Art*. Ithaca, N.Y., 1979

North, J. D. *Horoscopes and History*. London, 1986.

Novaes, G. de. *Introduzione alle vite de' sommi pontefici o siano dissertazioni storico-critiche . . . cominciando dall'elezione, coronazione, e possesso de' pontefici medesimi*. 2 vols. Rome, 1822.

Nussdorfer, L. "City Politics in Baroque Rome: 1623–1644." Ph.D. diss., Princeton University, 1985.

———. "The Vacant See: Ritual and Protest in Early Modern Rome." *The Sixteenth Century Journal* 18 (1987): 173–89.

O'Malley, J. W. *Praise and Blame in Renaissance Rome, Rhetoric, Doctrine, and Reform in the Sacred Orators of the Papal Court, c. 1450–1521*. Durham, N.C., 1979.

D'Onofrio, C. *Roma vista da Roma*. Rome, 1967.

———. *Le fontane di Roma*, 3rd ed. Rome, 1986.

Ost, H. "Borrominis römische Universitätskirche S. Ivo alla Sapienza." *Zeitschrift für Kunstgeschichte* 30 (1967): 101–42.

Ottonelli, G. D. and P. Berrettini. *Trattato della pittura e scultura uso et abuso loro*. Ed. V. Casale. Treviso, 1973.

The Oxford Dictionary of the Christian Church. Eds. F. L. Cross and E. A. Livingstone, 2nd ed. Oxford, 1974.

Panofsky, E. *Hercules am Scheidewege*. Leipzig–Berlin, 1930.

Panofsky-Soergel, G. "Zur Geschichte des Palazzo Mattei di Giove." *Römisches Jahrbuch für Kunstgeschichte* 11 (1967–1968): 111–88.

Paris-Berendsen [See Berendsen.]

Parronchi, A. "L'emisfero settentrionale della Sagrestia Vecchia." In U. Baldini and B. Nardini, *San Lorenzo: la basilica, le sagrestie, le cappelle, la biblioteca*. Florence, 1984, 72–79.

———. "L'emispero della Sacrestia Vecchia: Giuliano Pesello?" In *Scritti di storia dell'arte in onore di Federico Zeri*. Ed. M. Natale. 2 vols. Milan, 1984, 1: 134–46.

Partridge, L. W. "The Sala d'Ercole in the Villa Farnese at Caprarola, Part I." *Art Bulletin* 53 (1971): 467–86.

———. "The Sala d'Ercole in the Villa Farnese at Caprarola, Part II." *Art Bulletin* 54 (1972): 50–62.

———. "Divinity and Dynasty at Caprarola: Perfect History in the Room of Farnese Deeds." *Art Bulletin* 60 (1978): 494–530.

Pascoli, L. *Vite de' pittori, scultori, ed architetti moderni*. 2 vols. Rome, 1730–1736.

Passeri, G. B. *Die Künstlerbiographien*. Ed. J. Hess. Leipzig–Vienna, 1934.

Pastor, L. v. *The History of the Popes*. 40 vols. London, 1923–1953.

Paul, C. "The Redecoration of Villa Borghese and the Patronage of Prince Marcantonio IV." Ph.D. diss., University of Pennsylvania, 1989.

[Pauly-Wissowa]. *Paulys Real-Encyclopädie der classischen Altertumswissenschaft*. Ed. G. Wissowa. Stuttgart, 1894-.

Pecchiai, P. *I Barberini*. Rome, 1959.

Pérez Sánchez, A. E. *Real Academia de Bellas Artes de San Fernando: catálogo de los dibujos*. Madrid, 1967.

———. *I grandi disegni italiani nelle collezioni di Madrid*. Milan, 1978.

Petruccelli della Gattina, F. *Histoire diplomatique des conclaves*. 3 vols. Paris, 1864–1865.

Petrucci Nardelli, F. "Il Card. Francesco Barberini Senior e la stampa a Roma." *Archivio della Società Romana di Storia Patria*. 108 (1985): 133–98.

Philo Judaeus. *Iosephi Patriarchae Vitae*. . . . Trans. P. F. Zino. Venice, 1574.

———. *Il ritratto del vero et perfetto gentilhuomo espresso da Filone Hebreo nella vita di Gioseppe Patriarca*. Trans. P. F. Zino. Venice, 1575.

Picinelli, F. *Mundus Symbolicus*. . . . 2 vols. Cologne, 1694.

Pieralisi, S. *Urbano VIII e Galileo Galilei*. Rome, 1875.

Pietrangeli, C. "La Sala dei Capitani." *Capitolium* 37 (1962): 640–48.

Piola Caselli, F. "Aspetti del debito pubblico nello stato pontificio: gli uffici vacabili." *Annali della Facoltà di Scienze Politiche, Università degli Studi di Perugia*, n.s., 1 (1970–1972): 3–74.

Pisano, G. "L'ultimo prefetto dell'urbe, Don Taddeo Barberini, e le relazioni tra la corte di Roma e la Repubblica Veneta sotto il pontificato di Urbano VIII." *Roma* 9 (1931): 103–20, 155–64.

Poensgen, T. *Die Deckenmalerei in italienischen Kirchen*. Berlin, 1969.

Poirier, M. "Pietro da Cortona e il dibattito disegno-colore." *Prospettiva* no. 16 (Jan. 1979): 23–30.

Pollak, O. *Die Kunsttätigkeit unter Urban VIII*. 2 vols. Vienna, 1928 and 1931.

Ponziani, O. *Poesie nella elezione e coronazione di pp. Urbano VIII, con un parallelo tra Alessandro Magno e la Santità Sua, della colomba e delle api*. Rome, 1623.

Popham, A. E. and K. M. Fenwick. *European Drawings in the Collection of the National Gallery of Canada*. Toronto, 1965.

Posner, D. *Annibale Carracci*. 2 vols. London, 1971.

———. "Review of *Pietro da Cortona o della pittura barocca* by Giuliano Briganti." *Art Bulletin* 55 (1964): 411–16.

Posse, H. "Das Deckenfresko des Pietro da Cortona im Palazzo Barberini und die Deckenmalerei in Rom." *Jahrbuch der Preussischen Kunstsammlungen* 40 (1919): 93–118, 126–73.

———. *Der römische Maler Andrea Sacchi*. Leipzig, 1925.

Pozzo, A. "Breve istruzione per dipingere a fresco." In *Perspectiva Pictorum et Architectorum*. Rome, 1693–1702. Pt. 2, appendix.

Presenzini, A. *Vita ed opere del pittore Andrea Camassei*. Assisi, 1880.

du Prey, P. de la Ruffinière. "Revisiting the Solomonic Symbolism of Borromini's Church of Sant'Ivo alla Sapienza." *The Rensselaer Polytechnic Institute of Architecture Journal*. Vol. Zero (1986): 58–71.

Prodi, P. *Il sovrano pontefice*. Bologna, 1982 [Eng. trans., *The Papal Prince*. Cambridge, 1987].

Pugliatti, T. *Agostino Tassi*. Rome, 1977.

Quazza, R. "L'elezione di Urbano VIII nelle relazioni dei diplomatici mantovani." *Archivio della Società Romana di Storia Patria* 46 (1922): 5–47.

Quednau, R. *Die Sala di Costantino im Vatikanischen Palast*. Hildesheim–New York, 1979.

Quinlan-McGrath, M. "The Astrological Vault of the Villa Farnesina: Agostino Chigi's Rising Sign." *Journal of the Warburg and Courtauld Institutes* 47 (1984): 91–105.

Ranke, L. v. *History of the Popes*. Trans. E. Fowler. 3 vols. New York, 1901.

Rash-Fabbri, N. "A Note on the Stanza della Segnatura." *Gazette des beaux-arts* 94 (1979): 97–104.

Ratti, N. *Della famiglia Sforza*. 2 vols. Rome, 1794.

Reallexikon für Antike und Christentum. Ed. T. Klauser. Stuttgart, 1950-.

Réau, L. *Iconographie de l'art chrétien*. 3 vols., Paris, 1955–1959.

Recupero, J. *Il Palazzo Farnese di Caprarola*. Florence, 1975.

Regio, P. *La miracolosa vita di Santo Francesco di Paola*. Naples, 1581.

Reinhard, W. "Nepotismus: Der Funktionswandel einer papstgeschichtlichen Konstanten." *Zeitschrift für Kirchengeschichte* 86 (1975): 145–85.

Reinhardt, V. *Kardinal Scipione Borghese (1605–1633): Vermögen, Finanzen und sozialer Aufsteig eines Papstnepoten*. Tübingen, 1984.

Reist, I. J. "*Divine Love* and Veronese's Frescoes at the Villa Barbaro." *Art Bulletin* 67 (1985): 615–27.

Repgen, K. "Finanzen, Kirchenrecht und Politik unter Urban VIII." *Römische Quartalschrift* 56 (1961): 62–74.

Rhodes, D. E. "Rosichino and Pietro da Cortona: A Correction with Notes on the Printer Fabio de Falco." In *Studies in Early Italian Printing*. London, 1982, 333–34.

Rice, E. F., Jr. *The Renaissance Idea of Wisdom*. Cambridge, Mass., 1958 [rpt. Westport, Conn., 1973].

Richardson, J. *An Account of the Statues, Bas-Reliefs, Drawings and Pictures in Italy, France etc*. London, 1722.

Rietbergen, P.J.A.N. *Pausen, Prelaten, Bureaucraten*. Nijmegen, 1983.

Rieth, A. *Der Blitz in der bildenden Kunst*. Munich, 1953.

Ripa, C. *Nova iconologia*. Padua, 1618.

———. *Della più che novissima iconologia. . . .* Padua, 1630.

Rivadeneyra, P. de. *El príncipe cristiano*. Madrid, 1595.

Robert-Tornow, W. *De Apium Mellisque apud Veteres Significatione et Symbolica et Mythologica*. Berlin, 1893.

Rocco, P. *Laetitia Orbis in Creationem Gregorii XV, Poemata*. Rome, 1621.

Romanelli, P. *Palestrina*. Naples, 1967.

Roscher, W. H. *Ausführliches Lexikon der griechischen und römischen Mythologie*. 6 vols. Leipzig, 1884–1937.

Rosi, M. "La congiura di Giacinto Centini contro Urbano VIII." *Archivio della Società Romana di Storia Patria*. 22 (1899): 347–70.

Rosichino, M. *Dichiaratione della pitture della sala de' signori Barberini*. Rome, 1640; 2nd ed., Rome, 1670.

Rospigliosi, G. "Discorso del sig. Giulio Rospigliosi sopra *L'elettione di Urbano VIII*, poema del sig. Francesco Bracciolini dell'Api." In F. Bracciolini,

L'elettione di Urbano VIII. Rome, 1628, 484–93.

Rossi, E. "La fuga del Cardinale Antonio Barberini." *Archivio della Società Romana di Storia Patria* 59 (1936): 303–27.

Rossi, F. de. *Ritratto di Roma moderna*. Rome, 1645.

Rossi, G. "Le postille inedite del Tassoni a *L'elezione di Urbano VIII*." In *Studi e ricerche tassoniane*. Bologna, 1904, 67–222.

Rousseau, C. "Cosimo I de' Medici and Astrology: The Symbolism of Prophecy." Ph.D. diss., Columbia University, 1983.

Roveri, I. "Scoperto nel Palazzo del Quirinale: un affresco del seicento." *Costume* 9 (Feb. 1964): 55–57.

Running, P. D. "The Flagellation of Christ: A Study in Iconography." Ph.D. diss., University of Iowa, 1951.

Saavedra Fajardo, D. de. *L'idea de un príncipe político christiano*. Munich, 1640.

S.D.N.D. Urbani Divina Providentia Papae VIII. Confirmatio Bullae Gregorii XV. de Electione Romani Pontificis, & Caeremonialis Continentis illius Ritus. Rome, 1626.

Sandrart, J. v. *Academie der Bau-, Bild- und Mahlerey-Künste*. Ed. A. R. Peltzer. Munich, 1925.

Sandström, S. *Levels of Unreality: Studies in Structure and Construction in Italian Mural Painting During the Renaissance*. Uppsala, 1963.

Sarbiewski, M. C. *Poemata Omnia*. . . . Antwerp, 1632.

Saxl, F. *La fede astrologica di Agostino Chigi*. . . . Rome, 1934.

Schaar, E. *Italienische Handzeichnungen des Barock aus den Beständen des Kupferstichkabinetts im Kunstmuseum Düsseldorf*. Düsseldorf, 1964.

Schapiro, M. "The Joseph Scenes on the Maximianus Throne in Ravenna." *Gazette des beaux-arts* 40 (1952): 27–38.

Schiavo, A. "Melozzo a Roma." *Presenza romagnola* 2 (1977): 89–110.

Schiller, G. *Ikonographie der christlichen Kunst*. 4 vols. Gütersloh, 1976.

Schöne, W. "Zur Bedeutung der Schrägsicht für die Deckenmalerei des Barock." *Festschrift Kurt Badt*. Berlin, 1961, 144–72.

Schöner, J. *Opusculum Astrologicum*. Nuremberg, 1539.

Schröter, E. *Die Ikonographie des Themas Parnass vor Raffael*. Hildesheim–New York, 1977.

Schulz, J. *Venetian Painted Ceilings of the Renaissance*. Berkeley–Los Angeles, 1968.

Schwaiger, G. "Nepotismus." In *LTK* 7 (1957–1965):878–79.

Schwarz, K. L. "Zum ästhetischen Problem des 'Programms' und der Symbolik und Allegorik in der barocken Malerei." *Wiener Jahrbuch für Kunstgeschichte* 11 (1937): 79–88.

Scott, J. B. "Allegories of Divine Wisdom in Italian Baroque Art." Ph.D. diss., Rutgers University, 1982.

———. "S. Ivo alla Sapienza and Borromini's Symbolic Language." *Journal of the Society of Architectural Historians* 41 (1982): 294–317.

———. "The Counter-Reformation Program of Borromini's Biblioteca Vallicelliana." *Storia dell'arte* 45 (1985): 295–304.

———. "Papal Patronage in the Seventeenth Century: Urban VIII, Bernini, and the Countess Matilda." In *L'âge d'or du mécénat (1598–1661)*. Eds. R. Mousnier and J. Mesnard. Paris, 1985, 119–27.

———. "Pietro da Cortona's Payments for the Barberini Salone." *Burlington Magazine* 131 (1989): 416–18.

Servius Honoratus, M. *In Vergilii carmina commentarii*. Eds. G. Thilo and H. Hagen. 3 vols. Leipzig, 1881–1902.

Sestieri, G. "Giuseppe Passeri pittore." *Commentari* 28 (1977): 114–36.

Shearman, J. "The Chigi Chapel in Santa Maria del Popolo." *Journal of the Warburg and Courtauld Institutes* 24 (1961): 129–60.

———. "The Vatican Stanze: Functions and Decorations." In *Proceedings of the British Academy* 56 (1971): 369–424.

———. *Raphael's Cartoons in the Coll. of Her Majesty the Queen and the Tapestries for the Sistine Chapel*. London, 1972.

Shumaker, W. *Renaissance Curiosa*. Binghamton, N.Y., 1982.

Silvestri, R. *Il principe infante*. Frankfurt–Macerata, 1620.

Simoni, A. *Orologi italiani dal cinquecento all'ottocento*. Milan, 1980.

Sirén, O., *Nicodemus Tessin D. Y:S Studieresor: i Danmark, Tyskland, Holland, Frankrike och Italien*. Stockholm, 1914.

Sjöström, I. *Quadratura: Studies in Italian Ceiling Painting*. Stockholm, 1978.

Smith, G. *The Casino of Pius IV*. Princeton, 1977.

———. "Cosimo I and the Joseph Tapestries for the Palazzo Vecchio." *Renaissance and Reformation* 6 (1982): 183–96.

Spear, R. *Domenichino*. New Haven, 1982.

Specchi, A. *Il quarto libro del nuovo teatro delli palazzi in prospettiva di Roma moderna*. . . . Rome, 1699.

Spiegazione delle pitture della sala degli eccellentissimi signori principi Barberini coll aggiunta della volta detta della divina sapienza. Rome, n.d.

Spinosa, N. "Spazio infinito e decorazione barocca." In *Storia dell'arte italiana dal cinquecento all'ottocento: cinquecento e seicento*. Ed. P. Fossati. Turin, 1981, 1:278–343.

Stampfle, F. and J. Bean. *Drawings from New York Collections II: The Seventeenth Century in Italy*. Greenwich, Conn., 1967.

Stein, P. I. "La Sala della Meridiana nella Torre dei Venti in Vaticano." *L'illustrazione vaticana* 9 (1938): 403–10.

Steinmann, E. *Die Sixtinesche Kapelle*. 2 vols. Munich, 1901 and 1905.

———. "Freskenzyklen der Spätrenaissance in Rom I: die Sala Farnese in der Cancelleria." *Monatshefte für Kunstwissenschaft* 3 (1910): 45–58.

Stevenson, E. L. *Terrestrial and Celestial Globes*. 2 vols. New Haven, 1921.

Stinger, C. L. *The Renaissance in Rome*. Bloomington, Ind., 1985.

Strabus, W. *Glossa Ordinaria*. 2 vols. In *Patrologiae Cursus Completus, Series Latina*. Ed. J.-P. Migne. Vols. 113–14. Paris, 1879.

Stumpo, E. *Il capitali finanziario a Roma fra cinque e seicento*. Milan, 1985.

Suarez, F. *Theologiae R. P. Fr. Suarez . . . Summa. . . .* Paris, 1877–1878.

Talbot, M. " 'Ore Italiane': The Reckoning of the Time of Day in Pre-Napoleonic Italy," *Italian Studies* 40 (1985): 51–62.

Tarditi, L. "Villa Sora Boncompagni." in *Villa e paese*. Ed. A. Tantillo Mignosi. Rome, 1980, 208–14.

Tellini Perina, C. "La Camera dei Giganti: fonti letterarie ed interpretazioni simboliche del mito." In M. Belfanti et al., *I Giganti di Palazzo Te*. Mantua, 1989, 23–41.

Teti, G. *Aedes Barberinae ad Quirinalem*. Rome, 1642; 2nd ed., Rome, 1647.

Thelen, H. *Francesco Borromini, die Handzeichnungen I*. Graz, 1967.

Thieme, U. and F. Becker, eds. *Allgemeines Lexikon der bildenden Künstler*. 37 vols. Leipzig, 1907–1950.

Tierney, B. *Origins of Papal Infallibility, 1150–1350*. Leiden, 1972.

Tietze, H. "Programme und Entwürfe zu den grossen österreichischen Deckenfresken." *Jahrbuch der Kunstsammlungen des allerhöchsten Kaiserhäuses* 30 (1911–1912): 1–28.

Titi, F. *Ammaestramento utile e curioso di pittura*. Rome, 1686.

Trezzani, L. *Francesco Cozza, 1605–1682*. Rome, 1981.

Trionfi, A. [Augustinus Triumphus] *Summa de Potestate Ecclesiastica*. Rome, 1584.

Urbanus VIII. *Poemata*. Paris, 1620.

———. *Poemata*. Rome, 1631.

———. *Poemata*. Antwerp, 1634.

———. *Poesie toscane del Card. Maffeo Barberini hoggi papa Urbano Ottavo*. Rome, 1637.

———. *Poemata*. Paris, 1642.

Vallone, A. *Aspetti dell'esegese dantesca nei secoli XVI e XVII*. Lecce, 1966.

Vannugli, A. "Gli affreschi di Antonio Tempesta a S. Stefano Rotondo e l'emblematica nella cultura del martirio presso la Compagnia di Gesù." *Storia dell'arte* 48 (1983): 101–16.

Vasari, G. *Le vite de' più eccellenti pittori scultori ed architettori*. Ed. G. Milanesi. 9 vols. Florence, 1906.

Verdi, O. "Le fonti documentarie." In *Il voltone di Pietro da Cortona in Palazzo Barberini, Quaderni di Palazzo Venezia 2*. Rome, 1983, 91–98.

Verdizotti, G.M. *In Clementis VIII P.O.M. Coronationem Carmen*. Venice, 1592.

Victon, F. *Vita, & Miracula S.P. Francisci a Paula. . . .* Rome, 1625.

Villa e paese. Ed. A. Tantillo Mignosi. Rome, 1980.

Villalpando, A. *De Clavium Potestatis Existentia atque Natura*. Washington, D.C., 1921.

Vitaletti, G. "Intorno a Federico Ubaldini e ai suoi manoscritti." *Miscellanea Francesco Ehrle V: scritti di storia e paleografia*, Studi e testi XLI. Rome, 1924, 489–506.

Vitruvius Pollio, M. *The Ten Books on Architecture*. Trans. M. H. Morgan. Cambridge, Mass., 1914.

Vitzthum, W. "Current and Forthcoming Exhibitions: New York." *Burlington Magazine* 101 (1959): 466.

———. "A Comment on the Iconography of Pietro da Cortona's Barberini Ceiling." *Burlington Magazine* 103 (1961): 427–33.

———. "Review of *Pietro da Cortona* by Giuliano Briganti." *Burlington Magazine* 105 (1963): 213–17.

———. "Review of *Pietro da Cortona o della pittura barocca* by Giuliano Briganti." *Master Drawings* 1 (1963): 49–51.

———. "Review of *Tapestries from the Samuel H. Kress Collection at the Philadelphia Museum of Art: The History of Constantine the Great Designed by Peter Paul Rubens and Pietro da Cortona* by David DuBon." *Burlington Magazine* 107 (1965): 262–63.

Vocabulario degli accademici della crusca. Venice, 1612.

Il voltone di Pietro da Cortona in Palazzo Barberini, Quaderni di Palazzo Venezia 2. Rome, 1983.

Voragine, J. de. *The Golden Legend*. Trans. G. Ryan and H. Ripperger. New York, 1969.

Voss, H. *Die Malerei des Barock in Rom*. Berlin, 1924.

Waagen, G. F. *Die Gemäldesammlungen in der Kaiserlichen Ermitage zu St. Petersburg*. Munich, 1864.

Waddy, P. "Palazzo Barberini: Early Projects." Ph.D. diss., New York University, 1973.

———. "Michelangelo Buonarroti the Younger, Sprezzatura, and Palazzo Barberini." *Architectura* 5 (1975): 101–22.

———. "The Design and Designers of Palazzo Barberini." *Journal of the Society of Architectural Histori-*

ans 35 (1976): 151–85.

———. "Taddeo Barberini as a Patron of Architecture." In *L'âge d'or du mécénat (1598–1661)*. Eds. R. Mousnier and J. Mesnard. Paris, 1985, 191–99.

———. *Seventeenth-Century Roman Palaces: Use and the Art of the Plan*. New York, 1990.

Walker, D. P. *Spiritual and Demonic Magic from Ficino to Campanella*. London, 1958.

Walmsley, T. S. "Evidence and Influence of Venetian Models and Precedents on Pietro da Cortona's Frescoed Decoration of the Gran Salone of the Palazzo Barberini in Rome." Master's thesis, University of London, 1988.

Warburg, A. "Eine astronomische Himmelsdarstellung in der alten Sakristei von S. Lorenzo in Florenz." In *Gesammelte Schriften*. Leipzig–Berlin, 1932, 1:169–72, 366–67.

———. "Italienische Kunst und internationale Astrologie im Palazzo Schifanoia zu Ferrara." In *Gesammelte Schriften*. Leipzig–Berlin, 1932, 2:459–81.

Ward-Jackson, P. *Victoria and Albert Museum Catalogues: Italian Drawings*. 2 vols. London, 1980.

Wasserman, J. "The Palazzo Sisto V in the Vatican." *Journal of the Society of Architectural Historians* 21 (1962): 26–35.

Waterhouse, E. K. *Baroque Painting in Rome*. London, 1937.

———. "Tasso and the Visual Arts." *Italian Studies* 3 (1947–1948): 146–62.

———. *Roman Baroque Painting*. Oxford, 1976.

Weil, M. S. "The Devotion of Forty Hours and Roman Baroque Illusions." *Journal of the Warburg and Courtauld Institutes* 37 (1974): 218–48.

Weil-Garris, K. and J. F. D'Amico. "The Renaissance Cardinal's Ideal Palace: A Chapter from Cortesi's *De Cardinalatu*." In *Studies in Italian Art and Architecture 15th through 18th Centuries, Memoirs of the American Academy in Rome* 35 (1980): 45–123.

Weil-Garris Brandt, K. "Cosmological Patterns in the Chigi Chapel." In *Raffaello a Roma: il convegno del 1983*. Rome, 1986, 127–57.

Westin, J. K. and R. H. Westin. *Carlo Maratti and His Contemporaries*. University Park, Pa., 1975.

White, T. H. *The Bestiary*. New York, 1960.

Whitman, N. T. and J. L. Varriano. *Roma Resurgens: Papal Medals from the Age of the Baroque*. Ann Arbor, Mich., 1983.

Wilks, M. *The Problem of Sovereignty in the Later Middle Ages: The Papal Monarchy with Augustinus Triumphus and the Publicists*. Cambridge, 1963.

Winner, M. "Bernini the Sculptor and the Classical Heritage in His Early Years: Praxiteles', Bernini's, and Lanfranco's *Pluto and Proserpina*." *Römisches Jahrbuch für Kunstgeschichte* 22 (1985): 193–207.

Witcombe, C.L.C.E. "Giovanni and Cherubino Alberti." Ph.D. diss., Bryn Mawr College, 1981.

———. "An Illusionistic Oculus by the Alberti Brothers in the Scala Santa." *Gazette des beaux-arts* 110 (1987): 61–72.

Wittkower, R. "Pietro da Cortona's Project for Reconstructing the Temple of Palestrina." In *Studies in Italian Baroque Art*. Ed. M. Wittkower. Boulder, 1975, 116–24.

———. "Transformations of Minerva in Renaissance Imagery." In *Allegory and the Migration of Symbols*. London, 1977, 130–42.

———. *Art and Architecture in Italy 1600–1750*, 3rd ed. Harmondsworth, 1980.

Wood, C. H. "Visual Panegyric in Guercino's Casino Ludovisi Frescoes." *Storia dell'arte* 58 (1986): 223–28.

Würtenberger, F. "Die manieristische Deckenmalerei in Mittelitalien." *Römisches Jahrbuch für Kunstgeschichte* 4 (1940): 59–141.

Zanardi, B. "Il restauro e le tecniche di esecuzione originale." In *Il voltone di Pietro da Cortona in Palazzo Barberini, Quaderni di Palazzo Venezia 2*. Rome, 1983, 11–38.

Zucchi, N. *Optica Philosophia*. 2 vols. Lyons, 1652–1656.

Zurawski, S. A. "Peter Paul Rubens and the Barberini, ca. 1625–1640." Ph.D. diss., Brown University, 1979.

———. "Connections between Rubens and the Barberini Legation in Paris, in 1625, and Their Influence on Roman Baroque Art." *Revue belge d'archéologie et d'histoire de l'art* 58 (1989): 23–50.

INDEX

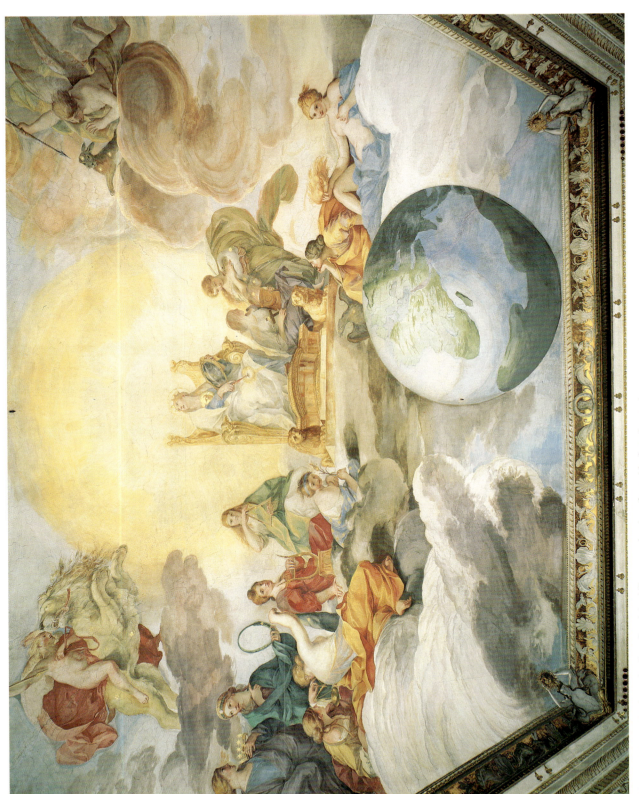

Plate 1. *Divine Wisdom*, Andrea Sacchi, oblique-angle view from ideal station point.

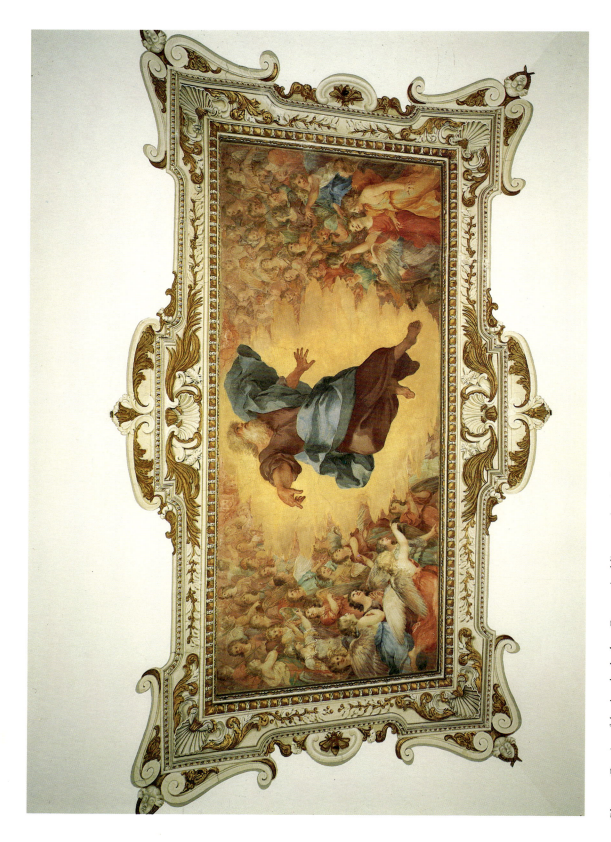

Plate II. *Creation of the Angels*, Andrea Camassei, oblique-angle view from ideal station point.

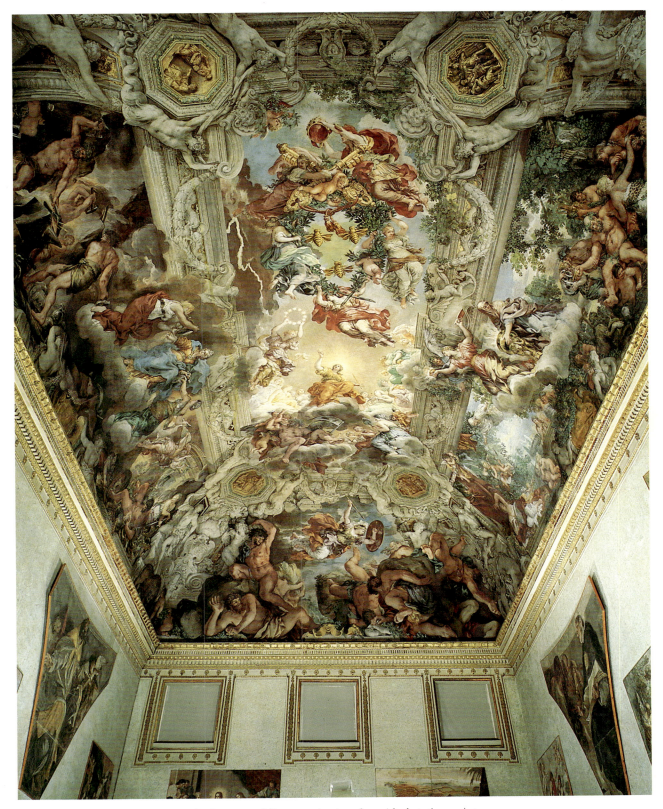

Plate III. *Divine Providence*, Pietro da Cortona, oblique-angle view from ideal station point.

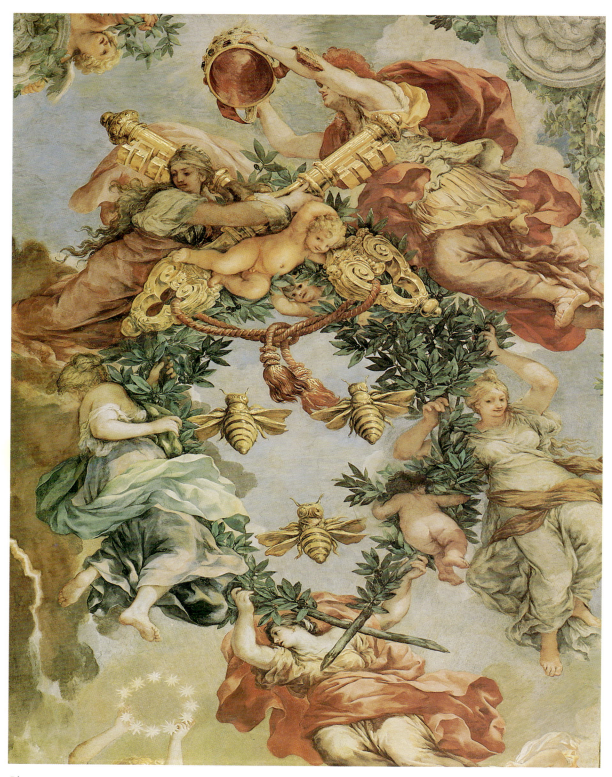

Plate IV. Coat of Arms of Urban VIII, detail of *Divine Providence*, Pietro da Cortona.

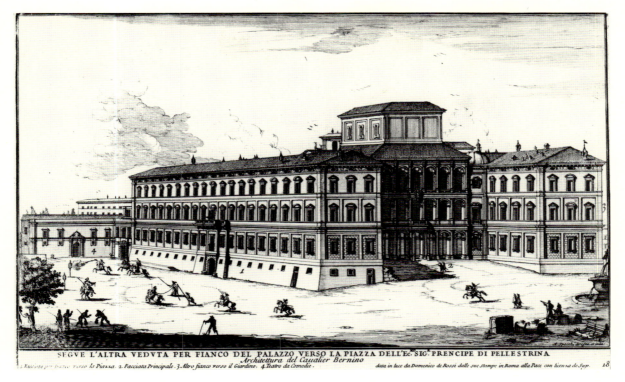

SEGVE L'ALTRA VEDVTA PER FIANCO DEL PALAZZO VERSO LA PIAZZA DELL'Ec. SIG. PRENCIPE DI PELLESTRINA
Architettura del Caualier Bernino

1. Ricouero per fuoco verso la Piazza. 2. Facciata Principale. 3. Altro fianco verso il Giardino. 4. Teatro da Comedie.   data in luce da Domenico de Rossi dalle sue Stampe in Roma alla Pace con licenza de Sup.   18

Fig. 1. Palazzo Barberini, view from the northwest, engraving. (Specchi, 1699)

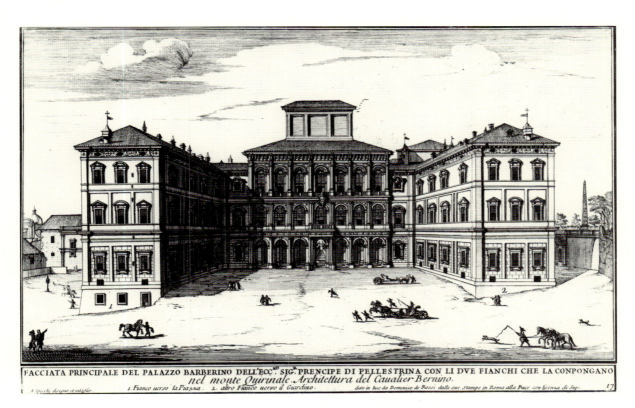

FACCIATA PRINCIPALE DEL PALAZZO BARBERINO DELL'ECC. SIG. PRENCIPE DI PELLESTRINA CON LI DVE FIANCHI CHE LA CONPONGANO
nel monte Quirinale Architettura del Caualier Bernino.

1. Specchi disegno et intaglio.   1. Fianco verso la Piazza.   2. altro Fianco verso il Giardino.   dato in luce da Domenico de Rossi dalle sue Stampe in Roma alla Pace con licenza de Sup.   17

Fig. 2. Palazzo Barberini, West Facade, engraving. (Specchi, 1699)

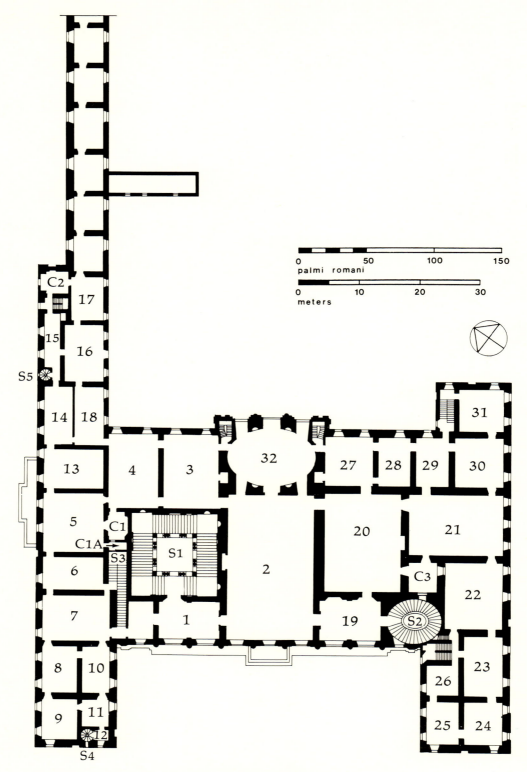

Fig. 3. Palazzo Barberini, Piano Nobile (PBN). (plan: Waddy, 1990)

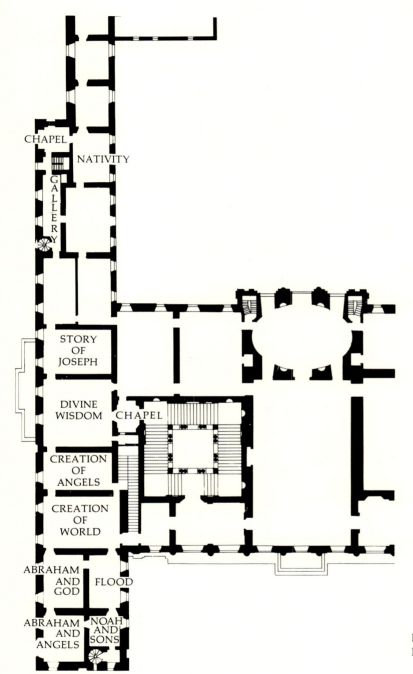

CHAPEL

NATIVITY

GALLERY

STORY
OF
JOSEPH

DIVINE
WISDOM

CHAPEL

CREATION
OF
ANGELS

CREATION
OF
WORLD

ABRAHAM
AND
GOD

FLOOD

ABRAHAM
AND
ANGELS

NOAH
AND
SONS

Fig. 4. Ceiling Paintings,
North Wing, Piano Nobile, 1632.

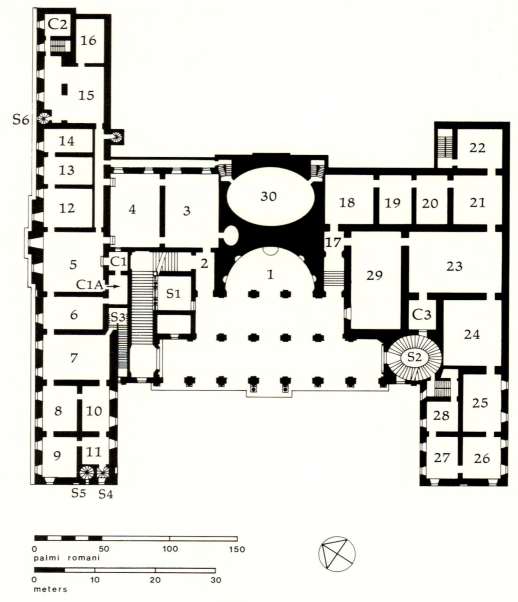

Fig. 5. Palazzo Barberini, Piano Terreno (PBT). (plan: Waddy, 1990)

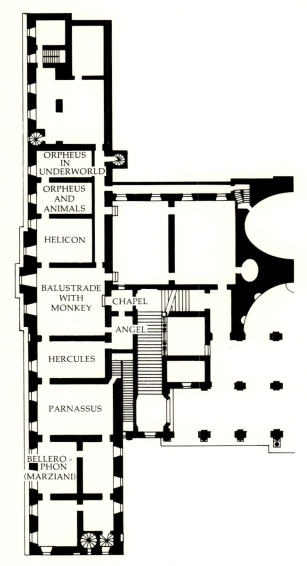

Fig. 6. Ceiling Paintings, North Wing,
Piano Terreno, 1632.

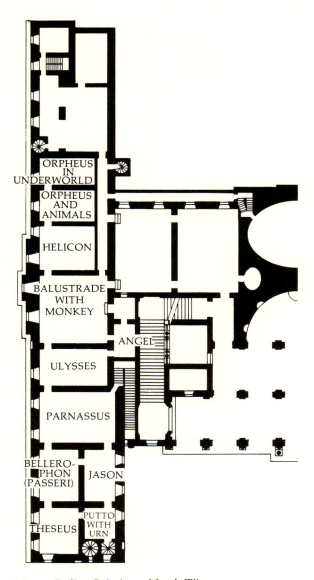

Fig. 7. Ceiling Paintings, North Wing,
Piano Terreno, 1678.

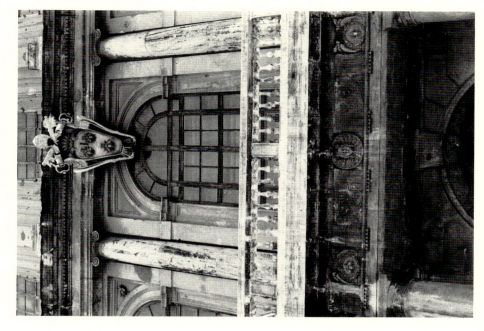

Fig. 10. Palazzo Barberini, detail of West Facade.

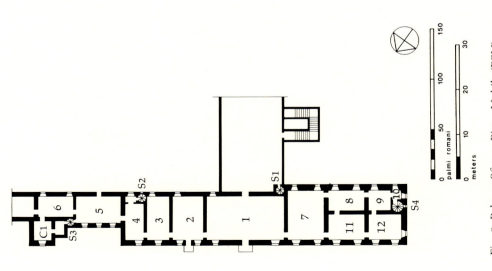

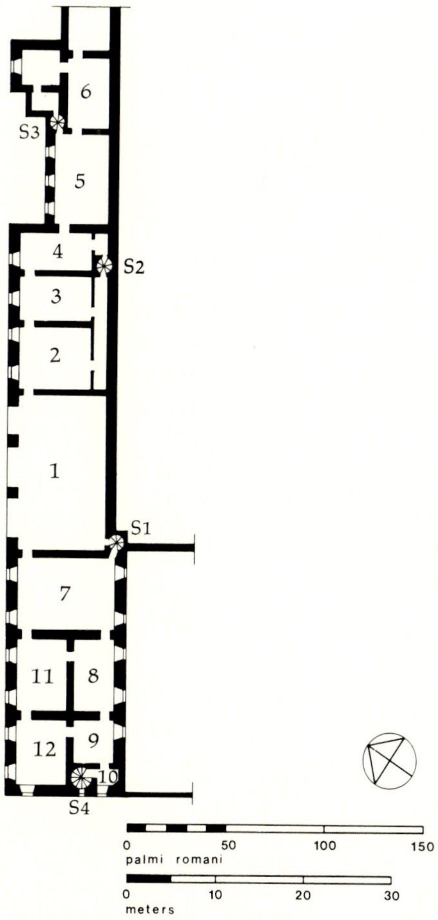

Fig. 9. Palazzo Sforza, Piano Terreno
(PST). (plan: Waddy, 1990)

Fig. 8. Palazzo Sforza, Piano Nobile (PSN).
(plan: Waddy, 1990)

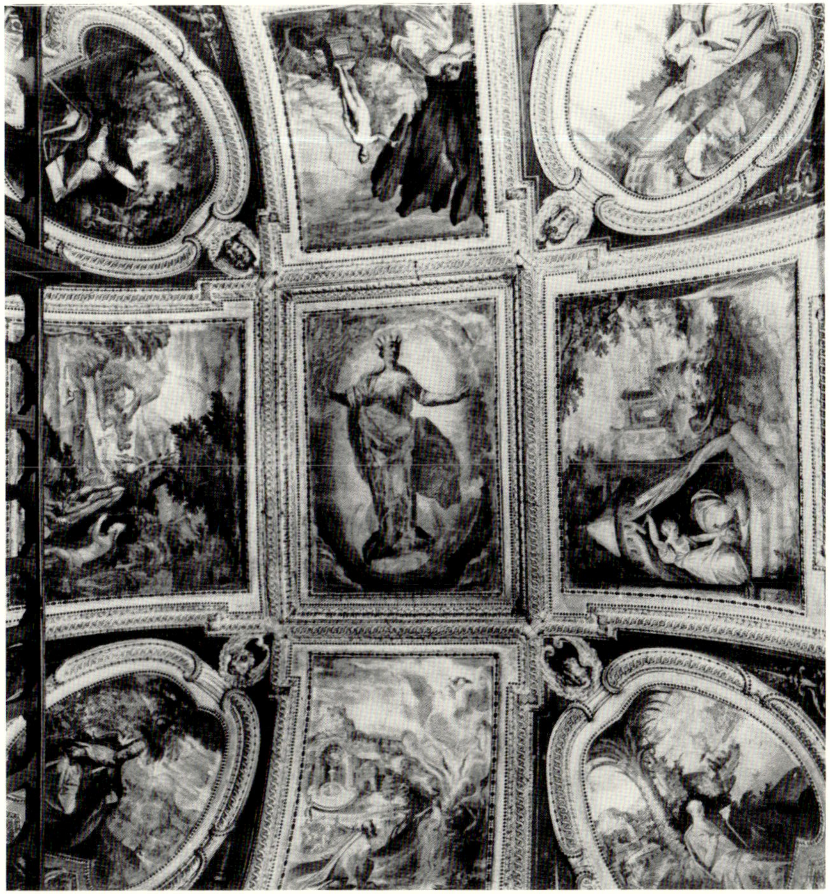

AMBROSE	JAEL AND SISERA	JEROME
DREAM OF NEBUCHADNEZZAR	VIRGIN IMMACULATE	MOSES AND BURNING BUSH
AUGUSTINE	CRUSHING OF THE SERPENT	GREGORY

Fig. 12. *Virgin Immaculate*, iconographic plan. (drawing: P. Westercamp)

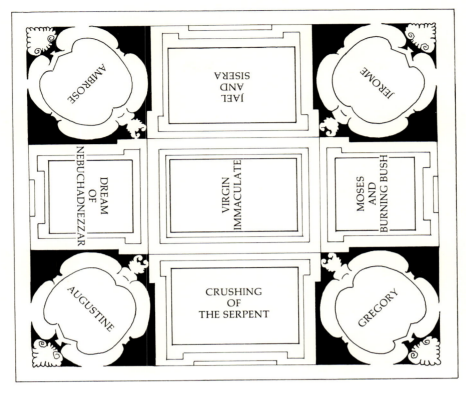

Fig. 11. *Virgin Immaculate*, Antonio Tempesta, fresco, Palazzo Barberini, North Wing.

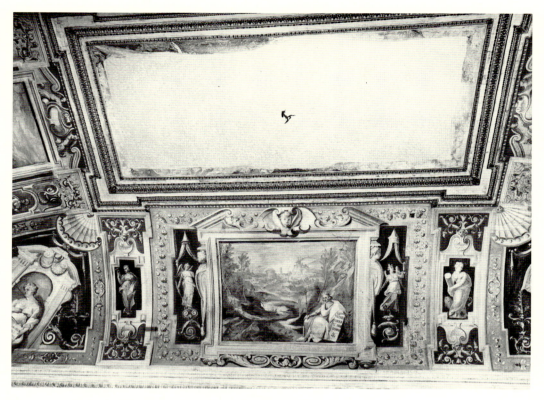

Fig. 13. *Nativity* (PSN 6/PBN 17), detail, fresco, Palazzo Barberini.

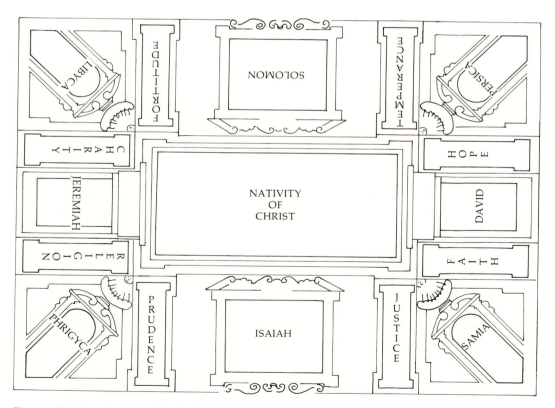

Fig. 14. *Nativity*, iconographic plan. (drawing: P. Westercamp)

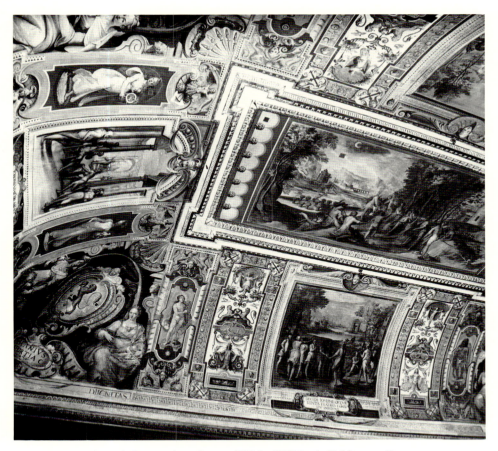

Fig. 15. *Story of Joseph* from point of entry (PSN 2/PBN 13), Baldassare Croce,
Nicolò Circignani et al., fresco, Palazzo Barberini.

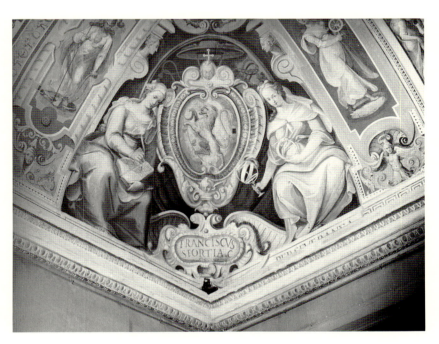

Fig. 16. *Clemency and Perseverance*,
detail of *Story of Joseph*.

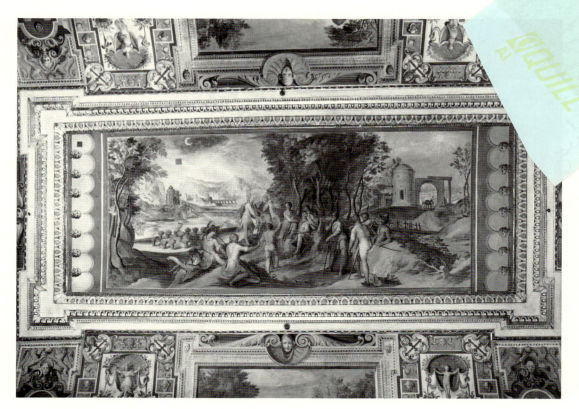

Fig. 17. *Joseph Interpreting His Dreams to His Brothers*, detail of *Story of Joseph.*

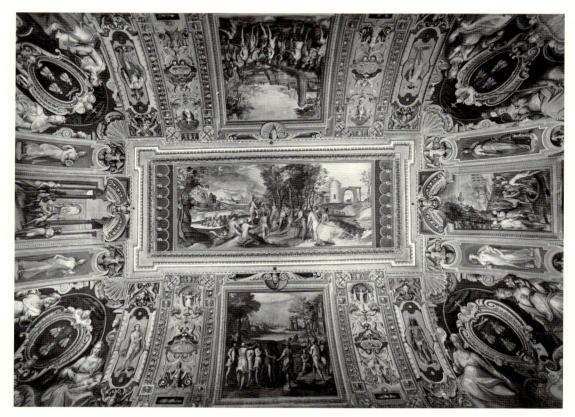

Fig. 18. *Story of Joseph* (PSN 2/PBN 13), prior to restoration.

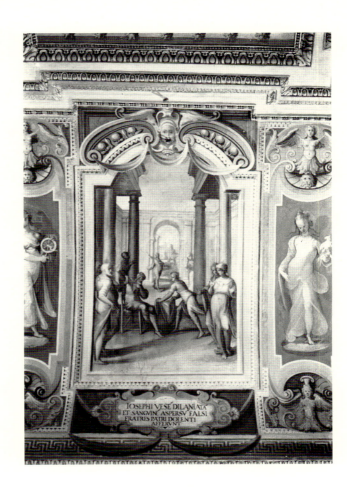

Fig. 20. *Jacob and the Bloody Coat of Joseph*, detail of the *Story of Joseph*.

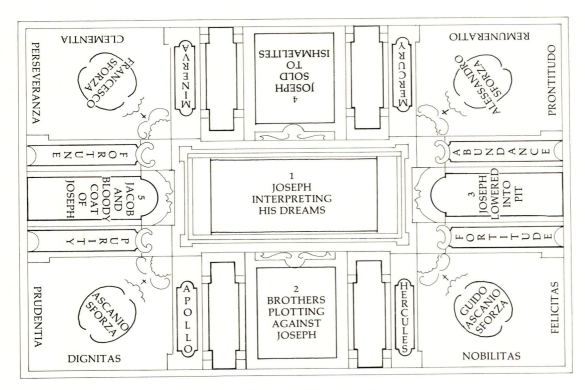

Fig. 19. *Story of Joseph*, iconographic plan. (drawing: P. Westercamp)

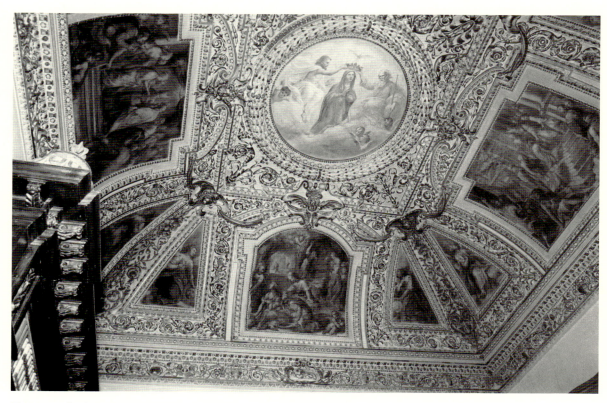

Fig. 21. *Life of the Virgin*, Antonio Viviani, detail, fresco, Sforza Chapel Antechamber, Palazzo Barberini.

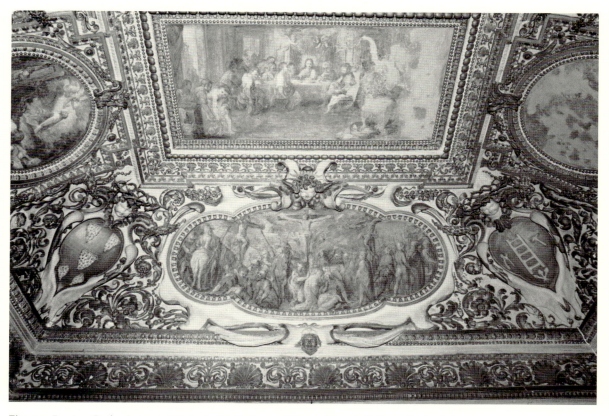

Fig. 22. *Passion Cycle*, Antonio Viviani, detail, fresco, Sforza Chapel, Palazzo Barberini.

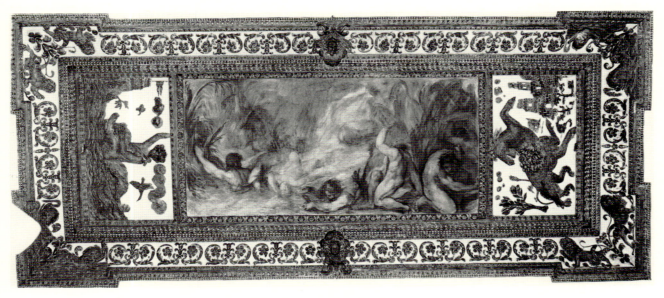

Fig. 23. The *Flood* (PSN 8/PBN 10), Antonio Viviani, fresco, Palazzo Barberini.

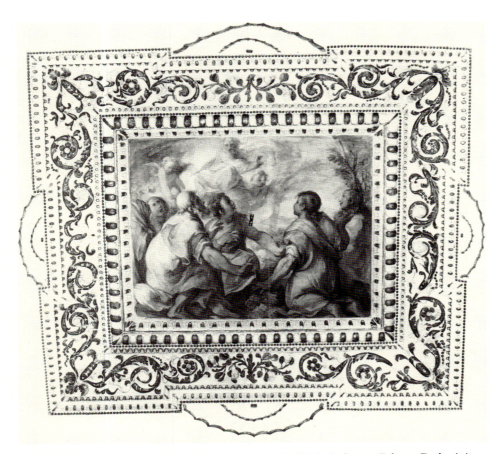

Fig. 24. *Noah and His Sons* (PSN 9/PBN 11), Antonio Viviani, fresco, Palazzo Barberini.

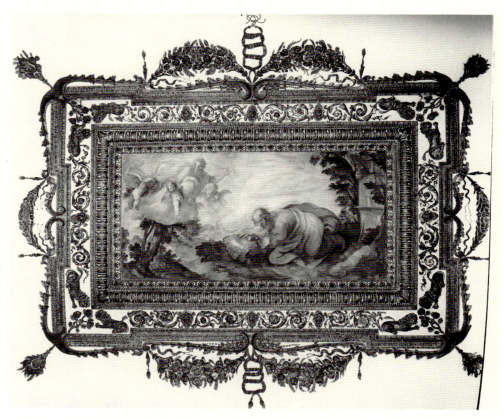

Fig. 25. *God Speaking to Abraham* (PSN 11/PBN 8), Antonio Viviani, fresco, Palazzo Barberini.

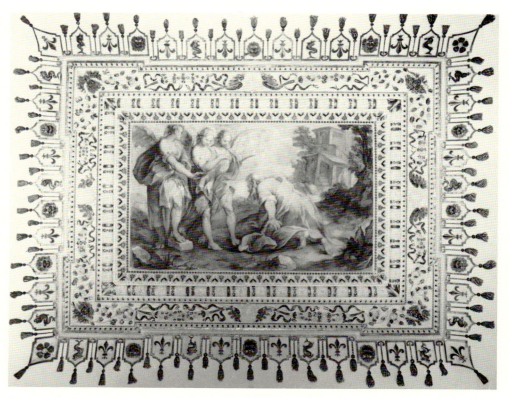

Fig. 26. *Abraham and the Three Angels* (PSN 12/PBN 9), Antonio Viviani, fresco, Palazzo Barberini.

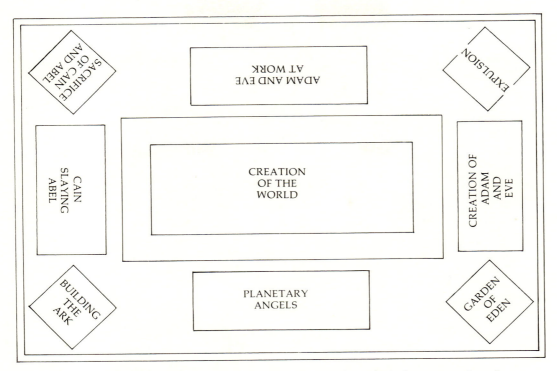

Fig. 28. *Creation of the World* (PSN 7/PBN 7), Antonio Viviani, hypothetical reconstruction of iconographic plan. (drawing: P. Westercamp)

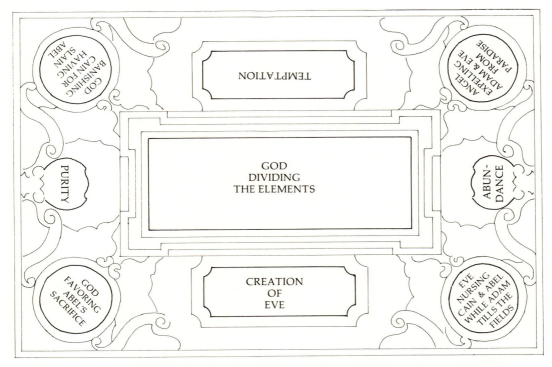

Fig. 29. *Creation of the World* (PBN 7), Niccolò Ricciolini and Laurent Pécheux, iconographic plan. (drawing: P. Westercamp)

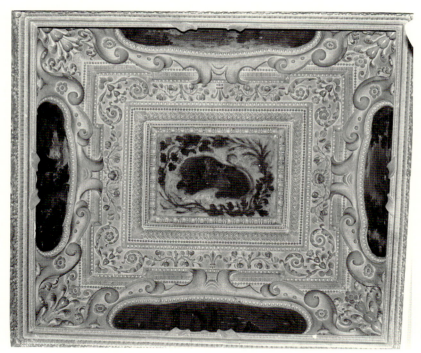

Fig. 27. *Sforza Lion* (PSN 10/PBN 12), stucco relief and fresco, Palazzo Barberini.

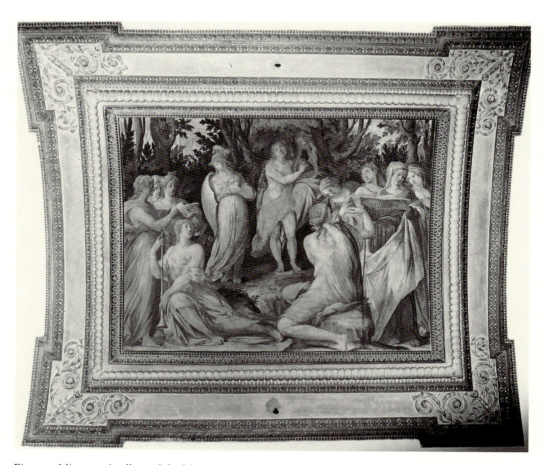

Fig. 30. *Minerva, Apollo, and the Muses on Mount Helicon* (PST 2/PBT 12), Circle of Giuseppe Cesare d'Arpino, fresco, Palazzo Barberini.

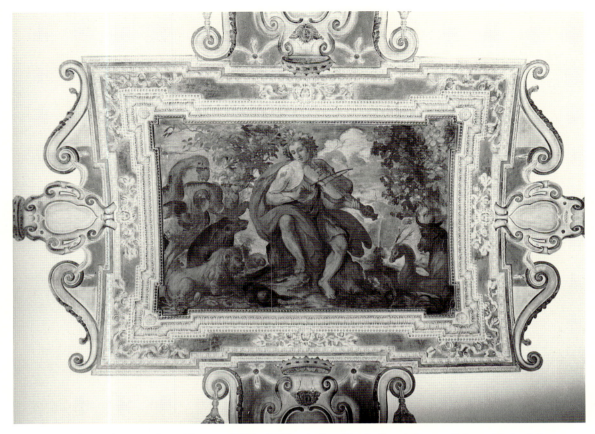

Fig. 31. *Orpheus Charming the Wild Beasts* (PST 3/PBT 13), Camillo Spallucci, fresco, Palazzo Barberini.

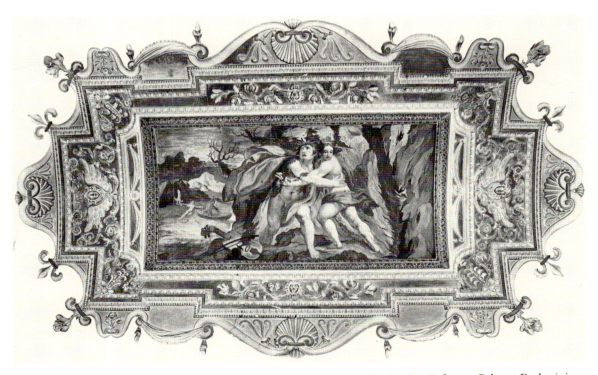

Fig. 32. *Orpheus and Eurydice in the Underworld* (PST 4/PBT 14), Camillo Spallucci, fresco, Palazzo Barberini.

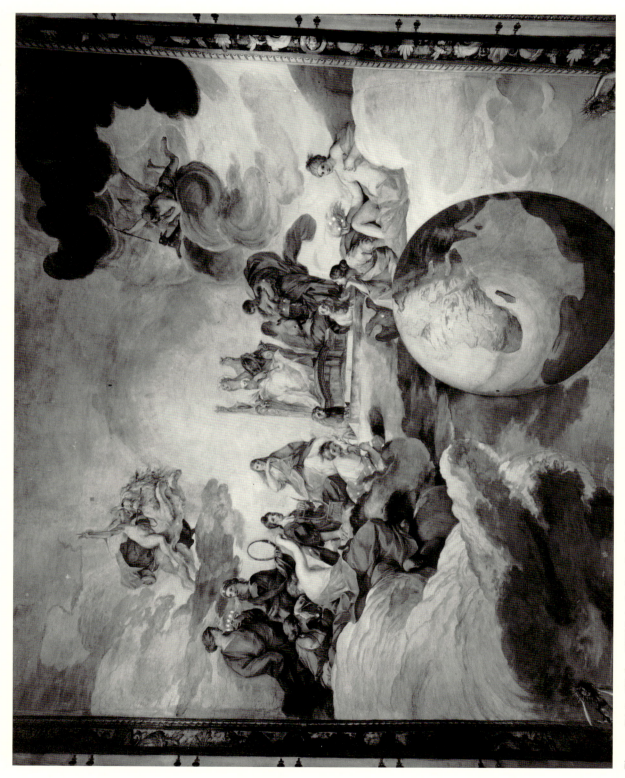

Fig. 33. *Divine Wisdom* (PBN 5), Andrea Sacchi, fresco, Palazzo Barberini.

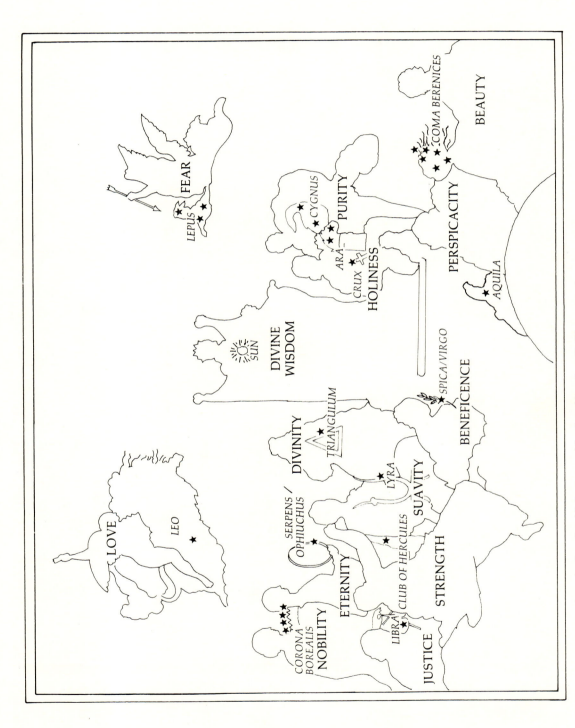

Fig. 34. *Divine Wisdom*, Andrea Sacchi, iconographic plan. (drawing: P. Westercamp)

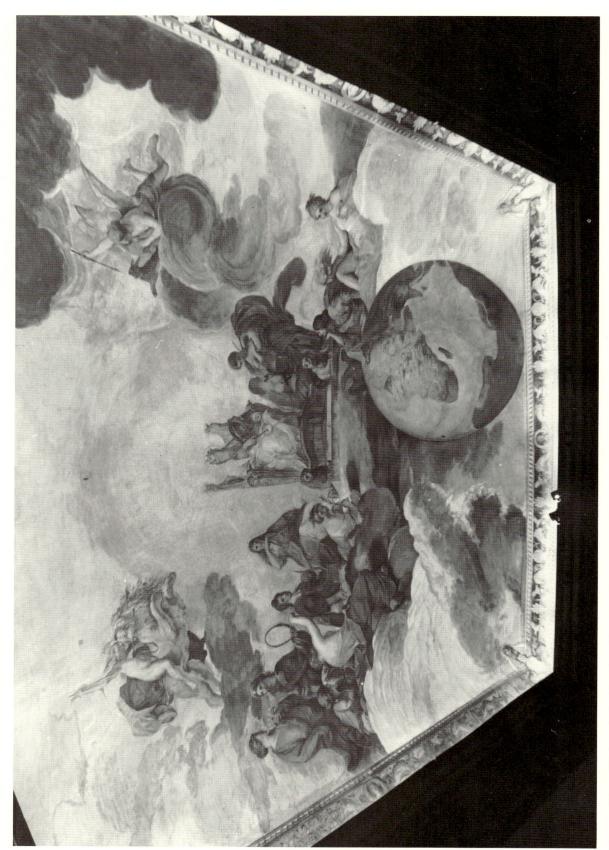

Fig. 35. *Divine Wisdom*, Andrea Sacchi, oblique-angle view from ideal station point.

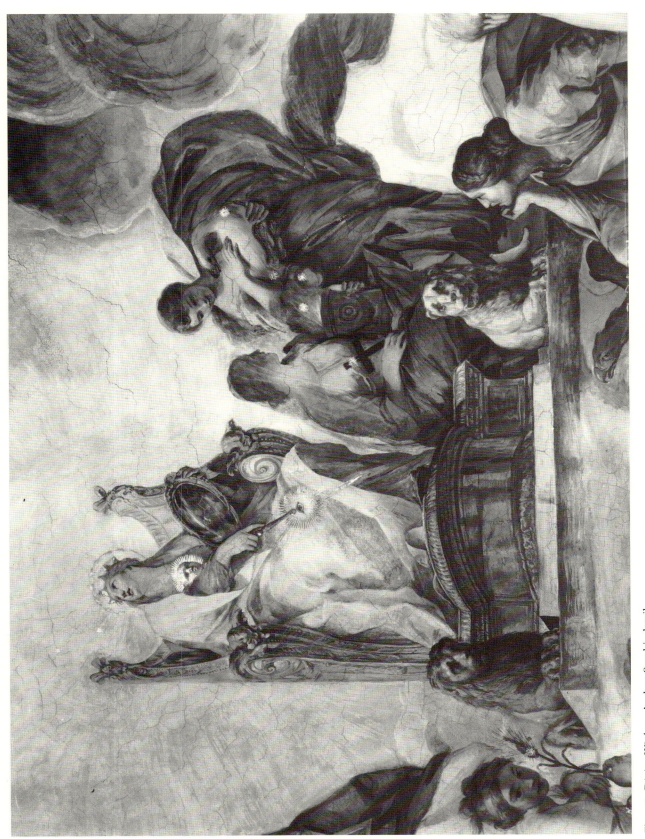

Fig. 36. *Divine Wisdom*, Andrea Sacchi, detail.

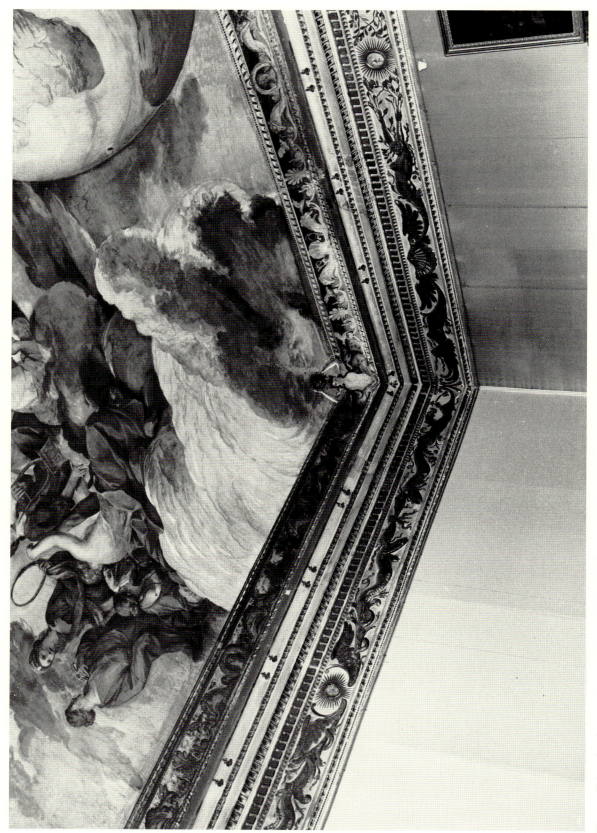

Fig. 37. Painted and stucco frieze (PBN 5), *Divine Wisdom*, Palazzo Barberini.

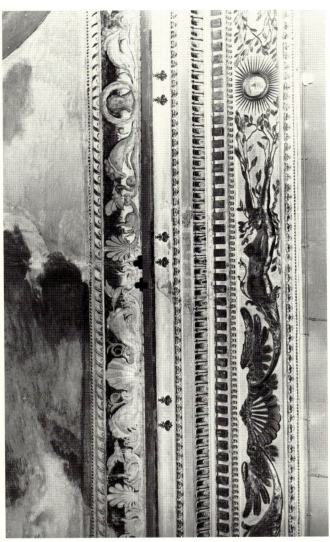

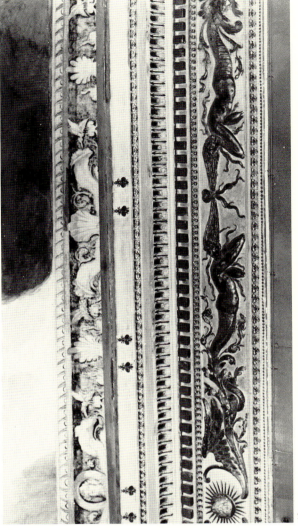

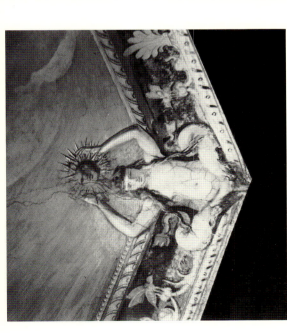

Fig. 38. Colonna Siren (PBN 5), detail of *Divine Wisdom*, Palazzo Barberini.

Fig. 39. *Daphne and Sun*, painted and stucco frieze (PBN 5), Palazzo Barberini.

Fig. 40. *Harpies and Apollo*, painted and stucco frieze (PBN 5), Palazzo Barberini.

39

40

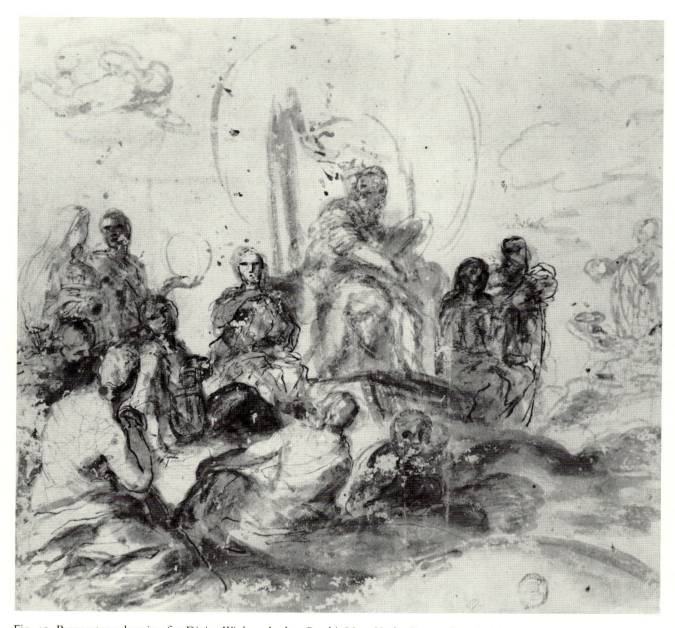

Fig. 41. Preparatory drawing for *Divine Wisdom*, Andrea Sacchi, New York, Cooper–Hewitt Museum of Design.

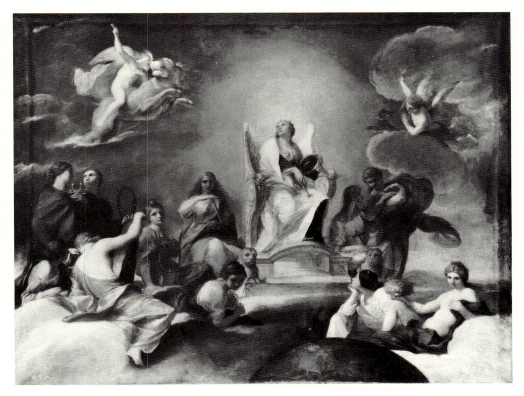

Fig. 42. Modello for *Divine Wisdom*, Andrea Sacchi, oil, Leningrad, Hermitage.

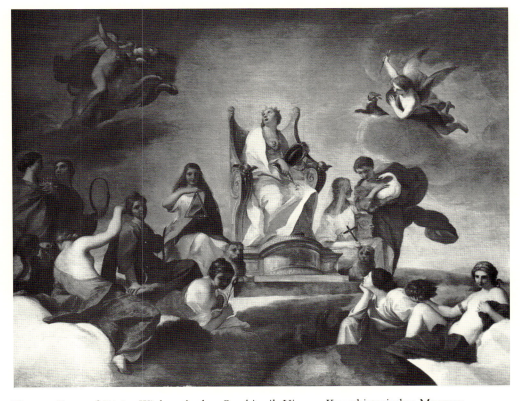

Fig. 43. Copy of *Divine Wisdom*, Andrea Sacchi, oil, Vienna, Kunsthistorisches Museum.

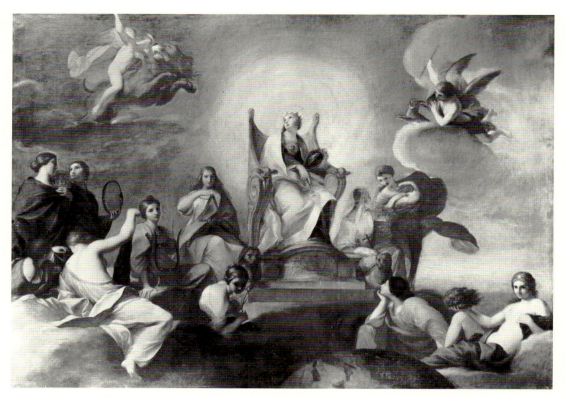

Fig. 44. Copy of *Divine Wisdom* with Chigi arms, Andrea Sacchi, oil, Rome, Galleria Nazionale d'Arte Antica.

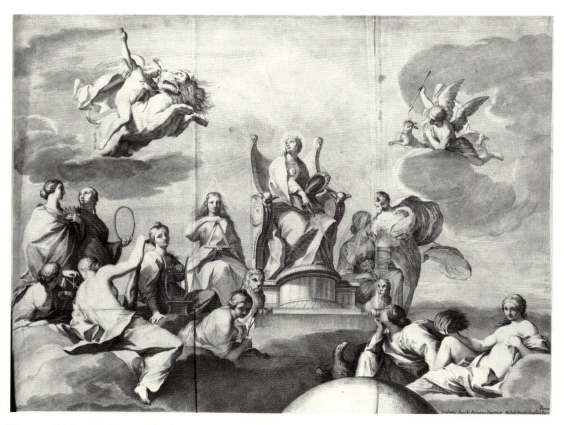

Fig. 45. *Divine Wisdom*, Michael Natalis after Andrea Sacchi, engraving. (Teti, 1642)

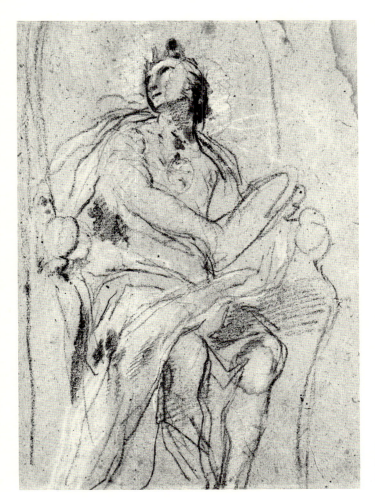

Fig. 46. Preparatory drawing for figure of Divine Wisdom, Andrea Sacchi, Düsseldorf, Kunstmuseum.

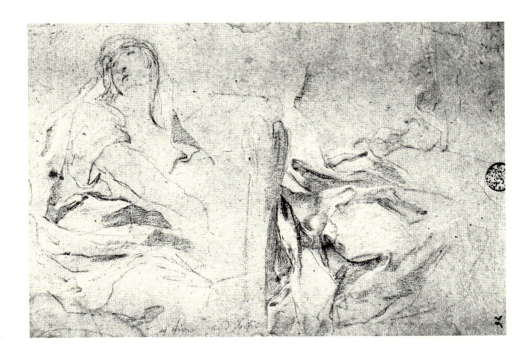

Fig. 47. Preparatory drawing for figure of Divine Wisdom, Andrea Sacchi, Düsseldorf, Kunstmuseum.

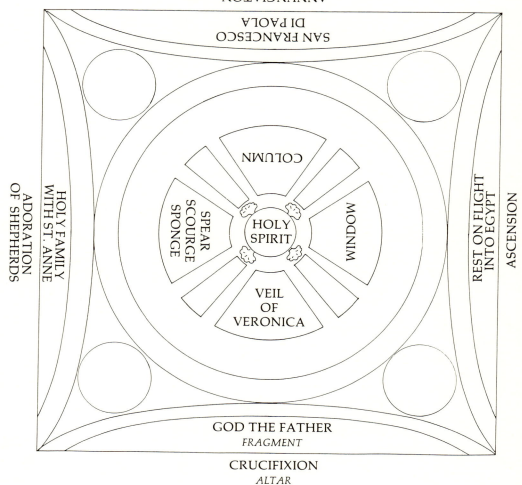

Fig. 48. Chapel Dome (PBN C1), Palazzo Barberini, iconographic plan. (drawing: P. Westercamp)

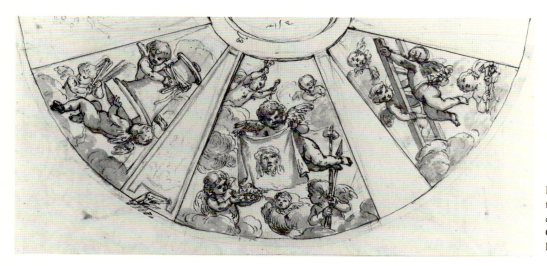

Fig. 50. Preliminary drawing for *Angels Holding Instruments of the Passion*, Pietro da Cortona, Windsor Castle, Royal Library.

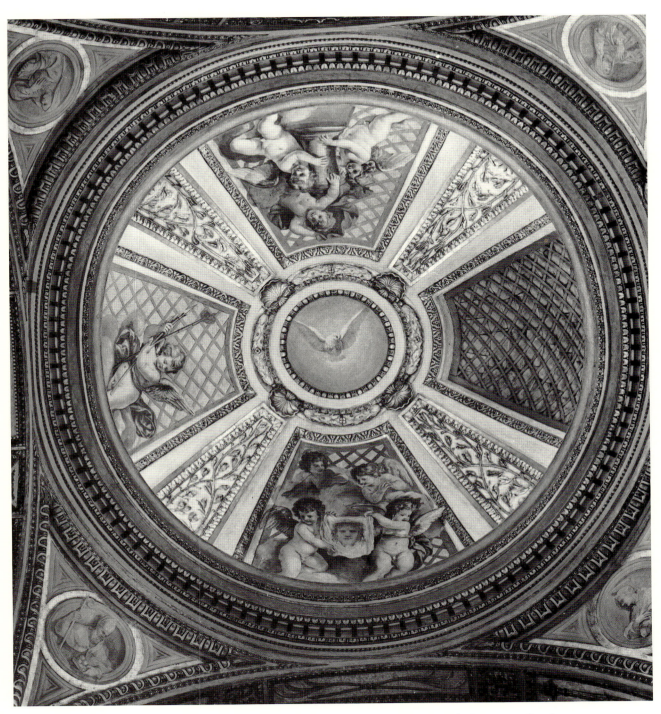

Fig. 49. Chapel Dome with *Angels Holding Instruments of the Passion* (PBN C1), Pietro da Cortona and assistants, fresco, Palazzo Barberini.

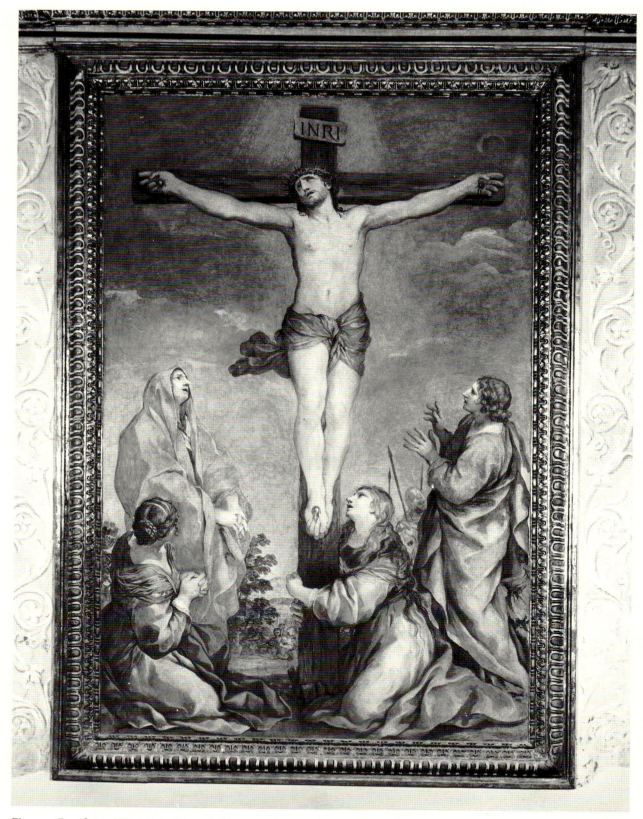

Fig. 51. *Crucifixion* (PBN C1), Pietro da Cortona, fresco, Chapel, Palazzo Barberini.

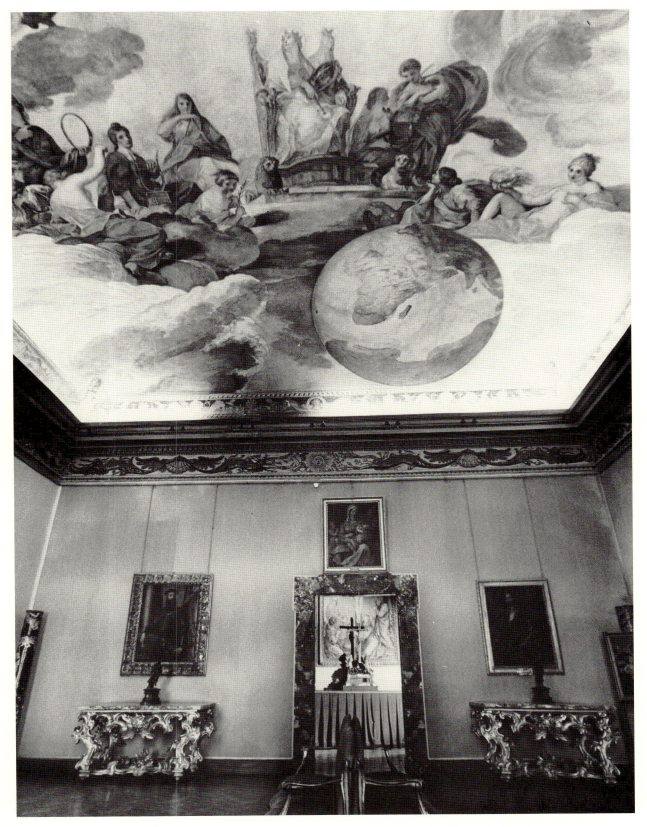

Fig. 52. *Divine Wisdom* and Chapel from ideal station point (PBN 5 and PBN C1), Palazzo Barberini.

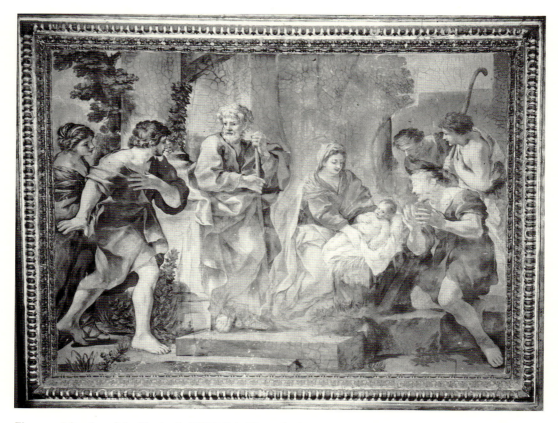

Fig. 53. *Adoration of the Shepherds* (PBN C1), Pietro da Cortona and assistant, fresco, Chapel, Palazzo Barberini.

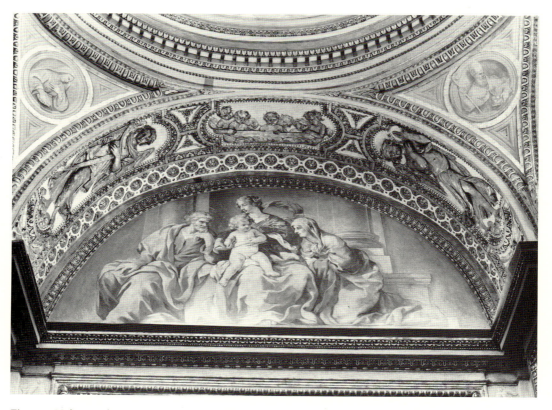

Fig. 54. *Holy Family with Saint Anne* (PBN C1), Pietro da Cortona and assistant, fresco, Chapel, Palazzo Barberini.

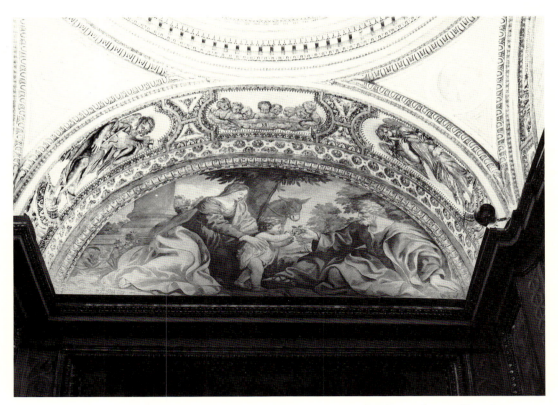

Fig. 55. *Rest on the Flight into Egypt* (PBN C1), Pietro da Cortona and assistant, fresco, Chapel, Palazzo Barberini.

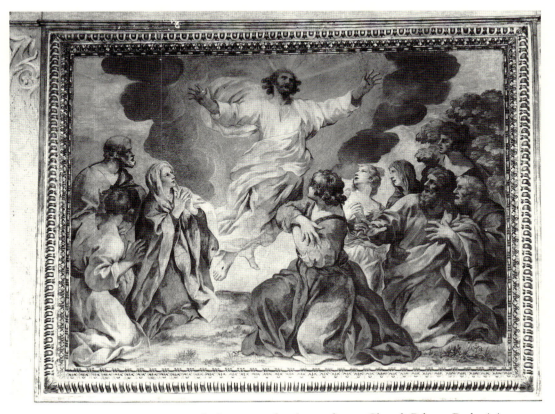

Fig. 56. *Ascension* (PBN C1), Pietro da Cortona and assistant, fresco, Chapel, Palazzo Barberini.

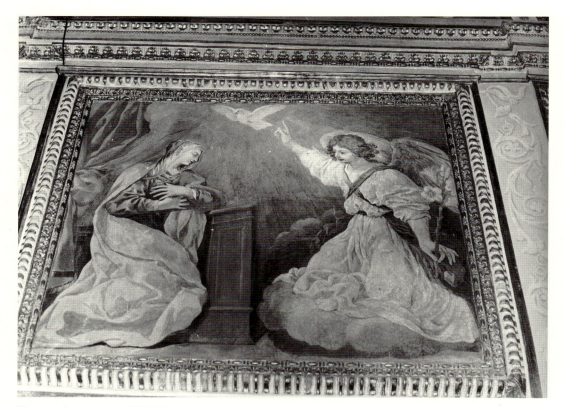

Fig. 57. *Annunciation* (PBN C1), Pietro da Cortona and assistant, fresco, Chapel, Palazzo Barberini.

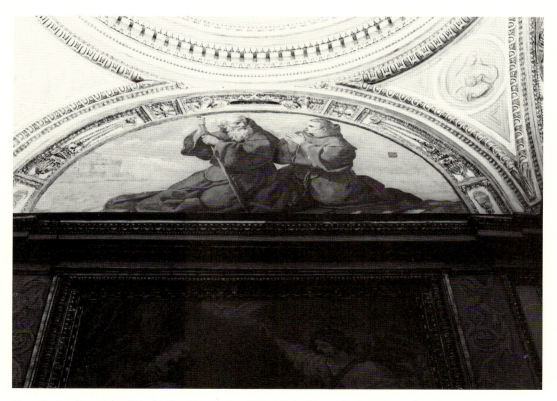

Fig. 58. *San Francesco di Paola Crossing the Sea* (PBN C1), Pietro da Cortona and assistant, fresco, Chapel, Palazzo Barberini.

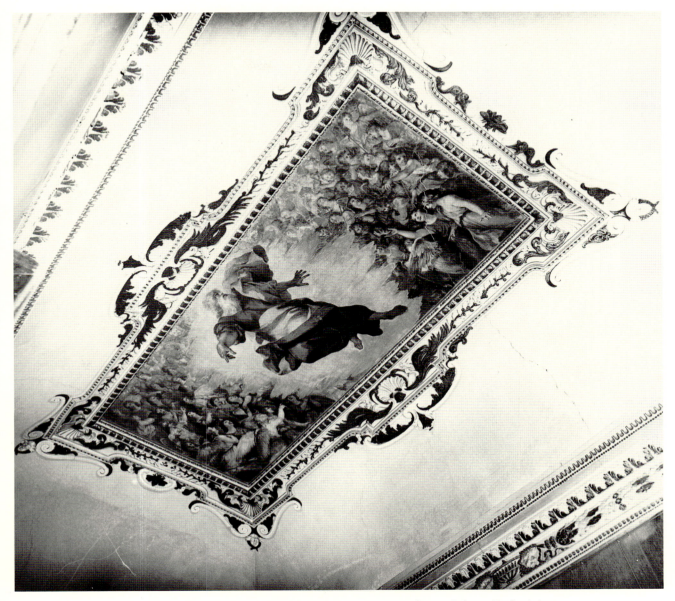

Fig. 59. *Creation of the Angels* from point of entry (PBN 6), Andrea Camassei, fresco, Palazzo Barberini.

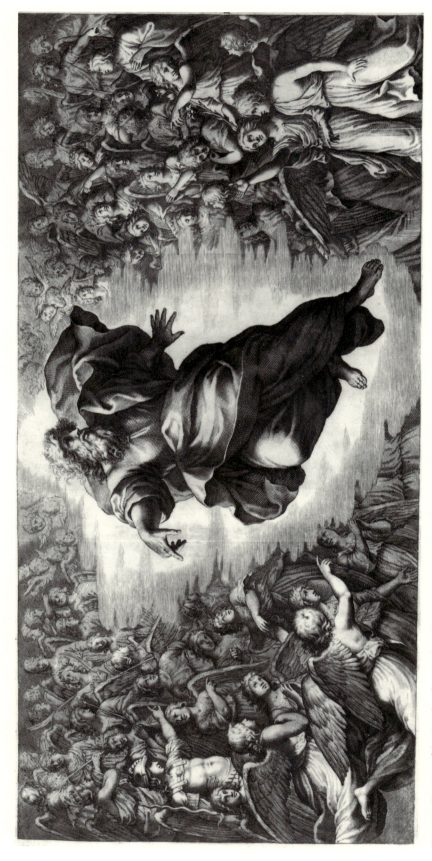

Fig. 60. *Creation of the Angels*, after Andrea Camassei, engraving. (Teti, 1642)

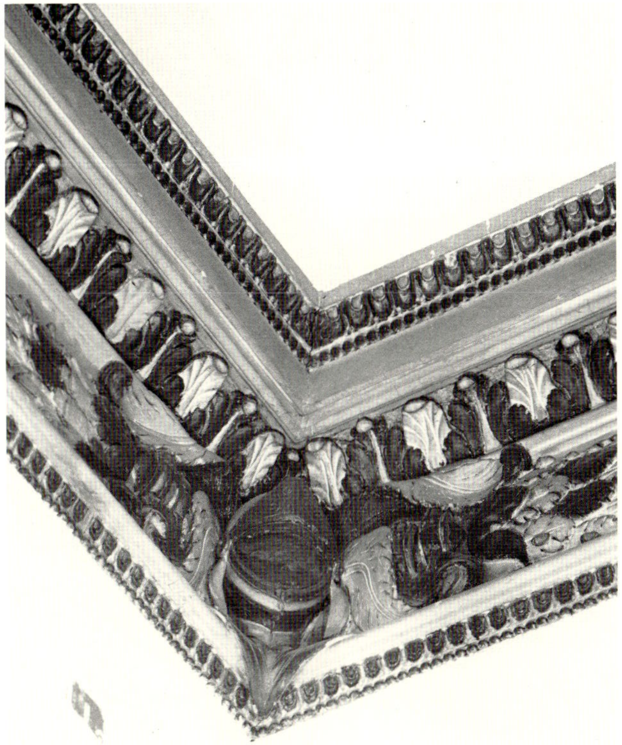

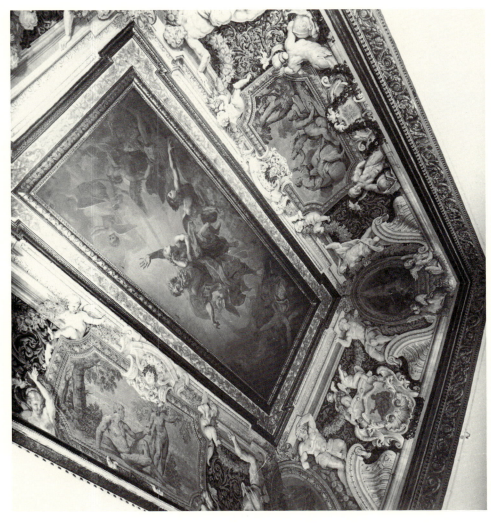

Fig. 62. *Creation of the World* from point of entry (PBN 7), Niccolò Ricciolini and Laurent Pécheux, fresco and oil, Palazzo Barberini.

Fig. 61. St. Michael's Helmet (PBN 6), stucco cornice, Palazzo Barberini.

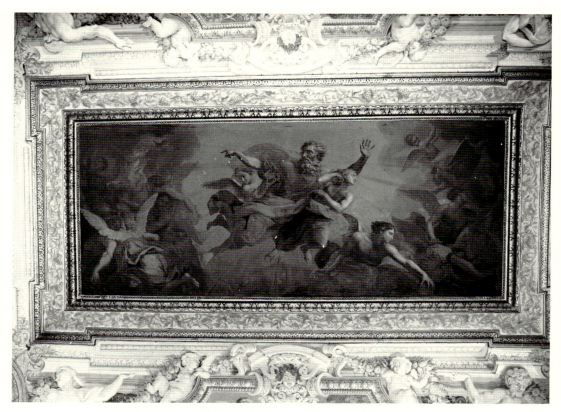

Fig. 63. *God Dividing the Elements* (PBN 7), Laurent Pécheux, oil, Palazzo Barberini.

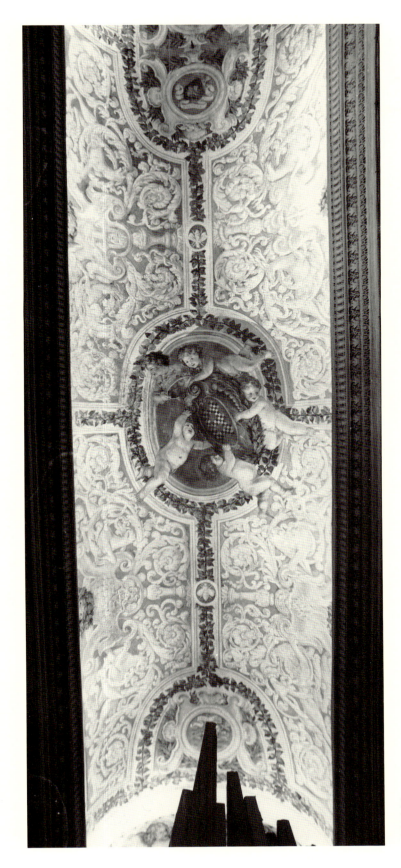

Fig. 64. Gallery Vault (PBN 15),
Pietro da Cortona and assistants, fresco,
Palazzo Barberini.

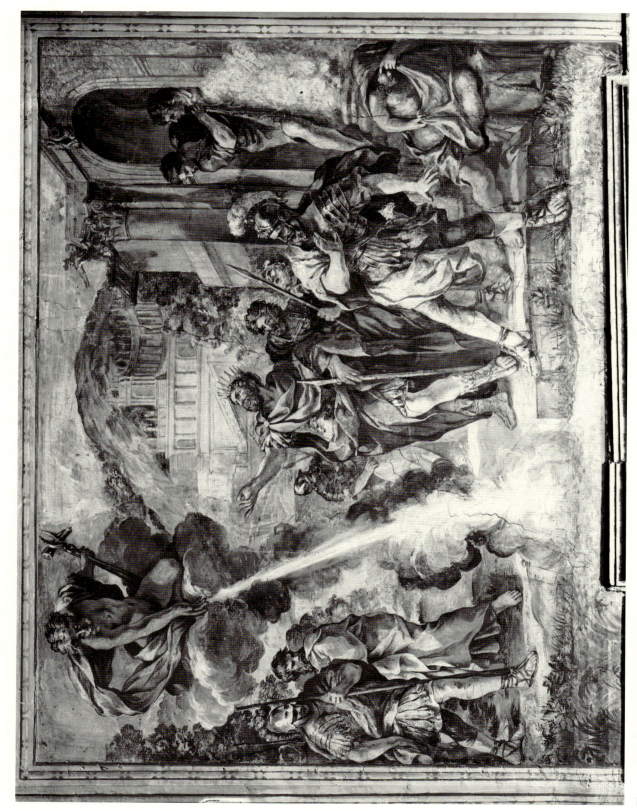

Fig. 65. *Founding of Palestrina* (PBN 15), Pietro da Cortona and Giovanni Francesco Romanelli, fresco, Palazzo Barberini.

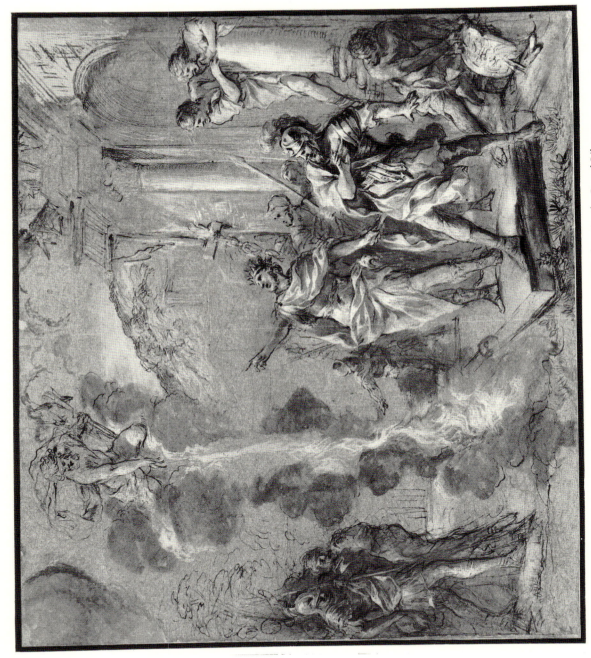

Fig. 66. Preparatory drawing for *Founding of Palestrina*, Pietro da Cortona, Windsor Castle, Royal Library.

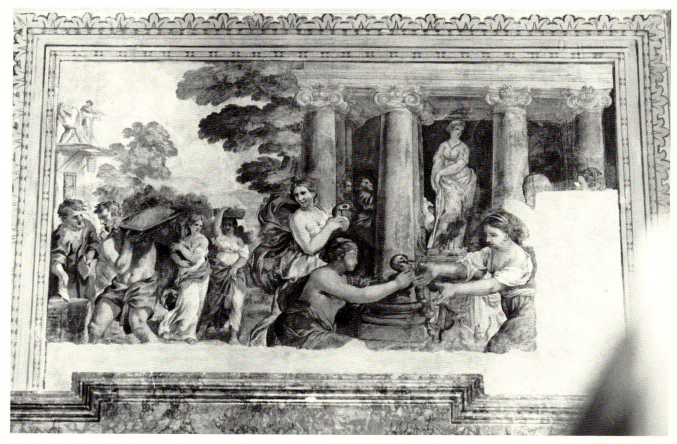

Fig. 67. *Sacrifice to Juno* (PBN 15), Pietro da Cortona and Giacinto Gimignani, fresco, Palazzo Barberini.

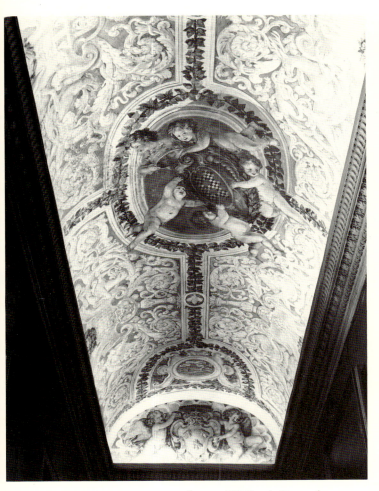

Fig. 68. Gallery Vault from point of entry (PBN 15), Pietro da Cortona and assistants, fresco, Palazzo Barberini.

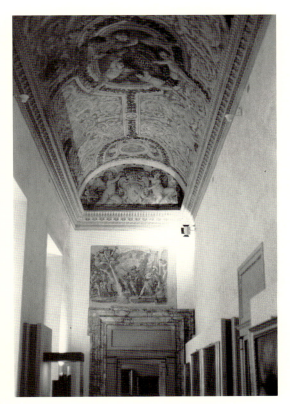

Fig. 69. Gallery from point of entry (PBN 15), Palazzo Barberini.

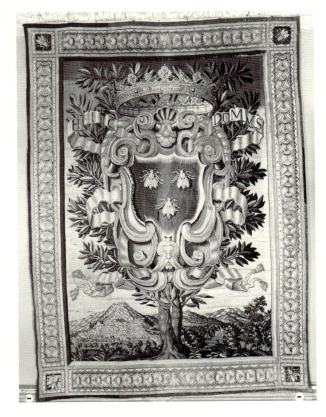

Fig. 70. *Hic Domus*, after Francesco Mingucci, tapestry, Barberini Collection, Rome.

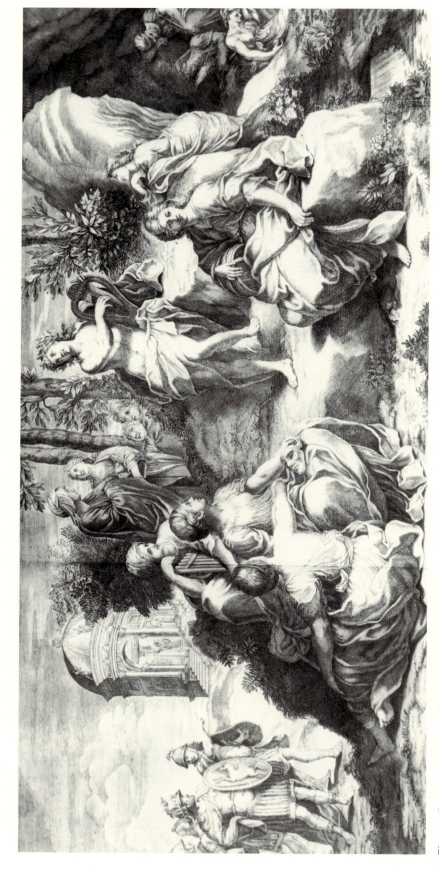

Fig. 72. *Parnassus* (PBT 7), after Andrea Camassei, engraving. (Teti, 1642)

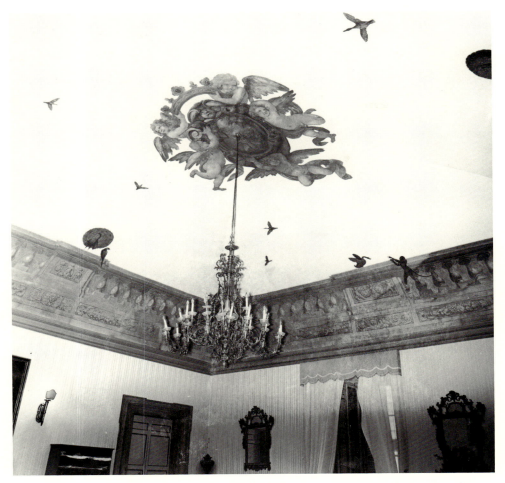

Fig. 71. *Balustrade with Monkey and Peacocks* (PBT 5), Simone Lagi and Agostino Tassi, fresco, Palazzo Barberini.

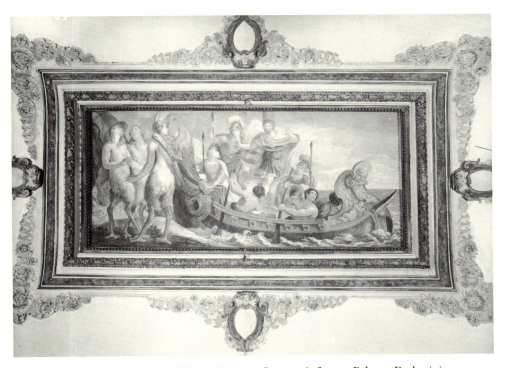

Fig. 73. *Ulysses and the Sirens* (PBT 6), Giacinto Camassei, fresco, Palazzo Barberini.

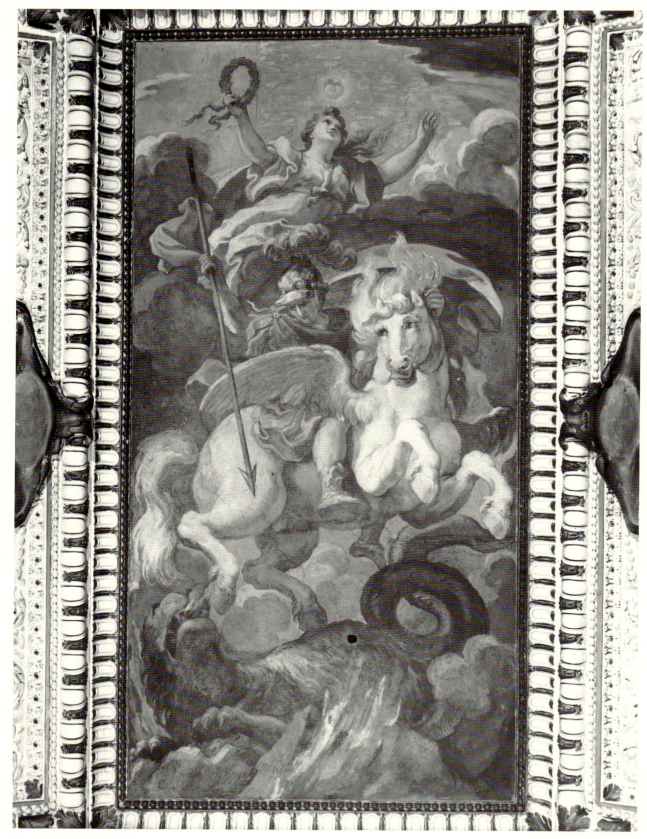

Fig. 74. *Bellerophon Slaying the Chimera* (PBT 8), Giuseppe Passeri, fresco, Palazzo Barberini.

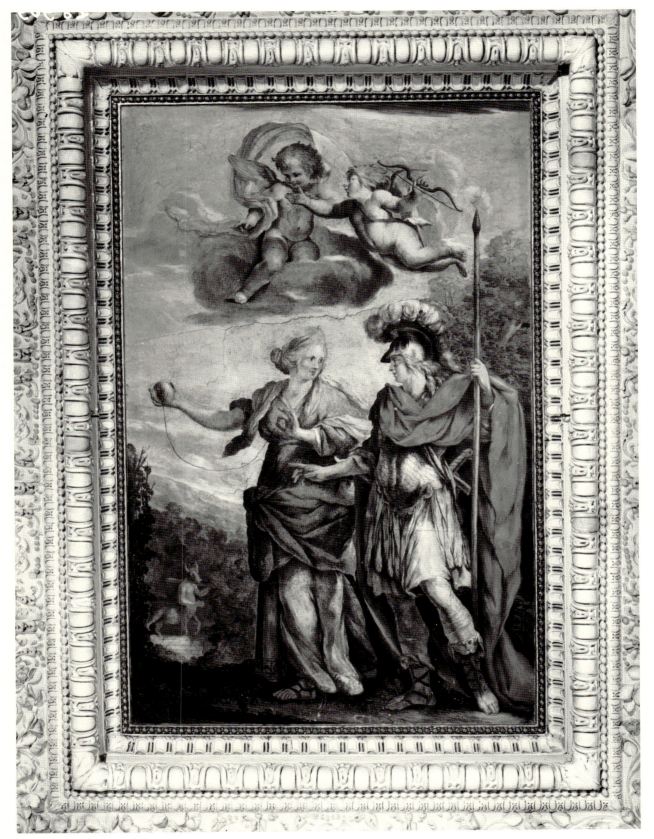

Fig. 75. *Theseus and Ariadne by the Labyrinth* (PBT 9), Urbano Romanelli, fresco, Palazzo Barberini.

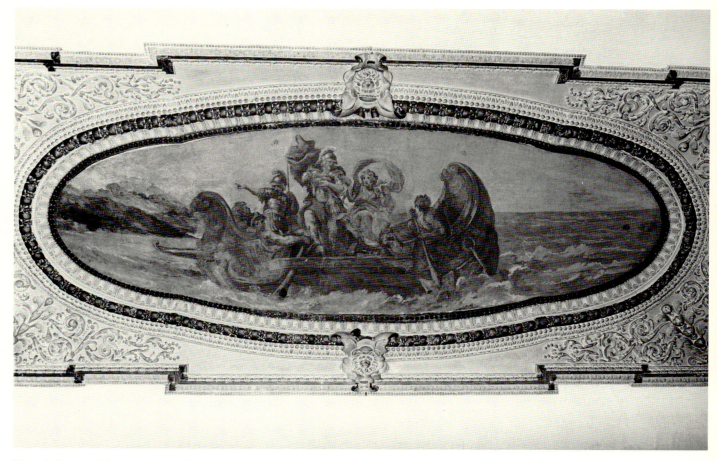

Fig. 76. *Jason and the Argonauts with the Golden Fleece* (PBT 10), Giuseppe Passeri, fresco, Palazzo Barberini.

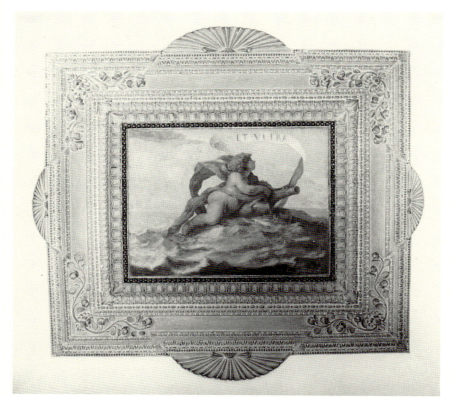

Fig. 77. *Putto on Amphora* (PBT 11), Urbano Romanelli, fresco, Palazzo Barberini.

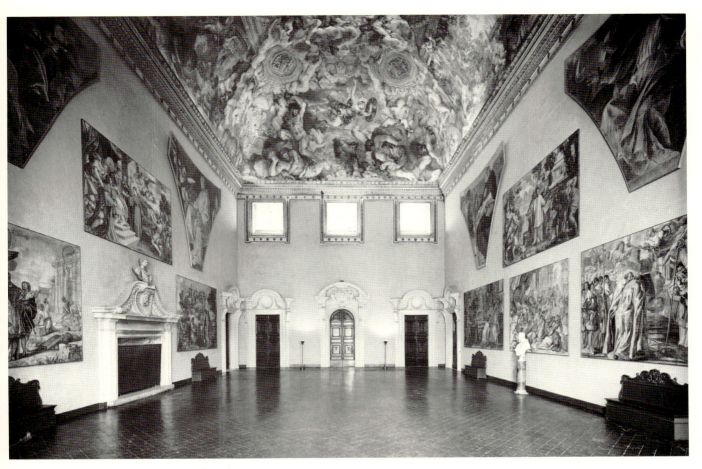

Fig. 78. Salone (PBN 2), Palazzo Barberini.

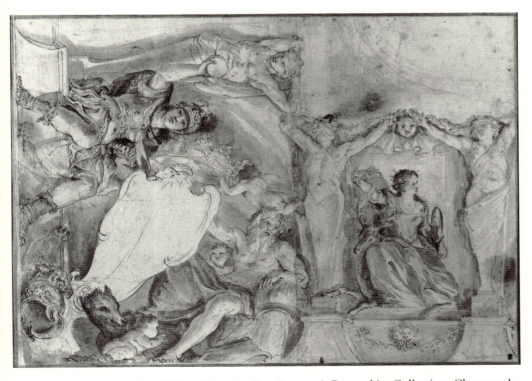

Fig. 79. *Drawing for Barberini Salone Vault*, Andrea Camassei, Devonshire Collection, Chatsworth.

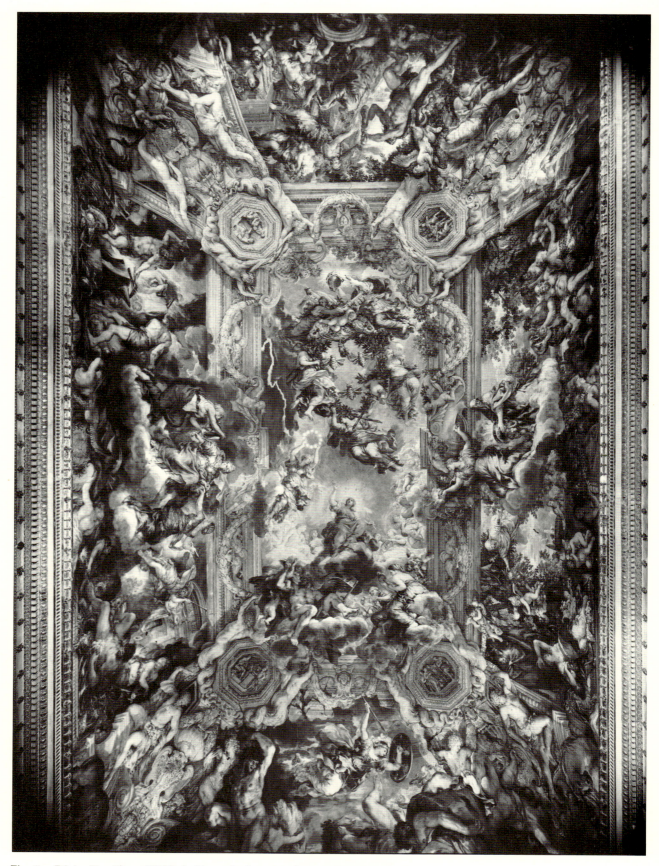

Fig. 80. *Divine Providence* (PBN 2), Pietro da Cortona, fresco, Palazzo Barberini.

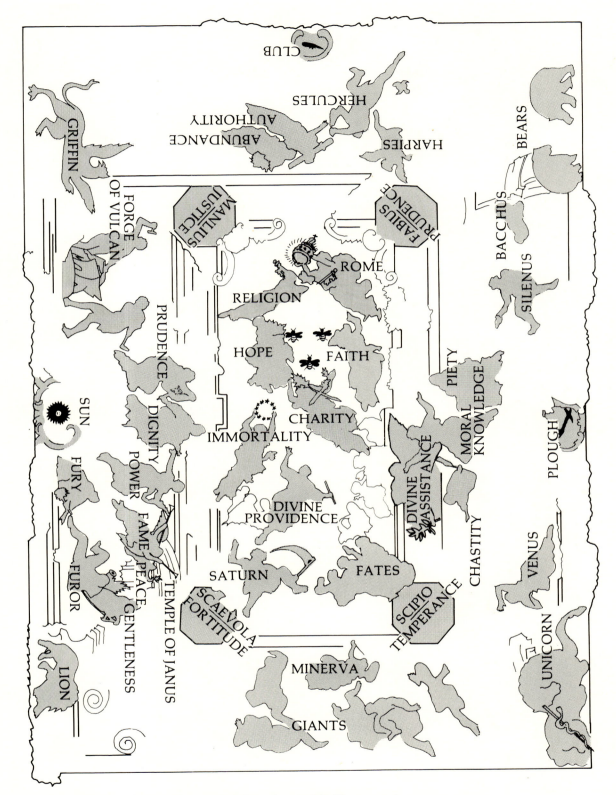

Fig. 81. *Divine Providence*, iconographic plan. (drawing: P. Westercamp)

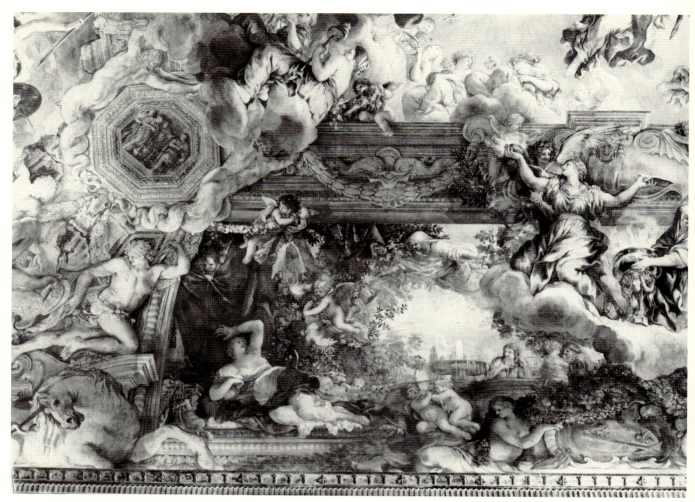

Fig. 82. *Venus*, detail of *Divine Providence*,
Palazzo Barberini.

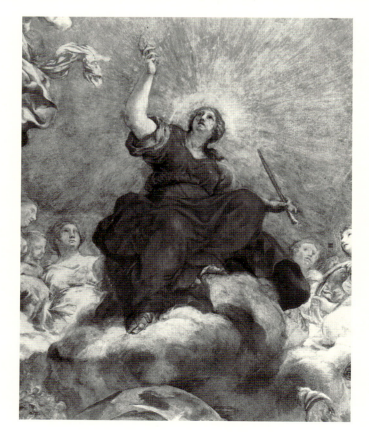

Fig. 84. Detail of *Divine Providence*, Palazzo
Barberini.

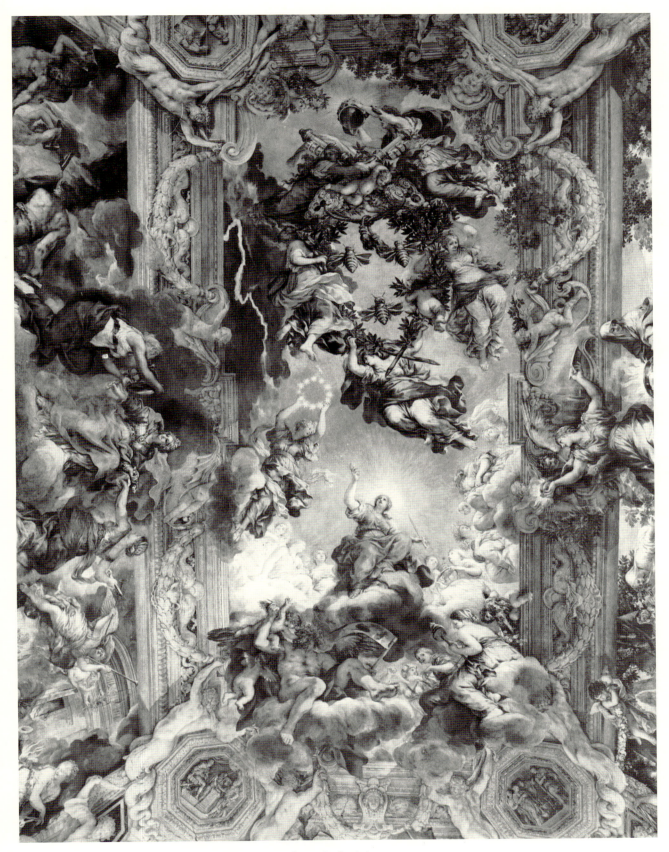

Fig. 83. *Divine Providence*, detail of central section, Palazzo Barberini.

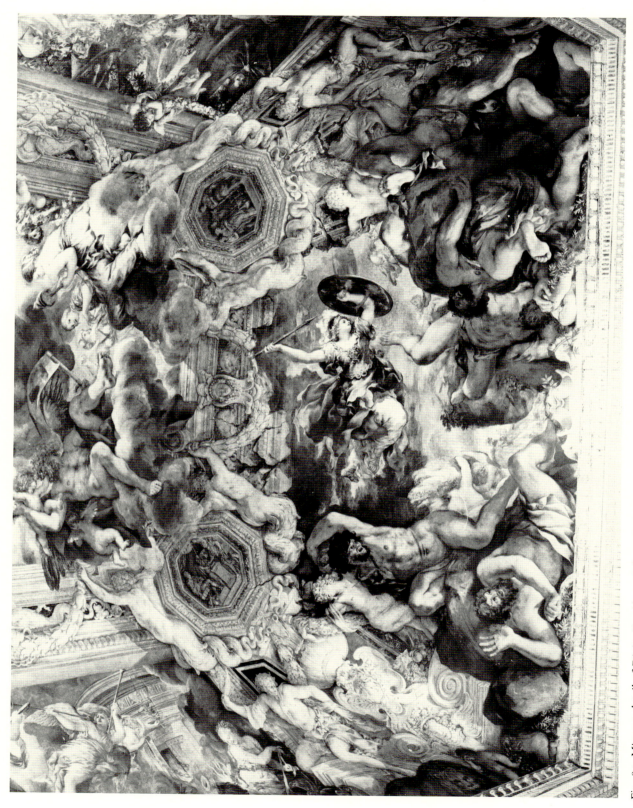

Fig. 85. *Minerva*, detail of *Divine Providence*, Palazzo Barberini.

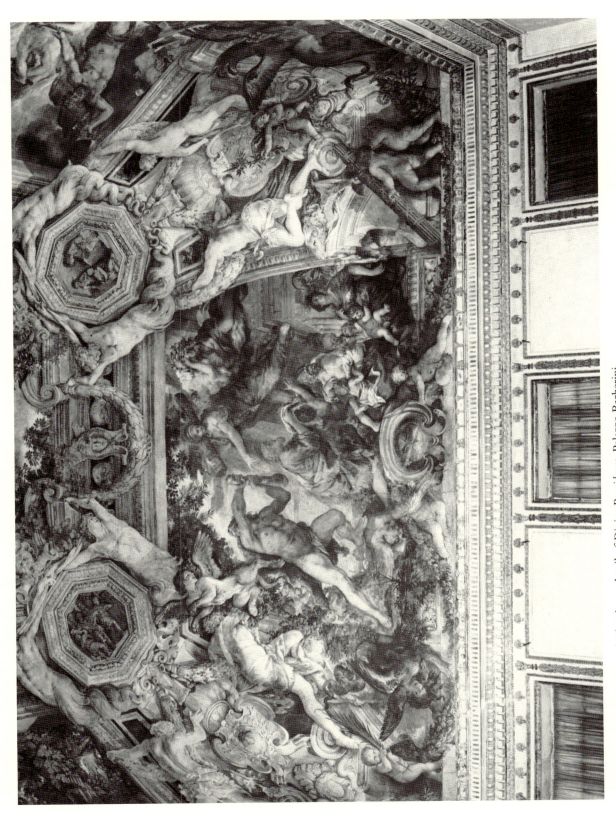

Fig. 86. *Hercules, Authority, and Abundance,* detail of *Divine Providence,* Palazzo Barberini.

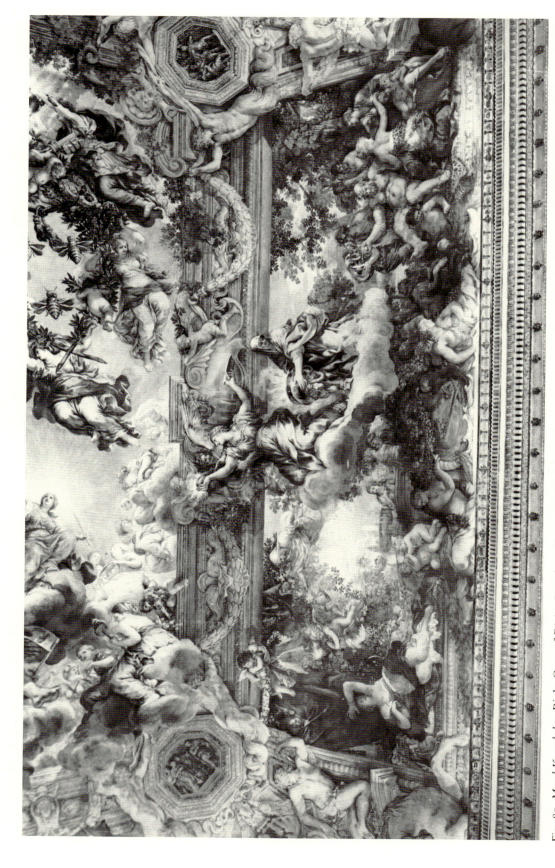

Fig. 87. *Moral Knowledge*, Right Cove of *Divine Providence*, Palazzo Barberini.

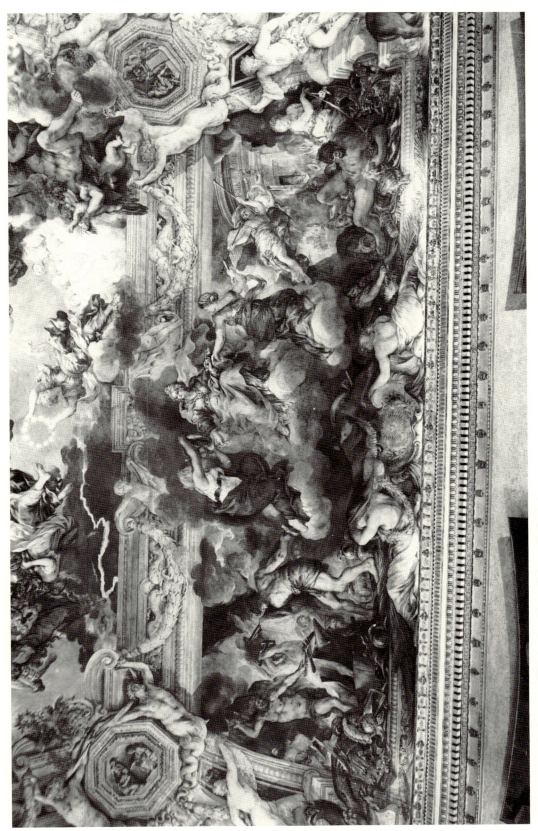

Fig. 88. *Dignity, Left Cove of Divine Providence*, Palazzo Barberini.

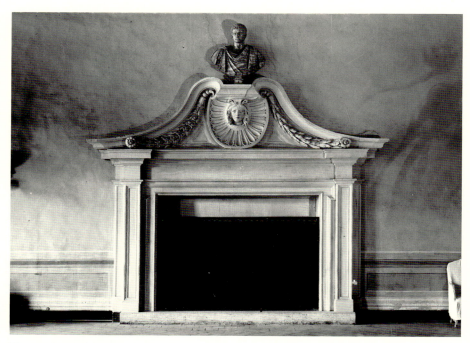

Fig. 89. Mantelpiece, Salone,
Palazzo Barberini.

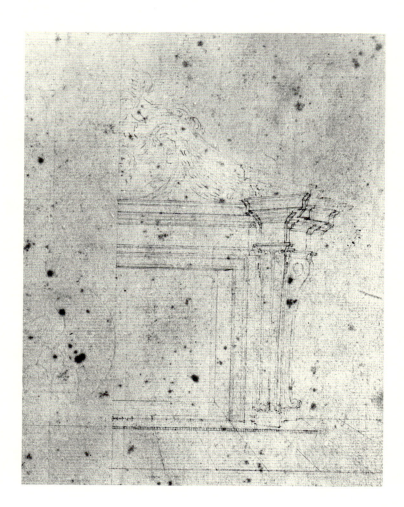

Fig. 90. Drawing for Mantelpiece,
detail, Francesco Borromini, Vienna,
Albertina.

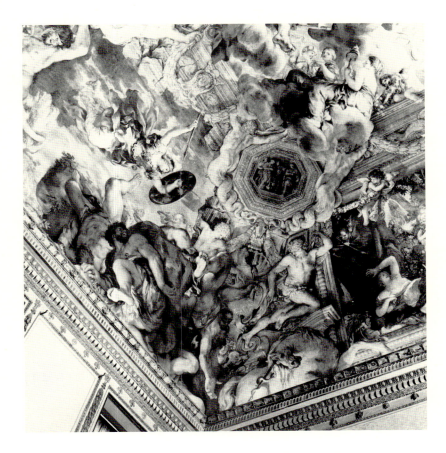

Fig. 91. *Scipio Africanus/Temperance*, detail of *Divine Providence*, Palazzo Barberini.

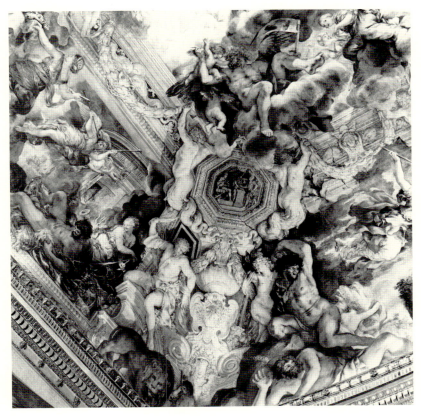

Fig. 92. *Mucius Scaevola/Fortitude*, detail of *Divine Providence*, Palazzo Barberini.

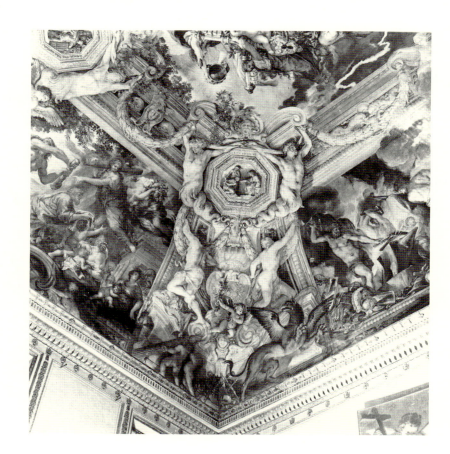

Fig. 93. *Titus Manlius/Justice*, detail of *Divine Providence*, Palazzo Barberini.

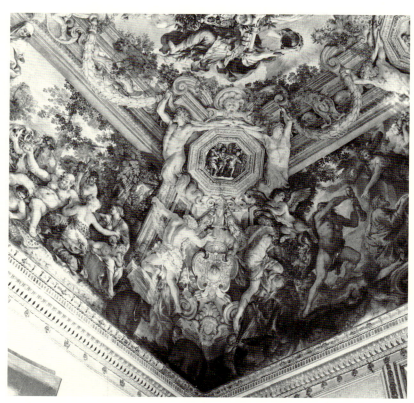

Fig. 94. *Fabius Maximus/Prudence*, detail of *Divine Providence*, Palazzo Barberini.

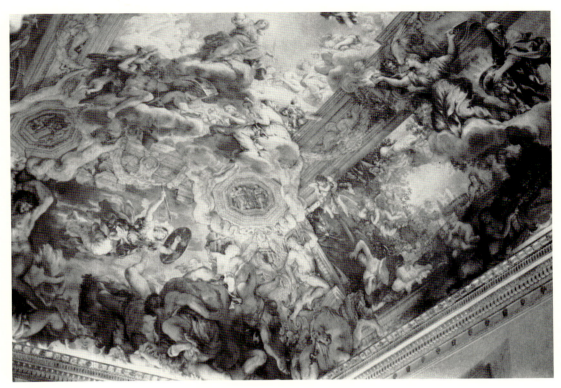

Fig. 95. *Divine Providence*, view from point of entry, Palazzo Barberini.

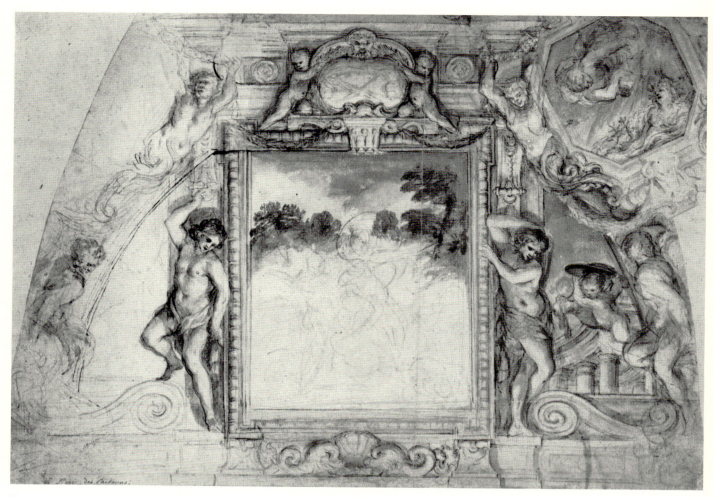

Fig. 96. Preparatory drawing for Hercules Cove of *Divine Providence*, Pietro da Cortona, Munich, Staatliche Graphische Sammlung.

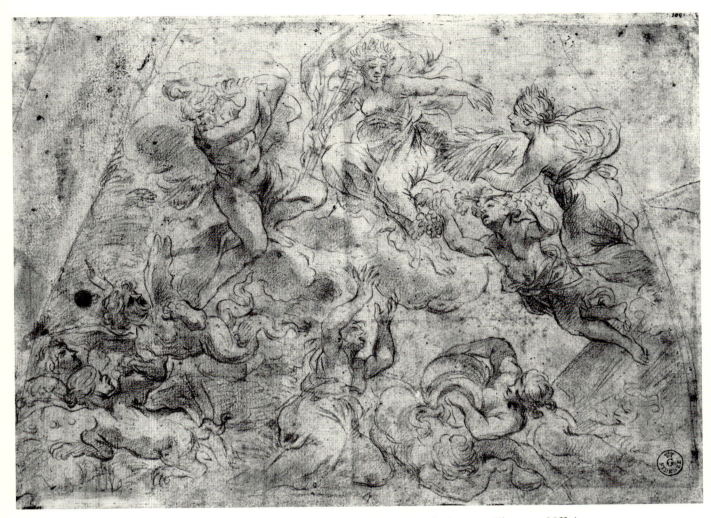

Fig. 97. Preparatory drawing for Hercules Cove of *Divine Providence*, after Pietro da Cortona, Florence, Uffizi.

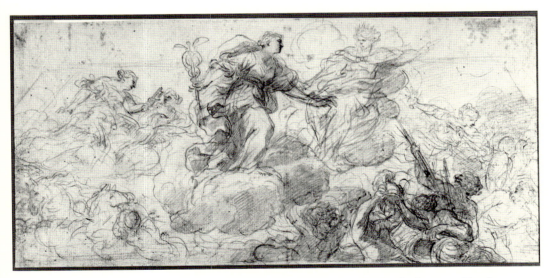

Fig. 98. Preparatory drawing for Dignity Cove of *Divine Providence*, Pietro da Cortona, Haarlem, Teylers Museum.

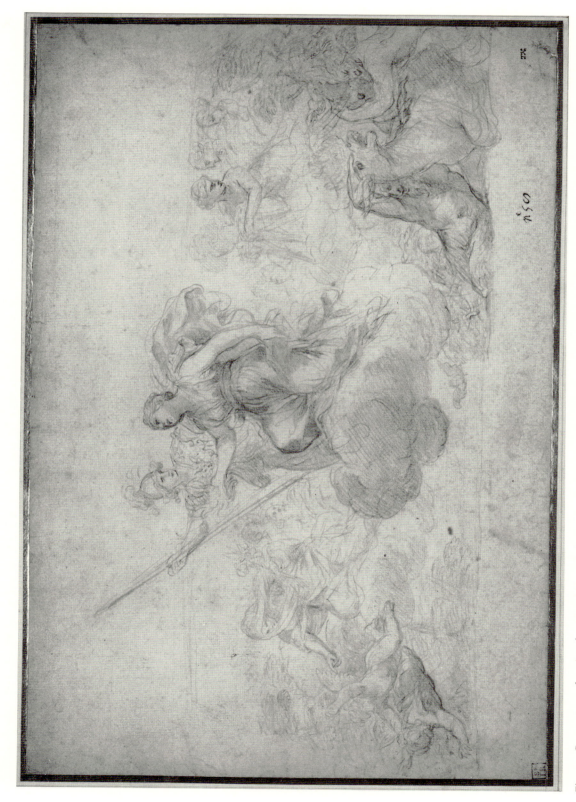

Fig. 99. Preparatory drawing for Moral Knowledge Cove of *Divine Providence*, Pietro da Cortona, Ottawa, National Gallery of Canada.

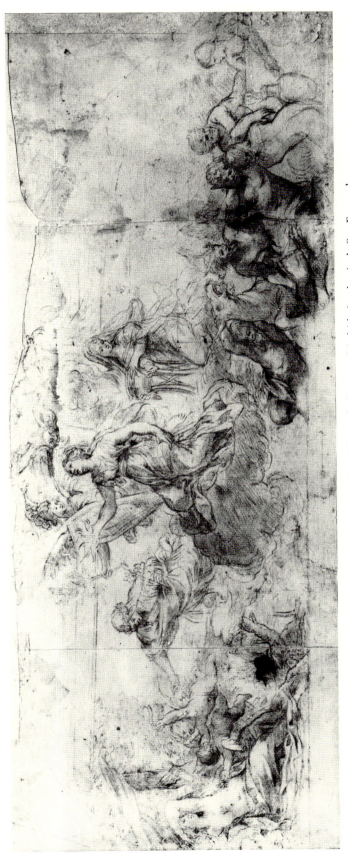

Fig. 100. Preparatory drawing for Moral Knowledge Cove of *Divine Providence*, Pietro da Cortona, Madrid, Academia de San Fernando.

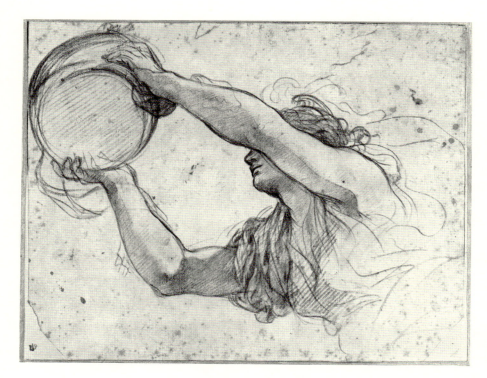

Fig. 101. Preparatory drawing for figure of Rome, Pietro da Cortona, New York, Pierpont Morgan Library.

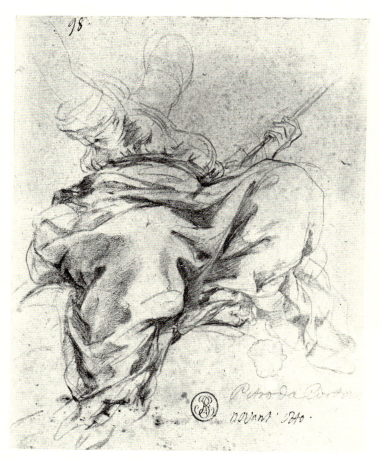

Fig. 102. Preparatory drawing for figure of Divine Providence, Pietro da Cortona, Paris, Louvre.

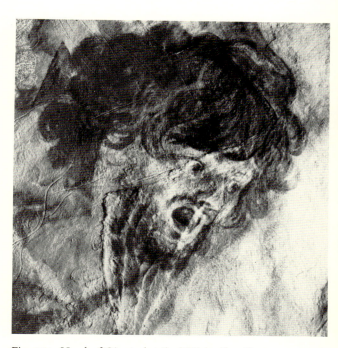

Fig. 103. Head of Giant, detail of *Divine Providence*, Pietro da Cortona.

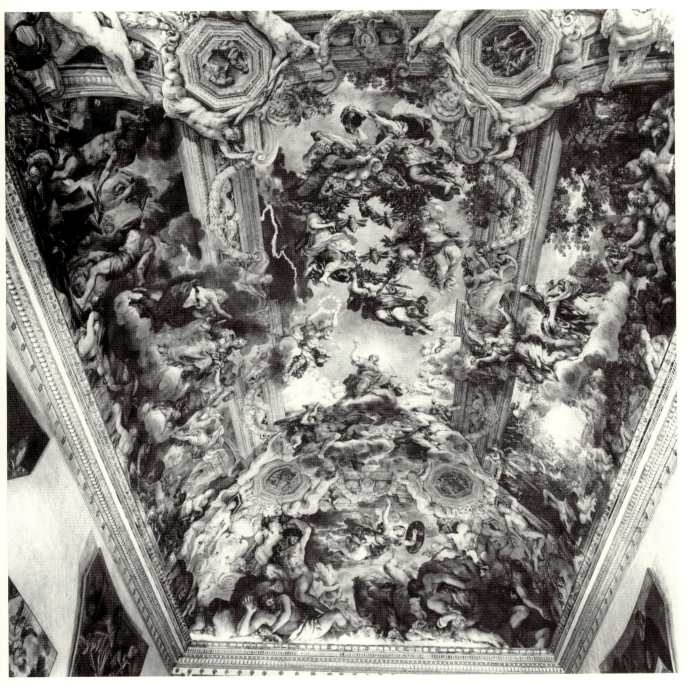

Fig. 104. *Divine Providence* from ideal station point (PBN 2), Pietro da Cortona, fresco, Palazzo Barberini.

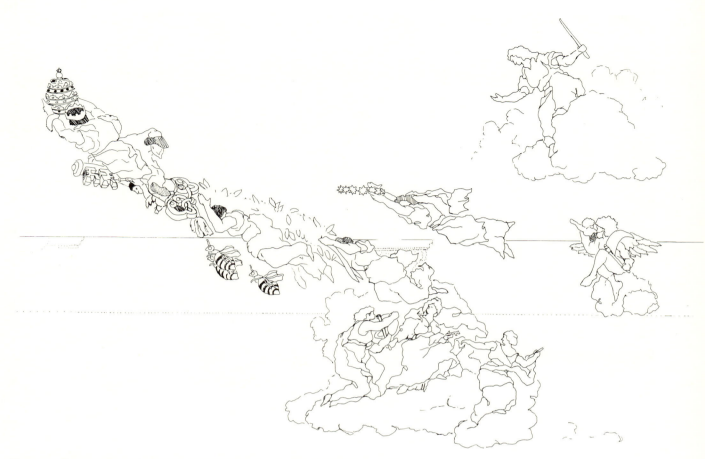

Fig. 105. Cross-section elevation of fictive space of *Divine Providence*. (drawing: P. Lawler)

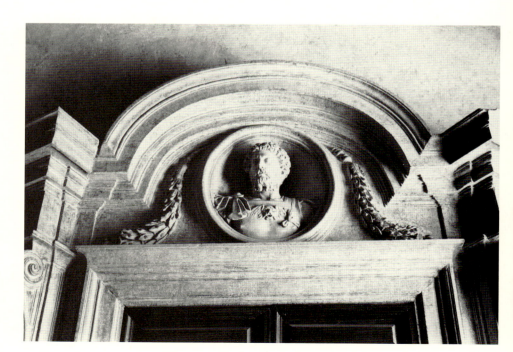

Fig. 108. Overdoor to elliptical
staircase, Salone (PBN 2),
Palazzo Barberini.

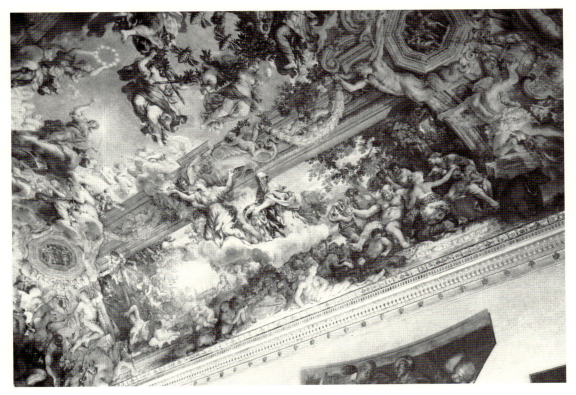

Fig. 106. Right Cove of *Divine Providence* from point of entry by square staircase (PBN S1), Pietro da Cortona, Palazzo Barberini.

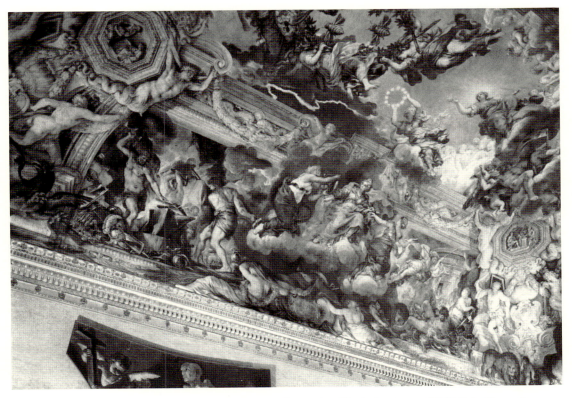

Fig. 107. Left Cove of *Divine Providence* from point of entry by elliptical staircase (PBN S2), Pietro da Cortona, Palazzo Barberini.

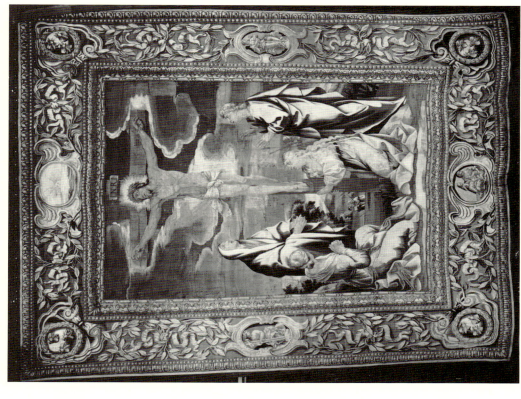

Fig. 110. *Crucifixion*, after Giovanni Francesco Romanelli, tapestry, New York, Cathedral Church of St. John the Divine.

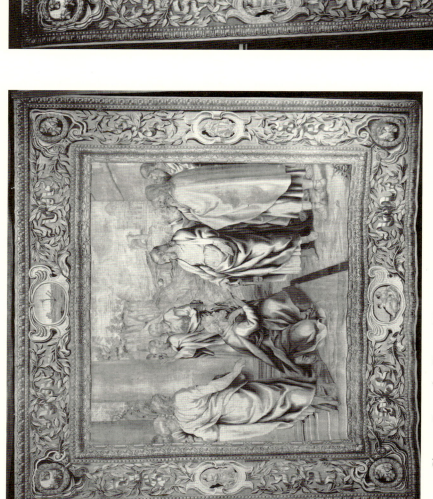

Fig. 109. *Charge to Peter*, after Giovanni Francesco Romanelli, tapestry, New York, Cathedral Church of St. John the Divine.

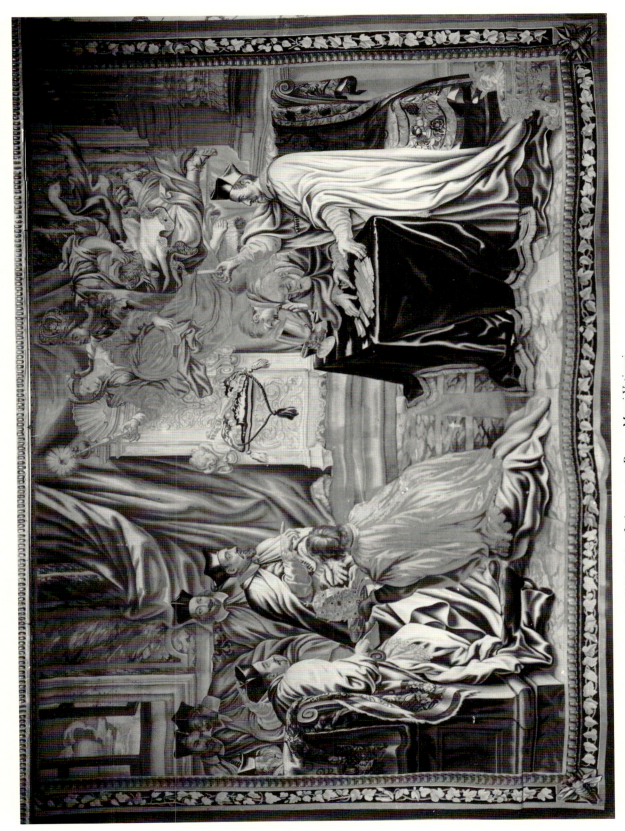

Fig. 111. *Ballot for the Election of Urban*, after Fabio Cristofani, tapestry, Rome, Musei Vaticani.

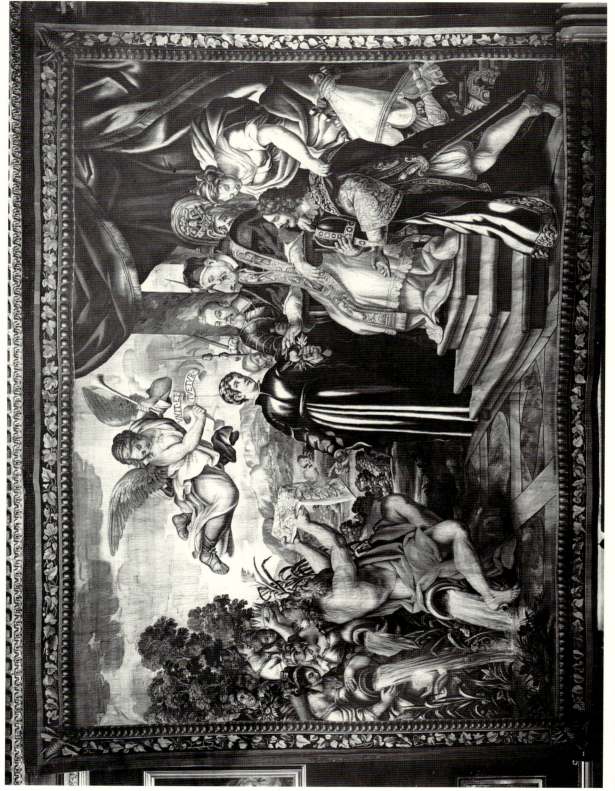

Fig. 112. *Urban and the Countess Matilda: Acquisition of the Papal States*, after Giuseppe Belloni, tapestry, Rome, Musei Vaticani.

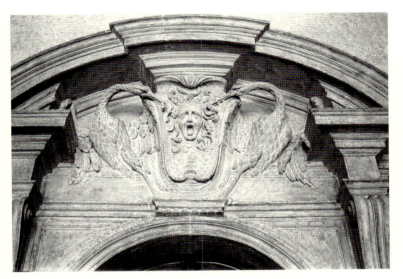

Fig. 113. Overdoor to Oval Room, Salone, Palazzo Barberini.

Fig. 114. Precedence and Preeminence of Titles, Cesare Ripa, *Della più che novissima iconologia*, Padua, 1630.

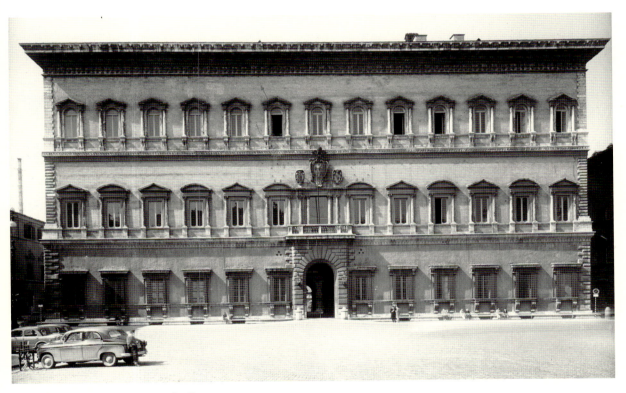

Fig. 115. Palazzo Farnese, Facade, Rome.

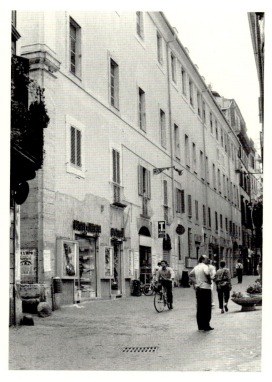

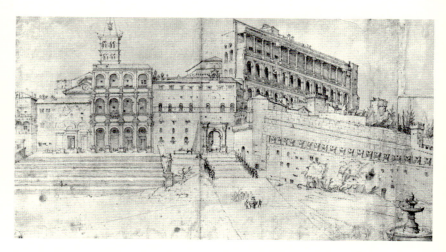

Fig. 116. Casa Grande ai Giubbonari, Rome, extent after 1624.

Fig. 117. Papal Benediction Loggia and Cortile di San Damaso, Vatican, Marten Van Heemskerck, drawing, ca. 1535, Vienna, Albertina.

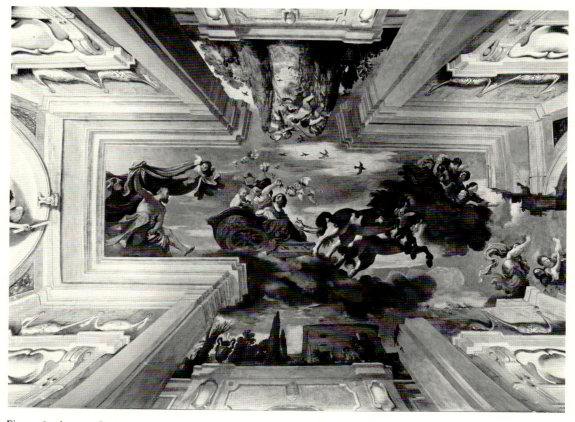

Fig. 118. *Aurora*, Guercino and Agostino Tassi, fresco, Casino Ludovisi, Rome.

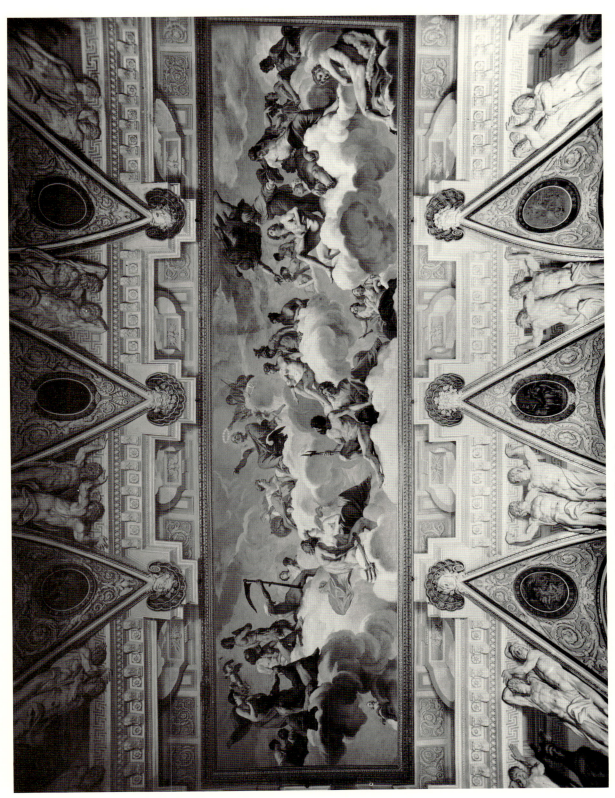

Fig. 119. *Council of the Gods*, Giovanni Lanfranco, fresco, Villa Borghese.

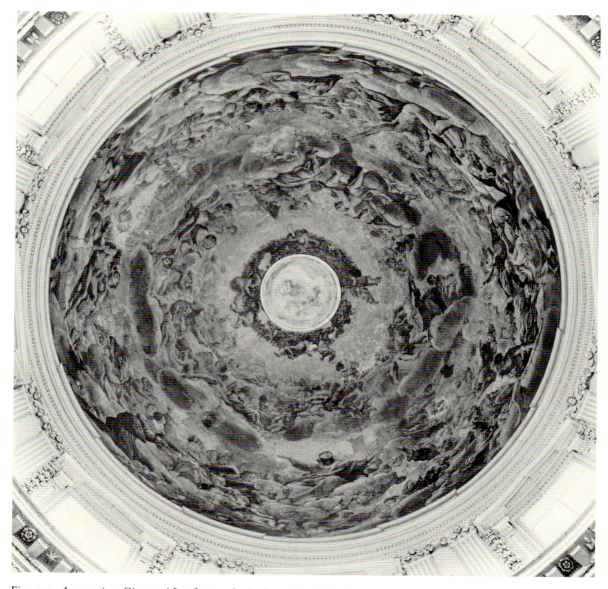

Fig. 120. *Assumption*, Giovanni Lanfranco, S. Andrea della Valle, Rome.

Fig. 122. Divine Wisdom, Cesare Ripa, *Nova iconologia*, Padua, 1618.

Fig. 123. *Divine Wisdom*, manuscript miniature, German, 13th century, Dublin, Chester Beatty Library.

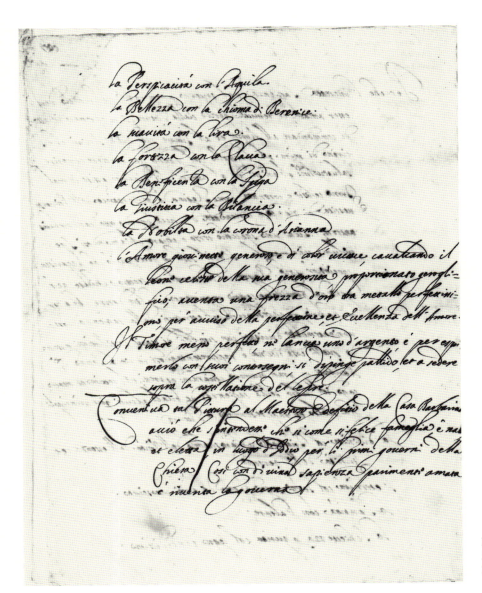

la Perspicacia con l'Aquila.

la Bellezza con la chioma di Berenice.

la suavità con la Lira.

la Fortezza con la Clava

la Beneficenza con la Spiga

la Giustizia con la Bilancia

la Nobiltà con la corona d'Arianna

l'Amore giouinetto, generoso, e di color uiuace, caualcando il
Leone centro della sua generosità, proportionato con gli
fig, auendo una frezza d'oro tra metalli perfezzi
oni per auuiso della perfezzione, et Eccellenza dell'Amore.

Il Timore meno perfetto n' lancia una d'argento è per esp
mento con i suoi contrassegni si dipinge pallido, et a sedere
sopra la cosa Massime del Tespr.

Conuentua col Pittore al Maestro desserio della Casa Barberina
auciò che s'intendono: che si come si felice famiglia è na
et eleua in luogo d'Idio per li primi gouerni della
Chiesa. Cosi con diuina sapienza parimenti amata
e riuerita la gouernà.

Fig. 121. Written program of
Divine Wisdom, BAV, Barb.
Lat. 6529, Misc. V, 52v.

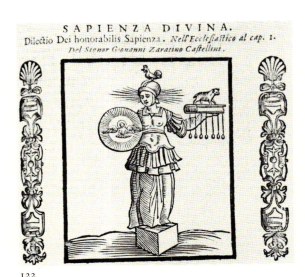

SAPIENZA DIVINA.
Dilectio Dei honorabilis Sapienza. *Nell'Ecclesiastico al cap.* 1.
Del Signor Giouanni Zaratino Castellini.

122

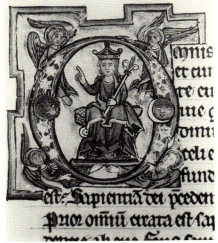

123

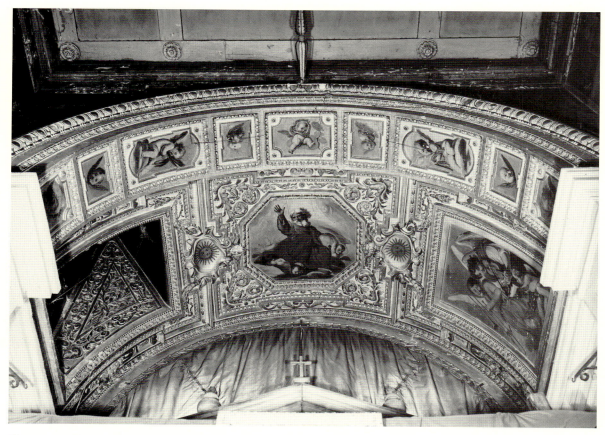

Fig. 124. Vault above Altar Aedicula, Bernini, S. Bibiana, Rome.

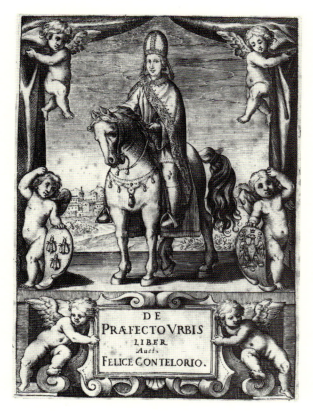

Fig. 125. Engraved frontispiece of *De Praefecto Urbis* by Felice Contelori, Rome, 1631.

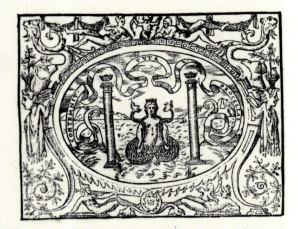

DEL S. STEFANO
COLONNA.

Côtemnit
tura procel
las.

Se bene irato & tempestoso è il mare,
Non perciò la Serena il suo furore
Teme: così l'huom pien d'alto valore
Suol'ogni caso auerso superare.

Fig. 126. Colonna Siren, woodcut impresa, *Le sententiose imprese* by Paolo Giovio, Lyons, 1562.

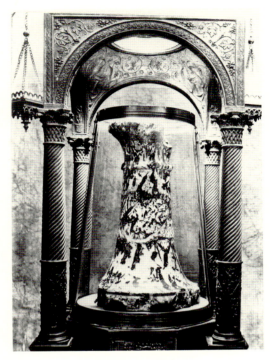

Fig. 128. Column of the Flagellation, S. Prassede, Rome.

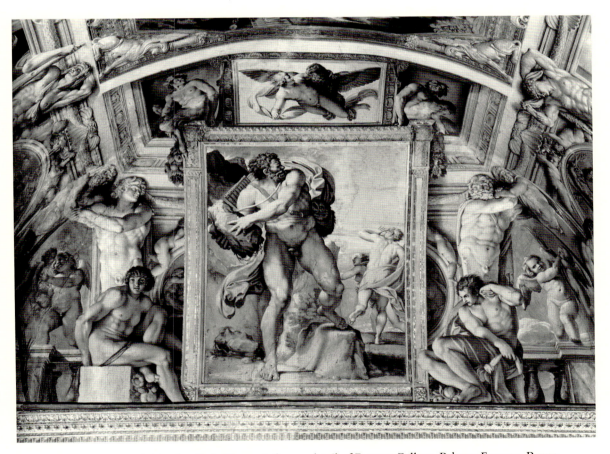

Fig. 127. *Polyphemus and Acis*, Annibale Carracci, fresco, detail of Farnese Gallery, Palazzo Farnese, Rome.

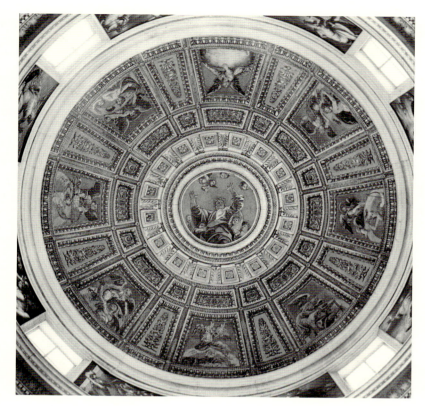

Fig. 129. Dome of Chigi Chapel, Raphael, mosaic, 1513–1516, S.M. del Popolo, Rome.

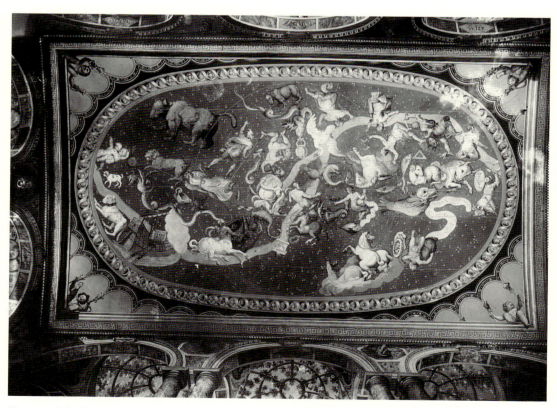

Fig. 130. Sala di Bologna, Giovanni Antonio Vanosino, fresco, Palazzo Vaticano, Rome.

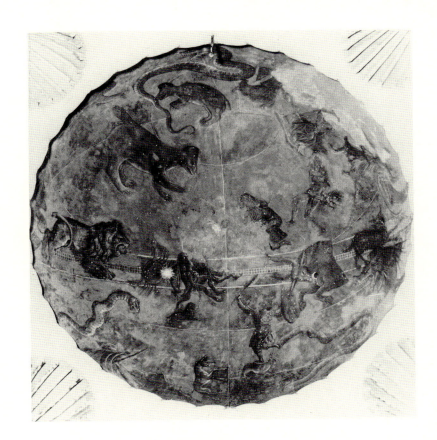

Fig. 131. Astrological Dome, fresco, ca.
1439, Old Sacristy, S. Lorenzo, Florence.

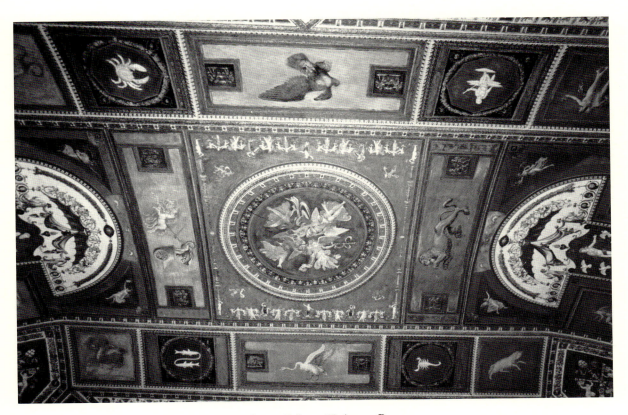

Fig. 132. Sala dei Pontefici, Perino del Vaga, fresco, Palazzo Vaticano, Rome.

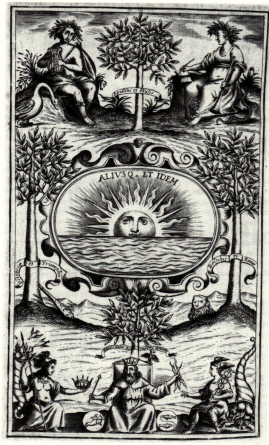

133

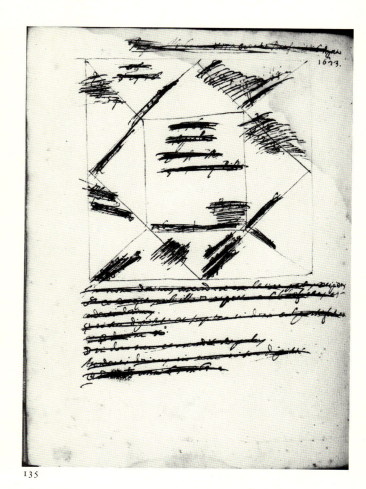

135

Fig. 133. Impresa of Maffeo Barberini, ALIUSQUE
ET IDEM, engraving, *Teatro d'imprese* by Giovanni
Ferro, Venice, 1623.

Fig. 134. *Apollo Pythius* and *Lion*, Palazzo
Barberini (PBN S1).

Fig. 135. Natal chart of Maffeo Barberini (Urban
VIII), BMF, Bigazzi 235, 36v.

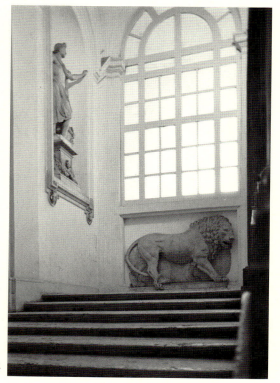

134

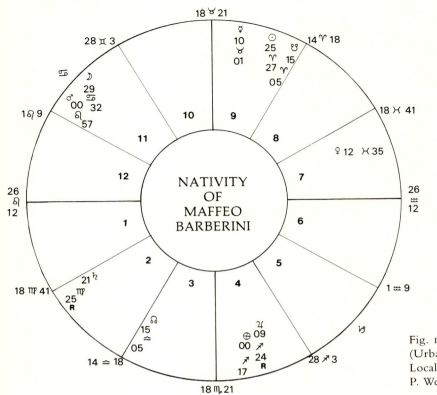

Fig. 136. Natal chart of Maffeo Barberini (Urban VIII), 5 April 1568, 1:29 P.M., Local Mean Time, Florence. (drawing: P. Westercamp)

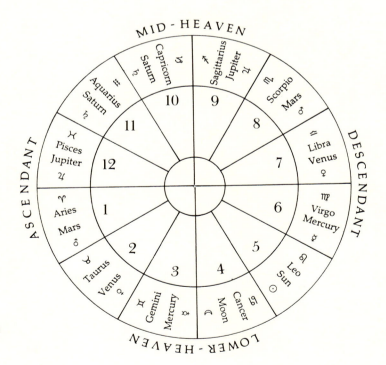

Fig. 137. Chart with Zodiacal and Planetary Glyphs and Archetypal Relationships. (drawing: P. Westercamp)

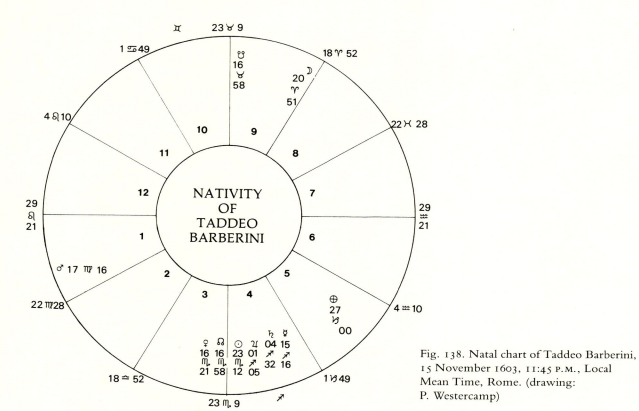

Fig. 138. Natal chart of Taddeo Barberini,
15 November 1603, 11:45 P.M., Local
Mean Time, Rome. (drawing:
P. Westercamp)

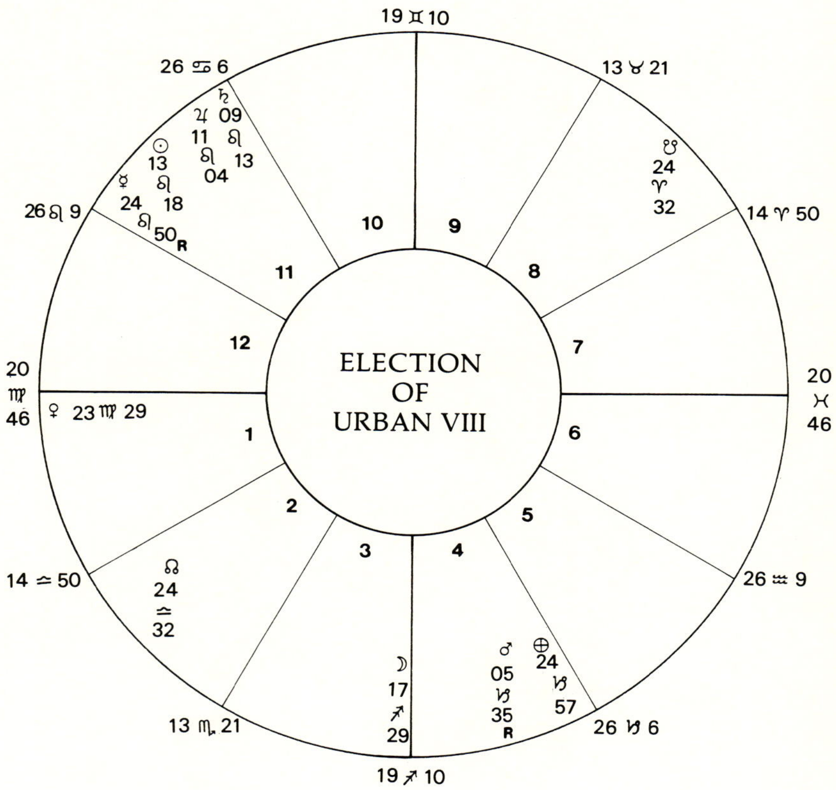

Fig. 140. Election chart of Urban VIII,
6 August 1623, 8:15 A.M., Local Mean
Time, Rome. (drawing:
P. Westercamp)

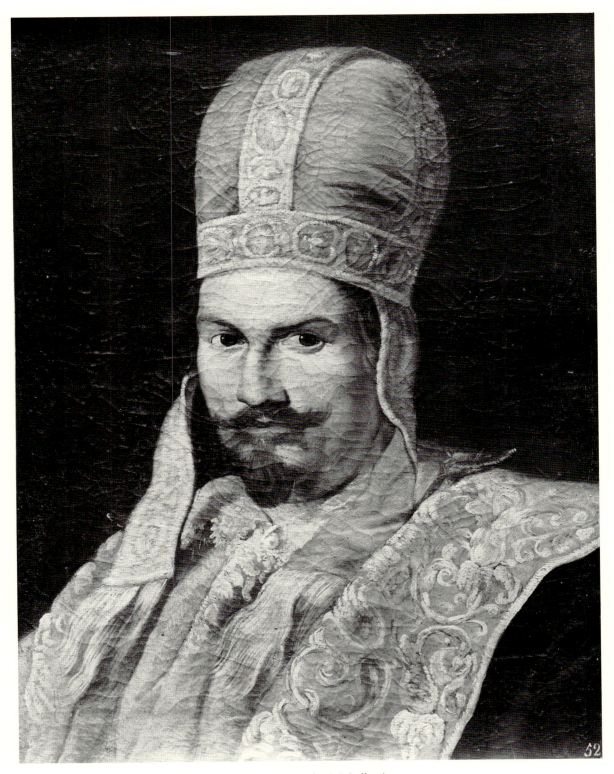

Fig. 139. *Taddeo Barberini*, Carlo Maratta, oil, Rome, Barberini Collection.

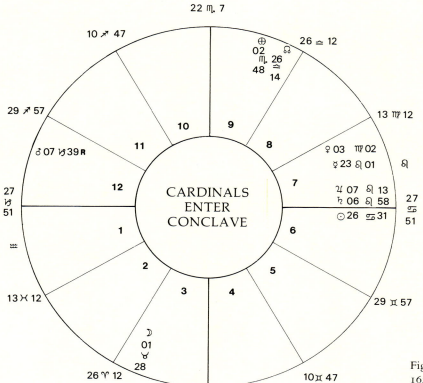

Fig. 141. Cardinals Enter Conclave, 19 July 1623, 7:30 P.M., Local Mean Time, Rome. (drawing: P. Westercamp)

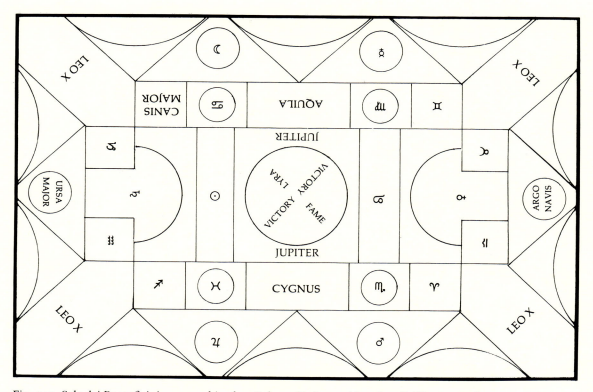

Fig. 142. Sala dei Pontefici, iconographic plan, Palazzo Vaticano. (drawing: P. Westercamp)

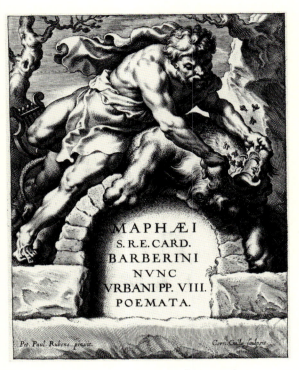

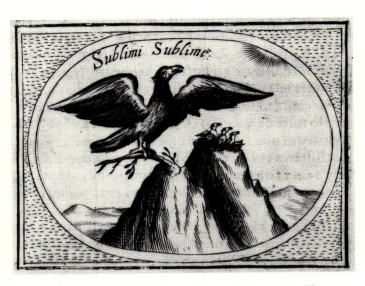

Fig. 144. Impresa of Maffeo Barberini, SUBLIMI SUBLIME, *Teatro d'imprese* by Giovanni Ferro, Venice, 1623.

Fig. 143. Frontispiece engraving of *Poemata* by Urbanus VIII, Cornelius Galle after Peter Paul Rubens, Antwerp, 1634.

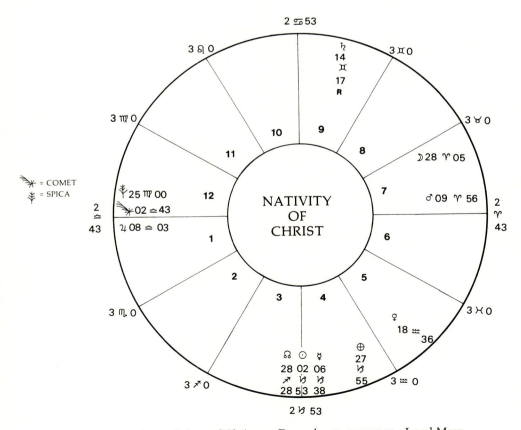

Fig. 145. Luca Cardano's natal chart of Christ, 24 December 0, 12:00 P.M., Local Mean Time, Bethlehem. (drawing: P. Westercamp)

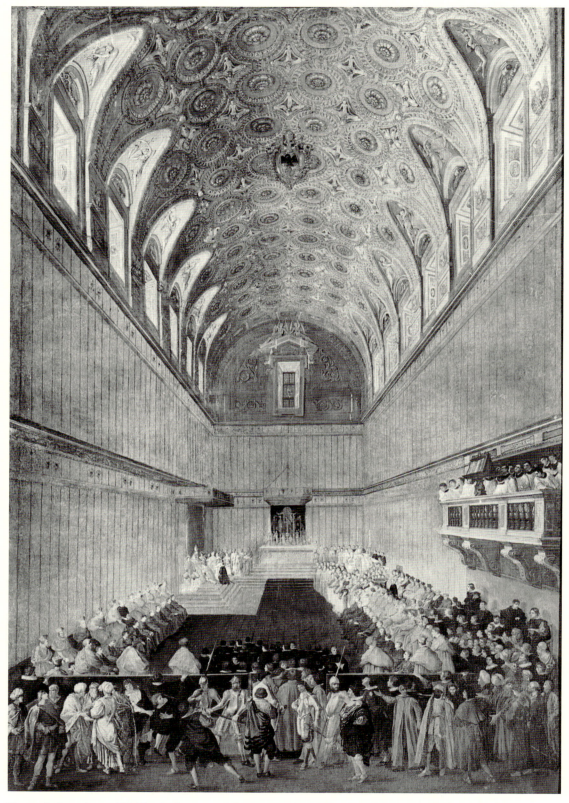

Fig. 146. *Investiture of Taddeo Barberini as Prefect*, Agostino Tassi, oil, Rome, Museo di Roma.

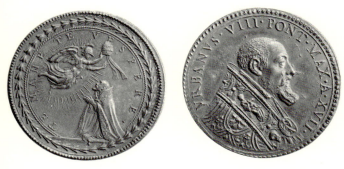

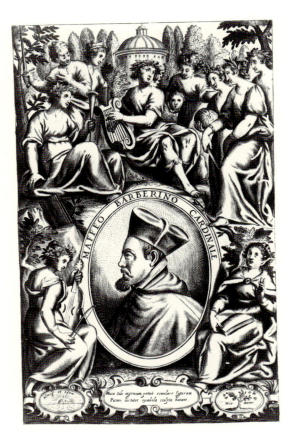

Fig. 147. TE MANE TE VESPERE, medal of Urban VIII, 1640,
London, British Museum.

Fig. 149. Dedication page engraving,
Teatro d'imprese by Giovanni Ferro,
Venice, 1623.

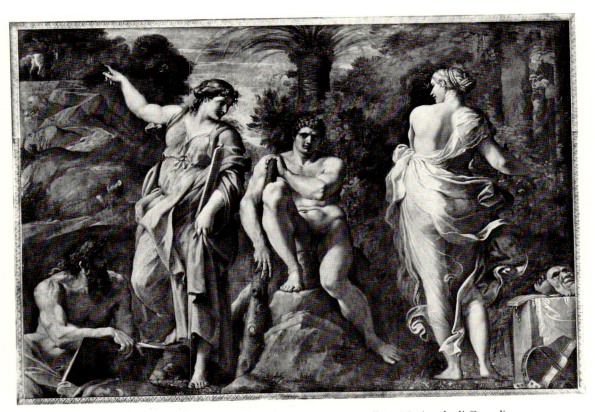

Fig. 148. *Hercules at the Crossroads*, Annibale Carracci, oil, Naples, Galleria Nazionale di Capodimonte.

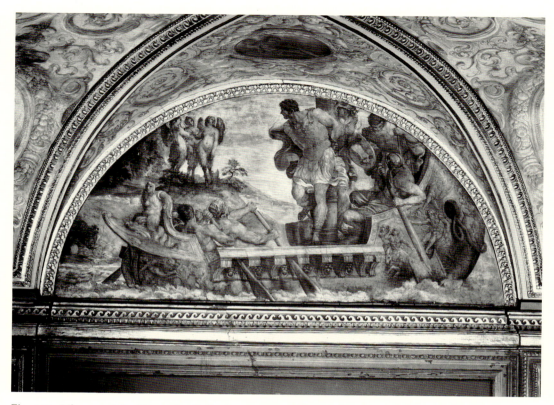

Fig. 150. *Ulysses and the Sirens*, Annibale Carracci, fresco, Camerino, Palazzo Farnese, Rome.

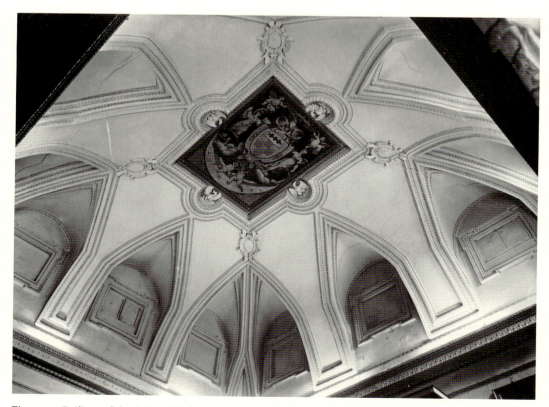

Fig. 152. Ceiling of the Sala dei Palafrenieri, Carlo Maderno, Borghese Garden Palace on the Quirinal (Palazzo Rospigliosi–Pallavicini), Rome.

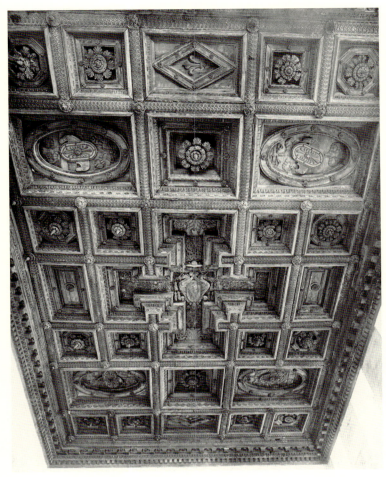

Fig. 151. Ceiling of the Sala dei Palafrenieri, Antonio da Sangallo the Younger, Palazzo Farnese, Rome.

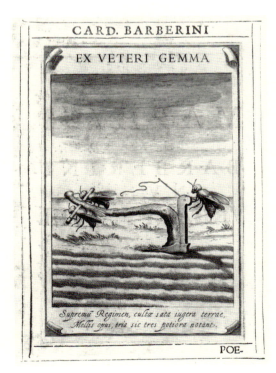

Fig. 153. Impresa of Urban VIII, frontispiece engraving, *Poemata* by Urbanus VIII, Rome, 1631.

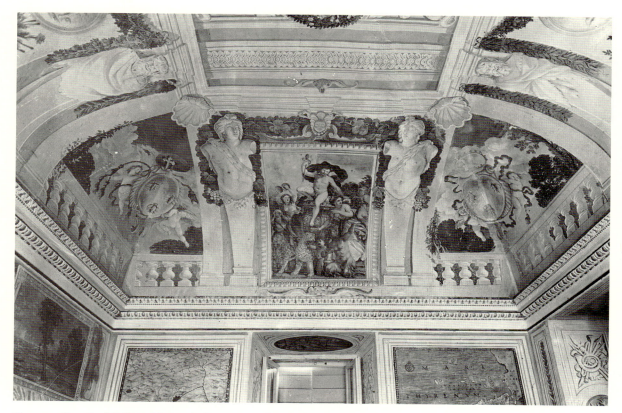

Fig. 154. Detail of Gallery, Pietro da Cortona, Villa Sacchetti, Castelfusano.

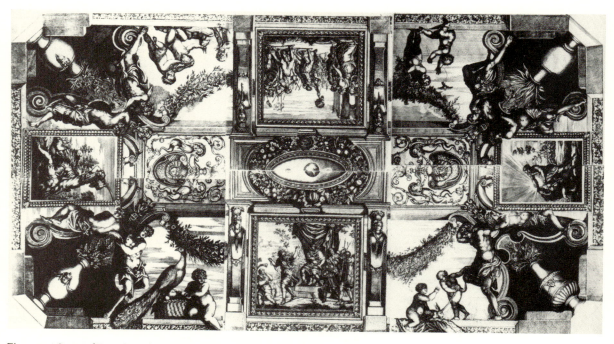

Fig. 155. *Story of David*, Federico Carocci, engraving, after Pietro da Cortona.

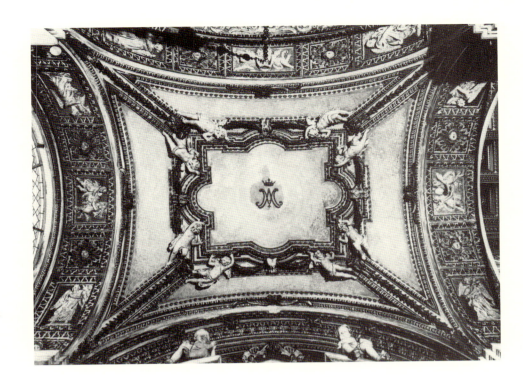

Fig. 156. Vault of the Cappella della Concezione, Pietro da Cortona, stucco, San Lorenzo in Damaso, Rome.

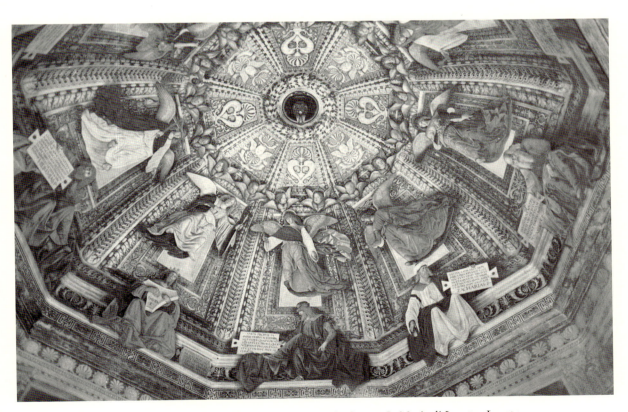

Fig. 157. Dome of the Sacristy of San Marco, Melozzo da Forlì, fresco, S. Maria di Loreto, Loreto.

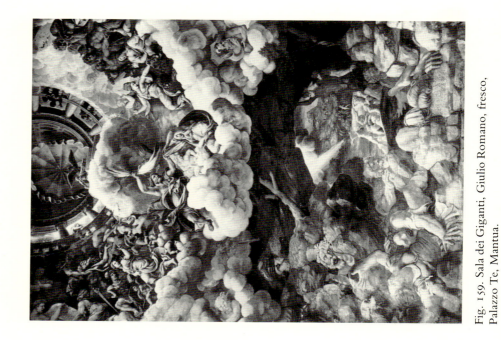

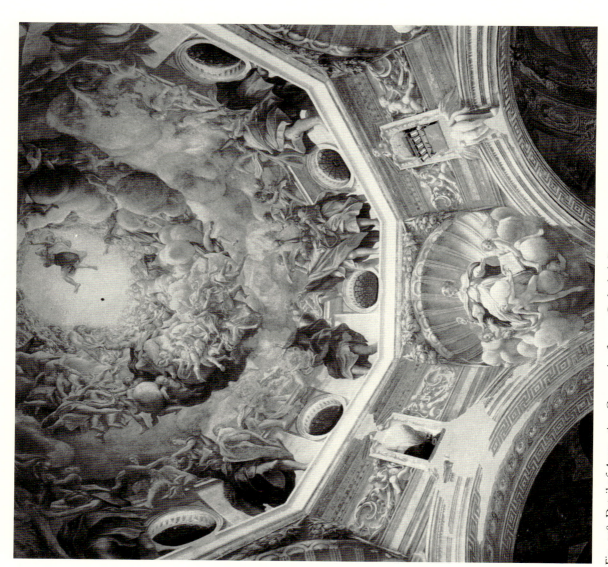

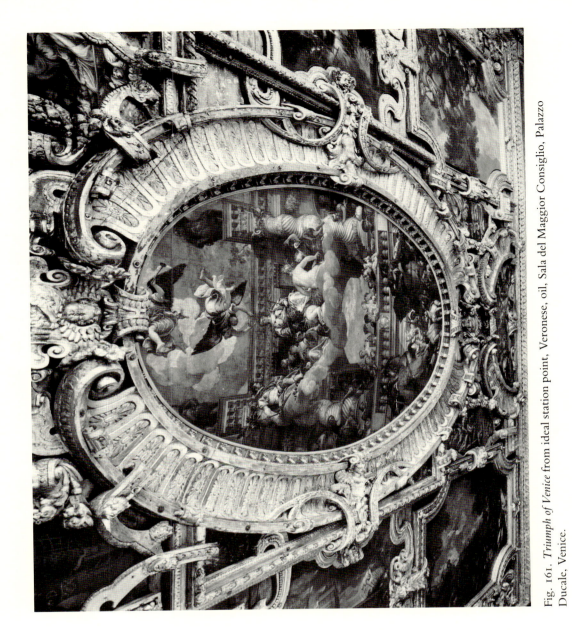

Fig. 161. *Triumph of Venice* from ideal station point, Veronese, oil, Sala del Maggior Consiglio, Palazzo Ducale, Venice.

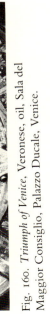

Fig. 160. *Triumph of Venice*, Veronese, oil, Sala del Maggior Consiglio, Palazzo Ducale, Venice.

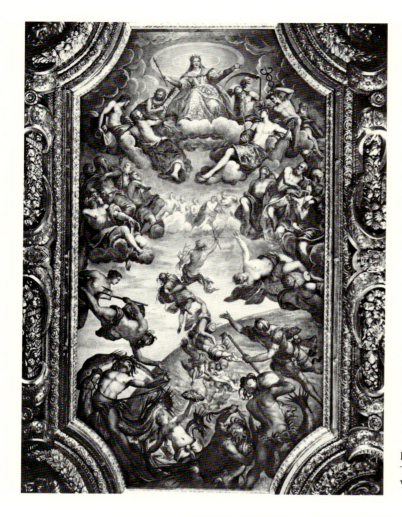

Fig. 162. *Venice Receiving the Tribute of the Sea*, Tintoretto, oil, Sala dei Pregadi, Palazzo Ducale, Venice.

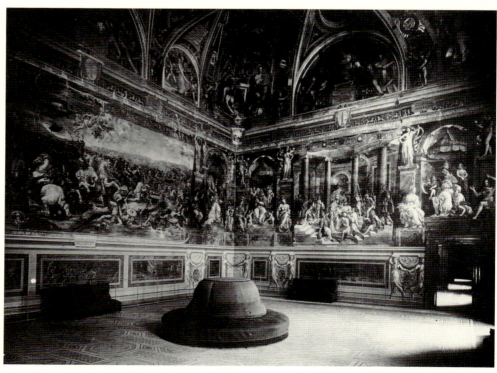

Fig. 163. Sala di Costantino, Giulio Romano and assistants, fresco, Palazzo Vaticano.

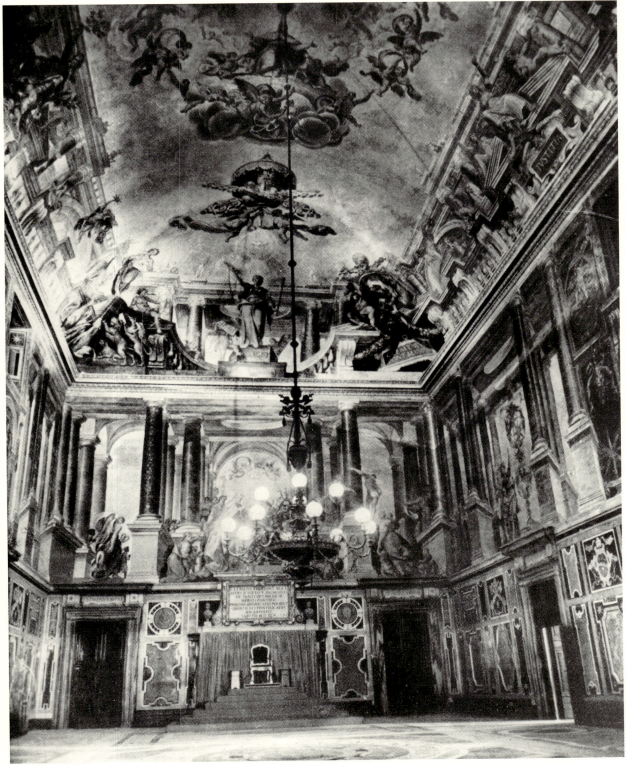

Fig. 164. Sala Clementina from ideal station point, Giovanni and Cherubino Alberti, fresco, Palazzo Vaticano.

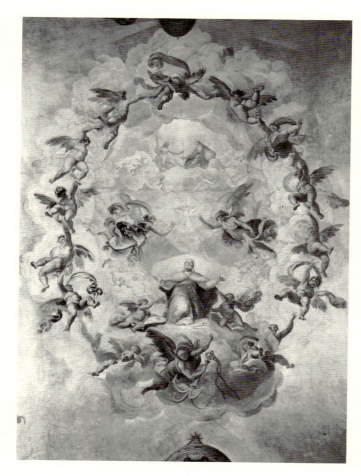

Fig. 165. *St. Clement Adoring the Trinity*, detail of the Sala Clementina, Cherubino Alberti, fresco, Palazzo Vaticano.

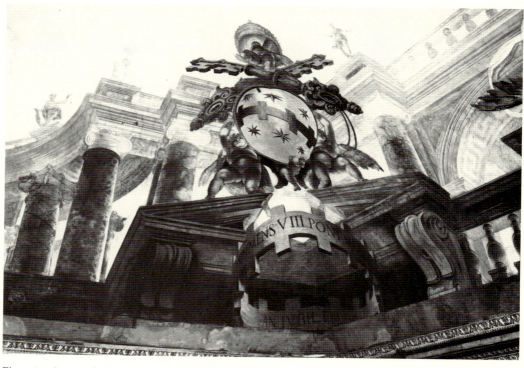

Fig. 167. Arms of Clement VIII Aldobrandini, detail of Sala Clementina, Giovanni and Cherubino Alberti, fresco, Palazzo Vaticano.

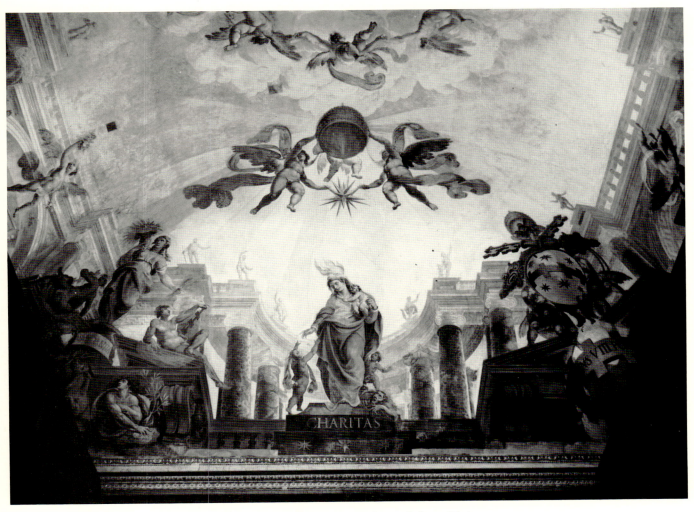

Fig. 166. Detail of Sala Clementina, Giovanni and Cherubino Alberti, fresco, Palazzo Vaticano.

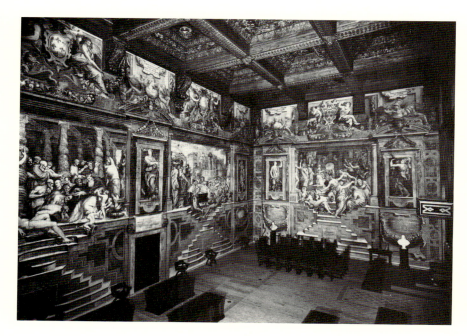

Fig. 168. Sala dei Cento Giorni, Giorgio Vasari, fresco, Palazzo della Cancelleria, Rome.

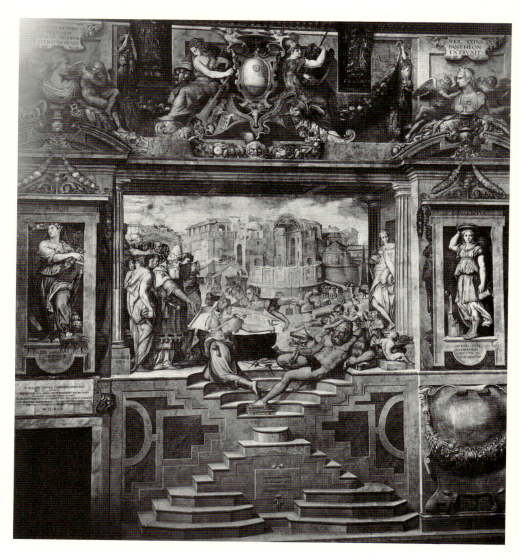

Fig. 169. *Paul III Ordering the Rebuilding of St. Peter's*, detail of Sala dei Cento Giorni, Giorgio Vasari, Palazzo della Cancelleria, Rome.

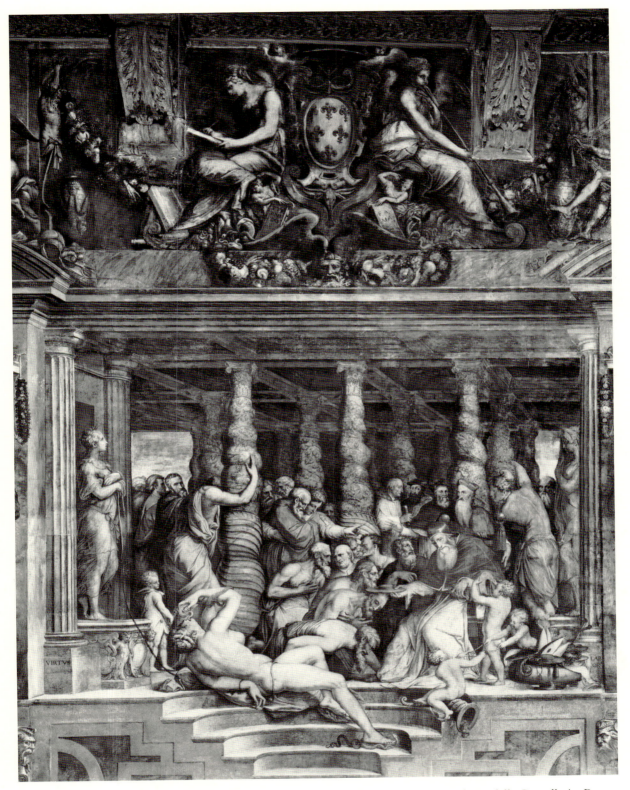

Fig. 170. *Paul III Awarding Benefices*, detail of Sala dei Cento Giorni, Giorgio Vasari, Palazzo della Cancelleria, Rome.

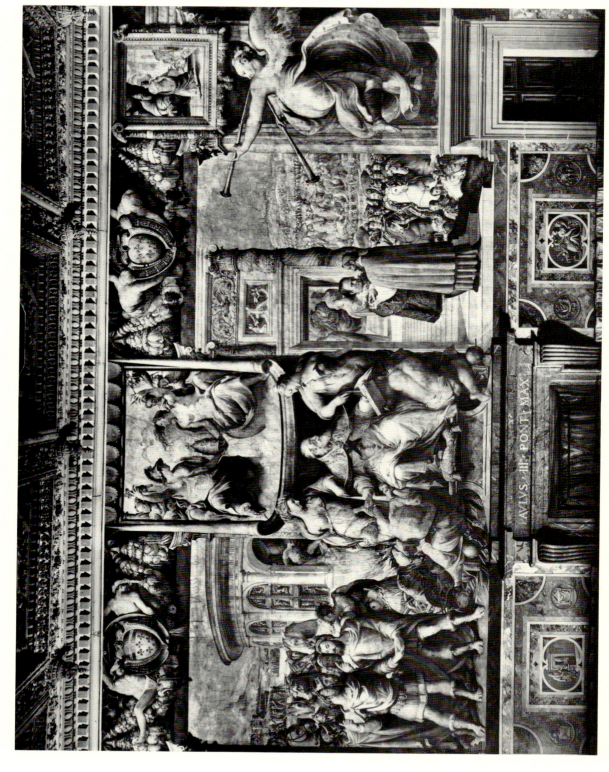

Fig. 171. *Paul III*, detail of the Sala dei Fasti Farnesiani, Francesco Salviati, fresco, Palazzo Farnese, Rome.

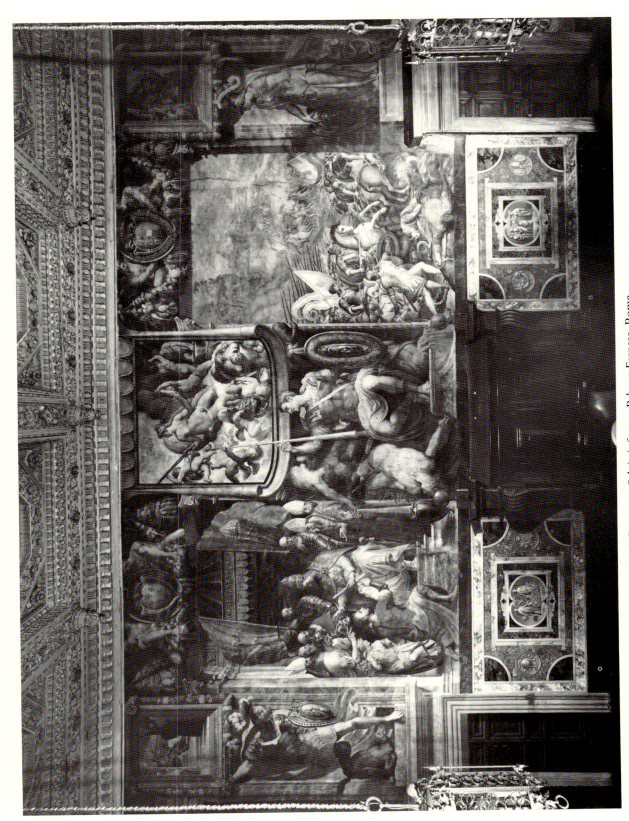

Fig. 172. *Aeneas*, detail of the Sala dei Fasti Farnesiani, Francesco Salviati, fresco, Palazzo Farnese, Rome.

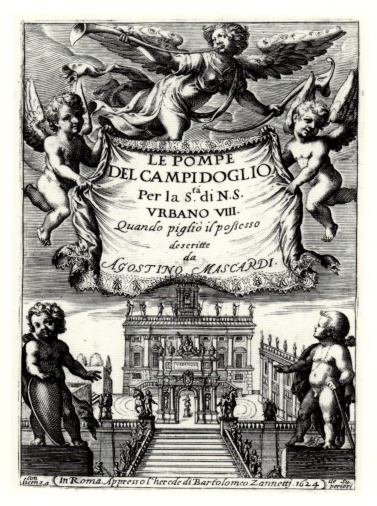

Fig. 173. Frontispiece engraving (Matthäus Greuter), Agostino Mascardi, *Le pompe del Campidoglio per la Santità di Nostro Signore Urbano VIII*, Rome, 1624.

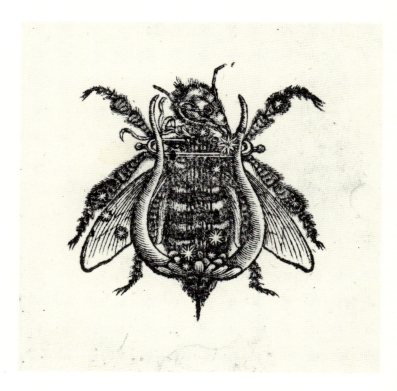

Fig. 174. Frontispiece of Rosichino's *Dichiaratione . . .* , Rome, 1670.